SALES MANAGEMENT
Teamwork, Leadership, and Technology

SIXTH EDITION

SALES
MANAGEMENT
Teamwork, Leadership, and Technology

SIXTH EDITION

CHARLES M. FUTRELL
Texas A&M University

Harcourt College Publishers

Fort Worth   Philadelphia   San Diego   New York   Orlando   Austin   San Antonio
Toronto   Montreal   London   Sydney   Tokyo

Publisher	Mike Roche
Acquisitions Editor	Bill Schoof
Market Strategist	Beverly Dunn
Developmental Editor	Bobbie Bochenko
Project Editor	Rebecca Dodson
Art Director	Brian Salisbury
Production Manager	James McDonald

Photo credits/Cover credit: Images courtesy of Photodisc.

ISBN: 0-03-031967-6
Library of Congress Catalog Card Number: 99-85958

Portions of the work were published in previous editions.

Address for Domestic Orders
Harcourt, Inc., 6277 Sea Harbor Drive, Orlando, FL 32887-6777
800-782-4479

Address for International Orders
International Customer Service
Harcourt, Inc., 6277 Sea Harbor Drive, Orlando, FL 32887-6777
407-345-3800
(fax) 407-345-4060
(e-mail) hbintl@harcourtbrace.com

Address for Editorial Correspondence
Harcourt College Publishers, 301 Commerce Street, Suite 3700, Fort Worth, TX 76102

Web Site Address
http://www.harcourtcollege.com

Printed in the United States of America

0123456789   043   987654321

Harcourt College Publishers

THE HARCOURT SERIES IN MARKETING

Assael
Marketing

Avila, Williams, Ingram, and LaForge
The Professional Selling Skills Workbook

Bateson and Hoffman
Managing Services Marketing: Text and Readings
Fourth Edition

Blackwell, Blackwell, and Talarzyk
Contemporary Cases in Consumer Behavior
Fourth Edition

Boone and Kurtz
Contemporary Marketing ^WIRED
Ninth Edition

Boone and Kurtz
Contemporary Marketing 1999

Churchill
Basic Marketing Research
Third Edition

Churchill
Marketing Research: Methodological Foundations
Seventh Edition

Czinkota, Dickson, Dunne, Griffin, Hoffman, Hutt, Lindgren, Lusch, Ronkainen, Rosenbloom, Sheth, Shimp, Siguaw, Simpson, Speh, and Urbany
Marketing: Best Practices

Czinkota and Ronkainen
Global Marketing

Czinkota and Ronkainen
International Marketing
Fifth Edition

Czinkota and Ronkainen
International Marketing Strategy: Environmental Assessment and Entry Strategies

Dickson
Marketing Management
Second Edition

Dunne and Lusch
Retailing
Third Edition

Engel, Blackwell, and Miniard
Consumer Behavior
Eighth Edition

Ferrell, Hartline, Lucas, Luck
Marketing Strategy

Futrell
Sales Management: Teamwork, Leadership, and Technology
Sixth Edition

Grover
Theory & Simulation of Market-Focused Management

Ghosh
Retail Management
Second Edition

Hoffman/Bateson
Essentials of Services Marketing

Hutt and Speh
Business Marketing Management: A Strategic View of Industrial and Organizational Markets
Sixth Edition

Ingram, LaForge, and Schwepker
Sales Management: Analysis and Decision Making
Fourth Edition

Lindgren and Shimp
Marketing: An Interactive Learning System

Krugman, Reid, Dunn, and Barban
Advertising: Its Role in Modern Marketing
Eighth Edition

Oberhaus, Ratliffe, and Stauble
Professional Selling: A Relationship Process
Second Edition

Parente
Advertising Campaign Strategy: A Guide to Marketing Communication Plans
Second Edition

Reedy
Electronic Marketing

Rosenbloom
Marketing Channels: A Management View
Sixth Edition

Sandburg
Discovering Your Marketing Career CD-ROM

Schaffer
Applying Marketing Principles Software

Schaffer
The Marketing Game

Schellinck and Maddox
Marketing Research: A Computer-Assisted Approach

Schnaars
MICROSIM

Schuster and Copeland
Global Business: Planning for Sales and Negotiations

Sheth, Mittal, and Newman
Customer Behavior: Consumer Behavior and Beyond

Shimp
Advertising, Promotion, and Supplemental Aspects of Integrated Marketing Communications
Fifth Edition

Talarzyk
Cases and Exercises in Marketing

Terpstra and Sarathy
International Marketing
Eighth Edition

Watson
Electronic Commerce

Weitz and Wensley
Readings in Strategic Marketing Analysis, Planning, and Implementation

Zikmund
Exploring Marketing Research
Seventh Edition

Zikmund
Essentials of Marketing Research

HARCOURT COLLEGE
OUTLINE SERIES

Peterson
Principles of Marketing

To my wife, Sue—
the lady who role-played as my buyer when I carried the sales bag

ABOUT THE AUTHOR

Charles M. Futrell is the Federated Professor of Marketing at Texas A&M University in College Station, Texas. He has a B.B.A., M.B.A., and Ph.D. in marketing. Dr. Futrell is a former salesperson turned professor. Before beginning his academic career, Professor Futrell worked in sales and marketing capacities for eight years with the Colgate Company, The Upjohn Company, and Ayerst Laboratories.

Dr. Futrell serves as a frequent reviewer for several academic journals. He is on the editorial board of *The Journal of Personal Selling & Sales Management* and the editorial advisory board of *The Journal of Marketing Theory and Practice.* His research in personal selling, sales management, research methodology, and marketing management has appeared in numerous national and international journals, such as the *Journal of Marketing* and the *Journal of Marketing Research.* An article in the summer 1991 issue of *The Journal of Personal Selling & Sales Management* ranked Charles as one of the top three sales researchers in America. He was also recognized in *Marketing Education,* Summer 1997, as one of the top 100 best researchers in the marketing discipline. His work has earned him several research awards and has resulted in his being associated with such groups as the national Bank Marketing Association's Sales and Professional Development Council and the Direct Selling Education Foundation's board of directors.

Professor Futrell served as the American Marketing Association's Chair of the Sales and Sales Management Special Interest Group (SIG) for the 1996–1997 Academic year. He was the first person elected to this position. Charles was elected Finance Chair for the Sales SIG's 1998–99 term. In 1999, The Association of Former Students awarded him the Lowry Mays College and Graduate School of Business Distinguished Teaching Award. In the spring of 2000 Dr. Futrell served as the Fulbright-Flad Chair in Marketing at the Portuguese Catholic University, Lisbon.

Dr. Futrell has written or co-written eight successful books for the college and professional audience. Three of the most popular books are *Sales Management: Teamworks, Leadership, and Technology,* sixth edition, The Dryden Press; *Fundamentals of Selling: Customers for Life,* sixth edition, and *ABC's of Relationship Selling,* sixth edition, both published by Irwin/McGraw-Hill publishers. These books are used in hundreds of American and international schools. Over 300,000 students worldwide have benefitted from Professor Futrell's books.

Professor Futrell has more than 25 years of teaching experience. Noted for being an excellent classroom instructor, he has developed numerous innovative instructional materials, including computer simulations, computerized classroom materials, video and CD-ROM exercises, and Web sites and sales Internet exercises.

In 1997 Dr. Futrell began using his Web site and group e-mails in his sales classes that often has 100 students in each section. Students sign up for both a lecture period and lab time. In each semester's six labs, students are videotaped in activities such as making a joint sales call, panel interview, selling oneself on a job interview, product sales presentations, and various experiential exercises.

TAMU's College of Business Administration and Graduate School of Business is one of the largest business programs in America, with more than 6,000 full-time business majors. Approximately 50 percent of the Marketing Department's 800 majors are in Charles's personal selling and/or sales management classes at various times. He has worked with close to 10,000 students in sales-related classes.

Professor Futrell's books, research, and teaching are based upon his extensive work with sales organizations of all types and sizes. This broad and rich background has resulted in his being invited to be a frequent speaker, researcher, and consultant to industry.

PREFACE

The best way to describe our sales world at the beginning of the 21st century is as a dynamic and changing place. The rapid growth in technology, the globalization of business, and increasing competition make sales and relationship skills more important than ever. In the sixth edition of *Sales Management: Teamwork, Leadership, and Technology*, my goal is to give students the information they need to compete in the 21st century. This edition has been updated to include more examples of sales teams, leadership, and selling in a global environment, more information about the technology available to every salesperson, and most importantly, more strategies on how to win customers for life.

Sales Management: Teamwork, Leadership, and Technology is written by a salesperson turned professor. For eight years I worked in sales with Colgate, Upjohn, and Ayerst. As a professor, I have taught selling and sales management to thousands of college students, business people, and industry sales personnel, developing and using the strategies, practices, and techniques presented in this text. In my classes and programs, I stress "learning by doing" examples and exercises and videotape role playing situations. This text is the result of these experiences.

When students ask me why I moved out of sales, I always reply, "I really haven't. I'm just selling a different product in a different industry." We are all selling, whether it's a product, an idea, parents, a friend, or ourselves—as when interviewing for a job.

PROVIDES THE BASIC

The sixth edition of *Sales Management: Teamwork, Leadership, and Technology* was conceived to provide ample materials for students to help them understand the basics of managing an outside sales force. Applicable material is also furnished for students to analyze the cases found at the end of each chapter.

The text is a blend of the academic side of our discipline and the real world—with heavy emphasis on the real world. This is truly an applied textbook. Much of the thanks for this goes to the many sales professionals who have reviewed, critiqued, and contributed to this edition. I have tried my best to present the basics on important sales management topics while illustrating them with real world examples from practicing sales managers.

BASIC STRUCTURE OF THE TEXT

The publisher and I worked hard to ensure that the sixth edition of *Sales Management: Teamwork, Leadership, and Technology* would provide students at colleges and universities with the basic foundation for understanding all major elements of sales management. The text presents sales management concepts and practices in a straightforward, easy-to-read manner, with enough depth and detail to challenge students to develop a solid understanding of this important aspect of a firm's marketing effort. The text is divided into six main parts:

- Part I, "Introduction to Sales Management," presents the sales manager as an administrator and emphasizes the important relationship among marketing and corporate objectives, strategies, and tactics. It also examines the social, ethical, and legal issues in selling.

- Part II, "Planning the Sales Team's Efforts," presents the relationship among sales force objectives, forecasting market demand, budgets, sales quotas, and the management of individual sales territories.
- Part III, "Staffing the Sales Team," discusses the important job of manpower planning and employment planning.
- Part IV, "Training the Sales Team," shows the sales manager as a teacher of product knowledge and selling skills. If a course in personal selling is typically taken before the course in sales management, the instructor may want to skip Chapter 11; if you want to emphasize selling, cover Chapter 11 early in the course.
- Part V, "Directing the Sales Team," adds a new dimension to current textbooks by discussing major concepts of motivation and leadership and how the sales manager can use the motivational mix to be an effective leader.
- Part VI, "Controlling the Sales Team," deals with evaluating sales and marketing costs and the individual salesperson's performance to determine whether objectives are reached.

THIS BOOK IS ALSO FOR PEOPLE EMPHASIZING PERSONAL SELLING

Although some schools offer both a personal selling and sales management course, many offer students only a sales management course. Approximately 20 percent of these instructors like to emphasize personal selling in their course. If you wish to treat personal selling as a main component, then cover Chapter 11, "Contents of the Sales Training Program: Sales Knowledge and the Selling Process," early in your course, perhaps after Chapter 4. Students are given enough information to develop a sales presentation and to role-play. Actual role playing could take place in the middle of the course after covering Chapters 5 through 9. This gives students several weeks to collect the necessary information and materials needed to make a sales presentation. Chapters 1 through 4 and Chapter 11 provide a solid background on personal selling.

Texas A&M, where I teach, offers both a personal selling and sales management course. Approximately 50 percent of the students taking sales management have taken the personal selling course. Even with this mix, I spend a lot of time explaining the many types of sales careers and activities done by salespeople and sales managers. Bringing in guest speakers, having students interview salespeople and/or sales managers, and giving students the opportunity to work for a day with a salesperson are a tremendous help in getting students to better understand the sales environment. How can you understand managing salespeople if you do not know what salespeople do?

WHAT'S NEW?

Lots! But the basic core of our sales management processes remains because reviewers, instructors, and students love it. Added is more information about:

- Technology in selling
- Relationship selling
- Sales careers
- Total quality selling
- Global selling
- The multicultural workplace
- Ethics

- Small business
- Services and not-for-profit selling
- Teams
- Leadership
- Industry examples

The following features have been expanded or are new to this edition:

SALES CAREERS   Career information has been expanded throughout so students will better understand that there are sales jobs in all organizations—business, service, and not-for-profit.

SALES MANAGEMENT EXPERIENTIAL EXERCISES   These end-of-chapter exercises help students better understand themselves and/or the text material. The exercises can be done within class or completed as homework and discussed within class. Two longer exercises appear at the end of the book.

SELLING AND MANAGING GLOBALLY   Many of these new boxed items were written by experienced friends and colleagues from countries around the world.

TECHNOLOGY IN SELLING   A new central theme shows the use of technology and automation in selling and servicing prospects and customers.

TEAMS   Emphasis has been placed on discussing the use of teams to sell, service, and oversee customers.

LEADERSHIP   Because it is essential for fielding a high-performing sales team, discussions and examples of leadership have been greatly expanded throughout the text.

INDUSTRY EXAMPLES   Over 50 new industry examples have been interwoven throughout the text, beginning with each chapter's new introductory example.

INTRODUCTORY CHAPTER EXAMPLES   Each chapter begins with a current example of real-world sales management practices.

CASES   Over 70 percent of the cases are new to the sixth edition. The first case of each chapter can be used for in-class discussion. Short discussion cases are at the end of each chapter. Comprehensive cases are in the back of the book.

SALES WORLD WIDE WEB DIRECTORY   This new resource contains the URLs for organizations with the largest sales forces in America. It is great for collecting information for research on finding a job, completing class exercises, and learning about careers in sales.

INTERNET EXERCISES   Class-tested Internet exercises are at the end of the book for ease of location.

TEXT AND CHAPTER PEDAGOGY

Many real-life features have been included in the fifth edition to stimulate learning. One major goal of this book is to offer better ways of using the textbook to convey sales knowledge to the student. The book includes numerous special features:

CHAPTER TOPICS AND OBJECTIVES   Each chapter begins with a clear statement of learning objectives and an outline of major topics. These devices provide an overview of what is to come and can also be used by students to see if they have understood and retained important points.

ART   Many aspects of sales management tend to be confusing at first. To enhance students' awareness and understanding, many exhibits have been included throughout the book. These exhibits consolidate key points, indicate relationships, and visually illustrate sales management practices.

MANAGING THE SALES TEAM   These boxes appear in each chapter and present interesting stories, practices, and concepts. Students feel these greatly add to their understanding and reading enjoyment of chapter material.

SELLING AND MANAGING GLOBALLY   These boxes introduce important and interesting global sales and selling concepts to the students. The boxes have been integrated throughout the text to illustrate the numerous global issues-related various aspects of sales.

CHAPTER SUMMARY AND APPLICATION QUESTIONS   Each chapter closes with a summary of key points to be retained. The application questions are a complementary learning tool that enables students to check their understanding of key issues, to think beyond basic concepts, and to determine areas that require further study. The summary and application questions help students discriminate between main and supporting points and provide mechanisms for self-teaching.

SALES MANAGEMENT EXPERIENTIAL EXERCISES   NEW! These application exercises have been added to the end-of-book material to further enhance the students' understanding of the chapter. Each exercise provides students with an opportunity to apply ideas and concepts learned in the chapter to situations faced in the sales world.

MANAGEMENT IN ACTION: ETHICAL DILEMMA   These end-of-chapter exercises provide students an opportunity to experience ethical dilemmas faced in the selling job. Students should review Chapter 2's definition and explanation of ethical behavior before discussing the ethical dilemmas.

FURTHER EXPLORING THE SALES WORLD   Students can move beyond the textbook and classroom to explore what's happening in the real world. Projects can be altered or adapted to the instructor's school location and learning objectives for the class.

GLOSSARY   Learning the selling vocabulary is essential to understanding today's sales world. This is facilitated in three ways. First, key concepts are boldfaced and defined where they first appear in the text. Second, key terms are shown at the end of each chapter. Third, a glossary summarizing all key terms and definitions appears at the end of the book for handy reference.

CASES FOR ANALYSIS   Each chapter ends with short discussion cases for student analysis and class discussion. These cases provide an opportunity for students to apply concepts to real events and to sharpen their diagnostic skills for sales problem-solving. Longer comprehensive cases are at the end of the text.

As you can see, the publisher and I have thoroughly considered how best to present the material to students for maximizing their interest and learning. Teacher, reviewer, and student response to this revision is fantastic. They are pleased with the readability, reasonable length, depth, and breadth of the material.

INTERNET EXERCISES   Internet exercises allow students the opportunity to improve their technology skills while learning. Several of the exercises might be appropriate as a class project, especially if the instructor combines two or more.

TEACHING AND LEARNING SUPPLEMENTS   Harcourt College Publishers has spared no expense to make *Sales Management: Teamwork, Leadership, and Technology* the premier text on the market today. Many instructors face classes with limited resources, and supplementary materials provide a way to expand and improve the students' learning experience. Our learning package was specifically designed to meet the needs of instructors facing a variety of teaching conditions and for both the first-time and veteran instructor.

INSTRUCTOR'S MANUAL   Loaded with ideas on teaching the course, chapter outlines, commentaries on cases, answers to everything—plus much more—the **Instructor's Manual** is a large, comprehensive time saver for teachers.

POWERPOINT SLIDES   New to this edition, this extremely user-friendly classroom tool is organized by chapter to enable instructors to custom design their own multimedia presentations using overhead transparencies, figures, tables, and key points from the text. These slides are available on the Internet at www.harcourtcollege.com.

TEST BANK   The most important part of the teaching package is the **Test Bank.** The **Test Bank** was given special attention during the preparation of this edition because instructors desire test questions that accurately and fairly assess student competence in subject material. Prepared by Dr. Thomas K. Pritchett and Dr. Betty M. Pritchett of Kennesaw State University and myself, the **Test Bank** provides hundreds of multiple choice and true/false questions. Professor Tom Pritchett also uses this book for his sales management classes. All test items have been reviewed and analyzed by Texas A&M University's Measurement and Testing Center and class-tested to ensure the highest quality. Each question is keyed to chapter learning objectives, has been rated for level of difficulty, and is designated either as factual or application so that instructors can provide a balanced set of questions for student exams.

COMPUTERIZED TEST BANK   The test items are also available in a computerized format, allowing instructors to select problems at random by level of difficulty or type, customize or add test questions, and scramble questions to create up to 99 versions of the same test. This is available in the Windows format.

REQUESTTEST AND ONLINE TESTING   The **RequestTest** phone-in testing service is also available to all adopters. Individual tests can be ordered by question number via fax, mail, phone, or e-mail with a 48-hour turn-around period. Also, Harcourt College Publishers can provide instructors with software for installing their own online testing program which allows tests to be administered over network or individual terminals. This program allows instructors to grade tests and store results with greater flexibility and convenience.

VIDEOS   This video package integrates the book's teamwork, leadership, and technology themes by presenting a real-world perspective of how sales professionals meet the challenges of business, especially in a new century. Each segment takes a problem-resolution approach by presenting challenges as well as results through key concepts taken directly from text chapters.

INTERNET SUPPORT   NEW! Visit the Harcourt Web site at http://www.harcourtcollege.com/ for the latest support material for our marketing list. Look for our useful instructor resources including annotated articles, resource links, cases, and other pedagogical aids which will be constantly updated.

DISTANCE LEARNING   For professors interested in supplementing classroom presentations with online content or who are interested in setting up a distance learning course, Harcourt College Publishers, along with WebCT, can provide you with the industry's leading online courses.

WebCT facilitates the creation of sophisticated Web-based educational environments by providing tools to help you manage course content, facilitate online classroom collaboration, and track your students' progress. If you are using WebCT in your class but not a Harcourt Online Course or textbook, you may adopt the *Student's Guide to the World Wide Web and WebCT* (ISBN: 0-03-045503-0). This manual gives step-by-step instructions on using WebCT tools and features.

In conjunction with WebCT, Harcourt College Publishers also offers information on adopting a Harcourt online course, WebCT testing service, free access to a blank WebCT template, and customized course creation. For more information, please contact your local sales representative. To view a demonstration of any of our online courses, go to **www.webct.harcourtcollege.com.**

THANK YOU FOR YOUR HELP   People who made a major contribution to this edition were the sales management experts who provided advice, reviews, answers to questions, and suggestions for change, insertions, and clarifications. I want to thank each of the colleagues for this valuable counsel:

Victor Clarke, Upper Iowa University; Elaine Lauffer, Limestone College; Lee Manzer, Oklahoma State University; Robert Roe, University of Wyoming; John Ronchetto, University of San Diego; G. Bernard Yevin, Fontbonne College.

Several highly respected professors provided excellent cases for this edition. They did a great job helping students to discuss the fundamental issues faced by sales managers. These professors are:

R. Keith Absher, *University of North Alabama;* **E. Edward Blevins**, *University of Dallas;* **Gerald Crawford**, *University of North Alabama;* **Tim Christiansen**, *Purdue University;* **William I. Evans**, *University of Dallas;* **David Gordon**, *University of Dallas;* **Tom F. Griffin**, *Auburn University at Montgomery;* **Jeffrey K. Sager;** *University of North Texas;* **William S. Stewart;** *University of North Alabama;* and **James L. Taylor**, *University of Alabama;* **George Wynn**, *James Madison University.*

A very special thanks goes to Crystal Goodman for editing and helping with the entire project.

The publisher's crew that produced the final package did a great job. Bill Schoof headed it. Bobbie Bochenko did the best job of overseeing the project over all the developmental editors I have had in my over 20 times of going through this process. I appreciate the efforts of the Harcourt College production and design staff: James McDonald, Production Manager; Rebecca Dodson, Project Editor; Brian Salisbury, Art Director; Linda Blundell, Picture and Rights Editor, and Lisa Kelley, Manufacturing Manager. Thanks also to the Harcourt College sales force that got the text to you and helped make the book so successful.

Let me know what you think of your book. I hope you learn from it and enjoy the text. I enjoyed preparing it for you. Best of success in your course, career, and life.

Charles M. Futrell
E-Mail: c-futrell@tamu.edu
Home Page: http://futrell-www.tamu.edu

BRIEF CONTENTS

CONTENTS

Sales Force Experiential Exercises   416
Sales Team Building Exercise   416
Sell Yourself on a Job Interview   416
What's Your Style—Senser, Intuitor, Thinker,
  Feeler?   420
Your Sales Aptitude   424

Exploring Sales Force Technology   430
Sales World Wide Web Directory   430
ACT! and Goldmine Help Create Customers
  for Life!   433
Sales World Wide Web Exercises   433
Planning Your Sales Call on Dell Computer:
  Location, Travel, Maps, and Research   436
Finding People, Organizations, Maps, Areas, Phone,
  and Address   436
What Is the Best Method to Determine
  Feedback?   437
Research Pays Off in the Sales Game!   437
Time Is Money, So Make Every Minute
  Count!   438
Comparing Places to Live for Your
  Salespeople   438
How Does Your Money Grow in a
  Retirement Fund?   438
Compensation Plan for College   438

Comprehensive Cases
  1 Zenith Computer Terminals, Inc. (A):
     Development of a Total Business Plan   441

  2 Zenith Computer Terminals, Inc. (B): Strategic
     Business Plans Fail—Sales Decline   444

  3 Zenith Computer Terminals, Inc. (C):
     Redesigning Sales Territories   445

  4 Zenith Computer Terminals, Inc. (D): Setting
     Quotas Facing Decreasing Sales   447

  5 Wallis Office Products: Defining New Sales
     Roles   449

  6 Briggs Industrial Supply Company (A):
     Determining Who and How Many
     to Hire   452

  7 Briggs Industrial Supply Company (B): Creating
     Recruitment and Selection Procedures   456

  8 United Cosmetics, Inc.: Creating a Staffing
     Program   460

  9 Farm Machinery for America: The Selection of a
     Salesperson   461

 10 Mead Envelope Company: Is a New
     Compensation Plan Needed?   468

 11 McDonald Sporting Goods Company:
     Determining the Best Compensation
     Program   470

 12 Burditt Chemical Corporation: Analysis of Sales
     and Marketing Costs   474

 13 Deer Tractors, Inc.: Analyzing Sales Data   477

 14 WESCO Distribution, Inc.   482

 15 SaleSoft, Inc. (A)   499

 16 Arrow Electronics, Inc.   514

 17 Aladdin Knowledge Systems   528

Notes   545
Glossary   553
Index   561

PART I
INTRODUCTION TO SALES MANAGEMENT

WELCOME TO the sales management course. Managers of sales personnel have a challenging job. They are the "spark plugs" that ignite salespeople to high performance levels. Part I includes Chapter 1, "Sales Management: Its Nature, Rewards, and Responsibilities," and Chapter 2, "Social, Ethical, and Legal Responsibilities of Sales Personnel."

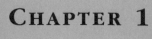

CHAPTER 1
SALES MANAGEMENT: ITS NATURE, REWARDS, AND RESPONSIBILITIES

CHAPTER OUTLINE

WHAT IS SALES MANAGEMENT?

THE FIVE FUNCTIONS OF SALES MANAGERS

SALES PERFORMANCE

MAJOR PARTS OF AN ORGANIZATIONAL SYSTEM

TYPES OF SALES MANAGERS

HOW DOES ONE BECOME A SALES MANAGER?

SALES MANAGEMENT SKILLS

PROMOTION FROM SALESPERSON TO SALES MANAGER

WHAT IS IT LIKE TO BE A SALES MANAGER?

LEARNING TO BE A SALES MANAGER

LEARNING OBJECTIVES

A career in sales management is exciting and unique and provides numerous opportunities. This chapter will do the following:

■ Provide you with an overview of a sales manager's job.

■ Introduce you to the various types of sales managers and the skills required of them.

■ Discuss what a new manager experiences when promoted from a sales job.

Harvey Mackay, a *New York Times* best-selling author and the planet's most sought-after business guru, says the major themes of all five of his books are twofold: "Prepare to win" and "do your homework." Taking a page out of football coach Lou Holtz's playbook, Mackay says that for a manager eager to produce a sales team that works, fairness may be the main ingredient. "One thing I learned from Lou Holtz is that for a team to perform up to its potential it has to have total, 100 percent committed loyalty to the head coach. But at the same time, the coach has to fight his or her guts out with management for that sales team. They've got to know that the coach is in their corner, no question about it," says Mackay.

Lou Holtz, a man with a vast knowledge of Mackay's first theme, "prepare to win," from his years as a college football coach, serves as an inspiration for sales managers. Mackay adds, "When a sales manager plays favorites, there goes the cohesiveness; there goes the teamwork. So not only is it important for a sales manager to introspectively ask, 'Am I treating everyone fairly?' but also to ask, 'Am I unwittingly contributing even to the perception that I'm playing favorites?'" Like a coach striving to lead his team into the championship game, sales managers must treat each person on their team not only as an individual, but also in a fair manner.

When it comes to the theme of "do your homework," Mackay believes in the importance of finding out about the customer as well as the role the manager plays in keeping his sales team informed. "In my early days as an envelope salesman, if I was calling on Pillsbury, General Mills, or 3M, the first thing I did was call the investor relations department. I would get all their annual reports and any papers they turned out. I would go to the library and get everything that was publicly available. So when I finally went to make the call on that person, I was prepared," says Mackay.

With today's technology, the only thing a salesperson has to do is click on the company's Web site. Mackay continues, "We live in an instant-information society, and with just a keystroke, we can come up with everything we want. So while the end of the goal is still the same—to acquire all the available information on a customer to build that profile—the tools that person uses to do so have changed. And it's the sales manager's responsibility to make them aware of all the tools at their disposal."

Managers must also use innovation to set their company apart from others, especially in today's selling environment where the differences in products have become nearly indistinguishable. Mackay believes that for a company to stand out, the sales manager needs to assume a leadership role. "The sales manager has to know all the tools that are being used—not just in the United States, but around the world. A sales manager has to think big, think bold, think quantum leaps, think vision, think customization, think flexible," states Mackay.

He stresses the importance of the sales manager's knowledge and the application of the ideas that exist in the surrounding world: "And it doesn't matter if you're running a two-person lemonade stand—today you must think globally. So as a sales manager, you have to first know what's up in your industry. But then you have to know what's going on in your country, across industries. Even if you're selling cars, for example, there are ideas you can adapt from people selling everything from nuts and bolts to securities to envelopes. The next step is being open to the world. If you can adapt just one idea from a sales organization in Madrid or Hong Kong or Toronto, that becomes an edge."[1] ■

This textbook introduces, explains, and provides examples of the process of sales management. By analyzing examples of successful managers such as Harvey Mackay and reviewing studies of sales management techniques and styles, you will learn the fundamentals of sales management. By the end of this book, you will have read about and understood fundamental sales management skills for planning, staffing, training, leading, and controlling (evaluating) a sales team or an entire sales organization. In the remainder of this chapter, we define sales management and look at the roles, activities, and challenges of managers in today's sales organizations.

WHAT IS SALES MANAGEMENT?

Any organization, large or small, that has customer-contact employees (salespeople) has sales managers. What do sales managers in these varied organizations have in common? They accomplish tasks through their people and organizations. One manager, John Rozurat of W. W. Grainger, described management as "the art of getting things done through people."[2] Michael Hammer and James Champy, noted management theorists who authored the revolutionary book *Reengineering the Corporation,* explain that managers decide how to use organizational resources, give direction to their organizations, and provide leadership to accomplish goals.[3]

Sales managers are responsible for generating sales, profits, and customer satisfaction levels that meet corporate objectives. They do this via a process called *management.* We define sales management as follows:

> *Sales management is the attainment of sales force goals in an effective and efficient manner through planning, staffing, training, leading, and controlling organizational resources.*

This definition covers two important ideas: (1) the five functions of planning, staffing, training, leading, and controlling and (2) the attainment of organizational goals in an effective and efficient manner. The sales management process of using resources to attain goals is illustrated in Figure 1.1. Although some sales management theorists identify additional management functions, such as organizing, communicating, or decision making, those additional functions will be discussed as subsets of the five primary functions in Figure 1.1. You will see that sales managers wear many hats; in a way, they need to be a jack-of-all-trades. They are planners, strategists, tacticians, organizers, forecasters, personnel specialists, trainers, communicators, motivators,

FIGURE 1.1   THE SALES MANAGEMENT PROCESS

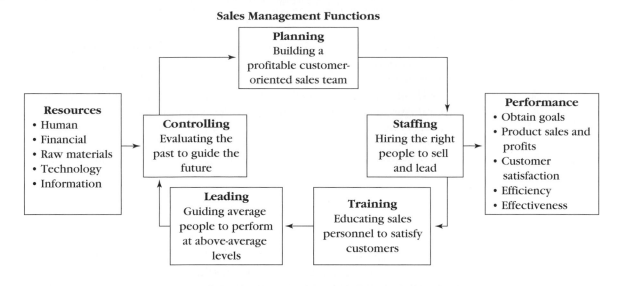

leaders, data analyzers, salespersons, employees, bosses, decision makers, and often spouses and parents. The specific functions and activities we will study include:

- Developing the strategy needed to reach sales goals.
- Properly designing and organizing sales forces around markets.
- Understanding the roles and activities of each sales job.
- Planning sales efforts.
- Examining the firm's market(s), forecasting, and budgeting.
- Staffing the personnel needs of the sales force.
- Training sales personnel.
- Directing people's efforts through effective motivation, compensation, and leadership.
- Analyzing and evaluating sales efforts.

Rather than viewing sales management as containing separate functions and activities (such as staffing, training, and motivating), we will view these as having systematic relationships with each other. For example, training can motivate people. All functions and activities are viewed as a dynamic process, composed of numerous interrelated parts, all aimed at helping the organization reach its sales objectives. Chapters in this textbook are devoted to the multiple activities and skills associated with each function, as well as to the environment, global competitiveness, and ethics, which influence how sales managers perform these functions. The next section begins with a brief overview of the five functions.

THE FIVE FUNCTIONS OF SALES MANAGERS

Sales managers work with and through individuals and groups in the company, in the sales force, and outside the firm to accomplish their goals. The sales manager's main goal is to achieve the levels of sales volume, profits, and customer satisfaction desired by higher levels of management. The factor underlying a manager's success in achieving this goal is the ability to influence the behavior of all parties involved, including the ability to influence salespeople to do what they would not do on their own. Part of a manager's job involves planning.

PLANNING

Planning defines where the organization wants to be in the future and how to get there. **Planning** is the conscious, systematic process of making decisions about goals and activities that an individual, group, work unit, or organization will pursue in the future and the use of resources needed to attain them. Each of the five functions shown in Figure 1.1 requires planning—even the planning function itself.

Managers develop plans for entire organizations, for specific work units, and for individuals. These plans may cover long periods of time (five years or more) or a short time horizon (days or weeks). They may be very general (for example, to improve profits through new product development) or very specific (for example, to reduce inventory of product X by 10 percent over the next month through an incentive system). In each case, however, managers are responsible for gathering and analyzing the information on which plans are based, setting the goals to be achieved, and deciding what needs to be done to achieve them.

A few years ago senior managers at Hewlett-Packard's (HP) computer systems unit (CSO) defined a plan, implemented it, and saw sales jump a whopping $7 billion. A major part of the plan involved organizing. *Organizing* includes the assignment of tasks, the grouping of tasks into departments, and the allocation of resources to departments.

The evolution of CSO's sales program began with a corporate reorganization that gave the company's various divisions greater independence. The changes took place because HP, after several years of steady growth, had become fat and slow moving. A large central bureaucracy had grown, and an emphasis on consensus management caused HP to delay products, miss targets, and watch its earnings slow—the same type of problems that have plagued IBM and Digital Equipment Corporation in recent years.

The reorganization that followed split HP into independent organizations, including the Computer Systems Organization, which could draw on the resources of the corporate giant but also could operate in a more entrepreneurial fashion. At the same time, each division became responsible for its own sales and marketing.[4]

STAFFING

Although a good plan is important, a manager usually cannot do the job alone. **Staffing** refers to activities undertaken to attract, develop, and maintain effective sales personnel within an organization.

PEOPLE ARE MOST IMPORTANT   People are the most important function in the management process. HP's top management helped increase sales $7 billion. Individual salespeople, such as David Greene, also are important to the team's success.

David Greene sells paper—cash register rolls and other total-commodity papers—for American Telephone and Telegraph Global Information Solution (AT&TGIS), formerly NCR Corporation. The industry profit margins are small for that type of product, perhaps 5 to 10 percent. Although the production of paper is a high fixed-cost endeavor, sales swing widely due to cyclical usage, while output is remarkably flat (except when a major plant starts up or shuts down). So it's hard to estimate a gross profit margin. Let's err on the conservative side and say that the profit on each additional dollar of sales revenue is about 7.5 cents.

Greene increased the sales in his district from $300,000 to $1.5 million. In doing so, he added an incremental $1.2 million in business to AT&TGIS's revenues. Using the conservative estimate of 7.5 percent profit margin on incremental sales, those sales are worth $90,000 per year to the firm in pure profit—that is, after accounting for the cost of David Greene himself!

This estimate completely ignores the fact customers tend to become less price sensitive when they become accustomed to dealing with a salesperson and receiving great service. Although this doesn't mean Greene can gouge his customers, he may be able to maintain a reasonable price when a particular competitor lowballs prices in his market in an effort to gain market share. Needless to say, that improves the margin on Greene's total basket of business and may push it above the 7.5 percent level we have estimated for the entire country. With total sales of $1.5 million, an increase of a single percentage point in profitability is worth $15,000—nothing to sneeze at.[5]

Staffing involves two activities: people planning and employment planning. The first determines how many—and the type of—sales personnel to hire. Employment planning consists of recruiting, selecting, and socializing people into the sales group. Thus, hiring salespeople who become high performers is very important to the success of an organization.

TRAINING

Sales managers spend much of their time training their salespeople. **Sales training** is the effort put forth by an employer to provide the salesperson job-related culture, skills, knowledge, and attitudes that result in improved performance in the selling environment. Some authors distinguish between training and development by noting that *training* usually refers to teaching people how to do their present jobs, whereas *development* refers to teaching people the skills needed for both present and future jobs. For simplicity, both will be referred to as *training*.

LEADING

The fourth sales management function is to provide leadership for sales personnel—salespeople as well as sales managers. **Leading** is the ability to influence other people toward the attainment of objectives. Leading means communicating goals to people throughout the sales group and infusing people with the desire to perform at a high level. For top corporate sales managers, leading involves motivating entire departments and divisions as well as those individuals working immediately with the managers.

CONTROLLING

A combination of comprehensive plans, good people, quality training, and outstanding leaders still does not guarantee success. It also takes understanding the organization's past and present situation. This involves controlling—the fifth management function. **Controlling** means monitoring sales personnel's activities, determining whether the organization is on target toward its goals, and making corrections as necessary. Sales managers must ensure continuously that the organization is moving toward its goals.

Specific controlling activities are to set performance standards that indicate progress toward long-term goals; to monitor performance of people and units by collecting performance data; to provide people with feedback or information about their progress; to identify performance problems by comparing performance data against standards; and to take actions to correct problems. Budgeting, cost cutting, and disciplinary action are just a few of the tools of control.

SALES PERFORMANCE

Another part of our definition of sales management is the attainment of sales goals in an efficient and effective manner. One reason sales management is so important is that organizations are so important and must generate revenues to stay in business.

FIGURE 1.2

THE SYSTEMS VIEW OF AN
ORGANIZATION

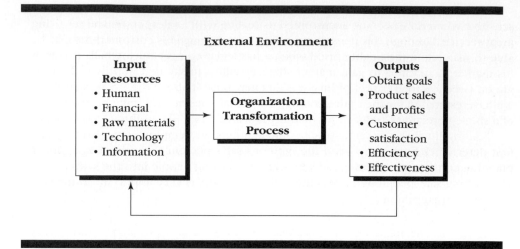

In our society, where complex technologies dominate, organizations bring together resources (people, money, raw materials, technology, and information) to perform tasks no individual could do alone. Without organizations, how could you go to school, eat, drive a car, go to a movie, or watch television? Organizations produce products (goods and services), and sales personnel sell them.

An **organization** is a social system that is goal directed and has a deliberated structure. **Social** means being made up of two or more people. As Figure 1.2 shows, a **system** is a set of interdependent parts that process inputs into outputs. **Goal directed** means an organization is designed to achieve some outcome, such as a profit (Xerox), educated people (college), meeting spiritual needs (Catholic church), or providing health care (hospital). **Deliberated structure** means that tasks are divided, and the responsibility for their performance is assigned to organization members. This definition applies to all organizations, including both profit and nonprofit. Sales personnel's primary task is to generate revenues by selling the products produced by the organization.

MAJOR PARTS OF AN ORGANIZATIONAL SYSTEM

Based on our definition of sales management, the sales manager's responsibility is to coordinate resources in an effective and efficient manner to accomplish the organization's sales goals. **Organizational effectiveness** is the degree to which the organization achieves a stated objective. It is an evaluation of whether the organization succeeds in accomplishing what it tries to do. Organizational effectiveness also means providing a good or service that customers value. **Organizational efficiency** refers to the amount of resources used to achieve an organizational goal. It is based on how much raw materials, money, and people are necessary for producing a given volume of output. Efficiency can be calculated by the amount of resources used to produce a good or service.

The ultimate responsibility of sales managers, then, is to achieve high performance, which is the attainment of organizational goals by using resources in an efficient and effective manner. Whether managers are responsible for the entire organization as a whole or a single sales group, their ultimate responsibility is performance—performance as defined by their individual organization. For profit organizations, performance usually involves sales volume, profits, and customer satisfaction. For not-for-profit organizations, performance, such as at a university or charity, involves fund raising (contributors) and getting people to use their goods or services (clients).

In times past, the most common solution to increasing sales was just to hire more people and spend more money, but companies can't afford that approach anymore. Instead of simply throwing more people at problems, organizations now throw fewer. They have to do more—faster and better—with less. This calls for highly committed people.

Organizations, particularly large ones, have many levels. The five sales management functions must be carried out at each level.

TYPES OF SALES MANAGERS

VERTICAL DIFFERENCES

An important determinant of the sales manager's job is an organization's hierarchical level. Three levels in the hierarchy are illustrated in Figure 1.3. **Strategic, or top, managers** are at the top of the hierarchy and are responsible for the entire organization. They have such titles as president, chairperson, executive director, chief executive officer, vice president of sales, national sales leader or manager, and vice president of worldwide sales. Top managers are responsible for setting organizational goals, defining strategies for achieving them, monitoring and interpreting the external environment, and making decisions that affect the entire organization. They look to the long-term future and concern themselves with general environmental trends and the organization's overall success. They also influence internal corporate culture.

Tactical, or middle, managers work at middle levels of the organization and are responsible for major groups. Examples of middle managers are zone and regional sales leaders. Middle managers have management levels beneath them. They are

FIGURE 1.3   SALES LEADER LEVELS IN THE ORGANIZATIONAL HIERARCHY

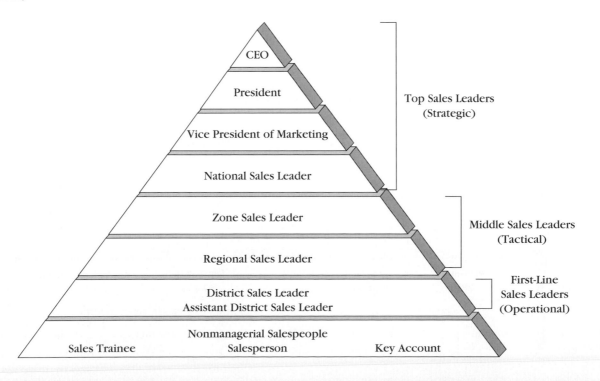

responsible for implementing the overall strategies and policies defined by top managers. Middle managers are concerned with the near future, are expected to establish good relationships with peers around the organization, encourage teamwork, and resolve conflicts.

Recent trends in corporate restructuring and downsizing have made the middle manager's job difficult. Many companies have become lean and efficient by laying off middle managers and by slashing middle management levels. Traditional pyramidal organization charts are flattening, allowing information to flow quickly from top to bottom and decisions to be made with the greater speed necessary in today's highly competitive global marketplace. These reductions increase the workload for remaining managers and contribute to job insecurity and a decline in opportunities for promotion. However, these cuts have improved the efficiency and performance of many corporations via improved responsiveness to customers, resulting in increased sales and profits.

Operational, or first-line, managers are directly responsible for sales of goods and services. They are the first level of management and have such titles as assistant district or district sales leader or manager. They are responsible for groups and nonmanagement employees. Their primary concern is the application of rules and procedures to achieve efficient sales, profits, and customer service and to motivate subordinates. The time horizon at this level is short, with the emphasis on accomplishing day-to-day objectives.

An illustration of how the five functional activities differ for the three management levels is shown in Figure 1.4. Managers at all levels perform all five functions but in different amounts. Planning for the organization is primarily the province of top managers, with time devoted to this task decreasing for middle and first-line managers. Staffing and training, in contrast, are highest for first-line managers and lowest for middle and top managers. Leading and controlling are similar for all three levels, with a little more time devoted to leading and controlling by middle and top managers.[6]

HORIZONTAL DIFFERENCES

The other major difference in sales management jobs occurs horizontally across the organization. Many firms have multidivisions, both domestic and international. Each division can have an organizational hierarchy similar to the one shown in Figure 1.3. Campbell Soup, for example, has consumer, industrial, and institutional divisions selling to retailers, businesses, and institutions such as schools. Black and Decker sells its tools to retailers and businesses using different divisions. General Motors has

FIGURE 1.4   PERCENTAGE OF TIME SPENT ON FUNCTIONAL ACTIVITIES BY ORGANIZATIONAL LEVEL

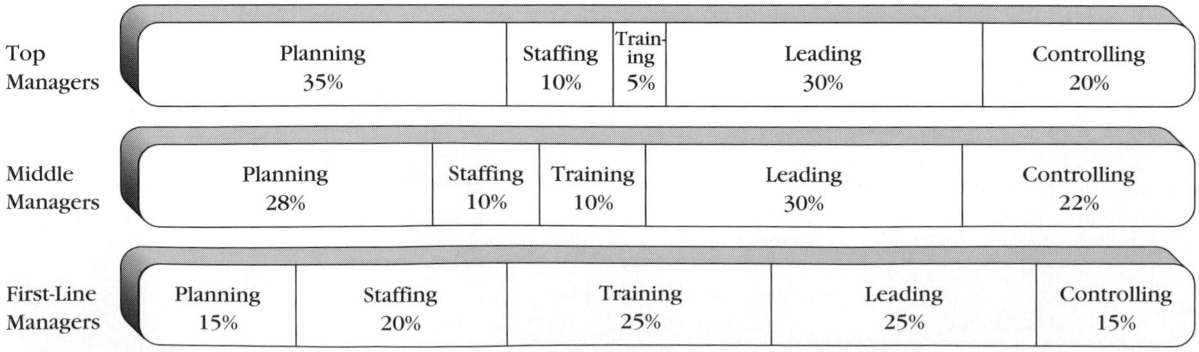

Top Managers	Planning 35%	Staffing 10%	Training 5%	Leading 30%	Controlling 20%
Middle Managers	Planning 28%	Staffing 10%	Training 10%	Leading 30%	Controlling 22%
First-Line Managers	Planning 15%	Staffing 20%	Training 25%	Leading 25%	Controlling 15%

divisions manufacturing and marketing different brands of vehicles such as Cadillac, Buick, Pontiac, GMC, and Oldsmobiles—each with its own sales force.

The path to a career in sales management begins with a position in sales 99 percent of the time, as shown in Figure 1.5. Most companies have two or three levels of sales positions, beginning at the trainee level. After training, a salesperson is given responsibility for a sales territory, thus moving up to a regular sales position. Within a few years, the salesperson can earn the status and financial rewards of a senior position, contacting the larger, more important customers. Some companies refer to this position as a **key account salesperson.** A person may choose to stop here and make selling his or her career or may choose to move into management. Although most recruiters today want to hire a person who can sell, they also want to hire a potential sales manager.

The beginning managerial level is usually the district sales manager's position. The **district sales manager** is responsible for usually three to ten salespeople in one district. From here a person may move into higher levels of sales management, such as that of the **regional sales manager,** responsible for three to five districts, and that of the **zone sales manager,** who oversees three to five regions. A person also may move from any of the management levels into the training, recruiting, product management, promotion, or marketing research areas.

Although individuals with no previous selling experience can be promoted into sales management positions, this rarely happens. Top managers usually feel that a person with sales experience has the credibility and the background to assume a higher position. Beginning as a salesperson allows a person to:

- Learn about the attitudes and procedures of the company's salespeople.
- Learn about customer attitudes toward the company, its products, and its salespeople.

HOW DOES ONE BECOME A SALES MANAGER?

FIGURE 1.5   A SALES PERSONNEL CAREER PATH

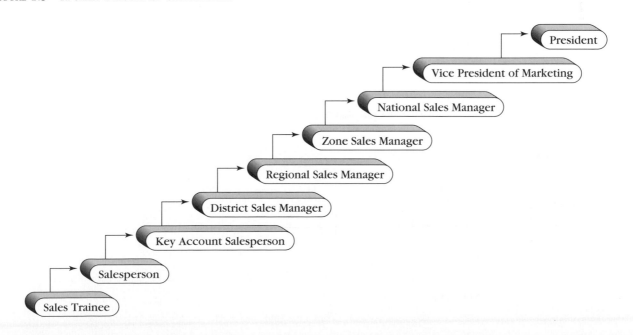

- Learn about the company's competitors.
- Gain knowledge of products and their applications, which is most important in technical sales.
- Become seasoned in the world of business.

Salespeople in small companies may advance more quickly than those in larger companies. However large or small, expanding firms tend to have more job openings and offer the opportunity for faster advancement in the corporate ranks. In years past, people felt that they should stay with a company until retirement. This is no longer true. Many have found they can progress faster by changing jobs. However, some companies prefer to promote from within, making it difficult to better oneself by changing jobs.

SALES MANAGEMENT SKILLS

A sales manager's job is diverse and complex and, as we shall see throughout this book, requires a range of skills. Although some management theorists propose a long list of skills, the necessary skills for planning, staffing, training, leading, and controlling can be summarized in three especially important categories: conceptual and decision, people, and technical. As illustrated in Figure 1.6, all managers need each skill, but the amounts differ by hierarchical level.

CONCEPTUAL AND DECISION SKILLS

Conceptual and decision skills refer to the cognitive ability to see the organization as a whole and the relationships among its parts. Conceptual skills involve the manager's thinking and planning abilities. They include knowing where one's group fits into the total organization and how the organization fits into the industry and the community. They mean the ability to think strategically—to take the broad, long-term view.

PEOPLE SKILLS

People skills involve the manager's ability to work with and through other people and to work effectively as a group member. These skills are demonstrated in the way a manager relates to other people, including the abilities to motivate, facilitate, coordinate, lead, communicate, and resolve conflicts.

FIGURE 1.6

RELATIONSHIP OF CONCEPTUAL AND DECISION, PEOPLE, AND TECHNICAL SKILLS TO SALES LEADER LEVEL

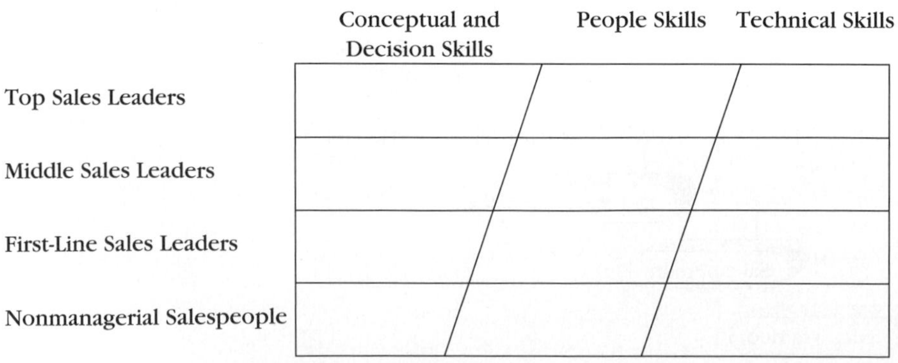

Managers spend well over half their time interacting with people. Because managers must deal with others, they must develop their abilities to lead, motivate, and communicate effectively with those around them. The ability to get along with diverse types of people and exchange information with them is vital for a successful management career. These skills are essential at all levels and in all parts of a sales organization.

TECHNICAL SKILLS

Technical skills are the ability to perform a specialized task that involves a certain method or process. They include mastery of the methods, techniques, and equipment involved in specific functions such as selling, training, and recruiting. Technical skills also involve specialized knowledge, analytical ability, the competent use of tools such as computers, and techniques to solve problems in that specific discipline.

Technical skills are most important at lower organizational levels. Many managers get promoted into their first management jobs by having excellent technical skills. However, technical skills are less important than people and conceptual skills as managers move up the hierarchy.

What happens when a salesperson is promoted into a management position? Often the qualities that make a good sales manager are significantly different from those needed by a salesperson, particularly in attitude toward the job and responsibilities. Many changes accompany a promotion from subordinate to boss. Some of these changes are immediate and apparent to everyone: a private office, a new title, a secretary, and a new supervisor. The more significant differences between the old and new jobs are less obvious and take longer to adjust to. The process of feeling comfortable with these changes is what "learning to think like a manager" is all about. The following are major changes that occur when a person becomes a new manager.

PROMOTION FROM SALESPERSON TO SALES MANAGER

1. *Perspectives change.* Most salespeople are largely concerned with doing a good job at their assigned tasks and planning how to get ahead. Managers, however, must keep the big picture in mind, considering the impact of plans and decisions on the goals and well-being of the group (sales district) and the organization as a whole.
2. *Goals change.* A manager is primarily concerned with meeting the organization's goals. In contrast, a salesperson's focus is on meeting personal goals.
3. *Responsibilities change.* A manager must supervise and speak for a group of people, in addition to completing administrative tasks. As a person moves up in the management ranks, more and more time is spent achieving results through others than on selling.
4. *Satisfaction changes.* Because a manager does less of the actual sales and customer work, satisfaction comes from watching others succeed rather than from the sales work itself.
5. *Job skill requirements change.* Technical competence is important for managers, but possessing additional skills is vital to success. Managers must become proficient at communicating, delegating, planning, managing time, directing, motivating, and training others.
6. *Relationships change.* A manager must develop new relationships with former peers, other managers, and a new supervisor. People quickly change how they act toward the new manager whether or not the manager alters his or her behavior toward them.

What Is It Like to Be a Sales Manager?

So far we have described how sales managers perform five basic functions that help ensure organizational resources are used to attain high levels of performance. These tasks require conceptual, people, and technical skills. Unless someone has actually performed managerial work, it is hard to understand exactly what sales managers do on an hour-by-hour, day-to-day basis, and, as we've seen, different managers—first-line, middle, top—perform similar but varied activities. Since five times as many first-line sales manager positions exist as middle or top, let's look at an example of a first-line sales manager's job.

First-Line Sales Management

After several years with Quaker Oats, Linda Baker became a district sales manager.[7] "My team was composed of seven full-time representatives and two part-timers," Baker says. "My district's annual sales volume was $16 million and I managed six direct accounts. The first week I started in my new position, I had to:

- Create a completely new district.
- Train four new employees.
- Set up my district office.

I was working out of my home and acting as my own secretary, typist, and receptionist."

The greatest challenge to Baker as a district manager was motivating her sales team. "First of all, I never really had managed people. During my two-and-a-half years as a district manager, I managed at one time or another 17 different people, promoted 3 into management, 7 into progressive field sales positions, and trained 10 new employees. I was constantly out in the field training employees about how to effectively sell Quaker products. My job sometimes began at 5:00 A.M. and sometimes ended at 3:00 A.M.! Since my people and I were constantly out in the field, the majority of our communication was done at night over the telephone. I listened to everything from car problems to direct account new item acceptances.

"One of my biggest challenges is finding the right people. Some candidates can come across so polished and confident in an interview, but after two weeks on the job, you see a totally different person. Sometimes an employee is certain about wanting a career in sales, but after six months on the job decides a career in an office is more desirable. After a couple of bad experiences, you learn how to spot a rehearsed interview. Hiring the right people is essential for ensuring smooth sailing in a district. If you can hire the best, it frees you for more pressing matters—such as sales volume.

"The district manager's number one accountability is increasing sales volume," Baker says. "Each quarter, the district was assigned a dollar volume quota for each product category. The quotas were then broken down at the territory level. The sales quotas plus additional merchandising and new item objectives were then written into a six-month sales incentive plan with assigned dollar amounts. An example of a sales dollar quota objective would be to sell the following quarterly dollar sales:

Division	Objectives 1st Quarter	Achieve Dollars	Objectives 2nd Quarter	Achieve Dollars
Human foods	$1,500,000	$1,400,000	$2,000,000	$2,400,000
Pet foods	1,000,000	1,200,000	1,300,000	1,200,000
Total	$2,500,000	$2,600,000	$3,300,000	$3,600,000

An example of a merchandising and new item objective would be:

- New Item: Sell Customer Z four sizes of Special Pet Dinners by July 1 and sell 2,500 cases on the introductory price deal. If the person met this goal, they would earn a bonus of $450.
- Merchandising: Sell Customer Z a four-inch column newspaper ad, forced-out displays (25 cases per store), and a temporary four-week price reduction on the Summer Vacation Sweepstakes promotion. Here, the salesperson would earn $400.

"It was my job, as district manager, to oversee development and execution of these objectives. These objectives were the key priority areas that had the greatest impact on the next six-month volume. To keep abreast, I traveled extensively in the field checking retail store conditions and constantly accompanied my salespeople on their sales calls."

THE PROMOTION EXPERIENCE

A new manager does not make an overnight transformation from thinking and behaving like a subordinate to thinking and behaving like a boss. Instead, when making the transition from one role to the other, the manager passes through several predictable stages. Although people seldom move neatly from one phase to the next, they generally experience all seven phases.

Phase One *Immobilization:* The person feels overwhelmed by the changes he or she is facing.

Phase Two *Minimization or denial of change:* This phase allows time for the individual involved to regroup and fully comprehend the change.

Phase Three *Depression:* Awareness sets in regarding the magnitude of the changes that must be made in one's habits, customs, relationships, and so forth.

Phase Four *Acceptance of reality:* Feelings of optimism return, and the person is ready to let go of the past.

Phase Five *Testing:* This is a time of trying out new behaviors and ways of coping with the new situation.

Phase Six *Searching for meanings:* The person's concern shifts to trying to understand both how and why things are different now.

Phase Seven *Internalization:* In this final phase the person incorporates the new meanings into his or her behavior.

PROBLEMS NEW MANAGERS EXPERIENCE

One of the biggest problems facing most new managers is their lack of preparation for the job. This happens for several reasons. For example, a salesperson is often selected for promotion to a management position because of his or her outstanding performance. The skills and abilities that help a salesperson become successful, however, are quite different from the skills needed by a manager. As a result, the new manager must acquire new attitudes, behaviors, and skills to succeed at managing others.

Adding to new managers' difficulties is the fact that companies generally expect them to step into the job and immediately function effectively. This expectation exists even though many organizations offer them little help or support. Even formal training programs that teach essential new skills are many times offered several months after the promotion into management. The "sink or swim" philosophy is still prevalent.

Finally, the new manager often lacks an immediate peer group. Former peers no longer regard the manager as "one of us." Other managers may hesitate to consider the person a member of their group until he or she has demonstrated the ability to think and act like management. This leaves the new manager belonging to neither group at a time when support from others is greatly needed. Given these and other problems, many new managers often feel inexperienced, uncertain, and overwhelmed by their new responsibilities.

MAKING A SUCCESSFUL TRANSITION TO MANAGEMENT

One key to making a successful transition into management is for the new manager to have a **learning attitude:** a willingness to learn, change, adapt, and seek help when needed. Managers with this attitude find the going much smoother than those who expect their job experience to remain relatively unchanged.

Having realistic expectations about what a management position is like plays a large part in determining how quickly new managers adjust. These newcomers can expect to face unfamiliar situations. They can expect their previous job expertise to be useful in some, but not all, situations. They also can expect to make mistakes, as this is an unavoidable part of learning a new job.

New managers must leave the old job behind and get off to a good start with peers, subordinates, and superiors. This means learning what responsibilities accompany the new job, not just continuing to work at the old job. It takes hard work—and much listening—to gain the loyalty and support of other people. A trap to avoid is making many changes quickly. Rapid changes likely will cause resentment among subordinates, and some changes may become inappropriate once the manager has gained a better understanding of the operation.

Finally, new managers would do well to remember one fact: They are the ones who have assumed a new role. They, not subordinates, other managers, or the surroundings, need to make the initial adjustments.

TECHNOLOGY SALES PERSONNEL USE

To better do their jobs and provide service to customers, sales personnel are becoming high tech. Talking computers, cellular phones, faxes, satellites, automated maps with driving directions for cars, and mobile offices are products rapidly becoming part of salespeople's selling arsenals. Throughout this book, you will learn about technology used by salespeople. Here's one example:

Imagine walking into a sales call with every piece of information needed to introduce a product to a customer: a record of the customer's sales history, up-to-date information about the customer's industry and competitors, detailed product spec sheets, current price sheets, and all the other information needed to close the sale. One way to do this would be to bring along a team of experts, each lugging cases filled with printed information. Another way would be to make a series of calls to the support team at the home office.

Or you could walk into the call carrying a seven-pound notebook computer containing all of the information just listed and with the capability of making a wireless real-time connection to data stored at the home office. This is state-of-the-art sales force automation.

Sales force automation is not a new concept. What makes it of interest today are the powerful information and communication tools now available. These include portable computers with an enormous amount of information capacity, high-speed modems, cellular and radio data networks that allow for wireless communication, and software that allows computers to easily share information.

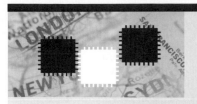

Selling and Managing Globally
When in Rome Do What the Romans Do

Imagine an American salesperson, Harry Slick, starting out on his overseas business trip. The following events occur on his trip:

1. In England, he phones a long-term customer and asks for an early breakfast business meeting so he can fly to Paris at noon.
2. In Paris, he invites a business prospect to have dinner at La Tour d'Argent and greets him with "Just call me Harry, Jacques."
3. In Germany, he arrives ten minutes late for an important meeting.
4. In Japan, he accepts the business cards of his hosts and, without looking at them, puts them in his pocket.

How many orders is Harry Slick likely to get? Probably none, although his company will face a pile of bills.

International business success requires each businessperson to understand and adapt to the local business culture and norms. Here are some rules of social and business etiquette managers should understand when doing business in other countries.

France Dress conservatively, except in the south where more casual clothes are worn. Do not refer to people by their first names; the French are formal with strangers.

Germany Be especially punctual. An American businessperson invited to someone's home should present flowers, preferably unwrapped, to the hostess. During introduc-

tions, greet women first and wait until they extend their hands before extending yours.

Italy Whether you dress conservatively or go native in a Giorgio Armani suit, keep in mind that Italian businesspeople are style conscious. Make appointments well in advance. Prepare for and be patient with Italian bureaucracies.

United Kingdom Toasts are often given at formal dinners. If the host honors you with a toast, be prepared to reciprocate. Business entertaining is done more often at lunch than at breakfast or dinner.

Saudi Arabia Although men kiss each other in greeting, they never kiss a woman in public. An American woman should wait for a man to extend his hand before offering hers. When a Saudi offers refreshment, accept; declining it is an insult.

Japan Don't imitate Japanese bowing customs unless you understand them thoroughly—who bows to whom, how many times, and when. It's a complicated ritual. Carry many cards, present them with both hands so your name can be read easily, and hand them to others in descending rank. Examine and acknowledge Japanese business cards handed to you. Expect Japanese business executives to take time making decisions and to work through all of the details before making a commitment.[8]

How do you learn to be a sales manager for the twenty-first century in an uncertain and rapidly changing world? More specifically, how does a course in sales management or even a college degree prepare you to become a sales manager ready to face the challenges of the twenty-first century?

Management of sales personnel is both an art and a science. It is an art because many skills cannot be learned from a textbook. Sales management takes practice just like tennis, golf, or basketball.

Sales management is also a science, because a growing body of knowledge and objective facts describes sales management and how to attain sales goals. Knowledge is acquired through systematic research and can be conveyed through teaching and textbooks. Systematic knowledge about planning, implementing, and evaluating, for example, helps sales managers understand the skills they need, the types of roles they must perform, and the techniques needed to manage sales personnel.

Books and classes can help you cultivate inherent leadership potential. "Years ago," Danka's Frank Pacetta says, "I read Jerry Kramer's *Instant Replay* and I was amazed by the energy, discipline, and vision that Vince Lombardi brought to bear on

Learning to Be a Sales Manager

the Green Bay Packers. Coach Lombardi was the guy who said, 'Winning isn't everything, it's the only thing.' When I read that, there was an immediate click. I could hear the button being pushed. I didn't rush right out and become a leader by any means. But I had permission from then on to use my own energy, discipline, and vision, characteristics that probably would have gone underutilized without Vince Lombardi's example."[9]

Pacetta reads, studies, and talks to other managers about what it takes to be a successful sales leader. "I'm still studying to be an effective leader," Pacetta says, "and it's a course I'll be enrolled in for the rest of my life. Just when I think I know it all, I discover I know nothing."[10]

Managing sales personnel also involves the use of numerous processes, a **process** being a series of actions or operations conducing to an end. Both staffing and training, for example, involve a process or series of actions. These can be explained in a book and tried by the sales manager. This textbook and your course will focus on the various processes used in managing sales personnel.

As you will learn, becoming a successful sales manager requires a blend of formal learning and practice, of science and art. Practice alone used to be enough to learn how to manage, but it is no longer. Formal course work in sales management can help a person become more competent and prepared for the challenges of the future. The study of sales management enables students to see and understand information about organizations that others cannot. Training that helps you acquire the conceptual, people, and technical skills necessary for sales management will be an asset.

MANAGEMENT IN ACTION: ETHICAL DILEMMA
WHO MADE THE SALE?

You are a sales manager of a highly successful firm that produces bricks for home and office builders. The territory's top seller, Steve Masters, is leaving for a month on a ski trip to New Mexico for a well-deserved vacation. You know that for the past three weeks Steve has worked relentlessly with one particular home builder, Tracey Gibson, in an attempt to sell bricks for a $500,000 home. Such a sale would have netted Steve a healthy $2,000 commission. Despite Steve's successful closing of more than 40 sales last month (beating your company's top sales record yet again), he was never able to close this particular sale even after meeting and negotiating with Gibson several times, who kept insisting on a "better deal."

Yesterday, Steve left on his vacation. Early this morning, one of your newest hires, Brian Lutrell, received a call from Gibson wanting to purchase the bricks at the price Steve had negotiated before his departure. Since Steve is staying in a remote mountain cabin with no phone, Brian was forced to handle the one hour's worth of paperwork in order to finalize the sale.

Later that afternoon, while reviewing the papers Brian had completed and left on your desk, you notice that in the blank marked "salesperson" Brian had written in his own name. The name of the individual who is in this blank will receive the $2,000 commission check. Thinking that Brian had simply made a mistake, you call him into your office to correct the error. However, you soon find that Brian had purposely written in his own name. He explained, "*I* made the sale. I wrote up the client, placed the order, and used my *own* selling time to do it. Steve sure doesn't need the sale. In fact, he was never actually able to make the sale when he was here. He wasn't even in town when the customer finally decided to place the order. He didn't work with the customer at all today—he's skiing! *I* did. *I* deserve credit for the sale." You know Brian is struggling to make his sales quota.

WHAT DO YOU DO?
1. Do nothing. Avoid conflict. Let Brian receive credit for the sale.
2. Split the commission in half by placing Steve's name and Brian's name in the blank to be fair to both individuals.
3. Place Steve's name in the blank. When Steve returns, instruct him to help Brian for an hour with his paperwork in return for the time Brian spent away from customers while helping Steve.

Skilled sales managers are the key to a successful organization. Through the process of management, sales managers are responsible for generating sales, profits, and customer satisfaction levels that meet corporate objectives. It is important to remember that sales management is the attainment of a sales force's goals in an effective and efficient manner by utilizing such functions as planning, staffing, training, leading, and controlling organizational resources.

Sales managers have five functions that, when combined, can allow them to achieve the goals desired by higher levels of management. Sales managers must be able to influence the behaviors of all involved. They accomplish this by considering people most important, by defining goals for future organizational performance, by providing adequate training for salespeople, and, moreover, by leading salespeople to accomplish their goals. Sales managers also must have the ability to monitor the activities of sales personnel and to apply this knowledge to determine if the organization is headed toward its target goals, making adjustments as necessary. The ultimate responsibility of sales managers, then, is to achieve a high level of performance.

The various types of sales managers can be broken down into the categories of vertical and horizontal. Appearing at the top of the vertical hierarchy in a sales organization are strategic managers. Tactical managers appear the next level down, and operational managers make up the first level of management. The salepeople themselves close out the hierarchy. Horizontal differences in a sales organization appear through multidivisions, which can be both domestic and international.

Most corporations hire a person who cannot only sell but who also shows the potential to one day become a sales manager. This person may follow the sales personnel career path, moving up the hierarchical chain of command. However, sales managers must have certain skills, including conceptual and decision skills, people skills, and technical skills. Their perspectives, goals, responsibilities, satisfaction, relationships, and job skill requirements will change. Although new managers may experience problems, solutions for making a successful transition into management exist; the key is to have a learning attitude.

THE BOTTOM LINE

■ KEY TERMS FOR SALES MANAGERS

Sales management, 4
Planning, 6
Staffing, 6
Sales training, 7
Leading, 7
Controlling, 7
Organization, 8
Social, 8
System, 8
Goal directed, 8
Deliberated structure, 8

Organizational
  effectiveness, 8
Organizational efficiency, 8
Strategic, or top,
  managers, 9
Tactical, or middle,
  managers, 9
Operational, or first-line,
  managers, 10
Key account
  salesperson, 11

District sales manager, 11
Regional sales manager, 11
Zone sales manager, 11
Conceptual and decision
  skills, 12
People skills, 12
Technical skills, 13
Learning attitude, 16
Process, 18

■ MANAGEMENT APPLICATION QUESTIONS

1. Sales managers have five functions. What are they, and why are they important?
2. One must start out as a salesperson and gain experience in that area before advancing on to management positions. How does one become a sales manager, and what are the different types of sales managers (citing both vertical and horizontal differences)?
3. What changes will one undergo when moving from a salesperson to sales manager position?
4. A first-line sales manager occupies a "linking" position in the firm. Explain why it might be termed this and why it is such an important and difficult position.
5. How will international/global selling affect the future for sales managers?
6. What are the most common problems experienced by sales managers?

■ FURTHER EXPLORING THE SALES WORLD

Interview a sales manager and ask questions about the job. Find out about the goals of the job and the major job activities used to reach these goals. Ask the sales manager what is best and worst about the job. If possible, have one or more sales managers come to class to discuss what it's really like to be a sales manager in that company and industry.

■ SALES MANAGEMENT EXPERIENTIAL EXERCISE

ARE YOU A GLOBAL TRAVELER?

Our global environment requires that American sales personnel learn to deal effectively with people in other countries. The assumption that foreign business leaders behave and negotiate in the same manner as Americans is false. How well prepared are you to live with globalization? Consider the following items, writing the numbers reflecting your views on another sheet of paper.

Are You Guilty of	*Definitely No*				*Definitely Yes*
1. Being Impatient? Do you think "Time is money" or "Let's get straight to the point"?	1	2	3	4	5
2. Having a short attention span, keeping bad listening habits, or being uncomfortable with silence?	1	2	3	4	5
3. Being somewhat argumentative, sometimes to the point of belligerence?	1	2	3	4	5
4. Being ignorant about the world beyond your borders?	1	2	3	4	5
5. Having a weakness in foreign languages?	1	2	3	4	5
6. Placing emphasis on short-term success?	1	2	3	4	5
7. Believing that advance preparations are less important than negotiations themselves?	1	2	3	4	5
8. Being legalistic and believing a deal is a deal, regardless of changing circumstances?	1	2	3	4	5
9. Having little interest in seminars on the subject of globalization, failing to browse through international topics in libraries or magazines, or not interacting with foreign students or employees?	1	2	3	4	5

Total Score _____

Add up your score. If you scored less than 27, congratulations. You have the temperament and interest to do well in a global company. If you scored more than 27, it's time to consider a change. Regardless of your score, go back over each item and make a plan of action to correct deficiencies indicated by answers of 4 or 5 to any question.

THE WILSON COMPANY
Is a Sales Manager's Job Really for Me?

Joy Gresham was still at her desk at 6 P.M. trying to tie up some loose ends with the hope that tomorrow might be a more productive day. Joy is the western regional sales director (a middle management position) in the Wilson Company. Wilson is a manufacturer of a well-known line of sporting goods. As she reads the mail she still has to answer and stacks the phone messages she still has to return, she wonders if being a middle manager is really her kind of job. Selling products, traveling, and meeting with clients seemed much more to her liking than the routine of her present job.

Today is a good example. Joy went to the office early so she could call Lewis Jackson, the eastern regional sales director, to confer on a joint sales forecast they are trying to prepare. Working with Lewis isn't the easiest of tasks. Compromise just isn't a word in Lewis's vocabulary. She also needs to call the production managers of two of the company's eastern plants to find out what is causing the delay in the receipt of the new product lines. Those production people don't seem to realize that a large inventory is needed to keep up sales. The new product lines were promised two weeks ago and still aren't here. The phone calls take longer than expected, but by midmorning Joy is finally able to settle into the major project she has planned for the day. After several days of perusing sales reports of the past several years, she concluded that total sales, as well as productivity of individual salespersons, can be improved if the region is redesigned and the territories of each salesperson are adjusted. This is a major project, and she must present it to her district sales managers at her monthly meeting tomorrow afternoon.

Joy is away from the office a little longer than expected because of lunch. When she returns, she finds a half dozen phone messages, including an urgent call from the corporate vice president of personnel, Wayne McDaniel. She returns Wayne's call, and, much to her dismay, she finds she is going to have to allocate a good portion of tomorrow's sales meeting to presenting the company's new benefits program. Wayne assures her that all the materials she needs will arrive late this afternoon and stresses the need for its immediate dissemination and explanation. After trying unsuccessfully to return several of the other phone calls, she returns to the territory redesign project. She finishes that project just before the 3 P.M. appointment she has with a candidate for district sales manager. Joy spends more than an hour with the candidate and is impressed enough with him to immediately make some follow-up phone calls.

Joy looks at her watch and realizes she hasn't enough time to make all the calls she'd planned. The whole day seems to have gotten away from her. She still has the materials from Wayne to review, and she has to prepare the agenda for tomorrow's meeting. She just has to figure a way to motivate better performance from those sales managers. The redesign of the territory was only a partial solution. Joy wonders what else she can do. "Oh," she thinks to herself, "I better call and cancel my date for tonight. It has been over three weeks since I've had any life other than work, and it feels like the only time I ever leave this office is to eat lunch!"

QUESTIONS
1. Compare Joy's present job to what you think her previous job as a salesperson was. How are they similar? How are they different?
2. What managerial skills are depicted in the case? Which skill is most important for Joy to possess? Why?
3. Why do you feel Joy might be disenchanted with her present job?

CASE 1.2

NABISCO
What They Didn't Teach Us in Sales Class

Rick Lester was depressed. He was cold and damp from the rain as he sat in his van in the parking lot outside a Food World supermarket. He had just telephoned the Nabisco division sales office and talked with Helen, the office secretary. Rick had asked her, "What are we supposed to do when it rains like this?" Rick could hear her repeat the question to William Brown, the division sales manager, who just happened to be in the office. Rick could hear the reply in the background: "Tell him to buy a raincoat!" When Helen repeated the response, Rick replied to her, "OK, have a nice day" with a slightly embarrassed tone in his voice. As he hung up the pay phone and sat back in his van, he thought, "What a heck of a way to make a living."

As a new salesman, Rick clearly had much to learn. He had been on the job for only one month, but he had already decided it was no "piece of cake." It all seemed so much easier when he watched Brown make calls during the two-week on-the-job training period. Now that he was making calls on his own, it was quite different and much more difficult. Interestingly, the sales class taken at the University of Alabama at Birmingham (UAB) last year had covered many reasons to go into selling but few disadvantages of pursuing a career in selling. Rick was now learning about these firsthand.

Rick's family, his parents and two younger sisters, had lived in Birmingham for many years. His father was a salesman, and his mother was a homemaker. Rick was an average student in high school, where he really majored in athletics and cheerleaders. After high school he accepted a partial athletic scholarship to Northwest Mississippi Junior College. His grades in college were about average overall but were low in basic math classes. The chief reason he selected business as his major was that it required no algebra. Following two years in Mississippi, Rick transferred to the University of Alabama at Birmingham and continued to work toward a bachelor of science degree in marketing. He later married when he graduated from UAB. He had three specific job opportunities, all in sales, but he chose the job with Nabisco because it was a big company with many benefits. He also thought highly of Brown, the local recruiter and division sales manager.

Rick started to work on September 1. The first week was spent reviewing sales training manuals and completing employment paperwork. He also stocked his new van with merchandise, advertising materials, and displays. The following two weeks were spent "working

the trade" with Brown, who made most of the calls while Rick learned by observing. Toward the end of the third week of employment, Rick started making the sales presentations while Brown observed. They would discuss each call after they returned to the van. During the fourth week, Rick worked alone. The present week had been difficult. He knew so little. On Friday it rained, and this was not helpful. It was about two o'clock when he called the office and was told to "buy a raincoat."

As he sat in the van waiting for the rain to let up, he began thinking about the situation in which he now found himself, and it was depressing. The rain was not the only reason for his low morale. He thought about his wife and how she had told her friends that Rick was in "public relations" rather than sales. Although they had not discussed it, Rick assumed she did not particularly like the title "salesman." Somewhere in the back of Rick's thoughts was clearly an image that selling does have low occupational status. Maybe it came from his father. He couldn't remember. Another troublesome aspect of the new job was the calloused way some retailers treat all salespeople. Others simply try to brush them off or avoid them altogether. This job certainly does not build up one's ego.

Other negative aspects of being in sales occurred to him. One is that selling is physically demanding. It is a requirement that the sales bag be carried into all calls. This properly loaded sales bag weighs 38 pounds and contains advertising materials, new products, sample merchandise, stapler, and the selling portfolio. For some calls, salespeople must transport cases of merchandise from the storage area to the shelves. A great deal of bending over and lifting are simply a part of the routine workday. By quitting time each day, Rick's clothing is wrinkled and damp from perspiration. Yesterday he had snagged a hole in the trousers of his new suit.

When each day is finished, reports must be prepared and mailed off to the home office. It is also necessary to reorganize and restock the van for the next day's work. Sometimes telephone calls must be made. By the time these chores are completed, it is almost bedtime. Rick has little time left to spend with his new wife. She had mentioned this a time or two.

The last annoying concern involves the knowledge that a good part of his success, or lack of it, depends on events over which he has no control. At several calls this week, a competitor had persuaded dealers to reduce shelf space for Nabisco products. These dealers reported that the competitor had a special promotion going on and the deal was "just too good to pass up." Rick could not find a way to recover the lost shelf space in those calls. This did not look good on the salesperson's daily report.

As the rain continued to come down, Rick felt very alone. Brown was not there to help or provide answers. The physical and emotional obstacles just seemed too big to overcome. The only way out of this mess, it seemed, was to quit this job and try to find another one that was not so depressing. "Maybe I could get a job in a bank where customers are always nice and the work is easier," Rick thought. As he started his van and drove away toward the division office, he felt relieved that he would soon be free of this impossible responsibility.

QUESTIONS

1. Should Rick Lester "turn in his keys"?
2. How should William Brown handle this situation? What should he say to Rick?
3. How can firms reduce high turnover among new sales personnel?
4. What can firms do to increase salesperson status?
5. What can professors do to better prepare students in sales classes?

Source: This case was written by Gerald Crawford and R. Keith Absher, Professors of Marketing, and William S. Stewart, Professor of Management, University of North Alabama, Florence, Alabama 35632.

CHAPTER 2

SOCIAL, ETHICAL, AND LEGAL RESPONSIBILITIES OF SALES PERSONNEL

CHAPTER OUTLINE

MANAGEMENT'S SOCIAL RESPONSIBILITIES

WHAT INFLUENCES ETHICAL BEHAVIOR?

MANAGEMENT'S ETHICAL RESPONSIBILITIES

ETHICS IN DEALING WITH SALESPEOPLE

SALESPEOPLE'S ETHICS IN DEALING WITH THEIR EMPLOYERS

ETHICS IN DEALING WITH CUSTOMERS

MANAGING SALES ETHICS

LEARNING OBJECTIVES

This chapter is one of the most important in this textbook. Understanding social, ethical, and legal issues helps build a solid foundation on which to base future decisions and to manage sales personnel. After studying this chapter, you should be able to explain the following:

■ Management's social responsibilities.

■ What influences ethical behavior.

■ Management's ethical responsibilities.

■ Ethical dealings among salespeople, employers, and customers.

■ The international side of ethics.

■ Managing sales ethics.

Age discrimination in the workplace has been a major issue. One case of age discrimination deals with a man named Philip Haun, a senior area sales manager for Ideal Industries. One year, Philip was credited with increasing sales in his division—which sold wire-splicing machines and other industrial products—140 percent. The next year, Haun was fired. His division's four-person team was about to merge with the seven-man sales force that sold wire strippers. Four people had to be let go, and Haun was one of them. His boss told him that his discharge wasn't performance related and that he was welcome to apply for other sales positions within the company. Haun, who was 51 at the time, thought the company still wanted to keep him. So Haun started combing the company for leads, but he had a tough time. Haun finally realized that Ideal didn't want him to stay on. He came to suspect that Ideal fired him because of his age. After he left Ideal, Haun filed suit against his former company, alleging age discrimination, and a U.S. Court of Appeals recently affirmed an earlier court decision in Haun's favor. Ideal executives deny the company fired Haun because of his age.

Haun's story is a familiar one in the sales profession. He is one of hundreds of salespeople who have sued their employers for age discrimination and won. Legal experts predict the number of workplace age-discrimination cases will skyrocket in the next five years as Baby Boomers become older. Some legal experts also say that sales managers are more likely to have negative stereotypes about older reps, and hire and fire based on those perceptions. Sales managers have a perception that older workers can't be energetic and learn new things as well as younger workers. Other sales executives get into trouble if it appears they simply don't want to pay older salespeople the hefty wages and benefits they have earned after years of hard work. Sales managers also tend to hold older workers to a different standard than younger ones, and they sometimes don't give older workers the same training opportunities.[1] ∎

As this example shows, sales personnel constantly are confronted with social, ethical, and legal issues. Yet if you think about it, everyone is—including yourself. If you found a bag full of $100 bills lying on the side of the road, would you keep it? Would you use the company car to run a personal errand? Have you ever broken the speed limit? Have you ever gone home with one of your employer's pens in your jacket pocket or purse? Would you cheat on a test?

These sorts of questions may be difficult for the average person to answer. Some people will respond with an unequivocal "yes" or "no." Others may mull it over awhile. Still others may feel compelled to say "it depends" and qualify their response with a "yes, but . . ." or a "no, but. . . ."

Newspapers, radio, and television frequently have news stories of individuals and organizations involved in both good and bad practices. This chapter addresses many of the important social, ethical, and legal issues in selling. It begins by discussing management's social responsibilities. Then it examines ethical behavior, followed by the ethical issues involved in dealing with salespeople, employers, and consumers. The chapter ends by presenting ways an organization can help its sales personnel follow ethical selling practices.

MANAGEMENT'S SOCIAL RESPONSIBILITIES

In one sense, the concept of corporate social responsibility is easy to understand; it means distinguishing right from wrong and doing right. It means being a good corporate citizen. The formal definition of **social responsibility** is management's obligation to make choices and take actions that will contribute to the welfare and interests of society as well as to those of the organization.

As straightforward as this definition seems, social responsibility can be a difficult concept to grasp because different people have different opinions on which actions improve society's welfare. To make matters worse, social responsibility covers a range of issues, and many of these issues have ambiguous boundaries between right and wrong.

ORGANIZATIONAL STAKEHOLDERS

One reason for the difficulty in understanding social responsibility is that managers must confront the question "Responsibility to whom?" The organization's environment consists of several sectors both inside and outside of the organization. From a social responsibility perspective, enlightened organizations view the internal and external environment as a variety of stakeholders.

A **stakeholder** is any group within or outside the organization that has a stake in the organization's performance. Each stakeholder has a different interest in the organization. As Figure 2.1 illustrates, eight important stakeholders exist. They are easily remembered using the acronym **CCC GOMES.** The first *C* refers to *customers,* and the last *S* refers to *suppliers. Owners', creditors'* and suppliers' interests are served by managerial efficiency, that is, the use of resources to achieve profits. *Managers* and *employees* expect work satisfaction, pay, and good supervision. Customers are concerned with decisions about the quality and availability of goods and services.

Other important stakeholders are the *government* and the *community.* Most corporations exist under the proper charter and licenses and operate within the limits of the laws and regulations from the government sector, including safety laws and environmental protection requirements. The community includes local government, the natural and physical environments, and the quality of life provided for residents. Socially responsible organizations pay attention to all stakeholders affected by their actions.

FIGURE 2.1

MAJOR STAKEHOLDERS IN
THE ORGANIZATION'S
PERFORMANCE

AN ORGANIZATION'S MAIN RESPONSIBILITIES

Once a company is aware of its stakeholders, what are its main responsibilities to them? Four exist: economic, legal, ethical, and discretionary. The responsibilities are discussed based on the order and frequency with which managers deal with each issue. Managers most frequently deal with economic issues.

ECONOMIC RESPONSIBILITIES   A company or any other business institution is, above all, a basic economic unit of society. Its responsibility is to produce the goods and services that society wants and to maximize profits for its owners and shareholders.

Quite often, corporations are said to operate solely to maximize profits. Certainly, profits are important to a firm, just as a grade-point average is important to a student. Profit provides the capital to stay in business, to expand, and to compensate for the risks of conducting business. Companies have a responsibility to make a profit in order to serve society. Imagine what would happen to our society if large corporations (for example, Wal-Mart, General Motors) did not make a profit and went out of business. Thousands of people would be affected.

LEGAL RESPONSIBILITIES   All modern societies lay down ground rules, laws, and regulations that organizations are expected to follow. Legal responsibility defines what society deems as important with respect to appropriate corporate behavior. Organizations are expected to fulfill their economic goals within the legal framework. Legal requirements are imposed by local town councils, state legislators, and federal regulatory agencies.[2]

ETHICAL RESPONSIBILITIES   Ethical responsibility includes behaviors that are not necessarily codified into law and may not serve the corporation's direct economic interests. To be ethical, organizational decision makers should act with equity, fairness, and impartiality; should respect the rights of individuals; and should provide different

MANAGING THE SALES TEAM
CATERPILLAR, INC.

Caterpillar, Inc., published "A Code of Worldwide Business Conduct and Operating Principles" that begins with a clear statement of corporate values. The code is 14 pages long and covers human relationships, disposal of waste, privacy of information about employees, product quality, sharing of technology, public responsibility, observance of local laws, and inside information. The initial statement of "Business Ethics," quoted next, indicates that Caterpillar expects its employees to display ethical behavior well above that required by law.

The law is a floor. Ethical business conduct should normally exist at a level well above the minimum required by law.

One of a company's most valuable assets is a reputation for integrity. If that be tarnished, customers, investors, suppliers, employees, and those who sell our product, will seek affiliation with other, more attractive companies. We intend to hold a single high standard of integrity everywhere. We will keep our word. We won't promise more than we can reasonably expect to deliver; nor will we make commitments we don't intend to keep.

The goal of corporate communication is the truth—well and persuasively told. In our adver-

tising and other public communications, we will avoid not only untruths, but also exaggeration and overstatement. Caterpillar employees shall not accept costly entertainment or gifts (excepting mementos and novelties of nominal value) from dealers, suppliers, and others with whom we do business. And we don't tolerate circumstances that produce, or reasonably appear to produce, conflict between personal interests of an employee and interests of the company.

We seek long-lasting relationships—based on integrity—with all whose activities touch upon our own.

The ethical performance of the enterprise is the sum of the ethics of the men and women who work here. Thus, we are all expected to adhere to high standards of personal integrity. For example, perjury or any other illegal act ostensibly taken to "protect" the company is wrong. A sale made because of deception is wrong. A production quota achieved through questionable means or figures is wrong. The end doesn't justify the means.

Source: Based on Caterpillar Annual Report, 1995.

treatment of individuals only when relevant to the organization's goals and tasks. Unethical behavior occurs when decisions enable an individual or company to gain at the expense of society.

DISCRETIONARY RESPONSIBILITIES **Discretionary responsibility** is purely voluntary and guided by a company's desire to make social contributions not mandated by economics, law, or ethics. Discretionary activities include generous philanthropic contributions that offer no monetary return to the company and that are not expected. Discretionary responsibility is the highest criterion of social responsibility, because it goes beyond societal expectations to contribute to the community's welfare.

HOW TO DEMONSTRATE SOCIAL RESPONSIBILITY

A corporation can demonstrate social responsibility in numerous ways. Actions that can be taken by all organizations include the following:

1. Taking corrective action before it is required.
2. Working with affected constituents to resolve mutual problems.
3. Working to establish industry-wide standards and self-regulation.
4. Publicly admitting mistakes.

5. Getting involved in appropriate social programs.
6. Helping correct environmental problems.
7. Monitoring the changing social environment.
8. Establishing and enforcing a corporate code of conduct.
9. Taking needed public stands on social issues.
10. Striving to make profits on an ongoing basis.

Economic, legal, ethical, and discretionary responsibilities to stakeholders will be important concerns organizations must face in the twenty-first century. Society is demanding more responsible action out of organizations, particularly regarding their ethical standards.

WHAT INFLUENCES ETHICAL BEHAVIOR?

Organizations are comprised of individuals. These individuals' morals and ethical values help shape those of the organization. Critical to making decisions in an ethical manner is the individual integrity of the organization's managers, especially those in top management positions. Thus, two major influences on the ethical behavior of sales personnel are employees and the organization itself.

THE INDIVIDUAL'S ROLE

All of us, employees and managers alike, bring certain ethical values to a job. Personality, religious background, family upbringing, personal experiences, and the situation faced are examples of factors that influence people in making decisions. Individuals usually can be placed into one of these levels of "moral development":

- *Level one:* **preconventional**—An individual who acts in his or her own best interests and thus follows rules to avoid punishment or receive rewards. Will break moral and legal laws if they conflict with what this type of person perceives as his or her best interests.
- *Level two:* **conventional**—An individual who conforms to the expectations of others, such as family, friends, employer, boss, society. Upholds moral and legal laws.
- *Level three:* **principled**—An individual lives by an internal set of morals, values, and ethics. These are upheld regardless of punishments or majority opinion. The individual would disobey orders, laws, and consequences in order to follow what he or she believes is right.[3]

The majority of managers, as well as people in general, operate at the conventional level. However, a few individuals are at level one, and, it is estimated that less than 20 percent of individuals reach the principled level.

THE ORGANIZATION'S ROLE

If the vast majority of people in our society are at the conventional level of moral development, it seems that most employees in an organization would feel they must "go along to get along"; in other words, they go along with rules in order to keep their jobs. At most, they will follow only formal policies and procedures.

How will sales personnel handle ethical dilemmas? What if no policies and procedures pertaining to some sales practices exist and a person is directed to do something by a superior that appears unethical? It is no wonder that radio, television, and newspaper reports frequently feature unethical business practices. Following the "hear no evil, see no evil, speak no evil" philosophy can create a preconventional- or conventional-level organizational climate.[4]

MANAGEMENT'S
ETHICAL
RESPONSIBILITIES

The concept of ethics is easy to understand but difficult to define in a precise way. In a general sense, **ethics** is a set of moral principles and values that governs the behavior of a person or group with respect to what is right or wrong. Ethics set standards as to what is good or bad in conduct and decision making.[5] *Principles* are the rules or laws that make up a code of ethics.

Many companies and their sales personnel get into trouble by making the assumption that "If it's not illegal, it must be ethical." Ethics and moral values are a powerful force for good that can regulate behavior both inside and outside the sales force. As principles of ethics and social responsibility are more widely recognized, companies can use codes of ethics and their corporate cultures to govern behavior, thereby eliminating the need for additional laws governing right and wrong.

WHAT IS ETHICAL BEHAVIOR?

Sales personnel are frequently faced with ethical dilemmas. **Ethical behavior** refers to treating others fairly. Specifically, it refers to:

- Being honest.
- Maintaining confidence and trust.
- Following the rules.
- Conducting yourself in the proper manner.
- Treating others fairly.
- Demonstrating loyalty to company and associates.
- Carrying your share of the work and responsibility with 100 percent effort.

The definition of ethical behavior, although reasonably specific and easy to understand, is difficult to apply in every situation. In real life, conflicting viewpoints, fuzzy circumstances, and unclear positions always exist. Though difficult, it is critical to cut through the smoke screen that sometimes exists in such a situation and to use "20/20 vision" to make an ethical choice.

WHAT IS AN ETHICAL DILEMMA?

Because ethical standards are not codified, disagreements and dilemmas about proper behavior often occur. An ethical dilemma arises in a situation when each alternative choice or behavior has some undesirable elements due to potentially negative ethical or personal consequences. Right or wrong cannot be clearly identified.[6] Consider the following:

- Your boss says he cannot give you a raise this year because of budget constraints, but he will look the other way if your expense accounts come in a little high because of your good work this past year.
- Stationed at the corporate headquarters in Chicago, you have 14 salespeople in countries all over the world. A sales rep living in another country calls to get approval to pay a government official $10,000 to approve the equipment purchase of $5 million. Such payoffs are part of common business practice in this part of the world.
- An industrial engineer, who is a good friend of yours, tells you three of your competitors have submitted price bids on his company's proposed new construction project. He suggests a price you should submit and mentions certain construction specifications his boss is looking for on this job.

These are kinds of dilemmas and issues that fall squarely in the domain of ethics. Because of their importance, an *ethical dilemma* situation appears toward the end of

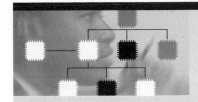

MANAGING THE SALES TEAM

QUESTIONS TO ASK YOURSELF IN ETHICAL DECISION MAKING

Here is a list of questions to ask yourself in determining if your decision is ethical. The questions will not guide you precisely on what to do but can help you evaluate a situation by examining your own values and those of your organization. The answers to these questions will force you to give serious thought to the social and ethical consequences of your behavior.

1. Is the problem/dilemma really what it appears to be? If you are not sure, find out.
2. Is the action you are considering legal? Ethical? If you are not sure, find out.
3. Do you understand the position of those who oppose the action you are considering? Is it reasonable?
4. Who does the action benefit? Harm? How much? How long?

5. Would you be willing to allow everyone to do what you are considering doing?
6. Have you sought the opinion of others who are knowledgeable on the subject and who would be objective?
7. Would your action be embarrassing to you if it were made known to your family, friends, co-workers, or superiors? Would you be comfortable defending your actions to an investigative reporter on the evening news?

No correct answers to these questions exist in an absolute sense. Yet, if you determine that an action is potentially harmful to someone or would be embarrassing to you, or if you do not know the ethical or legal consequences, these guidelines will help you clarify whether the action is socially responsible.

each chapter. In answering, refer both to this chapter and each ethical dilemma's chapter.[7]

Now let's turn to the three main ethical areas most frequently faced by sales personnel. These three areas involve salespeople, employers, and customers. Our discussion cannot be all inclusive but represents an attempt to give you a feel for some of the difficult situations faced by sales personnel.

ETHICS IN DEALING WITH SALESPEOPLE

Sales managers have both social and ethical responsibilities to their sales personnel. Salespeople are a valuable resource; they have been recruited, carefully trained, and given important responsibilities. They represent a large financial investment and should be treated in a professional manner. Yet occasionally a company may place its managers or salespeople in positions that force them to choose among compromising their personal ethics, not doing what is required, or leaving the organization. Certainly the choice depends on the magnitude of the situation. At times situations arise in which it is difficult to say whether a sales practice is ethical or unethical. Many sales practices are in the gray area between being completely ethical and completely unethical. Five ethical considerations faced by the sales manager in dealing with salespeople are the level of sales pressure to place on a salesperson; decisions concerning a salesperson's territory; whether to be honest with the salesperson; what to do with the salesperson who is ill; and employees' rights.

LEVEL OF SALES PRESSURE

What is an acceptable level of pressure to place on salespeople? Should managers establish performance goals that they know a salesperson has only a 50/50 chance of attaining? Should the manager acknowledge that goals were set too high? If circumstances change in the salesperson's territory—for example, a large customer goes out of business—should the manager lower sales goals?

These are questions all managers must consider. They have no right or wrong answers. Managers are responsible for their groups' goals and have a natural tendency to place pressure on salespeople so these goals will be reached. Some managers can motivate their people to produce at high levels without applying pressure, while others place tremendous pressure on their salespeople to attain sales well beyond their quotas. However, managers should set realistic and obtainable goals. They should consider individual territory situations. If this is done fairly and sales are still down, then pressure may be applied.

DECISIONS AFFECTING TERRITORY

Management makes decisions that affect sales territories and, in turn, salespeople. For example, a company might increase the number of sales territories, which often necessitates splitting up a single territory. A salesperson spends years building up a territory to its current sales volume. If it is cut, customers are taken away. If the salesperson has worked on a commission basis, this would mean a decrease in earnings.

Consider the situation of reducing the number of sales territories. What procedures do you use? Several years ago a large manufacturer of health and beauty aids (shaving cream, toothpaste, shampoo) reduced the number of its territories to lower selling costs. So, for example, three territories became two. Here is how one of its salespeople described it:

> I made my plane reservations to fly from Dallas to Florida to our annual national meeting. Beforehand I was told to bring my records up-to-date and bring them to the regional office in Dallas. Don't fly, drive to Dallas. I drove from Louisiana to Dallas with my bags packed to go to the national meeting. I walked into the office with my records under my arm. My district and regional managers were there. They told me of the reorganization and said I was fired. They asked for my car keys. I called my wife, told her what happened, and then caught a bus back home. There were five of us in the region that were called in that day. Oh, they gave us a good job recommendation—it's just the way we were treated. Some people had been with the company for five years or more. They didn't go by tenure but where territories were located.

Companies must deal with the individual in a fair and straightforward manner. It would have been better for the managers of these salespeople to go to their home towns and personally explain the changes to them. Instead, they treated the salespeople in an unprofessional manner.

One decision affecting a territory is what to do with extra-large customers, sometimes called key accounts. Should they be taken away from the salesperson and made house accounts? If so, responsibility for contacting the customer can be given to someone from the home office (house) or to a key account salesperson. The local salesperson may not get credit for sales to this account even though the customer is located in the salesperson's territory. A salesperson states the problem in this manner:

> I've been with the company 35 years. When I first began I called on these people who had one grocery store. Today they have 208. The buyer knows me. He buys all of my regular and special greeting cards. They do whatever I ask. I made $22,000 in commissions from their sales last year. Now management wants to make it a house account.

Here the salesperson loses money. It is difficult to treat the salesperson fairly in this situation. The company does not want to pay these large commissions, and 90 percent of the 208 stores are located out of the salesperson's territory. Managers should carefully explain this to the salesperson. Instead of taking the full $22,000 away from the salesperson, they could pay a 20 percent commission as a reward for building up the account.

To Tell the Truth?

Should salespeople be told they are not promotable, they are marginal performers, or they are being transferred to the poorest territory in the company in hopes that they will be forced to quit? Good judgment must prevail. In general, sales managers prefer to tell the truth.

Do you tell the truth when you fire a salesperson? If a fired employee has tried and has been honest, many sales managers will tell prospective employers that the person quit voluntarily rather than was fired. One manager put it this way: "I feel she can do a good job for another company. I don't want to hurt her future."

The Ill Salesperson

How much help do you give the alcoholic, drug-addicted, AIDS-infected, or physically or mentally ill salesperson? More and more companies require their salespeople to seek professional help for alcohol or drug abuse. If the salespeople honestly try to improve, companies offer support and keep them in the field. Yet the company can only go so far. The firm cannot have an intoxicated or "high" salesperson calling on customers. Once the illness begins having a negative effect on business, the salesperson is taken out of the territory. Sick leave and worker's compensation will cover expenses until the salesperson is cured. The manager who shows a sincere, personal interest in helping the ill salesperson can greatly increase the person's chances of recovery.

Employee Rights

Sales managers must be current on the ethics and laws regarding their employees' rights and develop strategies for their organizations in addressing employee rights. Here are several important questions to which all managers should know the answers:

1. Under what conditions can an organization fire sales personnel without committing a legal violation?
2. What rights do and should sales personnel have regarding the privacy of, and access to, their employment records?
3. What can organizations do to prevent sexual harassment in the workplace?

Employee rights are rights desired by employees regarding the security of their jobs and the treatment administered by their employer while on the job, irrespective of whether such rights are currently protected by law or collective bargaining agreements of labor unions. Let us briefly examine these three questions.

TERMINATION AT WILL   Early in this century many courts were adamant in their strict application of this common-law rule to terminate at will. For example, the **termination-at-will rule** was used in a 1903 case, *Boyer v. Western Union Tel. Co.,* 124 F 246, CCED Mo. (1903), in which the court upheld the company's right to discharge its employees for union activities and indicated that the results would be the same if the company's employees had been discharged for being Presbyterians. Later on, in *Lewis v. Minnesota Mutual Life Ins. Co.,* 37 NW 2d 316 (1949), the termination-at-will rule was used to uphold the dismissal of the life insurance company's best salesperson—even though no apparent cause for dismissal was given, and the company had promised the employee lifetime employment in return for an agreement to remain with the company.

Only recently have court decisions and legislative enactments moved the pendulum of protection away from the employer and toward the rights of the individual employee through limitations on the termination-at-will rule.

Although many employers claim that essentially all their rights have been taken away, they still retain the right to terminate sales personnel for poor performance, excessive absenteeism, unsafe conduct, and generally poor organizational citizenship. However, employers must maintain accurate records of these events for their employees and must inform the employees on where they stand. To be safe, employers should also have a grievance process for employees to ensure that due process is respected.

PRIVACY   Today it is more important than ever to keep objective and orderly personnel files. They are critical evidence that employers have treated their employees fairly and with respect and have not violated any laws. Without these, organizations may get caught on the short end of a lawsuit.

Although several federal laws influence record keeping, they are primarily directed at public employers. However, many private employers are moving on their own initiative to give their employees the right to access their personnel files and to prohibit the file information from being given to others without employee consent. In addition, employers are casting out of their personnel files any nonjob-related information and ending hiring practices that solicit that type of information.

SEXUAL HARASSMENT   **Cooperative acceptance** refers to the right of employees to be treated fairly and with respect regardless of race, sex, national origin, physical disability, age, or religion while on the job as well as when applying and regarding job security. Not only does this mean that employees have the right not to be discriminated against in employment practices and decisions, but it also means that employees have the right to be free of sexual harassment.

Today the right not to be discriminated against is generally protected under Title VII, the Age Discrimination in Employment Act, the Rehabilitation Act, the Vietnam Era Veteran's Readjustment Assistance Act, numerous court decisions, and state and local government laws. Though the right to be free of sexual harassment is addressed explicitly in fewer laws, it has been found in the 1980 Equal Employment Opportunity Commission (EEOC) guidelines that state sexual harassment is a form of sex discrimination. Defining sexual harassment as a form of sex discrimination under Title VII is also found in numerous court decisions.

Employers must prevent sexual harassment and discrimination. This can be done with top management support, grievance procedures, verification procedures, training for all employees, and performance appraisal and compensation policies that reward those who practice antiharassment behavior and punish those who do not.

REASONS FOR RESPECTING EMPLOYEE RIGHTS   Companies should recognize that important strategic purposes are served by respecting employee rights. The main ones are:

- Providing a high quality of work life.
- Attracting and retaining good sales personnel; making recruitment and selection more effective and their need less frequent.
- Avoiding costly back-pay awards and fines.
- Establishing a balance between employee rights and obligations and employer rights and obligations.

Both organizations and employees benefit from respecting employee rights. Organizations benefit from reduced legal costs, since not observing many employee rights is illegal. Their images as good employers increase, resulting in enhanced organizational attractiveness. This in turn makes it easier for the organization to recruit a pool of potentially qualified applicants. Although expanded employee rights, especially job security, may reduce needed management flexibility and thus profitability, they may be an impetus for better planning, resulting in increased profitability.

Increased profitability also may result from the benefits employees receive when their rights are observed: Employees may experience the feelings of being treated fairly and with respect, increased self-esteem, and a heightened sense of job security. Employees who have job security may be more productive and committed to the organization than those without job security. As employees begin to see the benefit of job security guarantees, organizations also gain through reduced wage-increase demands and greater flexibility in job assignments.

Salespeople, as well as sales managers, occasionally may be involved in some of the following issues.

SALESPEOPLE'S ETHICS IN DEALING WITH THEIR EMPLOYERS

MISUSING COMPANY ASSETS

The most often misused company assets are automobiles, expense accounts, samples, and damaged-merchandise credits. All can be used for personal gain or as bribes and kickbacks to customers. For example, a credit for damaged merchandise when no damage has occurred or valuable product samples can be given to customers.

In addition, a salesperson can misuse company assets by taking trade secrets to a future employer who is also the company's competitor. The salesperson also might be violating a noncompetition or nonsolicitation agreement he or she has signed. Many companies use these agreements to prevent employees from taking trade secrets with them. To avoid any future legal problems, the prospective employer should investigate whether or not the salesperson is subject to such a clause. Famous Fixtures, a Milwaukee company, asks candidates for sales positions what agreements they have signed with their current employers. It asks these questions early in the interviewing process to prevent future problems.[8]

MOONLIGHTING

Salespeople are not closely supervised; consequently, they may be tempted to take a second job, perhaps on company time. Some salespeople attend college on company time. For example, a salesperson may enroll in an evening master of business administration (M.B.A.) program and take off in the early afternoon to prepare for class. Employers find these practices unacceptable.

CHEATING

A salesperson may not play fair in sales contests. If a contest starts in July, the salesperson may not turn in sales orders for the end of June and then may lump them with July sales. Some might arrange, with or without the customer's permission, to ship unnecessary or unwanted merchandise that is held until payment is due and then returned to the company after the contest is over. The salesperson also may overload the customer to win the contest.

AFFECTING FELLOW SALESPEOPLE

Often the unethical practices of one salesperson can affect fellow salespeople. Someone who cheats in winning a contest is taking money and prizes from other salespeople. A salesperson also may fail to split commissions with fellow employees or may take customers away from them.

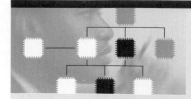

MANAGING THE SALES TEAM
ARE THESE SOCIALLY RESPONSIBLE ACTIONS?

Often it is difficult to determine whether actions taken by sales executives are for profit or social motives. For example, consider the following:

- Training and educational programs for salespeople.
- A company heavily dependent on government contracts hiring minority groups.
- Setting fair sales goals.
- Fairly rewarding salespeople's performance.
- Paying salaries above industry averages.

- Providing extensive medical and life insurance coverage.
- Holding sales meetings in resort areas.

Some people argue these are responsible acts done unselfishly, while others say these are good business practices that help maximize a firm's sales and profits. The argument is simply rhetorical. These are examples of good business practices carried out in a responsible manner. No longer can the sales function be carried out in a manner other than one fair to salespeople, customers, and society.

TECHNOLOGY THEFT

Picture this: A salesperson or sales manager quits, or is fired, and takes the organization's customer records to use for his or her, or a future employer's, benefit. How is that possible? Well, it's getting easier to do these days because more and more companies provide their sales personnel with computers, software, and data on their customers.

ETHICS IN DEALING WITH CUSTOMERS

"We have formal, ethical policies called 'business conduct guidelines,'" FMC's (an oil supply company) Alan Killingsworth says. "These guidelines thoroughly discuss business conduct and clearly state what is proper conduct and how to report improper conduct. All sales personnel review them and even sign a statement that they understand the guidelines."

Numerous ethical situations may arise in dealing with customers. All sales organizations should create specific business conduct guidelines, such as FMC's. Some of the more common problems faced by sales personnel include the following.

BRIBES OR GIFTS

A salesperson may attempt to bribe a buyer. Money, gifts, entertainment, and travel opportunities may be offered.[9] At times a thin line exists between good business and the misuse of a bribe or gift. A $10 gift to a $10,000 customer may be merely a gift, but how do we define a $1,000 gift for a $1 million customer? Many companies forbid their buyers to take gifts of any size from salespeople. However, bribery does exist. The U.S. Chamber of Commerce estimates that, of the annual $40 billion "white collar crimes," bribes and kickbacks account for $7 billion.

Buyers may ask for cash, merchandise, or travel payment in return for placing an order with the salesperson. Imagine you are a salesperson working on 5 percent straight commission. The buyer says, "I'm ready to place a $20,000 order for office supplies with you. However, another salesperson has offered to pay my expenses for a weekend in Las Vegas in exchange for my business. You know, $500 tax free is a lot of money." You quickly calculate that your commission is $1,000. You still make $500. Would it be hard to pass up that $500?[10]

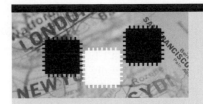

SELLING AND MANAGING GLOBALLY
CUSTOMER GIFT GIVING IN JAPAN

The highly ritualized practice of exchanging presents is paramount to cultivating long-lasting relationships in Japan. Gifts are exchanged with customers, between companies doing business together, and between employees and superiors within Japanese companies. As important as the gifts may be, so are the decorative wrappings and even the stores where the items are purchased.

As for presents, IBM's Vince Matal rules "the more lavish the better." Matal claims that he learned his lesson the hard way after returning from a few buying missions with totally inappropriate items, such as books, which are generally deemed too practical or unimpressive for the gift swap. Matal finds luxuries to be more on target, such as French chocolates, fine wine, or hard-to-come-by treats, such as the honeydew melon he once presented to a client. "It was a $55 melon," Matal says, "It was an imported melon from—possibly California—I don't know. But they sure don't grow them in Japan. It came in a beautiful wooden crate. And then we gave them a beautiful bottle of very nice champagne. Another $90. So we gave a $150 gift, easily, and that was regular."

Sources: Richard F. Beltramini, "Exploring the Effectiveness of Business Gifts: A Controlled Field Experiment," *Journal of the Academy of Marketing Science* (Winter 1992): 87–91; and Bristol Voss, "Eat, Drink, and Be Wary," *Sales & Marketing Management* (January 1992): 49–54.

MISREPRESENTATION

Today, even casual misstatements by salespeople can put a company on the wrong side of the law.[11] Most salespeople are unaware that they assume legal obligations—with accompanying risks and responsibilities—every time they approach a customer. However, we all know that salespeople sometimes "oversell." They exaggerate the capabilities of their products or services and sometimes make false statements just to close a sale.

Often buyers depend heavily on the technical knowledge of salespeople, along with their professional integrity. Yet both sales managers and staff find it difficult to know just how far they can go with well-intentioned sales talk, personal opinion, and promises. They do not realize that by using certain statements they can embroil themselves and their companies in a lawsuit and ruin the very business relationship they are trying to establish.

When a customer relies on a salesperson's statements, purchases the product or service, and then finds that it fails to perform as promised, the supplier can be sued for **misrepresentation** and **breach of warranty.** Companies around the United States have been liable for million-dollar judgments for making such mistakes, particularly when their salespeople sold high-ticket, high-tech products or services.

However, you can avoid such mistakes if you are aware of the law of misrepresentation and breaches of warranty relative to the selling function and follow strategies that keep you and your company out of trouble. Salespeople must understand the difference between "sales puff" (opinions) and statements of fact and the legal ramifications of each. Preventive steps exist for salespeople to follow, and they should work closely with management so they can avoid time-consuming delays and costly legal fees.

WHAT THE LAW SAYS   Misrepresentation and breach of warranty are two legal causes of action; that is, they are theories on which an injured party seeks damages.[12] These two theories differ in the kind of proof required and the type of damages that may be awarded by a judge or jury. However, both commonly occur in the selling context and are treated similarly for our purposes. Both typically arise when a salesperson makes erroneous statements or offers false promises regarding a product's characteristics and capabilities.

Not all sales statements have legal consequences, however. When sales personnel loosely describe their product in glowing terms ("Our service can't be beat; it's the best around"), such statements are viewed as "opinions" and generally cannot be relied on by a customer, supplier, or wholesaler. Thus a standard defense used by lawyers in misrepresentation and breach of warranty lawsuits is that a purchaser cannot rely on a salesperson's puffery, because taking these remarks at face value is unreasonable.

However, when a salesperson makes claims or promises of a "factual nature" regarding a product's inherent capabilities (for example, the results, profits, or savings that will be achieved, what it will do for a customer, how it will perform, and so on), the law treats these comments as statements of fact and warranties.

The subtle difference between sales puffery and statements of fact is often difficult to distinguish. No particular form of words is necessary, and each case is analyzed according to its circumstances. Generally, the less knowledgeable the customer, the greater the chances the court will interpret a statement as actionable. The following is an actual recent case and illustrates this point.

An Example   An independent sales rep sold heavy industrial equipment. He went to a purchaser's construction site, observed his operations, and then told the president of the company that his proposed equipment would "keep up with any other machine then being used and that it would work well in cooperation with the customer's other machines and equipment."

The customer informed the rep that he was not personally knowledgeable about the kind of equipment the rep was selling and that he needed time to study the rep's report. Several weeks later, he bought the equipment based on the rep's recommendations.

After a few months he sued the rep's company, claiming that the equipment did not perform according to the representations in sales literature sent prior to the execution of the contract and to statements made by the rep at the time of the sale. The equipment manufacturer defended itself by arguing that the statements made by the rep were nonactionable opinions made innocently by the rep, in good faith, with no intent to deceive the purchaser.

The court ruled in favor of the customer, finding that the rep's statements were "predictions" of how the equipment would perform; this made them more than mere sales talk. The rep was held responsible for knowing the capabilities of the equipment he was selling, so his assertions were deemed to be statements of fact, not opinions. Furthermore, the court stated that it was unfair that a knowledgeable salesperson should take advantage of a naïve purchaser.

PRICE DISCRIMINATION

Some customers may be given price reductions and promotional allowances and support, while others are not, even though under certain circumstances this is in violation of the Robinson–Patman Act of 1936. The act does allow sellers to grant what are called quantity discounts to large buyers based on savings in the cost of manufacturing, but individual salespeople or managers may not practice price discrimination to improve sales.

You need to be careful about charging different prices to customers who buy similar quantities of a product. Once a customer finds out he or she paid a higher price, you lose his or her business. The customer receiving the lower price may not trust you. In addition, your company may be sued, and you could lose your job.

TIE-IN SALES

To purchase a particular line of merchandise, a buyer may be required to buy other unwanted products. This is called a **tie-in sale** and is prohibited under the Clayton Act when it substantially lessens competition. Yet the individual salesperson or manager can do this. For example, the salesperson of a popular line of cosmetics might tell a buyer, "I have a limited supply of the merchandise you want. If all of your 27 stores will display, advertise, and push my total line, I may be able to supply you." That means the buyer will need to buy ten items never purchased before. Is this good business? It's illegal!

EXCLUSIVE DEALERSHIP

When a contract requires a wholesaler or retailer to purchase products from one manufacturer, it is an exclusive dealing. If it tends to lessen competition, it is prohibited under the Clayton Act.

RECIPROCITY

A salesperson says, "I can get my company to buy all of our office supplies from your company if you buy lighting fixtures, supplies, and replacement parts from us." Is this a good business practice?

Reciprocity refers to buying a product from someone if the person or organization agrees to buy from you. The Federal Trade Commission and the U.S. Department of Justice will consider such a trade agreement illegal if it results in hurting or eliminating competition. Most purchasing agents find this practice offensive. Because reciprocal sales agreements may be illegal, if not unethical, buyers are often afraid to even discuss this with sellers.

SALES RESTRICTIONS

To protect consumers against sometimes unethical sales activities of door-to-door salespeople, legislation exists at the federal, state, and local levels. The Federal Trade Commission and most states have adopted **cooling-off laws.**[13]1 This provides for a cooling-off period (usually three days) in which the buyer may cancel the contract, return any merchandise, and obtain a full refund. The law covers sales of $25 or more made door-to-door. It also states that the seller must give the buyer a written, dated contract or receipt of the transaction and must tell the buyer about the three-day cancellation period.

Many cities require persons selling directly to consumers to be licensed by the city in which they are doing business if they are not residents and to pay a license fee. A bond also may be required. These city ordinances are often called **Green River ordinances** because the first legislation of this kind was passed in Green River, Wyoming, in 1933. This type of ordinance helps protect the consumer and aids local companies by making it more difficult for outside competition to enter their market.

Both the cooling-off laws and the Green River Ordinance were passed to protect consumers from salespeople using unethical, high-pressure sales tactics. These statutes, and others, were necessary because a few salespeople used unethical practices in sales transactions.[14]

MANAGING SALES ETHICS

Over the years a number of surveys have been undertaken to determine managers' views of business ethics. In general, they found the following:

- All managers feel they face ethical problems.

- Most managers feel they and their employers should be more ethical.
- Managers are more ethical with their friends than with people they do not know.
- Even though they want to be more ethical, some managers lower their ethical standards in order to meet job goals.
- Managers are aware of unethical practices in their industry and company ranging from price discrimination to hiring discrimination.
- Business ethics can be influenced by an employee's supervisor and by the company environment.

Organizations are concerned about how to improve their social responsiveness and ethical climate. Managers must take active steps to ensure the company stays on ethical ground. Management methods to help organizations be more responsive include (1) top management taking the lead, (2) carefully selecting leaders, (3) establishing and following a code of ethics, (4) creating ethical structures, (5) formally encouraging whistle-blowing, (6) creating an ethical sales climate, and (7) establishing control systems.

FOLLOW THE LEADER

The organization's chief executive officer, president, and vice presidents should clearly champion efforts for ethical conduct. Others will follow their lead. Their speeches, interviews, and actions need to constantly communicate the organization's ethical values. The Business Roundtable, an association of chief executives from 250 large corporations, issued a report on ethics policy and practice in companies such as Boeing, Chemical Bank, General Mills, GTE, Xerox, Johnson & Johnson, and Hewlett-Packard.[15] The report concluded that no point emerged more clearly than the crucial role of top management in guiding the social and ethical responsibilities of their organization.

LEADER SELECTION IS IMPORTANT

Since so few individuals are at the principled level of moral development, it is critical to carefully choose managers. Only people who have the highest level of integrity, standards, and values should assume leadership positions.

ESTABLISH A CODE OF ETHICS

A **code of ethics** is a formal statement of the company's values concerning ethics and social issues. It states which values or behaviors are expected and which ones will not be tolerated. These values and behaviors must be backed by management's action. Top management support gives needed assurance the code will be followed.

Two types of codes of ethics exist: principle-based statements and policy-based statements. Principle-based statements are designed to affect corporate culture, define fundamental values, and contain general language about company responsibilities, quality of products, and treatment of employees. General statements of principle are often called corporate credos. Examples are GTE's "Vision and Values," Johnson & Johnson's "The Credo," and Hewlett-Packard's "The HP Way."[16]

Policy-based statements generally outline the procedures to be used in specific ethical situations. These situations include marketing practice, conflicts of interest, observance of laws, proprietary information, political gifts, and equal opportunities. Examples of policy-based statements are Boeing's "Business Conduct Guidelines," Chemical Bank's "Code of Ethics," GTE's "Code of Business Ethics" and its "Anti-Trust and Conflict of Interest Guidelines," and Norton's "Norton Policy on Business Ethics."[17]

CREATE ETHICAL STRUCTURES

Ethical structures represent the various systems, positions, and programs a company can undertake to implement ethical behavior. Nationwide Mutual Insurance Co. of Columbus, Ohio, for example, created an office of ethics and compliance to instill a system of values in its employees and sales agents. The first phase of the office's work was to assess the ethics environment of the company. Later, the company opened an ethics and compliance information resource center to answer concerns over the telephone.[17]

Numerous firms have ethics committees or an ombudsperson. An **ethical committee** is a group of executives appointed to oversee company ethics. The committee assumes responsibility for disciplining wrongdoers. Taking this responsibility is essential if the organization is to directly influence employee behavior. An **ethical ombudsperson** is an official given the responsibility of corporate conscience who hears and investigates ethical complaints and informs top management of potential ethical issues. For example, companies like IBM, Xerox, and Proctor & Gamble have ethics committees reporting directly to the CEO.

ENCOURAGE WHISTLE-BLOWING

Employee disclosure of illegal, immoral, or illegitimate practices on the employer's part is called whistle-blowing. Companies can provide a mechanism for whistle-blowing as a matter of policy. All employees who observe or become aware of criminal practices or unethical behavior should be encouraged to report the incident(s) to their supervisors, to a higher level of management, or to an appropriate unit of the organization, such as an ethics committee. Formalized procedures for complaining can encourage honest employees to report questionable incidents. For example, a company could provide its employees with a toll-free number to report unethical activities to top management. This "silent witness" program may be more successful than other procedures because it allows employees to report incidents without actually having to confront colleagues or supervisors. This program is especially valuable if the employee's own manager is involved in unethical practices. However, with programs such as these, careful verification is necessary to guard against the use of the program as a means of retribution against managers or other employees.

CREATE AN ETHICAL SALES CLIMATE

The single most important factor to improve the climate for ethical behavior in a sales force is the action taken by top-level managers. Sales managers must help develop and support their codes of ethics. They should publicize the codes and their opposition to unethical sales practices to their subordinate managers and their salespeople. They can achieve a stronger level of ethical awareness during sales meetings, in training sessions, and when contacting customers while working with salespeople.

ESTABLISH CONTROL SYSTEMS

Finally, control systems must be established. Methods should be employed to determine whether salespeople give bribes, falsify reports, or pad expenses. For example, sales made from low bids could be checked to determine whether procedures were correctly followed. Dismissal, demotion, suspension, or reprimand would be possible penalties (for example, commissions would not be paid on a sale associated with unethical sales practices).

Overall, management must make a concerted effort to create an ethical climate within the workplace in order to best serve customer and organizational goals.

MANAGEMENT IN ACTION: ETHICAL DILEMMA
IT'S JUST WHAT I NEED!

Jim Baker, your neighbor, is a regional sales manager for a large firm that manufactures consumer goods. Jim's company is repeatedly written up as one of the top ten sales forces in America in *Sales & Marketing Management* magazine. Jim's firm, in fact, grosses more than $20 billion per year in sales.

As a sales manager, you are always interested in what Jim is doing because it frequently gives you good management ideas. Since your company is not a competitor and is much smaller than Jim's, he freely shares ideas and sales training materials with you. He also knows you don't tell anyone about his help.

Tonight, Jim shows up at your door with a new piece of computer software his salespeople will use for such things as customer leads, reports, forecasting, callback reminders, and product and customer histories. You had been looking for a program like this for months, but none had offered this wide range of features together in one piece of software. Though you had considered having someone pro-

gram and create a customized software package that would include all of the features your sales force needs, estimates for this customized software package were well out of the range of your company's budget. However, Jim's package is similar to what the customized package would have offered you. It is exactly what you need. Unfortunately, this cost is also too high for you to buy it. Jim says you can make copies. He says, "Who cares about this stuff? No one gets caught anyway. You're not hurting anyone. It will be a great help to you."

WHAT DO YOU DO?
1. Duplicate copies for each of your salespeople and yourself.
2. Thank Jim, but decline his offer to copy or use the disk.
3. Ask Jim if you can simply use the disk from time to time. Since you are not actually *copying* the software, you are not breaking the law, but you can still use the software whenever you want.

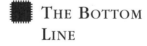

THE BOTTOM LINE

Ethics and social responsibility are hot topics for managers. Ethical behavior pertains to values of right and wrong. Ethical decisions and behavior are typically guided by a value system. For an individual manager, the ability to make correct ethical choices will depend on both personal and organizational characteristics. An important personal characteristic is one's level of moral development. Corporate culture is an organizational characteristic that influences ethical behavior.

Corporate social responsibility concerns a company's values toward society. How can organizations be good corporate citizens? The model for evaluating social performance uses four criteria: economic, legal, ethical, and discretionary.

Social responsibility in business means profitably serving employees and customers in an ethical and lawful manner. Extra costs can accrue because a firm takes a socially responsible action, but this is a part of doing business in today's society, and it pays in the long run.

Salespeople and managers realize that their business practices, including international dealings, should be carried out in an ethical manner. They must be ethical in dealing with their salespeople, their employers, and their customers. Ethical standards and guidelines for sales personnel must be developed, supported, and policed. In the future, ethical selling practices will be even more important to conducting business profitably. Techniques for improving social responsiveness include leadership, codes of ethics, ethical structures, whistle-blowing, and establishing control systems. Finally, research suggests that socially responsible organizations perform as well as—and often better than—organizations that are not socially responsible.

■ KEY TERMS FOR SALES MANAGERS

Social responsibility, 26
Stakeholder, 26
CCC GOMES, 26
Discretionary responsibility, 28
Preconventional moral development level, 29
Conventional moral development level, 29

Principled moral development level, 29
Ethics, 30
Ethical behavior, 30
Employee rights, 33
Termination-at-will rule, 33
Cooperative acceptance, 34
Misrepresentation, 37
Breach of warranty, 37

Tie-in sale, 39
Reciprocity, 39
Cooling-off laws, 39
Green River ordinances, 39
Code of ethics, 40
Ethical committee, 41
Ethical ombudsperson, 41

■ MANAGEMENT APPLICATION QUESTIONS

1. Which of the following situations represents socially responsible actions by firms?
   a. Creating recreation facilities for sales personnel.
   b. Paying for college courses associated with an M.B.A. program.
   c. Allowing sales personnel to buy company products at a discount.
   Do managers feel business ethics can be improved? Describe ethical situations that sales managers may face in dealing with salespeople.

2. Imagine yourself in a situation of being encouraged to inflate your expense account. Do you think your choice would be most affected by your individual moral development or by the cultural values of the company for which you worked? Explain.

3. Have you ever experienced an ethical dilemma? Evaluate the dilemma with respect to its impact on other people.

4. Discuss the difference between *sales puffery* and *misrepresentation* and how to avoid making mistakes that may prove costly to the firm.

5. Lincoln Electric considers customers and employees to be more important stakeholders than shareholders. Is it appropriate for management to define some stakeholders as more important than others? Should all stakeholders be considered equal?

6. Do you think a code of ethics combined with an ethics committee would be more effective than only leadership for implementing ethical behavior? Discuss.

7. It is often hard for a manager to determine what is "right" and even more difficult to put ethical behavior into practice. A manager's ethical orientation often brings him or her into conflict with people, policies, customers, or bosses. Consider the following dilemmas. How would you handle them?
   a. A well-liked member of your sales group with an excellent record confides to you that he has AIDS. Although his illness has not affected his performance, you're concerned about his future health and about the reactions of his coworkers. What do you do?
      (1) Tell him to keep you informed about his health, and say nothing to his coworkers.
      (2) Arrange for him to transfer to an area of the organization where he can work alone.
      (3) Hold a staff meeting to inform his coworkers, and ask them how they feel about his continued presence on your team.
      (4) Consult your human resources officer on how to proceed.
   b. During a reorganization, you're told to reduce staff in the department you manage. After analyzing staffing requirements, you realize the job would be a lot easier if two professionals, who are both over age 60, would retire. What do you do?
      (1) Say nothing and determine layoffs based purely on performance and length of service.
      (2) Schedule a meeting with both employees, and ask if they'd consider early retirement.
      (3) Schedule a meeting with all staff, and ask if anyone is interested in severance or early retirement.

        (4) Lay off the older workers.

c. One of your salespeople has recently experienced two personal tragedies: Her husband filed for divorce, and her mother died. Although you feel genuine sympathy for her, her work is suffering. A report you completed, based on inaccurate data she provided, has been criticized by your boss. Your manager asks you for an explanation. What do you do?

        (1) Apologize for the inaccuracies, and correct the data.

        (2) Tell your boss that the data supplied by your colleague was the source of the problem.

        (3) Say your colleague has a problem and needs support.

        (4) Tell your boss that because of your workload, you didn't have time to check the figures in the report.

d. Your firm recently hired a new sales manager who is at the same level you are. You do not like the man personally and consider him a rival professionally. You run into a friend who knows your rival well. You discover from the friend that your rival did not attend Harvard as he stated on his résumé and in fact has not graduated from any college. You know his supposed Harvard background was instrumental in getting him hired. What do you do?

        (1) Expose the lie to your superiors.

        (2) Without giving names, consult your human resources officer on how to proceed.

        (3) Say nothing. The company obviously failed to check him out, and the lie will probably surface on its own.

        (4) Confront the man with the information, and let him decide what to do.

e. During a changeover in the sales department, you discover your company has been routinely overcharging customers for services provided to them. Your supervisors say repayment of charges would wreak havoc on company profits. Your company is federally regulated, and the oversight commission has not noticed the mistake. Your bosses say the problem will never come to light, and they will take steps to correct the program so it never happens again. What do you do?

        (1) Contact the oversight commission.

        (2) Take the matter public, anonymously or otherwise.

        (3) Say nothing. It is now in the hands of the bosses.

        (4) Work with the bosses on a plan to recognize the company's error, and set up a schedule of rebates that would not unduly penalize the company.

f. In this morning's mail, you receive plans and samples for a promising new product from a competitor's disgruntled employee. What do you do?

        (1) Throw the plans away.

        (2) Send the samples to your research department for analysis.

        (3) Notify your competitor about what is going on.

        (4) Call the FBI.

■ FURTHER EXPLORING THE SALES WORLD

1. Contact your local Better Business Bureau, and prepare a report on local laws regulating the activities of salespeople.

2. The *Journal of Marketing* has a section titled "Legal Developments in Marketing." Report on several legal cases found in this section related to a firm's personal selling activities.

3. Talk to a sales manager about the social, ethical, and legal issues involved in the job. Does the manager's firm have

    a. A code of ethics?

    b. An ethics committee?

    c. An ethical ombudsperson?

    d. Procedures for whistle-blowing?

Get a copy of any of the manager's materials relating to topics discussed in this chapter. Report on your findings.

SALES MANAGEMENT EXPERIENTIAL EXERCISE

ETHICAL WORK CLIMATES

On a separate sheet of paper answer the following questions by writing down the number that best describes an organization for which you have worked:

		Disagree				Agree
1.	Whatever is best for everyone in the company is the major consideration here.	1	2	3	4	5
2.	Our major concern is always what is best for the other person.	1	2	3	4	5
3.	People are expected to comply with the law and professional standards above other considerations.	1	2	3	4	5
4.	In this company, the first consideration is whether a decision violates any law.	1	2	3	4	5
5.	It is very important to follow company rules and procedures here.	1	2	3	4	5
6.	People in this company strictly obey company policies.	1	2	3	4	5
7.	In this company, people are mostly out for themselves.	1	2	3	4	5
8.	People are expected to do anything to further the company's interests, regardless of the consequences.	1	2	3	4	5
9.	In this company, people are guided by their own personal ethics.	1	2	3	4	5
10.	Each person in this company decides for himself or herself what is right and wrong.	1	2	3	4	5

Total Score _____

Add up your score. These questions measure the dimensions of an organization's ethical climate. Questions 1 and 2 measure caring for people, questions 3 and 4 measure lawfulness, questions 5 and 6 measure rules adherence, questions 7 and 8 measure emphasis on financial and company performance, and questions 9 and 10 measure individual independence. Questions 7 and 8 are reverse scored. (That is, if you answered 5, your actual score to write down is 1; a 4 is really a 2, etc.) A total score above 40 indicates a very positive ethical climate. A score from 30 to 40 indicates an above-average ethical climate. A score from 20 to 30 indicates a below-average ethical climate, and a score below 20 indicates a very poor ethical climate.

Go back over the questions and think about changes you could have made to improve the ethical climate in the organization. Discuss with other students what you could do as a manager to improve ethics in future companies you work for.[18]

CASE 2.1

MISSISSIPPI LEASING, INC.
Is This Legal?

As the sales manager of a printing company in Oxford, Mississippi, you are about to invest in a car leasing program that involves 18 company cars for your sales staff. With your comptroller, you have examined several leasing programs. You have narrowed down your selection to two leasing companies that offer very similar terms. You are meeting with the president of Equilease, a company with which you have never done business before. You know from your own prospect files that one of your sales representatives has previously tried to call on the purchasing manager of Equilease to get some of the company's printing business; however, he could not sell the account.

As you meet with the president for lunch, you gently steer the conversation in the direction of printing services. Since he is very knowledgeable about printing services and prices, you ask him about ballpark prices charged by his existing supplier. You feel you could provide his company with higher quality service at a better price.

Since the president of Equilease is in a good mood, you think about setting up a win/win situation. You are considering an offer like "Let's make this a double win. I'll give you 100 percent of our leasing business if you'll consider giving us 50 percent of your printing business. Fair enough?"

QUESTION
As the sales manager, what would you actually do?

ILLINOIS OFFICE MACHINES, INC.
How Should You Handle Competition?

You are in the very competitive business of selling office machines. You and one of your salespeople have an appointment with the senior partner of a large medical center. This potential buyer already has studied several competitive products. Her "hot buttons" are low operating costs and low maintenance. You know that four competitors have demonstrated their product to your prospect. After you have shown her the benefits of your product, she asks you: "Tell me, what makes your machine better than brand X?" You restate some of your obvious product benefits, and she comes back with "The salesman with company X told me that they use a special kind of toner that is far superior to what you are using for your machine and that it will increase the lifetime of their machine by 20 percent."

You know that this is an obvious lie, so you ask: "What evidence did this salesperson give you to prove his claim?" She shows you a customer testimonial letter that talks about how satisfied they were with their machine, but it says nothing about longer lifetime. You reply carefully: "That's the first time I have ever seen a letter praising a brand X machine."

Next, she shows you another piece of paper, a chart that graphically illustrates the operating costs of five different brands. The chart says on the bottom "Marketing Research—Brand X, 2000." It shows your machine with the highest operating costs over a five-year period, and it shows brand X in the leading position with 50 percent lower operating costs. You are stunned by this unfair competitive comparison. You try to control your temper and think about saying "They always are much better than we are on paper, but when it comes to reality, we outperform them every time."

QUESTIONS

1. Is an ethical conflict occurring here? Why or why not?
2. Would you try to reverse your prospect's decision? Why or why not?

Part II

Planning the Sales Team's Efforts

Sales Managers are involved in planning, organizing, setting sales objectives, forecasting market demand, budgets, sales quotas, and overseeing the operation of individual sales territories. These activities form the bases of sales planning. Part II includes Chapter 3, "Building Relationships through Strategic Planning," Chapter 4, "The Market-Driven Sales Organization," Chapter 5, "Forecasting Market Demand and Sales Budgets," Chapter 6, "Design and Size of Sales Territories," and Chapter 7, "Sales Objectives and Quotas."

CHAPTER 3

BUILDING RELATIONSHIPS
THROUGH STRATEGIC PLANNING

CHAPTER OUTLINE

IMPORTANCE OF CORPORATE PLANNING

WHAT IS MARKETING?

MARKETING'S IMPORTANCE TO THE FIRM

ESSENTIALS OF A FIRM'S MARKETING EFFORT

RELATIONSHIP MARKETING

TECHNOLOGY BUILDS RELATIONSHIPS AND PARTNERS

RELATIONSHIP MARKETING AND THE SALES FORCE

STRATEGIC PLANNING AND THE SALES MANAGEMENT PROCESS

LEARNING OBJECTIVES

Strategic planning helps an organization build long-term relationships with its customers. This chapter will help you better understand:

■ The importance of corporate strategy.

■ How strategic planning differs from tactical operational planning.

■ The relationship between marketing and sales force strategies.

■ The role of personal selling in the firm's marketing relationship efforts.

Xerox noticed that it was missing out on a large amount of business when some of its largest users of high-end printers went to other companies for mid-range and low-end printers. They knew that they needed to develop a methodological plan to help them manage customer relationships across multiple products, often with different selling processes.

Many office managers do not prefer to buy low-end equipment through a direct sales force, and Xerox did not work with dealers and distributors. Because of this, Xerox had to allow its sales reps to deal with indirect sales channels in order to help customers buy the way that they desire most. The company made the transition from a purely direct sales model to one that mixes direct and indirect sales.

Using this strategy, Xerox sales reps are able to refer an account to a dealer for a lower-end product. Their sales quota and compensation are then both properly adjusted. In this way, Xerox is formalizing its policy of encouraging the cross-selling of one product line against another, even when these lines are distributed through conflicting channels.

A well-informed sales force can dramatically improve cross-selling techniques, enabling the company to realize the full potential of its customers, as in the case of Xerox. Cross-selling is one of the best ways to increase customer's profitability, but the organization of this selling effort is usually a problem for most companies. This is not difficult to imagine considering the divisions formed by cross-selling, where separate entities rarely communicate with each other or share customer information.

To prevent this, there must be a method to the madness. As in the case of Xerox, a little organization and planning went a long way in the terms of sales. By informing their sales force and making the transformations needed, their cross-selling efforts have definitely allowed them to realize the full selling capability of their sales force and the profit potential of their customers.[1] ■

For several decades, Xerox operated on the frontier of a planning field now called strategic management. Xerox continues to be a leader in this area. In this chapter, we examine the important concepts and processes involved in planning and strategic management as related to marketing and the sales force.

Top corporate management understands the tremendous importance of the sales force in the organization's business and marketing efforts. Marketing generates revenues for the firm. For many businesses, the sales force comprises the firm's total marketing efforts. When the sales force hits its sales target, the corporation achieves its profit goals. Unfortunately, the reverse is also true. Chapter 3 discusses the important relationships among corporate leaders, the marketing department, and the sales force. Let's begin by examining the importance of corporate planning.

IMPORTANCE OF CORPORATE PLANNING

Planning is the conscious, systematic process of making decisions about goals and activities that an individual, group, work unit, or organization will pursue in the future and the use of resources to obtain them. Planning is not an informal or haphazard response to a crisis; it is a purposeful effort, directed and controlled by managers and often drawing on the knowledge and experience of employees throughout the organization. Planning provides individuals and work units with a clear map to follow in their future activities, but at the same time this map may allow for individual circumstances and changing conditions.

STRATEGIC PLANNING

Strategic planning involves making decisions about the organization's long-term goals and strategies. Senior executives are responsible for the development and execution of the strategic plan, although they usually do not personally formulate or implement the entire plan. **Strategic goals** are major targets or end results that relate to the long-term survival, value, and growth of the organization. Strategic managers usually establish goals that reflect both effectiveness (providing appropriate outputs) and efficiency (a high ratio of outputs to inputs). Typical strategic goals include various measures of return to shareholders, profitability, quantity and quality of outputs, market share, productivity, and contribution to society. When appropriate, goals should be quantified and linked to a time frame. They should be acceptable to the managers and employees charged with achieving them, and they should be consistent both within and among work units.

A **strategy** is a pattern of actions and resource allocations designed to achieve the goals of the organization. The strategy an organization implements is an attempt to match the skills and resources of the organization with the opportunities found in the external environment; that is, every organization has certain strengths and weaknesses. The actions, or strategies, the organization implements should be directed toward building strengths in areas that satisfy the wants and needs of consumers and other key actors in the organization's external environment.

TACTICAL AND OPERATIONAL PLANNING

Once the organization's strategic goals and plans are identified, they become the basis of planning undertaken by tactical and operational managers. Goals and plans become more specific and involve shorter periods of time as planning moves from the strategic level to the operational level. **Tactical planning** translates broad strategic goals and plans into specific goals and plans relevant to a definite portion of the organization, often a functional area such as marketing or human resources. Tactical plans focus on the major actions a unit must take to fulfill its part of the strategic plan. A **tactic,** then, is the operational means by which an organization intends to reach its objectives. **Operational planning** identifies the specific procedures and processes required at lower levels of the organization. Operational managers usually develop plans for very short periods of time and focus on routine tasks such as sales, production runs, delivery schedules, and human resource requirements.

ESTABLISHING A MISSION AND VISION

The first step in strategic planning is establishing a mission and vision for the organization. The **mission** is the basic purpose and values of the organization, as well as its scope of operations. It is a statement of the organization's reason to exist. The mission often is written in terms of the general clients it serves. Depending on the scope of the organization, the mission may be broad or narrow.

The **strategic vision** moves beyond the mission statement to provide a perspective on where the company is headed and what the organization can become. Although the terms *mission* and *vision* often are used interchangeably, the vision statement ideally clarifies the long-term direction of the company and its strategic intent. **Values** represent the firm's mode of conduct toward others and itself. Figure 3.1 illustrates how Kodak has outlined its vision, mission, and value.

Strategic goals evolve from the mission, vision, and values of the organization. The chief executive officer of the organization, with the input and approval of the board of directors, establishes both the mission and the major strategic goals. The mission and the strategic goals influence everyone who has contact with the organization.

The company's mission, vision, values, objectives, strategies, and tactics are often referred to as a **strategic plan.** These six factors interrelate, ensuring the best allocation of the firm's resources to fulfill its mission and objective. This is achieved by answering four key questions:

1. Where are we?
2. Where do we want to be?
3. How should we get there?
4. Can we afford it?

FIGURE 3.1

KODAK'S VISION, MISSION, AND VALUES

VISION
"Our heritage has been and our future is to be the World Leader in Imaging."
MISSION
"Build a world-class, results-oriented culture . . .
by providing . . . solutions to capture, store, process, output,
and communicate . . . images to people and machines
anywhere, anytime . . . bringing differentiated, cost-effective
solutions . . . to the marketplace and with
flawless quality . . . through a diverse team of energetic
employees with the world-class talent and skills
necessary to sustain Kodak as the World Leader in Imaging.
In this way, we will achieve our
fundamental objective of Total Customer Satisfaction,
and our consequent goals of Increased Global
Market Share and Superior Financial Performance."
VALUES
(1) Respect for the Dignity of the Individual
(2) Integrity (3) Trust (4) Credibility
(5) Continuous Improvement and Personal Renewal

Source: Kodak's 1999 annual report.

FIGURE 3.2

RELATIONSHIP BETWEEN
THE ORGANIZATION'S
STRATEGIC PLAN AND
OPERATIONAL PLANS

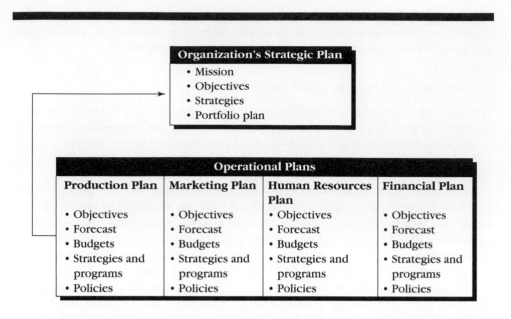

To answer these questions, planners must begin at the top of the organizational pyramid and work down. The reason for beginning at the top is clear. Top management's job is to make key assumptions, state the organization's purpose and philosophy, establish priorities, and draw up major policies. After—and only after—these factors are in place can strategic planners make specific objectives and action statements.

In well-managed organizations, a direct relationship exists between strategic planning and the planning done by managers at all levels. The planning foci and the time perspectives will, of course, differ. Figure 3.2 illustrates the relationship between the strategic plan and operational plans. It indicates that all plans should be derived from the strategic plan while also contributing to its achievement.

So who tells the marketing group what to do? The top management of the organization. And what is it that marketing does for the firm?

WHAT IS MARKETING?

To be successful in today's competitive marketplace, businesspeople realize they must first determine specific human needs and wants and then produce goods and services to satisfy them. A company, whether it is Ford Motor Company or a small retailer, is in business to create satisfying goods and services for its customers. The success of such goods and services is determined solely by the consumers who buy them. Goods and services that do not satisfy consumers are forced quickly from this competitive market because consumers do not buy them.

What does a business firm do in the U.S. economy? Reduced to a basic level, businesses have two major functions: *production* of goods or creation of services and *marketing* those goods and services. If you asked the general public what the term *marketing* means, many would say it means *selling*. Selling, in turn, usually implies public advertising and personal selling. Yet the act of selling is only one part of a firm's marketing activities.

DEFINITION OF MARKETING

Numerous definitions of *marketing* exist. This book will use the American Marketing Association's definition:

Marketing is defined as the process of planning and executing the conception, pricing, promotion, and distribution of goods, services, and ideas to create exchanges that satisfy individual and organizational objectives.[2]

This definition of *marketing* is the most widely accepted by marketing educators and practitioners. It indicates that marketing is more than advertising or personal selling. Marketing involves a diverse set of activities directed at a wide range of goods, services, and ideas. These activities involve the development, pricing, promotion, and distribution of satisfying goods and services to consumers and industrial users. Marketing activities are therefore very important both to the individual company and to the economy as a whole.

Marketing considerations should be the most critical factors guiding all short-range and long-range planning in any organization. Too often, unfortunately, American business has been oriented toward production. Products have been designed by engineers, manufactured by production people, priced by marketers, and then given to sales managers to sell. That procedure generally won't work in today's environment of intense competition and constant change. Just building a good product will not result in a company's success. The product must be marketed to consumers before its full value is realized.

As shown in Figure 3.3, the marketing group is the link between customers and the organization. Salespeople are part of marketing. They are in direct contact with customers.

Marketing people typically have these four basic objectives to accomplish:

1. Maximize sales of existing products in existing markets.

MARKETING'S IMPORTANCE TO THE FIRM

FIGURE 3.3   THE MARKETING GROUP—THE LINK BETWEEN CUSTOMERS AND THE ORGANIZATION

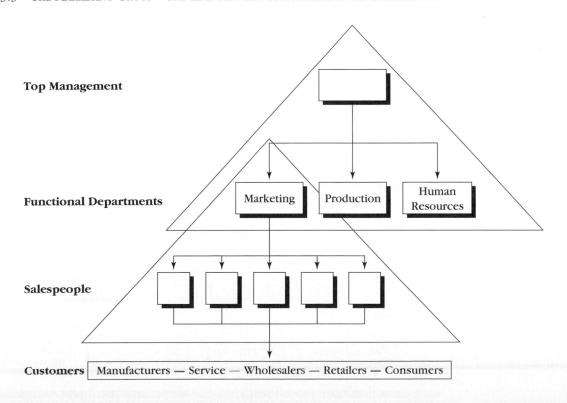

Top Management

Functional Departments

Marketing   Production   Human Resources

Salespeople

Customers | Manufacturers — Service — Wholesalers — Retailers — Consumers

2. Develop and sell new products.
3. Develop new markets for existing or new products.
4. Provide the quality of service necessary for customers to be satisfied with their transactions and to continue doing business with the organization.

MARKETING GENERATES SALES

As is apparent from the first three objectives, the main role of marketing in an organization is to generate revenues. Financial people manage the money that marketing generates, and production people use it to create goods and services. Marketing activities are therefore very important to the organization because they must generate sales to stay in business.

MARKETING PROVIDES QUALITY SERVICE

Marketing personnel also help make sure customers are satisfied with their purchases. Marketing provides more to the marketplace than a needed product. It helps generate sales by providing the quality of service customers expect.

Excellent service pays off because it creates true customers—customers who are glad they selected a product because of the company and its service performance. True customers are like annuities: They keep pumping revenue into the firm's coffers. Such customers return to buy more and influence others to buy from the company. Quality service thus helps the organization to maximize sales.

ESSENTIALS OF A FIRM'S MARKETING EFFORT

The essentials of a firm's marketing effort include its abilities (1) to determine the needs of its customers and (2) to create and maintain an effective marketing mix that satisfies customer needs. As shown in Figure 3.4, a firm's **marketing mix** consists of four main elements—product, price, distribution or place, and promotion—a marketing manager uses to market goods and services. It is the marketing manager's responsibility to determine how best to use each element in the firm's marketing efforts.

PRODUCT: IT'S MORE THAN YOU MIGHT THINK

A **good** is a physical object that can be purchased. A radio, a house, and a car are examples of a good. A **service** is an action or activity done for others for a fee. Lawyers, plumbers, teachers, and taxicab drivers perform services. The term *product* refers to both goods and services.

FIGURE 3.4

FOUR MARKETING-MIX ELEMENTS AND FOUR PROMOTION ACTIVITIES

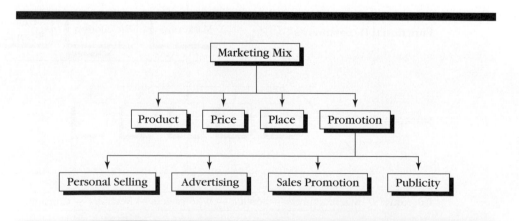

When you think of a product, most likely you imagine some tangible object you can touch, such as a radio or an automobile. However, a product is more than you might think.

A **product** is a bundle of tangible and intangible attributes, including packaging, color, and brand, plus the services and even the reputation of the seller. People buy more than a set of physical attributes. They buy "satisfaction," such as what the product will do, its quality, and the image of owning the product. Take a Polo shirt, for example. What is the difference (besides price) between a Polo shirt and a Sears-brand shirt? Both shirts perform the same function of clothing someone. So why do some people buy the Polo? For many people, image plays an important part in their decision to purchase a Polo shirt. So a seller of a product is selling more than what a product will do for people.

Two general types of products exist. Consumer products are produced for, and purchased by, households for their use. Industrial products are sold primarily for use in producing other products.

Firms spend enormous amounts of time and money creating the products they sell. They carefully research what customers want before developing a product, giving consideration not only to the product but also to its package design, trademarks, warranties, and service policies.

Research and development and strategies for selling new products are major corporate marketing department activities. Often, sales personnel have little input on what products should be produced. Their involvement in selling the product begins after the product has been produced.

SERVICES ARE PRODUCTS

Most people think of selling physical products, such as candy, cars, or copiers. Yet one of the biggest trends today is the phenomenal growth of careers in selling services. The government sector, with its schools, post offices, and military, is in the service business. The private, nonprofit sector, with its charities, churches, colleges, and hospitals, is in the service business. A good part of the whole business sector, with its airlines, banks, insurance companies, and law firms, is in the service business. Rock music bands and barbers perform services. As you see, the production of services may or may not be linked to a physical product.

Figure 3.5 shows a mix of goods and services on a continuum ranging from relatively pure goods to relatively pure services. Few truly pure goods or services exist because each usually requires the other. When taking a college course, for example, you may buy a textbook. Similarly, buying salt, soup, and toothpaste requires supporting services such as totaling up what you owe and sacking the good(s) at the cashier's checkout.

The special nature of services stems from several distinctive characteristics that create selling challenges and opportunities. Sales techniques for services are substantially different from those for goods.

FIGURE 3.5   A GOOD/SERVICE CONTINUUM

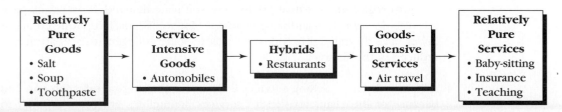

Intangibility   Because services are essentially intangible, customers cannot sample—taste, feel, see, hear, or smell—services before they buy them. This feature places some strain on sellers. Salespeople must concentrate on the benefits to be derived from the service, rather than emphasizing the service itself. An insurance salesperson thus may stress service benefits such as guaranteed payment of a child's college expenses or a retirement income of so many dollars per month. AT&T salespersons discuss how business users can cut selling costs by using AT&T's long-distance calling system.

Inseparability   Services often cannot be separated from the seller. Moreover, some services must be created and dispensed simultaneously. For example, dentists create and dispense almost all their services at the same time.

From a sales standpoint, inseparability frequently means that a direct sale is the only possible channel of distribution and that a seller's services cannot be sold in very many markets. These characteristics also limit the scale of a firm's operation. One person can repair only so many autos in a day or treat only so many medical patients.

As an exception to the inseparability feature, the services may be sold by a person representing the creator-seller. Travel agents, insurance brokers, and rental agents, for instance, represent and help promote services other institutions produce.

Heterogeneity   A service industry, or even an individual seller of services, cannot standardize output. Each unit of the service is somewhat different from other units of the same service. For example, an airline does not give the same quality of service on each trip. All repair jobs a mechanic does on automobiles are not of equal quality. The difficulty of judging the quality of a service is an added complication. (Of course, we can say the same for some goods.) It is particularly difficult to forecast quality in advance of buying a service. For example, a person pays to see a ball game without knowing whether it will be an exciting one, well worth the price of admission, or a dull performance.

Perishability and Fluctuating Demand   Services are highly perishable, and they cannot be stored. Unused electric power, empty seats in a stadium, and idle mechanics in a garage all represent business lost forever. Furthermore, the market for services fluctuates considerably by season, by day of the week, and by hour of the day. Many ski lifts lie idle all summer, and in some areas golf courses go unused in the winter. The use of city buses fluctuates greatly during the day.

Some notable exceptions to this generalization regarding the perishability and storage of services exist. In health and life insurance, for example, the service is purchased and then held by the insurance company (the seller) until needed by the buyer or the beneficiary. This hold constitutes a type of storage.

The combination of perishability and fluctuating demand creates product-planning, pricing, and promotional challenges for service company executives. Some organizations have developed new uses for idle plant capacity during off-seasons. Thus, during the summer, several ski resorts operate their ski lifts for hikers and sightseers who want access to higher elevations.

Advertising and creative pricing also stimulate demand during slack periods. Hotels offer lower prices and family packages for weekends. Telephone companies offer lower rates during nights and weekends. In some college towns, apartment rates are reduced in the summer.

A Tough Sell   Selling services is the most challenging sales job you could have because of the characteristics of services. Intangibles are often difficult for many prospects to understand; these include insurance, financial investments, car repairs, and health services such as surgery.

PRICE: IT'S IMPORTANT TO SUCCESS

The corporate marketing department also determines each product's initial price. This process involves establishing each product's normal price and possible special discount prices. Since product price often is critical to customers, it is an important part of the marketing mix. **Price** refers to the value or worth of a product that attracts the buyer to exchange money or something of value for it.

Companies develop varied pricing techniques and methods for their salespeople to use. For example, General Motors, Chrysler, and Ford have offered consumers cash rebates to increase automobile sales. Companies such as Quaker Oats, Kraft, and Lever Brothers send out discount coupons to consumers and offer special price reductions to retailers on their products so retailers will reduce their prices. Some salespeople use offers of a price reduction in their sales presentations to entice a retailer to purchase large quantities of a product. Getting large shipments to retailers and other types of customers leads to another element of the marketing mix.

DISTRIBUTION: IT HAS TO BE AVAILABLE

The marketing manager also determines the best method of distributing a product. **Distribution** refers to the channel structure used to transfer products from an organization to its customers. It is important to have the product available to customers in a convenient and accessible location.

DISTRIBUTION MOVES PRODUCTS TO CUSTOMERS   Customers can be individuals and organizations. Customers fall into one of three groups: households, firms, and governments.

A **household** refers to a decision-making unit buying for personal use. Every individual in the economy belongs to a household. Some households consists of a single person, while others consist of families or of groups of unrelated individuals, such as two or three students sharing an apartment.

A **firm** is an organization that produces goods and services. All producers are called firms, no matter how big they are or what they produce. Automakers, farmers, banks, and insurance companies are all firms. Firms can be for profit, such as General Electric, or nonprofit, such as the American Heart Association. They purchase goods and services to enable them to fulfill their production goals.

A **government** is an organization that has two functions: the provision of goods and services to households and firms and the redistribution of income and wealth. Examples of the goods and services supplied by the government are national defense, law enforcement, public health, transportation, and education.

Several examples of distribution channels for consumer and industrial products are shown in Figure 3.6. The manufacturer of consumer products may have its salespeople selling directly to the household consumer. Mary Kay Cosmetics and Tupperware, for example, sell only to household consumers.

DISTRIBUTION USES RESELLERS   Many manufacturers, however, sell directly to resellers—wholesalers or retailers. Wholesalers buy goods in large quantities and resell them, usually in smaller quantities, to retailers or to industrial or business users. Retailers buy goods from others and sell them to ultimate consumers for their personal use. Two main distribution channels for manufacturers of industrial products are selling directly to the industrial user, such as another manufacturer, or selling to a wholesaler, who in turn sells to another manufacturer or industrial user.

PROMOTION: PEOPLE HAVE TO BE TOLD

Promotion, as part of the marketing mix, increases company sales by communicating product information to potential customers. The four basic parts of a firm's

FIGURE 3.6   TYPICAL DISTRIBUTION CHANNELS FOR CONSUMER AND INDUSTRIAL PRODUCTS

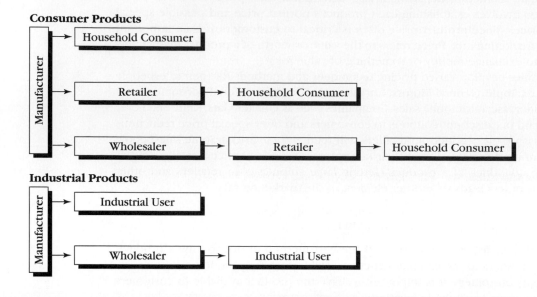

promotional effort are **personal selling, advertising, publicity,** and **sales promotion.** These are briefly explained in Table 3.1. The company's sales force is one segment of the firm's promotional effort. In addition to informing people about a product's existence, promotion educates consumers about the product's features, advantages, and benefits; tells them where to buy it; and makes them aware of its price versus its value. Marketers must ask themselves, "What are the best promotional elements to use in selling a product?" This decision is made only after consideration of the type of product and the customers who will buy it.

The marketing manager determines what proportion of the firm's budget to allocate to each product and how much emphasis on each of the promotional variables to give to each product. Firms typically spend more money on their sales force than on advertising and promotion. Organizations selling in industrial markets spend a

TABLE 3.1

PROMOTIONAL ACTIVITIES

- *Personal selling.* Personal communication of information to persuade a prospective customer to buy something—a good, service, idea, or whatever—that satisfies an individual's needs.
- *Advertising.* Nonpersonal communication of information paid for by an identified sponsor such as an individual or an organization. Modes of advertising include television, radio, direct mail, catalogs, newspapers, and outdoor advertising such as billboards.
- *Publicity:* Nonpersonal communication of information that is not paid for by an individual or organization. Information appears in media such as television, radio, and newspaper usually in the form of news releases, but is not paid for by the sponsoring company.
- *Sales promotion.* Involves activities or materials used to create sales for goods or services. The two types of sales promotion are consumer and trade sales promotion. Consumer sales promotion includes free samples, coupons, contests, and demonstrations to consumers. Trade sales promotion encourages wholesalers and retailers to purchase and to sell aggressively using devices such as sales contests, displays, special purchase prices, and free merchandise.

TABLE 3.2

EXAMPLES OF EACH
MARKETING-MIX
ELEMENT

PRODUCT	PRICE	PLACE	PROMOTION
Brand name	Credit terms	Channels	Advertising
Features	Discounts	Inventory	Coupons
Image	List price	Locations	Free samples
Packaging	Promotional allowances	Retailers	Personal selling
Quality level		Transportation	Product displays
Returns		Wholesalers	Publicity
Services			Sales management
Sizes			Trade shows
Warranties			

higher percentage of the promotional budget on their sales force than do consumer-goods manufacturers. Industrial purchasing agents do not see advertisements for their products on television and rely on salespeople to keep them informed.

THE GOAL OF A MARKETING MIX

The goal of designing a marketing mix is simple. The organization's marketing group strives to create a marketing mix for the right product, at the right price, at the right time, and with the right promotional effort.

COORDINATION IS IMPORTANT   No matter what marketing-mix activities are used, they must be coordinated with the marketing elements shown in Table 3.2. The most effective marketing effort considers the needs of customers and coordinates activities from all four elements.

Manufactured by 3M, Post-it Notes are a perfect example of a product that nearly failed under an ineffective marketing mix. Originally tested in several medium-sized markets, the product had drab sales results. Post-it Notes were successful only after 3M redesigned the marketing strategy to incorporate essential activities from all four marketing-mix elements. Concentrating on the Boise, Idaho, test market, management decided the flaws in the original marketing program were too little promotion and no demonstration of how the notes worked or what they were designed to do.

The redesigned strategy joined five activities from the original marketing mix with two more activities to increase the promotional element. The original components were, first, *product:* 3M recognized that a large market existed for note pages that could be peeled off and attached easily. Second, it capitalized on the pad's unique *feature,* a "totally imperfect" adhesive. Third, 3M made the pads available in a variety of *sizes.* Fourth, the company offered special promotional *prices.* And fifth, for *place,* 3M had local dealers available through which businesses could place orders. 3M added two components to increase promotion in the campaign: Sixth, for a *nonpersonal promotion,* 3M took out eight two-color inserts in the *Boise Statesman* newspaper illustrating the use of Post-it Notes; and, seventh, 3M increased the power of *personal selling* through a combined use of *free samples* and *demonstration.* 3M hired Manpower Temporary Services personnel to go from office to office in the Boise business section demonstrating the pads and leaving samples. Local dealers then dispatched salespeople to close the sales.

Following this campaign, Post-it Notes immediately caught on. Within four years they went into national production and were the most successful product in 3M's history. By overlooking the promotional element, 3M almost had had a failure on hand. Adding promotional activities coordinated the marketing plan and enabled Post-it Notes to succeed. You can see that coordination of all major elements is essential.

RELATIONSHIP MARKETING

Organizations today are starting to target new and present customers. The emphasis is shifting from selling to customers *today* to creating customers for *tomorrow*. Thus businesses are finally beginning to think more long term than short term.

Relationship marketing is the creation of customer loyalty. Organizations use combinations of products, prices, distribution, promotions, and service to achieve this goal. Relationship marketing is based on the idea that important customers need continuous attention.

An organization using relationship marketing does not seek a simple sale or transaction. It targets a major customer it would like to sell to now and in the future. The company wants to demonstrate to the customer that it has the capabilities to serve the account's needs in a superior way, particularly if a *committed relationship* can be formed. The type of selling needed to establish a long-term collaborative relationship is complex. General Motors, for example, prefers suppliers who can sell and deliver a coordinated set of goods and services to many locations, who can quickly solve problems that arise in their different locations, and who can work closely with GM to improve products and processes.

Most companies, unfortunately, are not set up to meet all of these requirements. The level of customer relationships businesses form still varies. Many organizations continue to sell to customers and then forget them. Other organizations develop a close relationship—even a partnership—with their customers.

LEVELS OF RELATIONSHIP MARKETING

What type relationship should an organization have with its customers? Is the cost of keeping a relationship worth it? To answer these questions, let's define the three general levels of selling relationships with customers:

- **Transaction selling:** Customers are sold to and not contacted again.
- **Relationship selling:** The seller contacts customers after the purchases to determine if they are satisfied and have future needs.
- **Partnering:** The seller works continually to improve its customers' operations, sales, and profits.

Many organizations must focus solely on the single transaction with each customer. When you go to McDonald's and buy a hamburger, that's it. You never personally hear from them again unless you return for another purchase. The same thing happens when you go to a movie, rent a video, open a bank checking account, visit the grocery store, or have your clothes cleaned. Each of these examples involves low-priced, low-profit products. Large numbers of geographically dispersed customers purchase them. This makes it very difficult and quite costly to contact customers. Such businesses often are forced to use transactional marketing.

Relationship marketing focuses on the transaction—making the sale—along with follow-up and service after the sale. The seller contacts the customer to ensure satisfaction with the purchase. The Cadillac Division of General Motors contacts each buyer of a new Cadillac to determine his or her satisfaction with the car. If that person is not satisfied, General Motors works with the retailer selling the car to make the customer happy with the purchase.

Partnering is a phenomenon of the 1990s. Businesses' growing concern over the competition not only in America but also internationally revitalized their need to work closely with important customers. The familiar 80/20 principle states that 80 percent of sales often come from 20 percent of a company's customers. Organizations now realize the need to identify their most important customers and designate them for their partnering programs. The organization's best salespeople are assigned to sell to and service these customers. Let's take a closer look at partnering since it is becoming so important to organizations.

Technology is the most dramatic force shaping an organization's marketing efforts today. Technology has released such wonders as antibiotics; CD-ROM computer hardware and software; cable television; and nonfattening, tasty, nutritious foods. Scientists today are working on a startling range of new technologies that will revolutionize our products and production processes. The most exciting work is occurring in biotechnology, solid-state electronics, robotics, medicine, and health.

In addition to having high-tech products to sell, salespeople are using technology in their jobs to sell and provide service to customers. Desktop and laptop computers, videocassette recordings, CD-ROM videodiscs, automatic dialers, electronic mail, fax machines, and teleconferencing are quickly becoming popular sales tools. Not only are sales and inventory information transferred much faster with high technology, but also specific computerized decision-support systems have been created for sales managers and sales representatives.

Computer technology helps salespeople increase the speed with which they can find and qualify leads, gather information prior to a customer presentation, reduce their paperwork, report new sales to the company, and provide service to customers after the sale.

Here is how computer technology works at Johnson Manufacturing. The company developed a laptop-computer-based software package consisting of several applications. The sales personnel expense program allows salespeople to easily and accurately record expenses and speeds up reimbursements. Using telephone modems, they send their weekly expenses directly to accounting for payment and to their managers for approval. Using the sales-inquiry function, the Johnson sales force can retrieve the latest account-specific information, including phone numbers, addresses, recent developments, and prices. Electronic mail allows the sales reps to rapidly receive and send messages to others. Various business forms, such as territory work plans and sales-call reports, are filled out faster and sent electronically. The Johnson sales force automation package includes an appointment calendar, a to-do list, a spreadsheet, and a graphics software package that helps salespeople prepare charts and graphs for customer presentations.

Technology is expensive. Hardware, software, and training are large investments. Yet companies believe technology is worth the cost because of decreased travel and paperwork, more productive sales calls, and better customer service.

TECHNOLOGY BUILDS RELATIONSHIPS AND PARTNERS

RELATIONSHIP MARKETING AND THE SALES FORCE

A major issue in an organization's relationship marketing program is the role of the sales force. Firms use salespeople in many ways. However, these four basic questions are guidelines that define the role of the sales force:

1. How much selling effort is necessary to gain and hold customers?
2. Is the sales force the best marketing tool, compared to advertising and other sales promotion methods, in terms of cost and results?
3. What type of sales activities—for example, technical assistance and frequent or infrequent sales calls—will be necessary?
4. Can the firm gain strength relative to its competition with its sales force?

The answers to these questions come largely from an analysis of competition, the target markets, and the firm's product offerings. These help determine (1) sales force objectives, (2) the level of resources—such as personnel and money—allocated to sales force activities, and (3) the importance of personal selling in the marketing mix. As illustrated in Figure 3.7, the sales force is becoming the center of the marketing universe for many organizations because of four reasons: relationships, revenues, service, and implementation.

FIGURE 3.7   THE SALES FORCE AS THE CENTER OF THE MARKETING SOLAR SYSTEM

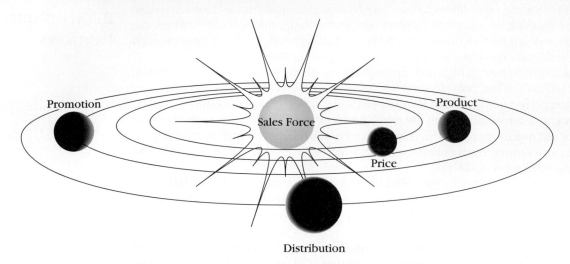

PERSONAL SELLING BUILDS RELATIONSHIPS

Personal selling is an essential element of any organization's marketing mix. The main functions of personal selling are to generate revenue and to provide service to help satisfy customers. These build relationships and are the keys to success in today's competitive marketplace.

SALESPEOPLE GENERATE REVENUE

Once a product or service has been developed, it must be sold. To generate profitable sales, the organization has to promote the product. In today's competitive marketplace, a firm has to make personal selling a main promotional method for selling the product.

Think about this! Virtually every product you see in any factory, office, school, or retail store was sold to that organization by a salesperson. The next time you are in a grocery store, stop and look around at the thousands of products. Salespeople are responsible for making those products available for you to buy.

Because they are involved in person-to-person discussions, salespeople can customize their sales presentations to the individual needs of specific people and organizations. Salespeople can observe a customer's reaction to a sales approach and make needed adjustments immediately. Advertising cannot do this.

It's true that advertising attracts the consumer's attention and arouses desire; however, ads don't close any sales. Personal selling does. In many cases, personal selling ends in an actual sale.

The promotional method of selling is, however, costly. The high cost is due to the expense of developing and operating a sales force. Yet this drawback is compensated for by salespeople's ability to contact specific individuals.

Organizations need a good personal-selling effort to compete in today's marketplace. Salespeople help make companies successful. Many of us feel salespeople have made America great!

SALESPEOPLE PROVIDE SERVICE

If an organization wants a customer to return—to be satisfied—it must provide an excellent level of service quality. **Service quality** is a subjective assessment that customers arrive at by evaluating the service level that they perceive being delivered.

Some customers may get the product they wanted but become unhappy because of poor service. In fact, many consumers feel they never really get service anymore. Take this story, for example. "Mom," the little girl said, "do all fairy tales begin with 'Once upon a time'?" "No dear," her mother said. "Sometimes they begin with 'The couch you ordered has arrived at our warehouse and should be delivered within five working days.'"

"Where is service today?" is a question frequently asked by customers. An organization's salespeople can help ensure that organizations' service standards are higher than customers' expectations.

SALESPEOPLE IMPLEMENT RELATIONSHIP MARKETING

Who better to help develop a relationship marketing program than the personnel constantly in contact with customers—salespeople? As noted earlier, relationship marketing is based upon the philosophy of being customer oriented. Organizations following this philosophy rely on their sales personnel to help implement customer-contact programs. Salespeople sell customers products; when customers are unhappy, salespeople take care of the problems.

Marketing links the organization with the customers. Salespeople who help customers find just the right products to satisfy their particular requirements are providing good service. Salespeople who are knowledgeable, who listen well and come up with answers, and who stand by their customers after the sales are made are also providing good service. Sales and service are inseparable in the formation of relationships.

Although sales does operate within marketing strategy, field sales management is not without its own strategic possibilities. Close coordination with marketing strategy is imperative, but the sales manager also has to define strategic goals for the selling organization, the selling program, and the selling effort.

STRATEGIC PLANNING AND THE SALES MANAGEMENT PROCESS

PLANNING A SALES STRATEGY

Planning a sales strategy requires that the sales manager begin with a mastery of the firm's marketing strategy. Then specific strategies for sales management of the selling organization must follow.

Remember, from prior sections, sales managers already know what the defined markets are, what the product mix will be, what new products are proposed to come on stream, what new additions to the business are planned, and what the policies for channels, distribution, pricing, and marketing information will be. If these are not done by a marketing department, such as might occur in a large firm, managers will need answers to the questions raised in the prior section before starting their field sales management strategies.

THE DEVELOPMENT OF SALES STRATEGIES

No one can sell his or her way to success with a weak product line, a dying market, or an ineffective pricing structure. Even if such problems do not occur, a well-thought-out sales strategy is needed to be successful in today's competitive marketplace. The following three areas of sales strategy are required:

1. A clear picture of the present situation, including the strengths, weaknesses, and problems of your sales and managerial staff, as well as the threats, risks, and opportunities that exist in your marketplace.

2. Well-defined strategies covering every major aspect of the selling units or departments, including territory, account, and call-management strategies by product line; this involves developing one-year and multiyear plans.
3. Income and expense budgets and a profit plan based on sound sales forecasts and a knowledge of pricing policy.

THE PRESENT SITUATION   A strategy for managing the sales effort starts with an honest definition of the present condition. This is to find some useful and productive objectives for the coming year and some strategies for the next five years. Both internal and external situations must be examined.

Managers have little room for self-deception or apathy when looking at their present organization, products, territories, and personnel. Strengths and weaknesses should be carefully examined. Strengths might include things such as (1) most of the salespeople are experienced; (2) the firm is a leader in technically innovative products; and (3) the company is financially sound. Weaknesses might be (1) the sales force is aging, and the firm cannot seem to attract and keep able young people; (2) products are priced higher than competitors'; and (3) competition is increasing, and the company's market share is slowly declining.

PREPARATION OF THE MULTIYEAR STRATEGIC PLAN   The next step is to develop a long-run, multiyear strategic plan for the sales force. A *sales strategic plan* includes the following four major questions:

1. What is the sales department's present condition? This is a final summary of the earlier statements of condition. The summary should not be an essay or a tome but a series of one-line statements of the major internal and external conditions important enough to be included in action plans for the coming years.
2. What trends are apparent? Here the sales manager looks at the situation and tries to project it into the future. If nothing is done differently, where would the sales force and the organization be in one year? Two years? Five years?
3. What are the most important objectives? These are missions over the next three to five years, not just next year. They might include such things as increasing salespeople's training, redesigning the compensation program, and developing computer software for field sales managers, plus providing them advanced educational programs.
4. What are the strategies for getting these objectives accomplished? This might require:
   - Increasing the budget and personnel for the sales training department.
   - Having an outside consulting firm overhaul the compensation plan.
   - Hiring one or more persons to develop software or contracting an outside vendor.

Each strategic statement should then be turned into an operational plan and put into the hands of responsible people who will make commitments to execute the plan. The whole idea is that times have changed—and will probably continue to change—and if the sales department does not adapt, ultimately the company will be a follower instead of a leader.

FINANCIAL PLANNING IS A PART OF THE SALES STRATEGY   All of the foregoing activities have been speculative. The pondering and studying precede taking any specific action. Next, the sales manager is ready to make some financial commitments and projections.

The sales department cannot do much about certain aspects of profit planning. It has no control, for example, over the cost of goods sold. Manufacturing cost accounting will define that element. It has no direct responsibility for general, administrative, and overhead expenses. Costs of materials and labor for producing the product are accountable elsewhere. Therefore, most sales departments have two principal concerns: (1) revenue produced, and (2) selling expense

The difference between these two is the contribution to the organization's profit from the sales effort. These calculations should be projected into the future, not only for a year ahead at budget time but also for several years in advance as part of the strategic field sales plan.

Chapter 5 discusses forecasting sales, so the important aspects of profit planning will not be fully discussed here. However, the accurate forecasting of sales and of the costs, or expenses, required to generate those sales is a major part of the sales strategy plan. Remember that sales managers are thinking strategically (in multiyear terms) for the field sales organization, so projection of these revenues and expenses beyond the first year should incorporate the manager's best estimates about the effect of changes in strategy, market plans, product innovations, enlargement in geographic markets, and sales forecasts.

When sales managers begin operational planning for field sales, they should define these in shorter terms, including monthly and quarterly estimates and forecasts for the single year ahead. They should not be unduly worried about the precise accuracy of future years. Managers will do a forecast of three to five years ahead every year and can adjust it based on what they learned and experienced in the current year.

These multiyear figures will help the firm find its best operating objectives. Thus, when top management sits down with the field sales managers, or sales reps if they are the next level down, they will have some specific targets at which to aim.

SETTING NEXT YEAR'S SALES PLAN

The basic objectives of the sales force are to make sales to customers and potential customers, to provide service to customers, and to transmit information received from customers to the firm. Given the general marketing plan, the sales manager's job is to define the activities of the sales force in support of each product or group of products. A sales force strategy will help the sales manager use the sales force efficiently to achieve the firm's market-share objectives.

Specific sales force objectives are usually derived from broader marketing and corporate objectives. Corporate objectives may be measured through market share, return on investment, or profit ratio, while the sales force might have objectives measured on the basis of the following:

- *Contribution to profits.* The sales force obtains the products from the company at cost or at a percentage markup above cost. The sales force then sells the products at a markup. This margin (cost minus selling price), minus all costs related to selling the product, represents the sales force's contribution to corporate net profit.
- *Return on assets (ROA) managed by the sales force.* The sales force makes capital investments in such things as automobiles, training materials, or demonstration product models. The return on these investments can be used as a measure of efficiency by subtracting current sales expenses—for instance, salary—from gross profit on sales volume.
- *Sales/cost ratio.* This is the ratio of sales force expenses to dollar sales volume.
- *Market share.* To use this measure, management must determine whether the sales force has the major impact on sales and not price, advertising, and so forth.

Objectives such as gross margins, or ROA, will not by themselves manage the sales organization. They must be broken down and converted into objectives that tell whether various sales units (for example, regions and districts) and individuals are contributing to those overall goals. The firm's top sales management make such conversions and communicate them to lower ranks.

For the field sales organization, dollar figures alone are of great value in measuring overall results. However, they are only one part of the data needed for the key sales areas dealing with territories, accounts, sales calls, and self-management.

The first class of objectives proposed—the regular, ongoing, and ordinary goals of the sales organization—consists mainly of experience-based numbers tailored to the person, the territory, the accounts, the calls, and personal self-management. Chapter 6 discusses in some depth the criteria for setting individual objectives. For now, objectives must be relative to an "output," not an activity. Also, a time period should be set for the completion of the objectives. Thus the salesperson who states his or her goals as "making calls" is stating an activity. "Making an average of seven calls per day" is an output-oriented objective. Some typical objectives a sales manager might use would include the following:

- Dollar volume per month
- Gross profit as percent of sales per month
- Dollar output per line per month
- Dollar output per salesperson per month
- Average order size per month
- Advertising as percent of sales per month

- Volume of returned goods per month
- Number of new accounts per month
- Share of market quarterly
- Number of complaints per month
- Amount of training per quarter (days)
- Days training per year
- Lost accounts per month
- Average monthly sales calls per rep

ESTABLISH KEY OBJECTIVES   From such a list, management determines the main goals for the sales force. With the key objectives identified and the environmental trends recognized, the sales manager is next in a position to lay out the objectives for the coming year. Properly defined, the objectives will be measurable (otherwise, how will the manager know when they are accomplished?), will require a certain amount of "stretch" (if they are too easy, they are not worth it), and yet will be achievable (the manager must believe they can be done). The objectives must state what is to be done but not how it is to be done. The "how" portion is what makes up the strategies and tactics.

Assume you have examined your organization, identified what you consider to be the key objectives, and thought about any ongoing market trends. As such, you feel your present situation to be as shown in Table 3.3.

Your environment is fairly stable, with the exception of a growing number of new businesses that could use your products. So far, no new competitors have appeared, the existing competition seems stagnant, and nobody seems to be raiding your sales force—hiring your people. Your sales force is relatively young, and although it is fairly proficient, a few individuals are weak in technical knowledge, a couple of

TABLE 3.3

WE MUST FIRST ANALYZE OUR PRESENT SITUATION

Sales volume	$150,000,000
Number of customers	400
Number of salespeople	20
Cost of sales (as a percentage of sales)	6%
Average calls per day per salesperson	5
Product returns as a percentage of sales	5%
Percentage of sales force with good technical knowledge	90%

the newer ones could further develop their selling skills, and one individual in particular is near promotability.

With this information, you now have a firm idea of "where you are," and accordingly you can develop the upcoming year's objectives. With the amount of new business moving into your area, you feel that a sales increase of $10 million (in constant dollars) is not unrealistic. You also realize that to achieve that increase, you will have to acquire new customers, because the existing ones will probably not increase their purchases that much.

To accomplish these objectives, you feel your sales force must become more productive (that is, make more calls per day), and the profitability figures would be helped immensely if you could hold sales expenses (travel, entertainment, and so on) to their present levels. Also, you will need more salespeople. Upper management has been somewhat concerned with the number of customers returning merchandise and has suggested you monitor the quality of sales your people are making. You feel you must coach them not to oversell a customer just to hit the sales objective. If this is done properly, you feel you can reduce your area's product returns by 2 percent. After scrutinizing the skills of your sales force, you feel that 10 percent of your people are rather weak in technical knowledge of the products. This is especially true of your new salespeople. A strengthening of their knowledge would assist them greatly in acquiring more sales.

COMPARE PRESENT WITH FUTURE   Given these facts about your sales organization, a comparison of your present key objectives versus your desired key objectives would appear as shown in Table 3.4. Therefore, these are your objectives for the coming year:

- Increase sales by $10 million.
- Acquire 50 new customers.
- Reduce sales expenses to 4 percent of sales.
- Increase productivity an average of one call per day per person.
- Reduce product returns by 2 percent.
- Achieve a 100 percent technically trained sales force.

With these as next year's objectives, everything you and your sales force do should be aimed at achieving them. This **objective-based thinking** should help you to separate the important activities from the unimportant ones and help you to prioritize (and legitimize) everything you do. To realize these objectives will take total commitment from you and your people throughout the year.

Reflecting back for a moment, you can see that two of the four basic questions involved in planning have been answered. "Where are we?" has been addressed by the present key objectives, and "Where do we want to be?" has been identified by the newly formed objectives. The next question to be answered is "How do we get there?" The answers to this question will make up the strategies and tactics for achieving the objectives during the coming year.

TABLE 3.4

Now We Can Determine Where We Want to Be

Key Indicator	Where Are We?	Where Do We Want to Be?
Sales volume	$150,000,000	$160,000,000
Number of customers	400	450
Number of salespeople	20	30
Cost of sales	6%	4%
Average calls per day per salesperson	5	6
Product returns	5%	3%
Percentage of sales force technically skilled	90%	100%

Allow Field Managers to Participate   As indicated earlier, achievement of your objectives will require a total, year-long commitment from both yourself and your sales force. When developing strategies and tactics, you have an excellent opportunity to engage your salespeople's commitment right from the beginning.

It is a time-proven fact that people are more committed to tasks, activities, or ideas they have helped create than they are to ideas forced on them. You will achieve more enthusiasm and much more commitment to your strategies if you allow the sales force a part in their development.

An excellent approach to this is used by Ford Motor Company's district sales manager Marnie Quinn. She uses a brainstorming session between her and her people—a session in which she outlines what must be accomplished (the objectives) but lets the sales force present and discuss ideas and methods by which they will be achieved. The resulting list of strategies and tactics means much more to them and commands much more commitment because it is from their ideas and not solely hers.

When you, as the manager (and leader), are developing your strategies and tactics with your sales force, first outline what the key objectives are at the present time, what those objectives are targeted to be one year hence, and thus what the objectives are for the team. Then, beginning with the first objective (in our example here, "Increase sales by $10 million"), ask "How can we accomplish this?"

Develop the Budget   Now we will answer the final question, "Can we afford to do it?" Will our plan generate enough sales and profits to cover the costs of implementing it?

To answer this requires a careful, and accurate, estimate of sales (see Chapter 5), plus the development of a projected sales and cost analysis financial statement. The sales, expenses, and profits for your company and each of its sales regions are estimated for the coming time period. Once approved by top management, this estimated financial plan will become the budget for your sales force and each sales region.

Establish Progress Checkpoints   All four of the concept questions have now been answered, and your plan is nearly complete. Still to be addressed is the determination of progress checkpoints during the year. This is best done by determining the degree of progress necessary during various time periods to ensure that your overall objectives are met by year end.

These time periods could be months or calendar quarters. For example, since your sales objective is to increase sales by $10 million, how much increase do you feel you should see each month (or quarter) to ensure a year-end total increase of $10 million? On a quarterly basis, it would be $2.5 million, assuming no seasonability in your sales. Therefore, if your sales are less than a $2.5 million increase at the end of the first quarter, you must increase sales efforts during the next three quarters to achieve the $10 million increase.

This same approach could be applied to each objective. A critical point to remember (and unfortunately many people do not) is that progress must be regularly monitored so minor problems are identified and resolved long before they become major problems.

Formalize Your Plan   Now that your plan has been fully developed, it should be committed to paper and actually published as your plan for the year. The printed copy should be distributed to all members of your management team so they are fully aware of the objectives and strategies to be followed during the year. As in football, your printed plan becomes your team's playbook, and every player must have one!

As noted earlier, the role of the sales manager in implementing the strategic plan is twofold. Up to this point, the first aspect—that of developing the overall objectives and strategies for the sales manager's respective sales force and area of responsibility—has been discussed. The second aspect is to coach each member of the sales force in developing a similar plan for his or her respective territory.

Convert Plans into Individual Objectives   Just as the objectives were set for the sales force and its subunits, regions, and districts, so too should they be set for each individual territory within the area. The sum of these territorial objectives should be the sales force's objectives. Each territorial objective also must be supported by viable strategies. Each member of the sales team must know exactly how his or her personal objectives will be achieved. The various strategies laid out for the area will have to be applied individually within each territory. Each member of the sales team must have a firm territorial plan by which to manage the territory during the year. As with the sales force plan, a schedule of periodic reviews should be established for each salesperson.

As we have seen, to manage a sales force in today's complex world requires much more than merely achieving the sales quota. The sales manager is in a vital position to have a direct impact on both the future of the business and the future of the sales staff. Such a position requires sound, fundamental leadership. Managing and leading the organization through objective-based thinking is one way to manifest and convey that leadership.

The sales manager who can step back and look at the organization from the aspects of "Where are we?," "Where do we want to be?," "How do we get there?," and "How much will it cost?" will be the individual who truly manages his or her business. Much like a coach with game plan in hand, the well-prepared sales manager will be able to enter the "game" with every confidence that his or her team will win.

Sales Objectives Direct Other Activities

The planning process and the eventual establishment of objectives for the various units and individuals within the sales force set in motion the program necessary to manage a sales force. (See Figure 3.8.) The *strategic sales force planning process* involves examining the relevant markets and determining the roles and activities of sales personnel necessary to service these markets. Next, the sales organization is designed and structured according to the needs of these markets. Sales, costs, and profits are projected for markets, products, and geographic areas. These forecasts lead to developing sales objectives for the sales force, for its various units (for example, sales regions and districts), and eventually for each salesperson. Finally, each salesperson develops specific plans for the sales territory. This involves segmenting prospects and customers based on sales volume and developing individual strategies for customers. Thus, a great deal of planning is needed to manage a successful sales force.

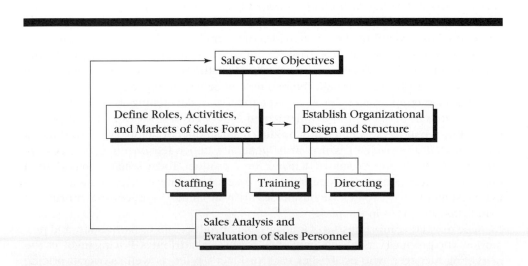

Figure 3.8

The Strategic Sales Force Planning Process

Successful implementation of these plans is critical to meeting sales objectives. The right people must be hired, properly trained, and directed to reach the various objectives. By carefully evaluating sales and cost, a sales manager can determine how each salesperson and sales unit has performed. As Figure 3.8 shows, managing is a continuous process involving planning, implementation, and evaluation.

Each of the sales managers' many activities, as shown in Figure 3.8, will be discussed in this book. For example, sales managers must constantly examine their marketplace and determine the job activities needed to compete in it. This and the proper design and structure of a sales force are the topics of the next chapter.

MANAGEMENT IN ACTION: ETHICAL DILEMMA
IT'S ALL RIGHT TO DO OVERSEAS!

Your group's sales performance has been less than what you hoped this year. As international sales manager based in San Francisco, your sales level is depressed because of a sluggish world economy. When Lucy called, you took a deep sigh of relief because now you have an excellent chance of making quota. She tells you she feels she has an excellent chance to sell $15 million of industrial machinery parts to a firm in Asia. However, one of that company's vice presidents indicates that a $10,000 donation to the company president would assure the sale. Although common in that country,

such a practice is against U.S. law and company policy. Your boss tells you, "We need the business. Do whatever it takes. It's up to you to make the sale. Don't lose it."

WHAT DO YOU DO?
1. Let your price stand without the donation.
2. Decrease your price by $10,000.
3. Make the $10,000 donation.
4. Withdraw the bid.

THE BOTTOM LINE

Strategic planning involves making decisions about an organization's long-term goals and strategies. Strategic goals are major targets, or end results, that relate to the long-term survival, value, and growth of the organization. A strategy is a pattern of actions and resource allocations designed to achieve the organization's goals. Tactical planning translates broad strategic goals and plans into those relevant to specific portions of the organization. Operational planning identifies the specific procedures and processes required at the organization's lower levels. The goals and plans that emerge from the overall planning process should be consistent and integrated. Planning is very important for the organization's marketing and sales group.

Most people today associate marketing with selling. Yet the act of selling is only one part of the overall marketing activities of a firm. The task of providing products that satisfy consumers forms the basis for current U.S. marketing systems. Marketing is an exchange process between buyers and sellers, the purpose of which is to satisfy buyers' needs and wants through the purchase of sellers' products.

This marketing concept evolved over the years, developing as American businesses matured. Initially, production-oriented American businesses assumed people would buy whatever was efficiently produced. This concept gradually evolved into a sales-oriented approach in which firms generally depended on effective sales approaches to stimulate consumer demand for a product. Today's marketing-oriented philosophy focuses on a firm's desire to increase sales while anticipating and satisfying consumer needs. Progressive businesses today are much more consumer oriented than firms have been in the past.

The marketing mix consists of four variables: product, price, distribution, and promotion. The product variable encompasses its physical attributes. Pricing involves the marketing manager, who establishes each product's price as well as overall pricing policies. Getting that product to the right place at the right time is the distribution variable. The promotion variable increases product demand by communicating information to potential customers via personal selling, advertising, publicity, and sales promotion.

Firms must carefully consider the role of the sales force in their promotional program or promotional aspect of the marketing mix. A firm has to decide if a sales force is a viable direct-marketing tool and, if so, which types of selling activities optimally promote its products.

KEY TERMS FOR SALES MANAGERS

Strategic planning, 52	Good, 56	Publicity, 60
Strategic goals, 52	Service, 56	Sales promotion, 60
Strategy, 52	Product, 57	Relationship marketing, 62
Tactical planning, 52	Price, 59	Transaction selling, 62
Tactic, 52	Distribution, 59	Relationship selling, 62
Operational planning, 52	Household, 59	Partnering, 62
Mission, 53	Firm, 59	Service quality, 64
Strategic vision, 53	Government, 59	Objective-based
Values, 53	Promotion, 59	thinking, 69
Strategic plan, 53	Personal selling, 60	
Marketing mix, 56	Advertising, 60	

MANAGEMENT APPLICATION QUESTIONS

1. How do strategic, operational, and tactical planning differ? How might the three levels complement one another in an organization?
2. A sales manager coming out of a sales meeting was heard to remark, "If we didn't have to waste our time with all this planning, we could spend our time on something productive like selling." What would you tell this sales manager about the purpose of planning?
3. Discuss the role of personal selling as it relates to a firm's marketing effort. What does the sales force do for the organization?
4. Discuss the four elements of a firm's marketing mix. Give several examples of how companies today have a marketing mix to compete in their industry.
5. Why is building a relationship important for a salesperson? What can an organization and its salespeople do to build relationships with customers?

FURTHER EXPLORING THE SALES WORLD

Interview the CEO, president, or other top-level executive of an organization to find out how the firm's corporate objectives relate to its marketing and sales force objectives. Almost any type of organization, such as a manufacturer, bank, hospital, car dealership, or retailer, could be used.

SALES MANAGEMENT EXPERIENTIAL EXERCISE

WHAT SHOULD YOUR CHILDREN'S COLLEGE MAJORS BE?

You are the parent of ten children and have just used your inheritance to acquire a medium-sized pharmaceutical company. Last year's sales were down 18 percent from the previous year. In fact, the past three years have been real losers. You want to clean house of current managers over the next ten years and bring your children into the business. Being a loving parent, you agree to send your children to college to educate each of them in one functional specialty. The ten children are actually five sets of twins exactly one year apart. The first set begins college this fall, followed by the remaining sets during the next four years. The big decision is which specialty each child should study. You want to have the most important functions taken over by your children as soon as possible, so you will ask the older children to study the most important areas.

Your task right now is to rank the functions to which your children will be assigned in order of priority and to give reasons for your ranking. Write this list on a separate sheet of paper. These are the functions:

_____ Distribution
_____ Manufacturing
_____ Market research
_____ New product development
_____ Human resources
_____ Product promotion
_____ Quality assurance
_____ Sales
_____ Legal and governmental affairs
_____ Controller

Analyze your reasons for how functional priority relates to the company's environmental/strategic needs. Now rank the functions as part of a small group. Discuss the problem until group members agree on a single ranking. How does the group's reasoning and ranking differ from your original thinking?

ALABAMA WHOLESALERS, INC.
Plans Don't Always Work!

It all started when the vice president for marketing and sales at Alabama Wholesalers, Inc., asked for a special fourth-quarter sales push. He selected you, the sales manager, to design a program that would enable the company to reach his goal of a significant increase in profits in this quarter over last quarter. You worked on the plan for five days and finally presented your proposal to the vice president: If the company added 8.5 percent to the promotional budget, your sales team would contribute an extra 17 percent to the profit.

Your plan would work through the raising of each salesperson's quota by 20 percent. This additional sales volume would generate enough revenue to increase profits to the goal level desired by the marketing vice president. The additional 8.5 percent requested for the promotional budget would be sent to motivate the sales force. Prizes would be awarded based on the percentage each salesperson sold above his or her quota. The prizes were fantastic. The top prize was a luxury-model car, and even the "worst" prize was a deluxe 35 mm camera set. Since this contest was based on percentage of improvement, each salesperson had the opportunity to enhance his or her best sales effort.

You felt your plan could not fail. You had used past sales history to determine projected profits and necessary supporting expenditures. You had even found a way to motivate all the members of your sales team. Unfortunately, the plan didn't work.

QUESTIONS

1. Why did you go over the expense budget, spending almost 10 percent more instead of the approved 8.5 percent increase?
2. Why did sales increase only 7 percent, instead of the 17 percent you had promised?
3. Was the plan bad, or was failure caused by poor implementation?
4. Now what are you going to do?

CHAPTER 4
THE MARKET-DRIVEN SALES ORGANIZATION

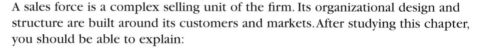

CHAPTER OUTLINE

FACTORS INFLUENCING ORGANIZATIONAL DESIGN AND STRUCTURE

MARKETING AND MARKETS

SALES JOBS ARE VARIED AND CAN BE CLASSIFIED

THE SALESPERSON'S JOB ACTIVITIES AS A TERRITORIAL MANAGER

SALES ORGANIZATIONAL DESIGN

SALES ORGANIZATIONAL STRUCTURE

NEW FORMS OF ORGANIZATIONS

COORDINATION AND TECHNOLOGY

LEARNING OBJECTIVES

A sales force is a complex selling unit of the firm. Its organizational design and structure are built around its customers and markets. After studying this chapter, you should be able to explain:

■ The type of markets in which salespeople work.

■ The major job activities of salespeople.

■ The various types of sales jobs.

■ Why sales jobs are designed for an individual organization's markets and customers.

■ The various types of sales force organizational structures.

■ Newer forms of organizations.

■ How coordination and technology improve customer service.

In January, leads were dropping, competitors were refocusing their efforts, and the number of new members had decreased significantly. This was the cue for Dave Mezzanotte, director of sales for SecureHorizons, a health plan for seniors, that some changes had to be made in the roles of his salespeople. He also realized that even the mention of words that start with *re*—like realigning and reorganization—could put many employees in a panic. So what did Mezzanotte do? He eased them into changes, preparing them every step of the way. "I wanted to get the organization into the mode of accepting quick change," he says.

Mezzanotte began by traveling extensively in the field, listening in on inside sales calls and speaking to top performers about difficulties they were having. He then met with his management team, and they came up with a vision of where the industry was headed and what SecureHorizons would have to do in order to adjust. By February, he had presented the company with "a graphic depiction of where we needed to go, what the problems were, what we needed to fix." He included anecdotes from his interviews about how employees were working harder for fewer results.

When the major realignment was announced in April, everyone was ready. On the day of the announcement, managers held individual meetings with their employees to address concerns. Management announced that people taking on new roles would undergo training in May. "I had to let them know when I presented this vision that I would never just let them hang out there," Mezzanotte says. He also made sure that information about compensation was available that day.

One year after his plan was implemented, Mezzanotte declares that SecureHorizons has maintained its market-leading position with the enrollment of 45 percent of all seniors who signed up for new health plans. However, some employees did struggle with their roles in the first few months, and Mezzanotte thinks that the company may require another restructuring in the near future. His expectations are that his employees will be ready.[1] ■

Companies such as SecureHorizons are trying to find ways to make the entire organization customer oriented. This approach allows more flexibility and responsiveness in today's competitive global environment.

Every company wrestles with the problem of organization. Reorganization often is necessary to reflect new strategies, changing market conditions, or innovative production technologies.[2]

These organizations are using the fundamental concepts of organizing. **Organizing** is the deployment of resources to achieve strategic objectives. *Deployment* is the division of labor into specific departments and jobs, formal lines of authority, and mechanisms for coordinating diverse organizational tasks.

Organizing is important because it develops from strategy. Strategy defines *what* to do; organizing defines *how* to do it. Organizational structure is a tool managers use to harness resources for getting things done. The design of a sales force requires establishing effective working relationships among the sales force, marketing, and other groups in the organization. The right organizational structure does not guarantee results, but the wrong structure can dampen results. As you will see in this chapter, the relationships among a company's markets, types of sales jobs, and salespeople's activities influence the design of various sales jobs and even the structure of the sales organization.

FACTORS INFLUENCING ORGANIZATIONAL DESIGN AND STRUCTURE

The operation of a sales force requires the coordination of numerous interacting or interdependent groups and activities. In deciding on the organizational design and structure of a sales force, managers:

- Examine customers in each market.
- Determine the types of sales jobs needed to serve a market.
- Note the job activities salespeople must do.
- Design sales jobs around customers.
- Set up the sales force organizational structure, which includes the various sales jobs and geographic territories.

These relationships are shown in Figure 4.1. As you will see later, properly designed sales jobs lead to higher performance and a better quality of work life for sales personnel. This chapter discusses each element of Figure 4.1. It starts with customers and markets.

FIGURE 4.1   THE RELATIONSHIPS AMONG MARKETS, JOBS, AND ACTIVITIES INFLUENCE SALES JOB DESIGN AND ORGANIZATIONAL STRUCTURE

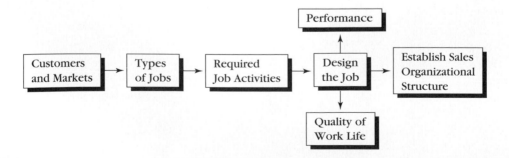

Marketing is the process of planning and executing the conception, pricing, promotion, and distribution of ideas, goods, and services to create exchanges that satisfy individual and organizational objectives. As you will see, these marketing activities take place basically in two markets.

MARKETING AND MARKETS

SALESPEOPLE WORK IN TWO MARKETS

Exchange takes place in two basic types of markets: consumer and business. Business markets are sometimes referred to as industrial or organizational markets. Each market has different characteristics, which means the salespeople working in each market must fulfill different roles.[3] Sales managers should understand the characteristics of their markets so they can identify the roles the sales force must play.

Sales activities are of infinite variety. A useful way to classify the many types of sales jobs is to place them among seven major categories.[4] These categories then can be arrayed on the basis of their complexity and difficulty:

SALES JOBS ARE VARIED AND CAN BE CLASSIFIED

Category One   Positions where the salesperson is predominantly an inside order taker, like the McDonald's hamburger salesperson standing behind the counter. Most of the customers have already made up their minds to buy. All the salesperson does is serve them. The salesperson may use suggestive selling by asking if the customer wants a large order of french fries rather than a small order, but opportunities for creative sales are few.

Category Two   Positions where the salesperson predominantly delivers the product, such as milk, bread, fuel, oil, and so forth. The person's selling responsibilities are secondary. Obviously, good service and a pleasant manner will enhance customer acceptance and hence lead to more sales. However, few do any truly creative selling.

Category Three   Positions where the salesperson is predominantly an order taker but also works in the field, such as selling soap, food, or health and beauty aids to retailers. In contacts with chain store personnel, these salespeople may even be discouraged from applying the hard sell. As with the delivery salesperson, good service and a pleasant personality may enhance personal acceptance, but these salespeople also do little creative selling. This description relates primarily to the entry-level job. Key account salespeople for these same companies often use creative selling techniques with their sizable customers.

Category Four   Positions where the salesperson is not expected or permitted to take an order but is asked only to build goodwill or to educate the actual or potential user—the textbook publisher's salesperson or the medical detailer representing an ethical pharmaceutical house. Some pharmaceutical manufacturers, however, do have their salespeople selling directly to physicians.

Category Five   Positions where the major emphasis is placed on technical knowledge, such as an engineering salesperson who is primarily a consultant. This person may become so preoccupied with the technical aspects of a project that he or she forgets to close a sale.

Category Six   Positions that demand the creative (specialty) sale of tangibles such as vacuum cleaners, refrigerators, house siding, encyclopedias, and so on. Here the salesperson often has a double task. First, the salesperson may have to make the prospect dissatisfied with his or her present appliance or situation. Only then can the salesperson take the second step and begin to sell the product. It is here that the hard sell becomes imperative.

Category Seven   Positions that require the creative sale of intangibles such as insurance or advertising services. This type of sale is ordinarily more difficult than that of tangibles. Salespeople can show, demonstrate, and dramatize tangible products but cannot do this with intangible products. Intangibles are often difficult for the prospect to comprehend. People cannot feel, smell, see, hear, or taste intangible products. This makes them more challenging to sell.

APPLICATIONS OF THE SALES JOB CLASSIFICATIONS

Rarely are these categories encountered exactly as described. Most sales positions are combinations or permutations of one or more of these categories. Thus, sales positions vary widely in their nature and requirements.

ORDER TAKERS   The salespeople in the first five classifications are often described as **order takers.** They wait for the customer to order. Although they must be employed to bring in additional business the employer would probably not obtain without their efforts, few truly create business. Many never attempt to close the sale.

The main problem with many order takers is that they create only one distinction in the customer's mind: price. So, once the sale is made, the order taker is vulnerable to other salespeople or telemarketers—all promising to save the customer money. If the competitor's price is lower, the customer is lost.

ORDER GETTERS   On the other hand, the creative selling of tangible goods or intangible services in highly competitive markets (or where the product has no special advantages) requires selling merchandise that cannot be sold in equal volume without a salesperson. These people are order getters. **Order getters** obtain, retain, and increase business with customers. They get new and repeat business using a creative sales strategy and a well-executed sales presentation. The salesperson has an infinitely more difficult selling task than does the representative in the first five categories mentioned earlier. In this sense, the tasks are those of a true salesperson, which is why this individual usually earns so much more than the order taker.

This salesperson has a double selling problem. First, the salesperson must often create discontent with what the prospect already has before beginning to sell constructively. Second, the salesperson often has to overcome the most powerful and obstinate resistance. For example, the prospect may never have heard of the product and, at the outset, has no desire whatsoever to purchase it. The prospect may even be prejudiced against it and may resent the intrusion of this "stranger." In other instances, the prospect may want it but wants competing products more. Frequently, the prospect cannot afford it. To meet such sales situations successfully requires creative selling of the highest order.

Creative salespeople are often faced with selling to numerous people to get one order. This is without a doubt the most difficult selling situation because the representative may have to win over not only the decision maker, the one who can say yes, but also other persons who cannot approve the order but each of whom has the power to veto it.

Order Getters Build Relationships   Happily, a growing number of salespeople do not sell by price and do not take orders. They distinguish themselves from their peers in their prospecting techniques, in their sales approach, and in their personal characteristics. They spend less time cold calling, record higher hit ratios, produce more new business, and have better retention rates.

What is their secret? They develop relationships with their customers. They know that the customer, tired of relentless sales pitches and products that all look alike, wants to be heard and understood. Price is important, but good salespeople also must identify and meet the customer's coverage and service needs. They establish rapport and determine whether prospects are interested in buying.

During the process, these salespeople do not pitch their products but instead enter into a dialogue. They listen more than talk, so they learn all they can about the customer's business and its needs. They ask good questions and take notes. When the time comes to present their products, they position them according to what the customer wants. They understand that objections are a natural part of the sales process, and they use them as opportunities to keep talking.

Their sales calls are more productive because order getters are smarter about developing prospects. Rather than making cold calls, they network among centers of influence, target specific accounts, and ask their clients for referrals. They are disciplined in their approach, constantly seeking new contacts and evaluating leads.

They also distinguish themselves in the way they prepare for a sales call. They have an objective in mind and are thorough in their information gathering, creating a professional impression that shows they value the customer's time.

After the account is sold, these salespeople further enhance the relationship by evaluating and responding to the customer's changing needs. Customers are contacted at routine intervals. Order getters realize that future sales will come from (1) selling present customers again and (2) getting customer referrals. Thus, follow-up and service after the sale are extremely important for making future sales.

In the final analysis, today's top salespeople reach a higher level of professionalism than order takers. They are well trained in their craft and are constantly practicing and refining their skills. They develop stronger relationships with their clients and the people who support their efforts. They understand the products they sell but also know something about their clients' businesses. Their customers, who consider them trusted advisors, gladly refer them to their business associates and friends.

TRUE SALESPEOPLE ARE HARD TO FIND

What does this statement mean? Although the first categories of sales positions (order taking) involve little actual selling, their members far outnumber those who engage in actual or creative selling. Thus, among the vast army of so-called salespeople, only a few actually create sales. Furthermore, competence in one type or class of sales does not guarantee equal competence in another. Success as an insider or route salesperson does not necessarily qualify a person for creative selling, or vice versa.

The significance of this classification is that each type of sales work requires its own unique combination of traits, attributes, and qualities in its practitioner. Because of this, if a sales manager is to establish a productive sales force, the first and most fundamental step is to determine the category of sales to be undertaken and to prepare precise specifications covering the qualities the incumbents will need to ensure success.

People with the prerequisite traits and attributes for success in creative sales are so rare that often 100 to 150 or even more applicants must be interviewed to find one qualified candidate. Therefore, continuous and intensive recruitment and sophisticated selection techniques are absolute prerequisites. Both these topics will be covered later in the text.

Sales managers examine their customers within each of the company's markets. The characteristics of a particular market—and the products sold—help determine salespeople's job activities. Knowing this information, in turn, results in organizing the sales force and developing its organizational structure based on job activities, customers, and markets.

THE SALESPERSON'S JOB ACTIVITIES AS A TERRITORIAL MANAGER

The salesperson's roles or activities can vary from company to company, depending on whether sales involve goods or services, the firm's market characteristics, and the location of customers. For example, a person selling Avon products performs similar, but somewhat different, job activities than the General Electric salesperson.

Most people believe a salesperson only makes sales presentations, but the job involves much more than person-to-person selling. The salesperson functions as a **territorial manager**—planning, organizing, and executing activities that increase sales and profits in a given territory. A **sales territory** is composed of a group of customers assigned within a geographic area. As manager of a territory, the salesperson performs the following seven functions:

1. *Provides solutions to customers' problems.* Customers have needs that can be met and problems that can be solved by purchasing goods or services. Salespeople seek to uncover potential or existing needs or problems and show how their products or services can satisfy those needs or solve those problems.

2. *Provides services to customers.* Salespeople provide a wide range of services including handling complaints, returning damaged merchandise, providing samples, suggesting business opportunities, and developing recommendations on how the customer can promote products purchased from the salesperson.

   If necessary, salespeople may even occasionally work at the customer's business. For example, a person selling fishing tackle may arrange an in-store demonstration of a manufacturer's products and offer to repair fishing reels as a service to the retailer's customers. Furthermore, a manufacturer may have its salespeople sell to distributors or wholesalers. Then the manufacturer's representative may make sales calls with the distributor's salespeople to help them sell and provide service to the distributor's customers.

3. *Sells to current and new customers.* The acquisition of new accounts is the lifeblood of a business; it brings new revenues into the company. This important job must be done if a salesperson's territory is to grow.

   Although new accounts are crucial, salespeople also strive to increase the sales volume of their current customers by encouraging them to purchase additional items within the same product line and any new products.

4. *Helps customers resell products to their customers.* A major part of many sales jobs is for the salesperson to help wholesalers and retailers resell the products they have purchased. The salesperson helps wholesale customers sell products to retail customers and helps retail customers sell products to consumers.

   Consider the Quaker Oats salesperson selling a product to grocery wholesalers. Not only must the wholesaler be contacted, but also grocery retailers must be called on, sales made, and orders written up and sent to the wholesaler. In turn, the wholesaler sells and delivers the products to the retailers. The Quaker Oats salesperson also develops promotional programs to help the retailer sell the firm's products. These programs involve supplying advertising materials, putting on store demonstrations, and setting up product displays.

5. *Helps customers use products after purchase.* The salesperson's job is not over after the sale is made. Often customers must be shown how to obtain the full benefit from the product. For example, after a customer buys an IBM computer system, technical specialists help the buyer learn how to operate the equipment.

6. *Builds goodwill with customers.* A selling job is people oriented, entailing face-to-face contact with the customer. Many sales are based, to some extent, on friendship and trust. The salesperson needs to develop personal, friendly, and businesslike relationships with everyone who may influence a buying decision. This is an ongoing part of the salesperson's job

and requires integrity, high ethical standards, and a sincere interest in satisfying customers' needs.

7. *Provides company with market information.* Salespeople provide information to their companies on such topics as competitors' activities, customers' reactions to new products, complaints about products or policies, market opportunities, and their own job activities. This information is so important to many companies that their salespeople are required to send in weekly or monthly reports on competition activities in their territory. Salespeople are a vital part of their employers' information retrieval system.

When combined and properly carried out, these seven sales job activities produce a successful sales performance. During a typical day, salespeople are involved in most of these activities.

Organizational design refers to the formal, coordinated process of communication, authority, and responsibility for sales groups and individuals. An effectively designed sales organization has a framework that enables the organization to serve its customers. Sales personnel then know what their responsibilities are and to whom they report and thus can concentrate on the activities needed to do their various jobs.

SALES ORGANIZATIONAL DESIGN

PURPOSES AND IMPORTANCE OF JOB DESIGN

Of the many purposes served by job design, the more important are to increase productivity and improve an individual's quality of work life. A person's work includes:

- *Content*—duties, tasks, behaviors, functions, responsibilities.
- *Qualifications required to perform it*—skills, abilities, experiences.
- *Returns and rewards for performing it*—pay, promotions, intrinsic satisfaction.

Quality of work life is a somewhat general concept referring to several aspects of the individual's work- and job-related experiences. Sales jobs should be designed to maintain a quality of work life that makes employment in the sales force a desirable personal and social situation. Quality of work life is an important part of an organization's culture in which salespeople experience feelings of self-control, responsibility, achievement, and self-respect. As you will see later in this chapter, this is why often numerous types of sales jobs exist in any one sales force.[5]

Organizational structure is the relatively fixed, formally defined relationship among jobs within the firm. Managers frequently must rethink structure and may reorganize to meet new conditions in the environment, new production technology, or changes in size. Structure is a powerful tool for reaching strategic goals. A strategy's success often is determined by the strategy's fit with organizational structure. Structure is reflected in a company's organizational chart.

SALES ORGANIZATIONAL STRUCTURE

Companies can structure their organizations in numerous ways. Most firms use a line organization or one of the many specialized designs based on functions, geographic markets, products, customers, or some combination of these factors.

THE LINE ORGANIZATION

In the **pure line organization,** the chief executive—usually the president—does the decision making for the firm. The president has complete authority. No specialists or advisers may exist within the firm. Many small sales firms have this structure. For example, the Compute Corporation is a Texas-based organization that sells used computers. Figure 4.2 shows the firm's line organization. The company was begun by its president 15 years ago. He and two salespeople did the selling and bookkeeping. Lewis Stoner buys late-model computers and sells them to companies currently without a computer or that need a large computer. As the business grew, Jake Preston was promoted to vice president of sales as a line assistant, and another salesperson was hired. An outside accounting firm maintains the financial records.

The advantages of this type of organization are that it is simple, it has low overhead, decisions are made rapidly and communicated quickly, and salespeople tend to feel they make a major individual contribution to the firm.

In this type of "one-man-show" organization, key people are difficult to replace. In addition, executives may be so busy with the day-to-day operations that little time can be devoted to planning. Also, because everyone is a jack-of-all-trades, lack of specialization can hinder the firm's growth.

SPECIALIZED DESIGN

The structure of an organization can be based on a variety of factors such as function, geography, product, customers, or a combination of these factors. Large companies commonly begin with a functional structure, develop geographic departments, split along product division lines, and end with a customer-focused structure. Although a firm may be organized along any one of these lines, typically a combination of these structural methods is used.

FUNCTIONAL SPECIALIZATION   The **functional organizational design,** sometimes called *line* and *staff organization,* is the grouping of work according to its characteristics. It is the most common organizational design. Firms need special expertise, so they develop advertising, sales, and marketing research units or departments and then group all related activities (such as sales and advertising) together, thus introducing specialization into the organizational design. This type of organization is often used by firms that have a small number of similar products.

No single chief executive, no matter how brilliant and dynamic, can effectively handle all of the responsibilities of a relatively large and complex organization. Figure 4.3 shows the functional organizational design of the sales and related units of Alarm System, a Kansas City, Missouri, industrial and home security firm. Note the difference between this figure and Figure 4.2. The line component of the organization still runs from the chief executive directly down to the salespeople. However, the staff reports directly to the vice president of marketing. The sales manager has staff authority equal to that of the advertising and marketing research managers. However, neither the advertising nor marketing research manager has authority over the salespeople. Persons in staff positions aid the vice president of marketing in marketing planning and operations.

FIGURE 4.2

COMPUTE
CORPORATION'S LINE
ORGANIZATION

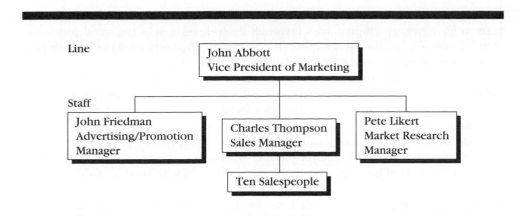

FIGURE 4.3

ALARM SYSTEM
CORPORATION'S
FUNCTIONAL
ORGANIZATIONAL DESIGN

The functional organizational structure is suitable when the organization outgrows the line organization and begins to add specialized positions. For example, as a firm grows, it adds more salespeople to call on an increasing number of customers; they sell a larger number of products or services and expand into multiple sales regions or a national market. This design is useful for medium to large organizations because it allows them to take advantage of the benefits of specialization.

However, the functional organizational structure also involves high overhead, because a large number of management positions must be created that are not directly involved in generating income. Such an organization operates more slowly than the line organization and takes longer to respond to changes in the business environment. However, these disadvantages are overshadowed by the advantages.

STAFF POSITIONS WITH LINE AUTHORITY   Occasionally a company may give staff personnel line authority or find staff personnel attempting to exert line authority outside of their areas of specialization. **Line authority** means that people in management positions have formal authority to direct and control immediate subordinates. **Staff authority** is narrower and includes the right to advise, recommend, and counsel in the staff specialists' areas of expertise. For example, a product manager might exert line authority by ordering salespeople to give away free samples of a product without first clearing the idea with sales management. Such outside line authority is almost always a mistake and causes problems in coordinating the selling effort. Primarily, it goes against a basic premise of organizational theory, that is, that an employee should report to only one person who has the power to direct that employee's activities and reward, discipline, or discharge. Managers of large national companies will fight to keep crossing line authority from happening, and thus it is not too common.[6]

A staff manager also can be given line authority within his or her area of specialization. For example, the sales training director can ask salespeople in a training class to perform certain activities such as role playing, obtaining product information, or taking quizzes on the information, and may even discipline a salesperson. However, although the training director can hire or fire people who are direct subordinates, he or she does not have the authority to fire, promote, or reward a salesperson.

GEOGRAPHIC SPECIALIZATION   Many large corporations are organized by geographic territory. This type of organization is generally used by companies with more than strictly local distribution of their products. Geographic organization is often combined with other methods of organization such as product or customer. With geographic specialization, each territorial unit can be treated virtually as a separate company or profit center. The sales manager of a given territory often has complete responsibility for meeting that unit's sales objectives. The unit can be called a division, region, branch, or district. Consider the organizational chart shown in Figure 4.4.

Textron Chemical primarily sells industrial chemicals used to manufacture plastics. Textron has three geographic sales divisions. Each division sells the same products. Each division is given the same support by the home office, and each has its own performance goals passed down from higher management.

Each regional sales manager works at a regional distribution or warehouse center. Having 18 regional distribution centers is a costly duplication of facilities. The cost is offset, however, by efficiency. For example, sales managers feel that this organization provides improvement in (1) control of activities, (2) market coverage, (3) customer service, (4) response to local conditions, and (5) direction of salespeople's efforts in achieving unit goals. Companies selling multiple product lines, with depth of assortment, often organize on the basis of geographic specialization combined with product specialization.

PRODUCT SPECIALIZATION   Another common type of organization in large companies is based on the firm's product. The entire company may be organized by product, with separate sales, advertising, marketing, and so on, along with staffs for each, or some functional units may remain centralized (for example, advertising) while a separate support staff is created for each product. With the former organization, for example, a separate sales force and sales management would exist for each product group. These sales divisions are treated as a separate company or profit center, as are geographic divisions. Large companies quite commonly use a combination of product and geographic departmentalization. In fact, it is difficult to find medium to large companies organized solely by product.

Product specialization is necessary, or at least useful, when (1) the products are very technical or of a complex nature, (2) a large number of similar but separate products exist, (3) products are relatively simple but completely different, (4) product lines are distributed through entirely different trade channels, or (5) different products are

FIGURE 4.4

TEXTRON CHEMICAL
CORPORATION
GEOGRAPHIC
SPECIALIZATION

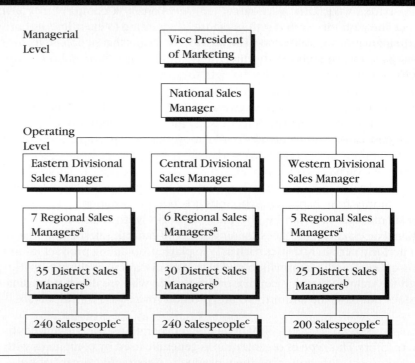

a. Different number of sales regions due to population differences.
b. Five district sales managers per region.
c. Approximately 8 salespeople per sales district.

sold to similar markets. When any combination of these factors is present, a company should investigate the possibility of product specialization of the sales force.

The advantage of product specialization is that each product receives close attention from the salesperson responsible for selling it. In the case of complex products, the salesperson can master the necessary information to sell the product effectively. The advantages of an organization based on geographic specialization also apply.

The drawbacks of product specialization, similar to those of geographic specialization, are the increased costs of executive personnel, sales personnel, and sales personnel time. A company organized by product specialization will often have different sales personnel calling on the same customers trying to sell them different products. This costs the company time for repeated calls by the salespeople and costs the customer time spent with each salesperson. Thus, if product specialization of the sales force can be avoided, either by hiring a higher caliber of sales personnel or by upgrading the training program, then these steps should be taken.

CUSTOMER SPECIALIZATION   Companies with several separate and distinct markets accounting for major portions of their sales often organize based on these markets or customers. Firms frequently shift from the product organizational structure to a structure based on customers. Markets then become the major sales emphasis. This seems to be the best specialization method for firms today.

COMBINATION OF DESIGN ELEMENTS   Many companies organize on the basis of some combination of functional, geographic, product, or customer design.

Figure 4.5 illustrates a company with production, marketing, and engineering functional specialists; the firm sells consumer and industrial goods in both U.S. and foreign markets. The consumer-goods division sells three categories of products through three geographically organized sales force divisions.

ORGANIZING FOR SELLING TO INTERNATIONAL CUSTOMERS

Many U.S. companies derive a substantial share of their total sales and profits from international operations. As shown in Figure 4.5, the international marketing and sales managers occupy a high organizational level. An international sales force is composed of personnel from the parent company, foreign nationals directed by a foreign sales or domestic sales manager operating abroad, or a group of individuals from both the parent company and the country in which business is being sought. Although the trend for large companies is to hire nationals to conduct sales, home-country salespeople remain important for a vast number of companies.[7]

ORGANIZING FOR SELLING TO MAJOR CUSTOMERS

Companies have realized the need to pay special attention to their major customers. Many organizations have 60 to 80 percent of their sales come from their major customers. Companies refer to these major customers with different terms such as house accounts, corporate accounts, headquarter accounts, key accounts, or national accounts. Whatever they are called, the loss of such customers would substantially affect a company's sales and profits. Companies use four basic organizational methods with their major customers:

1. A separate division to deal with major accounts.
2. Select members of the current sales force.
3. Sales managers.
4. A combination of 1, 2, and 3.

Senior sales personnel and sales managers are used when the regular sales force lacks the knowledge, selling and negotiating skills, coordinating abilities, and time

FIGURE 4.5   MULTIPLE DESIGN FACTORS

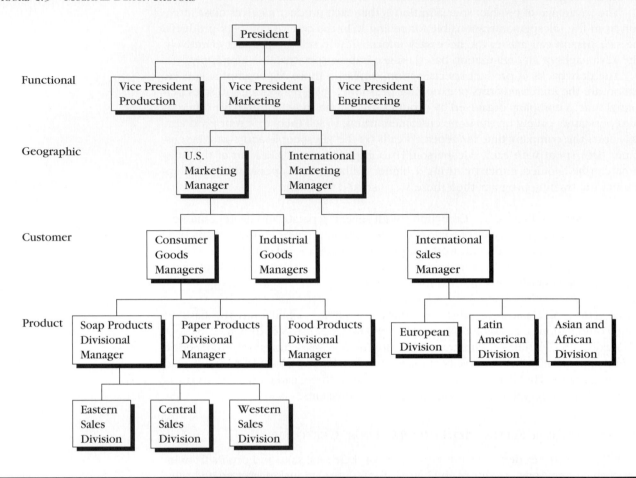

needed to deal successfully and profitably with larger accounts that purchase centrally. Key-account salespeople often bear heavier responsibilities than the general sales force because, under carefully worked out rules, they are delegated more authority to negotiate marketing packages, including price, quantities, promotional allowances, customer training plans, delivery arrangements for various field locations, and other special deals, and to provide assurance of any needed field follow-up service.

Key-account salespeople frequently cover the headquarters purchasing authorities of companies with decentralized ordering locations—or at least, plants where installation and service occur—which require the participation and follow-up of salespeople in distant locations. The key-accounts salesperson covering the headquarters obtains an "approved supplier" status; provides intelligence to other salespeople about when, where, and how much the company is likely to purchase; and coordinates national and local account coverage activities. He or she usually depends on the general sales force for local follow-up and service.

Some companies charge their district managers with responsibility for dealing with some or all key accounts rather than use a separate key-account sales force. However, use of district managers—particularly if they are given substantial incentives for key-account sales—may seriously undermine the quality of their sales management performance as recruiters, trainers, and supervisors of territorial salespeople.

If possible, firms should not give their managers direct sales responsibilities for individual customers. Sales managers need to be free from this pressure in order to manage people who are selling.

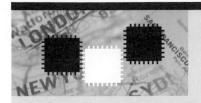

SELLING AND MANAGING GLOBALLY

A TYPICAL SALES DAY IN CHINA: WHAT TO EXPECT

- The workday begins around 8:15 or 8:30 A.M. Men wear suits and ties; women wear appropriate business attire.
- Travel is by taxi to most appointments. Many use bicycles for personal transportation, but chaotic traffic makes this hazardous.
- Mostly you call on men; women hold about 10 percent of the senior advisory or management positions.
- Use English on most business calls (it's the international business language), although Mandarin or Cantonese (in the southern part of China) are required on some. It's not necessary for foreigners to know the many Chinese regional dialects.
- When taking taxis, get someone to write out directions to your destination in Chinese. Negotiate the fare before you leave. If your prospect's office is off the beaten path or if your call is late in the day, pay extra to have the taxi wait for you. On-call taxis take hours to arrive, and you may have a long hike back to a main street to flag one down.
- Expect to conduct business at your client's office or at your office and after hours on the golf course, over cocktails, or at dinner. If you *must* conduct business at your office, send a car to call for your prospect or customer. However, if your customers prefer meeting in your office, sending a car is not necessary.
- Appearances can be deceiving; senior managers may show up at a trade show wearing overalls. One-on-one sales calls are not the norm. Expect to meet with two or more people. The Chinese are genuinely curious about your company and product line. They all want to learn more.
- Get right down to business. Although meetings can begin with personal discussions about your experiences in Asia, the Chinese are not prone to idle chitchat.
- Meals are important and can include 12 courses. If you plan to meet through lunch, you will likely send out for (surprise!) Chinese. Evening meals are divided equally between Asian and Continental cuisine.
- Sales calls usually last from 30 to 45 minutes; depending on the industry, they can last up to several hours.

- Because of traffic, four calls a day—two in the morning and two in the afternoon—make a great day. Group your calls geographically.
- Companies used to doing business with the West or Japan are fully automated with computers and faxes, albeit much older models than you are used to seeing. Not too many people carry portable phones or pagers, but this is changing almost hourly.
- Show that your company is serious about staying in China by printing bilingual order forms. Shaking hands and thanking the customer for the order are normal. Bowing is not required (unless your customer is Japanese).
- The business of business cards is serious. Take your customer's card in both hands, look at it carefully, and remark on something you see. Offer your card first at the beginning of the meeting. If you will be in China for longer than one meeting, print bilingual business cards. If you smoke, offer a cigarette. If the meeting is at your office, offer tea or coffee immediately.
- Business hours end at 6:30 P.M., but days end around 10 or 11 P.M. with dinner and then time at a club. Understand your customer's normal routine. Customers may transport key personnel to and from work in a company bus or other scheduled transportation. Don't get caught at closing with two-thirds of your meeting hurrying out to catch their group ride home.
- Be patient with yourself and the host country. Study before you go, so you won't be caught with egg foo yung on your face.

Sources: See John S. Hill and Richard R. Still, "Organizing the Overseas Sales Force—How Multinationals Do It," *The Journal of Personal Selling & Sales Management* (Spring 1990): 57–66; Cynthia R. Cautherm, "Moving Technical Support into the Sales Loop," *Sales & Marketing Management* (August 1990): 58–61; and Kate Bertrand, "Get Ready for Global Capitalism," *Business Marketing* (September 1990): 42–53.

In response to changing demands and new strategic requirements, new organizational forms are emerging. All represent efforts to become more responsive to customers. The new concepts include stragegic alliances and team-based organizations.

NEW FORMS OF ORGANIZATIONS

STRATEGIC ALLIANCES

The modern organization has a variety of links with other organizations. These links are more complex than the standard relationships with traditional stakeholders such

FIGURE 4.6

CROSS-FUNCTIONAL
SELLING TEAM

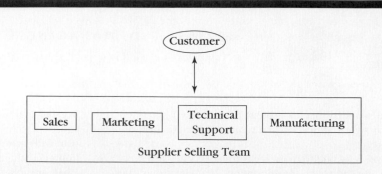

as suppliers and clients. Today even fierce competitors are working together at unprecedented levels to achieve their strategic goals.[8] For example, IBM and Apple have some cooperative arrangements, and GM, Ford, and Chrysler agreed to work together on "high-speed multiplexing," which improves the performance of a vehicle's electronic controls.

A **strategic alliance** is a formal relationship created with the purpose of joint pursuit of mutual goals. In a strategic alliance, individual organizations share administrative authority, form social links, and accept joint ownership. Such alliances are blurring firms' boundaries. They occur between companies and their competitors, governments, and universities. Such partnering often crosses national and cultural boundaries.

Companies form strategic alliances to develop new technologies, enter new markets, and reduce manufacturing costs. Alliances are often the fastest, most efficient way to achieve objectives.

TEAM-BASED ORGANIZATIONS

Many organizations are more responsive to their environment because they use work teams as their basic building blocks; that is, they are **team-based organizations.** Teams are made up of people from different functional units, such as manufacturing, technical support, marketing, and sales (see Figure 4.6). These **cross-functional teams** are composed of a defined group of individuals bringing together expertise from different parts of the supplier organization to capture, retain, and increase business with customers.

Cross-functional teams operate separately from traditional, vertical lines of authority. Moreover, cross-functional teams often are short lived. Teams form, complete their tasks, disband, and then new teams form. People may be members of more than one cross-functional team simultaneously.

Frequently, organizations form sales teams to make sales presentations. Salespeople set the appointment, develop sales objectives, and act as monitors during the discussions. However, other members of the sales team conduct the main discussions.

COORDINATION
AND TECHNOLOGY

As organizations grow and evolve, two things happen. First, new positions and departments are added to deal with factors in the external environment or with new strategic needs. As companies add these positions and departments, they grow more complex, with hundreds of positions and departments performing incredibly diverse activities.

Second, senior managers must find a way to tie all of these departments together. The formal chain of command and the supervision it provides is effective, but it is not enough. The organization needs systems to process information and to enable communications among people in different departments, at different levels, and often in different countries.

Coordination refers to the quality of collaboration across groups. Without coordination, a company's left hand will not act in concert with the right hand, causing problems and conflicts. Coordination is required regardless of whether the organization has a functional, divisional, or team structure. Employees identify with their immediate department or team, taking its interest to heart, and may not readily compromise with other units for the good of the organization as a whole.

Without a major effort at coordination, an organization (such as IBM) may find itself unable to properly serve its customers. One of Louis Gerstner's first moves as IBM's CEO was to restructure a sales force that had traditionally been built around selling mainframes. Under Gerstner's new structure, senior managers, organized geographically, acted as account executives for top IBM clients in their region. These executives could call on a pool of regional product specialists and service reps to help meet a customer's need. Sales reps were encouraged to push total solutions, not just products. Teamwork was a buzzword.

INTERNATIONAL COORDINATION

In the international arena, coordination is especially important. How can managers ensure that needed coordination will take place in their company, both domestically and globally? Coordination is the outcome of information—as will be discussed in Chapter 5—and cooperation. Managers can design systems and structures to promote communication. The most important methods for achieving coordination are information systems, task forces and teams, and integrating managers.

IBM executives, for example, realized their customers needed specialists from every corner of the world. Ned Lautenbach, IBM's senior vice president and group

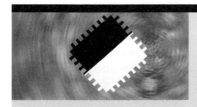

MANAGEMENT IN ACTION: ETHICAL DILEMMA
THIS REORGANIZATION CREATES LAYOFFS

You are a regional sales manager over five district managers and 50 salespeople. All sales personnel are paid a base salary plus quarterly bonuses of up to 50 percent of their salary. Company sales are seasonal with 40 to 60 percent of orders being placed October through December. To receive the bonus, each salesperson must be employed through December 31.

In March, your company merges with a competitor. In early June, you call one of your friends who works in the corporate payroll office. Your friend happens to let it slip that his office is under orders to determine how much money can be saved by laying off 30 to 50 percent of the entire sales force, including sales managers. The decision for these layoffs has been approved and finalized by top management and is scheduled for December 15. You wonder if this date was strategically selected by management to render employees ineligible for their huge fourth-quarter bonus. You are aware that few of your people could quickly find jobs once laid off.

WHAT DO YOU DO?
1. Say nothing. However, start looking for another job as soon as possible. Also take all of your vacation and sick leave before December 15.
2. Informally notify your managers to tell their people that if they have another job opportunity, take it!
3. Continue to do your best in your work and not let the upcoming layoffs worry you. Things will work out.

executive of worldwide sales and services, says the best customer solutions meshed resources from multiple countries and were customized to clients' individual needs. "Our solutions don't come in a box," he says. "We need to quickly move ideas, skills, and resources from one part of the world to another."

COORDINATION PROVIDES CUSTOMER SERVICE

Not being coordinated can become a serious problem when customer satisfaction is at stake. Bill Roberts, vice president of information technology for Ford Credit, a large IBM customer, says his company expects quick, complete service, regardless of location. As this Ford subsidiary continues to penetrate global markets (the company offers financial services to automotive customers in 31 countries), the pressure is on IBM to support its worldwide business objective. "IBM definitely has to be there when we want them," Roberts says. "Otherwise, it's not the partner we want."[9]

THE BOTTOM LINE

Markets, job types, and job activities influence the design of the various sales jobs and, consequently, even the structure of the sales organization. When designed properly, these sales jobs may result in better performance. Salespeople work in two types of markets: the consumer market and the business (or industrial) market.

Sales activities are very diverse and easier to understand if classified in one of seven categories. Although the boundaries of these categories are not distinct, most salespeople and their job types fit into one of them. The first five classifications can be identified as order takers, salespeople who rarely close a sale. Unfortunately, these order takers far outnumber their initiative counterparts, the order getters. The order getters are successful in that they build relationships with their customers—an important factor toward reaching sales goals. The creative salesperson has a much more difficult task, for his or her customers are unsure of what they want. Consequently, each type of sales work requires its own style of practitioner.

A salesperson's job activities involve much more than person-to-person selling. As the manager of a sales territory, a salesperson must give solutions to customers' problems, provide service, sell to new customers, help customers resell products, help customers use products, build goodwill, and provide the company with market information.

Companies can structure their organizations in numerous ways. Most firms, however, use line organization or a specialized design based on functions, geographic markets, products, customers, or a combination of these factors. Coordination is playing a larger role in sales organizations because companies are not only dealing with domestic markets but are also competing in the international arena. Coordination is especially important for acquiring satisfied, long-term customers.

KEY TERMS FOR SALES MANAGERS

Organizing, 78	Organizational structure, 83	Strategic alliance, 90
Order takers, 80	Pure line organization, 83	Team-based organizations, 90
Order getters, 80	Functional organizational design, 84	Cross-functional teams, 90
Territorial manager, 82	Line authority, 85	Coordination, 91
Sales territory, 82	Staff authority, 85	
Organizational design, 83		

MANAGEMENT APPLICATION QUESTIONS

1. Define the term *marketing* and the two different types of markets in which salespeople work.

2. Seven different categories of sales jobs exist. Which of these classifications contain salespeople that are most beneficial to business? What characteristics do the salespeople in these categories exhibit?
3. What functions does the salesperson as a territorial manager perform? Why are these important?
4. What is organizational design? What functions does it serve?
5. Give examples of why a firm might organize around functional, geographic, product, and customer specializations.
6. Discuss why some firms are beginning to organize around their key or major accounts.
7. What is coordination, and how are companies using it both domestically and internationally as a means of improving customer service?
8. What weaknesses can be found in a "one-man-show" organization, and how can these weaknesses be resolved?
9. How are order getters more successful as salespeople? What makes the order taker weak?

■ FURTHER EXPLORING THE SALES WORLD

1. Interview salespeople from organizations in three different industries such as in manufacturing of industrial or consumer goods or in financial services. Determine what they do and the main job activities they must accomplish to reach their job goals. Compare and contrast the information you gather.
2. Obtain the formal sales organizational structure of any firm. Evaluate the design and structure of the sales force. Interview a sales manager for the company to determine how its markets and customers influence the design of its sales force.

■ SALES MANAGEMENT EXPERIENTIAL EXERCISE

WHAT ARE YOUR PEOPLE SKILLS?

How well do you understand people, observe their behavior, and address their personal and professional growth? This self-test can help you see your skills. On a separate sheet of paper, write your score for each question. Write 4 if you strongly agree, 1 if you strongly disagree, or 2 or 3 if your feelings are somewhere in between.

	Strongly Agree			Strongly Disagree
	4	3	2	1

1. I think people often are unaware of their true motivation.
2. Psychological factors often play more of a role in job performance than in the job's required skills.
3. I make a conscious effort to understand the basic needs of others.
4. I am able to empathize with other people, even when I don't share their viewpoints.
5. I consciously try to organize my thinking around others.
6. People often reveal themselves by small details of behavior.
7. I am usually aware of people's strengths and weaknesses.
8. Most people aren't easy to read.
9. I notice when someone gets a new haircut, eyeglasses, or clothes.
10. After a meeting, I can usually accurately report how others responded to the discussion.
11. People may present themselves in a certain way that doesn't show who they really are.
12. I try not to read my own attitudes into other people's behavior.
13. I often think about the implications of my past impressions of people on the job.
14. When dealing with others, I try to consider how different they may be from me.
15. I don't judge someone until I have enough information to form a sound judgment.
16. I often think about ways to foster other people's personal and professional growth.
17. I see people for their potential—not how they can be of use to me but how they can fulfill their life goals.
18. You can't change someone else.

19. When making decisions about people, I deliberately consider a wide range of factors.
20. I consciously try to help people play to their strengths and address their weaknesses.

Total Score _____

What were your skills? If your score was
- 75–80: You're probably strong in solving people problems.
- 61–74: You have potential strengths in this area.
- 40–60: You have potential weaknesses in this area.
- 20–39: You have weaknesses to work on in solving people problems.

Now relate what you've learned to your work experiences by setting goals and intermediate targets. Then adjust!

ALASKA OFFICE SUPPLIES
Everyone Is Part of the Sales Team

Tyrone, one of your salespeople, calls the home office of Alaska Office Supplies and, sounding angry and righteous, blasts the factory and support people for not paying attention to a customer. He claims that they caused late delivery, didn't follow up, and shipped the wrong products. The imprudent home-office manager reacts angrily and says to Tyrone, "Who do you work for anyway? Me [meaning the company] or the customer?"

As tempers flare (as they can in telephone confrontations), the conversation ends with "Who the hell do you think you are?"

QUESTIONS

1. What do you suppose all that was really about?
2. What was Tyrone's motivation?
3. What emotions did his behavior disguise, perhaps unconsciously?
4. How should the home-office manager have evaluated the situation?
5. How should we read this whole situation?
6. What would you do as Tyrone's sales manager?

CASE 4.2

REYNOLDS & REYNOLDS
Team Selling

In the past, warranty work accounted for as much as 70 percent of an auto dealership's service load. That number is steadily dropping to around 30 percent. Because of this large decline, dealerships must now proactively target service retention and loyalty among new car buyers. That's where the sales team of Reynolds & Reynolds comes in.

Reynolds helps dealerships become more effective at retaining new car buyers as service customers and building loyalty among the customers to keep them coming back. They help dealers to better understand their customer base, figure out who their most profitable customers are, and then target them with focused incentives to get the customers back into the dealerships when service is needed.

THE OPPORTUNITY

Bob Sherman, a Minneapolis-area sales associate with Reynolds, and his regional sales manager, Tim O'Neill, along with Chuck Wiltgen, marketing specialist, met with representatives from Ben Frothingham's American Ford Dealership. American Ford was in need of a new retention plan to boost service sales, and Reynolds provided them with one. The group effectively presented their marketing strategies and tied up the deal successfully.

Sherman established the contact with American Ford's service department and discussed their options. His next call was more promising and he talked with them more about a new initiative from Ford called "Quality Care Maintenance." They gave him negative feedback, so he suggested that they meet with his boss, Tim O'Neill. By the close of the third meeting, American Ford agreed to have reports run on their customer retention rate and their database system.

PRE-CALL PLANNING

Before the call, Sherman, O'Neill, and Wiltgen discussed details of the opportunity, roles each would play, and any possible concerns that they anticipated. They decided that Sherman would discuss the reports with the customer, and Chuck would be the implementation guy. Tim would be there for backup. because they had been working together so long, they basically already knew how to present their information.

STAGE 1: REPORT

After two reports were run to determine just who the dealership's customer base was, the three met with Carol Bemis, the dealership's new parts and service director and

Brad Greenberg, service manager. Sherman opened the meeting by recapping the set of mutual expectations and handing out copies of the reports. Sherman had calculated that in the previous year, the dealership lost $144,000 for customers that did not return for service. Sherman calls this the "lost opportunity" for that year. He explained that if American Ford had done business with every one of its new car customers from the past five years, the service department would have brought in an additional $1.3 million. O'Neill and Wiltgen confirmed these figures, and Tim recommended that the company run these reports every 90 days to use as a diagnostic tool.

STAGE 2: ANALYSIS

Sherman then shared the database information with Bemis and Greenberg. He discussed with them the number of customers they have on the database that were considered active, meaning that they had been in for service in the previous six months. The report also divided the customers into where they come from, broken down into area codes and the top nine nearby ZIP codes.

They discussed problems they were having with their marketing strategies, and they all came to the conclusion that the dealership needed service reminders. In response to specific questions, the Reynolds sales team explained that (1) with more than 100 different coupons, mailers could be easily customized to suit changing needs; (2) mailings to customers could be sorted by area code, American Ford service advisor, or ZIP code; (3) the American Ford logo could be placed on the new mailers; and (4) copies of all the coupons available for use could be made available for Bemis and Greenberg to review.

STAGE 3: PROGRAM

The Reynolds team then helped them to figure out the best way to implement a "Preferred Customer Card" program. Sherman explained that in other dealerships with the program, they generally have the service advisors ask the customers up front if they have the card. If they do, the advisor knows that the customer is already in the database and does not need to be added to the list. Reynolds calls this "data hygiene," meaning they are helping companies cleanse their databases so that their service reminder program really hits the mark.

STAGE 4: RETURNS

The team then presented Bemis and Greenberg with Reynolds's "Direct Drive" program. This program allows the dealership to customize its mailings for the customers that are active and those that are inactive. It also sorts customers by vehicle so that each customer will receive a mailing that is specifically designed for his or her needs.

This suggestion rolled the conversation over to the topic of cost. Sherman went over the monthly fees for the Direct Drive program and the costs per mailer and phone call for service reminders. Greenberg and Bemis discovered that they were spending about the same amount on the poor results they were getting from their current vendor. Sherman then calculated that if the dealership did implement the program, they could gain $30,750 of additional business in a single month with only a 5 percent response rate.

STAGE 5: CLOSE

After Greenberg looked over the figures, he showed genuine enthusiasm for what Reynolds could do for American Ford. O'Neill added that his company's pro-grams cover all angles of the customer base—the actives, inactives, and new customers. Bemis and Greenberg agreed to move forward with the service reminder program for the entire database of active customers. They also decided to go with the Direct Drive program to target their inactive customers. This was more progress than the Reynolds team had expected from the account. The meeting closed with Greenberg and Wiltgen hammering out the fine print of the agreement, while O'Neill, Sherman, and Bemis set up a timetable for the next step in the process.

QUESTIONS

1. How is the effectiveness of team selling demonstrated by the Reynolds team, and what are some of the disadvantages to this method in this particular case?
2. How did the Reynolds team successfully execute the following critical roles in sales: client access, client education/persuasion, and fulfillment?[10]

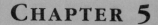

CHAPTER 5

FORECASTING MARKET DEMAND AND SALES BUDGETS

CHAPTER OUTLINE

MANAGING SALES INFORMATION

FORECASTING MARKET DEMAND

USES OF SALES FORECASTS

THE FORECASTING PROCESS

SALES FORECASTING METHODS

THE TOP BRASS APPROVES THE FINAL FORECAST

THE SALES MANAGER'S BUDGET

LEARNING OBJECTIVES

The process of forecasting helps an organization make decisions; it is necessary for determining information about future markets. This chapter should help you understand:

■ The importance of forecasting in a firm's marketing decision support system.

■ The uses and different categories of sales forecasts.

■ The two forecasting methods—survey and mathematical—and their different uses.

■ That the responsibility for approving the final forecast rests at the top management level.

■ The need for knowledge of computers because they are used in forecasting and developing sales budgets.

Forecasting and keeping tabs on competitors are a constant challenge. However, Steve Adolt, a business analyst for BOC Gases, likes keeping tabs on competitors. One rival was building a new plant in California, and Adolt wanted to find out what was going on, so he called the BOC sales manager in that territory. He found out that the competitor was entering a joint venture with one of BOC's competitors. BOC gathered this competitive intelligence (CI) only a few days before the information became public knowledge. But when CI is collected early enough, it can give companies the chance to build strategies around the information. CI exists to help senior management make better-informed decisions. By talking to customers and industry associates, and by reading publications and Web sites, companies can learn about their competitor's activities and industry trends. CI professionals have a difficult task of isolating vital information, especially through the Internet and published reports. So the human sources provide a better picture of what is happening.

Salespeople have the best opportunities to dig for competitive information. This is because sales and marketing people already have relationships with customers, industry experts, and other contacts throughout the supply chain. In addition, reps already possess the techniques for skillfully questioning their sources. Salespeople in remote locations, especially, may notice important developments. Ava Youngblood, head of the board of directors for the Society of Competitive Intelligence Professionals, advises that after CI professionals explain to the sales force what they're looking for, there should be a secure way to record the information—via phone, e-mail, or intranet. Ultimately, CI exists to help companies gain an edge on their competitors and learn of new industry trends.

The problem confronting many companies like BOC is obtaining useful information and using it to build strategies. The Internet and published reports are not always the best sources for useful information. Salespeople can find the competitive information, and this information can have remarkable benefits toward both improved control and improved competitiveness.[1] ■

All organizations such as BOC have the challenge of developing internal databases and information systems to help salespeople and the company keep track of inventory, customers, and sales activities. Two issues face all managers, whether running an entrepreneurial business or a large corporation: getting access to disorganized data and turning the data into useful information.

MANAGING SALES INFORMATION

"Our charge is to design, build, and implement decision support systems that help our field and marketing managers make business decisions," Dan McKee, marketing decision support systems manager for Marion Merrell Dow, Inc., says. "If it's computer based, especially if it's microcomputer based, then we tend to view that as a decision support system. However, rather than giving them the PC and saying, 'Here it is. Use it to solve problems,' we say, 'Here is the tool. We have also put together this collection of software to help you analyze this situation, your employees' job performances, and a variety of other issues like forecasting sales.'

"With the software we put together, we can monitor each rep that we have in the field and assess how well each is performing," McKee says. "The reason we call it decision support systems is because it's trying to maximize the capabilities of the PC and is also incorporating data from mainframes. We now have a couple of packages that link mainframes to PCs, and they pass data back and forth. For example, we have a salesperson customer-call reporting system. Information comes into a centralized agency, which then builds a database of call activities. All of our managers have decision support systems at their locations to help them assess their situations."

Dan McKee shared an excellent example of using information provided to corporate management from its field sales force and of applying it when planning marketing and sales programs. He also explained how their decision support systems evaluate plan implementation. An important use of a decision support system is to forecast market demand.

FORECASTING MARKET DEMAND

Today, we find companies centralizing their data collection, so forecasting is now part of a firm's marketing decision support system. A **marketing decision support system (MDSS)** is an ongoing, future-oriented structure designed to generate, process, store, and later retrieve information to aid decision making in an organization's marketing program. It involves problem-solving technology composed of people, knowledge, software, and hardware "wired" into the sales management process.

An organization generates and gathers much data in its day-to-day operations and has much more data available to it. However, unless the company has some system to retrieve and process this data, it is probably not generating its marketing information effectively. Without such a system, information flowing from these sources is frequently lost, distorted, or delayed.

In contrast, a well-designed MDSS can provide faster, less expensive, and more complete information flow for sales management decision making. Executives can receive more frequent and more detailed reports. The storage and retrieval capability of an MDSS allows the collection and use of a wider variety of data. Management can continually monitor product sales, markets, salespeople, and other marketing units in greater detail.

A marketing decision support system is of most obvious value in a large company where information is likely to get lost or distorted as it becomes widely dispersed. However, integrated information systems also can have beneficial effects on management's performance in small and medium-sized firms.

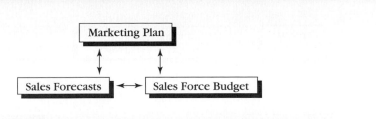

FIGURE 5.1

PLANNING/FORECASTING/
BUDGETING SEQUENCE

USES OF SALES FORECASTS

A **sales forecast** is the estimated dollar or unit sales for a specific future time period based on a proposed marketing plan and an assumed market environment. Today industry sales, total company sales, industry product categories, company product lines, and individual products are major elements that must be taken into account when estimating future demand for a company's products. Sales managers forecast customer, sales territory, regional, divisional, national, and, sometimes, world sales. They forecast short-range (for example, three to six months), medium-range (for example, six months to two years), and long-range (more than two years) demand.

A key factor to a company's success—sometimes to its survival—is how well the sales manager forecasts the company's future product sales. Forecasting the future is always a matter of probabilities, never of certainties.

A sales forecast is important for at least five reasons. Each reason has an impact on another business function.

1. A sales forecast becomes a basis for setting and maintaining a production schedule—manufacturing.
2. It determines the quantity and timing of needs for labor, equipment, tools, parts, and raw materials—purchasing, personnel.
3. It influences the amount of borrowed capital needed to finance the production and the necessary cash flow to operate the business—controller.
4. It provides a basis for sales quota assignments to various segments of the sales force—sales manager.
5. It is the overall base that determines the company's business and marketing plans, which are further broken down into specific goals—marketing officer.

The firm's sales forecast depends on many factors. The planned marketing activities of the firm have a major impact on the level of sales obtained in the marketplace. As shown in Figure 5.1, the firm's marketing plans have an influence on sales forecasts and budgets. Marketing plans can increase sales, which, in turn, can increase budgets and quotas. From sales forecasts, sales goals are generated for products and product lines, individual salespeople, or company divisions. Once plans have evolved into sales forecasts, the company develops its sales budgets.

THE FORECASTING PROCESS

The **forecasting process** refers to a series of procedures used to forecast. It begins when an objective is determined. This may be an estimation of dollar sales, unit sales, or the number of salespeople to hire. As shown in Figure 5.2, dependent and independent variables are selected next. Dependent variables refer to what is being forecasted such as sales or the number of salespeople to hire next year.

A **market factor** is an item or element that (1) exists in a market, (2) may be measured quantitatively, and (3) is related to the demand for a product or service. A **market index** is simply a market factor expressed as a percentage relative to some base figure. In general, as the market index rises, industry sales have a potential

FIGURE 5.2

THE FORECASTING
PROCESS

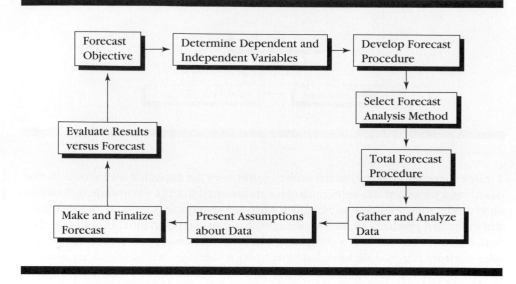

to increase and vice versa. If 2000 is the base year, it would have an index of 100. If 2001's market index drops to 75, sales are expected to be down 25 percent. If 2001 has a market index of 125, sales are potentially up and could increase by 25 percent. An index may be composed of multiple market factors such as price, population, and disposable personal income.

Next in the process, forecast procedures and methods for analyzing data are determined. If the procedures have not been used before, the firm may want to test them. Data are then gathered and analyzed. Often, assumptions must be made about the forecast, such as "We assume GNP will increase by 5 percent; no labor strikes will occur; our competition will not introduce a similar product; and our marketing budget will be $1 million." The forecast is made, finalized, and, as time passes, evaluated.

THE BREAKDOWN AND BUILDUP FORECASTING CATEGORIES

Two broad categories of sales forecasting exist: the "breakdown" and "buildup" methods. The basic steps in the *breakdown method* are shown in Figure 5.3. First, the manager studies the firm's internal and external environments to determine which factors may influence sales. Conditions within the firm, including pricing, product changes, distribution, promotion, financial resources, management skills, labor supply, technology, and plant capacity, as well as external factors, such as the general economy, industry activity, competitors' activities, and governmental actions, may be taken into account.

Next, the manager makes a sales forecast for the industry. **Industry sales forecast,** or market potential, is the estimated sales for all sellers in the entire market or

FIGURE 5.3

BASIC STEPS IN
BREAKDOWN METHOD OF
FORECASTING SALES

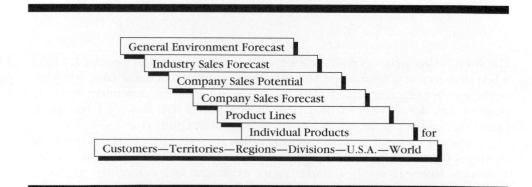

industry over a specified time period under given conditions: for example, total U.S. sales of automobiles during the next 12 months.

Company sales potential, the maximum estimated or potential sales the company may reach in a defined time period under given conditions, is then calculated. This is the company's share of the estimated sales for an entire industry. It is often referred to as **market share** and is usually stated as a percentage. In essence, the company is saying that, if everything goes well, it has the potential to sell, for example, $2 million in fishing lures, amounting to 10 percent of the market's total sales. Next, the manager makes a company sales forecast. At times, sales potential and sales forecast may be the same. However, a company's sales forecast is usually lower because numerous factors inside and outside the firm may cause sales to be less than the potential. Labor strikes or insufficient funds to allow expansion of the sales force are examples of factors inside the firm that may prevent the company from reaching its sales potential. Lack of raw material or fuel or an increase in competition are outside factors that may restrict a firm's ability to reach its sales potential. The main goal of forecasting is to maximize certainty and precision in business decisions.

The *buildup method* of sales forecasting is basically the reverse of the breakdown method. Individual forecasts are made by groups and units within the firm, and these are combined to make broader forecasts.

Companies with a large product offering serving multiple markets have difficulty using this method. Companies forecasting short-, medium-, and long-range sales for the industry, company, product lines, and individual products for divisions, regions, sales territories, and customers use more sophisticated forecasting methods, discussed next.

SALES FORECASTING METHODS

Two categories of sales forecasting methods exist, as shown in Figure 5.4. **Survey methods** are qualitative and include executive opinion, sales force composite, and customer's intention surveys. Examples of quantitative **mathematical methods** are test markets, market factors, naïve models, trend analysis, and correlation analysis.

The sales manager asks, "Which method should I use?" The answer is "It depends." This section describes several of the more popular forecasting methods. The statistical calculations of the mathematical methods will not be described, primarily because they cannot be adequately done in the few pages of one chapter. However, the basics of each method should be understood.

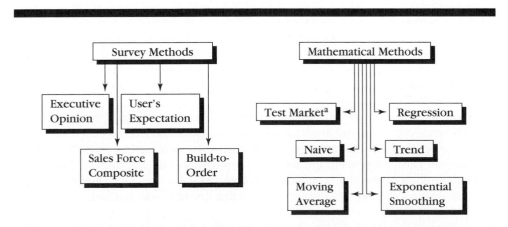

FIGURE 5.4

THE MORE POPULAR OF MANY FORECASTING METHODS

[a] With test market methods, experimental designs and multivariate statistical analyses may be used.

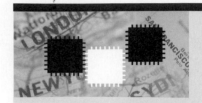

Selling and Managing Globally

Watch Out in Russia and China—They May Bug Your Room to Find Out Your Secrets

Computerized banking services are, at long last, coming to Russia and China—thanks in no small part to Hurston Anderson at Arkansas Systems Inc. in Little Rock. Over the course of several months Anderson, vice president of sales and marketing, and his colleagues worked out deals to supply the Central Bank of Russia and the People's Bank of China with software that will help bring their banking systems into the twentieth century. Arkansas Systems beat out a number of competitors, mostly foreign. In Russia and China, Anderson says, "this idea that because it's American, it's the best" still exists.

Negotiating in these countries can be dicey, Anderson says. "They bug your hotel rooms, for one thing." But then again, the stakes are huge. Although the initial deals have been in six figures, the long-term payoff could reach into the tens of millions.

One new deal is for automated-teller-machine (ATM) software and a check-clearing system in Siberia. In an earlier ATM deal in Moscow, Anderson recalls, "The guy from Central Bank pulled $130,000 out of a valise and wanted to pay us that way!"

The Chinese project includes check-clearing systems at 10,000 branch banks in three Chinese banking regions. Though the initial contract is for $500,000, Anderson notes that no fewer than 77 banking regions exist in China. "And 77 times $500,000 is what? About $40 million, I'd say. Boy, I hope they don't try delivering all that in a valise."

_____

Source: Arne J. DeKeijzer, "China: The Sales Doors Open," *Personal Selling Power,* March–April 1996, 12–22.

SURVEY FORECASTING METHODS

Four basic survey methods are the uses of executive opinion, sales force composite, user's expectations, and build-to-order. The simplest to use is the executive opinion method.

EXECUTIVE OPINION   This is the original sales forecasting method and is still the most widely used, regardless of company size. More-sophisticated methods, such as the time series projections and regression analysis discussed later in this chapter, gain new converts every day as forecasters learn how to use them, aided by data-processing facilities. However, the experienced executive's feel for the market—the "educated hunches"—plays a vital part in nearly every sales forecast, no matter how many mathematical techniques are also used. A sales manager once said. "We use some of the most sophisticated forecasting methods known to man, keeping busy a battery of economists and statisticians. But we find there's no substitute in this business for the seasoned sales executive's 'seat-of-the-pants' intuition—the advantage of close personal contact with distributors and dealers—which we rely on in assessing our technically derived forecasts."

Executive forecasting is done in two ways: (1) by one seasoned individual (usually in a small company) or (2) by a group of individuals, sometimes called a "jury of executive opinion." The group approach, in turn, uses two methods: (1) Key executives submit the independent estimates without discussion, and these are averaged into one forecast by the chief executive; or (2) the group meets, each person presents separate estimates, differences are resolved, and a consensus is reached.

Delphi Method   The well-known **Delphi method** consists of administering a series of questionnaires to panels of experts. Each new questionnaire depends on the responses from the previous questionnaire. This approach enables each panel respondent to have access to information contributed by other respondents but eliminates the "snowball" or "bandwagon" effect (that is, responses based on the replies of others).

SALES FORCE COMPOSITE   An example of a buildup approach to forecasting is obtaining the opinions of sales personnel concerning future sales. This method is often used to generate forecasts in the industrial equipment industry and is a common practice in the oil-field supply industry. Take, for example, a company selling drilling trucks that, when fully equipped, sell for $500,000. The firm cannot afford to carry a large inventory and requires that its salespeople contact all potential customers. So each salesperson gives an estimate of future sales, and his or her immediate manager reviews the estimates with each salesperson. The district manager then formulates a forecast that is passed up to the regional manager. Corporate management thus uses the **sales force composite** forecast to determine how many drilling trucks should be produced for the coming year. Many companies use the accuracy of the field sales manager's forecasts as a major part of their performance evaluation. The more accurate a manager's forecast, the higher the compensation the manager receives.

Should Salespeople Be Paid Bonuses for Accurate Forecasts?   Since salespeople have a reputation for misjudging their sales, managers ask, "How can we get salespeople to be more accurate in their forecasts?" Training is certainly a key here. Some companies pay bonuses when salespeople hit their sales forecast target.

USER'S EXPECTATIONS   Consumer and industrial companies often poll their actual or potential customers, ranging from individual households to intermediaries. Some companies employ consumer panels that are given products and asked to supply information on the product's quality, features, price, and whether they would buy it.

Consumers have difficulty predicting their future buying habits. Often they say yes in a survey but are not willing to pay for the product in the store. Forecasts based solely on this method tend to be overly optimistic. If the product has relatively few buyers; if buyers make a strong commitment, such as signing a contract or making a partial advance payment; or if specific customers have said yes and later bought, then this method is often effective. An example is an original-equipment manufacturer who sells to major automobile companies. The automobile companies indicate their needs two and three years in advance.

BUILD-TO-ORDER   Driven by recurring demand-forecasting nightmares and faced with a rapidly changing marketplace, major desktop computer vendors such as Dell have decided to build final products only after firm orders are placed, a practice called *build-to-order*.

MATHEMATICAL FORECASTING METHODS

Many types of mathematical methods can be used to forecast. This section describes the major mathematical methods in nontechnical terms and then discusses several variables and sources outside the firm that a sales manager should understand.

TEST MARKETS   **Test markets** are a popular method of measuring consumer acceptance of new products. The results from a test market are used to make predictions about future sales. Companies select a limited number of medium-sized cities (see Figure 5.5) with populations that they feel are representative of their customers in terms of such factors as age, income, or shopping behavior. A product is promoted just as if it were being sold nationally, and product features are then evaluated. Instead of spending hundreds of thousands of dollars on marketing the product nationally, the company spends a lesser amount simulating future sales. Companies may develop several different marketing strategies for different test markets to see which is more effective. Proper experimental design and mathematical analyses are important to correctly evaluate test market data.

One example of test marketing occurred in Beaumont, Texas, where Colgate-Palmolive tested a new deodorant. The product manager arranged for radio and TV advertising in the area. Promotional materials such as floor stands and advertising were

FIGURE 5.5   CITIES COMMONLY USED AS TEST MARKETS—RESIDENTS ARE MOST LIKELY TO SEE NEW PRODUCTS

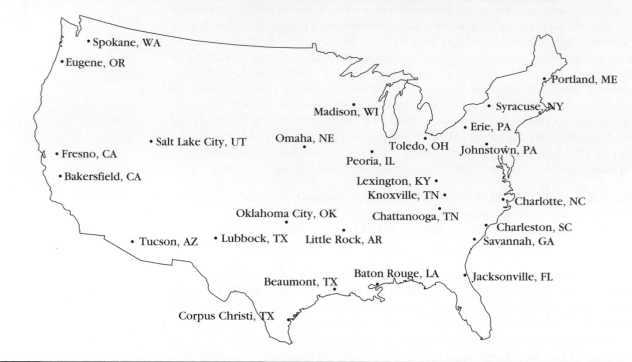

furnished to retailers. Consumers were not aware Colgate was testing the product. Salespeople called on all wholesale and retail customers within a 50-mile radius of the city. They delivered the product themselves, and product sales were closely monitored for six months. However, the product was never introduced nationally because sales forecasts based on the test market indicated that consumers would not buy enough of the product to make it profitable. Companies often change product features and promotional themes as a result of the data obtained in a test-market situation, as did Procter & Gamble when it test marketed Ivory shampoo and conditioner.

TIME SERIES PROJECTIONS   **Time series projections** are popular sales forecasting tools. Although numerous time series methods exist, we will concentrate on the naïve, moving-average, exponential-smoothing, trend, and regression methods; we also will concentrate on an explanation of the methods—not a technical discussion of the statistics involved.

Time series methods use chronologically ordered raw data. Historical data are used to project future events. For example, past sales are used to project future sales. However, future events are often different from past events, which makes the accuracy of such methods far less than 100 percent. Even so, past sales are useful as information input into the forecasting procedure. By studying the historical correlations of sales levels over time, a manager can find a general indication of the possible continuation of the time series. The primary advantage of time series analysis is its objectivity, because it is based on the established record of historical data.

The classical approach to time series analysis is that any given observation, such as sales for a given year, is made up of trend, seasonal, cyclical, and erratic components:

- The *trend* component may be defined as long-term growth or decline.
- The *seasonal* component is periodic variation that occurs with some degree of regularity.

- The *cyclical* component is a wavelike fluctuation about the trend. The length and the amplitude of the cycle are not regular—for example, a business cycle with a recession–boom sales trend.
- The *erratic* component is not predictable and depends on such events as strikes or floods.

Not all statisticians agree with this classification of components. Some would argue that more than four components exist; others feel fewer exist and that, for example, the trend and cyclical components are produced by the same factors. The basic premise of this classification is that a single data point (for example, company X's year 2000 sales of $6 million) was achieved due to various business and economic variables. Sales forecasters attempt to express these variables with statistical models that can be tested and verified in the hope of being able to predict future events.

Naïve Method   The assumption underlying the **naïve method,** often referred to as the *ratio method,* of forecasting is that what happened in the immediate past will continue to occur in the immediate future. The formula is stated this way:

$$\text{Next Year's Sales} = \text{This Year's Sales} \times \frac{\text{This Year's Sales}}{\text{Last Year's Sales}}$$

Assume, for example, that sales for period 6 were to be forecasted. Also assume this year's sales, period 5, equaled $450,000 and that last year's sales, period 4, were $350,000. Thus, next year's sales forecast equals $578,571.

This is a simple forecasting method and requires little data and statistical manipulation. It is a time series method of forecasting that often has been accurate for the short run, especially if trends are stable or are changing in a relatively consistent manner. As shown in the example sales figures, it is assumed that the percentage increase from period 4 to period 5, 22.2 percent, will remain the same for the next period—in this case, period 6.

Moving Average   **Moving averages** are used to allow for marketplace factors changing at different rates and at different times. With this method, both the distant past and the distant future have little value in forecasting. The moving average is a technique that attempts to "smooth out" the different rates of change for the immediate past, usually the past three to five years. The forecast is the mean of these past periods and is only valid for one period in the future. The forecast is updated by eliminating the data for the earliest period and adding the most recent data.

Take, for example, the data in Table 5.1. The sales volumes for periods 3, 4, and 5 are totaled and then divided by 3 to derive the mean of 366.6, which is the period 6 forecast. If the company operates in a stable environment, a short two- or three-period average may be most useful. For a firm in an industry with cyclical variations, the moving average should use data equal to the length of a cycle.

TABLE 5.1

EXAMPLE OF MOVING-AVERAGE FORECAST

PERIOD	SALES VOLUME	SALES FOR THREE-YEAR PERIOD	THREE-YEAR MOVING AVERAGE
1	200		
2	250		
3	300	750	
4	350	900	300
5	450	1100 ($\div 3$) =	366.6
6	?		

Period 6 Forecast = 366.6

Exponential Smoothing **Exponential smoothing** is similar to the moving-average forecasting method. It allows consideration of all past data, but less weight is placed on data as it ages. For example, last year's data has greater weight than data from five years ago. In other words, exponential smoothing is basically a weighted moving average of all past data. The method is used to forecast only one period in the future. When using this method, a probability weighting factor, or smoothing constant, is selected arbitrarily. This factor is usually between 0.1 and 0.5 but can range from something greater than zero to something less than 1.0. This value determines how sensitive the forecast will be to past data. For example, the larger the value, the more sensitive the forecasting values will be to recent changes in sales. The forecasting equation is

Next Year's Sales = a (This Year's Sales) + $(1 - a)$ (This Year's Forecast)

Assume that this year's sales were \$450,000 and that this year's forecast was \$300,000. The a in the equation is the smoothing constant. Assume that a was given a value of 0.2. The forecast for next year's sales would equal

$$0.2 \times (\$450,000) + (0.8) \times (\$300,000) = \$330,000$$

If sales change consistently, the smoothing constant should be small to retain the effect of earlier data. Rapid changes call for a large a. Several values for a may be applied to past forecasts and actual data to help determine the most appropriate a for the particular situation. The a value that proves to be most accurate then can be chosen for future forecasting.

Simple exponential smoothing is especially useful when the data have little trend or seasonal pattern. Versions of exponential smoothing can be used with trends in sales data.

Trend Projections—Least Squares Of two trend forecasting techniques, the least-squares, curve-fitting method is one step above the "eyeball-fitting" technique. **Eyeball fitting** is simply a plot of the data with a line drawn through them that the forecaster feels most accurately fits the linear trend of the data. In some respects the least squares method is a formalization of the eyeball-fitting technique. It is used to mathematically project the trend line to the forecasting period with time as the independent variable that influences the dependent variable—in this case, sales.

The **least squares technique** is more accurate than the eyeball-fitting method. However, it has the disadvantage that prediction is based on past sales (see Figure 5.6). The future may not be the same, causing the forecast to be inaccurate. Furthermore, time is not the factor causing sales to increase or decrease. Factors internal (for example, sales force size) and external (for example, competition) to the firm influence sales. Certainly forecasters must consider past sales data, especially if their firm operates in a stable, low-technology industry that has in the past (and is expected to in the future) experienced little change in its internal and external environment. However, to forecast sales accurately, factors that are closely related to sales should be taken into account to increase reliability. The use of standard or custom computer programs makes analysis of these factors easy for the forecaster.

Regression Analysis **Regression analysis** is a statistical method used to incorporate independent factors that are thought to influence sales (for example, population, advertising) into the forecasting procedure. Two or more variables are used to estimate the tendency of sales to vary. One variable required is the dependent variable, which in this case is past sales. *Simple* regression procedures use only one independent variable, such as population.

Multiple regression uses two or more independent variables, such as population and sales force size or population, income, and sales force size. The relationship between the dependent and independent variables can be one of two basic types. A *linear* regression assumes the relationship is a straight line, as shown in Figure 5.7(A). This simple regression example shows a direct relationship between sales and population. As population increases, so do sales. If population decreased, sales also would decrease.

FIGURE 5.6   A TREND FORECAST OF SALES

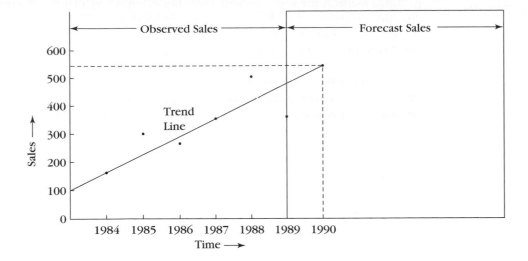

A *curvilinear* relationship is a nonlinear regression producing a line that is not straight. One example is shown in Figure 5.7(B). This line shows that sales increase as population increases until a point is reached at which sales begin to decrease. However, the line can take numerous shapes.

Sales managers rely on statisticians using computer programs to produce regression analyses. Future sales volume is predicted from regression analyses of such variables as past sales, economic indicators (such as population, income, and age), and market factors. It is important to find independent variables that have a direct causal relationship with sales. Often the independent variables also have to be forecasted because a reliable estimate of these variables is a prerequisite for forecasting sales.

Forecasting accuracy is influenced by many factors. Sales managers may ask their marketing research people to predict sales if, for example, (1) a recession occurs, (2) price is increased 5 percent, (3) sales force size is increased 10 percent, and (4) advertising is decreased 5 percent. They also may seek answers to questions about variations in the percentage increases or decreases of each factor. Answers to these questions must be obtained by statisticians trained in forecasting, simulation, and computer techniques.

FIGURE 5.7

REGRESSION ANALYSIS

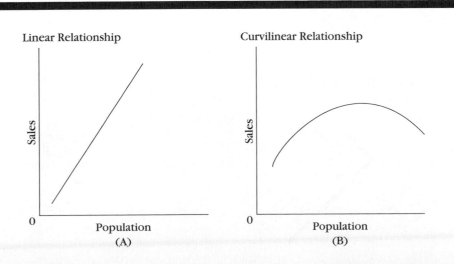

The Top Brass Approves the Final Forecast

The sales forecast has a major impact on planning for the company budgets and sales force budgets and or decision making. Because of its importance, final forecast approval is made at the top corporate level. For example, in a large industrial firm, the chairperson (who is the chief executive officer), the president (who is the chief operating officer), and the vice presidents of marketing and finance approve major forecasts. Often they review several forecasts to arrive at the final form. The final choice is usually a compromise between breakdown and buildup forecasts.

This process is epitomized by United Parcel Service (UPS), the Atlanta-based shipping and delivery company. UPS management uses a two-pronged approach in which the marketing group puts together a forecast based on economic indicators and historical sales data. Effort is then made to verify that forecast from the ground up. Local managers work with sales reps to create territorial forecasts, which are then aggregated into district, then regional, and, finally, a national forcecast.

A senior management team in the UPS corporate office than compares the two forecasts and works with the regional offices to reconcile the differences. This version goes back and forth between the corporate and regional offices until agreement occurs. Once this is finished, the management team makes the decision to send the marketing plan out to the sales force as a business plan in the form of goals and quotas.[2]

As we have discussed, numerous questions need to be answered to hit the forecasting "bull's-eye." Figure 5.8 presents some of the most important questions that need to be answered. Think about each one of them. Sales managers need to be knowledgeable about many things; that is why the job is so challenging and rewarding.

The Need to Overcome "Computerphobia"

Sooner or later, anyone who forecasts sales or uses sales forecasts in sales work will find the computer an essential tool. For instance, the vast amount of arithmetic used

FIGURE 5.8   Questions to Answer to Improve Chances of Hitting the Forecasting Bull's-Eye

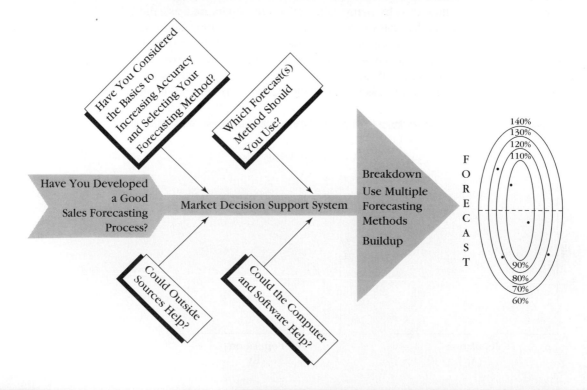

TABLE 5.2   GUIDE TO FORECASTING

FORECASTING METHOD	TIME SPAN	MATHEMATICAL SOPHISTICATION	COMPUTER NEED	ACCURACY
Executive Opinion	Short to medium	Minimal	Not essential	Limited
Delphi Method	Medium to long	Minimal	Not essential	Limited; good in dynamic conditions
Sales Force Composite	Short to medium	Minimal	Not essential	Accurate under dynamic conditions
User's Expectations	Short to medium	Minimal	Not essential	Limited
Test Markets	Medium	Needed	Needed	Accurate
Naïve Method	Present to medium	Minimal	Not essential	Limited
Moving Average	Short to long	Minimal	Helpful	Accurate under stable conditions
Exponential Smoothing	Short to medium	Minimal	Helpful	Accurate under stable conditions
Least Squares	Short to long	Needed	Desirable	Varies widely
Regression Analysis	Short to medium	Needed	Essential	Accurate if variable relationships stable

in time series analysis—especially in short-term forecasting—would be extremely burdensome and expensive without computers. The sales manager concerned with forecasting therefore must know a few basic facts about computers and how they fit into the forecasting process.

Sales managers are realizing they must overcome their "computerphobia." This can be helped by developing a guide to forecasting, as shown in Table 5.2, and then selecting the appropriate forecasting method. Training with the appropriate software will help counter a manager's reluctance toward using statistical forecasting methods and the computer.

Sales managers at Pepsico, for example, must overcome "computerphobia" because the computer plays a central role in developing forecasts based on the relationships between variables. Given the number of products, package sizes, and markets involved, Pepsico managers require the use of multidimensional analysis systems to build realistic, relatively accurate forecasts. Such systems provide the sales and marketing managers with suitable sales and marketing targets, allowing them to accurately plan marketing strategies.[3]

For Ault Foods Ltd., a major player in the food services industry, quick and ready access to customer and product information is a competitive necessity. However, tracking and analyzing data from 8,000 products, 30,000 customers, and 3 million customer orders each year is a daunting task. In 1994, Ault examined its paper-based approach to marketing and sales analysis and embraced a client-server approach to implementing organizational change, developing a comprehensive query and analysis computer system called the Sales Information System (SIS), which is accessible to employees throughout the corporation. SIS is based on the IBM AS/400 Advanced Server Model 140. It provides online access to sales and profit results, offering ad hoc query and analysis capabilities that help users understand business trends and solve specific problems. Since the majority of Ault's staff was unaccustomed to computers, training was a major component of the system's integration. A tiered approach was adopted, with in-house staff trained to become trainers.[4]

The **sales force budget** is the amount of money available or assigned for a definite period, usually one year. It is based on estimates of expenditures during that period and on proposals for financing the budget. Thus, the budget depends on the sales forecast and the amount of revenue expected to be generated for the organization

THE SALES MANAGER'S BUDGET

during that period. The budget for the sales force is a valuable resource that the sales manager redistributes among lower level managers. Budget funds must be appropriated wisely in order to properly support selling activities that allow sales personnel and the total marketing group to reach their performance goals. One marketing manager says:

> *I put my budget money where I get the most bang for the buck. To get extra dollars above their minimum operating budget, my sales managers must sell me that their plans will get the job done. If they can't do that, advertising, promotion, and my product managers end up getting more than their share of the marketing budget.*

BUDGET PURPOSES

The budget is an extremely important factor in the successful operation of the sales force. Top sales managers spend a great deal of time attempting to convince corporate management to increase the size of their budgets. Budgets are formulated for many reasons, including the major ones of planning, coordination, and control.

PLANNING   Corporations and their functional units develop objectives for future periods, and budgets determine how these objectives will be met. For example, alternative marketing plans, the probable profit from each plan, and the individual budget for each will be considered before management is able to decide on future marketing programs.

COORDINATION   The budget is a major management tool for coordinating the activities of all functional areas and subgroups within the entire organization. For example, sales must be coordinated with production to ensure that enough products are available to meet demand. The production manager can use sales forecasts and the sales department's marketing plans to determine the necessary production level. Budgeting allows the financial executive to determine the firm's revenues and expenses (for example, accounts receivable, inventory, raw materials, labor) and have enough capital to finance all business operations.

However, some flexibility must be built into the budget so that plans may be changed in response to market conditions. Many companies allocate a dollar lump sum to their sales managers, allowing the managers to invest in the selling activities dictated by the sales and marketing plans. Thus, each sales group (for example, division, region, district) has a budget.

CONTROL   Allocation of budgeted funds gives management control over their use. Sales managers estimate their budget needs, are given funds to operate their units, and then are held responsible for reaching their stated goals by using their budgets effectively. As the sales program is implemented and income and expenses are actually generated, managers assess results against the amount budgeted and determine whether they are meeting objectives.

SALES FORCE BUDGETING METHODS

How much money does the sales manager receive to operate the sales force? Although no fixed financial formulas exist to appropriate funds, firms use one of three general methods to determine how money should be allocated. First, some firms use an arbitrary percentage of sales. Second, other firms may use executive judgment. Third, a few companies estimate the cost of operating each sales force unit along with the costs of each sales program over a specified period to arrive at a total budget. Table 5.3 lists some typical costs entailed in operating a sales force. Whichever method is chosen, the actual amount budgeted will be based on the organization's sales forecast, marketing plans, projected profits, top management's perception of the sales force's importance in reaching corporate objectives, and the sales manager's

TABLE 5.3

SALES FORCE
OPERATING COSTS

1. Base salaries
   a. Management
   b. Salespeople
2. Commissions
3. Other compensation
   a. Social Security
   b. Retirement plan
   c. Stock options
   d. Hospitalization

4. Special incentives
5. Office expenses
6. Product samples
7. Selling aids
8. Transportation expenses
9. Entertainment
10. Travel

skill in negotiating with superiors. Budgets are often modified several times before the final dollar figures are determined.

FORECASTED BUDGET FOR SALES REGIONS

Sales forecasts are used to develop the sales budget. Again, the computer can be used to generate a projected *profit-and-loss (P&L) statement* similar to the one shown in Table 5.4. This P&L statement is divided by sales region for the second quarter of the year. Similar statements would be developed on monthly, quarterly, biyearly, and yearly bases. Then at the end of each reporting period, an actual P&L statement is generated, and a comparison is made between projected and actual results. Part of the manager's performance evaluation is based on the accuracy of staying within the budget.

TABLE 5.4   PROFIT AND LOSS PROJECTED, QUARTER 2

	COMPANY	SOUTH	SOUTHWEST	NORTHEAST	EAST
INCOME					
Sales revenue	$31,539,200	$9,907,200	$11,929,600	$1,459,200	$8,243,200
Less cost of goods sold	19,712,000	6,192,000	7,456,000	912,000	5,152,000
Gross Margin	$11,827,200	$3,715,200	$ 4,473,600	$547,200	$3,091,200
EXPENSES					
Marketing research	120,000	37,695	45,390	5,552	31,364
Advertising	300,000	94,237	113,474	13,880	78,409
Sales promotion	200,000	62,825	75,649	9,253	52,273
Sales support	200,000	62,825	75,649	9,253	52,273
Sales managers' salaries	245,000	70,000	70,000	35,000	70,000
Sales managers' commissions	157,696	49,536	59,648	7,296	41,216
Salespeople's salaries	1,120,000	300,000	360,000	200,000	260,000
Salespeople's commissions	1,576,960	495,360	596,480	72,960	412,160
PERSONNEL					
Training expense	43,000	15,000	1,000	15,000	12,000
Transfer expense	13,000	4,000	2,000	4,000	3,000
Severance expense	8,500	1,000	3,000	2,500	2,000
Total Expenses	$ 3,984,156	$1,192,477	1,402,290	$ 374,694	$1,014,694
Profit before Income Tax	$ 7,843,044	$2,522,722	$ 3,071,310	$ 172,506	$2,076,506
Less for Income Tax	3,921,522	1,261,361	1,535,655	86,253	1,038,253
NET PROFIT	$ 3,921,522	$1,261,361	$ 1,535,655	$ 86,253	$1,038,253
Percent Profit	12.43	12.73	12.87	5.91	12.60

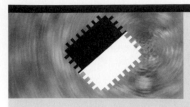

MANAGEMENT IN ACTION: ETHICAL DILEMMA
LET'S BUY IT!

You are asked to make a recommendation to your organization's president of what computer hardware and software to buy. You meet with Mike Stevens—another district manager like yourself—and your boss, George Sterns, to discuss the bids for 30 top computers and forecasting software for the sales force. The computers also require equipment to connect to telephones and software that would interconnect with the current marketing decision support system.

Mike reported, "The companies are close with respect to quality and reputation. The only difference is price, with Kentucky Electronics in the low end and Quantron, Inc., on the high end. I think we should go with Kentucky." George responded, "Are you sure that's the best choice? After all, the plant is over 300 miles away, which could mean problems with delivery and service. I'd prefer Quantron, whom we've used once before. They provided good service. Besides Frank Johns [one of their top people] and I go way back; we were fraternity brothers in college. I can count on him to smooth out any rough spots."

"But the extra 4 percent would put us over budget," Mike said. "The president won't like that."

"Don't worry. It's not such a big overrun. I'll explain the situation."

"But the purchasing regulations require us to accept the lowest bidder, unless there is a difference in quality or some other factor. I've also heard that Kentucky is hungry and has a staff of good programmers," Mike said.

George said, "A few extra pennies won't kill the budget. Hey, Frank is giving a barbecue next weekend. I'll give him a call and squeeze you in. He's a great guy, and you'll enjoy meeting him."

WHAT DO YOU DO?
1. Select Quantron, Inc. Personal contacts are better for the company than formal bids and company regulations. Enjoy the party.
2. Pass the bids to the head of purchasing. Selecting Quantron, Inc., violates regulations, and Kentucky Electronics should be given a chance to compete.
3. Try to persuade George to change his mind. Point out that he is using personal favoritism as his decision criterion. It's your obligation to do the right thing because you are responsible for this project.

BUDGETS SHOULD BE FLEXIBLE

Allocating exact dollar amounts to the sales group is difficult because market conditions may fluctuate. Sales, costs, prices, or the competition's marketing efforts are some factors that may be higher or lower than expected. The sales force should be able to react to market conditions, and therefore the budget should not be fixed in concrete.

Never ask of money spent
Where the spender thinks it went.
Nobody was ever meant
To remember or invent
What he did with every cent.

Robert Frost

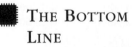

THE BOTTOM LINE

Because of the growing trend in business to centralize data collections, the job of forecasting has become an integral part of a firm's marketing decision support systems (MDSS). The MDSS is a structure that generates, processes, stores, and retrieves data used in a firm's marketing program. The most common data collected are the measurement of market potentials, market share analysis, determination of market characteristics, and sales analysis.

In a survey, 97 percent of the participating firms were involved with sales forecasting. Another survey indicated that company size was the basis for determining responsibility for forecasting. Because of the importance of sales forecasting, sales managers should at least understand the basics involved; their jobs and the jobs of their salespeople depend on accurate forecasting.

A sales forecast is the estimated dollar or unit sales for a specific future period based on a proposed marketing plan and an assumed market environment. The forecast impacts other business functions, including manufacturing, personnel, and purchasing. It depends on many factors that the sales manager must accurately interpret in order to be successful.

Firms know sales forecasting is never 100 percent correct. However, certain factors, when considered, can improve forecast accuracy. Formal training is the most important element; the sales data collected also play a major role, as do unbiased, nonjudgmental decisions. When selecting a forecasting method, a firm should consider several criteria.

Two categories of sales forecasting methods are survey methods and mathematical methods. The four survey methods—executive opinion, sales force composite, user's expectations, and build-to-order—are qualitative. The many mathematical methods are quantitative.

Because the sales forecast has a major impact on the company, the top executives give final approval. Often they review several forecasts before making the final selection. The final choice is usually a compromise between a breakdown and a buildup forecast.

To create a sales forecast, sales managers should know how to use a computer. Not only is it extremely helpful in building the forecast, but it also is used for developing the sales force budget, which is the amount of money available or assigned for a definite period. The budget is based on estimates of expenditures and, therefore, depends on the sales forecast. When the budget is determined, it should remain flexible to move with fluctuating market demand.

KEY TERMS FOR SALES MANAGERS

Marketing decision support system (MDSS), 100
Sales forecast, 101
Forecasting process, 101
Market factor, 101
Market index, 101
Industry sales forecast, 103
Company sales potential, 103

Market share, 103
Survey methods, 103
Mathematical methods, 103
Executive forecasting, 104
Delphi method, 104
Sales force composite, 105
Test markets, 105
Time series projections, 106
Naïve method, 107

Moving averages, 107
Exponential smoothing, 108
Eyeball fitting, 108
Least squares technique, 108
Regression analysis, 108
Sales force budget, 111

MANAGEMENT APPLICATION QUESTIONS

1. Discuss why Dan McKee and people like him are important to sales managers and what role they may occupy in helping a sales manager with forecasts and budgets.
2. Sales forecasting has two broad categories: the breakdown and buildup approaches. Compare these two methods, and discuss whether they should give the sales manager the same final figure.
3. Describe any one survey method of sales forecasting, and identify its strong and weak areas.
4. Using the following information, develop a sales forecast for the next year for this firm using the naïve method, the moving average method (using a three-year average), and a trend projection (using least squares if you know how). Do you think these methods should all give you the same estimate? Why or why not?

XYZ CORPORATION

YEAR	SALES
1995	$ 750,000
1996	825,000
1997	895,000
1998	975,000
1999	1,025,000
2000	1,100,000
2001?	

5. The sales forecast is used to create the sales force budget. What are the three major reasons a budget is formulated?

6. Savvy sales managers know how to use several different types of forecasts to check and recheck sales projections. Determine the method you would use in each of the following situations, and discuss why you would use the method.

    a. You're introducing a new product. Which forecasting method will best assess your short-range sales projections? (1) user's expectations, (2) industry forecast, or (3) test market.

    b. Your company operates in a market where competition is stable. One of the quickest and least expensive methods of sales forecasting for your organization is (1) industry forecast, (2) past sales figures, or (3) test market.

    c. Your actual sales consistently outstrip or fall well below projected sales. Which of the following forecast methods is more likely to produce these results? (1) market survey, (2) user's expectations, or (3) sales force survey.

    d. Your consumer durable or industrial product is used by a relatively small number of buyers. The most logical means of sales forecasting in this situation is (1) user's expectations, (2) statistical correlation analysis, or (3) survey of sales force opinion.

    e. Sales of your product are greatly affected by long-term trends and seasonal changes. The long-term forecasting method that may work best in this situation is (1) statistical correlation analysis, (2) trend and cycle analysis, or (3) market index.

 ## FURTHER EXPLORING THE SALES WORLD

Go to the library and find a recent annual report of a large national corporation that has sales of more than $1 billion. Generally, sales are reported for the past three to five years. Using the naïve and three-year moving-average forecasting methods, project the corporation's sales for (1) years for which you already know the answers and (2) the year after the latest year included in the annual report. If you can find out the sales for 1996, 1997, 1998, and 1999, then determine the accuracy of your forecast by projecting sales for 1997, 1998, and 1999. After using the two forecasting methods, compare your answers with actual sales. Then forecast for 2001 or a year that does not have sales data. Report on your findings. What conclusions can you make concerning the accuracy of your two forecasting methods.

SALES MANAGEMENT EXPERIENTIAL EXERCISE

IS ORGANIZATIONAL SELLING FOR YOU?

You are learning much about selling in this course. Let's find out how much you're learning and also better understand your attitude toward selling. *Three* of the ten statements are false. Which are the false statements? Please first cover the answers.

1. Dealing with customers is less exciting than the work involved in most other jobs.
2. Selling brings out the best in your personality.
3. Salespeople are made, not born; if you don't plan and work hard, you'll never be exceptional at selling.
4. Attitude is more important in selling positions than most other jobs.
5. Those good at selling often can improve their income quickly.
6. Learning to sell now will help you succeed in any job in the future.
7. In your first sales job, what you learn can be more important than what you earn.
8. Selling is less demanding than other jobs.
9. You have less freedom in most selling positions.
10. A smile uses fewer muscles than a frown.[5]

    False statements: 1, 8, and 9.

CASE 5.1

FLORIDA COMPUTER SALES
What Info Is Needed?

When Florida Computer Sales (FCS) opened its doors last year, the lack of information and control became apparent. Customers often wanted to return current equipment and buy new models. This transaction meant finding the new equipment in inventory, estimating trade-in value, handling the financing, and inserting the used equipment into stock. The record keeping involved phone calls back and forth among customers, salespeople, and FCS; filling out paperwork; reviewing sales slips; searching for inventory; and guessing well. Hiring more bookkeepers to keep track of things did not help. FCS's entrepreneurial business, which was growing rapidly until now, may peak soon. Product sales were increasing so rapidly it was almost impossible to avoid having out-of-stock items. Customers and salespeople were complaining, and FCS's business was being hurt.

QUESTIONS
1. What suggestions do you have for improving information and control at FCS?
2. How would a computer information system help FCS give better service to customers?

CHAPTER 6

DESIGN AND SIZE OF SALES TERRITORIES

LEARNING OBJECTIVES

The design, size, and operation of sales territories are critical to a firm's success because they allow the firm to provide service to customers. This chapter will help you to understand:

- The definition of a sales territory.

- Who is responsible for territorial development.

- The factors to consider when designing sales territories.

- The importance of reducing sales leakage.

- How computers can help design territories.

When Digital Equipment Corporation's account team in Connecticut needed to see what marketing manager Joe Batista and his team in Massachusetts had prepared for a client, Batista was able to present his ideas with the click of a mouse. Batista input his ideas into a PowerPoint presentation and uploaded it to Internet Conference Center, a Web-based presentation provided by Contigo Software. Within minutes the software converted the presentation into HTML (a language that prepares files for the Internet) and published it online.

The account team joined Batista via teleconference and used their own computers' Web browsers to log on to the Web site Batista specified. Once the team was logged on, Batista was able to take control of the browsers and lead them through the presentation in real time, highlighting and pointing out specific items as he went. The account reps used their more detailed knowledge of the client to add comments that would help refine the presentation. The client was then shown the presentation online. Batista and his team did not even have to leave their office.

"The use of [Web-based communication] clearly helps shorten our sales cycle," Batista says. Presentations are created and delivered much quicker, sometimes taking weeks less than the process would take face-to-face. "It's all about speed," agrees Julie Creed, a partner at the Chicago-based Financial Relations Board, which uses the same Web product to help clients. Salespeople invite potential investors to simply log on to the Financial Relations Board's Web site for a demo, supplemented by teleconference. If the prospect shows interest, the salesperson may then schedule an in-person meeting.

"They're reaching many more investors this way," Creed says, "because a salesperson who might not have an extra day to fly down to Dallas to give a demo can simply say to a prospect, 'Dial up this Web site and I'll show you what our company's all about.'" Creed says that salespeople are also allowed to have their manager or CEO sit in on an online demonstration—something that would rarely be possible if they had to travel to conduct an in-person presentation. Technology is helping both of these companies significantly reduce the length of their sales cycles, broaden their lists of prospects, and reach more people scattered across large geographical areas.[1] ■

The sales territory is an important business unit containing the organization's customers. Territory design and management are important to the success of the sales force. This chapter introduces you to the factors to consider when designing sales territories. First, let's examine the question "What is a sales territory?"

WHAT IS A SALES TERRITORY?

A **sales territory** is composed of a group of customers or a geographic area assigned to a salesperson. The territory may or may not have geographic boundaries. Typically, however, a salesperson is assigned to a geographic area containing present and potential customers.

As discussed in Chapter 3, companies analyze their total markets by looking at the various market segments, estimating their sales potential, selecting their target markets, and developing a marketing mix based on the needs and desires of the marketplace. Many of these practices also can be applied to a sales territory. In fact, the single sales territory should be considered as an individual market or segment of the company's total market.

WHO IS RESPONSIBLE FOR TERRITORIAL DEVELOPMENT?

Development of sales territories is usually the responsibility of the sales manager overseeing the larger sales units within the organization—for example, the divisional, regional, or zone sales manager. This person knows the markets, customers, and sales personnel needed to service these accounts. The manager makes recommendations to corporate management on whether to increase or decrease the number of sales territories. Often, however, the manager has the authority to change geographic boundaries without corporate approval. It is important that all field managers (for example, district, regional, divisional) affected by territorial change have a part in seeing that the needs of the company, customers, and sales personnel are served.

WHY ESTABLISH SALES TERRITORIES?   Companies develop and use sales territories for numerous reasons. Seven of the more important reasons are discussed here.

To Obtain Thorough Coverage of the Market   With proper coverage of its territories, the company can better achieve the sales potential of its markets. The salesperson can analyze the territory and identify and classify customers. At the individual territorial level, the salesperson can better meet customers' needs. Division into territories also allows management to realign territories easily as customers and sales increase or decrease.

To Establish a Salesperson's Responsibility   Salespeople act as business managers for their territories. They are responsible for maintaining and generating sales volume. Salespeople's job tasks are clearly defined. They know where customers are located and how often they should be called upon. They also know what performance goals they are expected to meet. This can have a positive effect on their performance and morale.

To Evaluate Performance   Performance can be monitored for each territory. Actual performance data can be collected, analyzed, and compared with expected performance goals. Individual territorial performance can be compared with district performance, district compared with regional performance, and regional compared with company performance. With computerized reporting systems, the firm can monitor individual territorial or area performance on a weekly, monthly, or quarterly basis to ascertain the success of its marketing efforts.

To Improve Customer Relations   Customer goodwill and increased sales can be expected when customers receive regular calls. From the customer's viewpoint, the salesperson is the company—for example, Procter & Gamble. The customer looks to the salesperson, not to Procter & Gamble's corporate office, when making purchases. Over the years, some salespeople build up such goodwill relations with their customers that customers will delay placing their orders because they know the salesperson will be at their business on a certain day or at a specific time of the month. Some salespeople even earn the right to order merchandise for certain customers.

To Reduce Sales Expense   Sales territories should be designed to avoid duplication of effort so lower selling costs can be realized and company profits improved. Fewer travel miles, fewer overnight trips, and contacting productive customers regularly can improve the firm's sales/cost ratio. In addition, by using the data collected, management can make decisions about the profitability of territories and determine whether to maintain, expand, or merge sales territories.

To Allow Better Matching of Salesperson to Customer   Salespeople can be hired and trained to meet the requirements of the customers in a specific territory. Indications are that the greater the similarity between customer and salesperson, the more likely the sales effort will be successful.

To Benefit Salespeople and the Company   Proper territorial design must aid salespeople in carrying out the firm's sales strategies. Thus the company can maximize its sales effort, while the salespeople can work in territories that afford them the opportunity to satisfy their personal needs (for example, good salary).

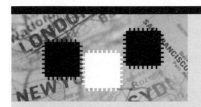

SELLING AND MANAGING GLOBALLY
SALESPEOPLE ARE MAKING IT HAPPEN IN CHINA

Today thousands of American companies are competing to take advantage of the booming market in China. Avon is selling cosmetics door to door. Texaco opened gas stations. Xerox has captured 45 percent of the photocopier market. AST computers hum away in schools and factories while Keystone valves are finding their way into infrastructure projects. Boeing keeps its assembly lines at peak capacity through lucrative aircraft sales to China. Experts estimate that China will purchase 50 to 60 large aircraft per year through 1998 to meet the rapidly growing demand. Motorola built a plant in China that produces 10,000 pagers a week that retail for $200 with a one-year service contract. The market for pagers is estimated at 4 million a year.

AT&T has publicly stated its Chinese business may eclipse its U.S. business after the turn of the century. Although most of the country's 400,000 entrepreneurs view cellular telephones as a necessity, 95 percent of the people in China look with envy at the communication toys used by their rich neighbors.

The insurance giant AIG has hired 140 salespeople who are knocking on doors in Shanghai. According to *The Wall Street Journal,* in eight months they sold more than 12,000 policies.

A few years ago, Diebold Inc., an Ohio-based manufacturer of banking equipment, learned that China was in the process of upgrading 100,000 bank branches. The company sent a lone sales representative, Edgar Petersen, on a two-week trip to China. He visited a number of banks, found a need for safe-deposit boxes, and returned with orders for safe-deposit boxes equal to a year's worth of Diebold's manufacturing capacity. Today, Diebold has captured 60 percent of China's ATM market. Diebold's chair, Robert W. Mahoney, estimates the Chinese market for ATMs will grow to 5,000 units per year within a short time. (That's about one-half the size of the U.S. market.)

Source: Sam Shaw, "Salespeople in China," *Business Week,* October 1995, 83.

Why Sales Territories May Not Be Developed   In spite of its stated advantages, developing sales territories does have disadvantages. First, salespeople may be more motivated if they are not restricted by a particular territory and can develop customers wherever they find them. In the chemical industry, for example, salespeople may be allowed to sell to any potential customer. However, after the sale is made, other company salespeople are not allowed to contact that client. Second, the company may be too small to be concerned with segmenting the market into sales areas. Third, management may not want to take the time, or may not have the know-how, for territorial development. Fourth, personal friendship may be the basis for attracting customers. For example, life insurance salespeople may first sell policies to their families and friends. As a general rule, however, assigning people to their own sales territory is best.

Factors to Consider When Designing Sales Territories

Sales force objectives may be based on factors such as contribution to profits, return on assets, sales/cost ratios, market share, or customer satisfaction. The attainment of sales force objectives is realized at the territorial level. These broad objectives are eventually converted into individual sales territorial goals based on factors such as sales increases, individual product sales, number of sales calls, and number of new customers obtained. Individual territorial sales are an important factor contributing to the achievement of corporate sales goals. For example, for an average territory, Procter & Gamble sales can be in the millions of dollars. Thus a single territory's sales can be greater than the total sales for many small companies.

The design of a firm's sales territory is an important factor in successful selling and in servicing various markets and customers. Figure 6.1 contains the major factors organizations should consider when designing sales territories. In the following example, note how these factors came into play when Kodak decided to realign 300 of its salespeople into a more effective sales organization.

Kodak's business research and marketing groups spent several months interviewing customers to try to discover how to best serve them. The feedback Kodak received prompted the company to reorganize its field force based not only on geography but also on customer needs and salespeople's expertise. Provided with a database of all existing accounts plus sales history data by product line and by customer segment, Kodak's top sales managers generated a new map of its territories using a geographic information systems (GIS) program called MapInfo.

Once these data were mapped out, they were aggregated at the county level, showing the concentration of sales dollars by county and metropolitan statistical area as well as where salespeople were located. The management team then analyzed each salesperson's workload. As a result of this analysis, the Kodak field force was reorganized into nine groups based primarily on the customer type. Salespeople were assigned to certain territories based on their strengths—technical knowledge,

FIGURE 6.1

Factors to Consider When Designing Territories

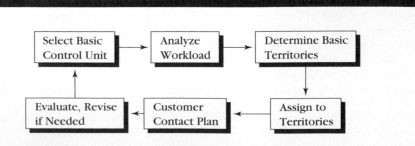

marketing skills, and so forth. With each salesperson focusing on one type of customer, Kodak hopes its salespeople will pay more attention to market trends and will be better able to solve customers' problems.[2]

SELECT BASIC CONTROL UNITS

Based on sales force objectives, sales managers can create, revise, or evaluate basic geographic control units and their territorial boundaries. Usually, territorial boundaries are based on:

- States.
- Counties.
- Cities and ZIP-code areas.
- Metropolitan statistical areas.
- Trading areas.
- Major accounts.
- A combination of two or more factors.

Industry and the type of products a firm sells usually dictate its basic control unit. Many firms use several control units. For example, a national pharmaceutical manufacturer now has 27 distribution centers with approximately 1,000 salespeople in the United States. The state of Texas is one of its sales units, with four sales districts employing 50 salespeople. The northeast Texas sales district has 13 salespeople, 4 of whom contact customers in the Dallas metropolitan area. The individual sales territories of the four salespeople living in Dallas are based on ZIP codes while the salespeople in northeast Texas living outside the metro area have their territories structured around counties.

No matter how a company divides its territories, however, it should always consider present and potential sales of the geographic areas. Customers and prospects become the nucleus around which sales territories are formed. Thus, the individual sales territory can be operated as a business or minimarket.

ANALYZE SALESPEOPLE'S WORKLOADS

It often seems that every company has a different territorial design. Because of differences in salespeople's workloads, firms in the same industry may even have different territorial designs.

Workload is the quantity of work expected from sales personnel. Three of the main influences on workload involve the nature of the job, intensity of market coverage, and type of products sold.

NATURE OF THE JOB   The nature of the job determines the job activities of salespeople. The salesperson who only calls on buyers and does no "missionary," or service, work can be responsible for a much larger geographic area than the salesperson who does both. Many companies selling consumer goods use both a senior salesperson and a service salesperson. The senior salesperson, for example, calls on buyers, while the service salesperson actually goes into the stores and services the accounts. In this way, a larger area can be covered by two salespeople.

INTENSITY OF MARKET COVERAGE   A key sales force strategy involves having the correct number of salespeople required to cover the firm's market. Each firm determines which of these distribution methods works best:

- *Intensive distribution:* Sell the product in every outlet where final customers might reasonably look for it.
- *Selective distribution:* Use a limited number of wholesalers and retailers in a given market.

- *Exclusive distribution:* Use only one wholesaler or retailer in a given market.

Firms using an intensive distribution strategy will require more territories than a firm using a selective or exclusive distribution strategy.

TYPE OF PRODUCTS SOLD   Whether the salesperson sells convenience, shopping, or specialty goods or services has an effect on call patterns and the amount of territory that can be covered. The salesperson who works for Frito-Lay selling snack foods to retail stores has to call on many more accounts than the Dell salesperson who sells computer networks to Fortune 100 organizations.

DETERMINE BASIC TERRITORIES

Once sales managers have selected the basic control unit or units and carefully analyzed salespeople's workload, they are ready to determine how to design the sales territories. Table 6.1 shows the six steps to consider when designing territories.

Step One   *Forecast sales and determine sales potentials.* Using the forecasting methods discussed in Chapter 5, the firm forecasts sales for its total market and for each geographic region. Sales potentials are also considered.

Step Two   *Determine the sales volume needed for each territory.* Next, management determines the level of sales needed to support each territory. Consideration must be given to all costs associated with the territory, including the salesperson's salary and expenses.

Step Three   *Determine the number of territories.* The following are several ways to determine the number of territories needed to sell and service a firm's market. The breakdown approach is the simplest. Steps 4 to 6 then will be discussed.

BREAKDOWN APPROACH   The **breakdown approach** uses factors such as sales, population, or number of customers. Assume a firm forecasts sales of $18 million. It feels that each territory must generate $1 million. Using the following formula, it finds that 18 territories are needed:

$$\text{Sales Force Size} = \frac{\text{Forecasted Sales}}{\text{Average Sales per Salesperson}}$$

The number of customers and population are frequently used to determine the number of territories. The Houston sales district of companies such as Quaker Oats has a guideline of one salesperson for every 100 to 120 retail stores. The population of an area determines the number of retail grocery stores. Thus, sales, population trends, and the number of retail stores help a district manager estimate the number of territories needed in the sales unit.

TABLE 6.1

SIX STEPS TO CONSIDER
WHEN DETERMINING A
FIRM'S BASIC TERRITORIES

1. Forecast sales and determine sales potentials.
2. Determine the sales volume needed for each territory.
3. Determine the number of territories.
4. Tentatively establish territories.
5. Determine the number of accounts for each territory.
6. Finalize the territories, and draw boundary lines.

EQUALIZED WORKLOAD   This method uses the number, location, and size of customers and prospects. Size refers to the amount of actual sales and sales potentials of customers and prospects. For many companies this information has already been collected by the time sales forecasts are made (Chapter 5) and by the time marketing costs and sales are analyzed (Chapter 15).

The firm knows where present customers are located. Field sales managers and their salespeople can provide information on prospects and new companies. Data also can be collected from places such as federal, state, and local governments, trade associations, telephone directories, and *Sales & Marketing Management* magazine's yearly publications on consumer and industrial buying power and sales potentials.

Once a firm determines the number, location, and size of customers and prospects, it needs to determine the frequency of sales calls and amount of time a call takes by using such data as:

- Time required for each sales call.
- Frequency of sales calls per given customers.
- Time intervals between sales calls.
- Travel time around territories.
- Nonselling time.

Here is how a firm can use this information: Sales managers first classify customers to identify the profitable ones. This, in turn, determines where the salesperson's time will be invested. One method of doing this follows:

KEY ACCOUNT	**UNPROFITABLE ACCOUNT**	**REGULAR ACCOUNT**
▪ Buys over $200,000 from us annually ▪ Loss of this customer would substantially affect the territory's sales and profits.	▪ Buys less than $1,000 from us annually ▪ Little potential to increase purchases above $1,000	▪ All other customers

The unprofitable accounts would not be called on; the key accounts and regular accounts become target customers. Once the accounts have been broadly classified, categories or types of accounts can be defined in such terms as extra large (key), large, medium, and small—this will be referred to as the *ELMS system.* For example, management may divide the 3,000 accounts in the firm's total market into these four basic sales categories, as shown in Table 6.2. As can be seen from the table, although relatively few extra large or large accounts exist, these quite often account for 80 percent of a company's profitable sales even though they represent only 20 percent of the total number of accounts. This is referred to as the **80/20 principle.** Eighty percent of a firm's sales comes from 20 percent of customers.

TABLE 6.2

EXAMPLE OF ACCOUNT
SEGMENTATION BASED
ON YEARLY SALES

CUSTOMER SIZE	YEARLY SALES (ACTUAL OR POTENTIAL)	NUMBER OF ACCOUNTS	PERCENT
Extra large	more than $200,000	100	3.3
Large	$75,000–200,000	500	16.7
Medium	$25,000–75,000	1,000	33.3
Small	$1,000–25,000	1,400	46.7
Total customers		3,000	

TABLE 6.3   DETERMINATION OF TOTAL NUMBER OF SALES CALLS

CUSTOMER SIZE	CALL FREQUENCY	(TIMES)	NUMBER OF ACCOUNTS	(EQUALS)	NUMBER OF CALLS PER YEAR
Extra large	1 per month (12)	×	100	=	1,200
Large	1 per month (12)	×	500	=	6,000
Medium	1 per month (12)	×	1,000	=	12,000
Small	1 per quarter (4)	×	1,400	=	5,600
Total			3,000	=	24,800

The number of key accounts in an individual territory varies, as does responsibility for them. Even if a key account is located geographically in a particular salesperson's territory, a key account salesperson may call on the customer. Typically this is done because of the account's importance to the company or the inexperience of the local salesperson.

The accounts with the higher sales or sales potential typically will be assigned to a higher number of sales calls. For example, extra large, large, and medium accounts are called upon once a month; small accounts are called upon every three months.

Assume the company has 3,000 real and potential customers. As shown in Table 6.3, the number of accounts multiplied by the call frequency equals the total number of sales calls the sales force must make per year. Assume a firm has determined that 24,800 calls per year must be made to service its 3,000 customers. It is estimated that the average salesperson works 46 out of every 52 weeks (considering time off for vacation, holidays, and illness). Taking into consideration travel time and nonselling time, the salesperson can make 6 calls per day, 30 calls per week, or 1,380 calls annually. This company needs 18 sales territories.

$$\frac{\text{Total Sales Force Customer Calls}}{\text{Individual Customer Calls}} = \frac{24,800}{1,380} = 18 \text{ Sales Territories}$$

This method is simple and straightforward. Its main drawbacks are that salespeople are not alike in their abilities and that all customers do not have similar characteristics and requirements. For example, all salespeople would not be able to average six daily calls. However, the method can be used in conjunction with management's knowledge of its market.

To revise the number of existing territories, some firms use the **incremental method.** It is based on the assumption that an additional territory can be added if profit contributions from sales in the territory exceed the costs of the territory. Thus, territories are added until the incremental profit contribution from the last additional territory equals the territory's incremental cost. To use this approach, management must know (1) the sales potential of an area, (2) the selling costs, and (3) the costs of production and distribution.

The following is an example of the incremental method applied to a sales district that currently has nine territories. First, assume a firm has estimated product- and distribution-related costs to be 70 percent of sales. The accounting department furnishes this information. This leaves a margin of 30 percent to cover a salesperson's costs, such as salary, car expenses, and profits. Management feels that sales volume is directly related to the number of salespeople. The more salespeople, the higher the district's sales will be. The question is whether increasing the number of territories will produce increased *profitable sales.* The data necessary to obtain an answer are presented in Table 6.4.

TABLE 6.4

PROFIT CONTRIBUTION OF NEW TERRITORY

Forecast sales for "proposed" 10 territories	$1,250,000
Forecast sales for "present" 9 territories	1,125,000
Sales from additional territory	$ 125,000

LESS COSTS

Cost of additional salesperson	$29,000	
Production and distribution costs at 70 percent	87,500	
Total costs		116,500
Profit contribution of additional territory		$ 8,500

TABLE 6.5   PROFIT CONTRIBUTIONS OF ADDITIONAL SALESPEOPLE

ADDITIONAL SALESPEOPLE	SALES INCREASE	(MINUS)	DIRECT SELLING COSTS	(MINUS)	COST OF GOODS SOLD	(EQUALS)	NET PROFIT CONTRIBUTION
10	$125,000	−	$29,000	−	$87,500	=	$8,500
11	100,000	−	29,000	−	70,000	=	1,000
12	80,000	−	29,000	-	56,000	=	−5,000

In this example, a territory can be added to the sales force because forecasted sales exceeded costs, leaving a profit contribution of $8,500. However, this conclusion is based on the assumptions that the increase in sales was due to the added salesperson and that the creation of a new territory would not affect other territories.

This method is particularly appropriate for the firm expanding its markets into previously uncovered or understaffed areas. The major element to consider is the territory's total incremental or marginal cost relative to its incremental or marginal revenue. Although it is assumed the cost of hiring an additional salesperson will be the same as the cost of the existing salespeople, the new salesperson's sales will be lower than those of other salespeople in the region. This is true because the region's sales potential will decrease faster than sales will increase as salespeople are added. Thus, as shown in Table 6.5, as salespeople are added, the profit generated by each new salesperson decreases. Personnel in this sales region could be increased to 11 salespeople for a net profit contribution of $1,000. Beyond this, a loss occurs even though sales are increasing. The addition of the 12th person increases sales by $80,000 but causes a profit loss of $5,000.

The drawbacks to using the incremental method center on the difficulties of estimating marginal sales directly produced by the added salesperson, marginal costs, and production and distribution costs. This method is theoretically attractive but sometimes impractical because of the difficulty of making these estimates.

Step Four   *Tentatively establish territories.* New territories now can be tentatively formed. If possible, each territory should have the same sales potential. This helps in properly evaluating and compensating salespeople.

The entire market can be divided into regions, regions into districts, and districts into sales territories. Contiguous territorial control units can be used to form one territory. If a company selling nationally has 18 salespeople, it might use states to form territories. If it is a regional office-supply firm selling in several states, it could use counties and cities as its basic control unit.

TABLE 6.6

DETERMINATION OF
CUSTOMER NUMBERS FOR
EACH TERRITORY

CUSTOMER SIZE	NUMBER OF ACCOUNTS	NUMBER OF CALLS PER MONTH
Extra large	5	5
Large	28	28
Medium	56	56
Small[a]	78	26
Total	167	115

[a]Contacted once every three months.

Step Five *Determine the number of accounts for each territory.* We determined earlier that using the equalized workload method, one salesperson could make 1,380 sales calls annually or approximately 115 a month. Using the information in Table 6.3, we simply divide the number of accounts by the number of salespeople, or 18, to help determine the number of accounts of each territory.

This was done to create the information in Table 6.6. Slight differences in the numbers occur due to rounding numbers. For example, a total of 500 accounts are classified as "large." Divide 500 by 18 salespeople, and rounded off you have 28 large customers. Each salesperson has a total of 167 accounts of all four sizes. This assumes all salespeople have the same ability and customers are geographically clustered together. This is typically not the situation, so adjustments are made to finalize the territories.

Step Six *Finalize the territories, and draw boundary lines.* Finally, the territories should be adjusted based on factors such as workload requirements, sales, sales potentials, number and size of customers, geographic distances between customers, and any other aspects that may influence territorial boundaries. Boundaries then can be drawn using one or more of the control units, such as states or cities.

ASSIGN TO TERRITORIES

Some salespeople can handle large territories and the travel associated with them; some can't. Some territories require experienced salespeople; some are best for new people. Some people want to live in metropolitan areas such as Chicago, Los Angeles, or Houston. Other people prefer territories with smaller cities. Someone born and raised in New York City may not want to be headquartered in Jackson, Mississippi, and vice versa.

These are a few of the factors a manager needs to consider when assigning new and experienced people to territories. Executive judgment based on past experience generally guides a manager in determining who should be assigned to a specific territory.

This is an important decision since a territory may generate millions of dollars in sales. The wrong person can cost the company in lost sales and bad relationships with customers. The right person can turn a poor territory into a winner. Hiring the right person is so important that the next three chapters involve staffing the sales force.

TABLE 6.7

WEEKLY ROUTE REPORT

TODAY'S DATE: DECEMBER 16		FOR WEEK BEGINNING DECEMBER 26
DATE	CITY	LOCATION
December 26 (Monday)	Dallas	Home
December 27 (Tuesday)	Dallas	Home
December 28 (Wednesday)	Waco	Holiday Inn/South
December 29 (Thursday)	Fort Worth	Home
December 30 (Friday)	Dallas	Home

CUSTOMER CONTACT PLAN

The fifth factor to consider in designing sales territories is the **customer contact plan.** This involves scheduling sales calls and routing a salesperson's movement around the territory.

Scheduling refers to establishing a fixed time (day and hour) when the salesperson will be at a customer's place of business. Routing is the travel pattern the salesperson uses in working a territory. In theory, strict formal route designs enable the salesperson to (1) improve territorial coverage, (2) minimize wasted time, and (3) establish communications between management and the sales force in terms of the location and activities of individual salespeople. When developing route patterns with their manager, salespeople determine the exact day and time of sales calls for each account; approximate waiting time; sales time; miscellaneous time for contacting people such as the promotional manager, checking inventory, or handling return merchandise; and travel time between accounts.

Typically, when the salesperson finishes the work week, a routing report is filled out. It is sent to the supervisor and indicates where the salesperson will be working in the future (see Table 6.7). In the example, today is Friday, December 16, and the salesperson is based in Dallas and planning, during the week of December 25, to call on accounts in Dallas for two days. Then the salesperson plans to work in Waco for a day, spend the night, drive to Fort Worth early the next morning to make calls, and arrive home Thursday night. The last day of the week the salesperson again plans to work in Dallas.

The weekly route report tells management where the salesperson is, and, if necessary, they can contact the salesperson. Some firms may ask their salespeople to specify the accounts they will call on and at what times. For example, on Monday, December 26, the salesperson may write "Dallas, 9:00 ante meridiem, Texas Instruments; Grand Prairie, 2:00 post meridiem, L.T.V." Thus, management also knows which accounts a salesperson will call on during a report period. If no overnight travel is necessary to cover a territory, the company may not require any route reports because the salesperson can be contacted at home in the evening.

CAREFULLY PLANNING ROUTES   At times, routing can be difficult for a salesperson. Customers do not locate themselves geographically for a salesperson's convenience. Also, getting around in large cities is becoming increasingly difficult. In addition, some accounts will see salespeople only on certain days and hours.

In today's complex selling situation, the absence of a well-thought-out daily and weekly route plan is a recipe for disaster. Salespeople cannot operate successfully without it. Imagine you are a salesperson planning your routes. How would you begin?

Start by locating your accounts on a large map. Mount the map on corkboard or foamboard, which can be obtained from an office supply store or picture framing shop. You can use a road map for large territories or a city map for densely populated areas. While you are at the office products store, pick up a supply of map pins with different-colored heads. Place the pins on the map, so you can see graphically where each account is located. For example, you could use:

- Red pins for extra large (EL) accounts.
- Yellow pins for large (L) accounts.
- Blue pins for medium (M) accounts.
- Black pins for small (S) accounts.
- Green pins for best prospects.

Once all the pins are in place, stand back and take a look at the map. Notice first where the EL accounts are located. This will help you determine your main routes or areas where you must go most frequently.

Now divide the map into sections, keeping about the same number of EL accounts in each. Of course, each section should be a natural geographic division; the roads should be located so you can drive easily from your home base to each section and get around readily once you are in a section. Generally, your L, M, and S accounts will fall into place near your EL accounts, with a few exceptions. For example, if you are working on a monthly or four-week call schedule for your ELs, then divide your territory into four sections, and work one section each week. In this way, you will be sure to get to all your ELs and also have the flexibility needed to get to your other accounts on a regular basis. If you had 31 EL, 57 L, 120 M, and 151 S accounts, your sections might look like this, but you would not be able to see all the accounts each week.

SECTION 1	SECTION 2
7 ELs	9 ELs
15 Ls	12 Ls
35 Ms	25 Ms
40 Ss	35 Ss

SECTION 3	SECTION 4
5 ELs	10 ELs
15 Ls	15 Ls
35 Ms	25 Ms
40 Ss	36 Ss

By setting up your geographic routes this way, you could call on all of your EL accounts every four weeks, half of your L and M accounts (making an 8-week call cycle), and one-quarter of your S accounts (making a 16-week call cycle). Allow time for calls on prospective customers, too. Use the same routing procedure as you would for your regular customers. The only difference might be that your prospects would be contacted on a less frequent basis than your customers, in most cases.

No "right number" of sections or routes is correct for all salespersons. The size of their territory, the geographic layout of that part of the country, and the call frequencies they want to establish determine the number of sections or routes. They should lay out the travel route so they can start from their home in the morning and return in the evening. If, however, they have a larger territory, they could make it a Monday to Friday route or a two-day (overnight) route. Remember, the critical factor is travel time, not miles. In some cases, using major nonstop highways may increase miles, but total travel time may decrease.

The actual route salespeople follow each day within each section can help maximize their use of daily prime selling hours. They should make long drives early in the morning and in the late afternoon, if possible. For example, if most of their accounts are strung out more or less in a straight line from their home base, they should get up early and drive to the far end of the territory before making the first call. They would then work their way back, so they end up near home at the end of the day. Figure 6.2 illustrates three basic routing plans, including the straight-line method just mentioned.

USING THE TELEPHONE FOR TERRITORIAL COVERAGE   The telephone has been described as simultaneously a great time-waster and a great time-saver. It all depends on how it is used. The increasing cost of personal sales calls and the increasing time spent traveling to make them are reasons for the efficient territorial manager to look to the telephone as a tool for territorial coverage.

With field selling costs still on the rise and no end in sight, more and more companies are developing telephone sales and marketing campaigns to supplement personal selling efforts. These campaigns use trained telephone communicators and well-developed telephone marketing techniques. Usually, they require a company-wide effort. Here, though, we will concentrate on how an individual territorial manager can use the telephone as a tool to save time on territorial coverage.

Telephone use in the individual territory may be grouped into three categories: sales generating, order processing, and customer servicing. The following are some applications of the telephone in each of these categories:

1. Sales generating
   ■ Selling regular orders to smaller accounts.
   ■ Selling specials, such as offering price discounts on an individual product.
   ■ Developing leads and qualifying prospects.

FIGURE 6.2   THREE BASIC ROUTING PATTERNS

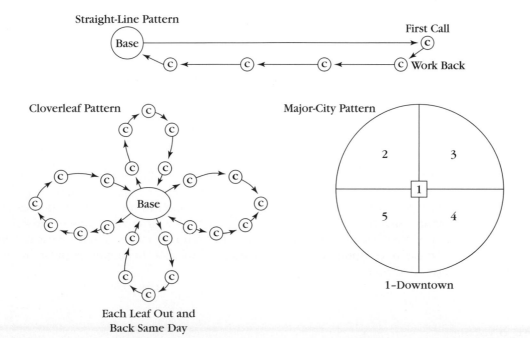

2. Order processing
   - Ordering through the warehouse.
   - Gathering credit information.
   - Checking if shipments have been made.
3. Customer servicing
   - Handling complaints.
   - Answering questions.

Although each salesperson has to decide which types of calls and which accounts may lend themselves to telephone applications, most people can benefit from adopting the following practices, as a minimum, in territorial coverage:

- Satisfying part of the service needs of accounts by telephone.
- Assigning smaller accounts, those that contribute less than 5 percent of business, substantially to telephone selling.
- Doing prospecting, market data gathering, and call scheduling by telephone.
- Carefully scheduling personal calls to distant accounts, replacing some of these personal visits with telephone calls, if possible.

As we have seen, the telephone and the computer are important selling tools for salespeople.

Evaluation and Revision of Sales Territories

Territorial control is the establishment of standards of performance for the individual territory in the form of qualitative and quantitative quotas or goals. Actual performance is compared with these goals for evaluation purposes. The salesperson can see how well territorial plans, strategies, and tactics were carried out toward meeting performance quotas. If quotas were not met, then new plans must be developed for the territory.

Many companies routinely furnish managers and individual salespeople with reports on the number of times during the year their salespeople have called on each account and the date of the last sales call. Management can monitor the frequency of—and time intervals between—calls for each of their salespeople.

As an example, a national pharmaceutical company supplies its sales force with the "net sales by customer and call report." The report lists each customer's name, address, and medical specialty. The desired number of monthly calls on a given customer and the actual number of calls to date are noted. Net sales are broken down into last year's sales, the current month's sales, and year-to-date sales. Finally, the date the salesperson last called on each customer is reported. Using this type of information, which might include 200 to 300 customers for each salesperson, management and salespeople can continually review sales call patterns and customer sales to update call frequency and scheduling.

REVISING SALES TERRITORIES   Management can follow the same procedures shown in Figure 6.1 when revising sales territories. Many companies continually evaluate their sales territories. Changes can be made, such as increasing or decreasing the number of territories or shifting geographic boundaries while keeping the same number of territories. These revisions help the company respond to business conditions. The use of computers to redesign sales territories is becoming popular and will be discussed later.

The Sales Territory Is a Business

Picture the individual sales territory as a business unit that incurs costs and generates revenues. The salesperson is the manager of that business—territory—responsible for improving sales.

TABLE 6.8   SALES LEAKAGE IS COSTLY!

1. If you have 30 salespeople and lose no one during the year:

    30 × 12 months = 360 yearly sales-months
2. If it takes an average of 4 months (hiring and training) to fill a territory and you lose 9 salespeople a year:

    9 × 4 months = 36 months of sales leakage
3. Now you're down to 324 yearly sales-months or a 3-year loss of sales time.
    - If the average $30,000-per-month territory lost $15,000 the first month and from $20,000 to $22,000 per month the next 3 months, then losses are about $75,000 until the vacancy is replaced with a new salesperson.
4. Many managers estimate a new salesperson sells only 50 percent of the industrial sales territory's potential in the first 6 months.

    This does not include
    - Recruiting costs—air, hotel, advertisements, or recruiters' fees.
    - Training—space, personnel, and travel.

THE RIGHT SALESPERSON PAYS OFF

Sales can go up or down within the territory, often depending on the salesperson. Take Jim Lane, for example, who sells for an electrical distributor in Dallas. Eighteen months after being assigned, Lane increased sales more than $1 million. In doing so, he created $110,000 of pure profit for his employer.

OPEN SALES TERRITORIES

Open sales territories are those left vacant until new salespeople are assigned to them. Jim Lane caused sales to increase in his new territory. However, vacant territories experience the following:

- Lost sales due to the vacancy.
- Lost sales due to the time needed for the new salesperson to build sales productivity—often five to six months to reach the entire sales force's sales average.

Sales leakage refers to the lost sales due to both the vacancy and the time required for the new salesperson to produce at average. Sales leakage can be very expensive, as shown in Table 6.8. The table information was provided by Texas Distributors, a wholesaler of construction materials.

USING COMPUTERS TO DESIGN TERRITORIES

A sales territory is a dynamic environment, constantly involving changes in customers, competitors, products, and sales force turnover. Although this creates imbalances in workloads and potential sales, managers are reluctant to realign their territories to reflect such changes because the tedious calculations consume time.

Marion Merrell Dow, Cincinnati, a Dow Chemical subsidiary, put an end to such reluctance with a PC-based mapping software that enables managers to realign territories and see an instant visual display of the effects of such realignment in a matter of minutes. Using the Maps III (Manpower Allocation and Planning System), a manager inputs criteria such as potential and actual sales, doctor and pharmacy counts, and travel time. Maps III combines this business data with geographic features, road networks, and five-digit ZIP codes to come up with the optimal territorial alignment.

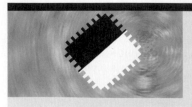

MANAGEMENT IN ACTION: ETHICAL DILEMMA
IS IT TOO EARLY TO TELL?

You and all of your firm's other regional managers recently met at your corporation's home office where the company's long-range sales plans, objectives, and quotas were discussed. Although no specific discussion on confidentiality occurred, you assumed the plans were to be kept a secret. One of your trustworthy district managers is determined to find out what happened at the meeting.

WHAT DO YOU DO?
1. Share the information, since no warnings were given. Besides, he works for the same company, and he would do the same.
2. Find out why he wants to know, or needs to know, before deciding what to do.
3. Treat the meeting as confidential, and refuse to discuss it with the district manager even if it jeopardizes your friendship.

The program was especially helpful when the company replaced its single sales force with two sales forces to get broader product coverage. One Marion Merrell Dow sales force promotes prescription pharmaceuticals, while a Lakeside sales force sells over-the-counter drugs. In all, the United States had to be redivided to create 400 Marion Merrell Dow sales territories and 250 Lakeside territories.

"Such a task," Dan McKee, manager of marketing decision support systems, says, "ordinarily takes a lot of time, hand-drawn maps, grease pencils, and plastic overlays. In addition, there are hours consumed in doing the arithmetic involved with the attributes assigned to individual sales territories and redrawing the boundaries. The PC does the arithmetic for a territory in a matter of seconds, and it creates a map of the realigned boundaries in two minutes."

Robert Mayne, sales operations manager, adds: "Human judgment still plays a role when the manager uses Maps III. However, the program gives him instant feedback on what he is thinking of doing, so that if his first realignment still leaves something out of balance, he makes further adjustments until he has the balance he wants. Thus he's able to try out more workable solutions until he is satisfied that he has the optimal territory alignment with regards to such factors as market potential and the experience level of sales representatives."

Computerized mapping is part of the company's effort to beef up its integrated planning. "Maps III, a new call reporting system, and mathematical models," McKee says, "will be rolled together to sharpen our marketing strategy. Because Maps III will be used with our management reports, we'll have a better idea of what's being done and where—and what's not being done."

THE BOTTOM LINE

According to salespeople, managing time and territory is the most important factor to be considered when carrying out their selling duties. This area of selling is emphasized heavily by companies and sales managers. The sales territory is a group of customers or a geographic area assigned to a salesperson; it is usually developed by the sales manager.

Developing sales territories has advantages as well as certain disadvantages. Salespeople may be more motivated if they are unrestricted, or the company may be too small to justify segmenting the market. Also, the manager may not want, or have the knowledge, to develop territories.

Sales force objectives are usually converted into individual sales territorial goals. The design of a territory is important to successful selling. Territorial boundaries are based on states, counties, cities, ZIP-code areas, metropolitan statistical areas, trading areas, or major accounts. The industry a firm belongs to determines its basic control unit.

The three main influences affecting the sales personnel's workload are nature of the job, intensity of market coverage, and products sold.

Before designing sales territories, managers must consider six factors. First, they must forecast and determine the sales volume needed for each territory. Next, they must determine the number of territories. They can use the breakdown approach or the equalized workload. Once the number and location of customers are determined, the key accounts must be established by their equal sales potentials. Managers determine the number of accounts for each territory by dividing the number of accounts by the number of salespeople in each territory. The last step is to finalize territories and draw boundary lines.

The customer contact plan includes scheduling sales calls and routing a salesperson's movement around the territory. Routes should be planned carefully so no time is wasted in traveling. The telephone also can be used to save time.

Territorial control allows actual performance to be compared with standards of performance for evaluation purposes. Companies want to avoid costly sales leakage. Computers can be programmed to design the ever-changing territories.

■ KEY TERMS FOR SALES MANAGERS

Sales territory, 120	80/20 principle, 125	Territorial control, 132
Sales force objectives, 122	Incremental method, 126	Open sales territories, 133
Workload, 123	Customer contact plan, 129	Sales leakage, 133
Breakdown approach, 124	Scheduling, 129	

■ MANAGEMENT APPLICATION QUESTIONS

1. What is a sales territory, and what may be some of the reasons a firm establishes sales territories? Can you think of a reason why a firm might not want to have sales territories?
2. What major factors do organizations consider when designing sales territories?
3. What are the six steps to consider when determining a firm's basic territories? Step number 4 has three methods—what are they?
4. Assume Music Express, Inc., has 6,000 prospects and customers. It is estimated that each salesperson can average 1,400 prospect and customer sales calls during a year. The entire sales force will need to make a total of 50,000 calls on prospects and customers. How many salespeople does Music Express need to have in its sales force? Explain your answer.
5. Use the following information to determine the sales force size for this company using both the equalized workload and the incremental methods. Should these two methods give the same result?

   The regional manager has asked you to decide if you should hire more salespeople for your district. Right now you have seven sales territories with one person assigned to each. The total number of real and potential customers in the district is 2,100. Present sales in the district are $750,000. Production and distribution costs are 60 percent of sales. If you add another salesperson, sales should go up 10 percent; two salespeople should increase it by 19 percent; and three salespeople would boost sales 24 percent. Of the 2,100 customers, 300 could be classified as A accounts, 700 as B accounts, and the rest as C accounts. It has been determined that A accounts need to be called on at least once every two weeks, B accounts once a month, and C accounts about once a quarter. Each salesperson should be able to make about ten sales calls in a day. Each salesperson added to the sales force will cost the firm another $25,000.

6. One of your salespeople has come to you for help. He is having trouble calling on his accounts. He says he feels his territory is too large and spread out, and he feels as though he is spending all his time in the car instead of making sales calls. What steps would you take to help him develop a more effective sales route?

7. Discuss why sales managers are using the telephone more in their work. For what kinds of applications might the telephone be useful?

FURTHER EXPLORING THE SALES WORLD

Contact any organization with two or more people in its outside sales force. Find out (1) who is responsible for determining the number of salespeople and sales territories, (2) the factors considered in designing sales territories, and (3) if accounts and prospects are segmented.

SALES MANAGEMENT EXPERIENTIAL EXERCISE

YOUR SELLING DAY: A TIME AND TERRITORY GAME

Your sales manager is working with you tomorrow only, and you want to call on your customers with the greatest sales potential (see Exhibit 6.1 below). Because you are on a straight commission, you will have the opportunity to maximize your income for that day. The area of your territory that you feel should be covered tomorrow contains 16 customers (see Exhibit 6.2 on the following page). To determine travel time, allow 15 minutes for each side of each small square. Each sales call takes 30 minutes. You can leave your house at 8:00 A.M. or later. Time for lunch must be taken in 15-minute blocks of time (for example, 15, 30, 45, or 60 minutes). Your last customer cannot be contacted after 4:30 P.M. in order to allow enough sales time. Your customers do not see salespeople after 5:00 P.M. Travel home can be done after 5:00 P.M.

Questions

1. Develop the route that gives the highest sales potential for the day your boss works with you.

2. For the next day, develop the route allowing you to contact the remaining customers in this part of your territory.

EXHIBIT 6.1

CUSTOMERS' SALES POTENTIALS

CUSTOMER	SALES POTENTIAL	CUSTOMER	SALES POTENTIAL
A	$4,000	I	$ 1,000
B	3,000	J	1,000
C	6,000	K	10,000
D	2,000	L	12,000
E	2,000	M	8,000
F	8,000	N	9,000
G	4,000	O	8,000
H	6,000	P	10,000

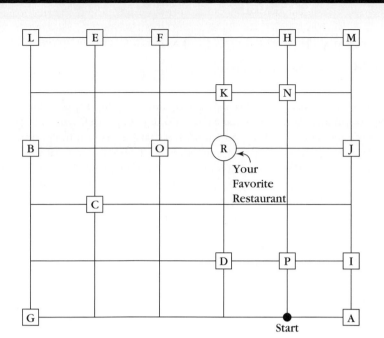

Start

EXHIBIT 6.2

PARTIAL MAP OF YOUR
SALES TERRITORY

CASE 6.1

ARIZONA ELECTRICAL, INC.
Is the Information Important?

Arizona Electrical sales reports prove that one of your salespeople is a top producer—creative, popular, and a super problem solver. Joe Jingle is almost the ideal member of your sales team. But not quite. The problem is with the quantity and quality of his written reports. For one thing, he never delivers them on time. If you do get them at all, it's only because you've nagged to the point of embarrassment. What's more, Joe's reports are downright cryptic—so terse, hasty, and abrupt they rarely contain useful information. The data they do contain read more like inadequately substantiated hints, rather than facts. Naturally, you hesitate to base your sales plans and forecasts on this top producer's "field intelligence."

Nobody really likes to write reports, especially when they have to be done every week within a specific deadline. Sure, it seems that just as you finish one report, you have to start another. That's the way of corporate life—your life and those of all the people who work in a hierarchical structure. The time has come for you to do something that, once and for all, will solve this problem and keep it solved.

QUESTION
What do you do?

SALLY MALONE'S DISTRICT
Development of an Account Segmentation Plan

Sally Malone sat patiently listening to her boss talk about the new time and territorial management program her company was implementing. Her boss was saying, "Since we wish eventually to establish priorities for our accounts in order to make time-investment decisions, we must classify the accounts into categories. A simple A, B, C, D, E designation of categories is the most commonly used approach, with A accounts the most valuable.

"The basis for setting the values or limits for each category is the distribution of sales, or concentration patterns, in most industries. In general, business in our company is distributed approximately as shown in Exhibit 1. Generally, the top 10 percent of the accounts will generate 65 percent, and the top 30 percent will generate 85 percent of the sales in any given territory. Salespeople may use this rule-of-thumb breakdown in determining the classification system for their accounts. Once the sales potential for all their accounts has been calculated, their territory should break down like this on the basis of that potential:

- A accounts = top 10 percent of the accounts, numerically
- B accounts = next 20 percent of the accounts, numerically
- C accounts = next 50 percent of the accounts, numerically
- D accounts = next 10 percent of the accounts, numerically
- E accounts = last 10 percent of the accounts, numerically

"Sally, I want you to have each of your salespeople take a close look at his or her sales call cycles. As I have explained, a call cycle is a round of calls in which all A

accounts are called on at least once and some, but not all, B, C, D, and E accounts are called on. When a salesperson has visited all of his or her A accounts, the cycle is completed. Then a new cycle begins, and the series of calls repeats itself. Since not all B, C, D, and E accounts are called on in every cycle, the specific accounts to be seen in these classifications differ from cycle to cycle. A call cycle, therefore, is established around the call frequency patterns of A accounts.

"Suppose a group of accounts is classified in this way:

ACCOUNTS	EXPECTED VALUE
A	$100,000 plus
B	50,000–100,000
C	30,000–50,000
D	20,000–30,000
E	Less than $20,000

"The call frequency patterns, therefore, based on potential and return on time invested, may be as follows:

ACCOUNTS	WEEKS BETWEEN CALLS	NUMBER OF ACCOUNTS
A	2	10
B	4	20
C	6	45
D	8	12
E	10	10

"Thus, a call cycle in this territory will cover two weeks. This means that in every two-week cycle the salesperson will call on these accounts:

- All of the As
- Half of the Bs
- One-third of the Cs
- One-fourth of the Ds
- One-fifth of the Es."

QUESTIONS

1. Develop a table showing a salesperson's call cycle using the call frequency patterns.
2. Discuss why this should be done.

EXHIBIT 1   DISTRIBUTION OF SALES

CUSTOMER CLASSIFICATION	PERCENTAGE OF CUSTOMERS	PERCENTAGE OF TOTAL SALES VOLUME
A	10	65
B	20	20
C	50	10
D	10	3
E	10	2
	100	100

CHAPTER 7

SALES OBJECTIVES AND QUOTAS

CHAPTER OUTLINE

LEARNING OBJECTIVES

Objectives and quotas are fundamental parts of a company because they provide the sales force with direction and goals. Selling by objectives (SBO) is a system that unites the sales force. This chapter should help you understand:

■ The relationship between sales objectives and quotas.

■ Why quotas are important.

■ The various types of quotas.

■ The methods for setting quotas.

■ Criteria needed for a good quota plan.

■ Major areas for establishing objectives.

■ How organizations set objectives.

■ The selling by objectives process.

Just as plants need sunlight and water to grow, to increase a company's revenues there must be organization and planning. One way that companies boost their revenues is through cross-selling, a process that takes careful planning and structure. When a company's product involves technical information, there must be even more organization. Automation can assist the sales force in this task, and the more automated they are, the more likely it is that there will be success in the cross-selling effort.

An example of a company that uses cross-selling to meet its marketing goals is Astra Pharmaceuticals LP. Astra is a company that looked at its marketing organization and came up with a system to increase its revenues. Through the use of technology, the company has been able to boost their power of customer interaction, and that has given them an increase in sales.

Astra uses a sophisticated customer database and sales automation system that has allowed them to facilitate and encourage cross-selling in their company. Cross-selling, which can be one of the best ways to increase the profitability of a customer, can sometimes turn out to be a tangled mess. Astra's database system has helped to prevent this from occurring.

This system enables the best practices to be shared across the enterprise, as the company deploys its "virtual teams" to address the specific needs of customers. For example, two Astra sales reps with technical expertise in two unrelated drugs can visit the same physician at different times and still coordinate their sales calls in ways designed to leverage the company's overall strength. The software that they use to meet their goals allows the sales calls to "mirror" each other in terms of the background each rep has about a specific physician.

This way, the company doubles its exposure to each physician and effectively enables the efforts of one product's sales force to leverage the efforts of another's. When that interaction is coordinated at an enterprise level with the use of this automation, the power of customer interaction is fully demonstrated.[1] ∎

Goals—such as those of Astra Pharmaceuticals—are based on the sales force's objectives and plans developed to reach them. Sales personnel live or die according to how they perform relative to their quotas. Quotas are the targets everyone shoots for. They are very important because if quotas are met, then sales forecast numbers are met, which makes top management happy.

This chapter introduces you to the procedures used to set objectives and quotas for the sales force. It discusses how managers develop plans, convert objectives into quotas, implement the plans, and then evaluate results. Let's examine how this is done by first defining the term *quota* and discussing why quotas are important.

WHAT IS A QUOTA?

A **quota** refers to an expected performance objective. Quotas are routinely assigned to sales units, such as regions and districts. Quotas also are assigned to individual salespeople.

Quotas are tactical in nature and thus derived from the sales force strategic objectives. Strategies stem from marketing and sales plans, sales forecasts, and budgets. Thus, quotas are guides for what needs to be done and a means of evaluating how well they were done.

WHY ARE QUOTAS IMPORTANT?

Quotas are of major importance because they establish the "end state"—the bottom line sought by the sales force. They are not static but are dynamic guides to sales force behavior. Quotas are ever-changing due to experience, feedback, and internal and external forces to the organization.

QUOTAS PROVIDE PERFORMANCE TARGETS

Quotas give direction to the sales force. Efforts and resources can be directed toward specific ends or targets the organization designates as important—for example, a 6 percent sales increase. Targets, in turn, provide incentives.

Because the organization tends to reward the type and level of behavior needed to reach corporate objectives, salespeople typically find financial rewards attached to the attainment of quotas. Job quotas represent the manager's expectations about the activities to be accomplished and about the level of accomplishment targeted for the time period.

QUOTAS PROVIDE STANDARDS

Quotas provide standards or means of determining job activities. They are a means of obtaining feedback and evaluating the salesperson's performance.

Management compares the salesperson's assigned quotas with actual accomplishments. These quotas become the primary basis for evaluating the performance of sales groups (that is, regions or districts) and individual salespeople. For example, sales quotas are used to evaluate the results of sales contests and to determine pay increases and promotions.

QUOTAS PROVIDE CONTROL

Quotas provide control because they serve to guide or direct the behavior of salespeople. *Authority* is the formal right to exercise control. When a new salesperson joins the company, he or she enters into an authority relationship with the superior.

The superior has the formal power to ask the salesperson to do something the person would not do otherwise and the right to punish for noncompliance. The salesperson's acceptance of this authority gives the organization a means by which to influence or control the salesperson.

Control can serve as an indirect supervisory technique. The superior has the authority to require the salesperson to average ten calls each day. The salesperson fills out call reports and sends them to the superior. Even though the superior is not working directly with the salesperson, the salesperson knows that ten calls must be made, so the salesperson's activities are indirectly monitored. Quotas may be set for total sales volume, individual products' sales volume, expenses, or the number of new accounts. The salesperson, therefore, concentrates efforts on these activities.

QUOTAS PROVIDE CHANGE OF DIRECTION

Quotas may serve to redirect the activities of the salesperson. For example, Colgate might emphasize only part of the product line during a sales period of two months.

At the beginning of a period, a company holds sales meetings to present the products to be emphasized to the customers. Sales quotas, possible contests, and selling techniques are discussed. Different behavior is achieved by placing sales quotas on different products. For example, salespeople slow up on selling a product the firm is not emphasizing during the current sales period and concentrate on selling a new product with a quota attached to it.

QUOTAS ARE MOTIVATIONAL

Quotas provide performance targets, standards, controls, and direction. Most important of all, quotas directly influence salespeople's motivational levels. Set a quota people believe in, promise them a reward for making quota, and then stand back and watch them work hard to reach their goal.

Quotas cause the entire sales team to turn their efforts toward common goals. Everyone gets excited about the challenge of making quota. One extreme example of this excited motivational style is Fred Thomas of Xerox Corporation, who is known to be so obsessed with quotas that he never turns off his drive. This leads to his selling at home, on vacation, and during other aspects of his personal life. Thomas motivates his fellow salespeople as he propels the excitement toward meeting the quotas. Quotas directly influence the amount of energy salespeople aim toward the sales target.[2]

TYPES OF QUOTAS

Organizations set many types of quotas. The most common quotas concern sales volume, gross margin or net profit, expenses, activities, and some combination of these four.

SALES VOLUME QUOTAS

Most, if not all, companies have sales volume quotas for their salespeople. **Sales volume quotas** include dollar or product unit objectives for a specific period of time. For example, General Mills uses dollar objectives, whereas Ford Motor Company's Marnie Quinn uses quotas based on the number of cars and trucks. Companies with relatively few items that carry high unit prices, such as cars, appliances, electronics, and airplanes, often use units instead of sales.

Total sales volume quotas are first set for the year. The yearly total volume quota is then set for shorter time periods such as six months, three months, two months, and one month.

BREAK DOWN TOTAL SALES VOLUME   Once salespeople know what their sales targets for the year are and how much they have to sell throughout the year to reach the total sales objective, they need to get down to the specifics. To do this, they ask themselves these questions: To whom are we going to sell? Where are they located geographically? Which products will be sold? Which products will sell the best? During what time period will these sales occur?

While answering these five questions, salespeople will establish sales volume quotas for the following:

- Product lines.
- Individual established and new products.
- Geographic areas based on how the sales organization is designed, which would include:
  - Sales divisions.
  - Sales regions.
  - Sales districts.
  - Individual sales territories.

Companies often establish sales quotas for each of the items for which they make a sales forecast.* Once set, these quotas become important sales targets and serve to evaluate job performance. Table 7.1 shows the total district sales volume quotas for a sales manager.† As you can see, the district did not make sales quota this year due to salesperson McNeal. Three of the four salespeople made quota. Later in this chapter, you will see other quotas and performance data used by this company.

PROFIT QUOTAS

Although sales volume is important, profits are more important. Today, sales managers are asked to generate profitable sales. Firms may set **profit quotas,** along with sales volume quotas, for salespeople, districts, regions, and even products and customers. Companies realize they must make a profit to stay in business.

THE TWO TYPES OF PROFIT QUOTAS   Companies develop profit quotas using either the gross margin or the net profit approach. The **gross margin quota** is determined

TABLE 7.1

COMPARATIVE TOTAL YEARLY SALES VOLUME FOR THE MIDWEST SALES DISTRICT

PERSON	SALES QUOTA (000)	ACTUAL SALES (000)	DOLLAR DIFFERENCE	PERFORMANCE INDEX[a]
Hise	$ 5,696	$ 5,792	$ 96	101.7
McNeal	5,584	4,842	−742	86.7
Young	6,012	6,046	34	100.6
Ford	4,310	4,334	24	100.6
Total	$21,602	$21,014	−$ 588	97.4[b]

[a](Actual Sales/Quota) × 100.
[b]Average of performance index.

*Refer back to Chapter 5 and review the basic steps and items in the breakdown and buildup methods of forecasting sales

†The names of people and products have been changed to provide anonymity for the sales personnel.

by subtracting cost of goods sold from sales volume. The cost of goods sold information is supplied by the firm's manufacturing department. It tells how much it costs to manufacture the product.

Some companies go one step further and determine net profit. The **net profit quota** is determined by subtracting cost of goods sold and salespeople's direct selling expenses from sales volume. This latter method is shown in Table 7.2. Cost of goods sold averaged around 80 percent of sales for this company. Salesperson Hise sold $5,792,000 with manufacturing costs of $4,633,600, or a gross profit margin of $1,158,400. Hise's salary was $45,600. Car, travel, entertainment, and administrative expenses were $22,400, leaving a net profit of $1,090,400 for the territory. This company uses a sales-to-net-profit ratio to evaluate profits. Hise's 18.8 percent ratio (net profit/sales) compares favorably to other salespeople in the district. An 18.5 percent ratio is considered acceptable by management. Salesperson Ford was asked to reduce his expenses so the ratio would rise above the 18 percent level.

One drawback to using profit quotas is that sales personnel generally do not set prices and have no control over manufacturing costs; therefore, they are not responsible for gross margins. Another problem arises when the net profit approach is used. Salespeople may cut back so far on expenses that it has a negative impact on sales. This may have happened with salesperson McNeal. He was asked to spend more on entertaining his prospects and customers. It was felt this might help his sales (see Table 7.1). The sales manager constantly must monitor expenses to make sure salespeople are spending enough, yet not too much, toward generating profitable sales.

EXPENSE QUOTAS

It is costly to operate a sales force. The cost of automobiles, entertainment, meals, and lodging keep going up and up. Many companies establish **expense quotas** aimed at controlling costs of sales units. Often expenses are related to sales volume or to the compensation plan.

A salesperson may receive an expense budget that is a percentage of the territory's sales volume. The salesperson must manage this expense dollar amount as if it were a bank checking account.

Other companies prefer to set upper dollar limits on items such as lodging, meals, and entertainment. These same companies often pay all expenses related to the car and office expenses. In this manner, they hope salespeople will avoid decreasing expenses to such a low level that they hurt sales.

	HISE	MCNEAL	YOUNG	FORD
Sales	$5,792,000	$4,842,000	$6,046,000	$4,334,000
Cost of Sales	4,633,600	3,873,600	4,836,800	3,467,200
Gross Margin	$1,158,400	$ 968,400	$1,209,200	$ 866,800
EXPENSES				
Salary	$ 45,600	$ 43,200	$ 40,800	$ 38,400
Other	22,400	28,800	23,200	49,600
Total Expenses	$ 68,000	$ 72,000	$ 64,000	$ 88,000
Net Profit	$1,090,400	$ 896,400	$1,145,200	$ 778,800
Sales/Net Profit Ratio	18.8%	18.5%	18.9%	18.0%

TABLE 7.2

CONDENSED COMPARATIVE PROFIT FOR MIDWEST SALES DISTRICT'S TERRITORIES

ACTIVITY QUOTAS

According to Jim Mobley of General Mills, the activities of a salesperson have a direct impact on sales. "There is no doubt about it," he says. "Certain activities create sales, so we put quotas on them."

"For example," he adds. "One additional sales call a day is 5 a week, 20 a month, and 240 calls a year. If the average salesperson sells an extra product to 10 percent of the people contacted, you have an extra 24 sales a year."

"Multiply that by the number of salespeople in the sales force," Mobley concludes, "and you're talking about big dollars."

Quotas cause salespeople to respond to them. If a sales force averages six sales calls a day and the manager wants to increase the average, chances are the manager can—by setting a quota of seven calls. The same thing can happen when quotas are set on the number of prospects contacted each day.

Activity quotas set objectives for job-related duties useful toward reaching salespeople's performance targets. They help direct salespeople toward performing important nonselling activities. For example, activity quotas are used in food sales where displays are built and products are straightened on the retailer's shelves. They are common in consumer and industrial sales where the salesperson must provide service after the sale.

Unfortunately, many salespeople do not view some activities as important. They prefer to do things resulting in sales today, not next month. Thus, salespeople may do the activity but infrequently or at a low-quality level. They have been known to falsify their activity reports on jobs not felt important.

Activity quotas typically should not be a basis for rewards. Rather, their attainment helps the manager better understand why salespeople do or do not meet their sales volume quota.

Table 7.3 shows how a company uses the sales call activity to compare salespeople. This company computerizes this information. It has determined that its "average" salesperson works 46 out of 52 weeks (considering time off for vacations, holidays, illness, and meetings) or 230 days each year. This salesperson works 5 days a week and makes 6 calls per day for a yearly total of 1,380 sales calls. Thus, three of the four salespeople shown in Table 7.3 are above the yearly company sales call average.

CUSTOMER SATISFACTION

Companies increase sales by reselling to current customers and getting new business through customer referrals. Thus, it is very important to keep customers happy.

TABLE 7.3   COMPARATIVE ACTIVITIES FOR THE MIDWEST SALES DISTRICT

PERSON	NUMBER OF CALLS	NUMBER OF ORDERS	ORDER/ CALL RATIO^	ACTUAL SALES (000)	AVERAGE SALES REP ORDER	TOTAL CUSTOMERS
Hise	1,900	1,140	60.0%	$ 5,792	$ 5,081	195
McNeal	1,500	1,000	66.7	4,842	4,842	160
Young	1,400	700	50.0	6,046	8,637	140
Ford	1,030	279	27.1	4,334	15,534	60
Total	5,830	3,119	51.0%	$21,014	$ 6,737	555

^Average of order/call ratio.

SELLING AND MANAGING GLOBALLY
WORKING A DEAL IN THE ARAB WORLD

Buyers in the Arab world are very hospitable and favorably disposed toward salespersons. Decisions there are frequently based on personal impressions supplemented by facts. The business climate and the tone of communication are very important. Arabs consider business transactions as social events; bargaining is an enjoyable and integral part of life.

Salespeople must respect all the religious and cultural customs of their Arab partners. They should remember that during the course of negotiations the Arabs may not be available at all times because of their religious customs.

One particularly aggravating practice to American businesspeople is that an Arab counterpart never says "no" directly; this custom avoids any loss of face on either side. By being aware of this, an American can respond accordingly.

At the end of the negotiation, an Arab counterpart signals agreement orally and commits himself firmly by giving his word. If circumstances change, however, an Arab buyer feels free to renegotiate a modification of the agreement.[3]

Source: Adapted from Sergy Frank, "Global Negotiation," *Sales & Marketing Management* (May 1996): 64-69.

Customer satisfaction refers to feelings about any differences between what is expected and actual experiences with the purchase. To measure customer satisfaction, organizations typically construct questionnaires that ask for customer feedback on factors such as the product purchased, price, after-sale follow-up, and the salesperson.

It can become very difficult to keep track of all the customer satisfaction data. Therefore, organizations find it easier to develop a **Customer Satisfaction Index** (or Rating). This index is usually a compilation of all scores into one number or percentage. For example, a company can ask customers to rate 50 items or factors related to their satisfaction, take an average of all those scores, and call it the index. A firm also can weigh the responses according to importance and then create an index from the weighted scores. However it is done, remember that the Customer Satisfaction Index is not each individual rating but an average or compilation of many ratings.

QUOTA COMBINATIONS

Many companies in all industries use a combination of these quotas. The two most common are sales volume and activity quotas. These quotas influence selling and non-selling activities.

One note of caution. It is important not to have too many quotas; otherwise, the salespeople may become confused as to what is expected. Several quotas should be used, but they should be on the most important activities, total sales volume, and the products that result in the most sales. "There are 15 items that we sell that comprise 70 percent of our business," Jim Mobley says. "We really concentrate on them by setting volume quotas on these items."

Sales quotas may be set in several ways. Let's survey several basic methods companies use most frequently for setting quotas and then examine how they actually set quotas.

METHODS FOR SETTING SALES QUOTAS

QUOTAS BASED ON FORECASTS AND POTENTIALS

For the large national corporations in the United States, the most common method for setting quotas is the use of sales forecasts plus market and territory potentials. The majority of sales managers profiled in this book use this method. Here is a general explanation of how it is used to set quotas.

The first step is generally a total volume or unit sales forecast for the company, product lines, and then individual products. Each of these three forecasts can be done on a geographic basis. For instance, let's assume the market potential of a given geographic area is related to factors such as population and buying power. A forecaster may find that Illinois has 5.79 percent of the total United States population and 8.28 percent of the buying power. The forecast can be based on one of these market indexes, or both can be combined into a multiple factor index. Assuming the forecaster comes up with a multiple factor index of 6.97 and that anticipated industry sales in the United States total $100 million, then anticipated industry sales in Illinois would be $6,970,000. The forecaster then would determine the company's estimated share of the market to come up with a final sales forecast. If the company has a 10 percent market share, the total sales volume quota for the Illinois salesperson would be $697,000. Now product line and individual product sales quotas can be set.

QUOTAS BASED ON FORECASTS ONLY

The prior procedure is common for the large national companies. Some firms, however, do not have the necessary information, data, money, and people to determine sales potentials for individual sales territories. This is especially true of companies that sell in small geographic areas.

Some firms set quotas in relation to their sales forecast or total market estimates. They then usually establish quotas based on past sales in a geographic area without regard for sales potentials. If a sales region sold 25 percent of the firm's past year's sales, its quota would be 25 percent of the forecasted sales for the next year.

QUOTAS BASED ON PAST EXPERIENCE

Some companies do not make sales forecasts for total sales volume, product lines, or individual products. They take the past year's sales for each geographic unit, add an arbitrary percentage, and use the results as their sales volume quotas. A few companies set quotas from an average of sales for several years. This average is preferred since it covers sales trends and the effects of exceptionally good or bad years.

Everyone's goal is to beat the past year's sales figures. This plan, however, ignores sales potentials. What if two territories have a potential of $500,000? Last year one salesperson had $400,000 in sales and another had $500,000. It is unfair to ask both people to increase sales 10 percent. It also does not consider a territory's past and present situations. If several new firms move into a territory and become customers, sales quotas are easier to reach. What if a territory was vacant for several months the past year? The addition of a salesperson can quickly increase sales above quota the next year.

Both of these examples occurred in a territory that this author was transferred into. My sales increased 50 percent one year. I received a midyear salary raise and an above-average year-end bonus. I took the money, but it never seemed fair to other salespeople within the district.

QUOTAS BASED ON EXECUTIVE JUDGMENTS

No matter what method a company uses for setting quotas, executive judgment should be a part of the process. Yet it is generally not recommended as the only method for deciding quotas.

Executive judgment is useful for setting quotas when little information exists. It may be impractical to determine the sales potential for a newly opened sales territory, for example, or impossible to estimate the acceptance of a new product. Frequently, managers have to rely on their past experiences to make future predictions.

QUOTAS SALESPEOPLE SET

How would you, as a salesperson, like to set your own quotas? It is not common, but it does happen, especially in companies expanding into new geographic areas or starting up a sales force. In each of these situations, it is difficult to project sales, even if sales potentials are available. No past sales exist on which to base future estimates.

In these situations, companies usually ask their own salespeople to set quotas for one or two years. This is long enough to collect the data needed to set quotas by one of the previously discussed methods. Most companies do, however, allow their salespeople to give input on the quota-setting process. "I sit down with each of my salespeople," Jim Mobley says, "and we set quotas for each phase of the operation."

Another company that uses sales force input to create sales quotas is Olympic Fasteners, which specializes in roof fasteners. In fact, this input is the main determinant of not only the quotas set for salespeople but also the production and manufacturing schedules. Salespeople's input is then combined with historical data and forecasting data to provide the final quota.[4]

QUOTAS RELATED TO COMPENSATION

Often salespeople are either promoted or not promoted within a company based on their meeting quota. Quotas represent the bottom line for a salesperson. For promotion, salespeople are usually judged on their attaining quotas over time. It is also very common to earn extra compensation by reaching sales volume quotas for total sales, existing products, and new products. For example, a salesperson may be paid a salary plus a bonus of 1 to 10 percent on all sales over quota. Typically, the quota for this situation is based on the past year's sales. If that total sales volume was $500,000, the salesperson would be paid a percentage of all sales over the $500,000 quota. The same thing can occur for sales of current and new products.

Quotas related to compensation are determined by any of the previously discussed quota-setting methods. Meeting quota is a way of life, the major job goal for many salespeople. Reaching quota means money in the bank for a salesperson, so how quotas are set is especially important. They have a direct influence on the motivation and morale of the sales force. Chapter 13 has an in-depth discussion of compensation plans that have incentive components and thus use quotas. Because quotas are so important, let's examine how some companies set sales quotas.

EXAMPLES OF SETTING SALES QUOTAS

The process of setting sales quotas is very similar for any type of organization. Whether the product is a good or a service, well-managed sales forces have standardized practices for setting quotas for each individual and group within the organization. Here are two examples.

HOW RESTAURANT SUPPLY CORPORATION SETS QUOTAS

"The extent to which quotas are reached," Jeff Lucas of the Restaurant Supply Corporation states, "had traditionally been related to the extent of our sales force's success.

"If quotas are reached," Lucas explains, "the sales force is successful. In our organization, broad, general objectives are refined into fairly specific and tangible objectives that are generally 'horizontal' in nature. In other words, they are objectives for major functional areas. At this point, the major functional areas of the organization, such as marketing and production, are assigned objectives."

He elaborates: "The second step is the translation of these organization-wide objectives into smaller, more-specific objectives for subgroups in the organization. These are 'vertical' objectives extending downward through various organizational levels."

Table 7.4   Levels of Organizational Sales Planning

Level	Purpose: What Is Planned	Who (Usually) Is Involved
1. Marketing	■ Organizational goals (increase in market share or penetration, increase in customers, increase in sales dollars and units sold) ■ Priorities (which regions, markets, and products to emphasize) ■ Dollar allotment (for promotion, advertising, new employees, sales incentives, and so on)	Upper management and sales and marketing executives
2. Regional plan	■ Goals for number of new customers and for increased business with old customers in each region and territory ■ Priorities (which accounts to emphasize) ■ Responsibilities (which accounts sales representatives will handle, what unit or dollar volume they will have to deliver)	Regional and district sales managers (with input from sales reps)
3. District plan	■ Goals to contribute to each customer's business, fulfill customers' needs, and solve customers' problems ■ Projected return on time invested and how much time to invest	District managers and sales representatives
4. Territorial plan	■ Precalls (research, setting objectives, strategies) ■ Each sales call ■ Evaluating results of each sales-call plan	Sales representatives

Table 7.4 and Figure 7.1 schematically depict the Restaurant Supply process of setting objectives for its sales force.

"How we conceptualize the type, or level, of plans is illustrated in Table 7.4," Lucas says. "These range from planning for the entire sales force to planning for an individual customer within a single sales territory. Plans also must be made for the entire product line as well as for individual products.

"Figure 7.1 shows how we develop specific plans for one of our major product lines—muffin mixes," he explains. "You see that I have a specific objective in mind: to increase our muffin sales by 10 percent. My marketing manager, national sales manager, and promotion manager now have objectives stemming from the general objective of increasing muffin sales."

Lucas continues: "The national sales manager now begins the vertical planning process. Regional and district sales managers examine the potential dollar sales in their areas. Figure 7.1 illustrates how the Midwest regional sales manager works with the District A sales manager in planning the overall account objectives and strategies.

"Then the District A sales manager involves each salesperson in the planning process," Lucas concludes. "In our example, Jim Clarke is asked to develop plans for each account in his territory."

How General Mills Sets Quotas

"Based upon past 14 months' sales," General Mills district sales manager Jim Mobley says, "the home office marketing group develops sales forecasts and forecasts the amount of money needed to spend to reach our sales goals. They provide each sales region with a sales program for the year. This would include how much product is to be sold during each of the four yearly sales periods."

Mobley continues his explanation: "The regional sales office feeds this information into a personal computer to arrive at individual sales territory quotas. At this time we can adjust a person's quotas. For example, if a buying office has moved into another

FIGURE 7.1 RESTAURANT SUPPLY SALES PLANS FOR MUFFIN MIXES

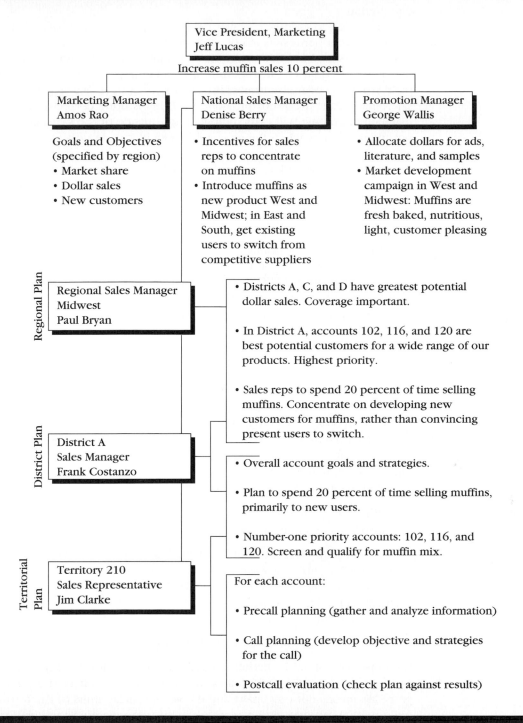

territory, we reduce one person's sales quota and increase someone else's quota." Mobley then sends the quotas by product to each salesperson and asks him or her to review and comment on them. "If no changes have occurred within the territory or if there are no errors, then typically these numbers become that person's quotas.

"Next we develop our quarterly action plans with each salesperson," he explains. "On a one-on-one basis, I sit down in a private place with each salesperson and plan what will be done in the next three months. Mobley adds that "objectives and quotas are set for every phase of each salesperson's operation. This includes such things as total volume, volume for established and new products, retail call patterns, and distribution."

According to Mobley, a General Mills salesperson is evaluated four times a year based on his or her results in obtaining quotas during the four previous action plans. "Each salesperson is evaluated on sales volume, major promotions, new product introductions, established distribution or maintaining our present business and trying to add to it, and administration of the territory." He adds, "We emphasize how well the salesperson sells the major promotions. If this is done correctly and distribution is maintained, volume will come unless things outside of the salesperson's control are occurring, such as when the geographic area is in a depressed state and customers are not buying as much."

Mobley also completes a personnel evaluation form on the salesperson's performance. "The salesperson comes to me four times a year and says, 'Based on the company's standards, here is how I did and here is the grade I feel I should get.' We negotiate this, and we then arrive at a performance evaluation that is fair to the person and the company.

"I take this to my manager of field sales and we discuss each salesperson's performance." He explains that this helps each district manager to grade salespeople using the same standards. "The regional manager does the same thing with the zone manager, who is over several regional managers," Mobley concludes.

As you can see, sales planning is a detailed, specific, action-oriented process. All organizational levels of the sales force become actively involved in this important process.

SELLING BY OBJECTIVES (SBO) SETS FUTURE TARGETS

From the overall sales strategies, the field sales managers chart out selling strategies for their sales units—regions and districts. All of this planning is necessary. Yet it is all ivory-tower foolishness unless management can get its salespeople turned on to making things happen during the coming year. Here are two basic steps to take toward successfully implementing sales strategies:

Step One   Organize the jobs
Step Two   Define annual objectives in important areas

Responsibility should be defined for four key organizational areas of concern (see Figure 7.2), not only for management and supervision but for every salesperson on the payroll. The four areas of organization are territorial, account, and call management and self-management.

TREATING THE TERRITORY AS A BUSINESS

Sales managers should schedule sales reps to come in for full discussions of the management practices they will follow while managing their territory for the coming year. This means not only managing the geographical limits of the territory but also the potential revenues and expenses, the customers within that territory, the development of leads and prospects, the market share within a territory and its growth potential, and trade and dealer relations within the territory.

MANAGING EACH ACCOUNT

An alternative way to look at the management of selling is to view the individual account as something to be managed. Estimates of the potential business to be produced from any account, the coverage of all of the accounts, and the generation of records to be analyzed for trends are all part of such management. The salesperson

FIGURE 7.2   THE FOUR MAJOR AREAS TO ESTABLISH OBJECTIVES WITH EACH SALESPERSON

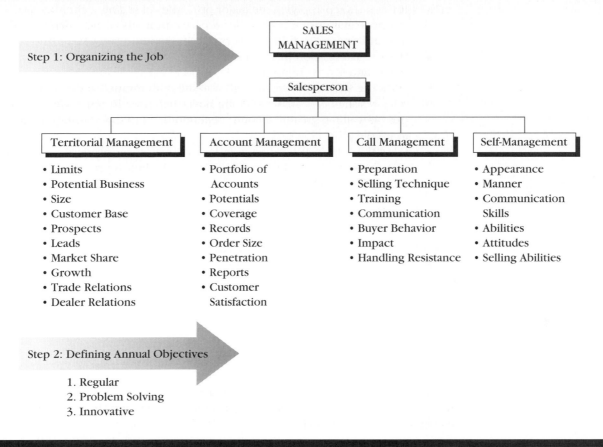

can define the dog, the star, the cash cow, and the problem child by assessing the account's potential growth and its current business share. This suggests a tactical plan for managing accounts.

1. *Build the stars.* Salespeople should spend more time, effort, energy, and expense building business that has a higher potential than its current sales.
2. *Harvest the cash cows.* Salespeople should make sure they maintain their present share of business from accounts.
3. *Fix the problems.* If a high-potential account does not seem to be giving all it possibly can, sales reps should put on their thinking caps and come up with a new approach and problem-solving tactic.
4. *Dogs.* Salespeople should divest accounts that have a low and declining potential, that occupy more time than could ever be justified, and that show no promise of improvement. It may seem like heresy to abandon an account, however small, but learning to bury the dead is nothing less than good tactics.

MANAGING EACH CALL

Although the sales manager obviously cannot go out with every salesperson and make every call—otherwise, why have a salesperson at all?—the management of the field sales department has a big stake in what is happening during each call. This means the sales manager should have some firm ideas about some of the following questions about the content of calls:

- Is the sales rep properly armed with information, leads, and materials before the call occurs?
- Is the sales rep applying the major principles of selling technique during the presentation? Or is the sales rep inventing his or her own and perhaps making every mistake every salesperson in history has made?
- Has the salesperson planned some coherent attack for the sales presentation, and is it working well?
- Does the sales rep have enough training in communication, in meeting sales resistance, in understanding buyer behavior, in improving call impact, in gaining greater account penetration, in follow-through methods to do the job?
- Does the sales rep have enough knowledge of the product and its applications, service and system backup, and technical problems to handle the toughest calling situation?

MANAGING ONESELF

When you look at the organizational charts in Chapter 4, you might think the salesperson is at the bottom of the organizational ladder. Yet a drastic difference exists between being at the bottom of the sales organization and being at the bottom of the organizational chart in other departments or organizations, such as manufacturing. The most important distinction here is that the sales rep is a "professional" and has many managerial functions, even when no direct-report employees are under his or her supervision.

In addition to the three functional approaches (territorial, account, and call management) to the sales job outlined thus far in this section, salespeople have a number of important self-management responsibilities, and these should be thoroughly aired and discussed when they are setting goals for the coming year. Self-management in selling includes the following:

- Since selling involves making contact with strangers, dress, style, demeanor, and personal decorum are part of the salesperson's tool kit.
- Communication skills, memory, logical speaking habits, and writing competence are vested in the person.
- Attitudes and outlook toward the job, the product, the company, and the customers all have an important bearing in the results to be achieved.
- The knowledge of selling techniques, what the various kinds are and how and when to use them, are personally vested in the sales rep and can be produced and polished by training.

BASIC LEVELS OF INDIVIDUAL OBJECTIVES

Now let's turn to the complete job of setting objectives with salespeople for the next year and the next quarter. These objectives will go beyond the ordinary and will include three types of objectives for each person:

1. Regular, ongoing, and recurring objectives.
2. Problem-solving objectives.
3. Innovative or creative objectives.

Of the many excellent reasons for having these three types of objectives, here are several important ones:

- The "regular goals" deal with such factors as sales volume, expenses, calls, territorial management targets, prospects, leads, market share, growth in order size, coverage, and reports. These goals ensure that the basic needs of the organization are in the hands of responsible people who have made commitments to produce a specific, tough, realistic, and measurable level of output for a specific period of time. Meeting these goals results in a "satisfactory" performance evaluation.

- "Problem-solving" goals are always distinctive with the individual salespersons. These goals deal with matters where deviations from norms have shown up, where things have gone wrong, where threats and changes are causing a breakdown of the ordinary flow of results, and where some specific commitments to fixing problems are needed. Obtaining these goals results in an "excellent" performance evaluation.
- "Innovative goals" are actions the salesperson states and commits to that are something new, creative, innovative, witty, wise, intelligent, and original in the territory or in another area of responsibility. These goals mean managing for breakthroughs and quantum leaps to new levels of performance. When they appear, they are evidence that the person is going beyond the ordinary requirements of the job. Accomplishing these goals results in a "superior" performance evaluation.

With these objectives, the manager is now equipped to make some fact-based judgment about the performance of his or her organization and each person in it. The people who are doing all of their regular work are achieving their regular, ongoing objectives. This entitles them to the same job at the same pay for another year. The people who are doing less than the ongoing, regular objectives are either trainees or failures, and in either case call for some special attention, training, and counseling by their supervisor.

The salespeople who are not only attaining all of the regular, ongoing responsibilities but also seeing, solving, and perhaps anticipating problems in their own territory are rated higher than the people who do not solve problems. This is a higher level of excellence than just doing the regular tasks.

The highest level of excellence is reserved for people who are doing all three: regular, problem-solving, and innovative goal setting and achievement. The highest rewards should be reserved for this third-level person. This scale is not arbitrary but is jointly established through a dialogue between the manager and salesperson at the beginning of each year and each quarter of that year.

To get maximum commitment, managers should establish objectives by personal, face-to-face discussion and not simply by an exchange of memoranda. You cannot get maximum commitment by writing to people; you have to talk to them. Managers should realize this from their selling experience. A sales rep needs to meet the customer to sell the product, and a manager needs to meet the salesperson to sell objectives and commitment. The verbal agreement worked out in negotiation and discussion then should be confirmed in writing with each party having a copy for reference during the year. This is a form of job contract, of accountability, and of commitment made by both sides.

Two major elements are at work here. The first is the "process" by which the objectives are set with the salesperson, and the second is the "product" that comes out of the discussion and is contained in the memo.

THE PROCEDURES FOR SETTING OBJECTIVES AND QUOTAS WITH SALESPEOPLE

The actual SBO process by which managers and salespeople, one-on-one, sit down and hammer out objectives for the coming year and quarter comprises four steps.

PREPARE THE WAY

Imagine you are a sales manager planning individual goal-setting meetings with your sales reps. Before you begin with individuals, especially new hires, conduct a meeting to explain the system and its reasons. Stress the benefits for the individual, and mention the benefits for the company. It is far better if the manager personally conducts the orientation briefing for the organization, because the authority and stature of the manager lend power and influence to what is being said.

At the end of the briefing, allow time for questions, and then announce that you will be seeking individual meetings with every salesperson to define objectives for the coming year. Distribute your "objectives" forms (see Figure 7.3) to everyone, and ask them to start working up "objective proposals" to bring to the goal-setting conference.

Schedule Conferences with Each Salesperson

Have the salespeople bring their working papers (forms) with them to the conference. You should allow enough time for a full discussion of everything the salespeople might want to bring up. Remember, you are going to go over the organization of their job in the four major areas first, before you start on the objectives and quotas. Discuss territorial, account, and call management and self-management, and get agreements on the organization of their job. Then start talking about specific commitments in each of the three areas, using the forms. You should:

- Ask them to suggest what they think objectives and quotas should be.
- Always review the recent past when discussing what the future might look like.
- Be realistic, which means using ranges in defining next year's goals.
  "What is a realistic target for this area?"
  "What is your stretch objective?"
  "What is a pessimistic level?"
- Listen fully to their statements and explanations, and then restate those statements to indicate that you understand them. You can then introduce any problems you see in their level of performance. "Joe, you suggest

FIGURE 7.3   Selling by Objectives Form

Name _____

For Year _____

List Your Responsibility Area _____

Output	Results Expected			
	Pessimistic	Realistic	Optimistic	Results
1. $ Volume/month				
2. $ Expense/month				
3. Gross margin/month				
4.				
5.				
6.				
7.				
8.				
9.				
10.				
11.				
12.				
Other				

Instruction: List the regular, ongoing, recurring objectives. Cover the ten major responsibilities of your job next year to manage territory, accounts, calls, and yourself.

$7,500 a month, and you have given some reasons why that seems realistic to you. I understand what you are saying. Now let me tell you my problem. The company objectives require a 10 percent increase, only half of which is due to price inflation. Let's see how we can work on this together to help solve my problem."

- Listen carefully to their reasoning, and avoid arguments and judgment before you have heard everything and proven that you understand by restating their sentences.

All three classes of objectives—the regular, problem solving, and innovative—should be covered. Often when salespeople get stuck on regular goals, they may be helped to raise them if they can be led into seeing problems blocking their growth or can be challenged to innovate and raise their levels of order size, market penetration, account management, call management, or self-management. Keep coming back to the basic organizational building blocks to get maximum challenge and completeness of coverage in the goals they agree to.

The purpose is not to win a contest but to have both sides win. Tell them this is your purpose. If the goals cannot be set in a single meeting, the salesperson should think more about innovation and problem solving, and another meeting should be scheduled.

Your goals meetings aren't casual but formal, planned, scheduled discussions. Cut off your telephone calls and any other interruptions. Make notes during the discussion, especially on agreements made. You should not do this over lunch. This is not an interruption of your job; it *is* your job, and it's the correct way to do it.

The time you spend getting people committed to their goals will buy you endless amounts of your own time during the coming year. All of the things you do within the SBO process will directly influence your success as a sales manager.

PREPARE A WRITTEN SUMMARY OF GOALS AGREED UPON

You can use the "objectives" form as a guide, but you don't really need forms. You can dictate goals or write them out and have typed copies—one for you and one for your salespeople. Ask them to go over their goals for errors in fact or understanding, and congratulate them on their commitment. The year ahead is now in their hands. They have five terrific conditions in their jobs.

1. They will know what is expected of them before they start.
2. They will know what resources and help are available.
3. They will know how much freedom they have and what reporting they need to do.
4. They will know how well they are doing in their work while they are doing it. This self-control aspect is an important motivator for salespeople.
5. They will know the basis on which rewards are given and how their annual reviews will be made.

OPTIONAL GROUP MEETINGS TO SHARE OBJECTIVES

Many firms follow this individual series of meetings with a group meeting. People stand up before their colleagues and make a brief presentation of their objectives for the coming year and the coming quarter. This has the advantage of building teamwork, eliminating conflicting jurisdictions and goals, and firming up the commitment.

Next, people might be asked to present (1) what they had said they would try to achieve that year, and (2) what they actually achieved and the reasons. The two parts could be reversed; each person could discuss his or her accomplishments and then goals.

A GOOD OBJECTIVE AND QUOTA PLAN IS SMART

For objectives and quotas to be fully accepted by the sales force, and thus to obtain maximum results, a quota plan should be SMART. Quotas and goals should be Specific, Measurable, Attainable, Realistic, and Time specific.

"Specific" quotas are a must. It is important that the quotas are clear and concise, leaving no doubt in anyone's mind as to what is expected. "Measuring" a salesperson's improvement in relations with customers is difficult; on the other hand, a specific dollar sales increase is measurable and specific.

"Attainable" goals are "realistic" yet challenging. If they are too easy to attain, salespeople may procrastinate or approach the goal lackadaisically. However, they may not accept a quota or objective that is too difficult and, thus, not try to meet it.

Finally, quotas should be "time specific." They should be developed for both the short run (for example, monthly, bimonthly, quarterly) and long run (for example, yearly). Most sales companies do this. Salespeople's lives revolve around month-to-month performance quotas, and their careers rest on their yearly performance quotas.

You, as sales manager, want to let people know what is expected of them and what they will receive when they reach their quotas. Properly setting quotas is one of management's most challenging jobs yet the most powerful motivational force a manager can use. The following is a simple, three-way test to judge how well quotas and objectives are written:

Test One Does this quota state exactly what the intended result is?

Test Two Does this quota specify when the intended result is to be accomplished?

Test Three Can the intended result be measured?

Statements of intention that fail one or more of these three test questions do not qualify as quotas or objectives and will tend to hinder rather than help the planning process.

SELLING-BY-OBJECTIVES MANAGEMENT

The district manager's job should be defined by the contribution the district makes to the sales department. Each manager should develop and set the objectives and quotas for his or her district. Upper management must reserve the power to approve or disapprove these objectives, but their development is part of a manager's responsibility; indeed, setting objectives and quotas is the manager's first responsibility. Today this is quite common.

At the individual level, **selling by objectives (SBO)** is the process elaborated on earlier whereby the manager and salesperson jointly identify common goals, define major areas of responsibility, and agree on the results expected. These measures are then used as guides for operating the territory and assessing the contribution of each salesperson.

Mutual understanding between a manager and a salesperson is of primary importance when setting objectives. The implication is that a salesperson will be motivated to increase performance if the salesperson is allowed to be involved in developing performance objectives and quotas.

THE BASIC MANAGING METHOD IS A TWO-WAY APPROACH

SBO is more than a philosophy; it is a method of managing that allows both managers and salespeople maximum involvement and participation in setting performance goals and in defining the methods of measuring accomplishments. SBO involves goal setting, job planning, management development, training, performance appraisal, and leadership.

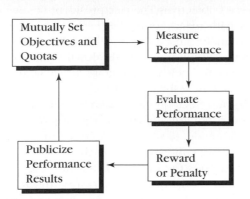

FIGURE 7.4

SETTING OBJECTIVES AND QUOTAS IS A TWO-WAY PROCESS BETWEEN MANAGER AND SALESPERSON

SBO is, then, a process involving a series of interdependent and interrelated elements, as illustrated in Figure 7.4. It includes an objective-setting element, a performance appraisal element, a reward element, and a feedback element, resulting in the development of new objectives and quotas. In most organizations, sales results are publicized throughout the district and company. Monthly, sometimes weekly, sales newsletters are mailed to all salespeople. Hence, this process has a major motivational impact on each salesperson.

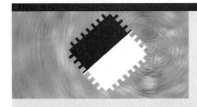

MANAGEMENT IN ACTION: ETHICAL DILEMMA
HAVE YOU LOST THE SALE?

You and one of your salespeople have been working for two months on an industrial account to obtain a firm commitment for a $185,000 computer system. Over the past three years, this particular firm has purchased $575,000 worth of computer systems from your company. If you can land the order today, you will become eligible for a quarterly commission bonus of $500. Your sales rep will earn $2,500. To meet your competitor's lower price, your manager decides to give you a special authorization to offer your client a $9,000 package consisting of free software, specialized operation training, and extended-service contract terms. Similar incentives have been offered on special occasions in the past. All customers are eligible for the package. You feel this sweetened offer will bring you below your competitor's rock-bottom price. You know your customer is a price buyer.

As you drive to your customer's office, you get tied up in a huge traffic jam. You call your client from your car phone and ask her secretary if it would be okay to come about 30 minutes later than scheduled. He tells you not to worry.

As you and your salesperson are ushered into the buyer's office, you greet your customer with a smile, ready to announce the good news. She informs you that she signed a contract with your competitor just ten minutes ago. Upon your insistence, she shows you the bottom line on the signed contract. You realize that by purchasing your system, she could have saved as much as $12,000.

WHAT DO YOU DO?
1. Compare the two offers for the buyer, and ask her to cancel the signed contract.
2. Tell her about your proposal, but do not suggest she cancel the signed contract.
3. Say nothing. Keep your cool—act professionally. Otherwise, you will lose the customer forever. Accept the loss in a gracious and courteous manner.

THE SALES
TERRITORY IS
WHERE QUOTAS
ARE MADE

A company tells marketing what is expected. Marketing develops its objectives, resulting in the sales force's objectives. The vice president of sales works out objectives, strategies, and tactics with managers in the field. They in turn establish objectives with each salesperson under their leadership. Plans are made; commitment is given. However, meeting these commitments comes down to how well these plans are implemented in each sales unit, such as the regions, districts, and territories.

The sales territory is "where the action is!" Committing salespeople to achieve organizational objectives and sales quotas is a challenging job. Setting objectives and quotas influences many other areas of the manager's job, such as recruitment, selection, training and development, rewards, and performance appraisal. These areas are so important that we devote entire chapters in the book to them.

The next chapter extends the discussion on how the sales manager and salesperson can effectively manage the individual territory to reach its objectives and quotas. The proper management of the salesperson's time and territory is critical to the success of the salesperson, manager, and company.

THE BOTTOM
LINE

Quotas are important to a company because they establish the "end state" sought, and they change according to external and internal forces. Quotas perform functions; they provide performance targets, standards, control, and change of direction, and they are motivational.

Many different types of quotas exist. They are divided into the categories of sales volume quotas, profit quotas, expense quotas, activity quotas, and Customer Satisfaction Indexes. Most companies combine these types of quotas to fit their needs; the sales volume and activity quotas are the most common.

Methods for setting quotas may vary. Larger corporations use quotas based on forecasts and potentials. Smaller corporations or corporations without as many resources employ quotas based only on forecasts. Other procedures include quotas based on past experience or on executive judgments, quotas set by salespeople, or quotas related to a form of compensation.

Setting a sales quota can be an involved process. Objectives must be well defined. Organizational objectives must be broken down for the sales force. This involves organizing the jobs and defining annual objectives. Four key areas of organization exist—territorial, account, and call management and self-management; and three types of individual objectives exist—regular, problem solving, and innovative.

Selling by objectives (SBO) is a common concept and is widely used by sales organizations. It is a method of managing that allows both managers and salespeople maximum participation in setting performance goals and in defining the methods of measuring accomplishments.

KEY TERMS FOR SALES MANAGERS

Quota, 142	Net profit quota, 145	Customer Satisfaction
Sales volume quotas, 143	Expense quotas, 145	Index, 147
Profit quotas, 144	Activity quotas, 146	Selling by objectives (SBO),
Gross margin quota, 144	Customer satisfaction, 147	158

MANAGEMENT APPLICATION QUESTIONS

1. Imagine you are one of Jim Mobley's salespeople. Discuss what you think of the way he turns the company's objectives and forecasts into your sales quotas.
2. What functions do quotas perform, and why are they so important to a firm?
3. Discuss whether the following is a good quota: "Our objective is to increase sales in the territory next quarter by making more effective sales calls through improved customer relations and better communication skills." How might you improve it?

4. What type of quota do you recommend for the following types of sales jobs? How long should the quota period be for each job?
   a. Selling General Mills grocery products
   b. Selling or leasing Xerox's products
   c. Selling Beecham's Aqua-Fresh toothpaste
   d. Selling Fritos to grocery stores
5. Mills, Inc. has two sales districts. For each district, determine its gross margin, net profit, and sales/net profit ratio. Why do the western and eastern districts' sales/net profit ratios differ? What does this ratio indicate to management?

	WESTERN DISTRICT	EASTERN DISTRICT
Sales	$10,634,000	$10,380,000
Cost of sales	−8,507,200	−8,304,000
Gross margin		
Expenses	−140,000	−152,000
Net profit		
Sales//net profit ratio		

6. Compare the yearly sales volume of these three salespeople. First, determine the dollar difference between their quotas and what was actually sold. Then calculate each person's performance index. What conclusions can you make based on your results?

	SALES QUOTA	ACTUAL SALES
a. Fahey	$1,000,000	$1,100,000
b. Jackson	750,000	720,000
c. Bush	1,200,000	1,050,000

7. Compute these three salespeople's orders-to-sales-calls ratios and average size of order for the year. Why might the three salespeople's performances differ?

	NUMBER OF CALLS	NUMBER OF ORDERS	ACTUAL SALES
a. Jackson	1,200	333	$ 6,000,000
b. Johnson	1,400	700	6,046,000
c. Sager	1,600	600	11,000,000

FURTHER EXPLORING THE SALES WORLD

Discuss with a sales manager the types of quotas he or she sets for salespeople. Ask to see sales reports that show quotas, sales, and possibly a performance index for a district's individual salespeople. Report on the sales manager's procedures for setting quotas and evaluating the results of people's performance.

SALES MANAGEMENT EXPERIENTIAL EXERCISE

CAN YOU MAKE THE GRADE?

Many high-performing students routinely set goals for each of their courses. These goals become their achievement targets and help guide their actions throughout the course. To help you develop goals for this course, answer the following questions.

1. What grade do you want to make in this course? _____
2. How many total points do you have to earn for this grade? _____
3. How many points do you now have in this course? _____
4. How many additional points do you have to earn for this grade? _____
5. Can you reach your goal? _____ Yes; _____ No.
6. On a scale of 1 to 10—with 10 being the maximum effort—how hard are you willing to work in this course to reach your goal? Be honest!
    My effort score equals: _____.
7. In the space below explain how you will reach your grade goal.

Arkansas Fishing Company
Are Quotas Accurate?

Carl Hess has an outstanding track record as a salesperson at Arkansas Fishing Company. His behavior toward customers is excellent and could serve as a role model. But with his peers and even with you—the sales group's manager—he is best described as offensive even though his ideas are good ones. He makes it clear he thinks any ideas or opinions presented by anyone else are worthless and inadequate. Carl seems to wear earmuffs with built-in filters—filters that allow only his own words to enter his thoughts for consideration. He never actually hears what others are proposing or suggesting. he is opinionated, argumentative, and downright unpleasant in the way he interacts with the group.

Carl laughs at the quotas you set for him. He says you don't know his customers and their buying potential. Your group has spent immeasurable amounts of time and energy trying to persuade him to consider other options and approaches to problems whose solutions are vital to the sales group. The group's resentment toward Carl is interfering with its growth and development as a team.

Questions

1. If you were Carl's manager, what would you do about his behavior?
2. What alternatives would you consider, and which course of action would you select?

Harrell Manufacturing
Elimination of Sales Budgets and Quotas

Wilson Harrell once owned a company that sold consumer products to American commissaries and military post exchanges all over the world. "We were exclusive representatives for companies like Kraft, Nabisco, Goodyear, and others, working strictly on commission," Harrell says. "Following standard practice, each year we sat down with our client companies and developed a master budget, which was, of course, last year's sales plus—plus. As CEO of my company, I had two objectives: (1) Meet this year's expenses and make a profit, and (2) stay in business next year.

"From sad experience, I knew that getting a big bonus from a client one year for beating my budget often meant I'd be in serious trouble the following year for not maintaining the same growth—maybe even get the boot. To avoid danger, I never willingly allowed big 'excess' sales over budget. To be sure, our company grew to $200 million, and I sold it for a whopping profit—but I cringe when I think of what sales might have been if we'd been free of vision-limiting, spirit-killing budgets.

"The real tragedy is that sales quotas actually dry up the greatest source of profits: incremental sales," Harrell continues. "And even worse, sales budgets install a corporate culture of 'just getting by' at every level.

"Let's look into the mind of a typical salesperson: 'If I exceed this year's sales budget, my next year's budget will be increased to equal whatever number I hit, plus another 10 percent or more. So if I go wild and exceed it by 100 percent, the next year I'll be looking at a target 200 percent of last year, plus some more. Wow! Maybe I could make those numbers; but if I don't, I'm risking my job. And I absolutely, positively will not do that. I'm not risking my job next year for a few pieces of silver this year.'

"What's the alternative?" Harrell asks. "Let's go back to the beginning of our entrepreneurial days, when we were small companies killing giants. Did you use a sales budget then? You bet you did: 'I want 100 percent of the market. Kill all competition. Sell everything to everybody and take no prisoners.' Let's go back to the time before we started running our sales forces by some banker's financial handbook. Stop penalizing performance and fostering mediocrity by telling your people how lousy they can be and still keep their jobs.

"Turn freedom loose, down where the salespeople live," Harrell suggests. "Tell everyone that the company's objective is to get all the business, in return for a share of the fruits of their contribution. Let each new year offer every one a clean slate of opportunity. Teach salespeople that 'job security' is all about the continual pursuit of excellence—about being the best they can be."[5]

Question
Discuss the advantages and disadvantages of quotas in relation to Harrell's views on not using quotas.

PART III
STAFFING THE SALES TEAM

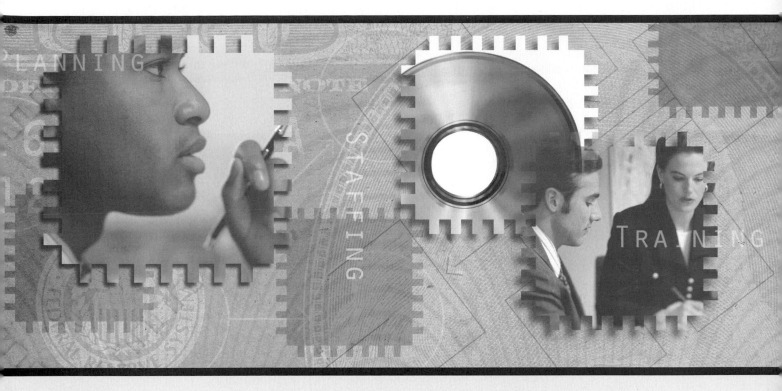

PEOPLE ARE the most important ingredient in a successful sales force. Staffing the sales force involves people and employment planning. Part III includes the following chapters: Chapter 8, "Planning for and Recruiting Successful Salespeople," and Chapter 9, "Selection, Placement, and Socialization of Successful Salespeople."

CHAPTER 8

PLANNING FOR AND RECRUITING SUCCESSFUL SALESPEOPLE

CHAPTER OUTLINE

WHAT IS SALES HUMAN RESOURCE MANAGEMENT?

PEOPLE PLANNING

PEOPLE FORECAST

DETERMINING THE TYPE OF PERSON FOR THE JOB

JOB DESCRIPTIONS AND SPECIFICATIONS FOR SUCCESSFUL PEOPLE

RECRUITMENT'S PURPOSE

LEGAL INFLUENCES

RECRUITMENT OF SALESPEOPLE

SOURCES OF RECRUITS—WHERE ARE THEY FOUND?

THE QUALIFIED APPLICANT POOL

RECRUITMENT EVALUATION

LEARNING OBJECTIVES

A successful sales force is determined by who is hired; this is the end result of sales human resource management. This chapter should help you understand:

■ What sales human resource management is and what its key relationships are.

■ The importance of planning for sales personnel needs.

■ What people planning and employment planning are.

■ What recruitment means and why it is so important.

■ The recruiting process: what it is, who does it, and where recruits are sought.

One issue comes up more than any other when sales managers are asked what area of their work they would like to learn more about: how to make good hiring decisions. With 38 years of experience building Mackay Envelope, Harvey Mackay understands this problem as well as anyone. Though he admits he has not totally mastered the art of hiring, he has developed a few guidelines to reduce the number of hiring blunders.

"Much more scarce than ability is the ability to recognize ability," he says. "So what can you do if this talent is not hardwired into you?" Mackay's answer to this is the fact that he has never hired anyone in 38 years without sending him or her to an industrial psychologist. Within a two to four hour testing time, the psychologist can zero in on concerns managers have with issues such as work ethic and motivation. Mackay adds, "I consider it a valuable investment. And remember, you're not giving the decision over to the industrial psychologist; you're just using the IP as another arrow in the quiver when making these critical decisions."

Other aspects of Mackay's hiring strategy may seem a bit unusual, but he defends them as essential to breaking through the formality of the traditional hiring procedure. "I've also never hired anyone without going into the home and talking to the spouse," he says. "I call it, 'Caring is contagious. Spread it around.' I want those people to know that I have a deep down, burning desire to make them successful . . . When they see that we go into the home to talk about the company and what we expect and what this is all about, then they understand that we care. I put the care into every hire we make, from switchboard operator to the shipping director."

Besides these two strategies, Mackay likes to have other people interview employment candidates as well in order to provide a different perspective. If he does not have much experience hiring for a certain position, he finds someone in human resources at another company who has hired 50 people for that type of job and has them interview the candidate.

Mackay has another approach he uses, especially when hiring possible salespeople: "When it comes to salespeople, I like to take the prospective hires out of the office. I'll interview them over a drink, over breakfast, I'll play golf or tennis with them, go out to a ball game or a movie." By doing this, Mackay says, "You really get to know what they're like." Mackay feels that this can eliminate the people that are "coached how to interview in an office situation" because "[employment candidates] can't keep up an act through a three-hour baseball game or over 18 holes of golf."

While he believes that these strategies can help an employer that is hiring for any position, Mackay reserves one test that has proven particularly effective when hiring salespeople. "The acid test of hiring a salesperson is as follows," he explains. "About five to ten minutes into the interview say to yourself, 'How would I feel if this person were working for my competitor?' And if you aren't worried, guess what? That's the end of the interview."[1] ■

Hiring the right person for the job is critical for the success of the sales manager and the sales force. Someone who becomes an above-average performer improves the overall performance of the sales group. Supervisors recognize and reward sales managers for their recruiting ability. Sales personnel—both salespeople and managers— are the most important ingredient for creating a high-performing sales organization. This chapter introduces you to the importance of planning and recruiting successful salespeople.

WHAT IS SALES HUMAN RESOURCE MANAGEMENT?

Sales human resource management (SHRM) refers to activities undertaken to attract, develop, and maintain effective sales force personnel within an organization. Some people refer to this as personnel management. However, SHRM is a phrase that recognizes the importance of a sales force as a vital human resource contributing to the organization's goals.

As shown in Figure 8.1, SHRM is composed of two elements: people planning and employment planning. As we will see, these two elements involve the entire process of determining how many people to hire and who to hire, as well as selection— matching these people to the right sales jobs and placing them in the right territory.

PEOPLE PLANNING

People are the most important ingredient in developing a successful sales force. "Your people," IBM's Matt Suffoletto says, "are more important than anything else, including training and compensation. If you don't have the right people, no amount of training and money can turn a 'sow's ear into a silk purse.'"

Why is people planning necessary? To develop a successful sales team, management should carefully plan for its sales personnel needs. **People planning** involves the number and type of people to hire.

More than ever, sales managers are moving to formal people planning systems as they discover that unsystematic approaches are inefficient in meeting their employment needs. Some reasons for formal planning are to achieve more effective and efficient use of human resources and improve sales force performance.

MORE EFFECTIVE AND EFFICIENT USE OF HUMAN RESOURCES

People planning precedes other sales personnel activities. How can you schedule recruiting if you do not know how many salespeople you will need? How can you

FIGURE 8.1

ACTIVITIES INVOLVED IN MANAGING A SALES FORCE'S HUMAN RESOURCES

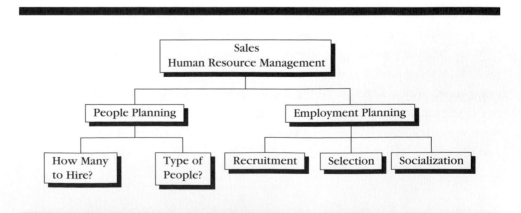

select effectively if you do not know the kinds of salespeople needed for job openings? How large a training program should you schedule? Careful analysis of many staffing activities shows that their effectiveness and efficiency depend on answers to questions about how many people with what talents are required.

INTERVIEW-TO-TERRITORY TIME LINE   The time from when the decision is made to hire someone to when the person is assigned to his or her territory can range from weeks to months to more than a year. Figure 8.2 illustrates this often lengthy time line.

Assume a sales organization like Xerox decides to hire 300 people. Also assume it wants to hire new college graduates. For the spring hiring period, the recruiters may begin interviewing in February, hire in April, and wait for May graduation to have the people report to work June 1. Training would last for months. Thus the person could be assigned to a sales territory the following year. An effective and efficient sales force requires people, coordination, and time.

IMPROVED SALES FORCE PERFORMANCE

As we have seen, the sales force is composed of many sales territories, each generating revenues. An empty sales territory can result in lost sales to the firm. If a company experiences a 20 percent yearly turnover in sales personnel, for example, vacant territories could be very costly. Anticipating how many people to hire helps to maximize the firm's sales, profits, and sales force performance. Hiring the right people also improves performance.

WHAT'S A SALESPERSON WORTH?   A salesperson's worth depends on what the salesperson costs to the company and on the profits from the products he or she sells.

David Greene sells paper—cash register rolls and other total-commodity papers—for AT&T Global Information Solutions (AT&TGIS), formerly NCR Corporation. The industry profit margins are small for that type of product, perhaps 5 to 10 percent. Although the production of paper is a high fixed-cost endeavor, sales swing widely due to cyclical usage, although output is remarkably flat (except when a major plant starts up or shuts down). So it's hard to estimate a gross profit margin. Let's err on the conservative side and say that the profit on each additional dollar of sales revenue is about 7.5 cents.

Greene increased the sales in his territory from $300,000 to $1.5 million. In doing so, he added an incremental $1.2 million to AT&TGIS's revenues. Applying the conservative estimate of 7.5 percent profit margin to the incremental sales makes them worth $90,000 per year to the firm in pure profit—that is, after accounting for the cost of David Greene himself!

Of course, this estimate completely ignores the fact customers tend to become less price sensitive when they are accustomed to dealing with a particular salesperson and receiving great service. Although this doesn't mean Greene can gouge his customers, he may be able to maintain a reasonable price when a particular

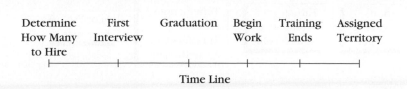

FIGURE 8.2

FROM INTERVIEW TO TERRITORY: A LONG TIme

competitor lowballs prices in his market in an effort to gain market share. Needless to say, that improves the margin on Greene's total basket of business and may push it above the 7.5 percent level we established for the AT&TGIS sales force in the entire country. For total sales of $1.5 million, an increase of a single percentage point in profitability is worth $15,000—nothing to sneeze at.[2]

As this example shows, the proper selection of productive salespeople is very important to the sales team's performance. What, then, should be the goal for hiring new salespeople in order to improve performance?

GOAL: HIRE ABOVE-AVERAGE PERFORMERS   Selecting someone who will become an above-average performer improves the overall performance of the sales group. David Greene, for example, made a major impact on sales for his sales team.

A *successful hire* is someone who performs above average. Think about it. Certainly, a sales manager does not want to hire a failure. But who wants to hire someone who ends up performing marginally or at an average level? Such a person does not help management improve the sales team's performance.

WHO DOES THE PLANNING?

Effectiveness in sales personnel planning requires the efforts and cooperation of the national sales manager and the field sales managers. Sales managers at the lower organizational levels, district and regional sales managers, are responsible for providing top management information on their staffing needs and for the actual recruiting and selection of new personnel.

Top management also has the important responsibility of selecting people for vacancies and new positions at higher levels in the sales organization. Thus, sales managers throughout the sales organization are responsible for the various activities involved in staffing the sales force.

The total number of sales personnel, or the size of the sales force, is basically determined by the number of sales territories and sales positions. Territorial design procedures were discussed in Chapter 7. Now, we need to know how to determine whether to hire new people and, if so, how many to hire.

PEOPLE FORECAST   The factors to consider when determining how many people to hire are shown in Figure 8.3. The sales force people-forecast model involves numerous elements. As the model indicates, the first step is for top management to set its objectives for the sales

FIGURE 8.3   SALES FORCE PEOPLE-FORECAST MODEL: FACTORS TO CONSIDER WHEN DETERMINING HOW MANY TO HIRE

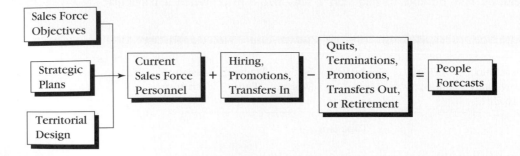

force, develop their strategic plans to reach the objectives, and design their sales territories around their customers. Each of these topics was discussed in earlier chapters.

So managers now know what the sales force is to do, how it will be done, and the total number of sales personnel needed to carry out company plans. The question now is "How many people should management hire to fill various sales territories?" Once managers know the answer to this question, they determine the types of people needed for the job openings.

The second component of people planning involves determining the type of person needed for the job. As you now know, sales forces are composed of many different types of jobs. These jobs should fit together, coordinate with one another, and link directly to the sales force's objectives. Thus, studying and understanding each job in the sales organization is a vital part of any staffing program.

DETERMINING THE TYPE OF PERSON FOR THE JOB

THE JOB ANALYSIS IS IMPORTANT

A **job analysis** refers to the formal study of jobs to define specific roles or activities to be performed in sales positions, for example, and to determine the personal qualifications needed for the jobs. The three steps in the job analysis are to:

1. Examine the total sales force and the fit of each job, and determine how each job relates to other jobs.
2. Select the jobs to be analyzed.

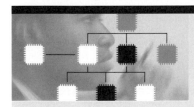

MANAGING THE SALES TEAM
WHY DO SALES PERSONNEL LEAVE THEIR EMPLOYERS?

Many managers do not know why their salespeople leave the job, according to a study of the causes and effects of business-to-business sales force turnover. Turnover is expensive. A company's direct cost of turnover could run in the millions of dollars a year.

Based on the survey results, these guidelines help managers develop a more effective and systematic approach to dealing with high turnover:

- Don't remain indifferent to the turnover problem. Try to find out why people are leaving, and work to bring about reforms that promote greater job satisfaction and stronger company loyalty. This may mean instituting exit interviews or employee attitude surveys to gain a better understanding of how salespeople feel about their jobs.
- Draw attention to the bottom-line impact of turnover as well as the hidden costs that can't be easily quantified, such as loss of company reputation and damaged morale.
- Adopt an open-door style of management. Experiment with innovative approaches such as weekly

gripe sessions, which allow salespeople to hash out what's bothering them about their jobs.
- Keep issues in perspective. Too many managers assume salespeople are concerned only about how much money they make. Don't ignore other work-related issues that, if tackled effectively, can be even more critical in helping to reduce turnover.
- Conduct a periodic audit to determine the extent and causes of job dissatisfaction among the sales force. Ask questions such as "Does your manager make enough coaching calls with you?" "Is your clerical support adequate?" "Do you feel your training is appropriate for the kind of selling you do?"
- Establish recruiting standards. Identify the capabilities and competencies that make a prospective employee an appropriate match for the company.
- Reevaluate the training strategy. Salespeople want to be well armed with product knowledge and sales skills before going out into the field.

Source: Survey taken by the author.

3. Collect the necessary information through observations of what people actually do in the jobs, interviews of people in the jobs, and questionnaires completed by job holders.

A wide range of information can be collected about a job. The types of information include work activities, performance standards, compensation ranges, and market characteristics.

Job Descriptions and Specifications for Successful People

As noted, firms use job analyses to develop job descriptions. **Job descriptions** are formal, written statements describing the nature, requirements, and responsibilities (for example, sales volume, territory, product line, customers, supervisory duties) of a specific sales position. They officially establish what the salesperson will do and how and why the person will carry out these duties, as well as indicate the salary range appropriate for the position.

Table 8.1 gives a partial job description for a position selling automotive replacement parts. This description has five basic parts. The "Nature of Job" section is a statement of the responsibilities involved. The next section, "Principal Responsibilities," states the specific end results or performance expected from someone holding the position. It is an explanation of how to implement the "Nature of Job" section. In the "Dimensions" section, job duties are discussed. Finally, the supervisory situation is explained.

Job specifications convert job descriptions into the qualifications (for example, abilities, behavior, education, skills) the organization feels are necessary for successful performance of the job. Often management determines specifications for a job in compliance with governmental regulations. This includes qualifications for initial employment and qualifications for jobs throughout the sales organization.

TABLE 8.1   FORMAL JOB DESCRIPTION, TRANSTEX AUTOMOTIVE SUPPLY CORPORATION

POSITION: SALES REPRESENTATIVE	ORGANIZATIONAL UNIT: REPLACEMENT PARTS
REPORTS TO: DISTRICT MANAGER	DATE: (WHEN JOB WAS DESCRIBED)

NATURE OF JOB

   Responsible for developing new accounts and reaching profitable sales goals in assigned territory.

PRINCIPAL RESPONSIBILITIES

   Meeting total sales goals for product lines and individual products.
   Maintaining an average of six daily sales calls.
   Maintaining an average of one monthly product presentation to wholesalers.

DIMENSIONS

   Develop strong promotional support from retail and wholesale customers.
   Plan effective territorial coverage resulting in high sales/call ratio.
   Inform management of activities by submitting daily and weekly call and sales reports to district manager.

SUPERVISION RECEIVED

   General and specific tasks are assigned for each sales period. Every two months work with supervisor for a minimum of one day.

SUPERVISION EXERCISED

   None

WHAT ARE JOB SPECIFICATIONS FOR SUCCESSFUL SALESPEOPLE?

We know the selling job is people oriented. Thus, salespeople must be able to positively and effectively deal with people. They must be able to build relationships. Successful salespeople should have the proper empathy and ego drive for specific types of sales jobs. They need empathy so they can identify and understand the customer's situation. Ego drive is the desire to make the sale, to overcome "no sales" and continue calling on customers, and to close the sale. Other reported desirable characteristics are shown in Table 8.2.

Each company should determine the individual job specifications and sales personnel characteristics necessary for successful performance. These should be continually updated. Most sales managers say the minimum components of a successful salesperson are:

1. *Intelligence*—the mental ability to perform at a high level.
2. *Education*—was an above-average student.
3. *Personality*—achievement oriented, self-confident, self-starter, positive outlook on life, tactful, mature, and has developed a realistic career plan.
4. *Experience*—will work hard, go beyond the call of duty; if a recent graduate, has participated in school organizations and created above-average class projects.
5. *Physical*—good first impression, neat appearance, good personal habits, and physically fit.

One method to use for locating potentially successful salespeople is to develop a profile.

PROFILING THE SUCCESSFUL CANDIDATE

Once a firm has designed a job, analyzed it, and reviewed the research on the characteristics that relate to successful salespeople, the next step is to answer the question "Who should we be looking for?" The person should be the one who potentially can do the best job for the organization. That individual ideally should possess the critical characteristics of the most successful salespeople.

To identify potentially successful salespeople, a firm must first establish the criteria for successful performance in its organization: that is, the standards by which performance is measured. Success in a company may include the following:

- Intelligence.
- Prospecting ability.
- Ability to create a follow-up system.
- Ability to influence people's decisions and opinions.
- Ability to cultivate long-term client relationships.
- Ability to negotiate contracts and prices.

TABLE 8.2

SELECTED CHARACTERISTICS OF SUCCESSFUL SALESPEOPLE

1.	High energy level	8.	Good physical appearance
2.	High self-confidence	9.	Likable
3.	Need for material things	10.	Self-disciplined
4.	Hardworking	11.	Intelligent
5.	Requires little supervision	12.	Achievement oriented
6.	High perseverance	13.	Good communication skills
7.	Competitive		

- Ability to determine prospects'/customers' needs (hot buttons).
- Computer skills.
- Selling ability.
- Conceptual ability.

A company need not identify more than five or six key traits when establishing its success criteria. It should give extra weight to the factor(s) that have the greatest influence on sales success. For example, in a highly technical environment, product and applications knowledge may be a key ingredient. Thus intelligence may play an important role in success there. In another environment, the ability to open new accounts might be the critical factor.

The American Computer Supply Corporation's Profile   American Computer Supply Corporation (ACSC)—it asked that its name be disguised—employs 550 salespeople throughout the United States. Turnover rates average 20 percent a year. Twenty percent sales increases over the past five years led to the projected need to hire 130 people in the next year.

Table 8.3 lists five characteristics ACSC uses to profile salespeople. The following steps show how the company develops and uses this information in order to help select successful salespeople:

1. ACSC identifies the characteristics based on success criteria established by its sales managers, as shown in Table 8.3.
2. Next, it determines the level of each characteristic in its top performers—people in the above-average and top-performer categories—using personality and intelligence tests.
3. ACSC then determines the level of each characteristic in the job applicants using personality and intelligence tests plus scored interview questions designed to collect information on each characteristic.

TABLE 8.3   Five Characteristics ACSC Uses to Select Salespeople

Characteristic	Why Important to Success	How to Identify
History of hard work	■ Understands the value of a dollar; otherwise, first job is a nightmare ■ Works hard with little supervision ■ Will exert whatever effort necessary to make something happen ■ Gets hands dirty/manual labor	■ Job *every* summer ■ Worked during school year (or played major college sports) ■ Financed part of education expenses ■ *Wants* a job ■ Type of past jobs
Perceptive	■ Must be able to *listen* to trade and manipulate a close ■ Must be able to anticipate trade ■ Must be street smart	■ Maturity level during interview ■ Answers questions well; no rambling ■ Plays off your questions during interview, looks for what you want ■ Discipline present
Intelligent	■ Must be a quick learner/think on feet	■ Test scores ■ Role-plays well
Communications skills	■ Must be able to sell ■ Must be able to write clearly	■ Observe in interview ■ Project tells you a lot ■ Clarity of application
Energy level high	■ Sales job is physically and mentally demanding ■ Salespeople must thrive on action	■ Ability to do more than one thing (i.e., school *plus* a job or sports) ■ Observe in interview ■ Observe on day in field

Figure 8.4   Major Influences and Components of Sales Recruitment

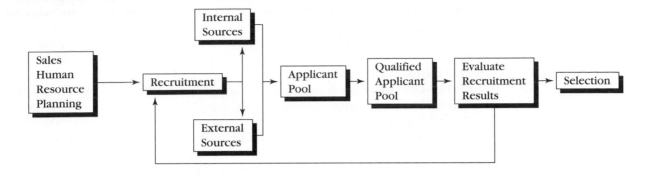

4. It hires applicants based on the characteristics.
5. ACSC tracks the performance of each rookie over time using the TAAMU performance system. Performance measures are averaged to create a performance index. These five TAAMU performance categories are usually present:

- Top performance.
- Above-average performance.
- Average performance.
- Marginal performance.
- Unacceptable performance.

Typically, a fairly constant percentage of people ACSC hires perform at each level or category, especially in the top two performance categories. Interestingly, these are usually the same people year after year. The company compares rookie performance to the veteran top performers twice a year, along with the trailing average for accumulated periods, such as 18 months, 24 months, and 30 months.

RECRUITMENT'S PURPOSE

Once plans have been made on the number and type of people to hire, it is time to create a recruitment strategy. **Recruitment** is the set of activities and processes used to legally obtain a sufficient number of individuals in such a manner that the recruits' and the sales force's best interests are taken into consideration. This definition reflects the relationship between recruitment and several other personnel activities. The general purpose of recruitment is to provide a pool of potentially qualified job candidates to select from. See Figure 8.4.

LEGAL INFLUENCES

Legal considerations, obligations, and requirements play a critical role in recruitment for most companies in America. Although much of the legal framework facing the sales manager is directed at employment decisions such as hiring, firing, and compensation, it essentially begins with the search for job applicants, whether the search is made inside the organization or outside. Although the equal employment opportunity laws and acts regarding staffing decisions (e.g., hiring, firing, demoting, transferring, and training) only specifically apply to selection, they have a direct impact on recruitment. Although we cannot deal with them in detail, the major laws and principles underlying legal employment guidelines are summarized in Table 8.4.

Although a number of federal agencies are involved, the **Equal Employment Opportunity Commission (EEOC)** is the principal governmental agency responsible for monitoring discriminatory practices. As such, the EEOC has a major influence on sales force staffing. Changing social values, attitudes toward minorities, women entering the workforce, and an increasing number of governmental regulations necessitated the creation of the commission.

The body of legislation affecting employment practices ranges from the Constitution itself to more recent laws, such as the **Equal Pay Act of 1963,** which specifically prohibits sex discrimination in pay. The provisions of this act were broadened under the **Education Amendments Act of 1972,** which states that "Any employee employed in bona fide executive, administrative, or professional capacity . . . or in the capacity of outside salesman" is entitled to equal pay. The most far-reaching, recent legislation in this context is the Civil Rights Act of 1964, especially Title VII of the act as amended by the **Equal Employment Opportunity Act of 1972,** which prohibits discrimination based on race, sex, religion, or national origin.

It is important to remember that certain types of discrimination are allowed if an employer can show that a given action is "reasonably necessary to the operation of that particular business or enterprise" and thus that employment decisions are based

TABLE 8.4   ANTIDISCRIMINATION LAWS AND ORDERS, UNITED STATES OF AMERICA

FEDERAL LAW	TYPE OF FEDERAL EMPLOYMENT DISCRIMINATION PROHIBITED	EMPLOYERS COVERED
U.S. Constitution, 1st and 5th Amendments	Deprivation of employment rights without due process of law	Federal government
U.S. Constitution, 14th Amendment	Deprivation of employment rights without due process of law	State and local governments
Civil Rights Acts of 1866 and 1870 (based on 13th Amendment)	Race discrimination in hiring, placement, and continuation of employment	Private employers, unions, employment agencies
Civil Rights Act of 1871 (based on 14th Amendment)	Deprivation of equal employment rights under cover of state law	State and local governments (private employers if conspiracy is involved)
National Labor Relations Act	Unfair representation by unions, or interference with employee rights, that discriminate on the basis of race, color, religion, sex, or national origin	Private employers and unions
Equal Pay Act of 1963	Sex differences in pay for substantially equal work	Private employers (state and local governments uncertain)
Executive Order 11141 (1964)	Age discrimination	Federal contractors and subcontractors
Title VI, 1964 Civil Rights Act	Discrimination based on race, color, or national origin	Employers receiving federal financial assistance
Title VII, 1964 Civil Rights Act (as amended by the Equal Employment Opportunity Act of 1972)	Discrimination or segregation based on race, color, religion, sex, or national origin	Private employers with 15 or more employees; federal, state, and local governments; unions and apprenticeship committees; employment agencies
Executive Orders 11246 and 11375 (1965)	Discrimination based on race, color, religion, sex, or national origin (affirmative action required)	Federal contractors and subcontractors

on a "bona fide occupational qualification." Included in this context are such things as age, testing, and preemployment background inquiries. However, this argument can be used against charges of discrimination in only a few cases.

WHAT RECRUITING INFORMATION CAN BE COLLECTED?

As suggested by the number of laws and governmental agencies concerned with employment, recruiters can get into trouble with the EEOC in many ways. One area of legal consideration is the information collected about an applicant. Recruiters are concerned about questions they feel they need to ask recruits but are hesitant to ask them given the present legal strictures (see Table 8.5 on page 178).

Information that some recruiters say they are cautious about includes race, national origin (birthplace), age, credit rating, general financial status, religious affiliation, membership in certain organizations, Social Security number, and military discharge status.

The government has many ways of influencing employment practices. Consequently, sales managers must continually update their information on government employment regulations and must have specific guidelines to follow. Broadly speaking, the equal employment opportunity criteria are based on two questions:

FEDERAL LAW	TYPE OF FEDERAL EMPLOYMENT DISCRIMINATION PROHIBITED	EMPLOYERS COVERED
Age Discrimination in Employment Act of 1967	Age discrimination against those between the ages of 40 and 65	Private employers with 20 or more employees, unions with 25 or more members, employment agencies, apprenticeship and training programs (state and local governments uncertain)
Title I, 1968 Civil Rights Act	Interference with a person's exercise of rights with respect to race, religion, color, or national origin	Persons generally
Executive Order 11478 (1969)	Discrimination based on race, color, religion, sex, national origin, political affiliation, marital status, or physical disability	Federal government
Revenue Sharing Act of 1972	Discrimination based on race, color, national origin, or sex	State and local governments receiving revenue-sharing funds
Education Amendments Act of 1972	Sex discrimination	Educational institutions receiving federal financial assistance
Rehabilitation Act of 1973; Executive Order 11914 (1974)	Discrimination based on physical or mental handicap (affirmative action required)	Federal contractors, federal government
Vietnam Era Veterans Readjustment Act of 1974	Discrimination against disabled veterans and Vietnam-era veterans (affirmative action required)	Federal contractors, federal government
Age Discrimination Act of 1975	Age discrimination	Employers receiving federal financial assistance
State laws/State fair employment practice laws	Similar to Title VII and Equal Employment Act of 1972	Varies by state; passed in about 85% of states
Americans with Disabilities Act of 1990	Discrimination based on physical and/or mental disabilities	Employers with more than 25 employees

TABLE 8.5   INTERVIEWING CAN AND CANNOT DO'S

SUBJECT	CAN DO OR ASK	CANNOT DO OR ASK
Sex	Notice appearance	Make comments or notes unless sex is a bona fide occupational qualification
Race	Notice general distinguishing characteristics to be used for identification purposes	Color of applicant's eyes, hair, etc., or other direct or indirect questions indicating race or color
Disability	Are you able to carry out necessary job assignments and perform them well and in a safe manner?	What is the nature and/or severity of any disabilities you have?
Marital status	Ask status after hiring, for insurance purposes	Are you married? Single? Divorced? Engaged? Are you living with anyone? Do you see your ex-spouse?
Children	Ask numbers and ages of children after hiring, for insurance purposes	Do you have children at home? How old? Who cares for them? Do you plan more children?
Physical data	Explain manual labor, lifting, other requirements of the job; show how it is performed; require physical exam	How tall are you? How heavy?
References	By whom were you referred for a position here?	Require the submission of religious reference
Criminal record	If security clearance is necessary, can this be done?	Have you ever been arrested, convicted, or spent time in jail prior to employment?
Military status	Are you a veteran? Why not? Any job-related experience?	What type of discharge do you have? What branch did you serve in?
Age	Ask age after hiring. Are you over 18?	How old are you? Estimate age
Housing	If you have no phone, how can we reach you?	Do you own your home? Do you rent? Do you live in an apartment or a house?

1. Are the employment practices equally applied, and do they have the same effect on all potential employees, regardless of race, sex, religion, national origin, or other personal characteristics?
2. Are the employment practices job related?

RECRUITMENT OF SALESPEOPLE

Recruitment of salespeople takes the proper recruiter, budget, and time to attract and hire quality individuals. To be an effective recruiter, a sales manager must have the answer to several questions, including

- How many people do I need to recruit?
- Who does the recruiting?
- Where do I find recruits?
- How can I develop a qualified pool of applicants?
- How can recruiting programs be evaluated?

The remainder of this chapter will help answer each of these questions. Let's begin with the first two questions.

HOW MANY RECRUITS DOES IT TAKE?

We have looked at determining the total number of salespeople to hire for the sales force. A big difference exists between the total number of people a firm needs to hire and the number of recruits it needs to generate to obtain its hiring goals.

Recruitment Pyramid		Ratio	Days
2	Report to Work	2:2	21
3	Offer/Hires	3:2	14
30	Interview/Offer	10:1	21
120	Leads/Interview	4:1	30

Recruiters have to estimate the number of applicants and interviews and the time needed to reach their recruitment goal. Figure 8.5 shows a recruitment plan for Mteck Industries, a manufacturer of oil field equipment. Starting at the top of the recruitment pyramid, Mteck management found that everyone who accepts a job actually reports to work. However, for every three job offers made, two were accepted. On the average, Mteck offers a job to 1 out of 10 people interviewed, so to hire 2 salespeople, it must interview 30 people. Furthermore, from the leads and applications received, it interviews 1 out of 4 people. So Mteck's recruiters must generate a list of 120 names to hire 2 people.

It takes Mteck 30 days to generate 120 leads and set up the interviews. Three weeks pass between the interview and when an applicant is offered a job. Another 14 days pass between the offer and acceptance of the job. Then it takes three weeks for the new person to begin work.

Certainly not all companies need 86 days to recruit and make a selection. Furthermore, interviewing 60 people to hire one person may not be necessary. However, recruiting does take time. Each type of sales force should set general guidelines on the time and number of interviews needed to hire a single salesperson.

Recruiting takes time, and time is money. The competition for a potential high-quality salesperson can be similar to the competition for recruiting college athletes. This requires a talented recruiter.

WHO DOES THE RECRUITING?

For the sales force's recruitment to be conducted using equal employment opportunity considerations, the sales manager must be aware of the relevant laws. The firm's human resources department is usually responsible for ensuring that the organization, including sales managers, is made aware of the organization's legal considerations for recruitment.

SOURCES OF RECRUITS—WHERE ARE THEY FOUND?

When companies have determined how many to recruit and who does the recruiting, they can examine the sources of potentially qualified job applicants and the methods used to recruit them (see Figure 8.4). After looking at the internal sources and methods, managers need to examine external sources and methods.

INTERNAL SOURCES

Internal recruitment sources come from inside the company. They include present employees, friends of employees, former employees, and former applicants.

Promotions, demotions, and transfers also can provide applicants for departments or divisions within the organization. Some companies pay a finder's fee to an employee for recommending someone who is later hired.

CURRENT EMPLOYEES   This is a source of job applicants in two respects: Current employees can refer friends to the organization, and they also can become applicants by applying for the job.

PROMOTIONS   Recruiting for positions above the initial entry sales position almost always comes from within the sales force. The case for promotion from within rests on several sound arguments. One is that present salespeople are better qualified. They know the company, and the company knows them. Another is that employees are likely to feel more secure and to identify their long-term interests with the organization that provides them the first choice of job opportunities. Availability of promotions within an organization also can motivate employees to perform well, and internal promotion can be much less expensive to the organization in terms of both time and money.

TRANSFERS   Another critical way to recruit internally is to transfer current sales personnel without promotion. Transfers are often important for providing salespeople with the more broad-based view of the organization necessary for future promotions.

EXTERNAL SOURCES

Recruiting internally does not always produce enough qualified job applicants. This is especially true for rapidly growing organizations with a large demand for salespeople. Therefore, organizations need to recruit from **external recruitment sources.** Recruiting from the outside has a number of advantages, including bringing in people with new ideas. Hiring an already trained salesperson is often cheaper and easier, particularly when the organization has an immediate demand. These are major external sources:

- Walk-ins
- Employment agencies
- Radio and television
- Newspaper advertisements
- Telephone-in advertisements

- The Internet
- Internships
- Colleges and universities
- Competitors

REALISTIC JOB PREVIEWS HELP BOTH COMPANY AND RECRUITS

A "realistic job preview" means that a person is given pertinent information about the job without distortion or exaggeration. In traditional job previews, the job is presented as attractive, interesting, and stimulating. Some jobs are all of these things. However, most jobs have some unattractive features. The realistic job preview presents the full picture—warts and all. Companies can expect these results from realistic previews:

- Newly hired salespeople have a higher rate of job survival than those hired using traditional previews.
- Salespeople hired indicate higher satisfaction.
- They can set the job expectations of new salespeople at realistic levels.
- They do not reduce the flow of highly capable applicants.

Realistic previews can inoculate salespeople against disappointment with the realities of a job. This could be an important technique for reducing costly turnover. The

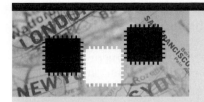

SELLING AND MANAGING GLOBALLY

CHINESE CULTURE: DON'T SHY AWAY FROM NEGOTIATING

To the Chinese, negotiation can be sport. "Negotiating? It's not esoteric," former U.S. Ambassador to China James Lilley, who is now a business consultant, says. "There's no arcane world of Chinese deviousness. Once you figure out what they want—and they telegraph their punches—you can make your deal. You've got to be willing to go to the brink. You've got to be willing to use them against each other; you've got to be willing to come in on top and bring pressure to bear." (In other words, use high-level pressure developed through relationships.)

The tough-love approach is suggested again and again: Be respectful; don't fly off the handle, but be resolute. Jim Stepanek, who spent years negotiating in China for Honeywell and other U.S. companies, says: "The only universal language is pain and anger. When they push down your price, and you calmly say no, they are going to delay the meeting another day and push you some more. When you finally get upset, and you ask to leave the room to control yourself because your blood vessels are popping out, and you come back a half hour later with steam still coming out your ears, then they know it is your lowest price."

Negotiating in China has advantages over negotiating in Japan, Craig McLaughlin suggests. "When you are negotiating with a Japanese organization, even when what you are presenting is totally unacceptable to the individual or company, they may not tell you. That is not a problem in China. They will be very direct. They're more likely to try and get you to negotiate against yourself. Instead of giving you a counterproposal they say, 'Go home and think about it, and come back with a better offer.'

"Another trait," McLaughlin continues, "is that quite often the people with whom you are negotiating do not have the authority to reach a compromise. The delegation of authority in China is not totally spelled out." Your best move? Tell them there is little point in going further with the meeting unless they are willing to reveal their chain of command. They may not necessarily give you a straight answer, and sometimes they may not even know themselves, but it is a step in the right direction.

Source: Jim Alexander, "Selling in China," *Business Week,* February 1995, 65.

best preview method is to have applicants work with an experienced salesperson for one day or more. This allows the person to see the job requirements firsthand and provides an opportunity to ask further questions of someone not in authority.

Ross Perot once said, "Eagles don't flock. You have to find them one at a time." Good people are hard to find. All-stars are even harder to find. This is why recruitment is so important.

As you saw in Figure 8.4, sales recruitment involves numerous influences and components. Everything discussed thus far concerns one goal—to develop an extremely qualified pool of applicants. The better the quality of people to choose from, the higher the probability of selecting a person who will be successful.

One method for improving the applicant pools is first to survey the applicants and next to survey those hired. That is, if the organization wants to attract candidates, it needs to know what attracts them and how to attract them. The organization should find out:

- How candidates obtain information regarding job availability.
- What attracts people to the job.
- What are the likes and dislikes about the job.
- Why the person took the job.

Answers to these questions help companies better understand recruitment. Also, companies should find out why people would not interview with them. This could change the total recruitment process.

THE QUALIFIED APPLICANT POOL

RECRUITMENT EVALUATION

Recruiting should always be evaluated, as shown in Figure 8.4. Remember that recruitment activity is supposed to attract people within legal limits, so people and organizations can select each other with their best interests in mind.

Job performance and turnover are benefit criteria for recruitment whose value should be assessed relative to recruitment. Another evaluation criterion by which to assess recruiting is legal compliance. Job applicants must be recruited fairly and without discrimination. In addition to assessing each benefit criterion for recruitment, companies can valuate or "cost out" each method or source of recruitment. This would require measuring the costs involved in using a recruiting method (for example, the travel, hotel, and salary expenses a recruiter incurs visiting a college campus). Then the financial benefits from the recruiting methods would be determined.

THE BOTTOM LINE

Sales human resource management (SHRM) is the use of several functions and activities for the benefit of the individual and the organization. SHRM is comprised of two elements: people planning and employment planning.

Developing a successful sales team requires the planning of personnel needs and analyzing the sales jobs to achieve more efficient use of human resources. Proper planning can improve sales performance by anticipating shortages, turnover, and profits. People planning involves analyzing the current supply of sales personnel in each position.

Job analysis is the definition of specific roles or activities to be performed in the sales positions. The three steps of job analysis are to (1) determine how each job relates to the others, (2) select jobs to be analyzed, and (3) collect information about the jobs. Job descriptions are formal, written statements describing the responsibilities and requirements of a position. Job specifications are the abilities, behavior, education, and skills necessary for successful job performance.

The goal of managing sales human resources is to hire above-average performers. The salespeople should have the right personal characteristics to succeed in the job. This is why job design and analysis are important for determining what kind of person is necessary for the job.

In order to hire the right person for the job, there must be a recruitment strategy. Recruitment is the set of activities and processes used to legally obtain a sufficient number of individuals in such a manner that the recruits' and the sales force's best interests are taken into consideration. Legal influences play a critical role in recruitment for most companies in America.

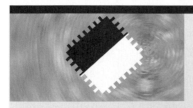

MANAGEMENT IN ACTION: ETHICAL DILEMMA
SHOULD I GO AGAINST THE COMMANDER?

Juan Gomez has been with your company six years. Last year he was transferred to your sales group. Juan has done an exceptional job. However, his previous manager, Larry Disney—a good friend of yours who was recently promoted to become your boss—had given him poor yearly performance evaluations prior to the transfer. A former U.S. Marine lieutenant, Larry is known for being a tough disciplinarian who expects people to be team players. Now that you are one of his subordinates, should you dare to contradict Larry's opinions of Juan?

WHAT DO YOU DO?
1. Give Juan an "exceptional" performance rating, even if it makes your friend and boss look bad and upsets him.
2. Compromise and reduce Juan's performance rating to "good."
3. Give Juan an "exceptional" rating but tell him to keep it confidential.

Recruitment of salespeople takes the proper recruiters, budget, and amount of time to attract and hire quality individuals. To hire the needed number of salespeople, companies must recruit, screen, and interview different numbers of individuals to find enough qualified candidates.

Recruits come from two sources. They can come from internal sources: friends of current employees, promotions, and transfers. Potential recruits can also come from external sources such as walk-in applicants; employment agencies; radio, television, and newspaper ads; internships, and colleges.

Recruiters should use site visits to give applicants a realistic job preview. These previews have been shown to increase job satisfaction and decrease turnover rates. To increase the number of qualified applicants and to attract the right applicants within legal specifications, companies should evaluate their recruiting programs. Recruitment procedures should be based on qualifications directly related to the job.

▓ KEY TERMS FOR SALES MANAGERS

Sales human resource management (SHRM), 168	Recruitment, 175	Equal Employment Opportunity Act of 1972, 176
People planning, 168	Equal Employment Opportunity Commission (EEOC), 176	
Job analysis, 171	Equal Pay Act of 1963, 176	Internal recruitment sources, 179
Job descriptions, 172	Education Amendments Act of 1972, 176	External recruitment sources, 180
Job specifications, 172		

▓ MANAGEMENT APPLICATION QUESTIONS

1. What are the major activities involved in planning sales personnel needs? Why are they so important?
2. What is the difference between a job description and a job specification?
3. Today, professional sports is big business. It provides entertainment to millions of people. Compare and contrast the importance of recruiting professional athletes to the importance of recruiting sales personnel. Include in your answer any similarities between developing a success profile for the athlete and developing one for the salesperson.
4. A manufacturer of consumer goods has a 500-person sales force. Each year, turnover equals 20 percent—100 people need to be hired. The five key characteristics the company uses to select salespeople are (1) aggressiveness, (2) perceptiveness, (3) intelligence, (4) high energy level, and (5) tenacity. What do you suggest the manufacturer should use to identify these characteristics in people?
5. A firm does not recruit within a vacuum. A number of factors, both internal and external to the firm, influence the recruiting process. Identify at least one internal and one external factor, and explain how it might affect the recruitment process.
6. A firm is attempting to estimate how many people it will have to recruit to find two salespeople and how long it will take. From reviewing its records, the firm finds it takes about one week after a person accepts the job to report for work. However, only 50 percent of the people offered the job accept one, and it takes a week for these decisions to be made. The interviewing process takes one week for every 20 people interviewed, and the firm only offers a job to 10 percent of the people it interviews. It interviews about two-thirds of the people that apply for the position, and it keeps applications open for two weeks. How many applicants should the firm have, and how long will it take to hire two salespeople?
7. Why is recruitment for the sales force such an important task for a firm?

▓ FURTHER EXPLORING THE SALES WORLD

Interview two or more sales managers and determine if they have a formal profile of characteristics they consider when hiring. If they do, ask how they identify the characteristics in a person. If they don't, ask what they look for in people. Chances are they have an informal profile. Find out the time it takes from the decision to hire someone to when the person is assigned to a sales territory.

■ SALES MANAGEMENT EXPERIENTIAL EXERCISE

PLAN YOUR INTERVIEW APPEARANCE

The most successful people in customer-contact jobs claim mental sharpness means communicating a positive self-image. Like an actor or actress, interacting with others requires you to be on stage at all times. Creating a good first impression is essential. Also important is understanding the direct connection between your attitude and how you look to yourself. The better your self-image when you encounter customers, clients, or guests, the more positive you are.

Rate yourself on each of the following grooming areas. If you write 5, you are saying improvement is not required. If you write a 1 or 2, you need considerable improvement. Be honest.

	Excellent	Good	Fair	Weak	Poor
Hairstyle, hair grooming, fingernails (appropriate length and cleanliness)	5	4	3	2	1
Personal cleanliness habits (body)	5	4	3	2	1
Clothing, piercings, and jewelry (appropriate to the situation)	5	4	3	2	1
Neatness (shoes shined; clothes clean, well pressed, etc.)	5	4	3	2	1
Fragrances, tattoos, and makeup	5	4	3	2	1
General grooming: Does your appearance reflect professionalism on the job?	5	4	3	2	1

When it comes to appearance on the job, I would rate myself as follows:

☐ Excellent   ☐ Good   ☐ Need Improvement

CONNECTICUT CANDY WHOLESALERS
An Unusual Cause of Turnover

Oh, Oh! Here comes trouble again! You are the regional sales manager of Connecticut Candy Wholesalers, and another salesperson has quit. Now your own chief wonders if you can hold onto staff. You don't think your personality, style, or demands have changed. Why is this happening?

In an exit interview five salespeople criticized the behavior of James, a staff member who has been with you the longest. This person always has seemed dedicated to you and the company. It's hard to believe, but facts you research support the salespeople's comments. James was the only one who claimed not to notice that many new hires were staying but a short time. Other pieces of the puzzle begin to fall into place. Each time you hired someone, James came to your office and asked to help break in the new group member. Very nice, you thought. Now you wonder why. He often reported negative information or complaints direct from the grapevine concerning the new hire's habits or behavior. James invariably asked how the new hire was going to affect his own job. Each time a new hire quit, he said, "I told you he wouldn't last very long in this company." Was it a self-fulfilling prophecy?

You ignored the fact that James was a loner, rarely joining the others for coffee or socializing. You rationalized that Connecticut Candy benefited from his intense dedication to work. You now remember the other group members' frequent comments: James literally hovered over every new hire's shoulder. He subjected all the new hires to personal putdowns and severe criticisms of their job performance. Every new hire was the victim of James's continuous and apparently cruel snipping. Even when a new hire handled a task very well or closed a tough sale, James crudely lectured the new hire about how the task should have been handled. He rarely, if ever, had a kind word to say or gave encouragement to the new hires during their break-in periods.

Clearly, James has driven new hires from the company. The more promising they are, the stronger James's efforts are to get them out. Now you have a duel dilemma. You can't fire him without hurting sales. He makes significant contributions, and you know your competitors want him. In fact, you know they've made offers to James. The other part of the dilemma is how to change James's behavior from destructive to constructive.

QUESTION
What will you do?

CASE 8.2

R. J. REYNOLDS
Selecting the Best Sales Team

Joe Miller had worked for R. J. Reynolds, a nationwide consumer goods company, for five years as a salesperson in the Oklahoma City sales division. He had been highly rated as a field sales representative and was recently promoted to assistant division sales manager in Memphis, Tennessee. This was his first step into field sales management. He was excited about his new position and the wider responsibilities that went along with the job.

His new boss, M. B. Wilson, was the division sales manager in Memphis. Joe had heard many good things about him over the years and was looking forward to gaining experience as a manager and being trained by Wilson. After Joe spent a few weeks becoming acquainted with the retail trade, key accounts, and the 12 sales representatives in the Memphis office, Wilson asked him to stop by the office on Friday morning for a short meeting. Joe learned that a sales representative in the division would soon be leaving to take a position with another company. The division manager explained the process used to find and employ sales representatives. Wilson also told Joe that he would need his help in locating and interviewing several applicants for the position that would soon be open. After Joe could locate 10 to 12 applicants, he would recommend 2 or 3 to Wilson for a second interview. The regional manager would later interview the top applicant and decide whether or not to make a job offer.

Joe was pleased to be involved in the recruiting process. From past observation, he knew that many young college graduates were seeking jobs, but finding applicants that matched the firm's job specifications would not be easy. R. J. Reynolds normally preferred to employ applicants with a college degree in marketing or business and a proven record of hard work. Furthermore, the right personality was important to the company. This means persons who are achievement oriented and self-confident and possess a positive outlook on life. Joe knew that he would need to talk with many applicants before finding two or three that would be acceptable to the company. Joe also knew that selling positions do not appeal to most graduating seniors. Furthermore, the cigarette and smoking tobacco industry had received a good deal of bad publicity over the past few years.

Wilson was in his late 50s and had been at his present job level for almost 20 years. He realized he would probably not go any higher in the company, so he was content to do the best job possible and play golf on weekends until retirement. He had attended college as a young man but had not graduated. His management philosophy was basically "to hire hard-working salespeople, treat them fairly, and most problems will take care of themselves." That philosophy had served him well over the years. The Memphis Division had a very high share of the cigarette and smoking tobacco market, excellent chain-store and dealer relations, and low employee turnover.

Joe had asked his new boss for advice on how he should go about finding applicants for the coming vacancy. Wilson explained how he had filled positions over the years. He liked to hire college-trained applicants from rural areas. The explanation was that young people who had grown up on a farm knew hard work and most understood and appreciated the value of money. Character and good communication skills were also important. But the two most important traits, according to Wilson, are one's motivation to be successful and one's persistence. Stressing this point, Wilson explained that after interviewing at the smaller colleges in outlying areas, he never followed up by contacting the applicants. "If they do not take the initiative to get back in touch with me, then they probably wouldn't make good salespeople anyway."

Wilson also had ideas about other staffing practices. He believed it was important to have a sales staff that included a good mix of women and minorities. Although he was careful in interviews to ask only questions that were work related, he seemed to prefer married applicants and persons from the local area. He also liked to hire women who had one or two children and a husband who held a job in the local area. His reasoning was that these applicants have more incentive to work hard and would want to remain in the area because of family ties. The seasoned manager was careful to remind Joe that this philosophy has paid off with high sales and low turnover in the Memphis Division.

As Joe thought about his responsibility for filling the position that would soon be open, he decided his new division manager's philosophy seemed to be basically logical. He was a little uncomfortable, however, with some of Wilson's ideas about recruiting from the smaller colleges and universities in rural areas. Joe had attended the University of Arkansas at Little Rock and had grown up in a fairly large city. He realized that Wilson would probably not have recruited him. He also wondered how many other potentially good sales representatives might be screened out by Wilson's criteria.

Joe remembered a lesson he had learned as a teenager while working in a supermarket. The manager had asked him to do some routine task. Joe told the manager, "I think there is a better way to do this." The manager replied, "You get paid to work, not to think." Maybe the present situation called for more work and less thinking. Joe started making plans to interview graduating seniors at some of the smaller colleges and universities within a 100-mile radius of Memphis. After all, his main goal as a new assistant division manager is to learn how to become a good division manager.

QUESTIONS

1. Discuss the strengths and weaknesses of the present staffing process R. J. Reynolds traditionally uses.
2. Discuss Wilson's personal recruiting philosophy. Is it good or bad and why?
3. What alternative sources of applicants are available?
4. How would you go about accomplishing Joe's current recruiting assignment?
5. Discuss the lesson Joe learned while he was a teenager and how it might apply in the present situation.

Source: This case was prepared by Professors Gerald Crawford and Professor R. Keith Absher, both of the University of North Alabama, and Professor Tom Griffin of Auburn University at Montgomery.

CHAPTER 9

SELECTION, PLACEMENT, AND SOCIALIZATION OF SUCCESSFUL SALESPEOPLE

CHAPTER OUTLINE

SELECTION AND PLACEMENT OF SUCCESSFUL SALES PERSONNEL

PREDICTORS FOR SELECTION DECISIONS

THE SELECTION PROCESS

EVALUATING SELECTION AND PLACEMENT DECISIONS

THE SOCIALIZATION OF SALES PERSONNEL

LEARNING OBJECTIVES

The selection, placement, and socialization of salespeople are extremely important to the sales force and the new individual. This chapter should help you understand:

■ The purposes, importance, and influencing factors of selection and placement.

■ The predictors used to make selection decisions.

■ The many forms of personnel selection, as well as their differences and similarities.

■ That evaluation of selection and placement decisions is very necessary.

■ With whom the final decision rests.

■ The need to effectively socialize new personnel into their jobs.

In a recent interview with James Weitzul, an industrial psychologist and president of Banks and Weitzul, a Princeton, New Jersey, consulting firm specializing in sales issues, he was asked, "Do you have any 'hire/no hire' questions when interviewing sales managers?" Weitzul responded by saying that, although no one can provide a simple question or questions suitable to every situation, certain questions can narrow down the number of potential employees interviewing for sales management positions. Weitzul pointed out that the single most important factor, however, is to find out if a candidate possesses strong qualities of self-discipline. "Evidence of this trait is best revealed by asking open-ended questions that allow interviewees to describe their own level of discipline without explicit prompting from the interviewer," he said.

Weitzul suggests four keys for determining an interviewee's level of self-discipline. An interviewer must first watch for applicants who need prompting on questions, because, according to Weitzul, the more prompting they need, the less self-discipline they have. For example, a question an interviewee might ask is "What do you mean by activities and accomplishments?" Such answers show a definite lack of self-discipline and a need for direction, structure, rules, and guidelines.

A job candidate's most recent employment situation is also critical to determining his or her level of self-discipline. If the interviewee is asked to describe a typical work week, the weak candidate will ask for more clarification, which Weitzul feels is demonstrative of a need for structure. Those who have a high degree of self-discipline will be very specific with their answers by providing information indicative of early starters and late workers, of who sets personal daily or weekly goals, of who establishes sales goals for their team, and of who monitors their team's performance.

Weitzul says he feels the most telling question involves sales numbers. For example, candidates who are unable to recollect their sales numbers for the past couple of years demonstrate a lack of self-discipline. On the other hand, the best candidates, whether just out of sales or a sales manager for another company, will be able to recall either individual production numbers or the sales numbers for each of their subordinates.

The final determining factor for individuals with strong self-disciplinary skills is what success means to them. If they feel success is defined by material possessions, then they will appear undisciplined. Self-disciplined candidates define success as achieving job objectives. They have solid goals for themselves and their company, and they know to what extent or in what amount of time they will accomplish them.[1] ■

Selection of personnel is not as easy as you would think. Employers consider several people for the job and select one. They use people's past accomplishments to predict their future success on the job. Will the selected person be successful? Only time will tell. People who become high performers increase sales for the entire group. Low or marginal performers have the reverse effect. Selection of all sales personnel is critical to the success of a sales group. This chapter examines the entire process involved in picking winners, assigning them to territories, and orienting them to their new jobs.

SELECTION AND PLACEMENT OF SUCCESSFUL SALES PERSONNEL

Selection of sales personnel refers to the process of selecting the best available person for the job. **Placement** is concerned with ensuring that job demands match an individual's skills, knowledge, and abilities, along with preferences, interests, and personality. Placement for entry-level salespeople involves which manager they will work for and their assigned individual territory. A company can hire qualified people, but if it places them in a territory they do not want or if customers have difficulty accepting the people, then the salespeople and the company suffer.

Placement for current sales personnel involves promotions, transfers, and demotions. Whenever a person changes assignments, the fit between the individual and job is important.

IS SELECTION THE MOST IMPORTANT ELEMENT IN FIELDING A SALES FORCE?

The selection of the right people is, without a doubt, extremely important to the success of the sales district, the region, and the total sales force. Few people would argue if you said it is the most important element in fielding a successful sales force.

IBM's Greg Gaston uses the simple analogy of a person and a lightbulb to illustrate why selection is so important to the success of a sales force. "A '60 watt' person has the capacity to generate relatively small amounts of light (productivity). When the '60 watter' is turned on—with training, rewards, and all the other motivational techniques discussed throughout this book—that person can reach only a limited level of productivity. The person restricts his or her own capacity to perform at an extremely high level. The '200 watter,' on the other hand, has a built-in, natural ability to produce relatively large amounts of light (productivity). This person brings above-average ability and motivational traits to the job."

We can say that input shapes output. The input of high-wattage people into the sales force produces above-average output (productivity). Thus, sales managers must strive to hire people with the preferences, interests, and personality for the job. Then they can use the various factors under their control to manage and lead their salespeople to high performance.

PURPOSES AND IMPORTANCE OF SELECTION AND PLACEMENT

Selection and placement procedures provide the fuel that runs the sales force. The correct selection and placement will improve organizational productivity. Since people have different levels of productivity, selection may result in substantial gains in productivity if the sales force has fewer staffing problems.

Sales managers want to improve productivity. They want to do it at a reasonable cost; doing it at a reduced cost would be fabulous. How can they do that?

The proper match between person and job can improve productivity and reduce operating costs. Often, selection costs equal 30 percent of a new hire's annual salary plus relocation costs. Cost savings would occur due to such factors as less turnover. Less turnover means lower training and staffing costs, not to mention saving the cost

FIGURE 9.1   MAJOR INFLUENCES AND COMPONENTS OF SALES FORCE SELECTION

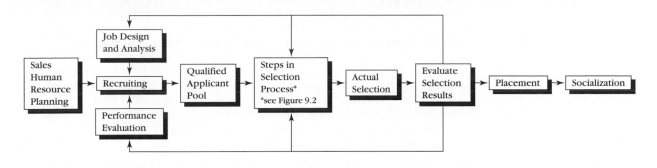

associated with sales managers' time. With lower turnover comes less downtime in sales territories, which results in higher sales.

FACTORS INFLUENCING SELECTION AND PLACEMENT

The success of a sales force's selection and placement procedures depends on their relationships with several staffing and management activities. As Figure 9.1 illustrates, selection decisions start with a pool of potentially qualified job applicants. As discussed in the previous chapter, this is directly related to the job design and job analysis, recruitment, and sales human resource planning activities.

Selection and placement also depend on performance evaluations as feedback, showing that the selection devices do indeed predict the performance of salespeople. As you will see later in this chapter, selection devices need to have the capability of predicting salespeople's performance. This ability allows firms to empirically validate their use of job-related procedures and devices to select their salespeople. The EEOC likes to see this because the proper selection of people is one of its prime directives.

In Chapter 5 we discussed the use of market factors and a market index for predicting sales. Sales managers want to have a single factor or several factors (index) that will predict sales well.

For hiring decisions, these sales managers want to have information to help forecast an applicant's future performance. Information about the individual forms the basis for predicting how successfully a job applicant will perform on the job.

To collect the proper information, managers must develop job-related performance criteria directly related to success at the job.* The performance criteria determine the type of information to obtain from the job applicants and to some extent the method used to gather the information. Remember that the job analysis is used to develop the criteria.

WHAT ARE PREDICTORS?

The various pieces of information about the person are often called **predictors.** They are referred to as **tests** when used to make selection decisions. The law, *Uniform Guidelines,* states:

PREDICTORS FOR SELECTION DECISIONS

---

*See Chapter 16 for a discussion on the development of job-related performance criteria.

[a] test is defined as any paper-and-pencil or performance measure used as a basis for any employment decision. The guidelines in this part apply, for example, to ability tests that are designed to measure eligibility for hire, transfer, promotion, membership, training, referral, or retention. This definition includes, but is not restricted to, measures of general intelligence, mental ability, and learning ability; specific intellectual abilities; mechanical, clerical, and other aptitudes; dexterity and coordination; knowledge and proficiency; occupational and other interests; and attitudes, personality, or temperament. The term "test" includes all formal, scored, quantified, or standardized techniques of assessing job suitability including, in addition to the above, specific qualifying or disqualifying personal history or background requirements, specific educational or work history requirements, scored interviews, biographical information blanks, interviewers' rating scales, scored application forms, etc.

Thus, the *Uniform Guidelines* includes all forms of information collection methods used to make selection decisions.

SOURCES FOR COLLECTING INFORMATION

Figure 9.2 presents the major steps in the sales personnel selection process used to collect information for hiring purposes. This information can be grouped into four categories: (1) skills, knowledge, and ability (SKAs); (2) preferences, interests, and personality (PIPs); (3) other category; and (4) other characteristics. The main sources for collecting information related to each category follow:

1. *SKAs:* employment tests for achievement, physical ability tests, interviews, weighted application blanks.
2. *PIPs:* employment tests for personality, interests, and preferences; interviews.
3. *Other category:* employment tests and interviews for collecting information on aspects such as aptitude, common sense, dexterity, level of education, experience, general mental ability, intelligence, and leadership.
4. *Other characteristics:* physical examinations, application blanks, reference checks, and interviews for collecting information such as ability to be bonded, driver's license number, ability to provide own automobile, and willingness to travel and relocate.

FIGURE 9.2

MAJOR STEPS IN SALES
PERSONNEL SELECTION
PROCESS

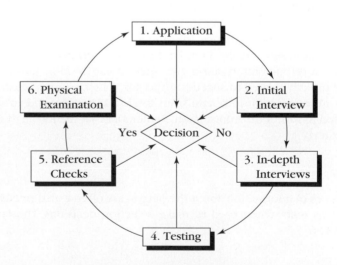

IS THE INFORMATION JOB RELATED?

Any information collected from the applicant should be related to the job. A low actual relationship may exist between the measured predictor and the job-related performance criteria. The grade point average of a college student, for example, may be related to success, yet other aspects, such as personality, interests, and preferences, also may be important for success. Because several factors can contribute to success, any one factor may be of little help in predicting sales success.

Because of these reasons, demonstrating job-relatedness for skill, knowledge, and ability predictors is generally easier than for predictors based on preferences, interest, and personality. Gathering the information is easy, but proving a strong relationship between the information and job performance can be a problem.

This also applies to information in the "other category," such as intelligence, general mental ability, aptitude, leadership, work experience, and educational level. Skills, knowledge, and abilities that can be learned in a reasonable time on the job or in training should not be used in making selection decisions. If applicants need only a minimum level of knowledge, skill, or ability, then only information showing whether the applicant meets these minimum requirements should be collected.

Information classified into the "other characteristics" category usually represents minimum qualifications for a job. They include factors such as requirement of a driver's license, grooming codes, and willingness to travel or relocate. Applicants either will or will not possess them. The level of a person's possession of these qualifications makes no difference. If an applicant does not have a needed qualification or is unwilling to comply with a required "other characteristic," the person can be disqualified from further consideration.

Craig Johnson, a regional manager for Duplex Products Inc., in Southfield, Michigan, tells of a screening process they have developed for finding possible interview candidates. This preliminary screening process consists of job-related qualifications including a college curriculum focused on sales and marketing, sales experience, and a desire to obtain a career in sales. It has worked well for college recruiting. Duplex recently obtained one of its best salespeople from this process.[2]

Let us examine each step of the sales personnel selection. Sales managers are expected to possess the skills, knowledge, and abilities necessary to successfully select top performers.

THE SELECTION PROCESS

In the past, selection of salespeople was often thought to be an easy decision. The sales manager interviewed applicants, sized them up, and let gut reactions guide the choice. Decisions were based on the sales manager's subjective likes or dislikes. **Selection tools**—procedures for helping in the hiring decision—were designed to aid this gut reaction. For most selection decisions, this was all the tools were intended to do; they were designed to increase the proportion of successful sales applicants selected. Today, selection is viewed as more than a simple reliance on intuitive feelings.

The selection decision is usually perceived as a series of steps through which applicants pass. At each step, a few more applicants are screened out, or more applicants accept other job offers and drop from the application list. Figure 9.2 illustrates a typical series of steps for the selection process.

This series is not universally used. Few organizations use all steps, for they can be time consuming and expensive, and several steps, such as 4, 5, and 6, may be performed at about the same time. Generally, the more important the job, the more likely each step will be used formally. Most organizations use the screening interview, application blank, and interview. A relatively small number of employers use tests. Background and reference checks and physical exams are used for some jobs and not others.

The reasons for these differences relate to the type of companies, their markets, and their size. For example, a regional wholesaler may use only the screening interview, application blank, and a follow-up interview; whereas IBM, Xerox, or Pepsi-Cola go through each step shown.

THE JOB APPLICATION BLANK

The first step in the process of selection is the application blank. It is, along with the interview, the most widely used selection tool.

The **application blank** is an orderly, convenient method of collecting necessary information for determining an applicant's minimum qualifications. Its format differs from company to company, often due to the differences in jobs.

Although firms can use the application blank to collect a wide range of information, legal constraints have lessened the amount and type of information an employer might actually be able to ask about an applicant. This is due to the difficulty in demonstrating job-relatedness and to discriminatory practices. Even with the various restrictions, application blanks still collect a great deal of useful information. When developing these forms, companies should follow the rule that questions not related to job qualifications should not be on the application blank.

INFORMATION TYPICALLY COLLECTED   Firms use application blanks to collect information about the applicant's education, work experience, physical and personal characteristics, and preferences. Much of this information can be directly related to the person's skills, knowledge, abilities, preferences, interests, and personality. When reviewing the application blank, the sales manager should look for the following:

- Does the applicant have the minimum job requirements?
- Account for all dates. If gaps occur, question them.
- Review the numbers of jobs and length of time spent on each job. Is the candidate a job-hopper?
- Analyze the reasons given for leaving jobs. Does a pattern occur? Does it pose a potential problem?
- Does a pattern of growth occur? Has the applicant shown a steady trend toward better jobs, more responsibility, greater earnings, and so forth?

How the form is filled out also counts. If it is messy, and if the applicant's appearance is the same, many recruiters may put the form in a rejection file after the applicant leaves the interview. This is especially true if a large number of applicants apply for the job.

Also, a professionally taken photograph left with or placed on an applicant's résumé greatly helps a recruiter remember the applicant. In a college recruitment center, for example, a recruiter may see 16 applicants in one day—one every 30 minutes. The photograph helps the recruiter relate written information to a person's appearance, personality, and general impression. It also is an indication the applicant is organized and interested in the job.

THE PERSONAL INTERVIEW—A ONE-ON-ONE SELLING SITUATION

The **personal interview** usually involves the one-on-one, face-to-face meeting of two strangers, both seeking to sell themselves to the other. Both the recruiter and the applicant are at the interview to see if a match exists between what the company is offering the applicant and what the applicant is offering the company. As illustrated in Table 9.1, interviews are important for both the sales manager and the applicant. Martha Hill of Hanes Knitwear states:

FOR THE SALES MANAGER	FOR THE APPLICANT
Act as a screening device to create the pool of qualified applicants	Act as a screening device to create a pool of qualified jobs
Confirm application blanks, written tests, and feedback from references relative to SKAs, PIPs, the other category, and other characteristics	Determine skills, knowledge, and abilities required
Judge if the applicant can be successful in the short and long run	Determine what will be received from the job, such as training, compensation, promotional opportunities
Meet the potential employee and determine if a match exists	Meet the potential boss and determine if a match exists

TABLE 9.1

INTERVIEWS ARE IMPORTANT FOR THE SALES MANAGER AND THE APPLICANT

My job as regional sales manager included responsibility for the hiring, training, and development of seven salespeople, in addition to analyzing our business and developing sales strategies to capitalize on our opportunities. Through many experiences in interviewing and hiring salespeople, I value this as one of the most difficult, yet important, aspects of my job. My general philosophy toward selection of candidates is to find the best person for the particular territory, and I systematically screen applicants before, during, and after interviews. I use a basic process to find people who are suitable, and I look for characteristics and/or experiences in an applicant's background that will either help to qualify or disqualify the person. I rely heavily on the use of personal interviews because face-to-face selling is exactly what our jobs involve, and the applicant must be able to sell me on hiring him/her in order to be successful at the job.

CRITICISMS OF INTERVIEWING   The nucleus of the staffing process is the interview. It is the principal way the interviewer and interviewee determine whether they have a mutual interest. Interviewing effectively is a challenge for both parties. The skill of the interviewer is a critical factor in the selection process.

Unfortunately, interviewers are sometimes untrained or unprepared and consequently conduct interviews haphazardly. This can result in poor content validity (incomplete information collected) and poor question validity (questions cause interviewee to answer according to perception of what recruiter wants to hear). The interviewer also must interpret information incorrectly, make snap decisions early in the interview, or make unreliable decisions. The untrained interviewer's techniques can result in the hiring of a "successful-looking failure" or the rejection of the "unsuccessful-looking success" (see Table 9.2). The real challenge is to correctly select the "unsuccessful-looking success."

How can a company help ensure it hires successful people? Noxell's Alan Baker has developed a solution:

We conduct a series of interviewing skills workshops throughout our entire sales organization at the management level. Everybody who goes to a college campus has completed this program. All of our hiring managers have the same orientation in terms of the goals, objectives, criteria, and the procedures of interviewing.

TYPES OF INTERVIEWS   Interviews are of three general types: structured, unstructured, and semistructured. In the patterned, or **structured interview,** the recruiter asks questions, often from a standard form. If it is highly structured, responses may

TABLE 9.2

THE INTERVIEW
QUADRANT

	SUCCESSFUL-LOOKING	
PERFORMANCE FAILURE	The successful-looking failure	The successful-looking success
	The unsuccessful-looking failure	The unsuccessful-looking success
	UNSUCCESSFUL-LOOKING	PERFORMANCE SUCCESS

be forced choice, that is, yes or no or multiple choice, and the applicant is usually not allowed to qualify answers. Managers may use the structured interview for initial screening, but it is not appropriate for gathering in-depth information, which often needs elaboration. Typically, applicants do not like to participate in this form of interview, nor do professional interviewers.

In an **unstructured interview,** the recruiter asks few preplanned questions and often begins with open-ended questions such as "Tell me about yourself" or "Why do you want to sell for IBM?" The applicant does 80 to 90 percent of the talking. A recruiter can effectively use this technique by asking probing questions and directing the conversation. Often the applicant leaves the interview wondering what was accomplished because the recruiter has given too little information. It takes a highly skilled interviewer to use this approach effectively. For that reason, and because applicants are often uneasy with this type of approach, the unstructured interview is usually not appropriate for a first interview.

The **semistructured interview** allows for interaction and collection of information of interest to both parties. Often only major questions are preplanned. It offers the greatest flexibility in allowing the interviewer to move from general to specific questions. The format allows recruiters to customize the interview for the individual. Applicants appear to prefer this type of interview. By following guidelines shown in Table 9.1, applicants can help ensure a successful interview for both parties.

The Stress Interview   Occasionally an interviewer may place the applicant in a stressful situation to ascertain how the person might cope with stress when selling. This interview technique has been used in the past but is seldom used today. Sales recruiters prefer not to place applicants in stressful situations, because they have found that applicants become defensive and a major reduction in communication occurs. Also, little, if any, correlation exists between how an individual might handle stress in an interview and stress on the job. Applicants tend to be less attracted to the job due to the negative image thus created. Furthermore, should a sales manager who used this approach hire and work with the applicant, friction may develop between the two due to the experience.

NONVERBAL CUES IN INTERVIEWS   An easterner who walked into a western saloon was amazed to see a dog sitting at a table playing poker with three men. "Can that dog really read cards?" he asked. "Yes, but he ain't much of a player," one of the men said. "Whenever he gets a good hand he wags his tail." In interviewing—as well as playing cards—nonverbal cues play an important part in the communication process. Body movements, gestures, firmness of handshake, eye contact, and physical appearance are all nonverbal cues. Often interviewers put more importance on the nonverbal cues than on the verbal.

It has been estimated that, at most, only 30 to 35 percent of the meaning conveyed in a message is verbal; the remainder is nonverbal. Similarly, for attitudes or feelings, one estimate is that merely 7 percent of what is communicated is verbal, while nonverbal factors account for the remaining 93 percent. Therefore, sales managers must be aware of nonverbal cues during interviews. One of the reasons nonverbal cues are so powerful is that, in most cases, interviewers are not aware of them as possible causal agents of impression formation. Interpretation of nonverbal cues, however, varies with each person.

INTERVIEWING PHASES   As shown in Figure 9.3, the sales interview has five main phases. These are preparation, opening the interview, the main body of the interview, closing the interview, and post-interview activities.

Interview Preparation   Just as the quarterback has a game plan and knows the first series of plays when beginning a game, so the interviewer must plan the interview. Interview preparation begins with a determination of the minimum requirements, traits, and background characteristics for the job. This should be kept to no more than six or seven factors. Applicants for sales jobs may be expected to meet salary, education, and travel requirements. If, for example, the job involves 50 percent travel, the interviewer must determine whether this is acceptable to the applicant. Suppose the applicant has no driver's license. This must be found out quickly. The application form should ask for this information. The interviewer should spend five to ten minutes reviewing the application form before beginning the interview. With preparation, a recruiter can formulate a checklist of critical requirements beforehand and standardize the interview.

Opening the Interview   The interviewer should greet the applicant with a warm, friendly handshake and give an introduction. After both are seated, the interviewer should state the purpose of the interview, mentioning the specific job involved and, if appropriate, the corresponding sales division of the company.

Many interviewers like to summarize what will be discussed during the interview. This adds structure and allows the applicant to ask questions. The introduction and summary should take about 20 percent of the interview time.

During the introductory stage, the interviewer can ask several short questions about the application form to clarify certain points. The interviewer's introductory techniques are extremely important to the success of the interview and to developing a friendly atmosphere. The attitudes of both the interviewer and the applicant evolving during the interview influence reliability. It is difficult to tell whether any

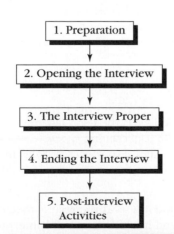

FIGURE 9.3

FIVE PHASES OF THE
SALES INTERVIEW

one technique is best. Interviewers often develop several standard questions from which one can be chosen as the applicant enters the room. Some interviewers prefer small talk on subjects ranging from the weather to sports at first. However, before they know it, this small talk can take 5 to 10 minutes of a 30-minute initial interview. So the interviewer should put the applicant at ease and get down to the basics quickly.

The Interview   Interaction is important during the interview. The interviewer can ask open-ended questions to allow the applicant to demonstrate communication skills and discuss career goals. A good interviewer/interviewee talk ratio would be 50/50. This allows time for the interviewer to discuss the job and its requirements and to determine whether the applicant should be invited back for a second in-depth interview.

Ending the Interview   After about 95 percent of the time allocated has passed, the interviewer should begin to end the interview. The closing of an interview is just as important as the closing of a sale. It is the portion of the interview that creates a good or bad image of the recruiter and the company and creates a desire for the job. Several basic topics should be covered.

First, briefly summarize what the job involves and other information discussed during the interview. Second, tell the applicant exactly what will happen in the future, that is, what the next step is, when the decision will be made to schedule another interview, and when the applicant will be notified. Third, give the applicant an idea of the chances of progressing to the next phase in the interview process. The recruiter should be cautious here. Too many applicants leave the interview feeling they have a 90 percent chance of getting the job, only to receive a rejection letter. Fourth, leave several minutes for the applicant to ask final questions.

Post-interview   As soon as the applicant leaves, the recruiter should record appropriate impressions. A tape recorder is helpful. Any promises made to the applicant also should be recorded; for example, send company literature or a letter within two weeks. The recruiter must stay with the timetable and honor what he or she promised to the applicant.

INTERVIEW GUIDELINES   Four basic guidelines to interviewing follow:

1. Collect information that relates directly to job performance.
2. Consciously wait until the interview is over to make a final decision. Consider all of the information.
3. Always remember that weaknesses can be offset by strengths and potential, so evaluate the whole person.
4. The interview is only one method of obtaining information on the applicant.

TESTS

EMPLOYMENT TESTS   As used here, the term *test* refers to a procedure, technique, or measurement instrument for ascertaining characteristics such as aptitudes, capacities, intelligence, knowledge, skills, or personality. Sales managers may approach the testing process in any one of several ways. They may decide the following:

- Not to use tests.
- To administer tests and interpret the results themselves.
- To administer tests and have someone else interpret the results.
- To turn the testing over to consulting industrial psychologists.

Sales managers should have the ability to judge the value of tests whether or not they ever use them.

The majority of sales managers use tests as only one part of the selection process. The purpose of testing is to determine whether applicants have traits the company feels lead to selling successfully. In turn, this results in advantages such as lower turnover and increased performance.

To be used successfully, tests must have *reliability* and *validity*. Sales managers must be cautious. A test may appear to be a good measuring instrument but may not have good predictive validity. One method of determining "concurrent" validity is to identify one or more factors common to the success of the specific firm's salespeople. These factors (for example, intelligence or high self-confidence) become the predictors. The applicant who scores within an acceptable range, based on present salespeople's scores, continues to be considered for the sales job. Sales managers can establish predictive validity by ascertaining the sales performance of these applicants after they are hired. However, a particular salesperson's performance can be influenced by factors outside his or her control, such as customers going into or out of business or an increase in product advertising. Actual sales performance must be used as the effectiveness measure.

Test subjects that are often used for selecting sales personnel include the following:

- *Aptitude tests* measure general suitability, learning ability, and natural ability for selling.
- *Intelligence tests* measure mental intelligence or intelligence quotient (IQ).
- *Interest tests* measure the level of interest in a sales career.
- *Knowledge tests* measure what is known about a subject, for example, computer programming when applying for a position in computer sales.
- *Personality tests* measure distinguishing character traits, attitudes, or habits, such as empathy, ego, self-confidence, and motivation.

Aptitude tests are very common. In fact, Caliper Corporation, a psychological testing and human resources consulting firm, has started giving sales aptitude tests to potential salespeople who want to sell for U.S. companies in the socialist Czech Republic.[3] See the Selling and Managing Globally box on page 200 for a more complete description of selecting Czech salespeople.

POLYGRAPH TESTS   The **polygraph test,** sometimes called the *lie detector test,* was developed in the 1920s. It measures blood pressure, respiration, heartbeat, and skin response and plots these on a graph. Questions such as "What is your name?" are first asked to determine a normal pattern. The tester looks for changes in response to questions such as "Have you ever stolen from your employer?" The changes are supposed to indicate the subject is lying.

Polygraph tests are seldom used to screen applicants for outside sales jobs for national companies and primarily are used by smaller companies. The federal government has placed strict limits on their application. Some people claim polygraph tests violate the Fourth Amendment to the Constitution in that they represent an invasion of privacy; they also may violate the Fifth Amendment by leading the applicant to incriminate himself or herself. A widely publicized objection is that polygraph tests are not reliable. Individuals actually telling the truth may become excited, and their response can be interpreted as lying. By the same token, individuals who lie may not elicit a measurable response. To use the polygraph test, a firm should select very carefully the person who administers the test in order to increase its reliability.

TESTING PROBLEMS   The major problems with testing are that tests are misused and not understood, causing many to say they are of little value for selecting successful

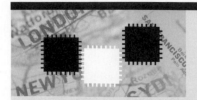

SELLING AND MANAGING GLOBALLY
SELECTING SOCIALIST SALESPEOPLE

No experience, no problem, says Dr. Herbert M. Greenberg, CEO of Caliper Corporation, a psychological testing and human resources consulting firm assessing the potential of Czech job candidates who want to sell for U.S. companies in the Czech Republic.

The Czech economy is booming, and many American companies with facilities in the country, including Warner Lambert, Kmart and Amway, are hiring. The problem is the local workforce—indeed, most of the country's 10 million people—are steeped in the traditions of socialism. "The challenge is that nobody has a track record in selling, servicing, and supervising in a free market economy," Greenberg explains, from Caliper's Princeton, New Jersey, headquarters offices.

So how does Caliper, which already has signed contracts with several U.S. firms operating in the Czech Republic, choose the right person for the job? Much the same way it does in the United States—with a sales aptitude test. Translated almost verbatim from the exam given to American candidates for positions there, the test looks for qualities such as ego drive, empathy, personal growth, and leader-

ship. "We're seeking the same thing that motivates people all over the world—getting the yes," Greenberg explains. "We also look at what happens when the person gets a no—is it a three-day holiday, a drinking binge, or does that person bounce right back?"

Caliper launched its Eastern European business partly because of the Czech Republic's similarity to Western culture and the country's pro-American attitude. Despite these positive factors, U.S. companies intent on hiring locals must be prepared to dispel long-held beliefs and to train seriously in a country that graduated its first M.B.A. in 1991. "Most Czechs are well educated, especially in technical fields, but there will be few people who know how to do the job," Greenberg notes. That means common hiring practices used in Philadelphia or New York won't work in Prague. "Companies will have to give up stealing from the competition and the typical age criteria they use here and hire on the basis of raw talent."

Source: Weld F. Royal, "From Socialist to Sales Rep," *Sales & Marketing Management* (August 1994):63.

salespeople. Consequently, tests are not used, or, if they are used, the results are ignored. Many sales managers only use tests because the home office requires them.

On the other hand, tests are often the sole screening criterion. If the applicant receives a low score, he or she will not be considered for employment. This may be acceptable if the score is extremely low; however, if the score is only slightly below the acceptable level, the recruiter could consider having the applicant retake the test or determine whether the applicant was very excited when taking the test. The test score, high or low, should not be the sole factor considered. It is only one portion of the information needed to make a hiring decision.

Applicants can become "test wise." For example, one widely used intelligence test is called the Wonderlich test. Because it is so popular, applicants may find that they take it often and that their scores improve each time. Applicants also can fake their responses, particularly to personality tests. For example, the Minnesota Multiphasic Personality Inventory (MMPI) is among the most widely used and respected instruments for assessing various personality traits. However, applicants may fake or alter their true feelings by responding to questions in a manner they feel is acceptable to the prospective employer. Take the following as an example:

1. I am happy most of the time. (Mood)
2. I am entirely self-confident. (Morale)
3. I would like to work outdoors. (Occupation)

An applicant's answers to these statements may not reflect his or her true feelings. For example, a positive response to statement 2 might be considered more "acceptable" from a male applicant. Scoring of a test such as the MMPI requires qualified interpretation of answers by individuals with considerable psychological sophistication.

Tests also can have a cultural bias and discriminate against certain groups. They may be valid predictors for one group of applicants but not for all groups, or different scores for different groups may be equally good indications of success on the job.

A single test or group of tests that would be the sole predictor of success in sales cannot be developed. Tests are only as good as the people who use them, but doing away with tests is like throwing the baby out with the bathwater. Some companies are doing away with tests because they feel the EEOC is placing too many restraints on their use. However, the laws are basically aimed at only one end: validity. The EEOC advocates a "systems" approach to hiring involving the collection of information related to job performance using interviews, tests, biographical data, and references. In the often-quoted *Griggs v. Duke Power* case, Chief Justice Burger stated, "What Congress has forbidden is giving these devices and mechanisms controlling force unless they are demonstrably a reasonable measure of job performance."

ESTABLISHING A TESTING PROGRAM   For a testing program to be effective, companies need to identify job factors related to success. Reliable, published tests that measure these specific factors should be selected. New tests can be constructed for the firm if no such tests are available. Before a test is given, the organization must determine the method of interpreting the results, how these will be used in the selection process, and administering and scoring procedures. Finally, the tests and procedures should be checked routinely to determine whether they are effective tools in selecting successful salespeople.

ASSESSMENT CENTERS

If an applicant makes it past the initial interview, some firms conduct steps 3 and 4 (Figure 9.2) at their assessment center. The **assessment center** is a centralized organizational unit within the firm. Its purpose is to evaluate all qualified applicants in a comprehensive and uniform manner.

Ford Motor Company's assessment center, for example, evaluates people through the use of interviews, tests, problem-solving exercises, and individual presentations. Highly trained personnel specialists test and evaluate applicants for several days.

Most companies report that the use of assessment centers results in dropping a high rate of applicants from further consideration for a job. However, the quality of the people selected significantly improves when an assessment center is used.

EMPLOYMENT REFERENCES

References are the names of persons from whom information can be obtained on an applicant's ability and character. References may be checked and recommendation letters requested to gain information about the applicant's past behavior and job performance. However, validity problems may arise. People tend to play down the faults of others, and they may not really know enough about the person to give a good recommendation, even though they feel they can.

In addition, a salesperson may be a low performer for one manager but a good performer for someone else. So a manager might give a reasonable recommendation even though the person was fired. In order to get an unbiased recommendation, recruiters should consider contacting people who know the applicant but were not given as references.

People giving bad recommendations have been sued and have had to pay damages. The Privacy Act of 1974 gives an individual the legal right to read reference letters. A person can waive this right, however, which would tend to increase the validity of the information and give the employer more trust in the references. One major study found that a low percentage of firms relied solely on written recommendations. Because many salespeople are bonded; given a car, expense checks, and sample merchandise; and make infrequent contact with their offices, firms really need to check their backgrounds. Personal references, past employers, past customers, and past and present teachers are used frequently. Past sales performance would appear to be the best indication of future behavior. However, little evidence exists to support this claim. Personal references appear to be the least reliable information collection method.

PHYSICAL EXAMINATIONS

Almost all companies require their prospective employees to undergo physical examinations. As a general rule, if the applicant gets this far in the process, he or she has the job unless health problems are discovered. The physical also may be necessary to enroll the applicant in the organization's various healthcare, worker's compensation, life insurance, and pension programs. However, physicals are not reliable for predicting the applicant's future health. Physical examinations are expensive and therefore are usually given toward the end of the selection process. A growing number of companies have applicants complete forms dealing with the state of their health without seeing a medical doctor.

EVALUATING SELECTION AND PLACEMENT DECISIONS

The quality and effectiveness of selection and placement decisions depend on sales managers hiring as many applicants as possible who turn out to be good performers. If sales managers can select and place applicants who do in fact turn out to perform well, sales force productivity will benefit. In addition, if sales managers do not select and place applicants who would have performed poorly, sales force productivity will also benefit.

When sales managers make selection and placement decisions that benefit sales force productivity, they are making decisions using valid predictors that serve legal considerations. Different agencies offer examples of valid selection criteria. For example, BC Company of Minster, Ohio, which sells various metal parts, has strict criteria that, taken together, single a candidate out.[4] These are good listening skills, a technical ability for working with a technical product, prospecting skills, and an ability to put customers at ease. All these are legal selection criteria because they can be justified as necessary for performing the duties the job requires. If a company uses predictors that do not result in selection and placement decisions that benefit productivity, its efforts are counterproductive and generally are not consistent with legal considerations. Thus, sales managers need to evaluate their predictors as well as their selection and placement decisions.

Sales managers also should consider the benefits of a selection and placement program versus the costs. Generally, procedures producing more successful salespeople require more time and personnel and thus are relatively more costly. The costs to consider include both actual and potential costs:

1. Actual costs (costs actually incurred in hiring applicants).
   a. *Recruiting and assessment costs:* salaries of all personnel associated with procedures, advertising expenses, travel expenses, and personnel testing evaluation costs.
   b. *Induction and orientation costs:* administrative costs of adding the employee to the payroll and salaries of the new employee and of those responsible for orienting the person to the new job.
   c. *Training costs:* salaries of training and development staff, salary of the new employee during training, and costs of any special materials, instruments, or facilities for training.

2. Potential costs (costs that might be incurred if a wrong selection decision is made).
   a. *Costs associated with hiring a person who subsequently fails:* record keeping; termination; costs of undesirable job behavior, such as materials or equipment damaged; loss of customers, clients, or patients; loss of goodwill, and so on; and costs incurred in replacing a failing employee.
   b. *Costs associated with rejecting a person who would have been successful on the job:* competitive disadvantage if person is hired by another firm (compare to the loss of a top sports star to a competing team) and costs of recruiting and assessing an additional applicant to replace the rejectee.

If an organization knows these costs associated with selection and placement procedures, it can select the procedures most likely to result in effective decisions. Some of the benefits of an effective hiring policy follow:

- Lowering the cost of turnover and absenteeism.
- Lowering training time.
- Meeting individual territorial sales potential.
- Increasing customer satisfaction by having the same salesperson call.
- Improving morale.
- Because of these benefits, increasing recruiting effectiveness and thus lowering the total costs associated with operating the sales force.

As mentioned earlier, the more thoroughly applicants are interviewed, the more costly the process. Yet many managers feel the six steps shown in Figure 9.2 are the minimum for the selection process. Cost can be outweighed by all the benefits of hiring successful salespeople.

PEOPLE MAY REJECT THE OFFER! WHY?

A sizable number of individuals who are offered a job do not accept it. Two reasons account for this rejection of the job offer. First, the person did not fully let the company know about his or her preferences, interests, and personality. From the individual's standpoint, no fit exists, even though the person is qualified to do the job.

The other reason is that the company makes the offer and waits for the applicant to accept the job. Many times qualified people take another job because another company makes them an offer and follows up with telephone calls, letters, and personal visits. The selection process is not over until the person actually reports to work. A few companies pay applicants a bonus if they take the job. This practice is similar to professional sports teams paying signing bonuses to get better players.

THE SOCIALIZATION OF SALES PERSONNEL

Recruitment and selection processes probably will not produce new salespeople who "know the ropes" (the values, norms, and behavior patterns) of the organization. Therefore, the organization must "socialize" new sales personnel. Socialization can be difficult, especially when organizational values differ from a new person's existing values. If the organization is not successful in socializing new salespeople, they may soon leave the organization.

Socialization is the process by which salespeople learn the sales culture and behaviors appropriate for their roles in the organization. It continues throughout a salesperson's employment. It involves teaching new employees, and even current ones, the appropriate values, norms, attitudes, and behaviors for the roles they play in the sales force. Socialization is primarily accomplished through the salesperson's interaction with others.

An important aspect of this definition is that socialization is concerned with the roles played rather than with the jobs salespeople occupy. Although people need specific skills to perform their jobs and are trained to perform them, they also need an awareness of the organization's basic goals, of the means to attain those goals, of their responsibilities, and of the acceptable behavior patterns for the roles they are expected to play. Salespeople acquire all this awareness by being socialized, formally and informally, through continuing contacts and experiences with others.

Salespeople also must be aware of what their roles are about and what skills are required. However, this awareness is generally acquired through job descriptions and job previews, which are predominantly preemployment activities. Properly done, the socialization process can help:

- Increase performance and job satisfaction.
- Reduce job anxieties and the fear of failure.
- Reduce turnover.
- Impart a positive image of the company, job duties, and future expectations.
- Save the manager's time and thus reduce costs.

As indicated, socialization is important for correctly and positively starting the salesperson on the job, and management cannot afford to overlook this. However, quite often the sales manager has one or more vacant territories and is interested in getting the salesperson to start selling in a hurry. At first, the new salesperson usually works a 12- to 14-hour day, calling on customers by day and studying and planning the next day's activities at night. Not only does the salesperson have to adjust to a new organization but also must frequently make personal adjustments that can be even more traumatic. For example, a move may mean changes for the entire family, including buying a home and sending the children to a new school. As Martha Hill of Hanes Knitwear explains:

Orientation of new salespeople is an important phase of a sales manager's job. It is crucial to get a new rep started on the right track in order to set the stage for future development. I encourage new reps to ask me their questions but also to try to learn independently by probing their accounts, consulting their reference materials, and then reporting to me what they have learned. The initiative taken by new reps often indicates their degree of interest and commitment. The application of what they learn is the key to progress; therefore, my training strongly encourages trial of newfound techniques.

So, from the very first, the new person must be treated like, and introduced as, a valuable addition to the sales force. Furthermore, if possible, the manager can make suggestions about schools, banks, shopping areas, doctors, and real estate agents in the new city. If the vacating salesperson is retired, transferred, or promoted, that person should introduce the new salesperson to the employees of important accounts and to personal friends.

The sales manager usually works with new people for a week or more initially. Thus, the manager also can make the important introductions. A good transition between the old and new salesperson is important, serving to create continued goodwill toward the company and its products. Managers like to work with, and stay in contact with, new salespeople as much as necessary to support their selling activities. Managers must set the standards for new salespeople and serve as a model the salespeople can strive to emulate. If a manager believes a new salesperson will do well, this belief should be conveyed to the person, who will be apt to live up to those expectations. This establishes the future expectations of the salesperson and is referred to as the **Pygmalion effect:** It is the self-fulfilling prophecy of telling someone he or she will succeed.

MANAGEMENT IN ACTION: ETHICAL DILEMMA
TERMINATING A SUCCESSFUL SALESPERSON

You are appointed district sales manager for a rapidly growing consumer-goods manufacturer with sales of $500 million. It hires new salespeople from college campuses across America. In training for your new job, you learn a 75 percent yearly turnover rate occurs in the beginning territorial manager's position. Thus, you will receive training on interviewing and hiring because it is your responsibility to replace these positions as they become vacant.

Three months after you take over the district, Carol Wilkerson—your regional manager—calls and says she will attend your district sales meeting next week. She wants you to rank all of your salespeople's performances. After the meeting you and she will determine whom to replace. She says it will probably be the two lowest performers. You are shocked. All of your salespeople are performing above quota.

After the meeting Carol says, "We are growing so rapidly that the company only wants to keep people with management potential. We look at people for six months. If they don't measure up, they are run off. We don't fire them. Severance pay costs too much. Five of your seven people have been with us more than nine months. We have to cut one, maybe two. It's what the home office expects. Who goes?"

WHAT DO YOU DO?
1. Try to talk Carol into going along with policy because your own performance review is coming up soon.
2. Refuse to recommend any employee to be "run off" because they are all performing above company standards.
3. Do your job, which requires that you recommend two people to be replaced. It's best for the company.

THE BOTTOM LINE

Establishing a sales force is a complex process that involves many variables. Correct selection and placement of personnel will improve a company's productivity.

Sales managers use predictors for hiring decisions; these are pieces of information about the applicant. Information can be collected by determining factors such as skills, interests, aptitude, and experience; also included are physical examinations and interviews. Any information collected must be job related.

The selection process is no longer based on intuitive feelings; it is a series of steps designed to test whether a person is right for a company and vice versa. The application blank is the most common tool used for hiring. Data collected within legal guidelines include such information as education, work experience, physical and personal characteristics, and preferences.

The personal interview is an important part of the selection process. Although it is a good method for obtaining factual information, it is often too subjective; however, it remains the most popular tool managers use when building a sales force. The three types of interviews are structured, unstructured, and semistructured. An interview consists of five main phases: preparation, opening, interview, ending, and post-interview.

Managers also can use certain employment tests for selecting personnel. Two major problems with testing are misuse and misunderstanding. To establish an effective testing program, companies need to identify desired job factors; select reliable tests; and develop methods for administering, interpreting, and scoring the tests. Some firms have assessment centers where they can evaluate qualified applicants in a comprehensive manner. Employment references and physical examinations are two additional methods used to gather information on an applicant.

Sales force productivity benefits with the selection of good employees. A selection procedure that produces a greater number of successful salespeople generally costs more and requires more time and personnel. Sales managers must weigh the costs with the benefits and determine if they at least balance.

▓ KEY TERMS FOR SALES MANAGERS

Selection, 190
Placement, 190
Predictors, 191
Tests, 191
Selection tools, 193
Application blank, 194

Personal interview, 194
Structured interview, 195
Unstructured interview, 196
Semistructured interview, 196
Polygraph test, 199

Assessment center, 201
References, 201
Socialization, 203
Pygmalion effect, 204

▓ MANAGEMENT APPLICATION QUESTIONS

1. A recruiter was heard to say she felt like a matchmaker at times rather than a representative for her firm. Why is this a perfectly acceptable way for a recruiter to feel?
2. Why is it important to collect information from all the areas discussed in the text to try to predict a person's sales performance?
3. The selection process consists of a series of steps that increases the information a sales manager has available to aid in the decision. What is the first step in this process, and what kind of information is usually obtained at this step?
4. Discuss the positive and negative features of a personal interview in the selection process.
5. An interview consists of phases, similar to a sales call. Discuss why it is important to plan for an interview, just as it is important to plan for a sales call.
6. What does the socialization process do for a salesperson, and why is it important?
7. The employment interview is one of the most critical steps in the employment process. It also may be an occasion for discriminating against individual employment candidates. The following questions represent what interviewers often ask job applicants. On a separate sheet of paper determine whether each question is legal, and be prepared to briefly explain your decision.

    You may want to meet in small groups during or outside of class and together determine your answer. After the class reconvenes, group spokespersons may present group findings.

Interview Questions

1. Could you provide us with a photo for our files?
2. Have you ever used another name (previous married name or alias)?
3. What was your maiden name?
4. What was your wife's maiden name?
5. What was your mother's maiden name?
6. What is your current address?
7. What was your previous address?
8. What is your social security number?
9. Where was your place of birth?
10. Where were your parents born?
11. What is your national origin?
12. Are you a naturalized citizen?
13. What languages do you speak?
14. What is your religious/church affiliation?
15. What is your racial classification?
16. How many dependents do you have?
17. What are the ages of your dependent children?
18. What is your marital status?
19. How old are you?
20. Do you have proof of your age (birth certificate or baptismal record)?
21. Whom do we notify in case of emergency?
22. What is your height and weight?
23. Have you ever been arrested?
24. Do you own a car?
25. Do you own a house?
26. Do you have any charge accounts?

27. Have you ever had your salary garnished?
28. What organizations do you belong to?
29. Are you available to work on Saturdays and Sundays?
30. Do you have any form of disability?

FURTHER EXPLORING THE SALES WORLD

Interview a sales manager about his or her selection process. Ask how the sales manager handles each step in the "sales personnel selection process" discussed in this chapter. Determine if some steps are not used and if this firm does other activities for its selection process. Find out why the sales manager uses the selection process discussed. Look to see if the company has a suggested selection process and how closely it is followed by the manager.

SALES MANAGEMENT EXPERIENTIAL EXERCISE

DO YOU LISTEN?

Instructions: Read the following questions, and write *yes* or *no* for each statement on a separate sheet of paper. Mark each answer as truthfully as you can in light of your behavior in the last few meetings or gatherings you attended.

	Yes	No
1. I frequently attempt to listen to several conversations at the same time.		
2. I like people to give me only the facts and then let me make my own interpretation.		
3. I sometimes pretend to pay attention to people.		
4. I consider myself a good judge of nonverbal communications.		
5. I usually know what another person is going to say before he or she says it.		
6. I usually end conversations that don't interest me by diverting my attention from the speaker.		
7. I frequently nod, frown, or whatever to let the speaker know how I feel about what he or she is saying.		
8. I usually respond immediately when someone has finished talking.		
9. I evaluate what is being said while it is being said.		
10. I usually formulate a response while the other person is still talking.		
11. The speaker's delivery style frequently keeps me from listening to content.		
12. I usually ask people's points of view.		
13. I make a concerted effort to understand other people's points of view.		
14. I frequently hear what I expect to hear rather than what is said.		
15. Most people believe I have understood their points of view when we disagree.		

According to communication theory, the correct answers are as follows: no for questions 1, 2, 3, 5, 6, 7, 8, 9, 10, 11, and 14 and yes for questions 4, 12, 13, and 15. If you missed only one or two questions, you strongly approve of your own listening habits, and you are on the right track to becoming an effective listener in your role as a salesperson. If you missed three or four questions, you have uncovered some doubts about your listening effectiveness, and your knowledge of how to listen has some gaps. If you missed five or more questions, you probably are not satisfied with the way you listen, and your friends and coworkers may not feel you are a good listener either. Work on improving your active listening skills.[5]

Case 9.1

Delaware Firearms
Is This the Correct Person?

Andre, one of your district sales managers at Delaware Firearms, was recently promoted from the field because he was so terrific with customers. Now he seems to have run into—or caused—quite a bit of trouble. Orders have fallen enough to make your own supervisors raise their eyebrows and wonder what's happening. They are asking questions you can't answer—not yet. But you know you had better develop an action plan. Of course, you have to define the problem before you can find a solution. So you tell the new manager you are paying him a district office visit to review the sales plan and quota.

While talking with the sales group during your visit, you soon discover that few of the district's salespeople really understand the sales plan, their individual quotas, the directions they should move in, or on which accounts they should concentrate. You review the district manager's file of memos and internal correspondence for the past quarter. Sure enough, there it is! Every single memo is filled with ambiguities, contradictions, and confused phraseology.

You hold a candid discussion with Andre. He admits concern about the way things are going, knows he needs help, and respects your managerial skills. He has sensed that the sales force doesn't always follow his instructions. The files you've read show how hard he has tried to communicate. Unhappily, his attempts have failed. Andre is being honest with you. He really doesn't understand the reason for the problem.

Questions
1. Have you selected the right person for the job?
2. What are you going to do now?

BOB JOHNSON
Searching for a Sales Job

The Thanksgiving Day atmosphere was so familiar to the Johnson family. There was the wonderful smell of turkey and dressing roasting in the oven and fresh cranberry sauce. One could sense the coolness in the air outside and the corn standing in the fields, ready for harvesting. The Johnson family had traveled to the farm for the annual Thanksgiving visit with parents, uncles, and aunts. More than 20 persons would soon arrive for the festivities and fellowship. Bob Johnson had driven to the farm in middle Tennessee from Nashville. He looked forward to a relaxing day and spending time with his dad, his grandfather, and three uncles and their families. It was also a good time to forget Vanderbilt University, term papers, and tests for a few hours.

Besides the normal concerns about college and grades, Bob was mentally preoccupied with graduation approaching in May and with the uncertainty about getting the "right" job. Bob's father and his Uncle Henry worked in sales for a progressive insurance company, Farmers Insurance Group. They were both quite successful financially and had encouraged Bob to apply for a position with Farmers. Uncle Frank also would be coming to the farm today. He managed a small industrial supply house and also had advised Bob to pursue a career in sales. Uncle John worked as a salesperson with Nabisco but would be retiring in a few years. He had mentioned he would be pleased to introduce Bob to the district sales manager at Nabisco. Bob had also contacted Muro Pharmaceutical Company through the University Placement Center. It had a sales position that would be opening in the Nashville area in May.

Bob had learned in classes that networking was the best way to find a position in the tight labor market and flat economy present in and around Nashville, Tennessee. Although none of the job leads were a sure thing, Bob was certain he would be favorably received. He was a hard worker, dependable, easy to talk with, and highly motivated and had excellent work references. Furthermore, Bob had good grades and work experience and likely would be a very competitive applicant. Bob was familiar with the field of selling and knew this was where he would best make his mark. His dad had further advised Bob to go with a large, well-known company so he could take advantage of its training programs. The exact words—"With the right training and three or four years of experience in the field, a young salesperson can work for almost any company and virtually name his or her price"—seemed to stick in Bob's mind. On this beautiful

fall day, he was anxious to discuss his job leads with people he trusted, his dad and his three uncles.

After the big Thanksgiving meal, the men were drawn to the football game on television, and the women were busy talking and visiting in another room. The grandchildren were outside playing under the big trees in the front yard. As the afternoon passed, Bob found time to talk with all three uncles about his job interests and to get their thoughts. He was especially interested in the training programs each company would provide. Several people had advised him to focus less on the starting salaries and more on what he would learn with each firm and on future opportunities.

On the two-hour drive back to Nashville, Bob thought about each job on the horizon. The Farmers Insurance Group is a well-established, full-line insurance company and employs more than 30,000 men and women in its sales force. It offers comprehensive property and casualty coverage; life insurance for individuals, families, and businesses; and highly specialized coverage for hospitals, automobile dealers, franchises, farms and ranches, restaurants, apartment houses, and small businesses of all types. Farmer's representatives use mail, door-to-door canvassing, and telephoning to identify prospects and write insurance policies. They use a soft-sell approach to establish good customer–agent relationships.

Farmers has a solid sales training program composed of a two-step process: the Reserve Agent Program and the Career Program. Most prospective career agents begin as part-time reserve agents. They begin under the direction of a district manager who is responsible for their training and development. They complete a series of four-hour classroom sessions and independent video and audio training programs. New salespeople then practice learned skills with the district manager in on-the-job sales calls. A major part of the training deals with handling rejection, even hostility, with grace. Many written and practical exams must be passed along the way. If all requirements are met, reserve agents are eligible to enter a two-year career agent training program. Career agent trainees attend a formal career school conducted by Farmers. During this period they continue to work under the district manager while acquiring additional knowledge and skills. On completion of this program, a career trainee can be certified as a Farmers Career Agent. New reserve and career trainees are paid on a drawing account basis, against earnings, for approximately six months. Trainee agents typically earn around

$20,000 at first, and experienced career agents typically earn $60,000 or more per year. Turnover in the insurance business tends to be higher than other entry-level management training programs.

Nabisco Biscuit Company was Bob's second possible job lead. It is one of the largest consumer food operations in the United States, with sales in excess of $2.7 billion each year. The 17,000 Nabisco employees bring more than 140 products and 70 brands to the marketplace. Outnumbering the nearest competitor by two to one, the company employs about 3,500 people in its sales force. With eight out of the top-ten-selling cookie and cracker products, Nabisco has more than 50 percent of the market. The Nabisco job possibility does not involve prospecting and making cold calls on consumers but instead involves selling to and servicing established retail accounts and developing new accounts within an assigned territory. The salesperson's role is to maintain present accounts, provide merchandising expertise, be professional in dress and demeanor, observe and report on competitors' activities, and develop new accounts. Nabisco's training program involves four days of video and personal instruction by company personnel training managers in areas such as the company and its history, packaging and baking processes, forms and paperwork, health and safety training, sales objectives, and the selling process. In addition, new salespeople spend about three days per month making calls on the job with division sales management. This one-on-one training decreases as salespeople gain experience.

Nabisco salespeople are provided with a late-model van to use for making calls and carrying merchandise and displays. Salespeople are allowed to use the van for personal transportation when off duty. New representatives are paid a straight salary, with later opportunities to earn bonuses when sales quotas are met. New salespeople are well paid for their efforts, typically starting at around $25,000 per year, depending on the employment region and the applicant's experience level. The work itself is not easy, especially at first. Calling on the retail trade always has been one of the toughest types of selling. Store managers see so many salespeople that they can become hardened to the many deals they are offered. New salespeople must develop a thick skin if they are to survive. Turnover is thought to be higher than most white-collar jobs but lower than typical commission-based positions.

Muro Pharmaceutical was a third possible job opportunity for Bob. He had signed up for an interview with Muro at the Vanderbilt Placement Center and had been told it would like to interview him within two weeks. Muro is a fast-growing, young company with headquarters in Lowell, Massachusetts. After doing some research, Bob learned that the company does about $50 million in sales each year. It currently has 160 sales representatives

who call on physicians to promote four major products in the allergy and asthma categories. Its two-phase training program consists of one week of intensive classroom indoctrination and learning in a nearby city. After that, new salespersons gain on-the-job experience calling on physicians in their assigned territories. A sales supervisor works with each new sales representative about once each month. Phase two of the training program begins after the new salesperson has been with the company from three to four months. It involves spending two weeks in classroom training at the home office in Lowell, Massachusetts. Representatives are taught basic pharmacology and are schooled in advanced selling techniques using role playing and simulated presentations recorded on videotape for review and discussion.

The company provides each representative with a company car that can be used for personal travel. The starting salary is between $28,000 and $32,000, depending on the applicant's qualifications and territory assignment. After applicants spend six months with the company, bonuses of $2,500 to $10,000 per year are typically available to those who meet their sales quotas.

Some uncertainties, however, exist in the pharmaceutical industry at the present time. Several larger companies have bought out or merged with smaller firms such as Muro. Another fear is that the trend toward managed health care will impact negatively on pharmaceutical sales practices. It is possible fewer sales representatives will be needed in the future. Physicians probably will have less latitude in prescribing specific drugs. Therefore, it may not be as important to attempt to influence individual physicians in their selection of drugs for patients. Bob liked what he had learned about Muro, but some things about the pharmaceutical industry concerned him at the present time.

As Bob Johnson approached the Nashville area after Thanksgiving, he realized his deep thoughts had made the trip back to school seem much shorter. This was probably the most important decision he had ever faced. But he still had not decided which position would be best for him.

Although he had not yet been offered any of the jobs, he knew he would be forced to make a decision in the months ahead.

QUESTIONS

1. What should be the primary basis for any job selection?
2. Discuss the positive and negative aspects of each job.
3. Which training program is the best? Why?
4. Which job would be the most interesting for you?
5. Which job do you think Bob Johnson will take, if offered?

Source: This case was written by professors Gerald Crawford and William S. Stewart, both of the University of North Alabama.

CASE 9.3

MARTIN, INC.
The First Woman Is Hired

To keep pace with the tremendous strides industrial firms have made in opening sales positions to women, Martin, Inc., a manufacturer of plastic products, has decided that more female sales representatives should be hired. The corporate office made this desire known to its field sales managers, almost to the point of applying pressure. The field sales managers, however, found it difficult to find and hire qualified women who were interested in a sales career.

Mike Butler, a division sales manager, was determined to locate a hardworking and qualified female sales representative. He knew this would both please the company and help to build a better sales division. Mike had been in his present position for only four years, but he was considered one of the "upwardly mobile" young managers. He is in his late twenties—a clean-cut, hardworking, company-oriented manager. He is trim and handsome, a former college football player at Alabama. He and his wife, a former cheerleader, and their two daughters live in Knoxville, Tennessee.

The Knoxville division has twelve sales assignments, which includes one vacant assignment in Huntsville, Alabama. Mike found and interviewed six prospective sales representatives—four males and two females. Nancy Bishop was subsequently hired to fill the vacant position. She was a marketing major in college and worked in public relations for three years at Delta Airlines before accepting the Martin position.

During the interview process, Nancy voluntarily indicated she would not be interested in marriage and children for several years and she liked to travel. Mike would have liked to ask her some things but did not feel he could safely bring them up. Nancy impressed him favorably because she was attractive, well dressed, easy to talk with, and very intelligent. She was qualified for the position and had a good attitude. She was not as qualified, however, as two of the male applicants.

Mike told his wife at breakfast one morning that he had hired Nancy and would introduce her to Martin customers in the north Alabama area after she completed some self-paced manuals in the division office. These manuals usually took about two weeks. He also indicated it would be necessary for him to be out of town

several nights during Nancy's three-week introductory training period. To his surprise, his wife did not like the idea of her husband traveling with this new member of the sales team.

A few surprises also occurred in the division office. The two secretaries were cool toward Nancy and not very helpful to her. Mike inquired about the problem, but no one had any comments to make. He hoped this would be a temporary situation and he would not have to say anything more about it.

After the initial two weeks in the office and during their first day together on the job, Nancy caught on quickly. They made calls in Decatur, Athens, and Sheffield. After their last call of the day, they checked into the Holiday Inn in Florence. As Mike unpacked his things and prepared for dinner, he thought through the events of the day:

> *Things went well today. Nancy was easy to work with. Although buyers were at first surprised to see the new salesperson, they seemed to like the idea of an attractive woman calling on them. . . . She just might be a real winner. Oh, there were a few things that confused me a little. One thing was opening and closing doors. . . . Should I do it or just treat her like another salesman? Should I carry the heavy sample case? What should we talk about while driving between cities? How can I forget that she is a woman . . . that smell of perfume . . . her nice figure that I couldn't help but notice out of the corner of my eye?*

The telephone rang in Mike's room. It was Nancy. "Hello, Mike, I was wondering if you would like to have dinner together. . . . It's no fun to eat alone." Mike could feel his heart beating faster than normal.

QUESTIONS
1. How would you describe the situation?
2. What actions would you take if you were Mike?

Source: This case was written by Professors Gerald Crawford and R. Keith Absher, Professors of Marketing, and William S. Stewart, Professor of Management, University of North Alabama, Florence, Alabama 35632.

PART IV
TRAINING THE SALES TEAM

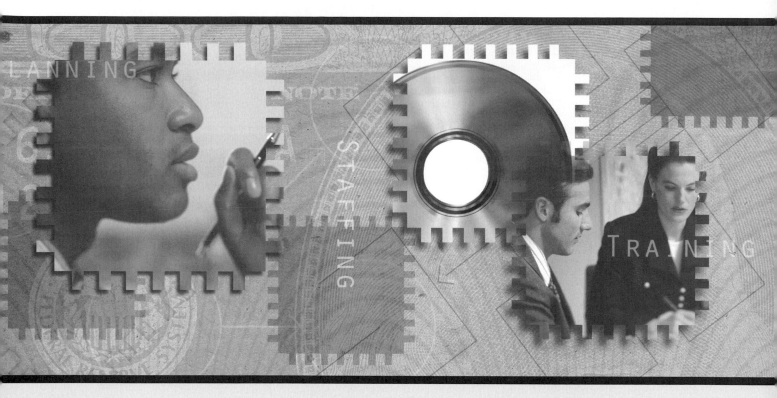

SINCE ALL sales managers are trainers of their salespeople, it is important for them to be familiar with planning, organizing, staffing, directing, and evaluating a training program. Additionally, managers are teachers of product knowledge and selling skills. Part IV includes the following: Chapter 10, "The Management of Sales Training and Development," and Chapter 11, "Contents of the Sales Training Program: Sales Knowledge and the Selling Process."

CHAPTER 10

THE MANAGEMENT OF SALES TRAINING AND DEVELOPMENT

LEARNING OBJECTIVES

To establish and maintain a productive sales force, an ongoing sales training program is essential. This chapter should help you understand:

■ What sales training is and what its purposes are.

■ How to plan a sales training program, including conducting a needs assessment.

■ That organizing a training program includes various training methods.

■ Who is involved in the staffing of a training program.

■ The motivating influence of a sales training culture.

■ The importance of an effective evaluation system.

Companies must sometimes spend an enormous amount of their travel budget paying for the expenses of sales strategy meetings. By conducting these sessions over the Web, Cisco Systems is saving about $1 million per month. This San Jose, California company, which provides networking solutions for the Internet, uses a virtual conference center product developed by Place Ware to hold its virtual meetings. "We're saving more money than we ever could have believed," says Mike Mitchell, the company's program manager for distance learning.

Whenever the company introduces a new product, Cisco has a Web meeting to update salespeople on the product's marketing and sales strategy, Mitchell says. The product manager or vice president of sales usually leads the meetings. They typically begin with a ten-minute slide presentation that spells out the planned strategy. The next 50 or so minutes are spent asking questions via teleconference. The leader of the conference can direct attendees' browsers to competitors' Web sites, and they can even be asked to vote on certain issues by using the product's instant polling feature. The technology's capabilities can hold up to 1,000 attendees, but Cisco likes to limit the meetings to about 100 salespeople to provide for maximum interaction.

Besides the money-saving factor, the new system is allowing salespeople to come in contact with each other much more frequently. "Our salespeople are actually meeting more online than they ever were face-to-face," Mitchell says, adding that some salespeople who in the past met with other reps and managers only a few times every quarter are meeting online nearly every day.

By increasing interaction between salespeople and managers, the virtual conference center is allowing for the exchange of ideas by people that would not normally be able to make recommendations. "That's very empowering for the sales force because they're able to make suggestions about where we're going with our sales and marketing strategies every step of the way."[1] ∎

This chapter will introduce you to the five phases of sales training and development. You will see that training must be carefully planned, implemented, and evaluated. Although many sales managers may never do corporate sales training, all will have the responsibility of training their own salespeople.

WHAT IS SALES TRAINING?

Sales training is the effort an employer puts forth to provide salespeople job-related culture, skills, knowledge, and attitudes that should result in improved performance in the selling environments.

John H. Patterson, founder of the National Cash Register Company and known as the "father of sales training," used to say, "At NCR our salespeople never stop learning." This philosophy is the reason that even today successful companies thoroughly train new salespeople and have ongoing training programs for their experienced sales personnel, even the most successful salespeople.

Basically, sales training is designed to change or reinforce behavior that makes salespeople more efficiently achieve their job goals. Salespeople are trained to perform activities they would not normally undertake. In addition, training is used to reinforce currently successful sales practices.

REENGINEERING TRAINING

The goal of building a successful sales culture in the changing global environment places new demands on training departments and requires organizations to develop innovative and comprehensive approaches that extend beyond geographic and time limitations. On-time training, one-on-one coaching, and behavioral-change training are just some of the strategies companies are applying to sales training curricula across the country. Many organizations have decided to reengineer the training process because of increased competition, a better understanding of the sales process, and new training techniques.

"Product knowledge and an understanding of the skills needed to make a good sale are not always enough to build a strong sales culture any more," MCI Communication's John Sally says. New markets and technologies have created the need to reengineer sales training.

"Sales training is an ongoing commitment," Micki Benz, director of sales at Honeywell, Inc., says. "There is no such thing as the spray and pray technique, where you spray [employees] with knowledge and pray that it takes."[2]

CHANGE BRINGS ABOUT TRAINING REENGINEERING

Things pass, and things change. The essential facts about change are these: First, change is happening more rapidly and dramatically than at any other time in history. Second, if sales managers don't anticipate change and adapt to it, they and their firms will not survive in a competitive business world. Third, sales personnel must be constantly trained on such topics as new products, changing technologies, competition, and the marketplace.

PURPOSES OF SALES TRAINING

Companies are interested in training primarily to increase sales, productivity, and profits, according to Allied Signal's Bob Baxter. "We're interested in state-of-the-art training equipment and procedures to help our people become experts in their field. That's why we invest millions of dollars into training."[3]

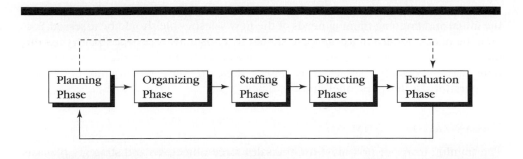

FIGURE 10.1

A SALES TRAINING
MODEL—DETERMINE
HOW TO EVALUATE
TRAINING WHEN
PLANNING

Many specific purposes of training involve more than improving general sales volume. These tend to relate to the type of training a company offers and include the following:

- Increasing customer satisfaction.
- Helping salespeople become managers.
- Orienting new salespeople to the job.
- Improving knowledge in areas such as product, company, competitors, or selling skills.
- Lowering absenteeism and turnover.
- Positively influencing attitudes in such areas as job satisfaction.
- Lowering selling costs.
- Informing salespeople.
- Obtaining feedback from salespeople.
- Increasing sales in a particular product or customer category.

Yet the primary purpose of training is an "investment" in the sales organization's most valuable resource—its salespeople. Training is an ongoing process and the responsibility of the trainee, trainer, and organization.

A SALES TRAINING MODEL

Imagine you have just been promoted to the job of director of your company's sales training. Now what do you do? How do you start? Eight national sales training directors were recently asked this question. They represented Ashland Oil, Avon, Bell & Howell, Cannon Business Machines, Marriott Corporation, Johnson & Johnson, TRW, Inc., and Unilever.[4] These companies differed in industry, markets, and training needs. However, their answers show they have a great deal in common.

Each of these trainers described the phases of planning, organizing, staffing, directing, and evaluating the training function as they are illustrated in Figure 10.1. As indicated by the dashed line in the figure, planning must take into account the evaluation phase. After management has determined the performance goals and implemented training to reach these goals, it must determine how to measure and evaluate the effectiveness of this training. In other words, the differences between desired performance and actual performance must be analyzed. Following the five phases of the training model can improve the odds of having a lasting effect. Let's discuss phase one: planning.

PHASE ONE: PLANNING FOR SALES TRAINING

The first step when developing or maintaining an ongoing sales training program is assessing needs. **Needs assessment** entails determining the training needs of the sales force and setting objectives for satisfying those needs. This process also involves identifying activities management feels the salespeople should perform to produce the desired sales results.

Needs assessment can deal with several different groups of sales personnel. First, the initial and ongoing training needs of the new salespeople should be assessed. Second, the needs of current salespeople should be constantly assessed. Finally, the sales manager's job requires constant reassessment to ensure these people are thoroughly trained. The necessary analysis for planning is done on four levels: organizational, task or operational, sales personnel, and customer.

ORGANIZATIONAL ANALYSIS

The training manager first must use the sales force objectives and strategic plans as guides for developing training goals. What are the objectives of the company? What strategies and tactics must the sales force implement to meet its objectives? With the answers to these questions, trainers can generate specific training goals for their salespeople. Bruce Scagel, previous training director for M&M–Mars and now a nationally recognized consultant, gives a good example of such goals.

Scagel attempts to adhere to four principles he believes ensure a successful training effort. They follow:

1. *Value:* Training should be focused on performance areas that offer the highest opportunity for payback. Often large performance gaps offer the greatest opportunity for improvement.
2. *Focus:* Training and development should be focused on a limited number of "big hitter" performance areas and should continue this focus over an extended period of time.
3. *Mass:* This is a key to bringing about maximum payoff through training and development. Strive to reach the most people with the most necessary development initiatives.
4. *Duration:* Training should be ongoing, using as many vehicles for reinforcing learning as possible. No one benefits in the long term with one-shot training and development.

To the extent firms adhere to these principles, Scagel believes training offers substantial payback.

One of the greatest challenges, as mentioned, is to integrate work as closely as possible with sales force operations. A simple framework Scagel is fond of using in discussions with sales management provides a clearer understanding of key training needs. It follows:

SALES OBJECTIVES/GOALS	KEY PERFORMANCE AREAS	CAPABILITY NEEDS	RESOURCES REQUIRED
X % increase in sales volume	Improve key account sales with Customer X, Y, Z	Knowledge, information, skill required to improve performance	People, dollars, equipment

This framework relates objectives and key performance areas to training and development or capability needs and offers both sales management and the training department a means to prioritize where resources should be applied to improve productivity.[5]

OPERATIONAL ANALYSIS

At the operational level, managers analyze job descriptions and specifications to determine the specific abilities that will be part of training. They also review performance to identify the successes and failures of the sales force and thus to determine where training is needed.

A **difficulty analysis** uncovers and analyzes problems salespeople experience. It might reveal that salespeople are having problems discussing aspects of their products with customers or that customers have begun to buy a new product from a competitor and the salespeople are having trouble convincing customers their product is just as good as the new product.

SALES PERSONNEL ANALYSIS

Analysis of the sales personnel's tasks is the definition of specific work-related behavior required of those who will be in the training program. The **behavioral objectives** identify the goals of the training program for both the trainer and the trainee. This applies to all sales personnel whether they are new or experienced.

CUSTOMER ANALYSIS

3M is an example of a company that has modified its training process to incorporate "the voice of the customer" into the training and development of each salesperson. 3M calls its customer-focused training A.C.T., an acronym that stands for the three steps in the process: assessment and analysis, curriculum content, and training transfer.

The 3M corporate training department developed a survey for customers to assess 3M's sales force and training needs in terms of specific key skills. The questionnaire is given to a select group of customers who are asked to assess the importance of each skill to the selling relationship and the salesperson's application of each skill. A feedback report for each salesperson summarizes customer perceptions, and the gap between perception and application suggests specific areas in which the salesperson can use additional training. The salesperson and his or her sales manager determine a training curriculum focusing on the three most significant gaps according to the customer survey.[6]

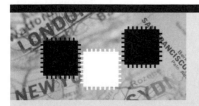

SELLING AND MANAGING GLOBALLY
LITTLE COLD CALLING IN JAPAN

Since it's customary in Japanese companies for a sales rep to be formally introduced to a prospect, the purpose of initial calls is understood but not discussed. The decision to do business together, if it occurs, results from the subtlety and patience of relationship building. "In America," Chuck Laughlin, coauthor of *Samurai Selling: The Ancient Art of Service in Sales,* says, "we may be into the middle of the sales process within days, hours . . . where a Japanese selling person can spend a year building the relationship before he begins to introduce his product."

"It's all a matter of time," IBM's Vince Matal, says. Then, after thinking again, he adds, "Proportion, I guess is what I'm saying. Where we might be 20 percent relationship, rapport, that kind of thing, and 80 percent selling the product, they're the opposite."

Now back in the United States as a consulting marketing representative for IBM in Raleigh, North Carolina, Matal re-

members the rules from his early days in sales. "You always try to develop a relationship and service your customers," he says, "but [the Japanese] do it to the exclusion—in my opinion—of actually trying to sell the product."

With years of relationship building before any deals get done, how do Japanese salespeople earn a living? The answer—a flat salary—is unusual in the United States but standard procedure in Japan. This compensation arrangement, which goes hand in hand with the tradition of lifetime employment, was the inspiration for the term *salarymen,* the unglamorous description of employees in a workforce that was once predominantly male.

Source: Carl Harper, "Selling Globally," *Travel* (May 1996):51–54.

MAKING THE NEEDS ASSESSMENT

The needs analysis serves as a guide to planning training programs. Figure 10.2 illustrates how this all comes together. The needs analysis is a continuous process aimed at constantly revising the training program to keep it current. This requires the following sequence:

1. Identify the requirements of the position (job description).
2. Determine the difference between performance objectives and results (evaluations).
3. Determine why a difference exists.
4. Revise the training program (if needed).
5. Develop training objectives.
6. Conduct the training program.
7. Evaluate the training program.
8. Revise the training program (if needed).

Then the process begins again. By constantly analyzing each job, the training manager can carefully plan for a well-trained sales force.

SOURCES OF INFORMATION FOR DETERMINING TRAINING NEEDS

How does the trainer determine what material needs to be included in training sessions? The best source is company personnel, but competitors and customers also can provide information concerning training needs. Here are some of the methods companies use to collect needed information on what to include in their training programs:

- Questionnaires.
- Interviews.
- Tests given during meetings for diagnostic purposes.
- Direct observation in the field.
- Analyses of sales, profits, and activity reports.

Lawyers Title Insurance Corporation, for example, has used questionnaires, interviews, and direct observation to design its training program. As James Hewitt, Lawyers's vice president and national sales manager, relates, they contacted "100 customers, sales managers, and sales reps to find out what everyone wanted to accomplish with the sales training program before designing it."[7]

Companies also may use failure analysis, success analysis, and exit interviews to assess training needs. **Failure analysis** determines the reasons low-performing salespeople fail to achieve their sales goals. Reasons for failing may be corrected through training. **Success analysis** is used to identify factors that appear to make salespeople successful. These factors may include making more sales calls, effective use of samples, or effective sales presentation techniques. The success factors then can be passed on to other salespeople.

FIGURE 10.2

REVISION OF TRAINING
PROGRAM BASED ON
NEEDS ASSESSMENT

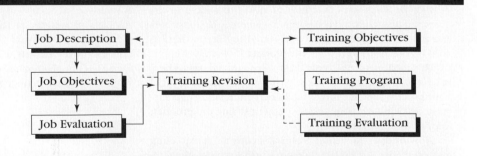

Exit interviews determine attitudes toward the job. They take place when people quit their jobs or shortly thereafter. Questions often asked include "What could this company have done to make you more successful?" "Could more training or a different type of training have helped increase your sales?" "Did your immediate supervisor regularly provide you with product information and selling ideas?" If the person leaving the job is honest in answering these types of questions, an exit interview can be a valuable tool. Often, however, people do not answer the questions truthfully because they have quit and no longer are concerned with the company's success. They also feel that to get a good job recommendation they should not criticize the company or their supervisors.

PHASE TWO: ORGANIZING FOR SALES TRAINING

The next step in the training process is to find out whether sufficient funds are available to carry out the needed training. If they are, organizing can proceed. Organizing sales training activities includes selecting training methods, media, materials, the location where training will take place, and when training should occur.

The training methods and aids that will best accomplish training objectives must be identified. The degree of trainee participation varies with the method used. Methods include panel discussions, case studies, gaming, and dramas or skits. The best method should be identified through one or more of the following factors:

- Training objectives to be accomplished.
- Number of trainees.
- Trainer's expertise.
- Each salesperson's understanding of the subject matter.
- Each trainee's ability to learn and past experience.
- Training materials available.
- The costs per trainee of each method.
- Extent of presession assignments.

Quite often salespeople come to training sessions unprepared. Trainers spend precious hours orienting them to the material, yet training plans are often made months in advance of the actual meeting date. Consequently, pre-session assignments are the key to ensuring that trainees begin to participate early in the sessions. Many companies send study material to their salespeople weeks before meetings, indicating assignments to complete before arrival. Study material may range from completely new information (for example, information on a new product) to a review of data the salespeople already possess.

TECHNOLOGY-BASED TRAINING METHODS

Classroom lectures, discussions, exercises, and role plays always have been some of the main training methods for salespeople. And sales trainers will continue to use them. Yet the power of multimedia computing to educate, inform, and entertain all at once is contributing to a revolution in training. Electronic methods range from innovative point-of-purchase sales demonstrations to electronic brochures on disks and CD-ROM.

INTERACTIVE MULTIMEDIA TRAINING   Interactive multimedia training is faster, more effective, and less expensive than conventional employee instruction. In many cases, it cuts classroom time by 50 percent. And since 72 percent of the more than $200 billion a year that U.S. companies spend on training goes to training-staff salaries, the potential savings with self-guided, computer-based instruction are enormous. Economy and speed are big draws these days, when companies are striving to trim overhead, and a growing number of firms are using temporary and contract employees who need to learn jobs quickly.[8] As businesses downsize, they are asking sales personnel to take on more responsibilities, which means retraining, often at the employer's expense. Interactive multimedia has emerged as an important tool for sales reengineering, and with today's more powerful PCs, the technology is available even to small companies.

Training is a natural application for interactive multimedia, which lends itself to self-paced instruction. Sales personnel can repeat or skip material as desired. Plus, interactive programs deliver immediate feedback and can adjust the material presented to the trainee's responses. The multimedia component further enhances training power. By combining text, graphics, sound, video, and animation, multimedia engages all the senses and makes use of proven learning theories.

ELECTRONIC PERFORMANCE SUPPORT SYSTEMS   The ultimate in interactive multimedia training and employee support, so-called electronic performance support systems (EPSS) improve on the traditional computer-based training that has been around for years. Old-fashioned computer-based training is really like a lecture in electronic format. By contrast, EPSS, or just-in-time training, is much more immediate and personalized. It supplies specific information on demand. Instead of completing a computer training program and later applying the information on the job, employees can access tutorials when the need arises in specific work situations. EPSS also puts large amounts of data at a salesperson's fingertips, so a user can simply point and click for immediate access to information, instead of slogging through manuals or asking someone else for help.

HIGH-TECH CUSTOMER SERVICE   Proponents maintain that interactive multimedia sales presentations are more informative, create a better image, and shorten the time it takes to close a sale. Laptops loaded with interactive multimedia presentations are fast becoming standard tools for salespeople. Well more than half the companies polled in one business survey use multimedia for sales presentations.[9] Thus, many training programs teach how to make such presentations. Several examples of how companies use multimedia sales presentations follow.

DISTANCE LEARNING   To implement a more personal training approach, some organizations operate their own television networks to deliver training messages, make their own videos, develop college-accredited courses and career certification programs, videotape employees in role-playing sales sessions, and use EPSS.

With 200 branches in 30 states, National Industrial Supply, for example, needed a training program that could transcend geographic boundaries and time constraints. The answer was to develop its own television network to transmit simultaneous broadcasts via satellite to its many branches. "We are aspiring to on-time training," Benjamin Bailey, an in-house training consultant, says. "Our employees need to learn bits of information they can immediately use." The system is interactive. Salespeople can question the experts and share information with their peers by calling toll-free numbers where the questions and answers are incorporated live into the broadcast. "It's kind of like *Larry King Live,*" Bailey says. "The single most important part of this system is to be able to answer questions; without it, you're still just pushing information."[10]

ROLE PLAYING

In **role playing** the trainee acts out an event such as the sale of a good or service to a hypothetical buyer. Often the trainee's presentation is videotaped and replayed for critique by a group, the trainee, and the trainer.

ON-THE-JOB TRAINING

The best and most frequently used training takes place on the job. On-the-job (OTJ) training may take several forms. New salespeople may accompany their manager and observe sales calls. At first, the supervisor makes all of the sales presentations for some period of time. Then, typically, an easier customer to call on is selected, and the trainee makes his or her first sales presentation with little or no assistance from the supervisor.

This is an exciting and important time for the trainee, and the experience must be critiqued in a positive manner to establish a good relationship between the salesperson and manager. If a sale was not made, the manager should reassure the salesperson that selling is based on percentages. If the manager maintains a positive attitude, so will the trainee.

For the experienced salesperson, on-the-job training includes observation and "curbstone" counseling by the sales manager. This way the salesperson gets immediate feedback. After the manager and salesperson leave the customer's office, the manager can critique the sales presentation. If needed, corrections are made. Imagine yourself making six critiqued sales presentations with your manager. The next day you can use what you have learned to make more effective sales presentations. On-the-job training is discussed more in Chapter 14.

TRAINING LEARNING CURVES

One of the first complaints many salespeople make about skills taught during group training sessions is "These skills sound just great, but I have to deal with the real world out there, and my customers simply can't be handled that way. I don't want to do it!"

Companies spend millions of dollars each year on training by the methods described so far. Some of this money is wasted because *no* follow-through occurs once salespeople return to the territory. Believe it or not, this is not uncommon.

Salespeople spend a few days, a week, or a few weeks in a training program. In many cases they return to their jobs using some of what they learned (maybe), but they slowly go back to past habits or develop new, unconstructive ones. No long-term behavioral change occurs because the knowledge and skills learned during training did not become a natural part of their behavior. Why?

A brief examination of the learning process as applied to sales training will help answer this question. When determining training methods, trainers must remember that true learning takes place in time. How people learn can be graphically illustrated using learning curves. Several important factors are required for salespeople to use what they have learned.

Hypothetical learning curves are a good way to visualize the learning process and why sales training must be ongoing if the trainee is to use it as a natural part of the job. The shape of the **learning curve** indicates the extent to which the rate of learning increases, levels off, or decreases with or without training and practice.

Both new and experienced salespeople often go through such a learning process. New product information and selling techniques are examples of knowledge and skills that at first may be learned relatively slowly. However, acceleration of the learning curve occurs as a salesperson begins to thoroughly understand the material and use it on the job. Attitudes can follow the same pattern. For example, at a sales meeting salespeople slowly become enthused, and before they leave they are motivated and excited.

However, what happens when those salespeople return to their sales territory? They must take what they have learned and apply it to their situations. Sales trainers feel that salespeople go through three phases of "usage" before true behavioral changes occur as a result of training. These follow:

1. *Awkward usage:* Trainees feel very awkward, maybe unsure or uncertain whether the training will work for them. They may not totally understand everything. Trainees do not know what their customers' reactions will be. They may know what has worked in the past. Will this work better?
2. *Conscious usage:* They begin to consciously use the training more and more, slowly becoming better at its application on the job.
3. *Natural usage:* Salespeople use the learned information, skills, or attitudes as a natural part of their day-to-day job. For example, the new questioning or closing techniques have become part of each sales presentation. They are very comfortable using the techniques—they come naturally. They do it on their own because they want to.

PLATEAUS   One common characteristic of a learning curve is illustrated in Figure 10.3. A plateau generally occurs during the awkward usage phase that follows the initial learning or training. No learning appears to take place. For example, the salesperson returns from a sales meeting where new product information was presented with suggestions on selling techniques to use. The salesperson needs time, as indicated by the plateau, to thoroughly study the information and practice the presentation. As the person consciously uses the product knowledge, learning continues. This moves the salesperson upward on the learning curve.

One goal of training is to move a salesperson from knowledge acquisition to the natural usage stage. A major barrier to this movement up the learning curve is the lack of reinforcement through follow-up and further on-the-job training. The rate of learning change will be influenced by factors such as:

- The nature of the material itself (technical or nontechnical).
- The manner in which the material is presented.
- Time intervals between training (frequency).
- The extent of follow-up and OTJ training.
- The trainee's attitude toward learning.

FIGURE 10.3

A HYPOTHETICAL
S-SHAPED LEARNING
CURVE WITH A PLATEAU

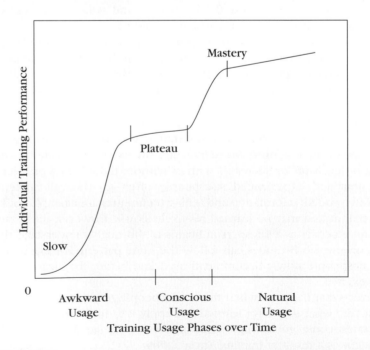

Of course, at any point a trainee may slow down or stop training usage, causing a downward slope in the learning curve. A salesperson may leave the training program on Friday afternoon fully intending to use what was learned yet on Monday morning continue to apply the same procedures used in the past. Habits are hard to break. If a salesperson's habits are to be changed, or if an inexperienced trainee is to retain learning, regular, on-the-job reinforcement is necessary.

WHERE DOES TRAINING TAKE PLACE?

A salesperson may receive training anyplace and any time of day or night. Sales training is continuous. In a broad sense, training occurs anytime a supervisor comments on a salesperson's reports, talks on the phone to the salesperson, works in the field with the salesperson, or conducts a meeting. The two broad categories of sales training are centralized and decentralized training. Companies use both of these training location procedures.

CENTRALIZED TRAINING   Training at a central location is referred to as **centralized training.** It is primarily intended for instruction of salespeople from all geographic areas the company serves. Programs typically are held at or close to the home office/manufacturing plant, in a large city, or at a resort. Centralized training programs are designed to supplement the basic training sales personnel receive in the field.

A salesperson may attend the firm's centralized training program when first starting work, after six months to a year of employment, or at other stipulated time intervals. The new salesperson initially may be trained in the field, then after one year be sent to the home office for training and to tour the firm's manufacturing facilities, and, finally, be sent back to the home office every five years for further training.

Centralized training programs usually have excellent facilities and equipment, such as classrooms, videotapes, computers, closed-circuit television, and sales laboratories designed for role playing. Trainees get to know each other and corporate executives. They are away from home and can concentrate on learning. Training content can be standardized so the entire sales force will have a common body of knowledge.

DECENTRALIZED TRAINING   **Decentralized training** may be conducted anywhere; it is the main form of sales force instruction. It can occur in a branch office, in the salesperson's car, at the customer's place of business, in a motel room, or at the salesperson's own home.

Decentralized training has numerous advantages. For one thing, costs are usually lower when compared with centralized training. For example, if a branch office is used as the training site, travel costs are less. The sessions are typically shorter, thus saving on motel and meal expenditures. Salespeople's geographic territories are such that often they see one another only during meetings and training programs. Many sales managers believe their salespeople receive as much knowledge and motivation from their peers in informal sessions as they do in regular formal training. Salespeople can informally discuss their problems in making sales and how they were able to overcome sales resistance. Their success stories can particularly benefit the inexperienced salesperson. These informal talks also occur when salespeople attend centralized training sessions. Finally, trainers can customize supplies, samples, and selling tools for salespeople to take home after the session.

Either type of training also has several disadvantages. A potential major weakness of decentralized training is that a branch manager may not be an able trainer, which can have a negative effect on the salespeople. Centralized training is expensive due to the cost of travel, meals, and facilities. Also, it is expensive for salespeople to be out of their territories, and trainees may not want to be away from their families for a prolonged period. A disadvantage common to both is that salespeople may come to the meeting unprepared, really only wanting to get away from work. Trainers understand this and overcome it by having well-prepared, interesting, informative, and participatory training sessions. Finally, customer sales may be lost as a result of either form. Thus, the cost of lost sales must be offset by increasing productivity and efficiency through training.

WHEN DOES TRAINING OCCUR?

For new sales personnel, training begins the first day they report to work. Basic company, product, and selling-skill information is usually given to the trainee to study. In a recruiting brochure, Procter & Gamble states: "Your training begins the day you join us and will continue throughout your career, regardless of your responsibility or job level." The firm gives new salespeople a two-day orientation that their immediate supervisor conducts. Company, product, and customer information is presented. Salespeople also receive a company car, equipment, and supplies. After the orientation session, the salespeople make sales calls on their customers with their manager. This procedure is not uncommon for selling consumer goods.

Training does not end with such an initial session but continues throughout the professional salesperson's career. Some firms want to train their salespeople thoroughly before assigning them a sales territory. Conversely, some firms feel salespeople can relate to and retain more from training if they work the sales territory for a short period.

SALES MEETINGS   Companies also provide salespeople with training at periodic sales meetings. Many companies have sales meetings once each month or every two months at the district level. They give salespeople information on products they will emphasize during the next month. Several days after the meeting, the division sales manager works with each salesperson as a followup to see that the person understands and uses materials presented at the meeting. These monthly meetings, and working with the DSM, serve as important training methods.

PHASE THREE: STAFFING FOR SALES TRAINING

Assume training plans have been determined, as have ways to evaluate the results of training. Training methods, media, materials, location, and times have been set. The next phase is to determine who actually will do the training.

WHO IS INVOLVED IN TRAINING?

Typically, three basic sources for sales trainers exist: corporate staff personnel, regular sales force personnel, and specialists from outside the company.

CORPORATE STAFF TRAINERS   Staff trainers are responsible for the creation, administration, and coordination of a firm's sales management and sales force training and development programs. Typically, the training manager and staff are separate from the personnel department. They have an ongoing relationship with all staff departments and the field organization. The training manager usually reports to someone at the upper corporate level, such as the vice president of sales.

SALES FORCE PERSONNEL   Senior sales reps and district and regional sales managers often are the main trainers of their firm's sales force. These people bring to the training program years of sales experience, which helps trainees relate quickly to their instructors and to the material the trainers present.

The trainer should not only be an effective salesperson but also a competent teacher. A company should select a senior salesperson as a trainer based on the

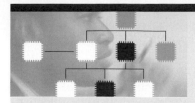

MANAGING THE SALES TEAM

JOB DESCRIPTION FOR SALES TRAINING MANAGER

1. *Broad function:* responsible for the development, administration, and coordination of the company's sales and sales management training and development programs.
2. *Reporting relationship:* reports to vice president of sales; responsible for communicating corporate sales and sales management activities and results accomplished.
3. *Duties and responsibilities:*
   - To assist sales management in identifying training needs.
   - To identify management problems to determine which are created in whole or in part by the sales sector and which of these sales training efforts can remedy.
   - To develop (or obtain) programs to meet the above needs.
   - To organize, coordinate, and schedule the training.
   - To determine who shall conduct the training and to provide such personnel with any necessary guidance.
   - To evaluate the training and report results to operating management.
   - To determine needs for followup to ensure continuing results and to plan, organize, conduct, and administer such training.
   - To coordinate with other personnel-development activities.
   - To develop any necessary long-range sales management training programs to aid operating managers with developing and maintaining an effective workforce.
   - To coordinate and use the training facilities within the organization and to procure outside consultant services when available, necessary, and appropriate.
   - To maintain an adequate system of records and progress reports.
   - To submit an annual budget for approval; the budget is to contain an explanation of the need for each training program and the operating problem(s) it seeks to avoid or eliminate.
4. *Relationships:* ongoing with all staff departments and the field organization.
5. *Education and experience required:* undergraduate college degree with a minimum of five years of sales experience, including sales management responsibilities.

ability to effectively communicate and teach, not on sales ability. People with both sales and teaching abilities usually can be found, but management must seek them out. An assignment as a trainer at the corporate level can be a step up the career ladder for a salesperson in the field.

OUTSIDE TRAINING SPECIALISTS   Trainers drawn from outside the company may be consultants specializing in sales training or representatives of programs such as Dale Carnegie Sales Courses and the Xerox Sales Learning Programs. Some universities also offer courses for salespeople and sales managers.

Smaller firms may rely heavily on outside trainers. This affords them the type of training they want without the cost of maintaining a training staff. Courses may be standardized or customized for the company. The company should carefully select outside trainers on the basis of individual needs.

Directing the sales training effort is the fourth step in the training model. Although not as much discussion space is dedicated to this phase as the other four phases in the model, it is just as important.

TRAINING CULTURE

Sales culture is the set of key values, ideas, beliefs, attitudes, customs, and other capabilities and habits shared or acquired as a sales group member. Culture defines

PHASE FOUR: DIRECTING THE SALES TRAINING EFFORT

what is important in an organization. It is the combination of attitudes and behaviors to which most members of an organization subscribe. Successful sales organizations have the cultural attitude that sales training is very important to their success.

SUPPORT FROM THE TOP

Top managers must support the company's training program if it is to be effective. They must provide the direction and budget for training. Direction involves encouraging the sales managers to create a climate that emphasizes the importance of training. Competent trainers, properly encouraged, motivated, and compensated, can make a valuable contribution to the success of sales personnel. Thus, companies must select the national sales trainer and those who are allowed to participate in field training programs with great care.

LEADERSHIP

Someone in the organization must have the persistence, energy, vision, and credibility to plan, steer, coordinate, and nurse the sales training program until it is implemented and refined. This leader is usually the national sales trainer.

For the development of a completely new program or the overhaul of an existing program, these trainers need persistence because early successes in a sales training program are hard to come by, and it is easy to become discouraged. They need energy because the main task is actually many tasks; at times the challenge will seem awesome. They need vision because a sustainable sales training program requires a master plan. Although trainers may roll sales programs out in stages, they should see the big picture from the start. This requires an analytical, conceptual approach; it requires vision.

Finally, these people need credibility, so top management will pay some attention to the requests for resources. It helps immensely if they have been promoted up through the sales ranks and thus understand the nuances of the firm's culture and the realities of running the firm's sales force.

PHASE FIVE: SALES TRAINING EVALUATION

The evaluation phase is critical to the success of the total training program. Training is an ongoing process, and one of the biggest challenges for a trainer is the evaluation of training over time. The question that must be asked is "What is the firm receiving in return for the money, time, and energy invested in training programs?"

The organization knows the cost of the program in salaries, materials, equipment, facilities, travel, room, meals, and entertainment. However, what tangible results can be measured in dollars? Too often, training objectives such as performance standards are established without the know-how to measure training results. Did productive learning occur, or did salespeople receive time off from regular selling duties only to have fun at the sales training meeting?

STEPS IN THE EVALUATION

What is involved in evaluating sales training? How can evaluations be made? If managers give thought to the evaluation process while designing a training program, evaluation can be an easier task. **Sales training evaluation** involves collecting data related to the program's objectives and tabulating and analyzing these data to determine the training's effectiveness. This is a four-step process:

1. Determine what should be measured.
2. Determine the information collection method.
3. Determine the measurement methods.

4. Analyze the data, determine the results, and draw conclusions for making recommendations.

WHAT SHOULD BE MEASURED?   When deciding what should be measured, sales trainers as a whole agree on the importance of evaluating the components, groups, and individual items related to training.

Components to Measure   Evaluation can be viewed as having the following components:

- *Reactions:* What did the participants say about the program?
- *Learning:* What knowledge, skills, or attitudes were learned?
- *Behavior:* Learning involves a change in behavior. Did the training actually result in a change of behavior?
- *OTJ results:* This is the most important—the bottom line. Did the training pay off? Did it really do what it was supposed to do?

Groups to Evaluate   To be effective and useful, evaluation must cover every element in the program—beginning with program design and continuing through to on-the-job performance results. This can be best accomplished by evaluating the following:

- *Program:* Should the topics contained in the program remain the same?
- *Presenter(s):* Did the presenter(s) do a good job?
- *Trainees:* What was their reaction to the program?
- *On-the-job results:* Did training actually influence trainees' performance?

Items to Measure   Specific items to be measured can be derived from training objectives. Whenever dollars are being spent, management thinks in terms of results related to dollar figures. Items will differ from company to company. However, most will measure training's influence on sales, profits, and customer satisfaction.

WHAT SHOULD BE THE INFORMATION COLLECTION METHOD?   This is the second step in evaluating training. Five basic data collection techniques are useful to trainers. They are questionnaires, interviews, tests, observation, and company data. Often all are used together to collect the information needed to evaluate training.

1. *Questionnaires* are the most popular instrument trainers use. They are easily administered. The value of questionnaires is that a trainer can collect data on the feelings, opinions, thoughts, and beliefs of the salespeople. People are often reluctant to express their views openly in a group but will do so quite willingly in writing—especially if they can do so anonymously.
2. *Interviews* are useful to gather in-depth information. The value of interviewing is its flexibility. The interviewer can alter the kind of questioning to respond to the interviewee's concerns. Focus groups of four to six salespeople are an excellent information collection method. If promised anonymity, salespeople will "tell it like it is!" This can provide a gold mine of information.
3. *Tests* are valuable for determining how much the trainee has learned. They should be designed to test comprehension and to evaluate individual program segments. Then, if needed, trainers can redesign segments.
4. *Observation* is one of the most valuable techniques trainers have. The trainer goes into the field to see if trainees are using their training. While out there, the trainer should ask the field managers their opinions.
5. *Company data,* such as performance evaluations, customer satisfaction scores, and sales data, are the best place to begin and end information collection for evaluation.

WHAT SHOULD BE THE MEASUREMENT METHODS? The method of information measurement is critical. This is the third step in accurately determining training effectiveness. Three common measurement methods are *after only, before/after,* and *before/after with control group.* For help in the discussion, T_1 will represent the pretest (before training), T_2 the posttest (after training), X the training program, and R the random selection of subjects.

The trainer should carefully weigh each measurement method's advantages and disadvantages. Selection should be based on the method's advantages in relation to the reason for measuring training. Trainers should ask these two questions: "Why should training be measured?" and "How should it be done?"

The *after-only method* is the simplest of all methods. It is also the least effective. As the name suggests, items are measured after training has occurred. The after-only method can be represented this way:

$$X\,T_2$$

This method is good for evaluating people's reactions to the program and presenters and for evaluating immediate learning if a test was given. It is not reliable for measuring changes in behavior or OTJ results. Only over time can the impact of training in these two areas be known. For this, trainers should use one of the other two methods that follow.

For the *before/after method,* the trainers measure the training objectives before and after training. With other variables held constant, the difference between the two is considered a measurement of the training effect. This method can be pictured like this:

$$T_1\,X\,T_2$$

Should sales begin to increase three months after training, management may say training has caused this sales increase. However, a number of other factors might have caused some, or all, of the increase, for example, an increase in advertising and sales promotion from the home office. Management must determine whether outside factors such as advertising are exerting an influence. Measurement of product knowledge or selling skills would be much easier with the before/after method than measuring sales.

One sales manager gave this example:

To gain a qualitative and quantitative analysis of results in telephone sales, we measured the "Sales Batting Averages" (the ratio of units sold to calls made) for a period of one month prior to a training program on telephone-selling techniques. We then measured the average for one month following the program. The batting average increased from .105 to .150 percentage points. This translated, roughly, into $2,700 additional gross sales per person per day.

The *before/after with control group method* is the best of the three methods for determining the impact training has on learning, behavior, and OTJ results. Here, two groups of salespeople are selected randomly by the trainer. Items to be measured are selected and tabulated. The first experimental group is given training; the second, or control group, is not.

Each group is analyzed to determine if items before (T_1) differ from after (T_2) the experimental group was given training.

Experimental Group *(R)* $T_1\,X\,T_2$

Control Group $\quad\quad T_1\,T_2$

For the control group, any differences between the before and after measurements must be the result of factors other than training. The company may begin to advertise more, for example. This may cause sales to increase, but it is not due to training. The effect of the training on salespeople in the experimental group is the result of the training plus the same outside factors, in this case advertising. A difference should exist between the two groups in the items measured if training had an effect. This difference (for example, increased sales in the experimental group) would indicate that training had a positive effect on the sales personnel.

ANALYSIS, CONCLUSIONS, AND RECOMMENDATIONS   Once trainers have collected the evaluation data, they can tabulate the results and determine their meaning. This may require a small or a great amount of time, depending on the number of respondents and the number of questions asked. The answers may be statistically analyzed, interpreted on the frequency of answers to questions, or both.

Trainers who use the correct method to collect the right information are then in a position to draw conclusions and make recommendations on future training. Quite often, no changes need to be made to a training program. Sales trainers use these positive results to reinforce the importance of their departments and to justify their existence and requests for larger operating budgets. By proving the company is earning a good return on investment, the sales trainer is in a position to improve the quality of the programs, thus further improving salespeople's productivity.

MANAGEMENT IN ACTION: ETHICAL DILEMMA
THIS TEST IS A PIECE OF CAKE!

Each year, all sales managers in your company complete a two-week training program at corporate headquarters. Before taking your present job, you worked in the corporate sales training office for 14 months. Now you are looking forward to visiting once again with the training staff at the upcoming program.

At the end of the training program, all sales managers will be given a comprehensive test covering all written and class materials. To qualify for additional training, you must score 92 percent or higher. The test is extremely difficult, with little margin for error.

It is not uncommon for two or three managers to score less than 92. Typically, these managers do not remain with the company for very long afterward, usually less than six months. As a result everyone feels a lot of pressure to perform well on the test. It can mean the difference between continuing your career with the company or having to search elsewhere for a job.

The topic to be covered on the test is "directing the sales force." This topic involves motivational theories, compensation, and leadership. In preparation for the training session, you carefully study all materials sent to you. In your files from your former position you have an old test on the "directing" training module. Since the test is fairly comprehensive, you decide to use it as a study aid and practice test.

On the morning of the test, you are told the exam is timed, and you are given one hour. As you open the envelope and pull out the test, you can't help smiling. This test is identical to the one you had in your files and used as practice.

WHAT DO YOU DO?
1. Nothing. The directors of the training program should have developed another test.
2. Ask the training instructor to come out in the hall, and explain to her that you have the test. Ask her what you should do.
3. Respectfully refuse the test on the grounds that your scores would not fairly reflect your performance as related to others. Politely request that you be given a different test.

THE BOTTOM LINE

Effective sales training provides the foundation for an effective sales force. Thorough and continuous sales training programs help not only the new members of a sales force but also the experienced salespeople who may need brushing up on their selling skills. Training is designed to increase sales, productivity, and profits; salespeople are seen as investments and should be trained in order to achieve their maximum potential.

A director of a sales training program can divide the program into five equally important phases. This sales training model includes planning, organizing, staffing, directing, and evaluating. Although evaluating is listed as the final step, it actually occurs simultaneously with the planning stage.

Planning the sales training program, step one, involves determining the sales force's training needs and establishing objectives to meet these needs. Not only do the newest recruits have basic training needs, but existing salespeople also have needs to be fulfilled. Constant observation ensures that the sales force is properly trained.

After the plans have been made, the next step is organizing the program. Organizing the activities includes choosing training methods, media, and materials, as well as the program's location and time. Trainers can arrange advanced preparation for salespeople. This precludes the waste of needed time and encourages early class participation.

Once the training plans, as well as evaluation procedures, have been developed and organized, the next step is to determine who will do the actual training. In general, three sources of training staff exist: corporate staff trainers who comprise an entirely separate personnel group, regular sales force personnel who sometimes train in addition to their own duties, and outside training specialists.

The fourth phase in the sales training program deals with directing the training effort. Constant support from a firm's top management personnel is vital to the successful training program. The trainers must be knowledgeable and competent and must themselves be motivated. The person in charge of the program should persistently observe its progress.

Evaluation is the fifth and final phase in a sales training program. As an ongoing process, evaluation involves determining what should be measured, the method of gathering information, the methods of measurement, and data analysis. Finally, the results can be studied, and any corrections or improvements can be considered.

▇ KEY TERMS FOR SALES MANAGERS

Sales training, 216	Success analysis, 220	Decentralized training, 225
Needs assessment, 217	Exit interviews, 221	Sales culture, 227
Difficulty analysis, 219	Role playing, 222	Sales training evaluation,
Behavioral objectives, 219	Learning curve, 223	228
Failure analysis, 220	Centralized training, 225	

▇ MANAGEMENT APPLICATION QUESTIONS

1. Discuss why a firm should not think of training costs as an expense but rather as an investment.
2. What is the first phase of sales training, and why is it so important?
3. Which training method has the highest trainee participation? Which has the lowest? Give an example of when you might want to use each of these methods.
4. Discuss the three phases of usage a person will normally go through when changing behavior after training, and show where they would occur on a learning curve.
5. Compare and contrast (through their advantages and disadvantages) centralized and decentralized training.
6. What are the three basic sources of sales trainers? Discuss how each source contributes to the training program.
7. Why is it so important for sales training to be part of a firm's culture?
8. Why is evaluation of sales training such an important step? How should this process be conducted?

FURTHER EXPLORING THE SALES WORLD

Chapter 10 discusses a five-phase sales training model. Interview one or more sales trainers or sales managers to find out if, and how, their sales force plans, implements, and evaluates sales training.

 ## SALES MANAGEMENT EXPERIENTIAL EXERCISE

WHAT'S YOUR CONFIDENCE LEVEL?

You may think you have a good attitude for sales, but if you do not have the confidence to meet customers and prospects you do not know, all is lost. This exercise can help you measure your self-confidence. Read each statement, and then, on a separate sheet of paper, write the number you believe best fits you.

	High				Low
1. I can convert strangers into friends quickly and easily.	5	4	3	2	1
2. I can attract and hold the attention of others even when I do not know them.	5	4	3	2	1
3. I love new situations.	5	4	3	2	1
4. I'm intrigued with the psychology of meeting and building a good relationship with someone I do not know.	5	4	3	2	1
5. I would enjoy making a sales presentation to a group of executives.	5	4	3	2	1
6. When dressed for the occasion, I have great confidence in myself.	5	4	3	2	1
7. I do not mind using the telephone to make appointments with strangers.	5	4	3	2	1
8. Others do not intimidate me.	5	4	3	2	1
9. I enjoy solving problems.	5	4	3	2	1
10. Most of the time, I feel secure.	5	4	3	2	1

Total Score

Add up the numbers to get your score. If you scored more than 40, you are self-confident enough to consider selling as a profession. If you rated yourself between 25 and 40, you need more experience dealing with people. A score of less than 25 indicates that you need to build your self-confidence, and another type of job probably would be better for you

CASE 10.1

GEORGIA AUTO SUPPLY
Does Training Work?

Brad has one way, and only one way, of handling every sales situation at Georgia Auto Supply—no matter which customer, prospect, product, or application. He tackles all in exactly the same way. It's almost as if he works according to a formula. He's totally confident! As his manager, you sincerely believe Brad's sales productivity could leap significantly if he didn't always have his mind fixed on one course of action. However, he has formed a behavioral pattern that has become a habit. From time to time his approach to selling works great. You don't understand why he doesn't take an adaptive selling approach, treating each customer uniquely. After all, your monthly sales meetings always stress this approach. Brad has participated in numerous role plays about treating each customer differently.

QUESTIONS
1. Why doesn't he use the training?
2. What are you going to do?

Toys and More, Inc.
Development of a Sales Training Program

Toys and More sells small toys and novelty items to variety stores and small food retail convenience stores. The company was started in 1990. Sales have increased rapidly, reaching $76 million in 1996. In fact, management feels that the company is growing too fast.

The Sales Force

James New was the first salesperson to be hired by his uncle, Ralph New. Ralph had been vice president of finance for a large manufacturer of children's toys. In 1987, he began to plan his own business. Ralph took his company retirement money, sold his stock in the company, and borrowed money from a local bank. He raised enough capital to lease a warehouse; buy merchandise; and hire a bookkeeper, three warehouse people, a secretary, and James as a salesperson. At first Ralph helped part-time with selling. Soon business matters were so great he spent all of his time in the office.

James hired Henry Haynes to sell. This was in 1991. By 1996 James, with the help of Henry, had hired more than 45 salespeople located in the southwestern and southern states. The area was divided into two regions. The southwestern region included Texas, Oklahoma, Arkansas, and Louisiana. The southern region included Mississippi, Tennessee, Alabama, Georgia, Florida, South Carolina, and North Carolina. Company sales were projected to increase 10 percent a year over the next three years. That meant about four to seven salespeople a year would be hired, considering the need for new salespeople and people leaving Toys and More. James felt it was time to develop procedures for training salespeople once they were hired. Also, he wanted to have three quarterly sales meetings and a national sales meeting in January. Ralph had never seen the importance of train-

ing or meetings. After all, the company sold simple products. It had little history to teach. James and Henry tried to hire older, experienced salespeople who already knew how to sell.

However, in May 1996, Ralph attended a one-week sales management program at a university. One afternoon of the meeting was devoted to how to conduct sales meetings, their costs, and what meetings could accomplish. James felt his company might benefit. Ralph agreed and asked James to develop a plan for the national and quarterly meetings. Ralph wanted the first sales meeting to be a national meeting in January 1997 and the first quarterly meeting to be sometime during the week of March 26, 1997. He told James to invite spouses to the national meeting. The only limitations were to hold it in the United States and not go overboard on costs. The national meeting budget, probably between $65,000 and $80,000, would have to be approved by Ralph. However, James had the authority to arrange everything else. Ralph asked James to present his plan to him the next month. After Ralph left, James drove to a local university library to look at current magazines, particularly the February issue of *Sales & Marketing Management,* and textbooks on sales meetings that the university instructor had shown him.

Question

Assuming the role of James New and using the sales training model in the chapter, develop a sales training program for the national meeting and the regional meetings.

Source: This case was developed by Professor Charles M. Futrell, based on information supplied by James New. The firm's name has been changed.

CASE 10.3

THE TELECOMMUNICATIONS CORPORATION
Training's Impact on Performance

The Telecommunications Corporation (TC) produces and markets telecommunications equipment. The typical TC system installation can service different geographic locations with a transceiver (transmitter and receiver in a single unit) at each location. The sending point contacts the receiving point via telephone lines. The time for traditional mail delivery for geographically remote locations is usually measured in days. Transmission by telecommunications reduces this time to minutes, hence the appeal of telecommunications equipment. The firm has enjoyed a competitive edge due primarily to its equipment features. Quality competition entering the marketplace is steadily eroding this edge. Consequently, TC has experienced a softening of its market position while the competition has been able to grow in their (combined) market share. Concerned about this deteriorating situation, top management formed a task force to analyze the situation. The essence of the task force findings is presented here.

THE SALES FORCE
The task force study revealed that the individual-customers segment had been producing according to plan, with the shortfall occurring in the major-account segment. The shortfall in the major-accounts segment was attributed to the following:

- A sales force that was not trained to capture the major-account business.
- A sales force that was not familiar with integrated systems selling.
- A sales force that was not familiar with the competitive situation in the marketplace.

In addition, the findings revealed that a high attrition rate among the sales force was a result of ineffective hiring. Those persons who were doing the interview were quite familiar with standard interviewing techniques but were not experienced with hiring salespersons who were specialized in the telecommunications market, resulting in frequent mismatch and attrition.

SALES STRATEGY
The principal sales strategy consisted of convincing prospects to lease several units for a trial period, usually around nine months, with the expectation that performance during the trial would encourage future

sales for a larger number of units. Initially this approach was successful due mainly to the product feature advantages that the TC equipment had over its competition. Problems became noticeable when the sales strategy no longer produced large orders after the trial period. Apparently, the competition had caught up, and the relative product strength TC had enjoyed was eroded.

It became obvious that the integrated system, not the individual pieces of hardware, must be sold or leased. During the same period management had exerted a great deal of pressure to reach short-term sales goals. This pressure turned the salespeople away from the long selling cycles characteristic of major accounts. The sales plan also had been unrealistic, resulting in goals that were too difficult to achieve, thus contributing to the high attrition rate.

SALES COMPENSATION PLAN
Managers put salespeople on 30-day quotas, requiring each to place "x" number of units per month. This month-to-month pressure tended to push sales activity farther away from major accounts due to the long selling cycle typically required for them.

Sales territories were designed without considering the number of major accounts contained in the geographic area. The salespeople were further frustrated with large, multiple-unit orders because they needed to have customers gather their own information from the geographically diverse locations. This information is used to demonstrate to the customer the cost advantages of employing the TC system. The process tended to slow down the selling cycle and placed a great deal of dependency on customers to obtain the required data. In addition, the compensation plan was geared to give more incentive to a sales, as opposed to a leasing, strategy. This factor also tended to retard major-accounts acquisition because of customers' desire for a system trial run before making a large dollar commitment. The compensation plan also favored

Source: This case was prepared by E. Edward Blevins, William I. Evans, and Dr. David Gordon, director of the M.B.A. program in Industrial Management, Graduate School of Management, University of Dallas.

equipment placements in new customer locations rather than expanding the number of units in an already existing account.

QUESTION

The major-account business is needed for TC to continue its growth. How does the firm take the existing sales force members and make them more effective selling the TC system to major accounts?

CHAPTER 11

CONTENTS OF THE SALES TRAINING PROGRAM: SALES KNOWLEDGE AND THE SELLING PROCESS

CHAPTER OUTLINE

LEARNING IS A LIFELONG JOURNEY

SHOULD IT BE CALLED TRAINING OR EDUCATION?

RELATIONSHIP OF TRAINING TO LEARNING

SALES KNOWLEDGE DEVELOPMENT

KNOWLEDGE OF TECHNOLOGY

SALES SKILLS DEVELOPMENT

THE SELLING PROCESS

RESEARCH REINFORCES CHAPTER'S SALES SUCCESS STRATEGIES

ADAPTING TO GLOBAL MARKETS

LEARNING OBJECTIVES

The training of a salesperson makes all the difference between a successful sales career and an unsuccessful one. This chapter should help you understand:

■ The connection between training and learning.

■ The importance of sales knowledge and how such knowledge is developed.

■ The use of computer technology to make the salesperson's job easier and to provide better customer service.

■ That persuasive communication is a fundamental aspect of sales skills development.

■ The selling process as a vital tool for the salesperson and the importance of each step.

■ That quality customer service is a necessity.

■ The research that reinforces the sales success strategies discussed in this chapter.

Picture this scenario: A salesperson, accompanied by the family dog, strolls into a training session wearing pajamas. This may sound strange, but it is not an unusual event for sales reps at Fisher Scientific International's sales training sessions. This New Hampshire–based chemical company's salespeople are not being trained in regular classrooms, but in the privacy of their own homes, hotel rooms, cars, or wherever else they can tote their laptops.

The company has been using the Internet to teach the majority of its salespeople—saving time in the process. "Web-based technologies are becoming really hot in sales because they save salespeople's time," says Tim Sloane, an analyst of Boston-based Aberdeen Group, a technology consulting firm. "If you're training your reps and conducting sales meetings on the Web, you're cutting down on their travel time and increasing their selling time."

These Web-based technologies have been keeping reps up to speed on their company's new products and sales and marketing strategies, while saving companies money on travel costs. Most of all, they can help reps do what they do best: sell.

Reducing the amount of time spent in a classroom is the main reason that Fisher Scientific continues to train its salespeople via the Web, according to John Pavlik, director of Fisher University, the company's training department. "It allows them to manage their time better because they are only getting training when they need it, in the doses they need it in," he says. If salespeople are not using the system, their manager will know. The system can track how long reps are online and in which area they're receiving training.

Fisher sales rep Scott Herring is a big fan of the new system. "Finally, we've got a way of getting good quality, ongoing training from the company that's very effective and very flexible," he says, adding that since he's able to access it at any time of the day or night, he's saving time during his busy work day.

So the idea of employees showing up for workshops and training sessions in their pajamas is not a far-fetched idea for Fisher Scientific and other companies that are integrating Web-based training. Because of this technology, salespeople are able to spend much less time training, and if sales people are spending less time on training, Pavlik says, they're able to spend more time on selling.[1] ■

The training department of Fisher Scientific knows that selling requires a lot—much more than most people think. In order for salespeople to tackle everything their field demands, they must be prepared. Preparation requires training, and Fisher Scientific utilizes an effective and efficient way to train their employees.

Salespeople's job performance is affected by the capabilities individuals bring to the job, the capabilities they develop once in the job, and their motivation for performing the job. Preparing personnel for selling responsibilities directly contributes to two of the three: capabilities development and motivation. Concerning motivation, preparation for selling is integral to a positive mental attitude, and attitude is integral to motivation. Individuals simply are not likely to feel motivated to do something they feel they are not prepared to do.

The costs of preparing people to sell may be burdensome to companies, but the costs of not taking this step are prohibitive: high employee turnover, employee ineffectiveness, poor customer service, lost business.

The previous chapter discussed how to set up training programs. This chapter examines their content.

LEARNING IS A LIFELONG JOURNEY

A father and his small son were out walking one afternoon when the youngster asked how electricity went through the wires stretched between the telephone poles. "Don't know," the father said. "Never knew much about electricity." A few blocks farther on the boy asked what caused thunder and lightning. "To tell the truth," the father said, "I never exactly understood that myself."

The boy continued to ask questions throughout the walk, none of which the father could explain. Finally, as they were nearing home, the boy asked, "Pop, I hope you don't mind my asking so many questions." "Of course not," the father replied. "How else are you going to learn?"

Sooner or later, of course, the boy will stop asking his father questions, and that will be unfortunate. Curiosity and the desire to learn should be encouraged and nurtured. Parents who want their children to do well in school but don't respect learning are deluding themselves. Not many children will be motivated to do it on their own.

The same is true in business. Managers and sales trainers must set the example for those working for them. If they have stopped learning and growing, they will be hard put to inspire their employees to do so, no matter how much they may pretend to encourage both.

SHOULD IT BE CALLED TRAINING OR EDUCATION?

The previous chapter defined sales training as the effort an employer puts forth to provide the salesperson job-related culture, skills, knowledge, and attitudes. We examined the big picture—the phases, and their components, of a sales training program. Chapter 11 emphasizes that a goal of training is to move a salesperson from knowledge acquisition to a point—or stage—where materials presented in training sessions become a natural part of the salesperson's job behavior. This means salespeople must learn new habits.

Learning is a relatively permanent change in behavior occurring as a result of experience. Training is included in one's experiences. Thus, training is part of an individual's total learning experience. Training tends to imply a short-term or one-time event. True learning for the salesperson takes place over time.

Sales trainers in America are beginning to use the word *training* to actually describe an educational (learning) process. A few actually view their programs as educational. One sales trainer made the point this way: "We've gotten away from the word *training*.... What we are trying to provide is the total education process which allows the individual basically to go from preschool all the way up to graduate school."

Should it be called training or education? This textbook will continue to call this process training; however, sales training is a part of the total educational process required to teach "old dogs" new tricks and young pups "the ropes." New sales managers may find terms like "educational sales training programs" being used instead of simply "sales training."

RELATIONSHIP OF TRAINING TO LEARNING

Chapter 10 discussed the five phases of a sales training program. Figure 11.1 incorporates these into a model designed to illustrate the way an organization attempts to influence a salesperson's learning. Sales training programs include sales and technology knowledge and sales skills. Sales trainers strive to create a positive mental attitude in a salesperson. They want to motivate this person to use the material on the job. Trainers want salespeople to leave their classes fully prepared and with full intention of using the knowledge and skills.

After returning to the sales territory, the salesperson begins to use the knowledge and selling skills. The district sales manager works with the salesperson to reinforce OTJ behavior. This reinforcement, along with further sales meetings and training materials sent to the salesperson, can eventually make the knowledge and skills a part of the salesperson's natural on-the-job behavior—habits.

The order of occurrence of knowledge, skills, attitude, intention, behavior, and habit is important for the sales trainer to understand. The model in Figure 11.1 shows that knowledge must form first. Salespeople have to have the knowledge before they

FIGURE 11.1

THE LEARNING PROCESS INVOLVED IN TRAINING THE INDIVIDUAL SALESPERSON

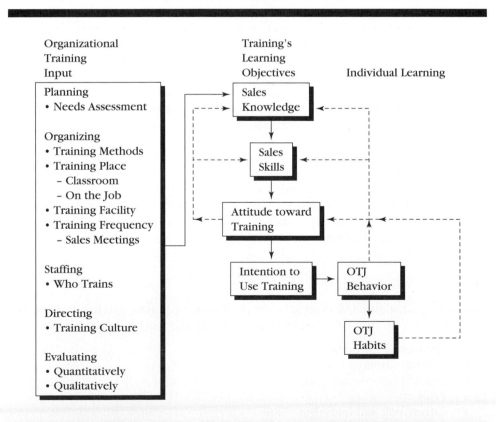

can properly use the sales skills. Once salespeople become knowledgeable and skill-ful and see the training as useful, they will apply it to their jobs.

ON-THE-JOB BEHAVIOR

The model's "feedback" lines (the dashed lines) show other important relationships. Let us begin in the lower right-hand corner of Figure 11.1. After receiving the training, the salesperson actually uses the knowledge and skills. If the salesperson perceives the training as worthwhile, the person is more receptive to further training and develops a positive attitude. The positive attitude and the OTJ experience result in the trainee (1) being receptive to new information, (2) looking forward to future training, and (3) possibly seeking new training.

If training is not perceived as worthwhile, the salesperson will not use it on the job. Or if the new knowledge and skills do not work, the person soon goes back to previous practices. In both cases, a negative attitude toward training is formed (or begins to form), and the chance the salesperson will seek out new training or be receptive to future training decreases.

OPERATIONAL AND BEHAVIORAL INFORMATION   Information can be of two types: operational and behavioral. The first type, **operational learning,** involves sales knowledge development such as new procedures, new product information, how to call in orders, new territorial forms to complete, new technology, and changes in the financial incentive program. This information is used to operate the sales territory or manager's unit. Operational types of procedures will be used instantly on the job and quickly will become a habit. Typically, operational training is in the area of sales and technology knowledge development.

Behavioral training involves the sales skills development area. It is often a challenge to change people's customer interaction habits—especially the veterans. Some typical trainee comments include "I've been doing it this way for five years. Why should I change?"; "You want me to close the sale two times. You're crazy. I'd get thrown out of the office"; and "I don't use visual aids in my presentations."

"You're going to do these things or else," a sales manager might think but not say. The manager knows the sales job is not like an office job where the boss can see the trainee using the sales skills. Thus, motivational and informative training programs and sales meetings, in addition to working with salespeople and providing them professionally developed company presentations, are extremely important for getting some salespeople to even use the information on the job. Firms must place continuous emphasis on employees using newly learned sales skills. Otherwise, salespeople will not form new, productive habits. Just because a company spends huge sums of money on training does not mean its salespeople automatically will use the skills on the job.

As noted earlier, sales training programs comprise mainly sales knowledge, knowledge of technology, and sales skills development. The remainder of this chapter discusses these three training components.

SALES KNOWLEDGE DEVELOPMENT

Properly trained salespeople need to be experts on their company and its competitors. Sales knowledge consists of numerous topics. Nine of the most important follow:

- Company knowledge.
- The sales role.
- Product knowledge.
- Prices.
- Advertising and sales promotion.
- Channels of distribution.

- Customers.
- Competition, industry, and economy.
- Territorial management skills.

COMPANY KNOWLEDGE

A newly hired salesperson first typically receives job-related information about the organization. The first day on the job, a salesperson is usually given company literature explaining the firm's history, development, and current operations. An organizational policy manual and fringe-benefits booklet are often distributed as well.

Company knowledge is easy to impart in a brief period. It is important to both new and experienced salespeople because it gives them a feeling of belonging and helps establish their company loyalty.

THE SALES ROLE

Salespeople also need to understand the sales role. Selling is unfamiliar to many new salespeople. Their lack of familiarity invokes discomforting images: hucksterism, canned spiels, hard selling, half-truths. Trainers must break down these images by presenting and reinforcing the role of a professional salesperson: serving the customer.

Professional salespeople help customers make better decisions about the business deal than they might make on their own. Professional salespeople listen, teach, clarify, and consult. They identify the products that fit the customer. They are the company's employee, but they are also the customer's partner. Sellers as partners is a role with which people can identify. Sellers as exploiters is not. Incorporating the true nature of professional selling into sales knowledge training is important in any industry.

PRODUCT KNOWLEDGE

Product knowledge is the foundation—the bedrock—of sales knowledge development. Sales personnel need in-depth understanding of the features, advantages, and benefits of what they are asked to sell. They have difficulty selling if they do not understand a product's features and advantages: They will not want to sell it if they do not understand its benefits. Such salespeople also will have trouble selling because they cannot use professional selling skills if they are not knowledgeable about their product.

Product knowledge may include these technical details:

- Performance data.
- Physical size and characteristics.
- How the product operates.
- Specific product features, advantages, and benefits.
- How well the product is selling in the marketplace.

The following quotations—all from salespeople mentioned in this book—convey the importance of product knowledge:

- "If you don't know the products, you can't sell them."
- "I want my customer to know that I know what I'm talking about."
- "We're cheating the customer if we don't know what we're talking about."
- "I've got to know what I'm selling. I'd better know my services. I'd better know the customer. I'd better have credibility."
- "Projecting the image of knowing what I'm talking about is very important."

Companies commonly use sales meetings to provide salespeople with sales knowledge. They can be a great method for providing all the information salespeople need to effectively sell a product.

PRICES

Salespeople find they have to constantly keep up with price changes. Existing products' prices vary constantly due to such factors as seasonal or promotional discounts. New products are often introduced. Some companies have hundreds, even thousands, of products. At times, keeping up is a challenge.

ADVERTISING AND SALES PROMOTION

Personal selling, advertising, publicity, and sales promotion are the main ingredients of a firm's promotional effort. Companies often coordinate these four tools in a promotional campaign. For example, the corporate marketing manager may ask a sales force to concentrate on selling product A for the months of April and May. Meanwhile, product A is simultaneously promoted on television and in magazines, and direct-mail samples or cents-off coupons for product A are sent to consumers.

Salespeople must keep abreast of their company's advertising and sales promotion activities. By incorporating these data into their sales presentation, salespeople can provide their customers with a world of information that customers probably knew little about and that could secure the sale.

CHANNELS OF DISTRIBUTION

Salespeople must understand the channel of distribution their company uses to move its products to the final consumer. Knowing as much as possible about each channel member is vital. Wholesalers and retailers often stock thousands of products, and each business may have hundreds of salespeople from a multitude of companies calling on its buyers. Some important information salespeople need includes:

- The likes and dislikes of each channel member's customers.
- The product lines and assortment each one carries.
- When each member sees salespeople.
- Each member's distribution, promotional, and pricing policies.
- What and how much of a product each has purchased in the past.

Although most channel members will have similar policies concerning salespeople, salespeople should keep abreast of the differences among them.

CUSTOMERS

Salespeople need to know about the market segments to which they will be selling. Demographic and institutional profiles and data on products used, undermet needs, and trends and changes over time need to be included in training programs. Building market research, such as test-market results, product and competitive sales, and buyer behavior findings, into sales knowledge development programs is one of the most valuable—and least used—applications of this information.

COMPETITION, INDUSTRY, AND ECONOMY

Salespeople are "boundary spanners." They are in the middle—between the customer and the employer. Salespeople must understand the big picture—competitive, social, economic, technological, and legislative/regulatory forces all impact the business. Credibility and effectiveness with the customer are jeopardized to the extent salespeople do not have this knowledge.

TERRITORIAL MANAGEMENT SKILLS

If salespeople were asked what they like least about their jobs, paperwork would probably be one of the top three items. They have to fill out forms for everything—

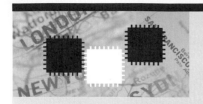

SELLING AND MANAGING GLOBALLY
RESPECTING THE TRADITIONS OF INDIA

Lisa Hendrick walked briskly through the low door; the soft, thick rugs on the floor muffled the sound of her heels. She greeted her customer, Babu Jagjivan, with a wide smile and an outstretched hand. Babu Jagjivan was clad in a long, khaki cotton shirt with swirls of white cloth wrapped around his legs. He took her hand rather tentatively and gestured her to take a seat. Hendrick sat on the nearest available chair and crossed her legs. She was ready to negotiate prices with the help of her interpreter, who spoke Hindi. However, Babu Jagjivan did not appear ready to conduct business. Instead, he summoned a boy with a clap of his hands. Immediately, the boy brought two steel containers filled with hot, steaming tea. Because it was a hot summer day with temperatures soaring to the 100s, Hendrick declined the tea. Babu Jagjivan seemed to be extremely reluctant to talk, let alone negotiate a deal. Hendrick was puzzled. She had thought she was adjusting to India very well. Only yesterday, she had negotiated a good contract with Rajan in Bangalore, a large metropolitan city in south India. But here, in Kanpur (a major city in north India), she was not meeting with much success. Hendrick wondered what could be wrong.

In India, customers vary from Westernized, urban sophisticates like Rajan to the earthy Babu Jagjivan. Although people everywhere seek to maximize economic benefits from a contract, the subtleties of negotiation and social mores cannot be overlooked. Babu Jagjivan was uncomfortable dealing with a woman. In the more traditional areas of India, it is not customary to shake hands with women—the traditional gesture of folding one's hands in respect (namaste) is the norm. The golden rule is to give the customer the pleasure of playing host, by accepting his or her tea and indulging in social pleasantries before getting down to business. Salespersons in India, as elsewhere, try to adapt to their customers by identifying with their customs. Hence, in urban India, the preferred language for business is English, and customers are more apt to be familiar with Western customs. In smaller towns, customers are more comfortable in the regional language (India has 15 official languages). People would be distrustful of salespersons who do not respect their customs. Certain weekdays (usually Fridays) are considered auspicious for signing business contracts, although this may vary from one region to another. For instance, even though people in many parts of south India would not commence new business on Tuesdays, this may not be true in the north.

Source: Developed by Pushkala Raman.

expense reimbursement, daily calls, orders, competitive activity, sample requests, new sales ideas, travel agendas, and to order more forms. Salespeople are running a business—their sales territory. They may sell millions of dollars each year in a territory. They have to learn how to do it. So initial training for new salespeople always includes a course on forms.

Throughout this book, other territorial management skills salespeople need to know are discussed. Forecasting, budgets, time management, sales-call planning, and customer-call recordkeeping are but a few of the many, many things salespeople must learn for managing their territories.

KNOWLEDGE OF TECHNOLOGY

The growing use of personal computers by sales personnel indicates the need to learn about computers and their use. To the nontechnical person—and that includes many of us—the PC may cause an uncomfortable feeling at first. People often feel apprehension about being able to use the PC and its software properly. However, combining the resources of computer manufacturers and software suppliers with company training programs quickly and effectively trains people while providing easy-to-use computer software.[2]

Sales personnel find PCs a valuable tool for increasing productivity within the sales force. The ten most widely used applications of PCs are shown in Table 11.1. Here are several major reasons to train salespeople to use a PC:

TABLE 11.1

TOP TEN PC APPLICATIONS

PC applications are focused on the customer. Here are the top ten applications in order of use:

1. Customer/prospect profile
2. Lead tracking
3. Call reports
4. Sales forecasts
5. Sales data analysis
6. Sales presentation
7. Time/territorial management
8. Order entry
9. Travel and expense reports
10. Checking inventory/shipping status

■ More effective management of sales leads and better follow-through on customer contacts. Computerization provides a permanent lead file.
■ Improves customer relations due to more effective follow-ups. This leads to greater productivity.
■ Improves organization of selling time. PCs help sales reps monitor and organize everything.
■ Provides more efficient account control and better time and territorial management. Sales reps are more aware of each account's status. This provides more time for customer contacts.
■ Increases number and quality of sales calls.
■ Improves speed and accuracy in finishing and sending reports and orders to the company.
■ Helps develop more effective proposals and persuasive presentations.

If you have little knowledge about the computer, start learning! Computers are here to stay. In your readings, look for how the computer is or can be used in your industry. Take a beginning computer course at a college or through your local public school's continuing education program. It is never too late to learn.

The rest of this section discusses sales force applications of technology. These should be included and updated in sales training programs.

SALES AND CUSTOMER SERVICE ENHANCEMENT

Computers are at the heart of salespeople's ability to provide top-quality customer service by receiving and sending out information efficiently.[3] Computers are impacting technology, advancing it at a rapid pace and affecting people—including salespeople—in all aspects of their lives. Providing quality customer service through technology rapidly increases salespeople's productivity.

A new wave of technology is going to sweep away computers as we know them and provide the ultimate in user-friendly tools that behave as associates. Within the next decade, many salespeople will have electronic secretaries similar to the one in the Managing the Sales Team box. This scenario illustrates how a computer can help handle the job that sales is all about—building and solidifying relationships.

Power is what stands between today's and tomorrow's systems—the ability to process vast amounts of data in a very short time. Today's portable computers simply can't do the calculations needed to take dictation or listen to voice commands, to understand most handwriting, or even to run most multimedia applications smoothly. A few more generations of technology should change all that.

In today's environment, sales force technology is already at work providing detailed, timely information that increases levels of productivity. Computers began going online as a way of setting themselves apart; now it is a required part of business to remain competitive.

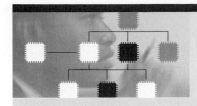

MANAGING THE SALES TEAM
THE COMPUTER AS A SALES ASSISTANT

It's 7:30 A.M., and you're getting ready to leave your hotel room. You turn to your computer and say, "System on."

"Good morning," the machine responds. " Are you ready to review your appointment calendar?"

"Sure. First, summarize E-mail traffic. I didn't have a chance to scan last night because I got in so late."

"You have received 37 messages in the past 24 hours. Twenty are low priority and have been filed in your home machine for review when your trip is over. Ten are medium priority and are stored in my memory for review at your convenience today. I suggest you scan the seven high-priority messages before you begin the day's activities."

"First, let's go over my day's schedule. I remember I had six appointments. Are they still on?"

"One was canceled. During the newswire scan you requested, I picked up serious traffic problems that should be resolved by late afternoon, so I contacted the electronic agents of two of your appointments and rescheduled. They have confirmed the new times. I interfaced with your car's mapping system yesterday, and the preferred routes are available in my memory."

"Any hot points I should remember?"

"Two of your appointments have had birthdays within the past two weeks. Winston of United Products sent a letter of complaint about a delayed shipment four months ago. My records state the issue was resolved to their satisfaction. A special promotion we began last week for American International appears to already have had a positive impact."

"Good. Let's sit down and go over the trends and analysis for each meeting. Sound off. I'll remember better if I just read the text."

Sales force technology and automation comes in a variety of sizes and applications. With technology doubling every six months, the desktop computer from a couple of years ago has become the notebook computer of today. But for those who prefer larger screens and keyboards for comfort, manufacturers are now including docking stations in desktop computers. These portholes enable downloading files in laptop computers to full-size, full-function computers after users return to the office.

Technology not only helps salespeople increase their productivity but also allows them to gather and access information more efficiently. They can use computer technology to improve communication with the home office, with others on their sales force, and with customers. Salespeople also use technology to create better strategies for targeting and tracking clients. Sales force automation breaks down into three broad areas of functionality covering (1) personal productivity, (2) communications, and (3) order processing and customer service.

PERSONAL PRODUCTIVITY

Many electronic programs can help a salesperson increase productivity through more efficient data storage and retrieval, better time management, and enhanced presentations. Let's discuss five of the most popular, beginning with contact management programs.

CONTACT MANAGEMENT   Contact management is a listing of all the customer contacts a salesperson makes in the course of conducting business. This file is like an electronic Rolodex and should include information such as the contact's name, title, company, address, phone number, fax number, and E-mail address. It also may include additional information, such as the particular industry, date of last order, name of administrative assistant, birthday, and so on.

A sales force automation system allows salespeople to retrieve this information easily in a variety of formats. They can sort contacts according to any one of the pieces of information they are tracking. For instance, a sales rep going to Dallas may want a list of area contacts that have made a purchase in the past six months. Though a person could sort this information manually, it would be extremely time consuming. Another example of sorted information salespeople may require is a list of customers by ZIP code for mailing labels or perhaps a list of clients with birthdays in October. All of these details are available and readily accessible through automation.

CALENDAR MANAGEMENT   As a salesperson, the most vulnerable asset you have to manage is time. Improvement of time management directly increases productivity. Electronic calendar management, as a part of sales force automation, can make time management easier and less prone to errors or oversights.

When a salesperson schedules appointments, telephone calls, or to-do lists on an electronic calendar, the system automatically checks for conflicts, eliminating the need for rescheduling. An electronic calendar can assign a relative priority to each item. It also can create an electronic link between a scheduled event and a particular contact or account, so the appointment or call information is accessible as both part of the salesperson's calendar and as part of the contact or account history. The information contained in the calendar is much more useful when it can be viewed from different perspectives.

For the sales manager, electronic calendar management automatically consolidates information on the whereabouts of the entire sales force. This improves on weekly or monthly calendars, which quickly become outdated. Information can be automatically generated when salespeople schedule their appointments. The system also allows salespeople to instantly update their appointments and schedules directly from the field.

AUTOMATED SALES PLANS, TACTICS, AND TICKLERS   Sales strategies often involve a sequence of events that can be identified and plotted. A traditional example is a thank-you letter sent immediately after an initial sales call and a follow-up telephone call three days later. In the real world, it may be difficult for busy salespeople to track all the details. Important follow-up items sometimes get overlooked. If this happens, a salesperson's diligent prospecting efforts become wasted, and valuable prospects are squandered.

A sales force automation system begins working as soon as the initial meeting is entered into the system. A few simple commands tell it to remind you to send a thank-you letter and schedule a follow-up call. It also can notify the sales manager if these actions are not taken.

Another sales situation might call for a regular follow-up every year or two after the sale, depending on the "itch cycle" associated with your product. It is particularly easy for follow-up calls like this to be neglected because of the long lead time involved. The problem becomes more apparent if the salesperson who made the original sale leaves the company or is promoted. When that happens, the customer often falls through the cracks, becoming an orphan. Automated sales tactics and "ticklers" prevent this from happening.

GEOGRAPHIC INFORMATION SYSTEMS   A geographic information system allows salespeople to view and manipulate customer and prospect information on an electronic map. This may be extremely useful if they are visiting an area for the first time. It also can be helpful for familiar areas. Customer information can be assessed directly from contact-management data and sorted accordingly, allowing sales reps to plan sales calls geographically and make the most efficient use of their time. Also, the system may reveal customer buying patterns that otherwise may not be apparent.

COMPUTER-BASED PRESENTATIONS   The computer can be a powerful presentation tool. With automation, sales reps can easily create dramatic and interactive computer-based presentations at relatively low costs. Moreover, they can customize their creations for a particular customer or prospect or to take advantage of a particular sales opportunity.

CD-ROM (compact disk read-only memory) technology enhances computer presentations. For example, John Darman, vice president of men's shaving products for Gillette, and the Jack Morton Company in Boston developed a CD-ROM sales presentation in about twelve weeks for their new Mach 3 ad campaign. One of the benefits of the CD-ROM is that it allows for a "presentation that couldn't be achieved in the world of paper," says Darman. Reps can take retailers through or allow them to use it themselves, to go in as much depth as they choose. They were able to go through the entire CD or point and click to their specific areas of interest. "Because you could so thoroughly go through the attributes everyone stayed [during sales calls] longer," says Paul Prebil, Gillette's director of food channel sales. The CD-ROM presentation was obviously a success. in the first six weeks of shipping, 80 percent of the food stores in the country had the razor on their shelves.[4]

COMMUNICATIONS WITH CUSTOMERS AND EMPLOYER

As we move into the twenty-first century, a company's success hinges on its ability to deliver information quickly to customers and employees. Today's most popular sales force automation systems involve word processing, E-mail, and faxes.

WORD PROCESSING Written communication plays a large part in the lives of most salespeople. Particularly important is the need for written communication with customers. A thank-you letter mailed immediately after an initial sales call often can make the difference between a favorable impression and one that is not as favorable. Sometimes it can make or break a sale. In spite of its potential impact, this simple task frequently is overlooked because the salesperson lacks an easy way to get it done. Other more pressing tasks always seem to take precedence. A sales force automation system can abbreviate the time it takes to accomplish this task to no more than a minute or two, the time it takes to execute a few keystrokes on a word processor.

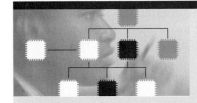

MANAGING THE SALES TEAM
THE SALES BUSINESS CARD—TELEPHONE, FAX, BEEPER, E-MAIL

Today's business cards often show multiple phone numbers; most now have more than one address. The technologically driven trend that puts fax, cellular, and beeper numbers on many cards has prompted the addition of electronic mail addresses.

E-mail addresses already are standard fare in the high-tech, communication, and academic fields. Other professions are beginning to add them as more and more people sign onto national and international online services that offer E-mail at home or the office.

Rocko Mitera, the marketing manager at Wace the Imaging Network, a graphics services company in Chicago, doesn't leave home without E-mail access or without the business cards that point the way to his electronic residence. "I've always maintained an electronic mail address," Mitera says, adding that it makes him more accessible to business contacts and friends.

"When you travel, you can receive and respond to messages very quickly," Mitera, who finds people respond faster to electronic mail, says.

Mitera uses a laptop computer to communicate with his office from out-of-town hotels; via E-mail, he can send documents and file reports. Mitera believes that without E-mail, the minute you walk out the door you lose your efficiency. E-mail beats phone tag, he contends, and predicts it will soon be a regular part of business communications.

Although an E-mail address may be the next step in having a well-dressed business card, it's not without its detractors. Steven Buckman, a Chicago marketing consultant, has E-mail but won't use it for his professional contacts. "E-mail is recreational; the fax is professional," Buckman says. "I'm in sales; I have to talk to [clients]."

Source: Kate Griffin, "Telephone-Fax, Beeper—E-Mail Address," *Marketing News* (September 1994):7–8.

Electronic Mail   Electronic mail (E-mail) allows messages to be sent electronically through a system that delivers them immediately to any number of recipients. Correspondence is typed into the computer and sent via telephone, cable, or satellite to an E-mail address, such as a telephone number. It is very easy to send or receive electronic messages from almost any location in the world and much more efficient than playing phone tag. For instance, a salesperson trying to contact a customer who is temporarily out of town may find E-mail is the best bet. E-mail also could be the mode of choice to send a quick note updating a manager and other salespeople on the team when a sales rep has only a few minutes to spare. For example, Barrett Joyner, the vice president of North American sales and marketing for SAS Institute, uses E-mail to connect himself with his large staff. He and his managers receive 80 to 100 messages a day and they respond to each one within 24 hours.[5]

Technology is having profound effects on corporate culture. For those who truly want to be close to their customers, electronic mail can have a tremendous impact. Remarkably, this is as true in a sales environment where salespeople rarely leave the confines of the office as it is when they are based in the field. (Your author's E-mail address is c-futrell@tamu.edu—let me hear from you.)

Fax Capabilities and Support   Next to the telephone, the fax machine is the most important piece of communication equipment in business. Notebook computers, equipped with fax modems, are unique time-savers for salespeople in the field. Options include the ability to prepare and fax a document—from a car, perhaps—without having to print a hard copy. Sales reps can receive documents in the same manner. This equipment can conveniently and inexpensively handle the great majority of a salesperson's written communication from the road.

Customer Order Processing and Service Support

The process of obtaining, generating, and completing an order is much more complicated than it may seem. The many steps involved in a manual system may take a number of days or even weeks to complete and confirm. Automated systems shorten the sales-and-delivery cycle. While in an office with a customer, salespeople can use a modem to access information and take action more efficiently. They can check the inventory status of merchandise on the sales order, receive approval for their client's credit status, and begin the shipping process immediately. Salespeople's automated order entries directly update the company computer, so they don't have to be reentered at the home office.

Salespeople's Mobile Offices   Salespeople have begun installing small offices directly into vehicles such as minivans. For salespeople who need to be constantly in touch with their clients, these minivans are a perfect solution for working through "dead" time. A vehicle can be equipped with a fully functional desk, swivel chair, light, computer, printer, fax machine, cellular phone, satellite dish, and remote phone. In their mobile offices, salespeople can stay in constant touch with their customers even when driving between cities or states. Jeff Brown, an agent manager with U.S. Cellular, uses a mobile office at least three or four times a week. "If I arrive at a prospect's office and they can't see me right away," Brown says, "then I can go outside to work in my office until they're ready to see me."[6]

E-Commerce and the Sales Force

An Internet site can be a help to salespeople in servicing and selling customers. The long-term benefits can be very rewarding. They are:

- **Builds Customer Loyalty**—A site that offers services people can't get from a competitor keeps customers coming back.

- **Saves Customers Money**—Online ordering and tracking reduces the customer's cost of processing a transaction.
- **Speeds the Sales Process**—Electronic sites offer the convenience, simplicity, and immediacy that customers demand.
- **Improves Relationships**—Successful commercial sites anticipate, and answer, routine customer problems—allowing salespeople to concentrate on the strategic issues that forge strong vendor–customer ties.
- **Lowers Sales Costs**—A site that lets salespeople spend more time selling and less time answering queries.[7]

GLOBAL TECHNOLOGY

The ability to access information anywhere is a valuable asset. We are in an era when corporate strategy relies on efficiency; it can make or break a business. Salespersons traveling far from home critically need the right information, at the right time, and in the right place. Increased worldwide interaction requires access and exchange of data on a global basis.

As technology solves problems, it presents new opportunities. For example, advances in mobile data collection and wireless data communications have dramatically increased the amount of data that needs to be collected, managed, stored, and accessed. Organizations that harness this information can maximize the level of service they offer, resulting in increased sales.

A salesperson in Europe, for example, can send information to a firm in America by satellite transmission. The information is stored in the organization's main computer database. A salesperson in Florida has access to the information and can send additional data to the database. Even a Texas salesperson in a customer's office can send and receive information to and from the same database using a telephone modem transmission or wireless communication.

Providing salespeople with both the knowledge and skills to transmit that knowledge to prospects and customers is extremely important to their performance. Sales knowledge without sales skills will mean far fewer sales than sales knowledge coupled with sales skills.

Sales skills development involves two key elements: (1) Persuasive communications and (2) the selling process.

Although these categories are not mutually exclusive, it is useful to think of sales skills training as a communications component of the complete selling process ranging from prospecting for customers to service after the sale. The selling process is complex enough to warrant its own section.

SALES SKILLS DEVELOPMENT

PERSUASIVE COMMUNICATIONS

Salespeople need not be "smooth talkers" to be effective, but they should be sensitive to factors that can enhance the persuasiveness of their message.

A new salesperson was sitting in a customer's office waiting for the buyer. His boss was with him. As they heard the buyer come into the office, the sales manager said, "Remember, a *KISS* for him." No, he was not saying to give the buyer a kiss but to use the old selling philosophy of *keep it simple, salesperson*.

The story is told of an elderly woman who went into a hardware store. The clerk greeted her and offered her some help. She replied that she was looking for a heater. So the clerk said, "Gee, are you lucky! We have a big sale on these heaters and a tremendous selection. Let me show you." So, after maybe 30 or 45 minutes of discussing duothermic controls, heat induction, and all the factors involved with a heater's operation, including the features and advantages of each of the 12 models, he turned to the woman and said, "Now, do you have any questions?" To which she replied, "Yes, just one, Sonny. Which of these things will keep a little old lady warm?"

An overly complex, technical sales presentation should be avoided when it is unnecessary. Salespeople should use words and materials the buyer can easily understand. A skilled salesperson can make a prospect feel comfortable with a new product or complex technology by subtly using nontechnical information and keeping a respectful attitude.

A complete list and discussion of the many persuasive communication skills taught to salespeople are really beyond the scope of this chapter. However, several of the main skills that should be included in every sales training program follow:

- Talking about product benefits to the prospect rather than the product's features and advantages. Procter & Gamble uses examples like this in its training: "The king-size Tide will bring you 'additional profits' (benefit) because it is the fastest selling size (advantage)."
- Nonverbal body language—learning to recognize a buyer's nonverbal signs and how to send out positive nonverbal body signals.
- Questioning or probing skills and courses in listening.
- Using visual aids, drama, and demonstrations in the sales presentation.

Trainers feel that these skills (1) capture the buyer's attention and interest; (2) create two-way communication; (3) get the buyer involved in the presentation; (4) provide a more complete, clearer explanation of the product and business proposition; and (5) increase a salesperson's persuasion powers. Salespeople's gains include positive attitudes, higher motivational levels, and increased sales.[8]

THE SELLING PROCESS

Certainly, no magic formula exists for making a sale. Many different factors may influence the purchase decision. Yet most sales trainers believe logical, sequential steps do exist that, if followed, can greatly improve the chance of making a sale. This is referred to as the **sales process.** This sequential series of actions by the salesperson leads to the customer taking a desired action and ends with a follow-up to ensure purchase satisfaction (Figure 11.2).

The feedback arrows to the left in Figure 11.2 illustrate that at times a salesperson may move back to the main presentation step. For example, say a salesperson has fully discussed the product with the buyer and asks for the order. The buyer says, "I need to think about this some more." The salesperson may ask, "What is it you need to think about?" "I'm not exactly sure how we can use this product in our present system," the buyer says. Now the salesperson must move back into the presentation to address the buyer's concern. The salesperson also may need to do this after a trial close, an objection, or the presentation. Thus, a salesperson's behavior should adapt to the situation in order to improve selling effectiveness.

Xerox's sales training philosophy embraces a similar sequential process. At Xerox's Document University trainees are brought through the process and learn what to expect from their customers and themselves during each stage. Although the process is sequential, sales trainees are taught to understand the buyer and to be willing to go to whatever stage the buyer is ready for.[9] Let's discuss each of the steps to see how today's professionals are trained to sell.

PROSPECTING FINDS CUSTOMERS

Prospecting is the first step in the selling process. A *prospect* is a person or business that needs the product a salesperson is selling and has the ability to buy it. Therefore,

FIGURE 11.2

THE SALES PROCESS

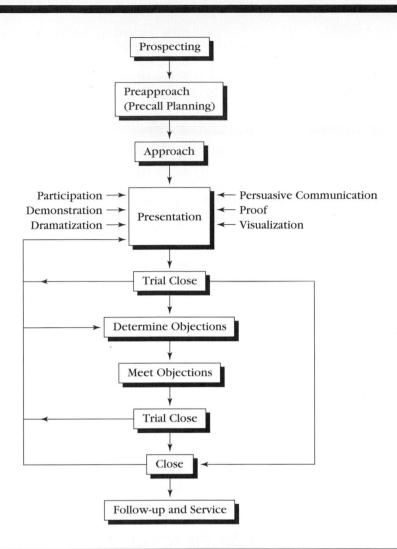

prospecting is the act of finding people who need and can buy the product. Prospecting is the lifeblood of sales.

A salesperson must look constantly for new prospects for two reasons. One is to increase sales. The other is to replace customers who will be lost over time. A prospect should not be confused with a lead. The name of a person or business that might be a prospect is referred to as a *lead.* Once the lead has been qualified as needing the product and as having the ability to buy it, the lead becomes a prospect.

Salespeople can ask themselves three questions to determine if an individual or organization is a **qualified prospect:**

1. Does the prospect have the *m*oney to buy?
2. Does the prospect have the *a*uthority to buy?
3. Does the prospect have the *d*esire to buy?

A simple way to remember this qualifying process is to think of the word *MAD.* A true prospect must have the financial resources, money or credit, to pay and the authority to make the buying decision. The prospect also should desire the product. Sometimes an individual or organization may not recognize a need for the product. It's the salesperson's job, then, to help create the need.

Table 11.2

Popular Prospecting
Methods

- Cold canvassing
- Endless chain—customer referral
- Orphaned customers
- Sales lead clubs
- Prospect lists
- Get published

- Public exhibitions and demonstrations
- Center of influence
- Direct mail
- Telephone and telemarketing
- Observation
- Networking

The actual methods by which a salesperson obtains prospects may vary. Several of the more popular prospecting methods are shown in Table 11.2.

Referrals Are Popular   Referrals come from prospects. Different sources of prospects form the prospect pool. The **prospect pool** is a group of names gathered from various sources. Your source, for example, may be a mailing list, telephone book, referrals, orphans, or existing customers. As shown in Figure 11.3, a prospect pool is usually created from four main sources.

1. **Leads:** people and organizations salespeople know nothing, or very little, about.
2. **Referrals:** people or organizations salespeople frequently know very little about other than what they learned from the referral.
3. **Orphans:** customers whose salesperson has left the company. Company records provide the only information about these past customers.
4. **Customers:** the most important prospects for future sales.

Most salespeople required to create customers through prospecting do not like to cold call—contacting strangers. They have the goal of using a prospect pool composed of customers, friends, and, when available, orphans.

Referrals from customers are the best way to increase the chances of selling to a stranger (prospect). Bob Burg, president of Burg Communications in Jupiter, Florida, strongly agrees. His experience tells him that "people want to do business with, and refer business to, people they know, like, and trust." Because this is true, "The days of the one-shot salesperson are over. The name of the game today is relationship building." Satisfied customers will provide the salesperson with a constant supply of prospects.[10]

Figure 11.3

The Prospect Pool

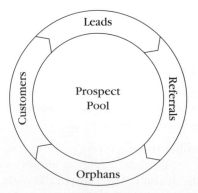

The John Deere Corporation has also found its prospect-pool database and customer communication most helpful. The database contains extensive information on the purchasing habits of tractor and farm-equipment owners. Those owners with 10- to 20-year-old equipment are called and offered information on John Deere's oil and filter products. Not only does the company sell more oil, but it also generates leads for its equipment dealers.[11]

PREAPPROACH IS PRECALL PLANNING

Once the prospect has been identified and qualified, the next step in the selling process is the preapproach. Prospecting and the preapproach are similar in that, for both, the salesperson is gathering information to use in the attempt to make a sale. During the **preapproach,** the salesperson investigates the prospect in greater depth and plans the sales call.

Harvey Mackay, founder of Mackay Envelope, is an example of someone that had to go through the process of preapproach quickly, and it paid off. Mackay's assistant notified him that the CEO of a large corporation he had been trying to set up a meeting with for almost a year would see him in two hours. That gave Mackay only two hours to prepare and do some background work on the CEO. Luckily, he had access to Lexis/Nexus. "Within 10 minutes I had 14 single-spaced sheets of paper on this person. I memorized it as best as I could in a cab going across town," says Mackay.

By the time he arrived at the appointment, Mackay had figured out the mutual interests the two could talk about and how he would tie in the information he wanted to talk to the CEO about. At one point in the interview, the CEO looked at him and said, "Boy, you really did your homework, didn't you?" Mackay's experience, in his words, "really goes to the heart of how crucial it is for a sales professional to know how to get information in a hurry, then to assimilate it and make use of it quicker than the next guy does."[12]

All sales trainers feel salespeople must carefully plan their sales calls. Although numerous reasons exist for planning the sales call, four of the most frequently mentioned are that planning:

- Helps build a salesperson's self-confidence.
- Develops an atmosphere of goodwill and trust with the buyer.
- Helps create an image of professionalism.
- Increases sales because people are prepared.

Figure 11.4 depicts the four facets for consideration when sales-call planning. These facets are (1) determining sales call objectives; (2) developing or reviewing the customer profile; (3) developing a customer benefit plan; and (4) developing the individual sales presentation based on the sales-call objective, customer profile, and customer benefit plan.

DETERMINING SALES CALL OBJECTIVES   Salespeople should have at least one objective in mind when they meet with a prospect or customer. Sales call objectives should be specific, measurable, and directly beneficial to the customer. For example,

FIGURE 11.4   STEPS IN PLANNING THE SALES CALL

| Determination of Call Objectives | → | Development of Customer Profile | → | Determination of Customer Benefits | → | Determination of Sales Presentation |

a Colgate salesperson might have the objectives of checking all merchandise, having the customer make a routine reorder on merchandise, and selling promotional quantities of Colgate toothpaste. Industrial salespeople develop similar objectives to determine if their present customers need to reorder and to sell new products.

DEVELOPING A CUSTOMER PROFILE   Salespeople should review as much relevant information as possible regarding the firm, the buyer, and the individuals who influence the buying decisions before making a sales call in order to properly develop a customized presentation.

DEVELOPING A CUSTOMER BENEFIT PLAN   Beginning with the sales-call objectives and what is known or has been learned about a prospect, the salesperson is then ready to develop the customer benefit plan. The customer benefit plan contains the nucleus of the information used in the sales presentation; thus, it should be developed to the best of the salesperson's ability. Creating a customer benefit plan can be approached as a four-step process:

Step One   Select the *features, advantages, and benefits* (FABs) of the product to present to the prospect. This activity addresses the issue of *why* the product should be purchased. The main reason a prospect should purchase a product is that its benefits fulfill certain needs or solve certain problems. Salespeople should carefully determine the benefits they wish to present. An example is shown in Table 11.3.

Step Two   Developing the *marketing plan.* If a salesperson is selling to a wholesaler or retailer, the marketing plan should include how, once the prospect buys the product, he or she will sell the product. An effective marketing plan would include suggestions for how a retailer, for example, should promote the product through displays, advertising, proper shelf space and positioning, and pricing. For an end user of the product, such as a company that buys manufacturing equipment, computers, or photocopiers, salespeople should develop a program showing how their product can be most effectively used or coordinated with existing equipment.

Step Three   Develop a *business proposition* that includes items such as the price, percent markup, forecasted profit per square foot of shelf space, return on investment, and payment plan. Value analysis is an example of a business proposition for an industrial product.

TABLE 11.3   FEATURES, ADVANTAGES, AND BENEFITS OF BIX BUCKWHEAT PANCAKE MIX

FEATURES	ADVANTAGES	BENEFITS
1. Traditional "farmhouse" recipe, with freshest ingredients; fortified with vitamins A, B, C, and D; no preservatives	Great tasting, fluffy, and light; highly nutritious	Provides an appealing item; expands breakfast menu; increases breakfast business
2. User needs only to add water, stir, and cook	Quick and easy to prepare	Requires minimal kitchen time and labor
3. Delivered weekly	No need to store large quantities	Requires minimal inventory space; keeps inventory costs low
4. Local distribution center	Additional orders can be filled quickly	Prevents out-of-stock situations
5. An experienced sales representative to serve account	Knowledge and background in food-service industry	Provides assistance for meeting changing needs and solving business problems

Step Four   Develop a *suggested purchase order* based on the customer benefit plan. A proper presentation of the analysis of customer needs and the product's ability to fulfill these needs, along with a satisfactory business proposition and marketing plan, should allow a salesperson to justify to the prospect how much of the product to purchase. Depending on the nature of the product, this suggestion also may have to include such details as what to buy, how much to buy, which assortment to buy, and when to ship the product to the customer.

The salesperson should create visual aids to effectively communicate the information developed in these four steps. The visuals should be organized in the order they will be discussed. The next step is to plan all aspects of the sales presentation itself.

DEVELOPING THE SALES PRESENTATION   Finally, the sales presentation must be planned from beginning to end. This process involves developing seven of the steps of the sales presentation described earlier in Figure 11.2. These are approach, presentation, trial close, determine objections, meet objections, additional trial close, and close of the sales presentation.

THE APPROACH—OPENING THE SALES PRESENTATION

The sales opener, or **approach,** is the first major part of the sales presentation. If done correctly, it greatly improves a salesperson's chances of making the sale. A buyer's reactions to the salesperson in the early minutes of the sales presentation are critical to a successful sale. This short time period is so important it is treated as an individual step in selling, referred to as "the approach." Part of any approach is the prospect's first impression of the salesperson.[13]

THE FIRST IMPRESSION IS CRITICAL TO SUCCESS   When a salesperson first meets a prospect, the initial impression is based on appearances and attitude. If this impression is favorable, the prospect is more likely to listen to the salesperson, but if it is not favorable, the prospect may erect communication barriers that can be difficult to overcome. Like an actor, the salesperson must learn how to project and maintain a positive, confident, and enthusiastic first impression no matter what mood the prospect is in when first encountering the salesperson.

APPROACH TECHNIQUES ARE NUMEROUS   The situation the salesperson faces will determine what approach technique should be used to begin the sales presentation. The most common approaches used in sales training programs follow:

- **Introductory approach:** The salesperson states his or her name and business. This is the most common approach and also the weakest. For example, "Hello, my name is Amy Firestone, representing the Barnhill Estate Company."
- **Product approach:** The salesperson places the product on the counter or hands it to the customer, saying nothing. The salesperson then waits for the prospect to begin the conversation. This is useful if the product is new, unique, colorful, or has been changed. If, for example, Pepsi-Cola completely changed the shape of its bottle and label, the salesperson should simply hand the product to the retail buyer and wait.
- **Customer benefit approach:** The salesperson asks a question that shows the product can benefit the prospect in some way, such as saving money. For example, "How would you like to save $100 on the purchase of your next IBM typewriter?"
- **Curiosity approach:** The salesperson asks a question to make the prospect curious about the product or service. For example, a textbook

salesperson might ask, "Do you know why 200 schools are using this book in their sales management courses?"

Most salespeople vary a combination of these techniques.[14] All but the introductory approach (the weakest) have three important characteristics in common: They capture the *attention* of the prospect; they stimulate *interest;* and they provide a *smooth transition* into the presentation.

Making a Great Presentation

The presentation itself is a continuation of the approach. What, then, should be the purpose of the presentation? Basically, the purpose of the **presentation** is to provide *knowledge* about the features, advantages, and benefits of the product, marketing plan, and business proposal. This allows the buyer to develop positive personal beliefs about the product. Such beliefs result in a *desire (or need)* for the product. The salesperson's job is to convert the need into a want and finally into the *belief* that this specific product is the best product to fulfill a certain need. Furthermore, the sales rep must convince the buyer that not only is this product the best but also that this seller is the best source from which to buy it.

Presentations filled only with a product's standard facts fall short of making the sale. Salespeople like L. Bryant Barry, from Sandoz Agro, Inc., realize they must captivate the audience to the point where the prospect is ready to close on the sale. Doing homework on the company's needs, associating the product with something the prospect does every day, adding relevant humor, and adding visual tools keep customers locked into a salesperson's presentation. Remembering these four tips enhances the presentation, and they also should be considered in the planning process.[15]

THE SALES PRESENTATION MIX   When developing a presentation, salespeople should consider which elements of the sales presentation mix (Figure 11.5) they will use for each prospect. The proper use of persuasive communication techniques, methods to encourage prospect participation, proof statements, visual aids, dramatization, and

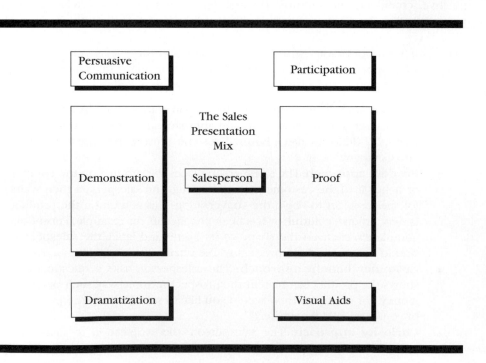

FIGURE 11.5

THE SALESPERSON'S PRESENTATION MIX IS TYPICALLY DEVELOPED BY SALES MANAGERS AND TRAINERS demonstrations can greatly increase a salesperson's chance of showing the prospect how the products will satisfy his or her needs.

As we know, it is often not what we say but how we say it that results in making the sale.[16] Persuasive communication techniques such as questioning, listening, logical reasoning, suggestion, and trial closes help to uncover needs, communicate effectively, and pull the prospect into the conversation.

Proof statements substantiate the claims salespeople make. They are especially useful for showing prospects that what they are saying is true and that they can be trusted. When challenged about a product statement, salespeople should "prove it" by incorporating into their presentation facts on a customer's past sales, guarantees the product will work or sell, testimonials, or company and independent research results.

To both show and tell, visuals should highlight a product's features, advantages, and benefits through the use of graphics, dramatization, and demonstration. This technique captures the prospect's attention and interest; creates two-way communication and participation; expresses the proposition in a clearer, more complete manner; and makes more sales. Careful attention to the development and rehearsal of the presentation is needed to ensure that it is carried out smoothly and naturally.

At any time salespeople should be prepared for the unexpected—a demonstration that breaks down, interruptions, questions about the competition, or the necessity for making a presentation in a less-than-ideal place such as the aisle of a retail store or the warehouse.

The presentation part of the overall sales presentation is the heart of the sale. It is where the salesperson develops desire, conviction, and action. By giving an effective presentation, the sales rep will have fewer objections to the proposition, which makes for an easier close of the sale.

SALESPEOPLE, MANAGERS, AND TRAINERS PREPARE PRESENTATION MIX   Salespeople are typically too involved in their daily activities to develop all of the needed visual aids and often even presentation ideas. The sales managers and trainers usually create and organize the presentation materials and then train salespeople to use them.

As the technological age continues, software companies have created user-friendly presentation tools that are easy to install on a laptop computer. Multimedia software provides a state-of-the-art presentation that enhances the salesperson–customer relationship. Presentation software that incorporates graphics, sound, and video into the standard presentation helps American Airlines keep ahead of its competition. At American, all sales reps are equipped with a high-powered laptop computer loaded with multimedia software to create their own presentations. The salespeople have found that using the software differentiates their presentation from the competition and delivers an impact that makes the sale.[17]

AT&T is another company using multimedia computer presentations. They are ideal for traveling salespersons with notebook computers, and the computers also allow two-way communication between the salesperson and the client. AT&T's sales force has fallen in love with this presentation style and looks to expand this concept.[18]

SALES PRESENTATION METHODS   The sales presentation involves a persuasive vocal and visual explanation of a business proposition. Although many ways to make a presentation exist, only three will be discussed here. They are the memorized or stimulus-response, formula, and need-satisfaction methods. The basic difference among the three is the percentage of the conversation the salesperson controls. The more-structured memorized and formula selling techniques normally give the salesperson a monopoly on the conversation, while the less-structured methods allow a much greater degree of buyer–seller interaction, in which both parties participate equally in the conversation.

Stimulus-Response Method   This method assumes that the prospect's needs can be stimulated by exposure to the product or already have been stimulated because the prospect has sought out the product. The salesperson does most of the talking. Only occasionally does the prospect get to talk. The salesperson does not know what the prospect needs, so all aspects of the product are first discussed, and then the prospect is asked to buy.

If no sale occurs, the presentation is begun again, and another attempt is made to close the sale. A "canned" presentation is an example of this approach. Everyone is told basically the same thing. If time is short, the unit price is low, or the salesperson confronts the prospect infrequently or only once, this approach might be considered. The salesperson goes directly to the presentation stage of the sales process and quickly asks for the order. This method is relatively ineffective for more-complicated selling situations. Here are some of the method's shortcomings:

- Talks about product features not important to buyer.
- Uses same "pitch" for different people.
- Assumes salesperson is in total control.
- Has little prospect participation, making it difficult to uncover needs.

Formula Method   This approach is like the stimulus-response method in that it is based on the assumption that all prospects are alike. However, here something is known about the prospect, so the presentation is slightly less structured than it is with the stimulus-response method. The salesperson may use a structured series of steps such as the **AIDA approach.**

AIDA stands for *attention, interest, desire,* and *action; conviction* may be added to form AIDCA, indicating the point at which the prospect feels the benefits outweigh the costs associated with the product. The approach is not complex and easily can be adapted to various situations.

The salesperson plans or "cans" the sales talk to quickly get attention and interest so the prospect will listen to the presentation. For the desire step, the salesperson translates the product's features and advantages into benefits for the prospect. Action or closing techniques are then used to make the sale. The AIDA method can be used if time is short, if prospects are the same, or if the salesperson lacks the ability to develop individualized sales presentations. The shortcomings of this approach are the same as those of the stimulus-response method.

Need-Satisfaction Method   The need-satisfaction method is different from the stimulus-response and the formula approaches in that it is designed as an interactive sales presentation. It is the most challenging and creative form of selling. The salesperson will typically start the presentation with a probing question: "What are you looking for in investment property?" "What type of computer needs does your company have?" This allows the prospect to discuss the company's needs.

As the salesperson is listening to the prospect, he or she mentally notes the product's features, advantages, and benefits in relation to the prospect's needs. If the salesperson is not clear on some things the prospect says, he or she should ask questions or restate what the prospect has said to make sure the prospect's needs and desires are completely expressed and understood. Once this stage is accomplished, the salesperson is ready to show how the products will satisfy the prospect's needs. The presentation can be personalized or concentrate on the specific features the salesperson's product can offer that will fulfill the prospect's needs.

This presentation method is the most challenging. Salespeople must be careful how they uncover the prospect's needs. Too many questions can alienate the prospect. Many prospects do not want to "open up" to a salesperson. Some salespeople are uncomfortable with this approach because they do not have the feeling of control over the situation that they have with a canned presentation. This is particularly true of new salespeople who have a few bad experiences with the method. They are reluctant to practice the technique until it is mastered. Eventually, a salesperson can learn to anticipate customers' reactions to the approach and learn to enjoy the challenge of interaction between buyer and seller.

TECHNOLOGY CAN HELP MAKE THE SALE   No matter what presentation mix or method salespeople use, they always should consider using technology. The latest technology can set a company's presentation apart from the rest, giving it a competitive edge. For example, Jim Lair, a senior sales consultant for Prism Solution Inc., decided to try using technology to save time and travel costs. By using software from PictureTalk Inc., a software company based in Pleasanton, California, he was able to make online sales presentations. The presentations ran on the company's Web site. Field salespeople logged on to the site from clients' offices, while Lair—teleconferenced in on the phone—controlled the presentations' slides and product demonstrations. During one week, Lair ran presentations for customers in Australia, Brazil, and England. Prism has been successful in cutting back on costs and time by using new technology and updating their means of communication.[19]

Overhead transparencies, 35mm slides, and black-and-white handouts are being replaced by dynamic software packages, interactive multimedia programs, active-matrix color screens, and multimedia projectors that bring computer images to life. Remember, it's often not what you say but how you say it that makes the sale.[20]

THE TRIAL CLOSE

The **trial close** involves checking the prospect's attitude toward the sales presentation. It may occur anytime during the selling process. However, it is especially useful (1) after making a strong selling point, (2) after overcoming an objection, or (3) once the presentation is complete (see Figure 11.2). It is used to check the buyer's "pulse" or mood to determine whether he or she is paying attention to the presentation and whether it is time to ask for a purchase.

"Some prospects are ready to buy early in the presentation, whereas others take longer. The reason a trial close is used centers on the psychological aspect of a prospect saying no when the salesperson attempts to close the sale. Once the prospect has said no, the salesperson may have difficulty moving from that position. So, to avoid this, salespeople may at any time use a trial close like one of these:

- How does that sound to you?
- What color do you prefer?
- If you bought this, where would you use it in your business?
- Are these features what you are looking for?

If the prospect responds favorably, the salesperson can move on to the close. However, if a negative response is received, the close can be postponed. The salesperson may need to completely start over with the presentation.[21]

OBJECTIONS ARE SALESPEOPLE'S FRIENDS

Theoretically, a salesperson's presentation should show the prospect that a need exists, that the product presented can best fill that need, and that further discussion should not be necessary. Very few presentations end that successfully, and very few prospects are that easily convinced. Usually, the prospect will raise some objections.

Experienced salespeople welcome objections. An **objection** is opposition or resistance to information or a request. It shows that the prospect is interested in the product and that if the objections can be answered to the satisfaction of the prospect, the sale will be made. If, on the other hand, the prospect simply sits quietly, making noncommittal sounds, and at the end of the presentation simply says, "That's nice. I'm not interested. Good-bye," the salesperson has no grounds for continuing, and the sale is lost.

Some salespeople and sales managers believe the art of selling does not begin until the objections are raised. This is when salespeople really begin to earn their money. Anyone can make a sale when no objections are raised. The ability to uncover and answer objections is a skill that should be mastered.

TYPES OF OBJECTIONS   Two types of objections occur: real or practical objections and hidden or psychological objections. *Real objections* are tangible, such as about a too-high price. If this is a real objection and the prospect says so, then the salesperson can show that the product is of high quality and worth the price or remove some optional features and reduce the price.

As long as the prospect clearly states the real objection to purchasing the product, the salesperson should be able to answer the objection and go into the close. However, prospects will not always be so agreeable and clearly state their objections. Rather, they will give some excuse about why they are not ready to make a purchase, thereby keeping their real objections hidden. Usually the prospect will not purchase the product until those *hidden objections* are somehow answered.

TECHNIQUES FOR MEETING QUESTIONS   Once the salesperson has uncovered all objections, he or she must answer them to the prospect's satisfaction. Naturally, different situations will require different ways to handle them. Here are a few methods that apply in many situations.

Postponing Objections   Often the prospect may skip ahead of the sales presentation. The salesperson then may want to postpone the objection until he or she has presented the background that would allow it to be met completely.

Prospect   "Your price is too high."

Salesperson   "In just a minute I'll show you this product is reasonably priced based on the savings you will receive compared with what you are presently doing."

Boomerang   One important selling skill to teach salespeople is how they can turn an objection into a benefit or a reason to buy. Take, for example, the wholesale drug salesperson who wants to sell a pharmacist a new type of container for prescription medicines. The salesperson hands the pharmacist a container.

Prospect: "They look nice, but I don't like them as well as my others. The tops seem hard to get off."

Salesperson: "Yes, they are hard to remove. We designed them so children couldn't get into the medicine. Isn't that a great safety measure?"

Asking Questions   Questioning the prospect is another selling skill salespeople can learn.

Prospect   "I do like this house, but it is not as nice as the one someone else showed us yesterday."

Salesperson: "Would you please tell me why?"

Real objections must be uncovered and properly dealt with in a straightforward manner. Objections can become a positive factor in the sales presentation if they allow the prospect to open up and participate in the dialogue.

The salesperson should not move to close the sale before handling sales resistance. However, if the objections appear to make the sale impossible, the salesperson has the option of not closing and waiting until another day or going ahead and asking for the business. Before closing or asking for the order, the salesperson may want to use another trial close.

THE CLOSE

All of the effort that has gone into the prospecting, preapproach, approach, and presentation has as its aim a successful close. **Closing** is the process of helping people make a beneficial decision. It is the part of the selling process that ultimately brings the sale to a conclusion. If all goes well, the conclusion will be positive; however, it can be negative.

DIFFICULTIES WITH CLOSING   The close can be difficult for some people. For numerous reasons, some salespeople fail to make a sale or even fail to attempt to close. First, a salesperson may not be confident in his or her ability to close. Perhaps numerous failures to make a sale have brought about this situation. Second, salespeople often determine on their own that the prospect does not need the quantity or type of merchandise or that the prospect simply should not buy. Finally, the person may be a poor salesperson. Quite often proper sales training and encouragement from management can greatly increase a person's selling ability.

CLOSING TECHNIQUES   A major key to making a sale is using effective closing methods. Different techniques work for different people. Here are several examples.

The Compliment   For this technique, the salesperson may compliment the prospect by saying something like "It is obvious you know a great deal about the grocery business. You have every square foot of your store making a good profit. Our products have the profit margin you want, and they sell like hotcakes, so you'll make an above-average profit. I suggest you buy one dozen mops and one dozen brooms for each of your 210 stores."

The Summary   Three or four benefits of interest to the prospect can be summarized in a positive manner so the prospect agrees; then the salesperson asks for the order. The salesperson emphasizes aspects in which the prospect has an interest.

Salesperson: "Mr. Stevenson, you say you like our fast delivery, profit margin, and credit policy. Is that right?" (Summary and trial close)

Prospect: "Yes, I do, Chuck."

Salesperson: "Then I suggest that you buy one dozen mops and one dozen brooms for each of your 210 stores."

Minor Decision   Agreement can be reached on minor, less important elements of the sale first. Commitment on the large dollar outlay is postponed until last. For example, an automobile salesperson would close on features such as color, interior, and accessories before closing on the final price.

Assumptive   The salesperson can assume the prospect will buy, making statements such as "I'll have this shipped to you tomorrow." If the customer has been called on for a long time, the salesperson can fill out the order form, hand it to the customer, and say, "This is what I'm going to send you." Many salespeople have earned the trust of their customers to such an extent that the salesperson orders for them. Here the assumptive technique is especially effective.

Salespeople should be trained to identify the common objections they will encounter and to develop closing approaches to overcome these objections. Salespeople must learn to adapt their presentation to each prospect and not to treat everyone the same—like a robot might do.

FOLLOW-UP AND SERVICE QUALITY ARE CRITICAL

Providing service to customers is critical to successfully managing a sales territory. Follow-up and service (the final step in the selling process as shown in Figure 11.2) create goodwill between a salesperson and the customer, which in the long run will increase sales faster than not providing such service. By contacting the customer after the sale to see that the maximum benefit is being derived from the purchase, a salesperson lays the foundation for a positive business relationship. Remember, it's easier to keep a customer than to find a new one.

RESEARCH REINFORCES CHAPTER'S SALES SUCCESS STRATEGIES

Although summarizing all of the sales success strategies a person should use may be difficult, one research report reinforces several of the key procedures—discussed in this chapter—to improve salespeople's performance. Xerox found that success involves learning and using each of the following skills:

1. Ask questions to gather information and uncover needs.
2. Recognize when a customer has a real need and how the benefits of the product or service can satisfy it.
3. Establish a balanced dialogue with customers.
4. Recognize and handle negative customer attitudes promptly and directly.
5. Use a benefit summary and an action plan requiring commitment when closing.

Training salespeople to develop these five selling skills plus others emphasized throughout the chapter and to combine them with their own natural ability and positive mental attitude will help them become successful, professional salespeople.

ADAPTING TO GLOBAL MARKETS

Personal selling involves verbal and nonverbal communication between seller and buyer. Unless a salesperson can communicate effectively in different cultural settings, sales will suffer. If a salesperson does not know that a Japanese "yes" often means "no" but that a Chinese "no" often means "yes," confusion will result. Perhaps more important than language are the silent languages of people from different cultures. They may think they are understanding one another when, in fact, they are misinterpreting one another. For example:

> *An American visits a Saudi official to convince him to expedite permits for equipment being brought into the country. The Saudi offers the American coffee, which he politely refuses (he has been drinking coffee all morning at the hotel while planning the visit). The American then sits down and crosses his legs, exposing the sole of his shoe; passes the documents to the Saudi with his left hand; inquires after the Saudi's wife; and emphasizes the urgency of getting the needed permits.*

In less than three minutes, the American unwittingly offended the Saudi five times. He refused his host's hospitality, showed disrespect, used an "unclean" hand, implied unintended familiarity, and displayed impatience with his host. The American had no intention of offending his host and probably was not aware of the rudeness of his behavior. The Saudi might forgive his American guest for being ignorant of local customs, but the forgiven salesperson is in a weakened position.

Knowing a customer in international sales means more than knowing the customer's product needs; it includes knowing the customer's culture. Here are five rules to teach salespeople for successful selling abroad:

1. Be prepared and do your homework. Learn about the host's culture, values, geography, artists, musicians, religion, and political structure. In short, do as complete a cultural analysis as possible to avoid mistakes.

MANAGEMENT IN ACTION: ETHICAL DILEMMA
NOW WHAT?*

Say you decided to do nothing and take the test. You waited the entire hour before turning it in, though it took only 15 minutes to complete. After rechecking each question several times, you know you have made a perfect score, which no one has ever done, so you intentionally miss one question.

As you leave the class the director of corporate training meets you in the hall and asks, "How did you do?" You reply, "It was a thorough test." She asks, "When you were working at the corporate sales training office, did you happen to help with the 'directing' module? I wanted to ask you yesterday but didn't get a chance."

WHAT DO YOU DO?
1. Say, "No, I really didn't have anything to do with that program," knowing that the director won't check—today she leaves on maternity leave, and it is rumored she is likely to stay home permanently with her new baby.
2. Say, "Yes, I did. Also, I should tell you that the test you gave me was exactly like the one I had in my files and used to study. I think that I should be given another test."
3. Say, "I did work with that program some." But mention nothing about the fact you have a copy of the test.

———————

*To answer, first read Chapter 10's ethical dilemma.

2. Slow down. Americans are slaves to the clock. Time is money to an American, but in many countries emphasis on time implies unfriendliness, arrogance, and untrustworthiness.
3. Develop relationships and trust before getting down to business. In many countries, business is not done until a feeling of trust has developed.
4. Learn the language and its nuances, or get a good interpreter. Too many ways exist to miscommunicate.
5. Respect the culture. Manners are important. As the guest, respect what your host considers important.

Anyone sent into another culture as a salesperson or company representative should receive training to develop the necessary cultural skills. In addition, the company should provide such employees specific schooling on the host country's customs, values, and social and political institutions. A variety of organizations offer intercultural trainings, and many companies do such training in-house as well.[22]

THE BOTTOM LINE

Sales training is now defined as part of a salesperson's overall educational experience. The knowledge taught during the salesperson's training period is absorbed and then used on the job as natural skills. Thus, training not only influences job behavior, but it also affects a person's total behavioral sphere. If the skills learned in training are successful on the job, the salesperson will have a positive attitude toward training; if they are unsuccessful, the salesperson will develop a negative attitude toward training.

Training can be divided into two categories: operational and behavioral. Operational information is used in the actual operation of the territory (for example, product information) while behavioral information involves the sales skills development area.

Companies are using and teaching technology more frequently than ever in the sales arena. Personal computers, for example, continue to offer more efficient ways to handle business. Although many people who are unfamiliar with PCs are apprehensive about using them, most software packages are easy to use and can make a sales professional's job much simpler. Computer technology also allows salespeople to provide better service to customers.

Sales skills development includes two key elements: persuasive communications and the selling process. A growing trend in persuasive communications is for salespeople to better understand themselves. To achieve this, companies can give their employees personality assessment tests. By better understanding their own personalities, salespeople can identify with and adjust to the different personalities of buyers.

The selling process is usually seen as a series of steps. Prospecting, the preapproach, the approach, and the presentation are the first four and involve the buyer's initial contact with the product. The trial close and meeting and overcoming objections are the next two steps; these help the salesperson learn the buyer's opinion of the product.

The close is the last step in the actual selling process. If all the previous work (prospecting, preapproach, approach, and presentation) results in a negative conclusion, several reasons may explain it. The salesperson may determine that the prospect does not need, or should not buy, the product. The salesperson may experience difficulty with closing, or the individual may be a poor salesperson. Four commonly used closing techniques are the compliment, summary, minor decision, and assumptive. Any of these are positive methods and should result in a sale. Once the sale is final, customer service becomes critical.

▪ KEY TERMS FOR SALES MANAGERS

Learning, 240	Leads, 254	Customer benefit approach, 257
Operational learning, 242	Referrals, 254	
Behavioral training, 242	Orphans, 254	Curiosity approach, 257
Sales skills development, 251	Customers, 254	Presentation, 258
	Preapproach, 255	Proof statements, 259
Sales process, 252	Approach, 257	AIDA approach, 260
Prospecting, 253	Introductory approach, 257	Trial close, 261
Qualified prospect, 253	Product approach, 257	Objection, 261
Prospect pool, 254		Closing, 263

▪ MANAGEMENT APPLICATION QUESTIONS

1. Why is it so important for salespeople's training to be viewed by salespeople as worthwhile and helpful for their job?
2. Why is behavioral information training not as readily acceptable and used by salespeople as operational information training?
3. The development of selling skills involves the two key elements of persuasive communications and the selling process. Discuss how these two work together to help increase sales.
4. A salesperson should ask four questions about any prospect, even before doing any recall planning. Discuss why a negative answer to each of these questions might lower the possibility of a sale.
5. The preapproach includes developing a customer benefit plan. What is a *customer benefit plan*, and why is it so important?
6. No one approach to a sales presentation is correct. The better approaches, however, do have three characteristics in common. What are they, and why is each important?
7. A large number of sales presentation techniques, such as the stimulus-response and need-satisfaction methods, exist. A good presentation for one product would not necessarily be a good presentation for another product. Choose two products that would need different sales presentations, and discuss why you would use different presentations.
8. What is the difference between a trial close and a close?
9. Why should a salesperson not be afraid of objections but indeed encourage them?
10. Discuss why a sale to a customer is not finished even when the signature is on the purchase order.

FURTHER EXPLORING THE SALES WORLD

Visit a sales trainer or sales manager, and determine the contents of his or her sales training programs for new and experienced salespeople. Ask if salespeople are trained to use a specific selling process. What steps in the selling process does this company follow?

SALES MANAGEMENT EXPERIENTIAL EXERCISE

DEVELOPING YOUR ROLE-PLAY SALES PRESENTATION

Instructions: You are ready to begin developing your own sales presentation. After selecting the product (good or service) you will sell, collect the necessary information. Then, on a separate sheet of paper, respond to the following:

1. State what you will sell.
2. Briefly describe the individual or organization to whom you will sell.
3. List several features of your product and each feature's main advantage and benefit. Refer back to page 256 for FAB definitions. These FABs would discuss your product, not your marketing plan or business proposition. You'll do that later.

FEATURE	ADVANTAGE	BENEFIT
a.		
b.		
c.		

4. Write down the name of the *approach* technique you will use in your presentation. After you review the various approach techniques in this chapter, select one technique to use in your role play based on what and to whom you are selling and your product's main benefits.
5. Now write out what you will actually say in your approach and include what the buyer will say. Relate your approach to your FABs so you will have a smooth transition into discussing your product.
6. Next write out what you will say in the first part of your presentation using your FABs. If appropriate, write the buyer's responses to each FAB.
7. Create your visual aids. Flip charts and notebooks are easy to develop, or you can place your visuals in a folder to pull out one at a time as you discuss them. Construct one or more proof statements.
8. Develop a demonstration of a product benefit. If possible, add dramatization. Remember, simply showing the product is not a demonstration. This may not be easy to do—especially if you're selling a service.
9. Practice using your visual aids. Hold the visual aids so your buyer can clearly see what is on each page. Rehearse your demonstration.
10. List several objections the buyer might give to your product.
11. Develop ways of handling each objection.
12. Each time you respond to each objection use a trial close to determine if you have overcome the objection or correctly answered the buyer's concern or question.
13. Select a closing technique such as the summary-of-benefits close. Write out your close.
14. Role-play this once or twice with someone to see if you are satisfied. If available, use a tape recorder to listen to your speed, voice inflections, phrases, and any unwanted mannerisms, such as frequently repeating "uh" or "I see."

CASE 11.1

HAWAIIAN NOVELTIES
Did You Make the Correct Choice?

You had high hopes for Carole, the person you selected for the key position of sales trainer for Hawaiian Novelties salespeople. But much to your dismay, she is perhaps the least dependable person on your entire sales staff. She has great credentials, including an M.B.A. with a major in marketing, and several years of productive field sales. She is articulate and intelligent and occasionally displays reasonably good powers of communication. What is she doing in an inside position? Why did she quit a productive career in field sales?

You believe the explanations: She could not be away from home or out of town for the length of time required to adequately cover a sales territory. She wants to stay close to salespeople, perhaps to vicariously share the excitement of "being out there, where the action is."

You quickly learn Carole is never on time. She never meets deadlines. She frequently pushes back the training program's starting date because of delays in getting training materials from the home office, because of unprepared instructors—so she says—or because she's unsure of what to include within the various training programs. Some of the training sessions are chaotic. Sales managers and salespeople have been complaining. The situation is getting out of hand. Some older salespeople are refusing to attend the training sessions.

What can be the matter? Carole puts in long hours. She takes few coffee breaks and never a long lunch. She is apparently diligent. She is entirely unlike most others in the office, rarely visiting or desk hopping, and frequently keeps her office door closed. Some of the work she produces is good.

QUESTIONS
1. If your assumptions are valid—if she truly is diligent and dedicated to her assigned tasks—just what is her problem?
2. Is something wrong with the way you are doing your managing job?
3. What will you do?

TASTER'S CLUB
Development of a Sales Presentation

Dick Shoemaker was getting very close to achieving his sales quota for the quarter, but he still had four weeks to go. He knew that if he could just get his major account, Best Value Markets, to increase its orders, he would have a very good shot at the top salesperson spot and win the sales contest his district was having.

Dick had just gotten a memo telling him that a 50-cent coupon was going to be running in the Sunday paper in two weeks. He knew that with the proper sales presentation and the coupon promotion to back it, he should be able to fill his quota next week with a sales call to Best Value. Dick sat down at his desk and started planning what he should do.

ACCOUNT INFORMATION
Best Value Markets is a large chain of stores (50 stores) that has an average weekly volume of $150,000 per store. It is the third-largest store chain in its market area and has an 18 percent market share. Last year was its best year with Dick's company brand, Taster's Club coffee. Sales were up 14 percent for Taster's Club overall, up 15 percent for ground coffee, and up 10 percent for instant coffee. The overall sales increase was double the overall volume increase of only 7 percent. Best Value sells an average of 114 cases of ground Taster's Club per week.

The average sales volume per square foot of space in the Best Value Markets is $6.00 per week. The overall profit margin that the chain operates with is 21 percent. The total store inventory turns over every three weeks. Best Value has used Taster's Club displays on previous occasions, and these have generated up to a 64 percent increase in volume, compared with the average volume.

Dick is a good friend of the coffee buyer, Fred Acosta, and of the merchandising manager, Doug Hendricks. Best Value has a new sales promoter, John Barringer, who reports directly to Doug Hendricks. John is the key decision maker on the monthly promotions made in the coffee area, as well as a number of other areas. Dick has been working with John, but he would not say they are friends at this point. John has recently transferred from the nonfoods area and does not have a great deal of grocery knowledge.

Best Value features the Taster's Club brand monthly with good ad space (food column inches) at competitive resale prices. Last year it ran 15 ground and 10 instant coffee features; however, it did not use any displays to back them up.

PRODUCT INFORMATION
With the memo Dick received telling him about the coupon was a description and a photo of a new display that Taster's Club had available, at no cost, for retailers. From the photo and description, Dick thought the quality of this display was the best he had seen in a long time. The display only takes up 2.4 square feet in a store, but it holds 12 cases of one-pound cans of Taster's Club. The company projects that this display should empty in one week.

Each case of Taster's Club contains 12 one-pound cans. These cases cost $43.44, but if the retailer pays in 30 days, $1.80 is deducted from the invoice. Most other items the retailers buy have to be paid for in 10 days to get any discount. The suggested retail price for each one-pound can is $3.99. If a retailer uses this pricing structure, each case of Taster's Club coffee should generate a 13 percent profit margin on sales, or $6.24 of profit per case.

Dick would really like to sell a feature and a display for each store in his sales call next week.

QUESTIONS
1. To whom should Dick make his presentation?
2. Develop a sales presentation outline showing the key facts about both the account and the product that would be useful for making the sale.

Source: This case was developed by Professor Charles M. Futrell and Tim Christiansen.

PART V
DIRECTING THE SALES TEAM

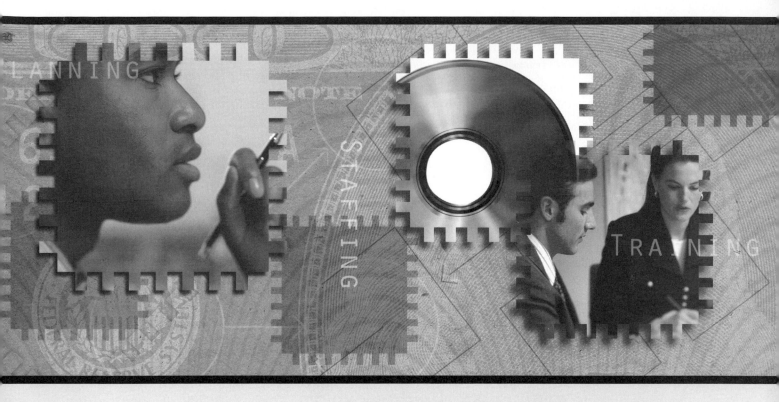

AN IMPORTANT part of the sales manager's job is motivating, rewarding, and leading sales personnel. After staffing, many experts feel this is the most important managerial function. Part V includes the following: Chapter 12, "Motivating Salespeople toward High Performance," Chapter 13, "Compensation for High Performance," and Chapter 14, "Leading the Sales Team."

CHAPTER 12
MOTIVATING SALESPEOPLE toward HIGH PERFORMANCE

CHAPTER OUTLINE

MOTIVATION AT EBBY HALLIDAY REALTORS©

UNDERSTAND WHAT MOTIVATION IS ALL ABOUT

DEVELOP A SALES CULTURE

KNOW SALESPEOPLE'S BASIC NEEDS

WHAT'S IN IT FOR ME?

A SALESPERSON'S BEHAVIORAL MODEL

GET TO KNOW THE PERSONAL SIDE OF SALESPERSONS!

MOTIVATIONAL COACHING IS NEEDED FOR HIGH-PERFORMANCE RESULTS

BE REALISTIC ABOUT MOTIVATING SALESPEOPLE!

LEARNING OBJECTIVES

An enthusiastic and motivated sales force is the best possible foundation for successful achievement of sales objectives. This chapter should help you understand:

■ That the definition of motivation includes the motivational mix and all of its various elements.

■ The powerful motivating influence of a high-performance sales culture.

■ The importance of realizing that salespeople have basic needs that, when met, are strongly motivating.

■ The model for a salesperson's behavior.

■ The benefit of knowing salespeople personally.

■ That not every member of a sales force can be motivated.

Staying at a private mansion in Mexico and spending an extravagant weekend in New York are just two of the incentives that motivate Chris Dillard, national account rep for Texas-based Monarch Business Systems. Though extra money is always nice, cash rewards are not the only prizes that inspire him to work hard. Monarch's "incentive trips" are one-of-a-kind experiences that have given him the opportunity to take part in adventures that he would have never been allowed otherwise. "For the money spent on some trips I've been on, you just can't beat it," says Dillard. "It makes me focused to go out and win."

Likewise, Sprint's small-business sales division in Kansas City, Missouri, finds it necessary to motivate employees in a unique way other than cash benefits. The office's spirit of playfulness and competition is what drives employees toward excellence. Nancy Diebler, small-business sales division manager, knows that it is necessary to keep a light atmosphere and offer recognition in order to keep employee turnover low and morale high.

When salespeople need a little inspiration the only thing they have to do is glance over to the "Happiness Is . . ." wall, where everybody placed a photo of whatever makes them come to work each day. The wall is adorned with pictures of their dogs, families, and anything else that motivates each individual. The managers also hang pictures of the top three salespeople where everyone can see them. When a rep turns on the computer in the morning, the first thing seen is a list of the top ten sellers from the day before. They also use other incentives such as movie tickets, casual days, trips, or trading jobs with a supervisor for the day. "In inside sales it's a stressful environment and a day can seem like a week," Diebler says. "It's essential to break it up with fun activities and feed [salespeoples'] competitive nature."

Many experts and salespeople agree that cash alone is not a top motivator, yet according to an Incentive Federation Survey, 63 percent of 968 respondents still rely on money rewards exclusively. Jim Kouzes, chairman of the Peters Group/Learning Systems in Palo Alto, California, and co-author of *Encouraging the Heart: A Leader's Guide to Rewarding and Recognizing Others,* says, "Rewards should be personal, special, and unique to the person who is receiving them. Goals themselves have no impact—people need feedback."

Managers who are constantly trying to entice their salespeople with boring beach photos or brochures of TV sets should consider following the example of Monarch and Sprint by pumping some creativity into their incentive programs. With today's competitive labor market, a good salesperson has many employment options, and if executives do not think of something motivating, then it is guaranteed that their competitors will.[1] ■

Motivation at Ebby Halliday Realtors©

Ebby Halliday oversees 25 offices in the Dallas/Fort Worth Metroplex with more than 1,000 independent contractors, sales associates, and 135 support employees for them. She describes here how she and her staff motivate sales personnel.

"Over the years, I've developed some guidelines for managing and motivating people that have worked well for us," Halliday says. "First is the proper selection of people who are motivated from within themselves. We also strive to create a vehicle composed of a positive climate and support program that will assist our people in becoming successful.

"We have not hesitated to do such things as to be the first with computers, the first with a nationwide referral service, and the first with first-class in-house training systems." Halliday continues: 'Our offices are state of the art both in technology and interior designs.

"We subscribe to the theory of excellence in performance and put service ahead of everything else. Service is number one. If quality service is given, everything else falls in line. We treat our people as associates, seldom referring to them as employees or even salespeople. We refer to them as associates because we are in a type of partnership relationship. Our associates respond to that type of treatment and that type of feeling toward them." She adds, "It helps our people feel as though they are part of a team. This is reinforced with our company slogan 'The Home Team.'"

Halliday also believes this helps to create a climate of success by giving them not only the tools to work with but also the atmosphere and history of success, as well as the dignity of having helped to create a successful company. "It creates a positive image within them of the company itself and our involvement within the community and industry. They can be proud of themselves and their organization.

"I don't believe you can truly motivate people," Halliday concluded. "I think they have to be self-motivated. They have to be in a work climate that has the facilities, the desire, and the know-how to incubate good people to bring out the qualities that are self-motivating."[2]

Motivating salespeople requires the skill of getting them to achieve their objectives while at the same time finding satisfaction from the job. This may sound easy, but in reality it is the greatest challenge any sales manager faces. In this chapter, a seven-part motivational program is presented. This program is based on concepts, research, and actual use with sales personnel. Your understanding of these components will help you to become a motivator and to design your customized motivational program for the individuals who will make up your sales team. The components of this motivational system follow:

- Understand what motivation is all about.
- Develop a high-performance sales culture.
- Know salespeople's basic needs.
- Realize that salespeople want to know what is in it for them.
- Get to know the personal side of salespersons.
- Always remember that motivational coaching is needed for high performance.
- Be realistic about motivating salespeople.

Understand What Motivation Is All About

To most people motivation suggests the level or amount of energy directed by someone toward a single task or goal. In business, motivation is sometimes used as a synonym for productivity. A salesperson is "motivated" if job performance exceeds the level expected by the firm. Can motivation be explained in these simple terms? Not really.

Motivation is a term originally derived from the Latin word *mover*, which means "to move" but has been expanded to include the various factors by which human

behavior is activated. In any discussion about the motivation of salespeople, the following four questions need to be considered:

1. What *arouses* salespeople's behavior?
2. What influences the *intensity* of the behavioral arousal?
3. What *directs* the person's behavior"
4. How is this behavior *maintained* over time?

As you can see, four words have been emphasized in these questions. These words allow us to develop our definition of motivation.

Motivation refers to the arousal, intensity, direction, and persistence of effort directed toward job tasks over a period of time. Thus, the sales manager seeks to influence salespeople to do certain activities, to work hard to reach activity goals, and to do so over the long haul, not just occasionally. The question arises, "What can sales managers use in their motivational program that will influence salespeople's behavior?" They can use a mix of motivational ingredients!

THE SALES MOTIVATIONAL MIX

Sales managers use various methods and techniques to motivate their salespeople. Yet all use, at least to some degree, seven broad classes of motivational ingredients to influence the arousal, intensity, direction, and persistence of people's behavior (Table 12.1). For this reason, these elements are referred to as the **motivational mix.** Although all ingredients within the mix should be part of the motivational program, management must determine the extent to which each element is emphasized for a particular sales force and individual.

Three of the seven motivational mix ingredients relate to rewards. Rewards fall into two major categories. First, individuals obtain rewards from their environment. These are called **extrinsic outcomes.** They include the basic compensation plan and special financial incentives. When salespeople perform at a given level, they can receive positive or negative outcomes from their manager, coworkers, the organization's reward system, or other sources.

A second type of outcome occurs purely from the performance of the task itself (e.g., feelings of accomplishment, personal worth, achievement). These are called **intrinsic outcomes.** In a sense, individuals give these rewards to themselves when they feel they are deserved. The environment cannot give them or directly take them away; it only can help make them possible.

1. Sales culture
   ■ Ceremonies and rites
   ■ Stories
   ■ Symbols
   ■ Language
2. Basic compensation
   ■ Salary
   ■ Commissions
   ■ Fringe benefits
3. Special financial incentives
   ■ Bonuses
   ■ Contests
   ■ Trips
4. Nonfinancial rewards
   ■ Opportunity for promotion
	■ Challenging work assignments
	   ■ Recognition
	5. Sales training
	   ■ Initial
	   ■ Ongoing
	   ■ Sales meetings
	6. Leadership
	   ■ Style
	   ■ Personal contacts
	7. Performance evaluation
	   ■ Method
	   ■ Performance
	   ■ Activity
	   ■ Publicity

TABLE 12.1

THE SEVEN COMPONENTS OF THE SALES MOTIVATIONAL MIX AND EXAMPLES OF EACH MOTIVATIONAL METHOD

As shown in Table 12.1, a wide range of motivational methods can be used to improve salespeople's productivity. Each of these is discussed in chapters you have read or will read. The purpose of this chapter is to provide you with the background information on how these motivational-mix items influence the individual salesperson. To have a successful motivational program, sales managers need to create the proper sales culture.

DEVELOP A SALES CULTURE

Sales culture refers to a set of key values, ideas, beliefs, attitudes, customs, and other capabilities and habits shared or acquired as a member of the sales group. Culture within the sales group has a major influence on salespeople's behavior.

IMPLEMENTATION OF A SALES CULTURE

The sales culture is an important tool for strategy implementation because management can directly influence culture through activities and symbols. Techniques managers use to convey the appropriate values and beliefs are ceremonies and rites, stories, symbols, and language.

CEREMONIES AND RITES   **Ceremonies and rites** are the elaborate, planned activities that make up a special event and often are conducted for the benefit of an audience. Managers can hold ceremonies and rites to provide dramatic examples of what the company values. Ceremonies are special occasions, such as a national sales meeting, that reinforce specific values, create bonds among people for sharing an important understanding, and celebrate heroes and heroines who do an outstanding job.

Like the awarding of medals at the Olympics, ceremonies and rites honor the "winners." This reinforces the main cultural value of any sales force: "reward for performance." The most effective places to implement this method are the monthly and yearly (national) sales meetings. This method results in the rapid creation of sales success stories that help fuel the motivational machine. Sales newsletters and training sessions also publicize sales success, further helping to spread stories about the company's sales champions.

STORIES   **Stories** are narratives based on true events that are frequently shared among salespeople and told to new sales reps to inform them about the organization. Some stories are considered legends because the events are historic and may have been embellished with fictional details.

Other stories are myths that are consistent with the organization's values and beliefs but that are not supported by facts. Stories are important because they keep alive the primary values of the organization and provide a shared understanding among all salespeople.

SYMBOLS   A **symbol** is one thing that represents another thing. In a sense, ceremonies, stories, slogans, and rites are symbols. They symbolize the organization's deeply held values. Another important symbol is a physical artifact of the organization (e.g., universities give diplomas; organizations give sales achievement awards).

Physical symbols are powerful because they focus attention on a specific item. At Mary Kay Cosmetics, Mary Kay gives Cadillacs to each year's top salespeople. The Cadillac is painted a distinctive shade, called "Mary Kay pink," to symbolize a successful sales year. The value of physical symbols is that they communicate important cultural values. If the physical symbols are consistent with the ceremonies, stories, values, and slogans, they are powerful facilitators of culture.

CULTURE	IMPLEMENTING CULTURE
Shared Values	**Shared Ceremonies**
■ Reward for performance	■ Annual awards for meritorius customer service
■ Customer service at any cost	
■ Employees are part of family	■ Monthly meetings to acknowledge people who attain 100% of sales targets
■ Attain sales targets	
Shared Beliefs	**Shared Stories**
■ Customer orientation	■ Sales managers who make salespeople successful; help with personal problems
■ We like this company	
■ We are a team	■ Heroic efforts to please customers by legendary salespeople
■ The company cares about us	**Shared Symbols and Slogans**
■ Quality work life	■ "Build bridges" to be in touch with customers.
■ We are professionals	
	■ "We don't stand on rank" (equality of family)
	■ Open offices for easy communication
	■ Special plaques for customer service and sales leaders

LANGUAGE   Many companies use a specific saying, slogan, metaphor, or other language form to convey special meaning to employees. **Slogans** can be readily picked up and repeated by company employees and customers.

Slogans are effective ways of communicating culture because chief executives can use them in a variety of public statements. Slogans enable the chief executive's philosophy to be disseminated widely. "IBM means service," "The eleventh commandment is 'never kill a new product idea'" (3M), and "Everybody at Northrop is in marketing" illustrate slogans used in organizations. They symbolize what the company stands for, both for employees and for people outside the organization.

Table 12.2 illustrates the relationship between culture and the means of communicating culture to the sales force. On the left side of the table, specific cultural values and beliefs are identified; examples of implementing culture using ceremonies, stories, symbols, and slogans are on the right. Managers and salespeople thus share a common belief system that reinforces organizational and sales strategy. Culture directly influences sales personnel's basic needs.

KNOW SALESPEOPLE'S BASIC NEEDS

Sales managers should realize that salespeople, like all people, are always trying to satisfy their inner drives and needs. That is why they took and keep the job. That is why they do what they do in their daily activities.

Sales managers can use the seven ingredients of the motivational mix to positively stimulate salespeople's inner drives and needs. It is hoped that the proper stimuli will positively influence their behavior, resulting in the attainment of job goals. Sales managers should regularly assess whether the company is successfully attending to these basic needs.

WHAT'S IN IT FOR ME?

Another important component of the motivational mix is rewards—pay, incentive, and nonfinancial rewards. Managers must realize that people want to know what is in the job for themselves. A major theory used to explain salespeople's work behavior is expectancy theory. It is a "process" theory (i.e., it seeks to explain why people choose a particular behavior), derived from the works of Tolman, Levin, Vroom, McClelland, and Atkinson.[3] **Expectancy theory** is based on the assumption that salespeople have expectancies about what they should receive from their employer as a result of their work efforts.

This theory views people as intelligent, rational individuals who make conscious decisions about their present and future behavior. People are not seen as inherently motivated or unmotivated. Rather, people's motivational levels are viewed as a function of their work environment: As long as that work environment is consistent with their goals and needs, they are motivated.

WHAT IS THE PROBABILITY OF SUCCESS?

Beliefs about the link between trying to perform a behavior and actually doing it well refer to a persons' expectancy about the future. **Expectancy,** then, is the salesperson's estimate of the probability that expending a given amount of effort on a task will lead to an improved level of performance on some dimension.

As shown in Figure 12.1, the first important question salespeople ask themselves is a variation of "If I work harder, what is the probability that my sales performance will improve?" Should the answer be "high," they are more likely to increase their job effort. This especially would be true if the answer to the next question is "highly."

As a student, you probably ask yourself a question similar to the first one: "If I study harder, what is the probability that my learning and grades will improve?" Figure 12.1 also can be applied to such a situation.

WILL I BE REWARDED FOR SUCCESS?

In expectancy theory, the salesperson's estimate of the probability that achieving an improved level of performance dimension will lead to increased attainment of a particular reward or outcome may be defined as **instrumentality.** Subsequently, the second question salespeople ask themselves might be "Will I be rewarded if my performance increases?" Take, for example, the salesperson on a straight salary. The salesperson might ask, "If I work four hours extra each day and my sales reach 130 percent of my quota, what is the probability I will get added pay?" In the short run, the probability of getting increased pay is zero. However, the yearly base-salary level might be increased. If the salesperson is on a straight commission, the probability of added pay, or instrumentality, is very high—up to 100 percent.

FIGURE 12.1   FOUR QUESTIONS SALESPEOPLE ASK TO DETERMINE HOW MUCH EFFORT THEY WILL DEVOTE TO THEIR JOBS

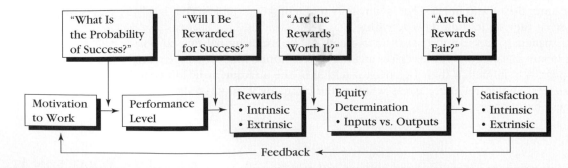

Again, you might ask yourself a question such as "If I increase the length of my studying for this course, will I learn more and receive a high grade?" Is your answer yes or no? What's the chance of your answer being correct? Your answer directly influences your effort in this course. The same is true for sales personnel.

ARE THE REWARDS WORTH IT?

Valence for rewards refers to the value the salesperson places on the reward. Therefore, the third important question salespeople ask themselves is "Are the rewards worth it?" For example, the salesperson might ask, "If I work 12 hours a day instead of 8 and win this sales contest, would it be beneficial to me?" If the prize is a pen and pencil set with the salesperson's name engraved on it, he or she may decide it is not worth the effort. However, if the contest prize is an all-expense paid trip to Paris for two, and the salesperson really wants to go, he or she may decide it is worth working the extra four hours a day. Valances can be positive (up to 1.0 in the theory's mathematical formulation) or negative (down to -1.0). For example, Chris Theodoras, a salesman for DoubleClick, received a positive valance for all of his hard work. He is now a proud owner of a blue BMW Z3, compliments of executives at DoubleClick. He received this reward for being the Internet advertising brokerage firm's top salesperson for the previous year.[4]

Once more, you might ask similar questions about this course. For example, some students in the class know that if they work longer hours and apply themselves, they will get better grades. Therefore, they answer yes to the first two questions. However, grades are not important to some students, so they say no to the question "Are the rewards worth it?" They only want to pass the course. The students who say no have low motivational levels, whereas the yes students have high levels of motivation.

Some salespeople have the same attitude. What is being offered as a "reward" may not be important, so they do only enough to keep their jobs. Often these people are not motivated by money. This is why the motivational mix must have a "nonfinancial" ingredient to help people develop intrinsic satisfaction.

The intrinsic satisfaction most people give themselves may be reward enough for doing a good job. Self-recognition of high performance and personally knowing you have done an above-average job can be a very rewarding experience. Intrinsic rewards can lead to some salespeople saying yes to each of these first three questions, resulting in high motivational levels. To maximize salespeople's motivational level, managers must try to ensure a yes answer for each question.

EXPECTANCY EXAMPLE   The following formula expresses expectancy theory:

$$\text{Motivation} = \text{Expectancy} \times \text{Instrumentality} \times \text{Valence}$$

Here is an example of applying the expectancy theory formula to a salesperson's motivation.

E (Expectancy) = A salesperson strongly believes that an increased number of calls per week will generate higher sales. This person would have a high effort–performance expectancy, such as a 95 percent chance of this occurring. *(Effort)*

I (Instrumentality) = If this same person also believes that such a sales increase will result in winning a sales contest, the person has a high performance–outcome expectancy. Assume a 99 percent chance of this outcome happening. *(Result)*

V (Valence) = If winning this contest is extremely important, a prize worth .90, for example, on a scale of 1.00, then the person is highly motivated. However, if the contest prize has little value for the salesperson, say .20, then the motivational force would be much lower. *(Value)*

As shown in Table 12.3, if any one of the three factors—expectancy, instrumentality, or valence—are low, a person's motivational level may drop dramatically. Thus, all three motivational components must be high for high motivational levels to exist. It's important to understand that expectancy theory helps explain a salesperson's motivation, not performance. A salesperson, for example, could work hard but not make sales quota, or vice versa. In a like manner, you could not study hard for your next test in this course, but you could make a high grade, or vice versa.

MANAGERIAL IMPLICATIONS OF EXPECTANCY THEORY   Expectancy theory is complex, but it helps sales managers zero in on key leverage points for influencing motivation. Three implications are crucial for managers:

1. *Increase expectancies.* Provide a work environment that facilitates the best performance, and set realistically attainable performance goals. Provide training, support, and encouragement so salespeople are confident they can perform at the levels expected of them. Charismatic leaders excel at boosting their followers' confidence.
2. *Make performance instrumental toward positive outcomes.* Make sure good performance is followed by personal recognition and praise, favorable performance reviews, pay increases, and other positive results. Also, make sure that working hard and doing tasks well will have as few negative results as possible. Finally, ensure that poor performance has fewer positive and more negative outcomes than good performance.
3. *Identify positively valent outcomes.* Understand what salespeople want to get out of their work. Think about what their jobs provide them and what is not, but could be, provided. Consider how people may differ in the valences they assign to outcomes. Know the need theories of motivation and their implications for identifying important outcomes.

As people realize the outcomes or consequences of their actions, they develop beliefs about how just or fair those outcomes are. Basically, they assess how fairly the organization treats them.

ARE THE REWARDS FAIR?

Once the salesperson has been rewarded for performance, he or she raises the question of whether the rewards are fair. According to the **equity theory,** a salesperson develops a ratio of job "inputs" to "outcomes" or what is received. This ratio is compared with the salesperson's perceptions of the ratios of other salespeople in the sales district, the region, and outside the organization. This comparison can be expressed as follows:

$$\text{My Own } \frac{\text{Outcomes}}{\text{Inputs}} \text{ versus Others' } \frac{\text{Outcomes}}{\text{Inputs}}$$

Inequity exists when the individual perceives that the ratio is comparatively inferior. A salesperson may develop an equity ratio on the basis of how hard one works

TABLE 12.3

SALESPERSON *A* VALUES THE CONTEST AND HAS A HIGH MOTIVATIONAL LEVEL; SALESPERSON *B* WILL NOT WORK HARD

SALESPERSON	EXPECTANCY		INSTRUMENTALITY		VALENCE		MOTIVATIONAL LEVEL
Salesperson *A*	.95	×	.99	×	.90	=	.846
Salesperson *B*	.95	×	.99	×	.20	=	.188

(input) versus the salary received (outcome) and compare this equity ratio with the ratios of other salespeople in the district. The salesperson would be more satisfied if his or her own ratio of inputs to outcomes is perceived to be the same as those of other salespeople.

If inequity is perceived, the salesperson may be motivated to restore equity using one of four methods.

- First, the salesperson may increase or decrease the level of input that may, in turn, influence outcomes. In other words, the salesperson may see other people working harder and receiving larger raises, so he or she works harder.
- Second, the salesperson could distort the facts by convincing himself or herself that equity really does exist even though it may not.
- Third, the salesperson could choose another salesperson with whom to compare the ratio of outcomes to inputs.
- Fourth, the salesperson could influence other salespeople to decrease the amount of effort they are putting into their job. For example, the salesperson might ask the supersalesperson or regular "quota buster" to slow down.

Equity theory contends that the salesperson would leave the job if he or she could not achieve an equitable relationship. Thus, the salesperson chooses a work/salary level that is equitable in comparison to that of some other salesperson.

Sales managers should be aware of equity theory because it points to a real need for management to evaluate salespeople's performance effectively and to reward them accordingly. The salesperson is concerned not only with the level of salary received but also with how that relates to fellow salespeople's salaries, including those of salespeople outside the company who work in similar situations.

HOW TO FACILITATE EQUITY

As shown in Figure 12.1, we can conceptualize the sequences of events leading from an individual's motivation to work to that person's determination of a level of intrinsic and extrinsic satisfaction about the various facets of a job. Frequently, the salesperson must experience several performance-evaluation cycles with the sales manager before knowing the answer to each of the four questions. Thus a feedback loop exists; if the salesperson first decides to work hard and later finds one of these following four situations, the individual will tend to reduce the level of effort.

1. Sales performance did not increase.
2. No important rewards were given for meeting quota.
3. The rewards given for meeting quota were not worth the extra work.
4. Treatment was not fair because one person's rewards were the same as another's who worked harder.

You may wonder about the discussion thus far and say to yourself, "Is this really true?" Yet if you look at your daily lives, you will often see examples of how various factors influence your behavior. For example, when this author's daughter (Amy) was 13 and his son (Greg) was 11 years old, their mother baked them some chocolate chip cookies. Each was given six cookies on a plate. Greg looked at Amy's plate and said, "That's not fair. Amy's cookies have more chocolate chips than mine." Greg's reaction is a good example of equity theory in practice. Life is not always fair, yet we all want it to be when it comes to how people treat us.

As noted earlier, motivating salespeople is not always easy; people are self-motivated and behave in their own self-interest. However, this behavior can be influenced by the sales management practices of their company and boss. Thus, sales managers need to be aware of the numerous factors that influence their salespeople's behavior.

JOB SATISFACTION AND WORK ATTITUDES   **Job satisfaction** refers to feelings toward the job. If people feel fairly treated from the outcomes they receive, they will be satisfied. A satisfied salesperson is not necessarily more productive than a dissatisfied one; sometimes people are happy with their jobs because they don't have to work hard. However, job dissatisfaction, aggregated across many individuals, creates a sales force that is more likely to exhibit (1) higher turnover; (2) higher absenteeism; (3) lower corporate citizenship; (4) more grievances and lawsuits; (5) stealing, sabotage, and vandalism; and (6) poorer mental and physical health (which can mean higher job stress, higher insurance costs, and more lawsuits). All of these consequences of dissatisfaction, either directly or indirectly, are costly to organizations.

Quality of Work Life (QWL) programs create a workplace environment that can enhance sales personnel's well-being and satisfaction. The general goal of QWL programs is to satisfy the full range of people's needs. QWL has eight categories:

1. Adequate and fair compensation.
2. A safe and healthy environment.
3. Jobs that develop human capacities.
4. A chance for personal growth and security.
5. A social environment that fosters personal identity, freedom from prejudice, a sense of community, and upward mobility.
6. Constitutionalism, or the rights of personal privacy, dissent, and due process.
7. A work role that minimizes infringement on personal leisure and family needs.
8. Socially responsible organizational actions (discussed in Chapter 2).

Organizations differ drastically in their attention to QWL. Critics claim QWL programs don't necessarily make employees work harder if the company does not tie rewards directly to individual performance. Advocates of QWL claim that it improves organizational effectiveness and productivity. The term **productivity** as applied by QWL advocates means much more than each person's quantity of work output. It also includes levels of turnover, absenteeism, accidents, theft, sabotage, creativity, innovation, and especially the *quality* of work.

VOLUNTARY TURNOVER   **Turnover** refers to someone leaving their present job. Promotions, transfers, and leaving the firm are examples of turnover. Exit turnover is when someone leaves the organization either voluntarily or involuntarily. Turnover is a consequence of unmet expectations and unfulfilled needs. How do sales managers know if the needs of their salespeople are being met? One way to find out is to ask them through anonymous mail surveys. These surveys can find out what salespeople have to say about all of the sales management program components—especially the seven motivational mix ingredients—and then adjustments can be made in the program.

Another way is to carefully examine turnover statistics by segmenting terminations according to the scheme shown in Figure 12.2. Nonvoluntary turnover occurs from firings or the manager and salesperson mutually agreeing that it is best for the person to leave. Of interest in these cases is why these people were hired.

Sales managers should mainly study the voluntary turnover—people who quit on their own. Again, managers should segment terminations into "desirable" to leave (these are the low performers) and "undesirable" to leave (these are the high performers). Next, they should carefully determine which "undesirable" turnovers were "controllable" and which were "uncontrollable." Some terminations are due to events such as a spouse being transferred and the employee having to quit or to a female salesperson becoming pregnant and not wanting to return to work. The company has no control over this type of turnover.

Controllable terminations are the ones where people quit because of something connected to the job. Typically, the reasons are associated with one or more

FIGURE 12.2

CLASSIFICATION OF TURNOVER

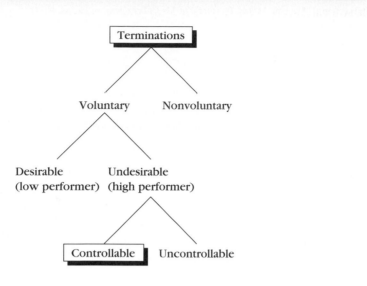

components of the motivational mix. High performers often leave because their expectations are not met concerning pay and promotional opportunities. Typically, they have mastered their present job and seek a more challenging job assignment. Pay is often secondary because they expect higher salaries will come with each promotion.

When an employee's expectations are not met, inequities are often perceived, and dissatisfaction with one or more facets of the job occurs. According to a survey on voluntary turnover by the HayGroup, dissatisfaction with an immediate manager is the leading reason (34 percent) a salesperson leaves a company. The other reasons were as follows: compensation (19 percent), career opportunity (12 percent), and quality of work life (10 percent).[5] The salesperson then begins to search for another job. If a better job is found, the salesperson quits, and the company has lost one of its most valuable resources—a high-performing salesperson.

A SALESPERSON'S BEHAVIORAL MODEL

We have seen that numerous factors influence salespeople's motivation. In this section elements of the previous discussion of motivation are brought together in a simplified model of a salesperson's behavior as it relates to motivation, performance, rewards, and satisfaction. This model is shown schematically in Figure 12.3.

The factors listed in the model may be defined as follows:

1. *Environmental factors* include such items as the economy and competition.
2. *Organizational factors* include motivational-mix factors such as the sales culture, compensation practices, nonfinancial rewards, training, leadership, and evaluation procedures.
3. *Personal factors* include intelligence, energy, ego strength, ego drive, empathy, individual needs, skill level, and aptitude.
4. *Motivation to work* is the effort the salesperson applies to the job. It includes the intensity, direction, and persistence of effort directed toward achieving sales goals. It is different from actual performance. The salesperson may work extremely hard, be highly motivated, and still not be able to meet the job's performance requirements. Here the salesperson

FIGURE 12.3   A SALESPERSON'S BEHAVIORAL MODEL HELPS ILLUSTRATE MOTIVATIONAL PROCESS

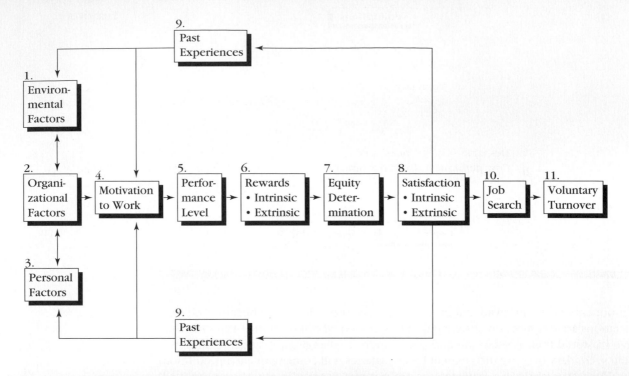

asks the three questions: (1) "If I work harder, what is the probability my performance will improve?"; (2) "Will I be rewarded if my performance increases?"; and (3) "Are the rewards worth it?"

5. *Performance level* is the salesperson's actual accomplishments such as increased sales by 10 percent or the number of new accounts opened. Based on performance, rewards are received and experienced by the individual.

6. *Rewards* are separated into intrinsic and extrinsic categories. Performance can lead to either or both types of rewards. This part of the model relates to actual rewards the individual receives. The organization gives extrinsic rewards. The individual experiences his or her own intrinsic rewards.

7. *Equity determination* is calculated by the salesperson by comparing inputs and outcomes to those of peers. At this point the salesperson asks, "Was I treated fairly?"

8. *Satisfaction,* both intrinsic and extrinsic, is derived from a comparison of what is considered a perceived equitable reward with the actual reward. If perceived equitable rewards exceed the actual reward, the salesperson is dissatisfied. However, if the reward is greater than the perceived equitable reward, the salesperson is satisfied. The larger the difference between what is expected and what is received, the greater the degree of satisfaction or dissatisfaction.

9. *Past experiences* serve to reinforce the link between behavior and its consequences. The salesperson would be motivated to expend a greater amount of work effort if previous effort is felt to have resulted in valued rewards. If, however, the salesperson sees work at a low level of performance leading to the achievement of these same valued rewards, the salesperson often will tend to lower the amount of effort.

10. With dissatisfaction often comes the *job search* for a better work environment. Often the person psychologically begins to withdraw from work, and motivational levels quickly decline.
11. *Voluntary turnover* results from finding another job that is expected to better fulfill the person's needs.

THE DYNAMICS OF THE MODEL

Here is how the model's variables relate to one another. Environmental, organizational, and personal factors, plus past experiences, influence the salesperson's decision as to the amount of effort he or she will apply to the job. The salesperson's motivation to work can be aroused, intensified, directed, and encouraged. High levels of motivation usually lead to relatively high performance levels. Motivation is viewed as the force working on an individual to expend effort. Motivation leads to the person's observed level of effort.

Effort alone, however, is not enough. Performance results from a combination of the effort that an individual puts forth and the level of that individual's ability. Ability in turn reflects the individuals' skills, training, aptitude, and talents. Effort thus combines with ability to produce a given level of sales performance. This is why performance is a function (*f*) of an individual's ability and motivation, or

$$\text{Sales Performance} = f\,(\text{Ability} \times \text{Motivation})$$

Performance then determines the rewards received. Once rewarded, the salesperson determines whether rewards are fair based on inputs into the job relative to those of other salespeople. This affects the salesperson's satisfaction with the various job facets. The "past experiences" feedback loop in the model illustrates the fact that these events are a continuous process. Satisfaction feeds back to the salesperson's motivation to work and environmental, organizational, and personal variables. The salesperson's behavioral process then begins again—reinforced by past experiences.

The model suggests that satisfaction is best thought of as a result of behavioral performance rather than as a cause of it. Strictly speaking, satisfaction does influence motivation in some ways. For instance, when satisfaction is perceived to come about as a result of behavior, satisfaction can increase motivation because it strengthens a salesperson's belief about the consequences of behavior. Also, it can lead to a decrease in the importance of certain rewards and, as a result, decrease the motivation for performances that are seen to lead to whatever rewards become less important.

As this performance versus reward process occurs time after time, the actual events serve to provide information that influences an individual's perceptions (particularly expectancies) and thus influences future motivation. This is shown in the model by the line connecting the performance outcome (satisfaction) with motivation. If expectancies are not met, the person changes jobs.

GET TO KNOW THE PERSONAL SIDE OF SALESPERSONS!

The first parts of the motivational program described in this chapter involve understanding the basic concepts involved in motivating people. Sales managers need to apply these concepts at the individual level. To do this they need to get to know the real person. This is the fifth component of the motivational program.

In today's sales force, the individual salesperson is important. One person can make a difference to the district's success. Thus, a salesperson is not simply a unit of work but a precious human being with vast potential. Managing the people of today means not only caring about people but also dealing with them at a deeply human level. That is not always a comforting experience for many of us.

A person's thoughts about life, work, friends, the world, oneself, and so forth are the nucleus of what motivates a person; these thoughts are influenced and altered by daily learning experiences. This thinking motivates behavior either positively or negatively. The salesperson reacts to the direction, training, guidance, and compensation put forth by sales management. The sales manager's job is to develop an awareness of how each salesperson views things. Then and only then does a manager have a chance to influence the long-term behavior of salespeople.

Understand the Salesperson's Motivational Behavior

All salespeople are different. Yet they have similarities that can help with understanding the individual and designing a highly personalized motivational plan of action.

Sales managers thinking about their salespeople might draw an analogy to the iceberg; One-tenth is above water. That one-tenth is the personality of the individual observed on and off the job. The other nine-tenths, not seen, are the individual's motives that are hidden and difficult to bring to the surface and out in the open where they can be dealt with.

Match People's Motives with Incentives They Value

Incentives are aspects of the environment that appeal to the salesperson's motives and have enough worth to motivate purposeful behavior to obtain them. Sales executives have the challenge of producing an incentive package that meets individual and group motives and yet remains within the constraints of company policy and costs. Policy and costs play a major role in what can and cannot be done with the incentive package.

Before structuring an incentive package, sales managers must recognize the two common categories of incentives. Incentives that motivate people to do their best are *high motivators*. Incentives that motivate little or not at all or, if incentives are absent, that demotivate are *low motivators*.

EXAMPLES OF HIGH MOTIVATORS

- Rewards for successes
- Recognition for achievement
- Job advancement
- Freedom to manage oneself
- Training and sales meetings
- Leadership
- Performance evaluation
- Incentive compensation plans

EXAMPLES OF LOW MOTIVATORS

- Company policy and procedures
- Fringe benefits
- Retirement programs
- More supervision

Low-motivator incentives prevent dissatisfaction; high-motivator incentives produce positive attitudes and the desire and motivation to get off dead center and win the rewards being offered. The value of particular incentives varies among salespeople. What one salesperson will strive for may not motivate action from another salesperson. The sales manager would do well to explore different aspects of incentives for each salesperson on the sales team. Here are several things to consider:

- Some salespeople like material incentives (money, car, office, bonuses) versus nonmaterial incentives (title, compliments, more authority, newspaper mention).
- The attraction to short-range incentives (special assignment, sales contest, three-month sales quota) versus long-range incentives (retirement, stock option plan, one-year sales goals) varies from person to person.
- Positive incentives (advancement, job enrichment, bonuses, larger territory, bigger accounts) in most instances motivate more successfully than negative incentives (demotion, reduction in salary, reprimands, threats).

The sales manager has to provide such a mixed bag of incentives that every salesperson will find in it something that satisfies his or her motives and therefore will be willing to put forth the effort to achieve those incentives that have personal appeal. Incentives, like motives, are highly personalized, and a group/community approach to the incentive package may produce little or no results.

EVERYONE VALUES MONEY   Throughout this chapter and the book, we discuss many factors that influence people's behavior. If asked what is the single largest factor that influences behavior, most people will say it's some type of extrinsic reward—particularly money.

"Certainly both intrinsic and extrinsic rewards are important," Ebby Halliday says. "Yet I feel the money people make as a result of the service they provide is the number one reward. Of course they also love the recognition of their successes.

"We have many types of formal recognition ceremonies" she explains, "such as our quarterly 'Breakfast of Champions' at which people in each office are recognized for their successes in numerous categories. These quarterly ceremonies allow us to recognize more people, especially those who might not be recognized at our annual awards ceremonies.

"At our annual awards program, people are called up in front of their peers as a band plays. The spotlight is on them. We present them with inscribed awards that they can proudly display.

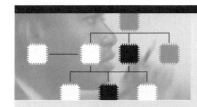

MANAGING THE SALES TEAM
HOW TO MOTIVATE YOURSELF AND OTHERS!

Here are ten factors that motivate this author and most people. See if any of these factors can help you. Add to the list.

1. *Enthusiasm encourages excitement.* We all love to be around people who truly enjoy what they do. Enthusiasm is a "sign of belief" in ourselves and what we are doing. People sense this in us. Enthusiasm is contagious. Spread it around!

2. *Self-esteem builds self-worth.* We need to appreciate that. Each of us is a miracle of life, and we are indeed something very special in the world. By respecting others, you build self-esteem and self-worth.

3. *Be positive.* We become what we think about most. So always be positive by replacing the negatives with positives. When asked how you're doing, always say "Great!" no matter how things are going for you.

4. *Setting and achieving goals.* Goals give us direction. Write out a "Want List" of everything you want to accomplish and assign a definite due date. Refer to the top ones each day. Continually keep working on meeting these goals.

5. *Dream big dreams.* Dreams are our direction. They move us to act and achieve. Dream about what you want to be and live your dreams.

6. *Accept responsibility.* Live by the saying "If it's going to be, it's up to me." We achieve in life when we are willing to accept total and unconditional responsibility for our own success or failure.

7. *Invest in yourself.* Invest time, money, and energy in yourself. Exercise routinely, eat correctly, live alcohol- and drug-free, read self-help and positive materials, and use positive cassette tapes, videos, music, and movies. Get to know yourself. Have time for yourself. Get high on life!

8. *Avoid comfort zones.* Almost everyone gets into comfort zones. Some people stay in them. To get out, learn something new each day, and immediately set a new goal after achieving one.

9. *The power of choice.* Choose to make each day of your life a good, productive one. Do something each day to accomplish your goals no matter how little. Anything is better than nothing. Always strive to give your best given the time, talent, and resources you have to work with.

10. *Have more fun.* We all take ourselves too seriously most of the time. Lighten up! Laugh at your mistakes. Learn from them. It's impossible to cry when we're laughing. Humor has a positive influence. If you have to worry, worry about what you can control, not what you can't control.

"Our compensation program incorporates a plateau system; the higher the salespeople's productivity, the higher the plateau, and thus, the higher their percentage on their overall commission rate," Halliday says. "If they reach a certain plateau at the end of the calendar year, they don't go back to zero again; they start on a certain plateau level. This is the best incentive of all—our very generous commission rate and incentive schedule."[6]

Whether they are selling real estate, toothpaste, copiers, computers, financial services, or breakfast cereals, people work primarily for money and the standard of living that income provides for them and their families. As you will see in the next chapter, money has various uses and meanings for companies and people. For example, suppose your company recognizes your higher performance by giving you a better raise than another salesperson. This tends to give you a good feeling about yourself (intrinsic rewards). Thus, the levels of rewards bestowed on a salesperson have a powerful influence on behavior.

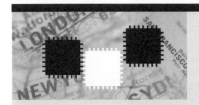

SELLING AND MANAGING GLOBALLY
FRENCH VERSUS AMERICAN SALESPEOPLE

Gerhard Gschwandtner, editor of *Personal Selling Power (PSP)* magazine, interviewed Jean-Pierre Tricard, a French sales trainer. The following excerpts from this interview discuss three important areas of a salesperson's job:

1. Differences between French and American salespeople

    PSP: How do you see the differences between French salespeople and American salespeople?

    Jean-Pierre Tricard: As you know, there are significant cultural differences between our two countries. For example, in our culture, the one thing that we tend to be afraid of is to talk about money. While the French are embarrassed to talk about how much money they make, Americans consider money as a concrete measure of success. In France, people who brag about how much money they make are looked on as thieves.

    PSP: How does this impact a sales negotiation?

    Tricard: When French salespeople get to the point of discussing the price, they start to panic. They literally don't know how to deal with that because they have not been trained to talk about money. In my opinion, American salespeople are better equipped to talk about price.

2. French salespeople focus on solving customer problems.

    PSP: Let's talk about the strong points of French salespeople.

    Tricard: First, most French salespeople love their company. They tend to love their product more than their bosses give them credit for. They tend to work hard for their company. Also, they have a great desire to be well thought of by their clients.

    PSP: How would you describe their relationship with their clients?

    Tricard: They go out of their way to help a customer solve a problem even when the problem has nothing to do with the sale. In other words, their aim is to be of service. Salespeople in France see themselves more as the client's team. For example, if a reseller has an inventory problem, the salesperson will help the customer move the inventory.

3. How Americans appear to the French

    PSP: What is a difference in selling between the two countries?

    Tricard: One difference would be that American salespeople are very direct. When you want something, you ask for it directly. In France, we're following different customs. We don't want to risk offending someone and we're afraid to show bad manners. As a result, we skirt the issues—we beat around the bush and it takes us much longer to make a request. Therefore, French salespeople tend to make more sales calls than necessary. They're often afraid of leading the prospect to the close.

    PSP: So you are saying that American salespeople who sell to a French prospect should plan on spending more time . . .

    Tricard: Yes, more time to listen to their clients, encouraging them to talk more, trying to get them relaxed and comfortable. French customers don't like to be pushed to a conclusion.

Source: Excerpts from Jean Gresham, "America vs. France in Selling," *Personal Selling Power* (January 1996): 17. Copyright © 1996 by SELLING POWER. Reprinted by permission of the publisher.

MOTIVATE THE TEAM   A popular trend for planning incentive programs is to plan for team-based rewards and goals. Kathy Bergquist from BI Performance Solutions suggests that implementing the transition to team incentives can be profitable.[7] Sales incentives tied to overall team sales can free companies to achieve a variety of their goals. If a company makes the switch, Bergquist says, clear communications must identify the firm's objective as well as what each individual can get out of the plan. She proposes six keys to managing a successful incentive program:

1. Identify the business goal you hope to target.
2. Communicate the business needs to your salespeople. They need to know what they're moving toward and why.
3. Listen to your salespeople. Ask what will motivate them, and then have them write down their goals and proposed rewards. This creates a motivational contact between you and your employees.
4. Make sure the goals are reachable. If your salespeople feel they don't have any chance of achieving the objective, the program will serve as a disincentive.
5. Don't repeat the same programs over and over. Change adds a greater measure of anticipation and expectancy.
6. Don't try to do everything at once. Target one business issue and do it well.

When sales managers get to know their sales personnel, they will know what turns on their motivation to work hard as a team.

MOTIVATIONAL COACHING IS NEEDED FOR HIGH-PERFORMANCE RESULTS

Motives are highly proprietary in nature and are only shared with another individual when respect, rapport, and confidence exist between the two parties. Salespeople do not openly or eagerly share their motives until their sales managers earn these three interaction ingredients.

As will be discussed in the chapters on leadership and evaluation of salespeople's performance, sales managers need to have ongoing motivational coaching sessions with each of their salespeople. This can occur when working with the salesperson, when talking by telephone, through written correspondence, and during formal performance-evaluation sessions. Thus, motivational coaching is another important component of the motivational program.

SALESPEOPLE HAVE BOUNDARY POSITIONS

Most of the time, salespeople work away from an office and by themselves. They commonly feel they are doing the job by themselves, often wondering if their manager and the company really know what they are doing and realize how hard salespeople have to work to be successful.

Salespeople are involved in meeting both the needs of their customers and the needs of their company. This places them in a **boundary position** between the customer and the company. Occasionally, salespeople are faced with the decision of whose interest to consider most—the customer's or the company's. This is especially true when the company is pushing hard for salespeople to meet their sales quota and the salesperson is asked to sell customers "a little extra" even if they do not need it. If ineffective coaching occurs, salespeople often experience misperceptions about their jobs. The two role perceptions sales mangers influence are *role ambiguity* and *role conflict*.

ROLE AMBIGUITY CAN INFLUENCE PERFORMANCE   Salespeople experience **role ambiguity** when they do not possess the information necessary to adequately perform

FIGURE 12.4

ROLE PERCEPTIONS
INFLUENCE PERFORMANCE

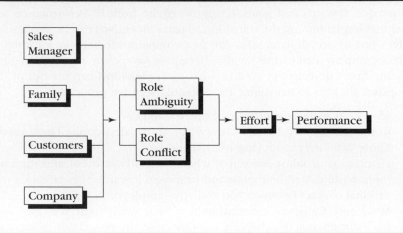

their jobs. They feel uncertain about what the company expects of them, about how to do their job, and about how their sales manager will perceive them. A major cause of role ambiguity is the manager's lack of effective coaching and counseling. This also can result in role conflict.

ROLE CONFLICT ALSO INFLUENCES PERFORMANCE   Salespeople experience **role conflict** when conflicting, inconsistent, or incompatible job demands occur from two or more people. The people and groups most involved in causing role conflict (and role ambiguity) are the salesperson's sales manager, family, customers, and company. As shown in Figure 12.4, role perceptions can have a direct influence on the person's performance. In general, the higher the salespeople's level of role ambiguity and role conflict, the lower their efforts and, thus, job performance.

Role perceptions can lower a salesperson's performance in numerous ways. The sales manager, for example, may not have enough time to properly train and work with the person. Thus, the salesperson may not know how to correctly do the job and thus may feel unimportant to the company. Another salesperson may have to travel, staying away from home overnight too frequently and causing unrest within the family. The job requires travel; the family does not like it. Or a customer may not have sold all of a product and wants to return it, but the company says no. Each of these situations can result in a salesperson experiencing internal conflicts that may lower performance.

At times even the best salespeople need advice and want to talk to their boss about situations that periodically arise. Coaching allows for personal contact between the salesperson and the sales manager. This is a great time for the manager to influence salespeople's behavior by recognizing and responding to their human needs.

BE REALISTIC ABOUT MOTIVATING SALESPEOPLE!

The last consideration when motivating individual salespeople is to be realistic about it. In the final analysis, all motivation is self-motivation. Sales management can only carry the task to a certain point, and then the individual salesperson takes over. This is another reason why hiring the right person is so important to a sales manager's success. Salespeople behave as they do for reasons of self-interest. They are motivated to put forth purposeful behavior because of a personal return—more money, a promotion, growth challenges, and so forth. If the individual perceives a lot of "what's in it for me" exists, the person is more motivated to take result-producing action. Motivation is a self-centered force.

Although many theories exist about how to motivate people, the following motivational T-E-C-H-N-I-Q-U-E-S for sales managers will help get the job done.

1. *Teach teamwork.* A sales manager should strive to create powerful sales teams. Salespeople, working together, can accomplish more than when they perform individually. Create incentive programs that promote teamwork and that do not force salespeople to compete with each other—too much.

2. *Empower.* Give salespeople all the essential authority to perform their responsibilities. Train them to make good decisions at the customer level.

3. *Communicate.* Explain your ideas and goals to salespeople. Sharing a common purpose with defined goals can greatly inspire them.

4. *Hear.* Listen attentively to salespeople. Ask about their short-term and long-term goals. Respond with respect. When they realize they are not alone, it will motivate them to succeed.

5. *Notice.* Managers need to acknowledge and compensate exceptional accomplishment. Salespeople will strive to achieve more when they are recognized for their efforts. Sincere recognition is a great motivational technique.

6. *Initiate integrity.* Set a good example. Don't change plans in the middle of a year. Establish win/win agreements. Always "walk your talk" and live up to your promises.

7. *Query.* Motivation is a continuing process. Be aware of the changes happening with your sales force. You may need to modify your motivational techniques to keep up with their development and growth.

8. *Unify.* A good sales manager will unite the sales team. You will demonstrate that cooperation among everyone will lead to more success for each individual. This type of motivation gives purpose and encourages understanding of the company goals.

9. *Exalt.* Giving inspiration to salespeople is a very important motivational method. Practicing professional selling skills will bring great success and true inspiration. Giving honest praise will inspire them. Never put salespeople down or demoralize them. Make them feel important by respecting their opinions. Be fair and honest.

MANAGEMENT IN ACTION: ETHICAL DILEMMA
SHOULD I OR SHOULDN'T I?

You are a sales manager for a high-tech electronics firm and have just accepted a job offer from a competitor of your current employer. Your new job will start in six weeks, and you are planning to give your employer a two-week notice of your decision. Today, your boss stops by to tell you that the company has just made an important technological breakthrough and that all managers will be briefed on this "top secret" new product the day after tomorrow. Your first thought is to tell your boss now about the new job. However, in the past when employees have given notice, they have been asked immediately to resign and were required to leave that day. Their salary was paid for two weeks from their last day on the job. If this happened to you, it would cost you one month's pay. You know your new employer cannot let you start to work earlier. Furthermore, you know this information would be valuable to you at your new job and that your current employer would not want you to have it if he knew you were leaving.

WHAT DO YOU DO?

1. Give only a two-week notice. After all, that's really all that is required of you by company policy.

2. Don't give notice until the day before you begin work for the new company. Since you know your boss will ask you to leave that day, you will get two weeks' pay even after you start work at your new job.

3. Resign immediately on the grounds that you can no longer act in your employer's best interest.

10. *Set standards.* Set high standards. Make salespeople understand they are working for an outstanding company. Salespeople will perform at a higher level when they represent high ethics and principles.

Remember that motivation cannot cure problems brought on by poor selection, ineffective training, lack of planning, product deficiencies, ill-conceived marketing programs, poor compensation programs, and management inadequacies. No cure-all managerial action plan exists for sure success.

These motivational guidelines should be considered in any motivational action you design and implement. This is not as easy as it seems. Remember, sales managers must consider the entire sale force ("the big picture") as well as the individual. The next chapter discusses one of the most powerful motivators—MONEY!

■ THE BOTTOM LINE

To achieve company and individual objectives, salespeople need to be motivated; this is the greatest challenge—and the most important job—for the sales manager. This chapter discusses a program of seven components to successfully motivate salespeople.

The first component involves an understanding of the motivational concept. A motivational mix consisting of seven broad categories is used; one very important category is that of rewards. Rewards can be divided into extrinsic outcomes (tangible compensation) and intrinsic outcomes (intangible compensation).

The second component in a motivational program is a high-performance sales culture. A sales culture refers to the integration of behaviors, values, ideas, and any other habits or capabilities shared or acquired as a member of a sales force. Individual salespeople in a high-performance sales culture have confidence in themselves and their jobs, cooperate with their colleagues, and compete within their group.

Salespeople have basic needs that influence behavior and lead to goal attainment. An understanding of these needs is the third part in the motivational program.

A realization that salespeople want to know "what's in it for them" is the fourth component. The expectancy theory is used to explain salespeople's work behavior. A salesperson explores behavioral options and advantages that result from choosing certain behaviors.

Knowing the theory of motivation is not enough. The fifth part of the motivational program involves managers knowing their salespeople personally; different salespeople will require different motivating techniques. Sales managers need to create an awareness in salespeople that their needs can be fulfilled by working for the company.

Proper motivational coaching is the sixth component of the motivational program. A lack of coaching or improper coaching can lead to a salesperson experiencing job misperceptions and role ambiguity and conflict. Coaching enhances personal contact between salespeople and managers and allows managers to influence salespeople.

Being realistic about motivating salespeople is the final part of the program. All motivation is ultimately self-evoked, so managers can do only a limited amount of extrinsic motivating. Also, individuals are motivated differently; therefore, managers cannot motivate all the members of a sales force at once. They should do their best for the greatest majority.

■ KEY TERMS FOR SALES MANAGERS

Motivation, 275	Expectancy theory, 278	Productivity, 282
Motivational mix, 275	Expectancy, 278	Turnover, 282
Extrinsic outcomes, 275	Instrumentality, 278	Incentives, 286
Intrinsic outcomes, 275	Valence, 279	Boundary position, 289
Ceremonies and rites, 276	Equity theory, 280	Role ambiguity, 289
Stories, 276	Job satisfaction, 282	Role conflict, 290
Symbols, 276	Quality of Work Life (QWL),	
Slogans, 277	282	

■ MANAGEMENT APPLICATION QUESTIONS

1. Does Ebby Halliday use extrinsic or intrinsic rewards to motivate her sales associates? Explain.
2. What is meant by motivation? Why is it such an important concept for sales managers to understand and learn how to use?
3. What is the difference between extrinsic and intrinsic rewards or outcomes? Give an example of each.
4. Can a sales manager develop a sales culture that would stimulate selling? How might a sales manager attempt this?
5. What do you feel is the difference between expectancy theory and equity theory? Which one do you feel motivates you the most?
6. Briefly describe the dynamics of the salesperson's behavioral model as it relates to motivation, performance, reward, and satisfaction.
7. Relate the salesperson's behavioral model to your behavior in this class. First consider the following questions. What factors cause you to increase or decrease the amount of effort—your motivation to work—you put into earning your desired grade? Your grade is your performance level. What intrinsic and extrinsic rewards do you receive from your grades? Do you consider how you are graded compared to your classmates? How do you determine if you are satisfied with the class? Do your test scores influence your motivation to work?
8. What does it mean when we say that salespeople occupy "boundary" positions? What kinds of problems can this type of position lead to?

■ FURTHER EXPLORING THE SALES WORLD

How do companies motivate salespeople? To find out, interview a sales manager to determine what methods he or she uses. This chapter discusses seven components of a sales motivational mix. Find out which of these the company uses. Remember, some companies may not think of sales training, leadership, and performance evaluation as motivational in nature. Use your questioning skills to uncover all the methods used to motivate people at the company.

■ SALES MANAGEMENT EXPERIENTIAL EXERCISE

WHAT MOTIVATES A SALES TEAM?

The two areas in which people find value in their work are the achievement of goals they have set for themselves internally and the attainment of objectives their managers provide them. See how well you understand motivation by taking this test.

	Agree	Disagree	Uncertain
1. People who are motivated perform better on the job than those who are not.	___	___	___
2. Some people are unmotivated, and a supervisor can do nothing with them.	___	___	___
3. In general, people won't work at something they don't like to do.	___	___	___
4. The attitudes a supervisor has toward team members can affect the work they do.	___	___	___
5. Most people work primarily for the money.	___	___	___
6. Management styles play a key role in employee motivation.	___	___	___
7. Few team members welcome criticism of their work.	___	___	___
8. People always want to be rewarded for doing a good job.	___	___	___

Your motivational know-how: Here's how to assess the above statements. **1.** *Agree.* **2.** *Disagree.* A good supervisor can make everyone's work rewarding. **3.** *Uncertain.* Urgency can motivate people for short periods of time. **4.** *Agree.* **5.** *Disagree.* Surveys show that challenge, interesting work, growth, and advancement rank ahead of money. **6.** *Uncertain.* No one style is effective with everyone. **7.** *Disagree.* Most team members realize criticism is vital to peak performance. **8.** *Agree.* Nothing is wrong with that. It's human nature.

CASE 12.1

IDAHO BAKERY SUPPLIES
How Can You Motivate This Salesperson?

Jackie, one of your salespeople at Idaho Bakery Supplies, has 30 accounts—some active, some dormant, some potential customers—yet, she spends her weekly business/social events with the same three people. Rarely do any other account names appear on her expense reports. You have personally met all of the key people of the 30 accounts. They're nice enough, the usual sprinkling of friendly people, grouches, and gripers. They represent important sales for the company and handsome bonuses and commissions all around.

You time a field trip with Jackie for the middle of the week, when the usual cocktails/golf/lunch series occurs. You observe her excellent relationships and superb rapport with the three key people. Unfortunately, they represent only about 10 percent of her account and produce a very small share of the territory's volume. The attention and the expense incurred "servicing" these three accounts do not seem justified.

You visit as many of Jackie's other accounts as time allows. Of course, she is with you on each call and, following your suggestions, leads the conversations. You are an interested observer who does not try to play "boss" or dominate the action during these calls. Could you have guessed what you see and hear?

The relationships between Jackie and the other accounts vary from good to poor. No serious conflicts or hostilities exist, yet none were as friendly or warm as the three whose names appear so often in her expense reports.

You get the clear impression that Jackie doesn't try very hard to develop a cordial relationship with most of her account reps. Maybe she did try hard at one time and didn't succeed. So now she merely makes routine calls, hoping to take an order rather than making an effort to sell.

QUESTIONS
1. Why is Jackie doing this?
2. What can you do to help improve her sales?

CASE 12.2

TELETRONIC ELECTRONICS
The First Woman Is Hired

Chris White was New Orleans's district sales manager. He was 51 years old and had been with Teletronic Electronics (TE) for 22 years. TE was a distributor of several thousand different types of small electrical parts, such as fuses, batteries, and wiring. In 1996 a company recruiter hired Judy Luby as a salesperson and assigned her to White. This made a total of nine salespeople White was responsible for, with accounts in Louisiana, Arkansas, and Mississippi.

THE FIRST WOMAN SALESPERSON
Luby graduated from Texas A&M University, majoring in industrial distribution. She was active in campus organizations while maintaining her 3.86 grade point average. Luby had worked in her father's business, an electronic distributorship like TE, located in Dallas, the past three summers. Luby wanted to be on her own, so she turned down her father's offer of a job after graduation. She was excited about her new job and felt she had a lot to offer. Even though she was the first woman to work for White, and one of only six women employed by TE, Luby felt she could do the job as well as any man.

SALES TRAINING
Luby attended a three-week training program, learning about products, policies, competition, and selling. Each week trainees were tested. Luby scored at the top of her class with a 97 percent average. Trainers rated her exceptionally high on her personality, motivation, ability to get along with others, self-discipline, and selling ability. She made several suggestions on sales techniques based on what she had learned while working at her father's business that were eventually used throughout the company.

When White received a summary of Luby's excellent training scores and comments from the trainers, he remembered a young man several years ago who wanted to tell him how to run his sales job. He thought "Why me? Why do I get stuck with these generous ones who know it all? And a female! Why, I'm old enough to be her father!"

WHITE DROPS BY
Luby was assigned the New Orleans sales territory and rented a very nice apartment. About three months after she began work, White stopped by Luby's apartment on a Friday to drop off some business forms she had requested. She was going out of town Monday and would not receive them by mail in time. White saw Luby talking to several people by the swimming pool in her building. She seemed very glad to see him. Luby was in her bathing suit, as were two of the four people—two males and two females—she was with and whom she introduced to White. White discovered they worked for two of their largest customers. Luby asked White whether he would like to go for a swim, but he said no, left the forms, and went back to his office steaming. The next week a letter went out to all salespeople reminding them to work a full day. That Friday Luby stopped by the office and said she had sold both customers a large order. White said it was not professional for a young woman to conduct business in that manner. Luby became so mad she began to cry.

WHITE WON'T PAY
Expense vouchers are sent to White for approval. Several small items, not normally approved, Luby had paid for by herself. For example, she had sent flowers to several buyers who had been in the hospital and had sent expensive birthday cards to several of her customers. Recently, however, she submitted vouchers for several dinner and entertainment expenses that were not approved. When Luby asked White to pay for two season tickets to the New Orleans Saints home games, he blew up. Luby explained that she had taken several customers to the games and felt that it had turned into business entertainment. White said no and told her he would pay for only standard expenses in the future.

It was not a week later when the wife of a buyer for one of their largest customers called the office requesting Luby's address. White took the call and was glad he did. The woman was upset because Luby had taken her husband to a football game, and he had come home late that night quite intoxicated. The buyer told his wife he had been out with a salesman from TE. His wife found out it was a saleswoman and she was furious. White called Luby that night and explained the situation. She apologized and said it would not happen again.

At that time Luby asked White whether the company would pay for her to take courses at a local university. White said no and told her he was not in favor of that because it would take time away from her job. After all, he did not even have a college degree and had been

---

Source: This case was developed by professor Charles M. Futrell and is based on several conversations with the person called Judy Luby. The name of the firm has been changed.

successful. Luby said she already had enrolled in an evening graduate-level sales management course that would count toward an M.B.A. For her class project she had collected sales data from the other salespeople in the district and developed a plan to geographically restructure sales territories and their accounts. Luby said the professor would have it graded in three weeks, and she would like to take his comments and present the final plan to White. "However," Luby said, "we'll have to meet at the university one morning because I have the data on their computer. There are some things I'd like to show you." White said he was not interested and told her she needed his approval to collect such information. He suggested she reconsider taking evening courses.

JOB PERFORMANCE

At the end of her first year on the job, Luby was fourth out of 295 salespeople in terms of percentage of sales increase. Corporate management wanted to move women into management and asked White whether Luby would be a good candidate. He said it was too soon to know and also commented that he personally had doubts that she would fit in and work as part of a team. White said she likes to do things on her own and that he did not think she could hold up under pressure.

LUBY'S SUGGESTION GOES TO THE HOME OFFICE

Two weeks later White received a telephone call from the national sales manager, Sam Moore. Moore said he had received Luby's report on realigning sales territories and felt it was excellent. In fact, he wanted to fly down next month and talk with White and Luby about realigning sales territories for the entire sales force using Luby's suggestions. Moore asked White whether he had read the report. White said, "No, because Luby has only been with us one year, and I don't feel she has the background to make such a suggestion."

After White hung up the telephone, he went into a rage. "That, that know-it-all has gone too far. She has bypassed me and made me look bad. I have put up with all I can stand. I am the boss, and I don't care what Moore says; she and I are going to have it out." White told his secretary to call Luby and have her at the office at 9:00 the next morning.

QUESTIONS

1. Why is White behaving this way?
2. Why is Luby behaving this way?
3. What will White do at the meeting? Is it the right thing to do?
4. Ideally, what should White do?

CHAPTER 13
COMPENSATION FOR HIGH PERFORMANCE

■ **CHAPTER OUTLINE**

COMPENSATION AT INGERSOLL-RAND

COMPENSATION IS MORE THAN MONEY

DESIGNING A COMPENSATION PROGRAM

PERFORMANCE-BASED PAY: PREREQUISITES AND OBSTACLES

TYPES OF COMPENSATION PLANS

THE MANAGER'S COMPENSATION

SALES FORCE EXPENSES

FRINGE BENEFITS

THE TOTAL COMPENSATION PACKAGE

FACTORS TO CONSIDER WHEN DEVELOPING A NEW PLAN

DEVELOPING AND INTRODUCING A NEW PLAN

■ **LEARNING OBJECTIVES**

Suitable compensation is a must for companies striving for a satisfied and high-quality sales force. This chapter should help you understand:

■ Why compensation is so important for establishing an effective sales force.

■ How to design, implement, and evaluate a compensation program.

■ The advantages and disadvantages involved in the three types of compensation plans: straight salary, straight commission, and combination salary.

■ The different types of sales force expenses and transportation.

■ The total compensation package and how to develop a proper compensation mix.

■ What is involved in designing a new compensation plan.

Glen Jackson, a 15-year veteran IBM rep, is the typical salesperson—he constantly counts his money. But instead of using a spreadsheet to estimate his stash, he simply logs onto IBM's Intranet site. This past January, IBM launched the site for its 9,000 salespeople. "We wanted to show employees very quickly how they can make a lot of money," says Steve Sams, director of incentive strategies for the $30 billion division of IBM. The site is very effective. It averages 100 visitors a day. Brad Brown, principal of Reward Strategies, a sales compensation consulting company in Sadbury, Massachusetts, expects more companies to put their pay plans online. "It's important in terms of keeping salespeople motivated and focused on selling," he says. "[Such tools] give reps instantaneous access to where they are versus their goals—it's like knowing the score of the ball game." The IBM site asks reps for their title, job description, and base salary. Depending on their answers, reps are taken to another screen that includes information on their particular incentive plan. Sams says, "We wanted every employee on a sales plan to see information as if they had a customized brochure just for them." Using a tool called an estimator, reps can determine what impact their performance will have on their specific incentive plan. The site has practical benefits, also. It cuts costs. Traditionally, IBM's compensation plan was published in brochures which were reprinted whenever management changed the plan. Each printing cost IBM approximately $10,000 more than the price of the Intranet site. "Even if the cost is comparable, I can use the same site next year—I can't use the same brochure next year," Sams says. Another benefit of the site is that "we're forcing our employees to use new technology, so they're experiencing what they're selling to their customers," states Sams. The process of putting the site together was a lot of hard work, but IBM believes it was well worth it.[1] ■

Sales is one of the few jobs where you earn your money—every day. If you do not sell something, you do not earn much—if anything—or you do not keep your job very long. Sales personnel have to be more productive on a daily basis. This requires hard work.

This chapter examines the important aspects of compensation plans for today's sales personnel. Let's begin by seeing how a manufacturer of industrial equipment compensates its sales force.

COMPENSATION AT INGERSOLL-RAND

Ingersoll-Rand's Power Tool Division primarily sells pneumatic power tool products for the automotive aftermarket and industrial market. These products include impact tools, grinders, sanders, assembly tools, percussive tools, and construction and demolition tools.

Compensation is one of the few tools a sales manager at any level has to influence the business, Larry Silber, the division's vice president of sales and marketing, says. "It is the most significant tool you have to influence people to accomplish the company's goals."

"Before actually determining how much we will pay people and the cost of a compensation program," Silber says, "we set our business strategy and direction we want our organization to take. This determines the type of compensation program we implement. Next, we determine the components of the program, and, finally, we carefully examine the cost associated with implementing it."

"At one time we had basically a 100 percent incentive program," Silber continues. "We compensated people with a low base salary and a high commission rate." Silber says he felt this did not provide much influence or control over people because they

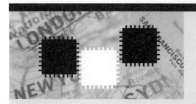

SELLING AND MANAGING GLOBALLY
THE JAPANESE TAKE RELATIONSHIP SELLING SERIOUSLY

The selling rules between Japanese clients and company representatives are highly ritualized. For instance, the president of one company might make a formal request of the president of another to introduce his sales manager, setting in motion the long process of establishing a relationship. But the Japanese are making some concessions in these recessionary times.

"You hear stories about Japanese companies just saying, 'Okay, it's a done deal and the price doesn't mean anything because it's just based on relationship,'" Daniel Wong, a salesperson for Japan Database, says. "Well, I think that's changing even now, because of the economic situation as it is."

A sales rep isn't likely to be able to break into a Japanese company without a proper introduction. "There are no hard-and-fast rules about anything," Wong says, "but [if you try it], your chances of success are limited. If you call on a traditional Japanese company, and you just cold call—I mean, myself [being a foreigner], I would have no chance whatsoever."

Because maintaining a relationship with a client is central to the Japanese concept of service, accounts, and territories are not generally shifted around, according to IBM's Vince Matal. In fact, it's the opposite. "Quite frequently," he says, "if there's a key account that [a sales rep] had a relationship with," the same rep will continue to call on the client as he moves up the corporate ladder, "even though [the original rep doesn't] have direct responsibility for the revenue from that account anymore."

Due to the often long process of obtaining new customers—and the concepts of service and long-term relationships—salespeople are most often paid a straight salary. However, there is a beginning trend of paying bonuses for customer retention and yearly sales to existing customers.

Source: John Bryan, "Selling the Japanese Way," *Fortune*, May 1995, 36.

primarily wanted to do what would maximize their income. They concentrated on getting orders today, not on planning how to manage their business. "We wanted our salespeople to manage their business for the future, 5, 10, 20 years down the road," Silber says. "So we changed the compensation program in order to influence their behavior."

The division's sales compensation plan is composed of three basic components. First, the base salary represents 60 percent of the total projected compensation level. Second, the sales incentive component, tied to the current year's goals, allows the salespeople to earn 40 percent of their compensation. The division calls the third component an objective bonus (approximately 10 percent), which it pays salespeople for reaching sales objectives for a particular quarter as assigned by their regional managers. This type of compensation gives managers the control needed to gain focus on specific projects.

"We also want our managers to manage for today, tomorrow, and the future," Silber says. "Their compensation is structured to accomplish this goal. The district sales managers have a 60 percent base, 30 percent commission, and 10 percent bonus structure. Regional sales managers are on a 70/20/10 program. We want the regional managers to be much more oriented toward managing their sales group, even though daily activity is very important to reaching their job goals."

Ingersoll-Rand also has a benefit program composed of features such as health and life insurance, stock, savings, and investment plans, and a fully funded retirement plan. "All of our people are provided with a company car plus a complete business expense reimbursement package," Silber says. "In addition, most of our salespeople have and utilize mobile telephones, fax machines, voice mail, and personal computers."[2]

COMPENSATION IS MORE THAN MONEY

Nothing that happens in a sales force has a more telling impact on its culture and success than the rewarded behaviors. The design and implementation of an effective sales reward system is directly related to the sales force's success level.

Any type of sales organization can reward sales performance in three fundamental and interrelated ways:

1. Direct financial rewards such as merit salary increases, bonuses, commission, contests, retirement programs, insurance, and other forms of financial incentives.
2. Career advancement such as larger account and sales territories and promotions upward in the organization; and personal development opportunities such as training and night school.
3. Nonfinancial compensation such as recognition dinners, small gifts, a certificate of achievement, features in sales newsletters, trophies, and membership in a special group (e.g., the million dollar club).

Although a **sales reward system** is not the only means of motivating salespeople, it is the most important. Measuring sales performance but not properly rewarding it severely limits the achievement level for salespeople.

PURPOSES OF COMPENSATION

Rewards are only one part of the salesperson's behavioral model. However, they are an important part. Compensation has six basic purposes for influencing motivation, described here.

CONNECT INDIVIDUAL WITH ORGANIZATION   In general, compensation provides sales personnel with a means of bridging the gap between sales force objectives and the individual salesperson's expectations and aspirations. The reward system must satisfy the individual needs of sales force members and must be tied directly to performance to maximize the possibility of obtaining sales force objectives.

INFLUENCE WORK BEHAVIOR   Compensation can directly motivate salespeople to behave in ways they otherwise would not behave. Sales managers often consider pay a major means of influencing salespeople's work behavior so they will improve their sales performance in the organization. Thus, this is the main purpose of compensation.

A large amount of research has been conducted on the relationship between reward and performance. Basically, it can be concluded that sales managers should reward equitably and tie rewards directly to performance. Further, as mentioned, the rewards should be valued by the salespeople.

ORGANIZATIONAL CHOICE   Any good compensation program should serve to help in recruiting and hiring qualified salespeople. It must also aid in retaining salespeople. The choice of joining or leaving an organization is often influenced by expectations of compensation.

An applicant examines the entire compensation program and compares it with those of other companies, also looking at how hard he or she will have to work (how much travel, amount of paperwork, hours worked each day) in relation to compensation.

INFLUENCE SATISFACTION   Compensation can affect a salesperson's satisfaction. Satisfaction with pay is both fairly simple and straightforward and complex. It is simple and straightforward in the sense that pay satisfaction is based on the difference between (1) what the salesperson perceives the pay "should be" as opposed to (2) the amount of pay actually received. Pay satisfaction is complex because of the large individual differences among salespeople. Take experience as an example. The new salesperson would probably perceive the job, including pay, differently than would an experienced salesperson. Thus, the reward system should take into consideration these individual differences.

Pay dissatisfaction can have costly consequences. As shown in Figure 13.1, pay dissatisfaction may create a desire for more pay, which in turn influences performance, absenteeism, grievances, job dissatisfaction, and turnover. In turn, job dissatisfaction can lead to psychological withdrawal from the job, stress, anxiety, and poor mental health.

FIGURE 13.1

EFFECTS OF PAY
DISSATISFACTION

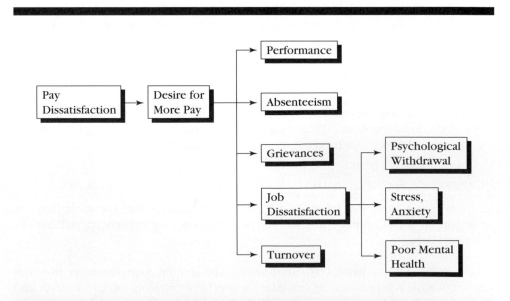

The results of research on the relationship between rewards and satisfaction have been summarized in five points. Individuals are satisfied with the rewards they receive in the following terms:

- How much reward is actually received in relation to how much was expected to be received. If the salesperson expected a $100-a-month raise and actually received $75 a month, dissatisfaction arises.
- How the rewards received compare with what others received. If salesperson Richard Nixon feels he has worked just as hard as Lucy Johnson but Lucy receives a larger raise, then Richard will be dissatisfied.
- Whether the rewards lead to other rewards. A salesperson is satisfied with rewards because he or she can buy a larger house.
- The level of extrinsic and intrinsic satisfaction from the rewards. A salesperson may receive satisfaction from winning a sales contest because of the money as well as the status and recognition the award entails.
- The value of different rewards. The company may offer salespeople fishing equipment or a fishing trip as a sales contest prize, but some salespeople may not like to fish. Reward preferences may vary with factors such as age, sex, stage of career, and situation.

FEEDBACK   Pay serves as direct feedback about the organization's valuation of the salesperson's performance. A sales manager may tell a salesperson that he or she is doing a good job, but the salesperson really does not know "how good 'good' is." However, assume the manager says, "Leslie, you are doing a good job. The average pay raise this year is $150 a month. Here is a $300-a-month raise for you." Leslie should have little doubt about how well he is doing in the job.

REINFORCEMENT   Pay can be viewed as reinforcing salespeople's behavior if it is tied to performance. In the previous example, Leslie was given an above-average pay raise for his performance. If Leslie values that pay raise and feels his hard work was worth the $300-a-month raise, then the pay raise reinforces Leslie's perception that he should continue to work hard in the future in order to receive another above-average pay raise.

DESIGNING A COMPENSATION PROGRAM

Taking into consideration the various factors influencing motivation and the purposes of compensation, we can now discuss how to establish or reevaluate a sales force compensation program.

DETERMINE SALES FORCE AND COMPENSATION OBJECTIVES

Figure 13.2 shows the major steps in a **formal compensation process.** As you have seen, compensation of salespeople requires forethought and planning. Sales managers must consider many factors when developing an effective reward system. They should always begin any reward system with establishing objectives. Compensation plans should have general and specific objectives for the individual performer. Examples follow:

- Attaining yearly sales volume and gross margins (general).
- Attaining monthly sales volume and sales on specific products (specific).
- Market penetration and exploiting the territory's potential (general).
- Call management and development of potential in key accounts as well as development of new accounts (specific).
- Introduction of new products (specific).

FIGURE 13.2

FORMAL COMPENSATION
PROCESS

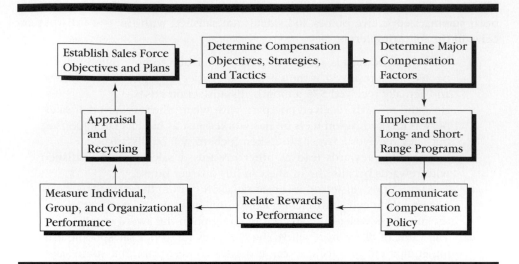

From these objectives the final package must be planned, administered, and evaluated for effect on the sales force's performance.

Larry Silber provided an excellent example of relating compensation objectives to sales force objectives. Ingersoll-Rand went from basically an incentive program to salary plus incentive. "This was done," Silber says, "to influence sales personnel to manage their area as a business rather than only sell. We needed salespeople to sell, service, and build customer's businesses. Our compensation program helps reach those objectives."

DETERMINE MAJOR COMPENSATION FACTORS

Once compensation objectives are determined, management should compare the compensation structure of the sales force with that of the competition, the industry, and the sales organization. After salaries are established, procedures for administering compensation should be determined. Four basic compensation decisions affecting how compensation is structured for the sales force are made at the corporate level: wage level, wage structure, salesperson's individual wage, and administration procedures.

WAGE LEVEL   First the **wage level** for salespeople in relation to compensation-paid salespeople in other organizations is determined. Managers realize that if their sales force receives salaries far lower than the industry average, salespeople may go to work for the competition. In fact, salespeople are often approached by competitors and offered jobs, and they see advertisements in newspapers that list salaries. They talk to salespeople with other firms about their jobs and salaries. So salaries for various sales positions should be established taking into consideration what other salespeople are paid in the industry.

WAGE STRUCTURE   After salaries are determined, the next step is to decide on the **wage structure** for the sales force. This is the pay differential among different sales levels within the organization. The job evaluation and description will indicate the extent to which the job contributes to organizational performance. A salary range is often set for each sales job. Salary for a new salesperson without any sales experience may be set at $20,000 to $28,000. A district sales manager's salary may be set at $45,000 to $60,000. The actual individual wage would be no lower than the minimum and no higher than the maximum. This range indicates what the job is worth to the organization.

INDIVIDUAL WAGE   Third, the **individual wage** for the salesperson is determined on the basis of his or her personal background and abilities as they relate to the job characteristics. The salary for individual salespeople will be within the wage range.

ADMINISTRATION PROCEDURES   Managers must make major decisions on when and how often to give pay raises, whether to give a cost-of-living raise, what criteria to use when determining raises, and how large to make a pay increase so it is meaningful. They also consider factors such as sales contests and cash bonuses. Many firms examine geographic cost-of-living information to give higher compensation to salespeople living in high-cost areas. A salesperson in New York might have a higher salary than one working for the same company in Oregon.

Budgets for compensation also must be considered at this time. Can the company afford this salary structure, benefits, commissions, contests, and so forth? Many companies do a return-on-investment (ROI) analysis to see, for example, if the results (e.g., sales and profits) of a contest are higher than its costs. They can do this by (1) examining sales before and after the contest, (2) determining results versus costs, and (3) checking to see if any factors other than the contest influenced sales. What did sales do during the same period the past two years? Were other factors, such as the economy, competition, and sales force size, different this year?

IMPLEMENT LONG- AND SHORT-RANGE COMPENSATION PROGRAMS

Both long- and short-range compensation programs must be developed and implemented. Long-range plans include promotions, retirement and disability benefits, and life insurance. Pay plans should have some degree of lasting value. They should be well thought out so few changes will be needed from year to year. Constant tinkering with or changing of the plan may cause complaints and dissatisfaction.

Short-range programs include bonuses and contests. These must be coordinated with both sales force objectives and the total marketing effort. If, for example, Bristol-Myers is coming out with a new hair spray, a contest for salespeople might be developed so the salespeople who sell the highest percentage in each sales district receive a cash bonus. Often, companies offer their salespeople extra compensation in each sales period throughout the year. A company may have two-month sales periods during which salespeople are to concentrate on selling several specific products. Managers must make their decisions on the bonuses or contests for each of these six sales periods months in advance.

COMMUNICATE COMPENSATION POLICY   One of the key elements in any compensation program is the communication process through which the sales force learns about the firm's compensation policy. Many prospective salespeople ask, "What will I be paid?"; "When do I get my first pay raise?"; and "What do I do to earn that pay raise?" Thus, compensation information is often communicated to the salesperson before he or she joins the organization. Accurate compensation information must be given to all sales personnel throughout their association with the company.

The salesperson's immediate supervisor is the key link in the compensation communication network. In the role as leader and disseminator of information, the manager is the first person salespeople look to for formal, accurate information. The communication process is so important to the success of sales personnel that sales management should carefully determine the compensation communication message the sales force is to receive. A two-way communication process in which salespeople have an active role gives them a feeling of control over their rewards, greater personal interest, and a feeling of distributive justice.

The **compensation message** should contain several elements. First, the salesperson needs to know what part the sales force is expected to take in attaining the organization's goals. Second, the salesperson's role in successfully achieving sales objectives should be thoroughly discussed. The sales manager must make clear to each salesperson that his or her future with the company depends on his or her sales ability. As the salesperson's performance improves, so will the performance of the sales group. Third, the limitations and weaknesses of the compensation program should not be hidden from the salesperson.

Relate Rewards to Performance

Rewards and promotions should be tied directly to the salesperson's individual contributions to sales force objectives. This phase of the compensation process is extremely important. Compensation is a direct indication of the salesperson's worth to the organization and is an objective measure of achievement. This will be discussed in more detail shortly.

Measurement of Performance

Companies need to regularly measure individual, sales group, and organizational performance to determine whether the compensation program's objectives are being met. This includes measuring factors such as sales improvement, new accounts obtained, and distribution of new products. Sales performance evaluation is discussed in detail in Chapters 15 and 16.

Appraisal and Recycling

Finally, management must determine whether the present compensation program is satisfactory. If it is not, a revision of the plan can be developed. Key questions in terms of the success of the plan follow:

- Are the compensation objectives being met?
- Is the firm able to attract new salespeople with this plan?
- What is the relationship of compensation to turnover?

The compensation process is continually changed to respond to new sales force objectives. Numerous compensation methods and methods of administering compensation exist. The key is to relate pay to performance.

PERFORMANCE-BASED PAY: PREREQUISITES AND OBSTACLES

People often say, "There is more to life than money." Well, most of us will agree. However, some people also say, "There is more to a job than money." Many of us do not completely agree with that statement. This is because money means numerous things to people, such as feedback on a job well done.

Money can be an extremely powerful performance motivator. If pay is going to influence salespeople's performance, the following factors are important:

- The salesperson must perceive a close relationship between performance and pay, as suggested by the expectancy model of motivation discussed in Chapter 12.
- Pay must be important to the salesperson.
- The salesperson must be able to perform what is necessary to achieve the pay.
- The salesperson must know what is expected.
- Performance must be measurable, and its evaluation must be fair.

For these conditions to exist for the salesperson, the organization must do its part, which means:

- Sales territories must have equal potential.
- The salesperson must know and understand how the pay program works.
- The performance appraisal system must be free from potential bias.
- Managers must be trained in giving feedback.
- The amount of money set aside for merit or incentive pay must be sufficiently large to make extra effort worthwhile.
- The job evaluation must be valid so the overall salary relationships are equitable.
- The sales culture must be such that the high performers (quota busters) are encouraged rather than discouraged by their peers.

Generally, not all of these conditions prevail simultaneously in organizations. Although performance-based pay plans are capable of substantially improving productivity, many obstacles in the design and implementation of these plans may suppress their potential effectiveness. These obstacles can be grouped into three general categories: (1) difficulties in specifying and measuring job performance, (2) problems in identifying valued rewards (pay being just one of many rewards), and (3) difficulties in linking rewards to job performance.*

Having considered the various motivational processes in the previous chapter, we can now determine the pay methods that will best stimulate the salesperson to maximize productivity. The basic compensation plans from which to choose are straight salary, straight commission, and a combination of salary and incentives, (e.g., commissions, bonuses, prizes).

Given the variety of combinations possible, sales management should design a plan that best suits the needs of the company, the sales force, and the customer. Most firms prefer to use a straight salary or salary-plus-incentive plan. The straight commission plan has been declining in popularity in recent years. Let's discuss each of these plans.

TYPES OF COMPENSATION PLANS

STRAIGHT SALARY

Of all the compensation plans, the **straight salary plan** is the simplest. The salesperson is paid a specific dollar amount at regular intervals, usually weekly, semimonthly, or monthly. For example, as shown in Figure 13.3 (A), the salesperson earns $22,000 annually regardless of whether that person sells $100,000 or $500,000 in merchandise.

ADVANTAGES TO THE SALESPERSON   This salary can provide a sense of security that a person may require for effective selling because it ensures a regular income. In theory, pay is independent of sales performance in the short run (one month, three months). However, if performance is low for a prolonged period of time, the company can take corrective action to improve sales or replace the salesperson. High sales performance can be rewarded by a periodic salary increase (every 6 or 12 months). New recruits and younger salespeople with little sales experience often prefer a compensation plan that gives them a known income.

From management's point of view, the plan is simple and economical to administer. Salespeople can be directed toward tasks the company believes are important

---

*Numbers 1 and 3 will be discussed in Chapter 16, and number 2 was discussed in Chapter 12.

FIGURE 13.3

TYPICAL COMPENSATION
PLANS

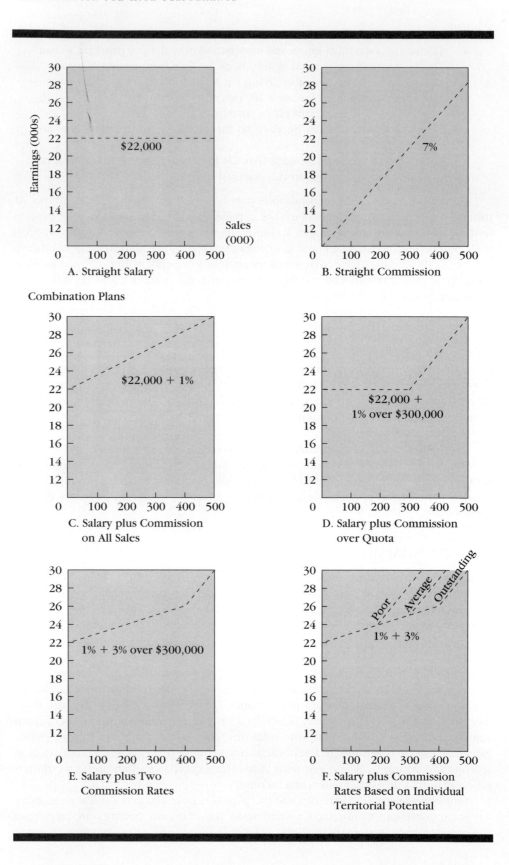

Combination Plans

much more easily than they could if they were on a straight commission plan. Management can direct selling duties that may not immediately result in sales, such as contacting nonproductive accounts or routinely calling on customers who purchase the company's products from a distribution center or wholesaler outside the territory.

Management also usually finds less resistance to reassignment of accounts and personnel transfers with this arrangement. Salespeople are less likely to use high-pressure selling tactics or to overload customers with merchandise that may be important to the salesperson but not best for the buyer or company. Finally, management can project compensation expenses for several years in the future because sales costs are relatively fixed. This can make salary budgeting much more accurate. However, because no direct relationship exists between salary and performance, estimating salary expenses as a percentage of sales is difficult.

DISADVANTAGES OF STRAIGHT SALARY PLANS   The straight salary plan has several potentially undesirable features. The major disadvantage is the lack of direct monetary incentive. If salespeople meet their job goals, they are rewarded by an increase in salary. However, managers usually make salary adjustments at specified intervals, so they may give the increase long after the goal was met.

In addition, salary adjustments are not always based on specific performance. Often managers give everyone the same salary increase or hardly vary the difference between the pay adjustment the high performers receive and that of the lower performers. Because salaries are usually kept secret, even if the top performers were given substantially higher raises, they may not perceive them as being performance reward related. This lack of incentive may cause better salespeople to change jobs.

The plan also can create a lowering of work norms within the sales group. Salespeople perceive that they are really in competition with their fellow salespeople and not with their firm's competitors. They only want to do an average job and meet or not greatly exceed sales goals. This arrangement thus can favor the less productive salespeople.

Another problem with the plan is that salary is not distributed in proportion to sales made. Salaries are a fixed expense of the firm and cannot be adjusted for downturns in the economy. This can increase direct selling costs more than other plans can. When sales decline, the firm may have to let people go. Salespeople who are kept on are often the people with the most job tenure and thus the ones receiving the larger salaries.

Salespeople may tend to emphasize the products that are easiest to sell, thus failing to have a balanced sales mix. A straight salary plan can compress the firm's salary structure because new trainees may earn almost as much as experienced salespeople do.

WHEN TO USE STRAIGHT SALARY PLANS   A straight salary plan is best for jobs in which a high percentage of the workday is devoted to nonselling activities and for which management finds it cannot effectively evaluate performance.

Companies can use straight salary effectively for routine selling jobs (selling milk, bread, or beverages), extensive missionary and educational sales (pharmaceutical selling), or sales jobs requiring lengthy presale and postsale service and negotiations (technical and complex products). See Table 13.1 for other characteristics. Firms

- Dominant market share in mature, stable industry
- Highly defined and stable customer base
- Strongly centralized and closely managed selling effort
- Significant number of house accounts
- Highly team-oriented sales efforts
- Service versus selling emphasis

TABLE 13.1

PROFILE OF A STRAIGHT SALARY COMPANY

sometimes use this method when the person is in training. For example, some insurance firms pay a salary the first year. After one year the salesperson is placed on a straight commission.

Straight Commission Plans

The **straight commission plan** is a complete incentive compensation plan. If salespeople do not sell anything, they do not earn anything. Two basic types of commission plans exist: (1) straight commission, and (2) draw against commission. The straight commission plan has three basic elements. First, pay is related directly to a performance unit such as a dollar value of sales or a type or amount of product units sold. Second, a commission percentage rate is attached to the unit. Third, a level at which commissions begin or change is established. For example, Figure 13.3 (B) shows a 7 percent commission on all sales. The salesperson must generate $314,300 in sales to earn the same $22,000 earned by the person under the straight salary plan.

Companies often use multiple commission rates. For example, at the start of each fiscal year, salespeople with Liberty Courier Inc., a $1.3 million delivery company in Woburn, Massachusetts, earn a 5 percent commission on volume generated within the area. The commission rises to 7 percent at the $75,000 revenue mark and to 10 percent at $100,000.[3]

A *regressive* plan could be used in which 12 percent is paid on the first $100,000 and 10 percent on sales over that amount. For sales of $300,000 the salesperson would receive $32,000. Commission rates decrease as sales increase. The regressive system is used to help place an upper limit on salesperson's earnings and to encourage top producers to accept management positions if they want to increase their earnings beyond the level attainable in a sales job.

Drawing Accounts   One version of the straight commission plan is known as the **drawing account.** It combines the incentive of a commission plan with the security of a fixed income. The firm establishes a monetary account for each salesperson. The amount may be based on the salesperson's individual needs, on a base level the company sets, or on a base level that takes into consideration the individual salespersons' needs, background, and selling potential.

The salesperson may believe that $2,000 is needed to meet base expenditures for one month. Thus, at the beginning of the month a "draw" of $2,000 against commission for that month is given. If sales for a particular month resulted in commissions of $2,100, at the end of the month the company would pay $100 in commissions. Conversely, if commissions earned for that month amounted to $1,300, the salesperson would owe the company $700.

Management must monitor each salesperson closely to prevent a negative balance on salary from becoming so large it is difficult, if not impossible, to repay. Should the balance become large, the prospect of repayment may be so discouraging the salesperson might quit the job. Though many firms have contractual agreements calling for repayment of negative balances against a draw account, collecting an overdraft can be difficult. Some firms use a guaranteed drawing-account plan in which the salesperson does not have to pay back overdrafts. Such a plan is actually a salary plus commission.

Advantages of Straight Commission Plans   Many sales managers believe the commission plan provides maximum incentive for their salespeople. The employee knows that earnings are contingent on selling the firm's goods or services. This expectancy of a performance reward should direct the salesperson to use sales time wisely and should motivate the person to perform at maximum capacity. It is the reason many people are attracted to commission sales jobs. Only their own abilities limit their earnings, and management cannot make arbitrary earnings decisions.

Salespeople under this plan often feel they are in business for themselves. If they are fired or leave their employer voluntarily, they often can continue the same business relationship with their customers after taking a job with another company. In addition, more and more people are attracted to part-time commission sales jobs, such as selling real estate or consumer products (e.g., Mary Kay Cosmetics) because of the earning potential. They can call on accounts that they feel are productive, determine their own work schedules, and set their own hours.

Many organizations prefer to use the commission plan because it is simple to administer and selling costs are in proportion to sales made, with allowance for a constant or average cost ratio. This is very important to a new firm that cannot afford to pay a portion of its salespeople a salary if they are not profitably productive, or in case of an economic recession that could cause sales costs to severely affect profits. A firm with limited capital can hire as many salespeople as needed with no cash outlay until sales are made.

The company pays the salesperson at the time of the sale, when the order is shipped, or when the order is paid for. For some types of sales, the salesperson may continue to receive payment in the future as long as the customer purchases the product or service; commissions for life-insurance policy premiums are an example.

DISADVANTAGES OF COMMISSION PLANS   Straight commission plans have several potential disadvantages. One, particularly for the person who has never sold before, is the uncertainty and insecurity of the plan. The salesperson must sell in order to be paid. This is fine for the company but may discourage people from seeking sales careers.

With some big sales volume items, a long period of time may elapse before a person makes a sale. For example, in commercial real estate, a person may make only one, two, or three sales a year. These sales often result in large commissions, but the individual must have enough funds to live on between commissions. For firms, the uncertainty and insecurity of straight commission sales jobs can lead to high turnover and thus high expenses and sales costs for activities such as recruiting, selection, and training.

Often, salespeople on commission develop little loyalty toward the company. Because they may, in fact, feel they are in business for themselves, the company may have difficulty controlling or channeling their efforts. The salesperson selects the customers, the products, and, in a few cases, the territory to call on and may not consider the customers' or the company's needs, particularly in one-time sales situations. In such cases the salesperson may use high-pressure techniques to close the sale because the customer will not be seen again. This practice has somewhat damaged the image of the sales occupation and is one of the reasons for the enactment of the cooling-off law, which allows customers three days to back out of any sales agreement involving more than $25.

Under the straight commission plan, salespeople are much more reluctant to split or change territories. They may have spent time building up a rapport with their customers and do not want to relinquish it. In addition, with straight commission, service after the sale may be neglected.

The cost of sales may be somewhat greater with a straight commission plan compared to other plans, even though a greater sales volume is produced. The salespeople can earn more pay per dollar of sale on straight commission than they can on salary plans. Commissions can fluctuate greatly. In good times, the salesperson may earn large commissions, but in a recession earnings may drop drastically, especially if sales ability is low.

The firm using the straight commission plan must establish a good evaluation system. Management must work with the salespeople to set realistic goals that will allow the salesperson and the firm to meet their objectives. Because performance or sales activities are dictated by the salesperson's marketplace or customers, managers must reward the behavior or selling activities they seek from the sales force. For example, differential commission rates could be used to deter the salespeople from concentrating on the easy-to-sell, low-profit margin items. A lower commission rate could be placed on these products. Higher commission rates and bonuses also could be established for the products on which the company wants the sales force to concentrate.

Today's complex distribution channels and exchange processes can make the proper allocation of commissions to salespeople difficult. The company must carefully examine the process through which the sales exchange is made to determine the commission compensation policies. Such factors as the possibility of split commissions, mail and telephone sales, house account sales, bad debts, trade-in sales, sales returns and allowances, and installment sales must be considered where applicable.

Each type of sale has unique characteristics. Administrative policies must be developed for each of these circumstances to provide proper compensation of sales personnel and to prevent morale problems.

WHEN TO USE STRAIGHT COMMISSION PLANS   Salespeople who must not only uncover their own leads but also turn them into prospects and then into buyers need to be highly paid. These people are the key ingredient in producing company revenue. Firms should use every form of direct compensation in this type of job, including commissions, bonuses, prizes, and awards. Table 13.2 lists characteristics of a straight commission firm. Other situations where commission plans can be used follow:

- Little nonselling, missionary work is involved.
- The company cannot afford to pay a salary and wants selling costs to be directly related to sales.
- The company uses independent contractors and part-timers.

Many companies use a straight commission plan, but they are in the minority. Today, most sales personnel are paid using one of the combination salary plans.

COMBINATION SALARY PLANS

Under a **combination salary plan,** a proportion of the salesperson's total pay is guaranteed, and the rest is incentive pay. These are some key questions management must answer when designing a salary-plus-incentive plan:

- What should be the split between the guaranteed salary and the average or maximum incentive payment?
- On what basis should the incentive be calculated?
- Who should participate in the plan?
- How is the salary administered?
- When should incentives be paid?

WHAT IS THE SPLIT?   The salary should constitute a living wage. The salesperson should be able to get by on salary alone in bad times. As to the incentive, the top

TABLE 13.2

PROFILE OF A
COMMISSION PLAN
COMPANY

- Low barriers to entry into the job
- Limited corporate cash resources
- Small entrant into an emerging market or market segment
- High risk reward sales force culture
- Undefined market opportunity or customer base
- Inability to set quotas or other performance criteria
- Volume-oriented business strategy

performers should be able to earn somewhere between 25 and 50 percent of their salary in incentives. Smaller amounts simply do not motivate them and thus constitute a mere handout on which the company may get no return.

HOW TO CALCULATE   Essentially, the incentive can be either (1) a commission, calculated as some percentage of the dollar volume or gross profit on products sold, or (2) a bonus, calculated either in fixed-sum increments or as a percentage of salary and based on sales volume, profit contribution, or the attainment of other specified marketing objectives.

In either case, the incentive is often calculated only on sales over some quota. This quota, which may be negotiated with the salesperson or set by the company, can be based on one or more of these factors:

- The past year's sales.
- The sales force's forecast of the coming year's sales.
- Corporate marketing targets.
- A specific net profit target.
- Geographic market potentials.

Since no quota can be set with complete accuracy, it is usually desirable to start incentive payments as 90 or 95 percent of quota to minimize the unintentional penalty imposed by too high a quota.

Set an Upper Limit   It is dangerous to calculate incentives as some percentage of base salary given for percentage increases in sales over the previous year. A large windfall sale can result in one happy salesperson getting 200 or 300 percent of salary and the rest of the sales force feeling underpaid.

For that matter, managers must give some thought to runaway incentives, however calculated. Sometimes, a cap is placed on incentive earnings or a limit placed on the credit awarded for sales to any one customer.

The incentive can be scaled upward so outstanding performers are rewarded more generously than they would be with a straight-line increase in incentives. This helps retain the star personnel.

Consider Profitable Products   When products vary in profitability, it is important that the plan contain built-in rewards for the extra effort needed to sell those products. Firms can do this in several ways:

- The profitable products can carry a higher commission or incentive reward than the run-of-the-mill products.
- The more profitable products can be weighted so one of them counts as much as two or three of the routine products.
- Separate quotas can be set for each product line, with the sales force receiving some reward for each line over quota but a significantly greater reward if all or most quotas are met.
- Salespeople can be paid on the basis of their individual contribution to profit. This is calculated by figuring the gross profits on sales and subtracting direct sales costs like salary, expenses, communication costs, and, sometimes, credit costs.

If the incentive plan is scaled upward to pay higher rewards as sales increase over quota, the plan must be designed so salespeople aren't tempted to manipulate the order flow. It is often possible to postpone a sale from one month to the next, or to oversell customers in a month, to maximize incentive payments. To avoid this, managers can set quarterly quotas with lower incentives for sales reps who do not make quota every quarter.

WHO SHOULD PARTICIPATE? The question of who gets incentive payments has two aspects. They involve split credit and support people.

Split Credit First is the question of **split credit** for sales. Often, one sales rep must get authorization for purchases at the customer's national headquarters, but each local plant or distribution center makes its own buying decisions and must be sold to by the local salespeople. In such cases, some formula is worked out by which credit for the sale is split 25/75, 50/50, 75/25, or whatever the relative importance and difficulty of the national and local selling tasks suggest.

Support People Sometimes the question arises of whether support people such as design engineers, application engineers, or proposal preparers should participate in the incentive plan. This is almost invariably unwise. Although their contributions to the ultimate sale may be just as great as that of the sales force, the environment in which they work and the nature of their motivation does not require the reward stimulus that is effective with the sales force.

SALARY ADMINISTRATION Effective salary administration is just as important under an incentive plan as it is under a straight salary. Some companies in which the sales force can steadily increase its volume tend to keep both salaries and quotas low so incentive payments can be high. In most companies, though, the salary is considered a form of recognition and is adjusted upward to reflect both cost-of-living increases and merit increases.

When these across-the-board cost-of-living adjustments ("COLA" in the jargon of personnel administrators) occur, it is important to adjust both the base salary and the incentive amount. If only salary is adjusted, the incentive program becomes relatively smaller each year and its motivational impact decreases.

WHEN TO PAY? As to frequency of payments, the general principle is to pay as frequently as practical, provided the sums do not become so small they seem trivial. In that case, it's better to accumulate larger amounts before payout. When this is done, it's a good idea to report monthly to each sales force member on the amount he or she has accumulated in the past month. Most companies pay quarterly, although with commission plans payments are at least monthly, sometimes even weekly or daily.

Numerous types of combination salary plans exist. The more popular plans are:

- Salary and commission.
- Salary and bonus: individual or group bonus.
- Salary, commission, and bonus: individual or group bonus.

Salary and Commission Figure 13.3 (C–F) illustrates four salary and commission plans. One (C) is a salary plus commission on all sales. The salesperson earns $22,000 regardless of sales, with an additional 1 percent commission. If the salesperson sells $300,000 of merchandise, an extra $3,000 is earned. Another plan (D) is a base salary plus a commission on everything sold over a sales quota. Once the salesperson sells $300,000, he or she earns 1 percent on all additional sales. The $300,000 may be based on meeting the past year's sales quota, or it may represent a sales quota above the past year's level. A third plan (E) is a base salary plus two commission rates. The salesperson earns 1 percent on all sales up to $300,000 and 3 percent on all sales over $300,000.

A firm using the final plan can take into consideration the potential of the individual sales territory in determining the compensation. Managers may decide they have three basic types of territories in terms of potential and then base the commissions on the territorial rating. Thus, in a territory with poor potential, 1 percent is paid on all sales up to $200,000, and 3 percent is paid on sales above that figure. The territory with average potential must generate $300,000 in sales before the salesperson begins earning 3 percent on sales above that level. Likewise, the "outstanding" territory must generate $400,000 in sales before the salesperson is compensated at a 3 percent commission rate. This plan is an attempt to equalize the commissions on the basis of the individual territories. The salesperson in the "poor" territory may have just as good, if not better, selling abilities than the salesperson in the "outstanding" sales territory. Many companies, therefore, believe the person's earnings should not be restricted because of the individual territory but should be based on sales abilities and skills.

Bonus: Individual or Group   In addition, to combination plans based on salary and commissions, many firms use a **bonus system.** Bonuses can be used with any basic compensation plan. A bonus is something given in addition to what is usually earned by the salesperson. Typically, it is money earned over an extended time period such as one year. Two types follow:

1. *Nonproductivity bonus.* One type of bonus includes the Christmas or year-end bonus and profit sharing, which is money given to all salespeople regardless of their productivity. An equal lump sum of money may be paid to each salesperson, or the bonus may be based on present salary and tenure with the organization. A firm may pay a Christmas bonus of 1.5 percent of salary to salespeople who have been with the firm for one to two years and 2 percent to those who have been with the firm for two to three years. The percentage may go as high as 10 percent. The bonus is paid on an individual basis.
2. *Productivity bonus.* The second type of bonus is related to productivity. Numerous bonus plans of this type can be devised, but they can be grouped into two general categories according to whether they are awarded on an individual or group basis. Bonuses can be awarded not only on the basis of sales or units sold but also on the basis of gross margins, on sales performance appraisals, on new accounts acquired, and on company or geographic earnings or sales.

SALES CONTESTS   Another compensation variable used to influence salespeople's performance is the sales contest. **Sales contests** are special sales programs offering salespeople incentives to achieve short-term work goals. The incentives may include items that indicate achievement recognition (e.g., certificates, cash, merchandise, or travel). However, do not always rely on money for the incentive. According to the results of a recent survey conducted by *Incentive* magazine, money is a poor choice to motivate salespeople. Even though most respondents say they prefer a cash incentive, the recipient of a cash reward is just as likely to feel unrewarded as rewarded. On the other hand, those who preferred travel or merchandise awards did feel justifiably rewarded—53 percent of those who chose merchandise reported feeling happy about their compensation rewards. With this in mind, Randy Davis, vice president/financial specialist with First Union Corporation says "that a mix of incentive awards is the best recipe for success."[4] Occasionally, contests may run for as long as a year; examples include the insurance or real estate industry's "Million Dollar Club." The incentives are given in addition to regular compensation.

The sales contest is an effective motivational method that companies can use to intensify, direct, and make persistent the salesperson's work effort over a given period of time. Salespeople will tend to intensify their work effort to meet contest goals and thereby earn rewards. Management can direct salespeople to sell specific products or to perform activities they would not normally do with contest incentives. Contests can cause salespeople to work harder for longer periods of time (persistence) to achieve the contest goals and earn extra rewards. As one executive in the cosmetics industry stated, "Our incentive program allows us to apply no direct sales pressure

Table 13.3

Profile of a
Combination-Pay
Plan Company

- Established company with growth potential, many products, and active competition
- Need to direct a complex set of behaviors
- Need for a variable pay component that will ensure top performers are rewarded commensurately

while motivating the salespeople and to reward those who reach company-approved goals. Contests have helped this company increase sales from $7.8 million to over $31 million in five years."

When to Use a Combination Salary Plan   Companies using salary-plus-incentive plans say that their chief advantages are that they (1) motivate the sales force, (2) attract and hold good people, and (3) can direct the sales force efforts in a profitable direction. Such a plan's main purpose is to provide a salary for directing behavior and an incentive for motivating people. Table 13.3 gives the characteristics of companies that offer combination plans.

The Manager's Compensation

It is customary and effective to have the first-line field sales managers participate in the incentive plan, although the method of calculating their incentive payments is different from that of salespeople. Managers' compensation should be based on some combination or weighting of two factors: (1) total district performance and (2) the performance of individual members of the sales force as measured by the number who exceed quota, the total amount of incentives earned, or some similar yardstick.

If compensation were based solely on total district sales, any sensible manager would be motivated to concentrate efforts on territories where the sales volume, or volume over quota, is potentially greater. If it were based solely on the number of individuals attaining quota or earning incentives, too much time would be spent on marginal territories and individuals in order to maximize the manager's incentive payment. Some combination of district performance and the proportion of salespeople who meet a goal will motivate the manager to allocate time fairly between nurturing the low performers and capitalizing on the potential of the star performers.

Sales Force Expenses

Daily expenses of field salespeople are a major part of the sales force budget. One study has shown that many companies incur from $50 to $60 in daily expenses for each of their salespeople. Assuming 20 working days exist in a month, then expenses would be more than $1,000 per month for each salesperson. This includes food, lodging, travel, entertainment, and auto expenses.* Reimbursement of business expenses allows the salesperson to maintain a good "business" standard of living.

Expense plans have the same basic objective as a compensation system, that is, to motivate the salesperson's behavior in terms of membership, performance, and attendance. Here are several criteria suggested for an effective expense plan:

---

*See the most recent yearly special issue of *Sales & Marketing Management* for data on selling costs.

1. *Fair for the salesperson:* It should pay for all business activities the company requires.
2. *Fair for the company:* It should not allow the salesperson to "pad" expenses.
3. *Cost effective:* Coverage of expenses should not be excessive and should be affordable to the company.
4. *Understandable:* It should be simple to understand and easy to administer.
5. *Convenient:* The salesperson should have a convenient and fast method of receiving reimbursement for expenses.

TYPES OF EXPENSE PLANS

Three general types of expense plans exist:

- The company pays all expenses.
- The salesperson pays all expenses.
- The company partially pays expenses.

COMPANY PAYS ALL EXPENSES   When the company pays all expenses for the salespeople, it makes handling expenses relatively simple and easy. The salespeople basically follow an honor system in which the company pays for all business-related expenses. To be successful, such a plan should involve a low level of conflict between management and salespeople over which expenses are legitimate.

Also, geographic cost differences should not be an issue. For example, the cost of lunch in New York would be higher than it would be in College Station, Texas. Some companies might allow only a set amount, such as $4 for lunch. The New York salesperson would lose money, while the College Station person would break even or maybe make a few pennies.

When a firm covers all expenses, it eliminates the time needed to survey costs across the country to set expense limits. The major advantage of the plan is that it allows the salesperson freedom from psychological concerns over money that might have to be spent to make the sale.

The company plan of paying all expenses has several disadvantages. For example, often salespeople will not try to economize on expenses. Some managers do not use the plan because it allows salespeople to make money. Companies often develop guidelines to circumvent possible abuses, such as specifying which business activities can be included as expense items. Of course, it is common to have a company complain that a salesperson is not spending enough.

SALESPERSON PAYS ALL EXPENSES   As is true of the plan just discussed, having salespeople pay their own expenses is very simple for the company. However, the salesperson has to keep an accurate record of expenses for income tax purposes. Many salespeople feel that paying their own expenses gives them a better overall tax situation. This arrangement also gives salespeople more of a feeling of being on their own. It often is used when the salesperson is on a straight commission. Some companies prefer to pay a little higher commission rate and have their salespeople pay all expenses.

The disadvantage to this arrangement is that the company has little control over salespeople's activities. Should the company want salespeople to entertain, go long distances for company training, or contact customers, the salespeople may say no or begrudgingly do these things. Salespeople also may try to economize and cut back on other selling activities they would otherwise do if the company were paying for expenses.

PARTIAL PAYMENT OF EXPENSES   Companies can use two basic methods to partially pay salespeople's expenses. One method is to give the salesperson a lump sum that he or she can spend over a specified time period such as a day, week, or month. For example, the company may allow $30 for room and food each day the salesperson stays away from home overnight. If the salesperson can be home each night, the company might pay for lunch and allow no more than $4.

With the second method, a maximum amount of reimbursement is set and itemized. The company might pay up to $15 for meals and $30 for a motel room when a salesperson stays overnight and $4 for lunch when he or she is home at night. It also might give an allowance for monthly expenses such as telephone, postage, parking, or washing the car.

A company plan of contributing to expenses has numerous advantages. It is much easier for the company to project and budget selling expenses. Salespeople know their expense limits, so it is difficult for them to make a profit on expenses. Management is less likely to question expenses, which should help reduce conflicts. Management can control salespeople's activities by allowing or disallowing expenses. If the company wants salespeople to take clients out to lunch and the company pays for it, then salespeople are willing to have business lunches or participate in other activities their company pays for.

The company plan of partially paying expenses has several disadvantages. The arrangement is inflexible, requires time to administer, and may not reimburse salespeople for expenses necessary for the job. Often, the expense amounts allocated are the same for the entire sales force. Geographic differences such as varying costs for meals, transportation, and lodging are not considered.

TABLE 13.4 SALARY AND FRINGE BENEFITS FOR A NEW SALESPERSON (BASED ON STARTING SALARY OF $2,200 PER MONTH WITH AUTOMATIC INCREASE TO $2,500 AFTER TRAINING COMPLETION)

STARTING SALARY BEFORE TRAINING COMPLETION (ANNUAL)

$26,400.00	Base salary ($2,200/month)
2,376.00	Company contribution to pension plan for future service only (9%)
1,000.00	Company contribution to group health insurance, major medical, and life insurance plans
100.00	Telephone allowance
3,500.00	Estimated value of having a car at salesperson's disposal
$33,376.00	Salary including fringe benefits ($2,781.33/month)
	Plus an Incentive Bonus Plan determined on relative attainment of sales forecast

Additional benefits that are not measured in dollars but that contribute materially to your standard of living, as well as to your security and development.

1. Under 5 years, two weeks of vacation; after 5 years, three weeks of vacation; after 15 years, four weeks of vacation; after 25 years, five weeks of vacation
2. Seven paid holidays
3. Christmas furlough
4. Pension plan that is rated as one of the best in the industry
5. Group health insurance and major medical plan cover not only the salesperson but also a spouse, unmarried children under age 19, and student children to age 26; continuance of 20% of life insurance after retirement at age 60 or later without cost to employee
6. Liberal sick-pay plan
7. New long-term disability (LTD) plan; LTD provides financial security for the salesperson and family for period of continuous total disability extending beyond the benefits provided under the sick and accident plan or the company worker's compensation supplement
8. Employees' education fund pays half the tuition for approved courses successfully completed, if the salesperson is employed less than 1 year; 75% of tuition after 1 year
9. Twenty weeks of intensive training followed by constant supervision and guidance by district sales manager
10. Regular reviews of job performance for salary consideration

FRINGE BENEFITS

Sales managers provide certain benefits and services to the sales force in addition to the types of compensation discussed. These are indirect compensation in that they are tax-free income, or the income is deferred for tax purposes until after retirement. In fact, benefits and services have become major costs to the employer. Five basic classifications of salespeople's benefits and services follow:

1. Benefits that are required legally, such as social security, unemployment compensation, and worker's compensation.
2. Pension and retirement programs.
3. Nonworking time such as vacations and holidays.
4. Insurance such as life, health, and accident.
5. Miscellaneous services such as education, recreation, and personal and financial counseling.

Table 13.4 is a summary of benefits a major corporation provides its salespeople.

THE TOTAL COMPENSATION PACKAGE

At the beginning of this chapter, compensation was defined as everything the salesperson receives in return for his or her work. People are attracted to a job for many reasons; pay is only one. The sales manager can better "sell" the job to prospective and present salespeople by determining the dollar value of fringe benefits and presenting pay and benefits as a total compensation package.

Table 13.4 is an example of how a manager can present salary and fringe benefits to a prospective employee. The salesperson in the example receives $581.33 a month in fringe benefits. The $2,781.33 monthly salary, including fringe benefits, is more attractive than the $2,200 base salary. Also, benefits that are difficult to measure in dollar amounts (e.g., sick leave, paid holidays, educational funding) can be specified, indicating what an employee actually receives from the job.

FACTORS TO CONSIDER WHEN DEVELOPING A NEW PLAN

Industry and company traditions usually dictate the basic type of pay plan to use. This includes factors such as the nature of the job, the market, channels of distribution, the caliber of the salespeople, a company's financial condition, and suggestions of sales personnel. Rarely does a firm make a complete shift from one type to another, with two exceptions:

1. Companies with a sales force on a straight salary may find it highly advantageous to move to a salary-plus-incentive plan. Such a plan is a happy medium between the security offered by a straight salary plan and the motivation of a straight commission plan.
2. Companies with a sales force on straight commission may sometimes adopt a salary-plus-incentive plan to gain more control over the sales force. This has been occurring among some types of distributors and wholesalers.

Aside from these exceptions, it would be difficult, if not impossible, to switch a sales force from any kind of commission or incentive plan to straight salary and equally difficult to switch from any plan that includes a salary to a straight commission plan. Developing and introducing a new plan requires several important considerations. Before this can be done, however, some information needs to be collected.

INFORMATION TO COLLECT

It is important for companies designing a new plan to collect information on competitors' plans, product profitability, and sales force activities.

COMPETITORS' PLANS   What is the minimum, median, and maximum amount each competitor pays in the way of salary, incentive payments, and total income? The American Management Association, *Sales & Marketing Management,* the Dartnell Corporation, and various industry associations collect such figures for various industries. They are useful if the tasks of a company's sales force are similar to that of the average salesperson in the industry. A sales force selling electric trains, however, may work quite differently from one selling marbles and stuffed animals, although statistics on both will be lumped together under the "toys" category.

Managers should compare their sales force with the kind of competitors they compete against every day. If necessary, they can make their own survey of competitors' plans. They can simply phone them, explain what figures they need, and offer to give them the survey results—without identifying individual companies, of course.

PRODUCT PROFITABILITY   If some product lines are more profitable than others, exactly what is the profit from each? This information is needed when firms are designing an incentive to promote the more profitable products. The procedure for developing these statistics is known as *distribution cost analysis* or *product line profitability analysis* and is covered in Chapter 15.

SALES FORCE ACTIVITIES   Managers need a firsthand picture of the sales force's activities and problems, which are not always accurately reflected in job descriptions. The best way is to spend two days each with a cross section of the sales force, interviewing them about their functions and problems and observing their activities.

DEVELOPING AND INTRODUCING A NEW PLAN

The sales manager of an electrical equipment manufacturer was puzzled and frustrated. Sales were below quota, two of its best salespeople had quit to go with competitors, and a promising new product was dying on the vine. It couldn't, he thought, be the fault of the generous compensation plan. The sales force received good salaries and substantial bonuses when sales were over quota.

Yet an analysis revealed the plan was largely to blame. The plan incorporated the three faults that make many current compensation plans obsolete:

1. Bonuses were based on sales volume, not on the relative profitability of products. Hence, the sales force pushed the low-margin, high-volume products instead of investing effort in the harder-to-sell but more profitable new product.
2. To make matters worse, bonuses were pooled. To the extent that an entire district went over quota, all sales force members in that district received bonuses. This meant that if any sales rep devoted missionary effort to the new product, he or she might increase corporate profits but would receive a smaller bonus and would indeed be reducing the bonuses of other sales reps in the district.
3. Although the company made cost-of-living adjustments in the base salaries, the bonus structure remained the same. The total pretax compensation the sales force received had just about kept pace with inflation, but they were now in higher tax brackets. As a result, the take-home portion of bonuses was actually smaller, and its purchasing power was smaller still.

Many of today's compensation plans don't motivate the sales force to push the more profitable products, don't reward individual effort, and don't provide bonuses large enough to motivate adequately. Managers should be aware of the signals of possible compensation problems listed in Table 13.5. Because an effective compensation

1. Declining revenues
2. Declining market share
3. Declining profitability
4. Insufficient premier accounts
5. High sales force turnover
6. Uneven sales force performance
7. Inadequate servicing of customers
8. Concentrating on easy-to-sell and unprofitable products

TABLE 13.5

KEY INDICATORS FOR POSSIBLE SALES COMPENSATION PROBLEMS

plan can enhance profits in normal times and cut losses during a recession, the design and updating of the plan should be of concern not only to the sales manager but to the marketing manager, financial head, and top management as well. When developing and introducing a new pay plan, managers should consider pretesting, selling, and evaluating it.

PRETEST THE PLAN

Before a new plan is introduced, it should be pretested with a computer or calculator using past sales, and possibly forecasted sales, to determine what happens to company profit and to the top, median, and marginal performers

1. In boom times.
2. During a recession.
3. If a runaway market occurs for one product.
4. If old products are dropped or new ones added.

SELL THE PLAN TO THE SALES FORCE

The company must carefully "sell the plan" to the sales force. If it introduces the plan at a national or regional sales meeting, it should explain the plan's rationale and then show the sales force what the average member would earn for a good job and for a superior job. Even more convincing, managers should give each salesperson a chance

MANAGEMENT IN ACTION: ETHICAL DILEMMA
HEALTH CARE BENEFITS DON'T COVER THIS

One of your top salespeople has a lengthy illness that will exceed the maximum 90-day sick leave allowance by 15 days. He cannot afford to lose two weeks of pay without extreme financial hardship.

WHAT DO YOU DO?

1. Do your job and follow the policies given to you. You shouldn't really involve yourself in your employee's personal life anyway.
2. Cover for him, and see that he gets paid for the 15 days. The company can afford it.
3. Don't cover for him, but try to help him out some other way.

to calculate what the incentive payments would be for the person's salary, territory, and various sales levels.

After it is in effect, the plan should be continually promoted or resold to the sales force. One chemical firm got additional mileage out of its quarterly incentive plan by sending to each sales force member, at the end of the second month of each quarter, a statement showing how much incentive was earned so far and a formula for calculating how much of each product would have to be sold in the remaining month to reach whatever incentive target the person had set.

CONSTANTLY EVALUATE THE PLAN

"Did the sales force reach its objectives?" "Why?" These are two questions managers should ask when evaluating any pay plan. If the answers are positive, then they should keep the plan. If objectives were not reached, they should find out why and determine if the reasons are related to pay. It could be that some minor adjustments need to be made in one of the plan's components.

If the plan is working, managers should still continually evaluate it. Mergers, new technologies, organizational structure realignments, and changes in channels of distribution are but a few of the many factors that can cause a firm to rethink its present compensation package.

▪ THE BOTTOM LINE

Compensations given for certain behaviors have major influences on a sales force's culture. Not only must sales performance be measured, but it also must be properly rewarded. Three interrelated elements of a compensation program are direct financial rewards, career advancement, and nonfinancial compensation.

Compensation is one part of the salesperson's behavioral model. Managers should design a sales force compensation program by considering the factors influencing motivation and the purposes of compensation. Compensation should be related to performance, which is determined by specific, known objectives.

Money can be an extremely powerful performance motivator if used with the right compensation program. The three basic plans are straight salary, straight commission, and a combination of salary and incentives. In addition, to direct compensation plans, companies can provide indirect, tax-free, or tax-deferred income. These can include fringe benefits such as vacation pay and legally mandated benefit programs such as Social Security. All benefits should be planned to provide the highest possible support for employees at a reasonable cost to the firm.

Under a combination salary plan, a proportion of the salesperson's total pay is guaranteed, and the rest is incentive pay. The salary should be a living wage, and top salespeople should earn between 25 and 50 percent of their salary in incentives. Incentives are usually calculated on sales over quota, and an upper limit should be set. It is important not to lower salaries just so incentives can be made higher. The advantages of combination salary plans are that they motivate the sales force, attract and hold good people, and can direct the sales force efforts in a profitable direction.

Daily expenses of field salespeople are a major part of the sales force budget. Consequently, expense plans should motivate the salesperson's behavior in terms of performance and attendance. An effective expense plan should be cost effective, understandable, convenient, and fair to both the salesperson and the company. Managers can select from three general types of expense plans; once the decision is made, an expense payment procedure must be developed. The company pays all expenses in the first type of expense plan; this releases the salesperson from concern over how much money is spent, but it often results in the salesperson not trying to economize. Under the second plan, the salesperson pays all expenses, which can result in the exact opposite situation—salespeople may economize too much. The third plan involves a partial payment of expenses by the company.

When developing a new pay plan, managers must consider the nature of the job, the market, channels of distribution, the caliber of the salespeople, a company's financial condition, and suggestions made by sales personnel. It is also important they consider the competition's pay plan.

The sales manager can better "sell" the job to prospective salespeople by determining the dollar value of fringe benefits and presenting pay and benefits as a total compensation package. The combination of pay and benefits a company chooses is called the compensation mix. Managers should consider the sales force's overall contributions to the company when establishing a sales compensation mix.

■ KEY TERMS FOR SALES MANAGERS

Sales reward system, 301	Compensation message, 305	Combination salary plan, 312
Formal compensation process, 303	Straight salary plan, 307	Split credit, 314
Wage level, 304	Straight commission plan, 310	Bonus system, 315
Wage structure, 304	Drawing account, 310	Sales contests, 315
Individual wage, 305		Expense plans, 316

■ MANAGEMENT APPLICATION QUESTIONS

1. What conditions at Ingersoll-Rand motivated management to change its compensation program? Did the original straight commission program have any faults?
2. What are the three ways to compensate performance? Which of these has the most impact and why?
3. Managers must consider a number of factors when designing or reevaluating a sales force compensation package. What is probably the most critical factor to consider and why?
4. Which salary plan allows an organization the most control over sales personnel, and which is better for motivation of high sales?
5. A company is considering the following three compensation plans for the salespeople listed in the table. Which of these will be the most expensive? Which will be the least expensive? Is the monetary cost the only consideration for a company?

   Plan A: Give each salesperson a commission of 10 percent on the first $250,000 of sales made each year and 12 percent on the next $250,000.

   Plan B: Give each salesperson a salary of $10,000 a year and 5 percent commission on all sales made each year.

   Plan C: Give each salesperson a salary of $25,000 a year and a bonus of 4 percent commission on all sales made over $250,000 in a year.

SALESPERSON	ESTIMATED SALES FOR NEXT YEAR
Herndon	$300,000
MacLean	270,000
Menon	190,000
Baker	290,000
Hand	225,000
Zank	325,000
Smith	310,000

6. What is the difference between a sales bonus and a sales contest?
7. Compare the three general types of expense plans. What is the major advantage of each of these? What is the major disadvantage of each of these?
8. Discuss what is meant by a "total compensation package."
9. When managers determine the proportion of incentive salary in an organization's compensation package, it is important they ask what the field sales force's contribution is to the organization's overall revenue and profits. Why?

■ FURTHER EXPLORING THE SALES WORLD

What is the best way to motivate salespeople? Most, if not all, sales managers will say compensation is the best motivator. Interview a sales manager to find out his or her view of the importance of pay as a motivator of people. Determine that firm's type of compensation plan and why it is used.

■ SALES MANAGEMENT EXPERIENTIAL EXERCISE

YOU DECIDE THE PAY RAISE

Sally Hise is the new district sales manager. It is time for her to make base-pay raise allocations for her salespeople. She has been budgeted $30,000 to allocate among her seven salespeople as pay raises. Past allocations have caused some ugly grievances in other sales teams, so Sally has been advised to base the allocations on objective criteria that can be qualified, weighted, and computed in numerical terms. After she makes her allocations, Sally must be prepared to justify her decisions. All of the evaluative criteria available to Sally are summarized in the table on page 325.

Instructions: Working in a small group, review the performance worksheet information. Determine how to allocate the $30,000. Select a group spokesperson to present group findings after the class reconvenes.

PERFORMANCE WORKSHEET

PREVIOUS MANAGERIAL RATINGS

SALESPERSON	EEO STATUS	SENIORITY	SALES PERFORMANCE[a]	ABSENTEE RATE	SELLING SKILLS	INITIATIVE	ATTITUDE	PERSONAL
David Bruce	Caucasian male	15 yrs.	90%	0.5%	Good	Poor	Poor	Nearing retirement; wife just died; having adjustment problems
Eric Cattalini	Caucasian male	12 yrs.	115	2.0	Excellent	Good	Excellent	Going to night school to finish his B.A. degree
Chua Li	Asian male	7 yrs.	112	3.5	Good	Excellent	Excellent	Legally deaf
Marilee Miller	Black female	1 yr.	88	10.0	Poor	Poor	Poor	Single parent with three children
Victor Muñoz	Hispanic male	3 yrs.	94	2.5	Poor	Average	Good	Has six dependents; speaks little English
Derek Thompson	Caucasian male	11 yrs.	98	8.0	Excellent	Average	Average	Married to rich wife; personal problems
Sarah Vickers	Caucasian female	8 yrs.	100	7.0	Good	Poor	Poor	Women's activist; wants to create a union

[a]Percent to quota. For example, 110% means a performance of 10% over quota for the past 12 months.

CASE 13.1

ILLINOIS SATELLITE
Selling Your Top Salesperson

It's time to put into action a change in the Illinois Satellite compensation program you have been thinking about for a long time. On paper, it is well planned. To the best of your knowledge, you haven't overlooked many details. Senior management supports the new program. As a good sales manager, you have set benchmarks and quantitative checkpoints for evaluating the effectiveness and merits of the change. Since this program is your design, it is also a measurement of your own effectiveness.

Most of your salespeople have agreed with the program. However, Lisa, one of your top producers, stubbornly resists it. For reasons unknown to you, she opposes the new program's changes. To make matters worse, her complaints to all involved are long and loud.

Since Lisa is one of your top producers, you are reluctant to transfer her out of your group. She is a valuable asset, and you don't want to lose her, but you certainly would like her to see the plan your way. Lisa's attitude is having a negative effect on her work. Even colleagues are feeling the impact of her griping. Whether or not they agree with Lisa, she has caused noticeable changes in their performance. The controversy will hinder the plan's effectiveness. During this period of transition, you need to keep sales moving, above all else. But sales have slowed. The finger of blame points clearly at Lisa. You must take an action that will have long-term benefits.

Ideally, you'll convert her from a resister to a supporter. Then the change can stand on its intrinsic merits.

QUESTION
1. What would you do?

CASE 13.2

COMPUTERBYTES, INC.
Should It Use a Draw Compensation Plan?

As a new company in the computer industry, ComputerBytes's (CB) corporate strategy is shaped by the tight-fisted doctrines of founder Barbara Krymsky, who's committed to making it grow rapidly through an aggressive direct sales effort rather than spending heavily on advertising and promotion.

Sales vice president Ed Thompson, however, has run into problems with paying his sales force. Like many entrepreneurial ventures, CB traditionally has kept salespeople on straight commission, paying them only when they make a sale. But, because the company's sales have no consistent pattern, salespeople's earnings have been fluctuating dramatically from month to month, and a lot of grumbling in the ranks has occurred.

To remedy this cash-flow situation, Thompson introduced a recoverable draw program that provides $500 a month to each sales rep. Here's how it works for Don Pierce, who's just been assigned to a territory in Georgia:

MONTH	COMMISSION EARNINGS	MONTHLY PAYCHECK	DEFICIT DRAW BALANCE
January	$ 0	$ 500	($500)
February	600	500	(400)
March	2,000	1,600	0
April	900	900	0
May	200	500	(300)

As shown, Pierce gets off to a slow start in January, earning no commissions at all, so he receives a recoverable draw payment of $500. The next month, he earns $600 in commissions, but he owes the company $500 as a result of his previous draw. Thus he nets $100 for the month. Since the program provides for a minimum cash flow of $500 per month, however, Pierce gets a $500 paycheck for February. He now owes the company $400.

March is a different story. A number of tough accounts that Pierce has been working on for weeks come through with orders. He earns $2,000 in commissions and, after paying the company back $400, is left with a paycheck of $1,600 for that month.

Sales go reasonably well in April, and Pierce brings in $900 in commissions. He keeps the full amount because he no longer has a deficit draw balance.

The following month, business tapers off. Pierce earns only $200 in commissions and receives the minimum $500 draw. He now is running a $300 deficit, which he hopes will be erased by higher earnings in the months ahead.

But what if those heftier commissions fail to materialize? Krymsky and Thompson worry that a general slowdown in the computer business may put their new sales reps in a bind, so the following year they decide to try a nonrecoverable draw program for three months. It is not a bad idea, but their first effort is a disaster.

The problem lies not with the draw itself but with how it's calculated. Instead of reconciling a salesperson's balance at the end of the three months, Thompson chooses to do it on a monthly basis. The following table, based on the performance of Bob Loder in the central Ontario region, shows why this is inappropriate.

MONTH	COMMISSION EARNINGS	NONRECOVERABLE DRAW	MONTHLY PAYCHECK
January	$ 200	$ 500	$ 500
February	1,200	500	1,200
March	0	500	500
Total	1,400	$1,500	$2,200

In January, the minimum earnings guarantee means that Loder receives a $500 paycheck, even though he earns only $200 in commissions. Since the nonrecoverable draw is reconciled at the end of the month, the company simply writes off Loder's $300 "debt" instead of carrying it forward.

This kind of reckoning can make a big difference in the eventual cost of a nonrecoverable draw program, as shown in the succeeding two months. When business picks up in February, for instance, Loder earns $1,200 in commissions and is paid the entire amount because his $300 shortfall from the previous month hasn't been carried forward.

In March, Loder's fortunes turn sour, and his commissions drop to zero. He gets another $500 paycheck, however, raising his total for the quarter to $2,200. That's fine for him but costly for CB. The total pay is $800 more than Loder's actual commissions and $700 more than the intended nonrecoverable draw.

Realizing that this arrangement isn't producing the kind of results they want, Krymsky and Thompson meet hastily over breakfast one morning at a coffee shop in the Nashville airport. "Is this the only way we can attract sales talent, Ed?" Krymsky asks, reminding him of why they'd introduced the nonrecoverable draw in the first place.

"We can tinker with it, Barbara, No problem," Thompson responds. "The concept is sound. We just need to change the timing of when we reconcile."

"Speak English, please."

"Well, when we got into this, we agreed that it was advisable to guarantee new salespeople an income of $1,500 for their first three months. This was the best way to attract potentially successful people who might have some concerns about surviving the initiation period, right?"

"Okay," Krymsky replies, "but another one like Loder, and we're all going down the tubes. Reconcile that!"

"I will, if you give me a chance. Let me show you what would've happened if we'd reconciled Loder's nonrecoverable draw at the end of the quarter instead of doing it monthly." Thompson takes a paper napkin and writes down some figures among the coffee stains.

Month	Commission Earnings	Nonrecoverable Draw	Monthly Paycheck
January	$ 200	$ 500	$ 500
February	1,200	500	500
March	0	500	500
Total	1,400	$1,500	$1,500

"By keeping the monthly paycheck to $500, we don't overcommit ourselves," Thompson continues. "The salesperson gets enough to live on, and, at the end of the draw period, we even things up. In this case, since Loder's earnings fell short of the total draw, we would've written off $100. That's not first choice, but it sure beats $800. And you can look at it as a one-time investment because after that you'll put the new salesperson on your main program, which is based on earned commissions and a recoverable draw."

"All right, but what happens if the new person's commissions for the three months are larger than the total nonrecoverable draw?" Krymsky asks.

Thompson takes another napkin and draws the following table:

Month	Commission Earnings	Nonrecoverable Draw	Monthly Paycheck
January	$ 800	$ 500	$ 500
February	600	500	500
March	900	500	1,300
Total	$2,300	$1,500	$2,300

"This is what you hope happens with everyone," he says. "At the end of the three months, the new salesperson's commission earnings exceed her nonrecoverable draw. We simply pay her the $800 she's due and send her on to our main program. She obviously won't suffer from a recoverable draw."

QUESTIONS
1. Should ComputerBytes use a draw compensation program? Why or why not?
2. Should further changes be made if it decides to use Thompson's plan? If yes, what changes would you suggest?

CHAPTER 14
LEADING THE SALES TEAM

CHAPTER OUTLINE

THE NATURE OF LEADERSHIP

AN INTEGRATIVE SALES MANAGER'S MODEL OF LEADERSHIP

THE SALES MANAGER

THE SALES MANAGER'S BEHAVIOR AND ACTIVITIES

THE SALESPERSON

THE SALES GROUP

THE SITUATION

THE SALESPERSON'S BEHAVIOR

LEARNING OBJECTIVES

The leader of *a sales* force must have a firm grasp of his or her power and of the leadership behaviors from which to choose. This chapter should help you understand:

■ That leadership is an influence process.

■ The many sources of a leader's power and their differences.

■ The many facets involved in an integrative sales manager's model of leadership.

■ That supervision, coaching, and counseling are important leadership activities.

What would cause the CEO of a company to jump into a freezing cold and dirty pond outside of his office? For Jack Kahl, CEO of Manco Inc., which manufactures self-adhesives, it was a bet with his employees that he would do just that if his reps achieved a goal of $60 million in annual revenues. A year after this challenge, Kahl, adorned in a bathing suit with rhinestones that spelled out $60 million, found himself taking a leap into the 45-degree water and beginning what would become an annual tradition at Manco. Over the years it has become an honor for salespeople to join Kahl in the annual dip because the event recognizes superior executives, sales reps, and other star employees.

When Manco's offices were relocated to Avon, Ohio, there was no pond on site, so Kahl had to come up with a new plan. "A maintenance supervisor who was losing his hair came into his office one day," says John Kahl, Jack's son and president of Manco. "Jack said, 'That's it! I'll shave my head if we make more than $100 million.' He really didn't think we could do it."

About 400 employees gathered a year later for Duck Challenge Day, the name given to the annual celebration of the company's accomplishments. After bonuses and awards were given, skits were performed and the moment of truth prevailed: Jack Kahl was seated in a barber's chair on stage while people took turns shaving off his hair. Manco surpassed every expectation that year by making $167 million, 13 percent more than the previous year.

Jack Kahl is a CEO that is able to influence his employees in a way that pushes them toward the accomplishment of goals. This is what makes him such an outstanding leader. His ability to motivate salespeople has increased sales dramatically over a short period of time and given his company a family atmosphere that is displayed through the teamwork used to reached the goals Kahl sets for the company every year.

Kevin Krueger, national account team leader, says that the best incentives at Manco are team based, which reinforces that the company is a family business. "What keeps me here as a salesperson is the environment," he says. "When we're recognized, we're recognized as a team—I've never been part of such a tight group of people. The incentives are intrinsic." By binding his team together, Jack Kahl has been able to bring his company to a place it would have never been able to reach without his superior leadership skills.[1] ■

In 1958 the Green Bay Packers, an American professional football team, ended their season with one win and ten losses. In 1959 new life was injected into the struggling football team. Vince Lombardi became their new coach and in the next nine years led the Packers to a 75 percent winning record. The Packers accumulated five national Football League championships, including the nation's first two Super Bowls.

Lombardi was an effective leader. In sales—as in football—leadership is one of the most important elements affecting people's performance. Whether working with new salespeople or high-performing veterans, managers face challenging situations daily.

For the manager, leadership is the focus of activity through which sales objectives are accomplished. This chapter will examine leadership, how leadership influences salespeople's behavior, and important leadership activities.

THE NATURE OF LEADERSHIP

Among all the ideas and writings about leadership, three words stand out—people, influence, and goals. Leadership occurs among people, involves the use of influence, and is used to attain goals. Influence means that the relationship among people is not passive. Moreover, influence is designed to achieve some end or goal. Thus, our formal definition of **leadership** is the ability to influence other people toward the attainment of objectives.

This definition stresses that leaders are involved with other people in the achievement of objectives. Leadership is a "people" activity, distinct from administrative paper shuffling or problem-solving activities.

LEADERS VERSUS MANAGERS

Management is the attainment of organizational goals in an effective and efficient manner through planning, organizing, staffing, directing, and controlling organizational resources. A **sales manager** is a person whose job is the management of sales resources—people and budgets. Leading is part of the manager's directing function.

As you have read throughout this book, traditional managers clarify salespeople's roles and job requirements, provide them appropriate rewards, and try to be considerate to them and meet their social needs. They help their people to improve productivity. Traditional managers are hardworking, tolerant, and fair minded. They take pride in keeping activities running smoothly and efficiently. The traditional leaders often stress the *impersonal* aspects of performance, such as plans, schedules, and budgets. They have a sense of commitment to the organization and conform to organizational norms and values.

To effectively operate a sales force in today's competitive marketplace, however, one must be more than just a traditional manager. One must be a leader—a leader who transcends traditional managerial techniques.

Leaders have the capacity to motivate people to do more than what is normally expected. Leaders raise people's consciousness about new outcomes and motivate them to overstep their own interests for the sake of the department or organization. Leaders tend to be less predictable than managers. They create an atmosphere of change, and they may be obsessed by visionary ideas that stimulate other people to work hard. Leaders have an emotional impact on people. They stand for something, have a vision of the future, communicate that vision to others, and motivate them to realize it.

CHARACTERISTICS OF THE VISIONARY LEADER

Sales managers have a challenging and often demanding job. The great responsibility of generating sales for the company plus the many facets and activities of the job require a talented person. They require a leader.

Harvey Mackay, who built the company of Mackay Envelope from the ground up, knows what it takes to be an effective leader. "The most important trait in a successful manager is leadership ability," Mackay says. "And some people, even if they're great sales reps, just don't have the talent for leading." He adds that many executives confuse leadership with authority and that leadership doesn't mean barking orders and yelling at people. "No, a leader has to provide a vision for where the organization is going and then inspire people to follow, even if that path may not lead to every individual's personal best interest," says Mackay.

Mackay realizes that every company conducts its business differently and has its own method of deciding how territories are allocated or how to determine machine time. He continues, "These are tough decisions. But I believe the sales manager should make these calls because he or she knows the price structure, knows the potential. And this is where the leadership comes in. The sales manager has to explain ... that it's a team effort, and it doesn't matter who you are. Make decisions that are in the best interests of the organization." He believes that there is a lesson that every sales manager who wants to be successful has to learn, and it's found in the words of Grace Hopper, the first woman admiral in the U.S. Navy: "You manage things, but you lead people." This a lesson that Mackay says should be learned—"the sooner, the better."[2]

The effective leader has the ability to turn a dream of the future—such as sales, profits, and other accomplishments—into reality. A leader does this through the willing cooperation of other people.

Figure 12.3 presented a comprehensive behavioral model to help illustrate what is known about the process individuals go through when deciding on their motivational levels—how hard they will work. An important organizational factor shown in the figure is the manager's leadership behavior and activities. This is further illustrated in Figure 14.1. Sales managers' behavior and activities directly influence their salespeople's motivation to work.

The material in this chapter shows that leadership is an extremely complex process. It is difficult, if not impossible, for the leader to know and understand all the factors involved in motivating people and then to choose the most effective behavior.

The study of leadership has, however, identified six factors that are important for the attainment of acceptable performance levels. An integrative model, presented in Figure 14.2, attempts to identify these important factors: (1) the sales manager himself or herself, (2) the sales manager's behavior and activities, (3) the salesperson, (4) the sales group, (5) the situation, and (6) the salesperson's behavior.

AN INTEGRATIVE SALES MANAGER'S MODEL OF LEADERSHIP

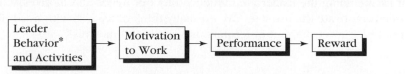

*Leader behavior is part of the organizational factors shown in the motivational model in Chapter 12, Figure 12.3.

FIGURE 14.1

THE SALES MANAGER'S BEHAVIOR IS AN IMPORTANT INFLUENCE ON THE SALESPERSON'S DECISION ON HOW MUCH EFFORT TO PUT INTO THE JOB

FIGURE 14.2 A SITUATIONAL MODEL OF LEADERSHIP FOR SALES PERSONNEL

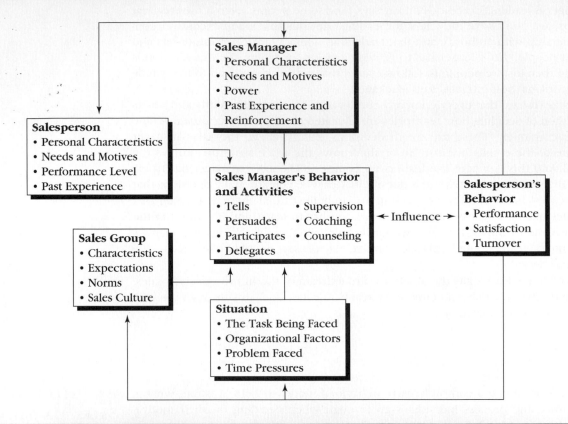

THE SALES MANAGER

The sales manager's behavior is greatly influenced by his or her personality characteristics, needs and motives, power, and past experience. Each of these four elements contributes to a sales manager's leadership style. Let us see how by first providing examples of the four personal characteristics of the sales manager and then relating these to leadership style.

PERSONALITY CHARACTERISTICS

Personality has an influence on the sales manager's leadership behavior. For example, how much confidence does the manager have in his or her ability to be a leader? Does the sales manager have the disposition, intelligence, and capabilities to be an effective leader?

NEEDS AND MOTIVES

All of us, including the leader, are influenced by our needs and motives. What particular needs motivate the manager? We normally think of leaders with needs for power and control, but what about other personal needs and motives?

POWER

Power is the ability to influence the behavior of others. Power represents the resources with which a leader effects changes in people's behavior. Leadership is the actual use of that power. Within organizations, leaders typically have five sources of power: legitimate, reward, coercive, expert, and referent.

LEGITIMATE POWER   **Legitimate power** comes from a formal management position in an organization and the authority granted to that position. For example, once a person has been selected as a district manager, most salespeople understand that they are obligated to follow the new manager's directions with respect to work activities. Salespeople accept this source of power as legitimate, which is why they comply.

REWARD POWER   **Reward power** stems from the leader's authority to bestow rewards on other people. Leaders may have access to formal rewards such as pay increases or promotions. They also have at their disposal rewards such as praise, attention, and recognition. Leaders can use rewards to influence salespeople's behavior.

COERCIVE POWER   **Coercive power** is the opposite of reward power. It refers to the leader's authority to punish or recommend punishment. Leaders have coercive power when they have the right to fire or demote employees, to criticize, or to withdraw pay increases. For example, if Paul, a salesperson, does not perform as expected, his manager has the coercive power to criticize him, reprimand him, put a negative letter in his file, and hurt his chance for a raise.

EXPERT POWER   **Expert power** is the result of a leader's special knowledge or skill regarding the tasks followers perform. When the leader is a true expert, salespeople go along with recommendations because of the manager's superior knowledge.

REFERENT POWER   **Referent power** comes from the leader's personality characteristics that command followers' identification, respect, and admiration, so they wish to emulate the leader. When salespeople admire and respect a manager because of the way the manager deals with them, the influence is based on referent power. Referent power depends on the leader's personal characteristics rather than on a formal title or position.

THE USE OF POWER   Leaders use the five sources of power to affect the behavior and performance of followers. But how do followers react to each source?

When leaders use legitimate power and reward power, the most likely outcome will be compliance. This means salespeople will do as they are told as long as the leader can reward them and has a legitimate company position. However, salespeople may not agree with or be committed to the course of action.

Coercive power is most likely to produce resistance. People hate to be forced to do things through punishment and will resist at every opportunity. They will try to avoid carrying out the instructions and to dodge the punishment.

Expert power and referent power have a positive impact because they lead to commitment. Salespeople will comply because they trust the leader's knowledge and ability or because they believe in and identify with the leader. They will perform as instructed because they want to.

PAST EXPERIENCE AND REINFORCEMENT

The leader's past experience also influences behavior. In many cases, leadership tendencies may be a function of the manager's cultural (personal and organizational) background. Past experience may dictate the manager's current leadership style. A manager who matures (organizationally) under a task-oriented manager may believe that this style is the only behavior to exhibit to salespeople in all situations.

Past successes (reinforcement) in dealing with salespeople in certain situations guide the manager in how to handle each person and the sales group. The sales manager's ability to diagnose a salesperson and the situation correctly is a key to successful leadership. Another important key to success is the manager's behavior and activities.

THE SALES MANAGER'S BEHAVIOR AND ACTIVITIES

The sales manager's personality characteristics, needs and motives, power, and past experiences have a direct influence on the person's natural leadership style. In this case the word *natural* refers to how the person really would prefer to behave toward a salesperson. However, the way one might prefer to behave is not always the best choice of action. It is therefore useful to study what is known about leadership and to suggest guidelines for sales managers to consider in their attempts to influence salespeople's behavior. Indications are that the manager should exhibit both "task" and "relationship" behavior in different situations.

BEHAVIOR INFLUENCES SALESPEOPLE

A leader exhibits **task behavior** when describing the duties and responsibilities of an individual or group. This includes telling people what to do, how to do it, when to do it, and who is to do it. Additionally, the people are closely supervised to make sure the job is done correctly.

Relationship behavior is the extent the leader uses two-way communication, not the one-way communication of task behavior. It includes listening, providing clarification, getting to know the individual's motives and goals, and giving positive feedback to help reinforce characteristics such as a person's self-image, confidence, and ego. Relationship behavior can involve delegating a high degree of authority and responsibility to salespeople for developing their own goals and how to meet these goals. The sales manager is available to assist and give guidance if necessary. However, it is up to the salesperson to accomplish the job's various goals. This is a very democratic leadership approach toward motivating people.

To help illustrate the use of leadership styles in different situations, four different styles were developed, based on past research. These four styles form the leadership continuum shown in Figure 14.3. On one extreme, the leadership approach is task oriented, and on the other extreme it is people oriented.

Next, four quadrants were developed to position these four basic leadership styles (Figure 14.4). The following examples illustrate different situations in which these styles can be used.

STYLE 1: TELLS   This leadership is characterized by above-average levels of task behavior and below-average levels of relationship behavior.

- *Example of an appropriate use:* A new salesperson is unsure of how to develop a sales presentation. The manager instructs the person.
- *Example of an inappropriate use:* The manager tells an experienced, high-performing salesperson how to develop a sales presentation.

The sales manager makes all the decisions here, exhibiting task behavior.

STYLE 2: PERSUADES   This leadership style is characterized by above-average amounts of both task and relationship behavior. The sales manager makes the decision but seeks the salesperson's cooperation by explaining what needs to be done and then persuading the salesperson to carry out the decision.

FIGURE 14.3   FOUR BASIC LEADERSHIP STYLES THAT INFLUENCE SALESPEOPLE

- *Example of an appropriate use:* A salesperson is promoted to a key account position and is motivated to do the new job but is presently unable to carry out the job's various activities. The manager instructs the salesperson on the procedures to use.
- *Example of an inappropriate use:* A new product will be introduced on the market. The salespeople are experienced at selling new products. However, at the sales meeting the manager instructs people on the procedures they should use to sell the new product and gives them an opportunity to ask questions and clarify the instructions.

STYLE 3: PARTICIPATES   This leadership style is characterized by above-average levels of relationship behavior and below-average levels of task behavior.

- *Example of an appropriate use:* A salesperson needs to do more service work in the sales territory but does not see how it will improve sales. The manager provides reasons for increased service and discusses the idea with the salesperson. The salesperson presents his or her viewpoint and, based on what is discussed, is allowed to continue present activities without increasing the level of service work.
- *Example of an inappropriate use:* Salespeople are experiencing declining sales due to the introduction of a competitor's new product. At a sales meeting the manager asks people how to handle the problem, praises their past work, and encourages their future efforts. The manager provides little direction and few suggestions on what should be done to improve sales.

STYLE 4: DELEGATES   This leadership style is characterized by below-average levels of both task behavior and relationship behavior.

- *Example of an appropriate use:* The salesperson is a high-performing, seasoned veteran who is highly motivated to be a top performer. The sales manager lets the person do the job with little direction.
- *Example of an inappropriate use:* A newer salesperson asks for help with selling to several customers and what would be the best way to routinely contact customers within the territory. The manager says, "You handle it. It is your responsibility."

This delegating type of leadership provides little direction, low levels of personal contact, and little supportive behavior. Styles 3 and 4 are different from Styles 1 and 2 where the sales manager provides the directions and makes the decisions. As you can see, quite often the chosen leadership style is based on the salesperson.

Activities Influence Salespeople

A job in sales is different from many other occupations. Other employees usually work under close supervisory control, whereas sales personnel operate with little or no direct supervision. A salesperson may see the boss only one day a month. Sales jobs frequently require a considerable amount of traveling and much time spent away from an office or home.

How do managers lead or influence if their salespeople are not around? They must go into the field and work with salespeople. Three important activities that direct the behavior of sales personnel are (1) supervision, (2) coaching, and (3) counseling.

THE SUPERVISION ACTIVITY   **Supervision** refers to the actual overseeing and directing of the day-to-day activities of salespeople. Supervision is the part of leadership concerned with the direct relationship between the manager and the sales force. A manager can supervise salespeople in two ways: indirectly and directly.

Indirect Supervisory Methods   A sales manager may be responsible for 3 to 12 salespeople. This is a lot of people to oversee. Most sales organizations employ the following methods to indirectly help their manager stay abreast of their people's day-to-day activities:

- Call reports let the manager know which customers and prospects were contacted and on what day. Many call reports have a brief description of the salesperson's activities and accomplishments for each sales call.
- Expense reports show where the salesperson spent the night, how much traveling was done, entertainment activities, and how much money was spent.
- Compensation directs sales personnel's activities. Commissions, bonuses, and contests influence the time and effort salespeople invest in their jobs.
- Sales analysis reports show what was sold and how much was sold.

These four indirect supervisory methods influence people to work toward reaching their job goals. The best way to supervise people, however, is with direct methods.

Direct Supervisory Methods   Three common methods for directly supervising people are the telephone or e-mail, sales meetings, and working with each salesperson.

1. The telephone and e-mail are essential tools for contacting salespeople and for salespeople to talk with the manager. Both are faster and cheaper than traveling to see a salesperson.
2. Sales meetings take place frequently, often once a month. This is a great time to provide information, training, and inspiration.

3. **Work withs,** often occurring once a month, refer to the manager's routine visits with each salesperson. The manager meets with each person in his or her sales territory for reasons such as:

   - Troubleshooting—calling on a specific account to handle a specific problem.
   - Joining the sales pro in a team effort in which both combine their selling talents to close a certain account.
   - Breaking in a new salesperson.
   - Training a seasoned sales pro to sell a new product or an established product in a new way.
   - Introducing a seasoned salesperson to a new territory.

   These are cases where the sales manager accompanies a sales pro on a sales call. "Work withs" are a necessary part of operations, but they do not constitute coaching, which will be defined next.

THE COACHING ACTIVITY   Coaching has been described as the single most important training technique available to the sales manager. Coaching is also an important leadership activity.

Coaching refers to intensively training someone on the job through instruction, demonstration, and practice. The purpose of coaching is to help the person be more efficient. Nothing will improve performance more than a manager's regular on-the-job coaching.

The main element of a coaching session is the **joint sales call.** This is where the manager accompanies a person on a sales call. By observing what occurs face-to-face with customers, the manager can discuss immediately after the sales call any strengths and opportunities to improve. With regular coaching sessions, the manager can reinforce good selling habits and improve selling skills.

Coaching involves special objectives and techniques. It is specifically planned for strengthening selling skills, reemphasizing or reinforcing formal training exposure, pointing out opportunities to improve, or expanding on selling skills already developed. Coaching, then, is the most important link in the continuous sales training process discussed in Chapter 10. Coaching involves these four important activities: presession preparation, the joint sales call, post-call discussion, and summary and critique.

Presession Analysis and Planning   Before actually making calls with anyone, you, as the sales manager, should familiarize yourself with all significant aspects of the person's past and current performance. This preparation is done for the same reason a good salesperson prepares for every important call. Here are six things to do:

1. *Review records.* Many companies have found that a "work with" file on each person is essential to an effective coaching program. This file need be nothing more than a folder containing a simple fact sheet on coaching sessions held with the particular individual. These fact sheets should cover the five key areas related to each coaching session:

   - *Background:* a brief description of the situation that prompted the coaching session.
   - *Objective:* the specific goal you hope to achieve in this session.
   - *The session itself:* a brief description of what occurred during the session, including details such as accounts called on, persons talked to, what was sold, and so forth.
   - *Developmental action:* a written record of the action you and the salesperson agreed should be taken as a result of what you discovered during this session.
   - *Follow up:* a record of whether or not the action has been taken.

Selling and Managing Globally
Europe and IBM—Changes Had to Be Made

On a crisp, sunny September 1993 morning, Lucio Stanca, the new chief of IBM Europe, greeted his top 100 managers in the basement of the company's Paris headquarters. The 52-year-old Italian promised to give all his energy and passion to speeding up change. Between the lines, the message was clear: Anyone who lagged behind just might be left there.

Following the abrupt departure of IBM Europe chief Hans-Olaf Henkel, Stanca and his top executives at the Paris operation were racing to implement Chief Executive Louis V. Gerstner Jr.'s vision of a more nimble global company. Deadlines to create a new management organization had been pushed forward, and efforts to think globally redoubled.

Stanca's first job was to assuage wounded egos and get IBM's troops marching together. "The biggest challenge is getting everyone sorted out and creating a new mind-set," Robert Dies, an executive vice president at IBM Europe, says.

IBM could not have avoided a serious shakeup. The old model of doing business—local operations complete with a chairperson and board, financial staff, sales force, a full complement of technical experts, and unquestionable say over all aspects of the company—was passé. Now a debilitated Big Blue struggled to control costs, to cater to a global clientele, and to serve its markets across industry groups and regions. That meant breaking down its once sacrosanct national boundaries.

It also meant shifting clout from country managers to centralized groups of experts, each focused on a key region of the world. According to Dies, 70 to 80 percent of IBM Europe's business would be handled by new industry sector teams.

The main goal of the remake was to globalize control over product development, sales, and marketing. Before, multinationals found it impossible to do business with IBM as a single entity. Now, a single contract could cover the world. "Getting a global buying arrangement remains one of the hardest problems," William R. Hoover, chair of Computer Sciences Corp., an IBM customer, says.

One reason for Gerstner's sense of urgency was to improve IBM's overseas performance. The previous year, European revenues fell 12.8 percent to $21.85 billion. Europe showed a profit on operations of $714 million but posted a net loss of $1.7 billion as a result of charges for restructuring. In Japan, IBM lost $240 million on sales of $12.6 billion. In 1993, both regions' revenues rose by 18 percent, but efforts to cut expenses abroad lagged those in the United States. Gerstner's new team in Europe said he left the execution up to them. They'll need Stanca's passion—and more—to make it work.

Source: Amos Bryant, "Big Blue Changes," *Fortune,* June 1995, 71-72.

The written coaching record is the means of achieving continuity from one "work with" to the next. This record prevents forgetting points discussed when working with someone. It provides useful written information and evidence of a salesperson's progress and achievements.

2. *Notify salespeople.* It is usually best to give notice of the coaching session. However, at times a surprise visit is useful or even necessary. Of course, whether or not you give advance notice, you can choose the day or days of the coaching session yourself. But a mutually agreed on date is generally more desirable, because most salespeople prefer to have some control over such matters. They will appreciate your respect for this fact.

3. *Schedule calls.* The particular accounts called on are important factors in coaching. Few salespeople enjoy calling on difficult prospects when their manager is along. Thus you should let the salesperson do the scheduling whenever possible. With thorough knowledge of the salesperson's accounts, you will have little difficulty determining whether the salesperson is choosing "setups" or is arranging calls with you that give the overall picture of how the person operates in various situations with various types of customers.

4. *Set length of coaching session.* It is generally accepted that coaching sessions lasting a full day are the most productive. Indeed, sometimes even one day may not be enough time to establish the rapport necessary for effective coaching. The job involves too many factors to get an accurate view of a person's effectiveness in just one or two calls. Also, in shorter sessions, too little time is available for the postcall discussions that lead to sound corrective action. Of course circumstances may limit the amount of time you can devote to the session. However, keep in mind the benefits of longer sessions.

5. *Prepare coaching checklist.* Throughout the joint sales call, have in mind a checklist of details to watch for (Table 14.1 is an example). This checklist should include evidence of attitude and habits, such as attire, grooming, condition of car, and voice loudness, as well as basic selling activities such as making and confirming appointments, planning the call, using selling aids, handling objections, and securing an action.

6. *Set the mood.* It is important to establish the mood for the coaching session by maintaining a spirit of enthusiastic anticipation. If your salespeople seem unduly nervous, you can put them at ease by letting them know you are aware of the pressure they are under—that you are aware the calls you are about to make are not "just like any other." Explain that it is quite natural to be somewhat apprehensive. Further, give them an opportunity to say anything important that may be on their mind in relation to the coaching process. Impress them with the fact that coaching is not spying, nor does it imply criticism of the job. It has one purpose: to help the salesperson become more professional.

The Joint Sales Call   When you, as the sales manager, have completed your presession discussion, you are ready for the first sales call. Before making it, however, review the precall planning. Usually you can do this on the way to the customer's place of business. A call-planning sheet will be helpful to both of you. Use it to plan what should be said and done; then use it as a checklist as you review the precall preparation. In fact, the items on the call-planning sheet can be made a part of your coaching checklist. These items include the following:

- Choosing an objective for the call.
- Selecting the major appeal to help achieve the objective.
- Analyzing the prospect's needs.
- Determining the most attractive benefits.
- Anticipating objections.
- Deciding on closing tactics.

The manager must make two decisions: the manager's role for the sales call and how best to observe the salesperson in action.

1. *The manager's role.* Usually, the supervisor plays a subordinate role during the joint sales call; the salesperson does the selling, while the manager simply observes from the sidelines. The salesperson must learn that in the coaching session you are not acting merely as a spy, troubleshooter, or supersales rep who steps in to save a particular sale. It is, of course, important to close as many sales as possible. But as sales manager, your primary responsibility is not to close sales; it is to multiply your selling effectiveness through your salespeople! Get *them* to close sales.

2. *Observe the salesperson.* One of the obvious benefits of making calls with salespeople is the chance it provides you to observe how each of them conducts him- or herself when face-to-face with customers and prospects. You can observe the obvious selling skills in a real selling situation—skills such as documenting benefits and handling objections.

Table 14.1

An Industrial Wholesaler's Field Coaching Sheet

Date _____

Sales Manager's Field Work-with Report

_____

Salesperson _____ District _____

_____

Territory Number and Job Title   Years of Experience

Personal
Appropriate dress, appearance, etc.   _____
Condition of car   _____
Material organization: briefcase, visuals, etc.   _____

Call Plans
Reviews the situation   _____
Analyzes problems/opportunities   _____
Sets specific objectives   _____
Plans the presentations   _____
Dresses up suggested order forms   _____
Knows who to see   _____
Keeps sales organizer up to date   _____

Review Plans
Reviews selling plans   _____
Reviews call record   _____

Personnel Greeting
Friendly greeting to all personnel   _____

Approach
Secures undivided attention   _____
Appeals to dealer's interests   _____
Takes control of interview   _____

Presentation
Presentation logical, clear, and interesting   _____
Lets dealer talk   _____
Presents from dealer's viewpoint   _____
Uses basic sales presentation framework   _____
Uses sales tools   _____

Close
Presents suggested order form and remains quiet   _____
Asks for the order   _____
Handles objections   _____

_____

Evaluation Key
1 = POOR—Does not meet expectations; 2 = FAIR—Meets minimum expectations; 3 = GOOD—Meets standards of performance; 4 = VERY GOOD—Close to top; exceeds expectations; 5 = EXCEPTIONAL—Outstanding contribution

---

You also are able to evaluate skill areas that are not quite so overt and explicit but that reveal themselves only indirectly. The salesperson's use of positive nonverbal skills during the presentation is a good example.

In addition to allowing you to observe salespeople in action and help them to work more effectively, the coaching session also give you an opportunity to help an individual plan a campaign to close a particular account. Never be reluctant to pass along specific ideas and information that might help with an especially tough customer. It is a common complaint of salespeople that their managers know more about their accounts than they do, but don't take the time to pass on the information.

Once you are face-to-face with the customer, note how the salesperson handles the introductions. Protocol dictates that you should be introduced to the customer or prospect. Thus, the salesperson will say, "Mr. Jones, I'd like you to meet Sam Smart, my manager. He is accompanying me on calls to learn more about my territory."

On calls where you have agreed to take a back seat but the customer insists on bringing you into the sales interview, you can gracefully redirect the discussion to your salesperson with comments such as "Charlie had a good thought on that subject earlier today. Why not tell Mr. Jones about it, Charlie?" or "I think Charlie can answer that question better than I can, Mr. Jones, since he is more familiar with your situation."

Postcall Discussions   After a joint sales call, it is almost impossible for you not to discuss what took place. Certainly the salesperson expects some comment from you. Remaining silent or ignoring the call entirely in your conversation will be interpreted as an indication of disapproval. Nevertheless, your comments need not be lengthy or involved. Sometimes it is enough to say no more than "Charlie, you handled that call very well," or "Boy, isn't that purchaser a tough nut to crack?" This approach is particularly useful late in the day when both of you may be tired and are perhaps just a call or so away from holding the overall critique in which you review and summarize the whole day's activities.

However, during many calls something particularly instructive—good or bad—occurs. In these cases it is useful to discuss the matter immediately after the call while it is still fresh in the salesperson's mind. Such **curbstone conferences,** usually held in the car, are brief postcall discussions about what has just occurred in the customer's place of business. The most effective coaching is to present what just happened as a learning experience, which will help on the next call. You can reinforce your discussion with compliments on what was done well.

"Formal" conferences need not be held after every call. Sometimes nothing worthy of such a discussion takes place, and sometimes you have no time for a conference. Besides, holding curbstone conferences too frequently causes them to become routine and to lose much of their impact.

It is always good to end the curbstone conference on a note of encouragement. This does not mean saying something good if nothing good can be said. Rather, it means saying something constructive. Thus, if you have had to discuss a weakness, point out how valuable it is just to get it out into the open and talk about it; point out that the biggest hurdle to overcome in correcting any weakness is simply recognizing it exists.

Summary and Critique   After all the joint sales calls have been completed, the time has come to sit down with the salesperson and review the entire coaching session. In this review, you should do the following:

- Define the sales rep's problems or opportunities for development.
- Outline the action you expect to be taken to overcome the problem or to take advantage of opportunities.
- Set up a time schedule, where applicable, for taking corrective action you suggest.
- State the results you expect to be achieved.

Write down your suggestions. To make certain the salesperson understands exactly what is to be done, prepare a copy. You can further check understanding by having salespeople tell you in their own words what they think you have asked them to do.

These suggestions for corrective action make up the material you will enter on the coaching fact sheet referred to earlier. You can write your suggestions directly on the fact sheet during this summary and critique stage of the coaching session, or you can use a separate piece of paper you later staple or clip to the fact sheet so it becomes a part of the permanent coaching record.

Before leaving, once again go over the purpose of the coaching session. Try to instill a receptive attitude toward the coaching experience so the salesperson will look forward to taking part in future sessions. Let it be known that your coaching effort is only a part of the continuous efforts a sales manager must make in leading his or her people.

Let the salesperson know you are aware of his or her abilities and that you are concerned with his or her needs. If appropriate, say that in addition to discovering areas in which difficulty occurred, you also have been reminded of his or her strengths.

When summarizing with the salesperson, make as many suggestions as you can to help day-to-day efforts, especially with those customers you visited together. You also should remind the salesperson of the many ways the company can help selling efforts, either by providing special training materials and opportunities or by giving specific support on certain accounts.

THE COUNSELING ACTIVITY   The purpose of coaching is to help salespeople to be more efficient. **Counseling** helps a person become a better-adjusted human being within the work environment. All managers are involved in counseling their employees. Often managers must deal with the petulant complainer, the organizational conniver, the isolated loner, the self-important know-it-all, the abrasive troublemaker—the list is virtually endless.

Managers should avoid two extremes of response. One is to maintain that the personal difficulties of employees are none of the manager's business. People are paid to perform. As long s they do so, according to this extreme belief, they can take their private problems to experts in or outside the organization. The other extreme is the missionary reaction, seen in managers who are tempted to run a clinic on company time, prying indelicately into matters beyond their capabilities and legitimate concern. It is a fact that human dilemmas reduce people's efficiency. To ignore them is folly; to probe into them unprofessionally is self-defeating and potentially dangerous.

A middle ground is defined by questions such as these: What principles should guide the supervisor's efforts to counsel people? What approaches should the manager take to appropriate job-related counseling? What kinds of counseling are relevant to the manager/leader's job?

Some Counseling Principles   Any salesperson with a disruptive personal problem is bound to feel uncertain, anxious, ashamed, or angry. If the manager cannot be supportive in attitude, then the manager should not even try to counsel. Additionally, the manager must be nonmoralistic and shockproof. The employee needs empathy and understanding more than sympathy and reassurance. The person looks for someone who will help work through the difficulty. Thus, the leader needs to establish a climate in which open, truthful communication can flow freely. The manager's role is to help the salesperson gain insight and learn. The manager is not expected to be a therapist or psychoanalyst.

The purpose of counseling is not merely to deal with the immediate problem but also to help the employee learn methods for coping with future difficulties. Thus, the manager should think and feel as the employee thinks and feels through the conflict or frustration. Although the salesperson is the overt leader, dominating the talk, the manager subtly guides the person to analyze the difficulty, to discover and evaluate possible courses of action, and to reach a realistic solution the person finds acceptable.

Three Categories of Problems   All problems can be classified into three general categories. First are those that fall surely within a manager's competence and responsibility. A bright, aggressive young person who seeks to move ahead faster than the organization can possibly permit has a problem a manager can legitimately take up. A manager also can handle problems such as a good person who has been passed over for a promotion and is turning sour.

The second class of problem is clearly beyond a manager's ability to handle, such as alcoholism, drugs, and deep, prolonged depression. In such cases, the most expert assistance available in the company or community is needed. Here the danger is that the subordinate may feel the manager is giving the brush-off. The person must be shown that the leader will continue to be concerned about the problem and that the person is being referred to another resource only to ensure the best help available.

The third classification is the most troublesome to handle: cases in which a manager is not sure whether he or she is going too far. How deeply should the manager become involved? The manager can listen until—and only until—he or she gets the drift of the difficulty. If the manager then thinks the problem cannot be dealt with personally, the manager can refer the person to a competent department such as personnel or medical. In gray areas, it is better to err on the side of caution than to blunder into a counseling relationship that may prove hurtful to both parties.

Possible Counseling Approaches   Conceptually, counseling may be thought of as ranging along a continuum.

The following approaches are to the negative end:

- *Threatening* promotes fear rather than learning.
- *Exhortation* appeals to the use of common sense, willpower, self-respect, and the like. It pressures the person to shape up and "fly right" without helping the person discover how to improve the situation.
- *Lecturing* makes the manager feel good but ordinarily is useless to the person. More often than not, the latter already has tried most of the gems presented but to no avail.

These three approaches are not counseling at all. They are merely forms of coercion and pressure.

Next on the continuum are the following:

- *Reassurance* tends to prop up the employee. Although reassurance has a part to play in counseling, comforting phrases are hardly a substitute for rational programs for improvement.
- *Advice giving* or *suggestions* also have a place in counseling. The manager must be wary, however, that they are only suggestions. The employee may find them rather impractical. Too many suggestions render the subordinate deaf to the counseling.
- *Social reinforcement* relies on the social nature of people, with the manager capitalizing on the behavior of reference groups the employee esteems, pointing out how others succeed, the social rewards that will be forthcoming, and so on. The manager reinforces the employee's positive comments and actions with praise and approval.

These three techniques have a function to play in counseling, but they do not constitute interaction as such. At best, they are likely to give only short-term results. If overdone, they get in the way of the employee's efforts to cope with difficulty.

The following approaches are at the positive end of the continuum:

- **Directive guidance** gives the manager an active role. The manager makes suggestions, proposes alternatives, asks directive questions, and sees to it that the employee considers practical solutions. The manager dispenses knowledge and experience to attain mutually acceptable solutions.
- **Problem solving,** again, makes the manager rather active in suggesting ways out of the problem. Yet the manager works with the employee

toward reaching a rational solution. The manager does not overdirect the person's thinking, but, together, they weave through the dilemma.

- **Nondirective guidance** asks open-ended questions, provides non-directive leads, reflects the feelings the employee has expressed, and restates the content of the person's remarks. A manager is far from passive when supplying such nondirective guidance. The manager strives to serve in an active, but subtle, encouraging role as the employee arrives at a subjectively meaningful resolution of the difficulty, that also will be socially and organizationally acceptable.

These three approaches can be called counseling in the strict sense. The manager uses one or another, singly or in combination, according to the needs of a given employee and the problem. It should be emphasized that merely listening, offering a person opportunities to vent a difficulty, is not counseling. It is a form of uninvolved politeness. However, at one time or another it may be necessary to listen quietly as a person discusses the situation.

Types of Counseling   Among the numerous types of counseling, here are five main types employed by sales managers.

1. **Performance counseling.** Overachievers and underachievers exist in most organizations. When a salesperson is lacking in motivation or when attitudes are negative, counseling is called for. Aimless and goalless salespeople who have superior talents are also good subjects for counseling. On the other hand, a person who is working so hard to achieve that burnout is likely to occur probably also requires some guidance. A third appropriate type of candidate for performance counseling is the employee whose views of and reactions to the firm's normal regimen or its authority figures are self-damaging in the long run. Any counseling effort expended in changing these attitudes may be energy well invested.

2. **Career counseling.** Some of the most perplexed salespeople are those who have so many talents they cannot decide which way they should advance. Helping such a person formulate a practical career plan is more than charity; it may well be the best way to keep the person with the firm. If the employee sees where it is possible to go in the organization and how to get there, he or she may not only be more satisfied in the job but also may strive to grow and learn.

   At the opposite extreme is the person who is nearing retirement. More and more, retirement is becoming a problem that should be handled by the personnel department. With the far longer span of active years often promised by greater life expectancy, counseling with regard to a second career is becoming increasingly necessary.

3. **Job adjustment counseling.** Every firm has built-in organizational frustrations in the form of requirements, policies, rules, procedures, customs, and taboos. Pressures, some of them unfair, exist in every sales force. If salespeople are to derive an element of psychic income from daily work, they must learn to adjust to such realities within the limits of personal convictions. Help in this area is needed by everyone at some time or other.

4. **Social adjustment counseling.** Organizations are composed of groups of people with whom one must interact. Some are easy to live with; others tend to annoy or disturb a given employee. A great deal of the executive's time will be spent helping people relate to one another. The manager's task is to build a cohesive, cooperating work team. It would be a miracle if the group developed such a character without the manager counseling some of its members on how best to deal with their peers and customers.

5. **Personal adjustment counseling.** Managers must decide the extent to which they can or should become involved in the strictly personal frustrations

and conflicts of people in terms of the possible approaches already presented. Frequently, however, a manager must be prepared to counsel some people through personal situations in their lives. As discussed earlier, managers should provide counseling only in areas in which they are qualified.

In summary, working with people, coaching, and counseling are great opportunities to establish a manager as a leader. A person's leadership ability is seldom on better display than it is during these sessions. The salespeople note just as carefully what is done and how the manager does it as managers note what they do. The quality of "work withs," coaching, and counseling is a reflection of the quality of the manager's leadership ability.

THE SALESPERSON

Before deciding on a particular leadership behavioral style, the sales manager should consider the individual characteristics and behavioral patterns of each salesperson. Factors to consider, as shown in Figure 14.2, include their personality characteristics, needs and motives, performance level, and past experience.

PERSONALITY CHARACTERISTICS

Personality may have an effect on how the salesperson will react to the leader's influence attempts. For example, will a high-performing, self-confident salesperson accept a sales manager who is very task oriented?

NEEDS AND MOTIVES

Just as needs and motives motivate leaders, a salesperson's need levels may dictate how the salesperson will react to a manager's influence attempts. For example, salespeople with dominant low-level needs may readily accept a task-oriented leader. A relationship leadership style may be more effective with people with dominant high-order needs.

PERFORMANCE LEVEL

Possibly the most important factor within the "salesperson" set of factors shown in Figure 14.2 is the individual's performance level. Remember that Chapter 12 said two important elements of performance are the person's ability and motivation. These two components help explain how different performance levels influence the choice of a leadership style. Let us review their meanings.

- **Ability** is the skills, knowledge, and experience of the individual.
- **Motivation** is the arousal, intensity, direction, and persistence of effort directed toward job tasks over a period of time. Included in this definition are the effort/performance and performance/reward relationships.

Performance thus involves a salesperson's ability and motivation to do the task. Performance levels refer to the different combinations of ability and motivation a person brings to the job. The sales manager has to separately judge these two performance components to select one of the four leadership styles. Let us apply this concept by examining the four main combinations of ability and motivation.

Performance Level 1 (low, low) Here the salesperson has "low" ability and "low" motivation. It would be proper to use the "tell" leadership style. Take, for example, a new salesperson who is unsure of how to develop a sales presentation for a new product. He asks for help. The sales manager develops it for him, has him memorize it, and has him role-play it. Then the two of them call on the customer together.

Performance Level 2 (low, high) Consider a salesperson with "low" ability but "high" motivation. Typically, this is a person on the job less than one year. The sales manager works with her on the presentation, making sure all of the important parts are included in it. She is allowed to adjust the presentation for a specific customer. However, the sales manager stresses the reasons to stay with the planned script. After they make the sales call, the manager critiques the sales presentation by changing the sequence of product benefits discussed with the buyer. They continue contacting customers with a critique afterward and feedback on how the salesperson can improve the sales call.

Performance Level 3 (high, low) Consider a salesperson who has been on the job for three years. He has the ability to do the job. However, he has not been properly servicing customers after the sale. Here the sales manager should first discuss the situation with the sales rep and then ask him to give his viewpoint. The sales manager's goal is to persuade the salesperson to change his behavior.

Performance Level 4 (high, high) With an experienced salesperson who is performing above average, the sales manager would let her know what is expected and provide feedback but would give her the authority and responsibility to carry out various tasks.

As shown in Table 14.2, the sales manager's leadership style is based on the salesperson's performance level. Sales managers should diagnose each salesperson's ability and motivation and then adjust their style. They should even change styles on the same person. For example, once the salesperson at Performance Level 2 (low ability, high motivation) learns the job, the manager could change to a delegation style, thus treating the person at Performance Level 4 (high ability, high motivation). The following is a guide to leadership selection:

- "Tell" the salesperson with low ability and low motivation.
- "Persuade" the salesperson with low ability but high motivation.
- Use "participation" with the salesperson having the ability but little or no motivation.
- "Delegation" works well for the salesperson having the ability and motivation to do the job.

How each salesperson's performance level will influence a sales manager's behavior varies. The high-performing salesperson doing a great job may require only delegation behavior by the sales manager. The average and low performers would require the sales manager to exhibit more task behavior. Predicting the exact behavior is difficult here, since other factors may come into play. For example, how should the manager handle the high performer who needs continual reinforcement? This may require participative behavior. Past experience with a salesperson will help the manager select the appropriate behavior.

TABLE 14.2

GUIDELINES TO CONSIDER WHEN SELECTING A LEADERSHIP STYLE BASED ON PERFORMANCE LEVEL

| | SALESPERSON'S PERFORMANCE LEVEL | | | |
| | ABILITY | | MOTIVATION | |
SALES MANAGER'S LEADERSHIP STYLE	Low	High	Low	High
Tells	✓		✓	
Persuades	✓			✓
Participates		✓	✓	
Delegates		✓		✓

EXPERIENCED SALESPEOPLE ALSO NEED LEADERSHIP   Because of factors such as tenure on the job, age, and being in the same territory for a length of time, experienced salespeople often have special management requirements. Some of the more common needs of experienced salespeople follow:

- *To be treated equally.* At times they feel forgotten, unloved, and neglected by the company. (Don't we all?) This often occurs because their manager must give more time to trainees and lower performers. The star salespeople can be the most neglected, since their performance is constantly outstanding. However, knowledge and skills of these salespeople may begin to decline. The manager must provide programs to keep everyone up to date. Trainers should routinely work with these people. Often trainers can spot problems in the field and alert the manager. Trainers also can stress the importance of district sales managers (DSM) maintaining a fair balance of attention to the needs of these individuals.

- *Help with performance problems.* Due to a lack of challenge, motivation, knowledge, and skills, often some experienced salespeople reach a performance plateau. Sales level off (or drop), the number of customer calls declines, paperwork is late getting to the DSM's office, and a change in attitude is noticed.

  To keep the salespeople on track, motivational principles and techniques should be main ingredients of all sales management programs. Motivational programs and knowledge and skills evaluations, along with training updates, can play an important part in reversing (and even preventing) performance plateaus.

- *Help overcoming the "greener grass" syndrome.* Because salespeople are achievement oriented, it is easy to see why they always are wanting to better themselves. They frequently compare their present jobs with other jobs—even interview with other companies. Often the "grass looks greener on the other side of the fence." They wonder, "Should I change jobs?"

  As they gain seniority, veterans see the increasing number of new salespeople entering their company. Some of them become outstanding performers and move ahead quickly. Some veterans experience self-doubts (can they continue to perform?) when they are above-average performers. Frequently, they are disappointed with the lack of promotional opportunities.

The manager's responsibility is to identify activities veterans could do. Many companies make them responsible for conducting one or more courses in their training program. Some companies have a sales training committee, headed by the national sales trainer, with several veteran salespeople as members. These salespeople provide feedback from the field to the home office. They often are asked to help evaluate the present training program. New salespeople work with experienced people as part of their training. Sales managers must keep the veterans involved; otherwise, they may lose them.

PAST EXPERIENCE

The salesperson's past experience and reinforcement may affect the leadership process. For example, a group of salespeople in a sales district may have adapted well to the sales manager's participative style. If, after a number of years, this manager is replaced by a more task-oriented manager, adjustment problems may develop.

The importance of a sales manager's diagnostic ability with salespeople cannot be overemphasized. Doctors make diagnostic judgments prior to prescribing treatment and so must the sales manager. Managers need to develop a rational process based on past experience and what was learned from it. Managers must not only know the four leadership styles, but they also must know how to use each one.

Leadership Style Selection Requires Power

The sales manager needs to understand the relationship between particular leadership styles and power. If a manager does not have the power base needed for a particular style, then its use will not produce the desired results.

As noted earlier, salespeople with low performance levels generally require a "tell" or "persuade" leadership style. This means a sales manager must have position power. The manager needs to have the authority to reward for success or penalize for noncompliance. If the manager does not have the power, then salespeople may not follow the directives.

The Sales Group

All sales groups (for example, district and regional) differ, even within the same company. The differences may be slight, but they do exist. Due to the various personality characteristics, needs and motives, performance levels, and past experience of individuals within a group, each sales group tends to take on its own personality. As shown in Figure 14.2, the sales group's characteristics, expectations, norms, and sales culture can affect the leader's effectiveness. They certainly can influence the needed leadership style.

Characteristics

If a person becomes a manager and in that capacity has a personality clash with one or more salespeople, that manager's effectiveness may decrease. On the other hand, the new manager's personality and leadership style may be well matched to the group, helping the sales manager to be effective. The sales manager should consider the characteristics of the salespeople and try to anticipate their reactions to attempts at influencing them. For example, if the salespeople and the group possess the following characteristics, the manager may delegate authority to them:

- They have the ability to deal with the sales situation.
- They are interested in the situation.
- They have a relatively high need for independence.
- They have a relatively high tolerance for ambiguity in the job.
- Past experience indicates that they can do a good job.
- They expect to participate in decision making.

If the group does not possess these characteristics, then the manager needs a more authoritative leadership style. Many sales groups do not have these characteristics. Typically, this is due to either high turnover or rapid growth of the sales force. Both cases cause the group to be composed of low-tenured, inexperienced people.

Expectations

The degree to which the leader meets the expectations of both salespeople and the group as a whole has an influence on the leader's effectiveness. The current generation of salespeople wants their managers to do the following:

- Help them be successful.
- Hire competent coworkers.
- Provide adequate training, including conducting effective sales meetings.
- Set responsible performance standards.
- Provide feedback on how they are doing.
- Give rewards based on performance.

The manager who is able to accomplish these tasks has a better chance of meeting the group's expectations.

NORMS

The group's norms also can influence the sales manager's effectiveness. **Norms** are the standards the group establishes. All groups develop norms that serve to regulate members' behavior and move that behavior toward conformity. Norms can define what is "appropriate" behavior and what are the "limits" of behavior. As a salesperson approaches these limits, signals may be received from other members that group norms are being violated. For example, a group without a sales culture may have members trying to convince high-performing salespeople ("quota busters") to reduce their sales efforts. A group with a true sales culture would encourage those all-stars to keep improving their performance and encourage low performers to pick up the pace.

Task-related norms can have a great effect on performance. The more important the norm is to the group, the more likely it is that members' behavior will be guided by the norm and the more likely the group will place pressure on members to conform. A positive performance norm (for example, to be the top sales district in the company) can greatly influence the leader's chances of success. However, a negative performance norm intended to reduce or limit performance may create difficulties for the leader in achieving success by making the group less productive. The sales manager's job is to develop positive group norms that will maximize productivity. To obtain the effort and cooperation desired from the group, the leader must have its confidence and trust.

SALES CULTURE

A group's sales culture, as discussed in Chapter 12, has a major influence on the group. A sales district with a true, positive, professional sales culture typically is managed by a successful leader who has pride in the group and enthusiasm for the job.

This manager uses a situational leadership style. The leader's actions are usually described by his or her salespeople as those of a parent. The leader supports the winners and helps others catch up. The leader runs interference; creates an atmosphere of understanding, trust, and love; and instills within each person the feeling that he or she is needed to help the company. Besides describing their leader as a parent, salespeople are often heard using the following descriptors:

- Enthusiastic
- Cheerleader
- Creator of champions
- Coach
- A professional

What can a sales manager do to create a sales culture with a group? The first things to do are listed in Table 14.3. These are the minimum building blocks for constructing a high-performance sales culture.

TABLE 14.3

THE MINIMUM REQUIREMENTS FOR BUILDING A SALES CULTURE

1. Hire people who possess the fundamental personal characteristics needed for top performance.
2. Eliminate roadblocks and chuckholes to each person's success.
3. Provide a good sales training program.
4. Provide performance standards.
5. Provide performance feedback.
6. Provide appropriate rewards for outstanding performance.

The Situation

The situation itself can influence the sales manager's behavior and effectiveness (Figure 14.2). Four primary factors that influence the leader's effectiveness are (1) the task faced, (2) the organizational factors, (3) the problem faced, and (4) the various time pressures.

The Task Faced

Task refers to the extent to which the job is simple or difficult and vague or specific. Sales managers should use task behavior techniques to provide structure if the job is vague and should reduce structure, using supportive or participative behavior techniques, if the work is specific. For example, assume salespeople sell basically the same products to the same customers month after month. They know what is expected of them. A sales manager may tell salespeople exactly who to call on and to use a canned sales presentation. In this highly structured selling job, some salespeople may resent the manager's techniques, which will cause less performance and job satisfaction than if they could develop their own sales pattern and presentation. This occurs particularly with salespeople who have been with the company for several years.

The Organizational Factors

The organization can influence the sales manager's actions because of factors such as (1) the amount of pressure it places on salespeople to reach goals, (2) the procedures to follow (for example, amount of paperwork), and (3) the amount of uncertainty in the job (for example, what is expected from management, job security). Task leadership techniques can help the salespeople understand what is expected of them and thereby improve the leader's effectiveness. A task style is often called for when the home office tells the sales force members they must meet certain goals within a certain time period (for example, the next two months).

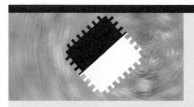

MANAGEMENT IN ACTION: ETHICAL DILEMMA
PERSONAL PROBLEMS AFFECT WORK

Al McDonald is 53. He has worked for your company for 30 years and for the past two he has worked under you. Life has been difficult for Al recently. His wife is terminally ill, and he has turned to alcohol to help him through these tough times. Between college costs for his two children, medical expenses for his wife, and his own personal problems, he has no money. He is considering selling his home for extra cash.

Sales have steadily decreased in his territory and, except for the customers who are his drinking buddies, few want to see him. Though he has never come to work "under the influence," his use of alcohol is still seriously affecting his work. For months you have urged him to get help, but he says, "I do not have a problem. Leave me alone. It's none of your business." Your boss has told you that you have two

months to increase the sales volume for Al's territory, or he will find another sales manager who can.

WHAT DO YOU DO?

1. Fire Al immediately. Keeping him on is simply too risky. You know you could lose your job if he doesn't clean up his act.
2. Follow the formal procedures set forth by your company for employees who are not meeting their expected sales quotas. Write him up and require him to attend a special "remedial" sales training class.
3. Force him to join a rehabilitation program; make it a requirement for keeping his job. Also have him report to you daily regarding his sales progress.

THE PROBLEM FACED

The problem or circumstances can determine the extent of authority to delegate. If individual or group sales are good, the manager can be relaxed, informal, and easy-going and can adopt participation and delegation techniques. However, if sales are low, the manager may adopt a more task-oriented approach to increase productivity.

THE TIME PRESSURES

The time pressure involved in a situation may make it more difficult to involve other people. The sales manager may be forced to tell salespeople what to do or do the job himself or herself. Here participation and delegation may be impractical or unsuccessful.

Sales managers are busy people. Time is a valuable resource for them. They are often faced with having too much to do in too little time.

THE SALESPERSON'S BEHAVIOR

We have defined leadership as an influence process, a process impacted by the sales manager, salesperson, sales group, and situation. As illustrated in Figure 14.2, it is also influenced by the salesperson's behavior.

For years sales managers have spoken of leadership as the one-way process of the supervisor influencing the salesperson's behavior. Today, we must recognize that leadership involves a two-way influence process. The salesperson's behavior influences the sales manager's behavior just as the sales manager's behavior influences the salesperson's behavior. As you review this chapter, note that many of the examples emphasized that the sales manager's behavior is often based on a reaction (diagnosis) to the salesperson's behavior.

The leadership process leads to actual outcomes related to the behavior of salespeople. Performance, satisfaction, and turnover are three major outcomes influenced by the sales manager's behavior. The criteria for evaluating these outcomes include analyzing the group's sales and marketing costs and reviewing salespeople's performance. These topics will be discussed in the next two chapters.

 THE BOTTOM LINE

As one of the most important elements affecting sales force performance, leadership is defined as a process by which one individual attempts to influence the activities of others on matters of importance in a given situation. Whether sales managers effectively influence salespeople depends on their knowledge of motivation, their ability to predict how individuals will respond to their leadership, and their capacity to adjust their influencing techniques as the situation changes.

Power is a tool sales managers use to influence the sales force. Within organizations, leaders typically have five different sources of power: legitimate, reward, coercive, expert, and referent. Followers react differently to these types of power. When a manager employs legitimate or reward power, followers usually comply. Coercive power produces resistance. The most effective powers, expert and referent, lead employees to commitment.

The choice of leadership behaviors to use depends on the relationships involved in the integrative leadership model, which consists of six important factors: the sales manager, the sales manager's behavior, the salesperson, the sales group, the situation, and the salesperson's behavior. Each of these six factors is individually composed of many elements.

The sales manager's behavior is based on that individual's personality, needs and motives, power, and past experience. These traits directly influence the leadership style the manager chooses to use in a given situation. A good manager should show both task behavior and relationship behavior when working with salespeople. Leadership style also should be considered when supervising, coaching, or counseling.

The appropriate leadership style depends a great deal on the individual salesperson. Like the sales manager's behavior, the salesperson's behavior is based on personality, needs and motives, and past experience. However, managers should examine a fourth element when studying the individual salesperson: performance level.

The sales group is the third factor in the integrative leadership model. Four elements combine to form the personality of the sales group: characteristics, expectations, norms, and sales culture. These four also influence the leader's effectiveness. The leader must take into consideration the individual salespeople who compose the group and behave accordingly.

Circumstances surrounding an individual situation, such as the task faced and the amount of time allotted to complete the task, also can affect a leader's management style.

Organizational factors also have a bearing on a leader's effectiveness. Factors such as pressure to achieve goals, proper procedures, and job uncertainty are inherent to the company and thus applicable to all employees.

The final factor in the integrative leadership model is the salesperson's behavior. Leadership is a two-way influence process, with the manager's behavior often a reaction to the salesperson's behavior. Three measures of a leader's effectiveness are employee performance, satisfaction, and turnover. These measures can be analyzed, and the manager's leadership can be changed based on the outcomes.

■ KEY TERMS FOR SALES MANAGERS

Leadership, 332	Supervision, 338	Career counseling, 346
Management, 332	Work withs, 339	Job adjustment counseling, 346
Sales manager, 332	Coaching, 339	
Power, 334	Joint sales call, 339	Social adjustment counseling, 346
Legitimate power, 335	Curbstone conferences, 343	
Reward power, 335	Counseling, 344	Personal adjustment counseling, 346
Coercive power, 335	Directive guidance, 345	
Expert power, 335	Problem solving, 345	Ability, 347
Referent power, 335	Nondirective guidance, 346	Motivation, 347
Task behavior, 336	Performance counseling, 346	Norms, 351
Relationship behavior, 336		

■ MANAGEMENT APPLICATION QUESTIONS

1. Discuss how a sales manager acquires different kinds of power to influence salespeople. Which of these powers are most important for a manager to have?
2. Leadership research has not found any single best leadership style. A situational approach suggests that a number of appropriate leadership styles exist, and which one may be best will depend on the situation. Describe the four major leadership styles discussed in the text, and give an example (other than those in the text) of when that leadership style would be appropriate.
3. Discuss what kind of leadership style a sales manager should use when working with a salesperson who is highly motivated and enjoys making calls on customers. Does it make a difference whether this is a new recruit or a veteran salesperson?
4. Discuss what other factors may influence a sales manager's choice of leadership styles, besides the sales manager and individual salespeople.
5. As a sales manager responsible for eight salespeople, what kind of personal and business relationship would you try to have with each of them?
6. Assume you discovered one of your salespeople was abusing alcohol and drugs yet was doing a great job. What would you do?

7. Imagine yourself a manager with a 54-year-old salesperson who consistently had poor performance for the past two years. This person has worked for the company 25 years. The person has two children in high school and one in college. The person's spouse recently quit work due to bad health. How would you handle this situation?

FURTHER EXPLORING THE SALES WORLD

Interview a district sales manager to determine what methods he or she uses to supervise, coach, and counsel salespeople. Ask the manager to describe "work withs." Does the manager complete a "work-with" report? What factors and activities does the manager evaluate when working with a salesperson?

SALES MANAGEMENT EXPERIENTIAL EXERCISE

WHAT MOTIVATES YOU?

Recently employees and their managers were asked, "What motivates you?" Survey results are shown below.

Ranked by Employees	Ranked by Managers
1. Interesting work	1. Compensation
2. Appreciation by management	2. Job security
3. Being well informed	3. Growth opportunities
4. Job security	4. Good working conditions
5. Compensation	5. Interesting work
6. Growth opportunities	6. Company's loyalty to employees
7. Good working conditions	7. Tactful discipline
8. Company's loyalty to employees	8. Appreciation by management
9. Tactful discipline	9. Help with personal problems
10. Help with personal problems	10. Being well informed

Instructions: Do you agree with the ranking of factors motivating both employees and managers? Why or why not? Why would employees rank compensation fifth? Which factor relates to leadership? Rank each of the ten factors for what motivates you.

CASE 14.1

INDIANA RESTAURANT EQUIPMENT & SUPPLIES
What to Do with the Guerrilla

You're the boss—the sales manager at Indiana Restaurant Equipment & Supplies. You have the title, rank, experience, authority, and the accountability that come with the job. So what's the gripe?

You have the feeling your salespeople aren't following your instructions. Instead, your group is modifying or even ignoring many of your orders. It happens too often to be coincidental. No sales manager can create and activate sales plans under conditions that appear so uncontrollable. To make matters worse, the sales force has a certain togetherness, a camaraderie that, under other circumstances, would be most desirable. However, your salespeople too often march together in directions that bear little resemblance to your instructions and that don't necessarily fit in with your overall strategy and tactics.

You wonder if you are becoming paranoid. What's happening? You suspect that, although you are the sales group's formal leader, an informal leader has emerged. Deliberately or not, that leader has become influential and is playing a more dominant role in the group than you. And, what's more, you think you know exactly who that informal leader is—Li Chen, one of your top salespeople.

Li is one of the most productive members of your sales force. But he is behaving like an underground rebel, a guerrilla fighter, a gang leader. He is quite intelligent but has a big ego and a tremendous need for recognition and achievement. You once thought Li considered you a favorite teacher, but it seems he is really working to undermine you. The group's performance against sales quota has declined. Does a connection exist between the sales drop-off and the informal leader? Why did Li emerge as the group's informal leader? Did you drop the ball somewhere, somehow? You must correct the situation. Your first impulse is to confront Li. Tell him they can have only one sales manager, and you are the one. Li can like it or move on!

Oops! Cool it. What if Li does move on and take his skills to your competitor? That's not good at all. You lose his powerful selling skills, and your competitor gains them. Besides, you really do like Li as a person. You also could lose the sales group's respect.

QUESTIONS
1. How can you turn the situation around?
2. What should you do with Li?

R.J. REYNOLDS TOBACCO COMPANY
Beyond Field Sales ... The Home Office

Becoming a really good all-around salesperson frequently involves a move into sales management. Several traditional levels in sales management exist that one can move through as skills and experience permit. Some exceptional sales managers, however, look for wider opportunities at the real nerve center of marketing, the home office. This is where the best and brightest can apply their successful marketing backgrounds. In large companies, line and staff positions are available in marketing research, advertising, public relations, product management, human resource development, or on the home office sales staff. Successful selling or sales management experience is often the proving ground for many of these jobs, especially in consumer goods companies. In the following case, Kerry Gatlin finds himself in a training position at the home office. It is proving to be a real challenge.

Dr. Colgin, staff psychologist for R.J. Reynolds Tobacco Company, greeted Kerry Gatlin as he came into his office at corporate headquarters in Winston-Salem, North Carolina. After receiving a phone call earlier in the day from the troubled Gatlin, Dr. Colgin agreed to meet with him after hours to accommodate Gatlin's urgent request for an appointment. Dr. Colgin knew only that Gatlin's wife had asked for a separation and left with their two small children the evening before but did not know what had precipitated this problem.

"Come in, Kerry," Dr. Colgin said. "I know how upset you are and I want to help. Why don't you start from the beginning and tell me what you feel led up to this unfortunate situation?"

"Well, I've been with the company for eight years," Kerry began, "and right now I feel like everything I've worked so hard for is going up in smoke. I started to work with RJR right out of college in my hometown—Little Rock, Arkansas. My wife, Beverly, was a schoolteacher. We had never thought of living anywhere else. But when I completed my six-month probationary period, I attended the orientation meeting for new salespeople at the home office here in Winston-Salem. I was very impressed by the caliber of people who spoke to us as well as the beautiful facilities and manufacturing plants. I made up my mind on the plane back to Little Rock that I was going to have an office at headquarters some day. I was going to do whatever it took to be where the action was."

Two and one-half years later Kerry had completed an M.B.A. at night while maintaining his position as the top performer in the Little Rock sales division. Within six months he was named assistant divisional sales manager in Atlanta, Georgia. He liked the managerial responsibility, but the new position required long hours away from his wife and new baby. The pressure to achieve his goals through others, rather than through his own efforts, created new and different problems. But, just as he had done before, he rose to the challenge and gave his job the long hours and hard work necessary to keep his career on track. As he was completing his first year and beginning to feel a little more comfortable as assistant divisional sales manager, his boss retired due to a heart condition. Kerry was named divisional sales manager and was made responsible for 18 sales reps. The job pressures became even more intense. These demands on his time and skills brought a renewed commitment to the "whatever it takes" philosophy he had followed successfully in the past.

Eighteen months after becoming divisional manager in Atlanta, Kerry was promoted to the home office. His position was assistant to the national advertising manager, a training slot for upwardly mobile, young management people. The position had been created three years before in an attempt to foster better understanding between the advertising and field sales organizations. The position could be filled only by someone approved by the sales manager and vice president of marketing. Kerry now reported to Bob Johnson, a top marketing executive who had moved up through advertising-agency and product-management experience, rather than field selling. Johnson, who was on a fast track himself, had made no secret of his desire to fill the slot with someone from within the national advertising department who could "carry their own weight." He had submitted the names of Joan Duville and Reilly Slickworth for the position, but Kerry was selected instead.

The job was everything Kerry had hoped it would be. Johnson, in spite of his reservations about someone from field sales, gave Kerry virtually all of the "glamour" trips—meeting and entertaining field sales managers

Sources: This case was written by Gerald Crawford, Professor of Marketing, University of North Alabama, Florence, and Tom F. Griffin, Lowder-Weil Eminent Scholar, Auburn University at Montgomery, Alabama.

and meeting and being entertained by advertising agency people. "It's just as well," Kerry said. "I don't think anyone else in the department could handle the demands of this travel schedule as well as I can." Kerry knew Johnson felt "maintaining relationships in the field" was important and that Kerry was "uniquely qualified" for this role due to his sales experience. However, due to his religious upbringing, Kerry was increasingly uncomfortable with the daily pattern of drinking alcohol that seemed to be an expected part of the glamour trips.

Kerry also admitted that his heavy travel schedule left him feeling "out of the loop." He never seemed to be a part of the strategy and planning sessions Johnson held with Duville, Slickworth, and other members of the national advertising staff. This was compounded by the fact he had not been trained to use his personal computer, which he knew could be used to produce the many written reports that were his responsibility and to analyze data on which planning was based. However, he did find the PC's clock and calendar functions to be very useful when he was in the office.

"It's not like they (Johnson, Duville, and Slickworth) don't want me to be a part of the planning," Kerry explained to Dr. Colgin. "Why, just two weeks ago, they asked me to join them for golf and lunch on Saturday to have some informal discussions about the coming year's promotion and sales strategy. Unfortunately, I was already scheduled to make a presentation in Denver that day. It would have been very informative for me. I understand that Johnson's boss, Elaine Cofield, director of advertising, also joined them."

Even though he was frequently called on to speak at large field sales meetings and explain the company's advertising support for new brands and promotional programs, Kerry never felt that he knew enough to speak authoritatively, or even accurately. Although he was considered an excellent speaker, anxiety and gastrointestinal problems would predictably begin to overtake him several days before each presentation. Kerry began to feel he was put in the position of defending advertising programs to the field sales organization. The tension between sales and advertising added to Kerry's anxieties. Sales always wanted more effective advertising or more control of the promotional budget. Advertising wanted more control of the promotional budget and better follow-up support from the field sales organization.

Kerry had discussed his feelings with Johnson, who assured him he himself would be able to spend more time with Kerry after the current round of marketing programs was in place. But, for the time being, Kerry's role in the field was indispensable to the national advertising organization. Johnson told Kerry, "We are a team, and we have made some impressive improvements in national advertising, which have not gone unnoticed at the top. I'm proud of what we have accomplished, and it will certainly be a feather in your cap when you return to the field sales organization. Right now we must continue to push ahead. I've set some impressive goals for our organization, and if we play as a team I know we can achieve them. Right now our back is to the wall. We really don't have any flexibility in our schedule if we want to get everything accomplished.

In addition to the job problems and stress, personal concerns now seemed to take precedence. Kerry's wife Beverly had not been happy and had mentioned divorce several times during the past few years. The couple now had two children, and it was clear that Kerry had not spent enough time with them or with his wife since moving to Winston-Salem. After returning from the ten-day business trip to Denver, Colorado, Kerry had been told by his wife that she wanted a legal separation in order to "think things over." The following day she left with the two children.

Kerry Gatlin looked at Dr. Colgin and asked, "What can I do now?" Clearly, he could not continue on the same course. His motivation and determination did not seem adequate to carry him through the present crisis.

QUESTIONS

1. What role does a mentor play in this case?
2. How could some of the present problems have been avoided?
3. What alternatives are open to Kerry Gatlin?
4. Which problems need immediate attention?
5. Can the marriage be saved?
6. Can this young man's career be saved?

OHIO BIOTECH, INC.
Night Work and Travel Have to Stop

Ellen Peters has asked to see you about a "personal matter." Having recently reviewed her sales record, you know she has been at or over quota for the past six months. In fact, Ellen was able to achieve this while still finding time to attend the annual sales rally as well as two educational seminars. You have just finished reading a memo from your boss, Al St. Aubin, the district sales manager at Ohio Biotech, inquiring as to Ellen's potential as a sales manager when she approaches your door.

"Come right in, Ellen, and have a seat. What can I do to help you?"

"Well, Ron, . . . it's my husband, Jack. He is very upset because he sees so little of me lately. He said he would call you if I didn't talk to you."

"Well, that's a surprise, Ellen, when I talked with Jack on Spouse's Night at the sales rally he seemed really proud of your award."

"I know, Ron, but then I went to the two seminars over at State College, and I've been working long hours on my accounts. Also, Jack has had to go out of town two or three times to show his cars."

"I understand, Ellen, but what can I do? What do you want me to do?"

"Ron, I need to know that I won't have to work at night or go out of town overnight anymore. That's what Jack wants. He wants me home where he knows I'm safe."

In thinking about how to respond, you note that Ellen and Jack have been married for 16 months. Plus, when Ellen started working for Biotech, you told her that job duties would require working some evenings and some traveling.

QUESTION
What would you say to Ellen?

Source: This case was written by Dr. Jeff Sager, Professor of Marketing, University of North Texas, Denton, Copyright © 1999.

C & D FOODS, INC.
Leadership: Who Is Best for the Job?

C & D Foods is a stable, old-line, family-owned food broker located in Birmingham, Alabama. The firm was started in 1948 by Marty Wilson and later managed by his sons, Steve, William, and John Wilson. C & D carries some top food brands, most of which are found in the frozen-food cases in supermarkets and in neighborhood grocery stores. Almost 200 salespeople sell to retail and wholesale accounts in Alabama, Mississippi, Georgia, and the Florida Panhandle. Some brands C & D sells are Pillsbury Frozen Food Products, Green Giant, Mrs. Paul's, Ore-Ida, Weight Watchers, Totino's and Gino's Pizzas, Minute Maid, and Hot Pockets. Sales have grown steadily over the years, and the sales forecast predicts continued yearly increases of approximately 12 percent.

Tom Pirkle has been with C & D foods for almost seven years and has been in the top 10 percent of sales producers over the past three years. He started with the company directly out of college and has earned the reputation of being easy to work with and professional in every way. Not only has Tom been a top salesperson at C & D, but also he has become a leader in the Birmingham business community. He had applied for an area sales manager's position with C & D that would soon be opening in Birmingham because of an upcoming retirement. In the past few months, however, Tom had become uneasy about his chances for promotion and had talked with his retiring area sales manager, Bob O'Brien. He had thought about talking with the general sales manager, Don Hendon, but had not yet gotten around to it. O'Brien told him he was truly appreciated and respected by the company and would be given "full consideration" for the upcoming vacancy. But the area sales manager was not very encouraging about Tom's chances of getting the position. Tom knew Bob O'Brien well enough to know that he was not being up front with him and that something else was probably going on privately.

In 1987 an inside salesperson, Mary James, filed a discrimination suit against C & D Foods. She made the allegation that her employer had not promoted her to an outside sales position, which involved significantly more pay, because she was a woman. The company quietly resolved the dispute, and Mary was given a territory in the Birmingham metro area. Within two years Mary James had become a top producer in the company. The company was so pleased with her success that it apparently began to show preference for female applicants. Eight female salespeople now work at C & D. Eight of the past ten persons hired have been women. The two new male salespeople were both African American. Mary James was promoted in 1992 to area sales manager in Columbus, Georgia.

This is the background for Tom's current concerns. He wants to become the next area sales manager in Birmingham when his friend retires, but he has heard through the grapevine that Barbara Howard, who has been with the company only three years, will probably get the job. It is true she is a good salesperson, but not in the same league with Tom Pirkle in sales volume or leadership qualities.

Tom talked with his friend George Montgomery, a management professor at the university, about his predicament. George explained that owners Steve, William, and John Wilson were probably so frightened by the 1987 lawsuit that they may have decided to push the affirmative action and equal opportunity programs beyond their intent. It is possible that Tom is now in a "reverse discrimination" situation. However, his chances in litigation would be about zero, according to Dr. Montgomery. He did agree it was an unfortunate turn of events for Tom, who had never been a part of any discrimination or sexist activity. George's parting words to Tom were "You just happen to be in the wrong place at the wrong time."

Tom thought to himself as he walked to his car, "I studied hard in school and took my marketing classes seriously. Since then I have tried to be the best salesman that I could possibly be, and I have worked so hard in my territory and in the community. This window of opportunity will soon pass, and my chances of promotion will disappear. What can I tell my friends and my family? Where do I go from here?"

QUESTIONS

1. From the facts available in the case, who would make the best area sales manager, Tom Pirkle or Barbara Howard?
2. Is Tom Pirkle being objective in this matter?
3. Was Professor George Montgomery's thinking objective?
4. Should performance be measured by other standards?
5. What else can Tom Pirkle do to get more facts or to resolve his present situation?
6. What risks does the company take if it promotes Barbara Howard over Tom Pirkle?
7. What can Tom say to his friends and family?

Source: This case was written by professors Gerald Crawford, Eminent Scholar, School of Business, and William S. Stewart, Dean, School of Business, both at the University of North Alabama, Florence.

PART VI
CONTROLLING THE SALES TEAM

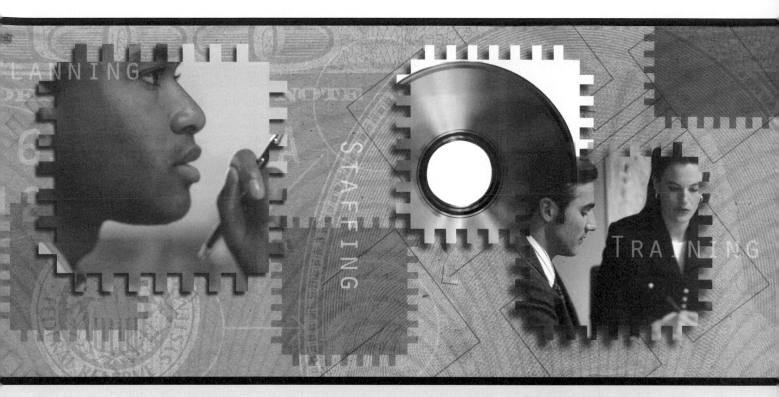

ANALYZING AND evaluating sales and marketing costs and the individual salesperson's performance to determine whether objectives have been reached are vital to the success of a sales force. Part VI includes the following: Chapter 15, "Analysis of Sales and Marketing Costs," and Chapter 16, "Evaluation of Salespeople's Performance."

CHAPTER 15
ANALYSIS OF SALES AND MARKETING COSTS

CHAPTER OUTLINE

MARKETING AUDIT

NET SALES VOLUME ANALYSIS

MARKETING COST ANALYSIS

LEARNING OBJECTIVES

Control of the marketing program is very important and is partially achieved by an analysis of net sales volume and marketing costs. This chapter should help you understand:

- The importance of marketing and sales audits and how they differ.

- That misdirected marketing effort can result in a loss of sales and profit.

- What sales analysis is and what it is used for.

- The important elements involved in marketing cost analysis.

Recently, Bristol-Myers Squibb decided to electronically reengineer the logistics of its customer service operations for the Clairol and Bristol-Myers product lines into one centralized support service. A project goal was to create a single data repository that would support finished goods through better computer-based management and tracking of accounts, promotional campaigns, and sales information.

When the company reengineered its service operations, the strategic goals were to reduce operating costs, streamline distribution efforts, and enhance customer services. "Our principal technology goals were to update our system so information would be fresher and more accurate and to focus more on the customer than we had in the past," Pat Cunningham, vice president of customer development, says.

The new Bristol-Myers sales and marketing cost system tracks sales, costs, and promotional campaigns, and provides sales information for product planning. The software supports accounts receivable and provides sales and analysis information, as well as historical information for forecasting and planning the manufacturing process.

"The system provides us with a simple but effective way to manage marketing funds for promotions and to monitor a promotion fund's performance," Cunningham says. "You can track the balance of a particular promotion fund, its budget, what has been committed by a customer, and what has yet to be done. With promotion funds management, we can assess whether a specific promotion achieves its sales management, we can assess whether a specific promotion achieves its sales goals, allowing us to make more-informed decisions."

The system also has automated the pricing process for Bristol-Myers, providing order-entry representatives with more information regarding accounts and more control over variables related to orders. For instance, it offers sales promotion and agreement data automatically so a representative is aware of a customer's promotion eligibility when an order is placed.

Coupled with electronic data interchange (EDI), the entire pricing, ordering, and invoicing process has been accelerated. "EDI is resident in the system, not an add-on," Cunningham says, "which helps ensure data integrity. That advantage gives us the ability to check inbound information from a customer order before it goes into the system, preventing any outbound errors from occurring in shipping, invoicing, or collection.

"Now our internal customer service representatives and field sales representatives—equipped with notebook computers and modems—have access to the system." Order turnaround time has been reduced by almost 50 percent and order management costs by 35 to 40 percent. Cash flow also has improved.[1] ■

Salespeople and their managers must plan, implement their plans, and then analyze their sales data to determine if they reached their sales objectives. Their past and current sales are used to set future marketing and sales plans. With today's computers and software, organizations such as Bristol-Myers Squibb can generate more data than that available about a professional football or baseball player.

The effectiveness of the sales force and of the overall marketing effort is reflected in the sales volume generated by each segment and the corresponding profit that results. A firm cannot stay in business, at least in the long run, unless profits are earned, no matter how efficiently the sales force is managed.

Profitability of territories, products, customers, and other units can be determined using sales and marketing costs analysis. This information is of great interest to sales executives and can affect the decisions they make. More and more firms are using this information in marketing and sales audits in a manner similar to Bristol-Myers Squibb.

The first part of this chapter is devoted to the analysis of net sales volume, describing what common bases are used to break down aggregate sales volume into smaller, more controllable segments; the problems incurred in sales analysis; and the uses for this type of study. The second part of the chapter is concerned with marketing cost analysis, what it is, and how it is used. Varying techniques are examined, and some problems are discussed.

Sales and cost analyses will not actually identify problems for the sales or marketing manager, but, if done properly, will indicate the presence of problems. The discovery of problem areas may result in changes that may improve sales and profits.

MARKETING AUDIT

The **marketing audit** is an evaluative tool designed to appraise the entire marketing operation in a systematic and comprehensive manner. It is used to evaluate the degree the marketing function is integrated with company operations by examining corporate marketing objectives, procedures, and methods and by tracing areas of responsibility for their implementation. Just as the auditing function attests to the accounting system operations as a whole, the marketing audit is designed to evaluate the total marketing operation, as opposed to singling out individual departments and programs or breaking down components of the marketing mix.

A marketing audit is not accomplished at a single point in time; it is most frequently an ongoing process, designed to uncover opportunities for improving marketing methods and activities as a whole and for increasing the firm's understanding of new marketing concepts and how they may be applied. Six aspects of marketing should be covered by the audit: objectives, policies, organization, methods, procedures, and personnel. The firm's effectiveness in each of these areas depends mainly on how the firm uses the marketing concept (for example, Is it totally consumer oriented?) and how the marketing strategy is adjusted to social, cultural, legal, and political environments.

The marketing audit should be performed by independent persons who do not have direct control or the responsibility for carrying out marketing activities. Often a separate department within the company, such as a marketing controller, may conduct the audit. Outside sources, such as management consulting firms, are sometimes employed to do the audit in order to achieve a degree of impartiality.

SALES FORCE AUDIT

The marketing audit can be applied to a smaller entity such as the sales force. A **sales force audit** involves the same six factors the marketing audit measures but is designed to evaluate selling strategy and to improve overall sales force effectiveness.

Once again, emphasis is on a systematic, unbiased review of the system (in this case, the sales force) as a whole. Some questions a sales force audit answers follow:

1. Are motivational techniques contributing to overall goals?
2. What are the target market's characteristics, and how is the company/ the competition responding to them?
3. What are the product line's characteristics, and how competitive are the product lines and sales policies of salespeople?
4. Are adequate controls available to direct the selling effort?
5. How well defined are the sales strategies, and how effectively are they contributing to the sales division's objectives?

THE 80/20 PRINCIPLE   The marketing effort should emphasize the subdivisions of categories as well as the aggregate total. The **80/20** or "concentration" **principle** states that the majority of a company's sales (or profits) may result directly from a very small number of the company's accounts, product or price lines, or geographic areas. For example, 80 percent of a company's sales may be coming from only 20 percent of its customers; accounts more than $2,000 may result in 75 percent of total sales; or one product line may contribute 65 percent of company net profit. With appropriate marketing sales and cost analysis, the marketing manager can identify profitable and high sales volume areas but must take care that a sufficient number of relevant breakdowns of the total sales or profit figures are available.

Many times a firm must carry marginal or unprofitable products to complement the existing product line, thus supplementing the more profitable sales areas. Equally, unprofitable or low-profit geographic areas often must be covered to contribute effectively to consumer perception and loyalty.

The 80/20 situation may exist even in well-managed firms. Management is often unaware of the true cost of serving unprofitable accounts and areas and cannot identify the particular percentages of sources that account for given sales. This problem is also complicated by salespeople's quotas. The quota is an incentive to increase sales in any way possible, including sales to unprofitable accounts, when greater corporate profit could be realized by concentrating sales effort on more-profitable accounts.

DIRECTING THE MARKETING EFFORT

Large capital expenditures on marketing are necessary to better isolate the specific needs and wants of target segments, to educate the target customers as to how they may fulfill those desires, and, ultimately, to stimulate consumer demand. For this reason, the marketing dollar must be allocated in a way that best generates high sales volume and net profits by concentrating marketing effort in the most profitable areas. Too often, management relates marketing expense to *total* sales volume or *total* net profits, with little regard for identifying the market segments that produce the majority of the sales and profit. Company management often will divide the total marketing allocation arbitrarily or equally among departments, product lines, geographic areas, price lines, or other easily identifiable segments.

Because different net profits, or unit sales, are contributed by different product lines, price lines, and geographic areas, the managers should direct the majority of marketing expenditures to areas for which the profit return per marketing dollar spent is the highest or for which the highest sales volume is generated. If a company manufactures cassette tapes that make a high contribution to profit and also markets cleaning cartridges (a complementary line) that make a very low contribution to profit, it would be inefficient to assign the same promotional effort to both product lines. The cassette tapes should receive the heaviest emphasis, because they possess the highest market potential. To illustrate the point another way, if an auto manufacturer sells 18 percent of annual production output to consumers in California but sells only 2 percent to Idaho, Montana, Wyoming, and Utah, the marketing effort should be much more intensely developed in California than in the other four states combined.

One might ask whether, if sales are comparatively low or unprofitable in certain areas, those areas should be eliminated completely and the firm's entire effort concentrated on the most productive segments. A firm will not normally choose to move in this direction for two reasons. First, fixed costs may be such that they will not have to be increased to produce additional product volume. In effect, if the product can be sold for more than its variable production cost, the sales dollars generated help contribute to fixed expenses, which are incurred whether or not the product is produced. Therefore, although the product itself is unprofitable, the company's overall profitability is increased by producing it. Second, and most important to the marketing manager, some product lines must be carried to complement a line or to provide a selling feature that will enhance sales in more profitable areas. The consumer might be more willing to buy the firm's cassette tapes if cleaning cartridges are offered as well, and the California consumer may be more inclined to purchase a car when assured that, if he or she gets transferred to Idaho, parts and service from a local dealer will still be available. However, the company cannot fulfill its objectives by relying on low sales areas or low profit lines, and the marketing effort in such cases should be minimal.

High sales volume and the resulting market share, without regard to profit, in individual segments are often the basis for heavy marketing emphasis. This is somewhat sound because high sales and market share help the company achieve visibility by promoting a high level of consumer awareness. However, profit should be the determining criterion because low sales with a large amount of total net profit contribute more to a company than does high sales volume with low contribution to net profits.

Marketers should take care to direct the marketing effort toward the person who most influences the decision to buy. They must determine whether it is the purchaser, the user, or a third party who will decide to make the purchase. While Jif peanut butter targeted the homemaker/mother in its ads ("Choosy mothers choose Jif"), Peter Pan aimed at the primary user, showing a child who says, "Although Mommy buys it, I eat it, and I choose Peter Pan."

The marketing effort must be based on the actual or potential sales volume, gross margin, or profit, not directed arbitrarily by territory, customer, product, or other division.

ICEBERG PRINCIPLE   Problems usually arise when marketing and sales activities are evaluated using aggregate, or very general, sales figures. An overall favorable volume or profit picture may cover up individual problem areas that may be overshadowed by more-profitable segments. Just as only 10 percent of an iceberg is visible above the surface, very few underlying causes of sales performance are apparent to the sales analyst using generalized performance figures. The **iceberg principle** refers to the effect that averaging, summarizing, and aggregating data can have on presenting the true sales or profit picture and underlying problems. The danger lies in assuming a favorable overall picture is indicative of a successful operation in each of the company's segments; therefore, it promotes a false sense of security in relation to company operations.

To illustrate, assume the following sales for Ajax machinery:

	1999	2000
Sales	$1,840,000	$1,916,000

At first glance, it appears Ajax is managing its operations effectively. Sales have increased by $76,000 over the previous year. However, further examination uncovers the number of units sold.

	1999	2000
Sales (units)	21,450	20,068

Now it is clear that sales, in units, have dropped off. This might indicate that higher-priced units were sold, and the company's sales increase would still look promising; conversely, it might indicate that the increase in sales is due only to rises in the consumer price index. Note that the iceberg principle is at work here. To find out where the problem lies, auditors must break down the sales figures into smaller units such as territories, accounts, product/price lines, and time periods.

Although Ajax dollar sales appear to be increasing at a satisfactory rate, a comparison with the entire industry also should be made. Assume the following total industry sales:

	1999	2000
Industry sales	$198,342,000	246,890,000

These indicate that Ajax was indeed experiencing a decline in market share (93 percent in 1999 compared with 78 percent in 2000), and that it was growing at a much slower rate than the industry as a whole.

Next, suppose the following breakdown of sales was supplied to the marketing analyst:

AJAX MACHINERY 2000 SALES

REGION	QUOTA	ACTUAL	VARIATION
NW	$134,000	$104,000	$−29,500
SE	328,000	328,500	+500
SW	286,000	285,000	−1,000
NE	398,000	402,000	+4,000

Further analysis is necessary to uncover the reason for the poor performance in the Northwest district. These questions should be answered:

1. Was the quota set too high?
2. Are salespeople having trouble with a particular product line?
3. Can the problem be narrowed down to a particular salesperson, sales district, product, or price line?
4. Do any sales divisions or districts have poor management?

When analysts investigate questions like these using a breakdown of the sales figures, they can identify the specific problem areas and take remedial action. If the problem is a lazy salesperson servicing large accounts in the Northwest region, the sales manager should aim at motivating that salesperson specifically, rather than designing a sales contest to increase Northwest region sales.

In addition, it cannot be assumed that other regions that met their assigned quotas are producing acceptably. As noted earlier, it is possible that poor performance for a particular product line is overshadowed by record sales for other major product lines. The competent market analyst continues the breakdown until the following have been ascertained: (1) where weak performance exists and (2) what controllable factors contribute to the problem. Computer-generated data can assist the sales analyst in virtually every area desired: breakdowns by salesperson, product, account, or territory.

NET SALES VOLUME ANALYSIS

WHAT IS SALES ANALYSIS?

Sales analysis is the detailed examination of a company's sales data and involves assimilating, classifying, comparing, and drawing conclusions. Although the extent of sales analysis varies from company to company, all companies collect sales data in the form of customer sales invoices or cash register receipts, which are necessary to maintain their accounting records. Management relays its requirements for sales information to the sales analyst, who collects data from external and internal sources, records them, and aids management with interpreting the data. Managers use sales analyses to evaluate current performance, for future planning, and to direct the sales effort.

ACCUMULATION OF SALES ANALYSIS INFORMATION   Sales are classified into many categories that serve as a basis for management's analysis. Sales figures may be reported in dollars, shipments, or sales orders and can be broken down into any of the following categories:

- Product lines
- Geographic areas
- Customer classes
- Order sizes
- Time periods
- Methods of sale
- Organizational units
- Salespeople

The criteria for categorization depend on what breakdown will provide management the most relevant and meaningful sales information. Categories are subdivided to provide enough detailed information to uncover problem areas. A firm's aggregate net sales figure may be broken down by geographic region, and, in turn, each region may be subdivided according to product line. The extent of the subdivision and the amount of data generated depend largely on the time and the money available for the analysis. Clearly, this is a situation in which the cost of generating the information desired should not exceed the benefits derived.

USES OF SALES ANALYSIS   The major use for sales analysis is to detect strengths and weaknesses in the sales effort. It shows who the largest customers are, how much is being sold, and where sales are most likely to occur. Sales data also can alert management to changes in market demographics and in the nature of the competition. Most important, sales analysis lays the foundation for more extensive analysis of marketing costs, from which performance efficiency and profitability can be determined. Several major broad applications of sales analysis follow:

- Establishment of the sales forecasting system.
- Development of sales performance measures.
- Evaluation of market position.
- Production planning and inventory control.
- Maintaining appropriate product mixes.
- Modifying the sales territory structures.
- Planning sales force activities.
- Evaluation of salespeople's performance.
- Measuring the effect of advertising and other sales promotional activities.
- Modifying channels of distribution.
- Evaluating channels of distribution.

ANALYZING SALES VOLUME

TOTAL SALES VOLUME   The beginning point in a net sales volume analysis is the total volume of the company's sales. **Total sales volume** is the first indication of how the company is faring in the marketplace. Total sales volume refers to the total sales for a specific period for a company, region, product, or customer. To measure this, three trends must be noted. First, is company sales volume increasing or decreasing over time? If sales volume is measured in dollars, an increase might indicate either increased unit sales or relatively constant sales paid for with inflated dollars. Next, what is happening to industry demand at this time? If company sales volume is increasing while industry demand is decreasing, the company might be doing exceedingly well; but if industry demand is increasing while company sales are increasing, the analyst needs to further investigate how fast each is increasing. Only then can the company determine whether it is retaining its share of the market. Third, what is the trend in the firm's market share? Is it maintaining a constant portion of industry demand, or are competitors eroding its market potential? Market share is determined by dividing company sales volume in dollars by industry demand in dollars.

Information used in the analysis of total sales volume for a hypothetical firm, the Imperial Home Appliance Corporation, is listed in Table 15.1. The firm manufactures six major product lines: washers, dryers, microwave ovens, ranges, refrigerators, and dishwashers. The company distributes nationally and divides the country geographically into the Midwest, Southwest, southern, eastern, and Pacific regions.

Annual sales, which have increased every year since 1994, were $181.3 million in 2000. It appears from Table 15.1 that the sales picture for Imperial is satisfactory; sales volume is increasing at a more rapid rate than industry demand, which is also increasing, and the company's share of the market has been steadily rising. At this point, the sales manager could be proud of a job well done and explore the issue no further.

TABLE 15.1

IMPERIAL HOME APPLIANCE CORP.: TOTAL SALES VOLUME (MILLIONS)

YEAR	COMPANY SALES VOLUME	INDUSTRY DEMAND	SHARES OF MARKET (%)
1994	$143.5	$ 8,644.6	1.66
1995	147.2	8,710.1	1.69
1996	151.7	9,029.8	1.68
1997	157.6	9,270.6	1.70
1998	168.7	9,868.1	1.71
1999	170.4	9,964.9	1.71
2000	181.3	10,419.5	1.74

Aggregate figures, however, hide individual problem areas. The marketing manager would do better to examine further breakdowns and uncover the iceberg effect.

Sales by Region: District   Table 15.2 is a regional breakdown of company sales volume. Here it is advantageous to compare regional sales with some other performance standard. Table 15.2 uses the retail sales index, but many other relevant indexes are readily available and may be more suited to the firm's individual needs—for example, *Sales Management's* Buying Power Index. The **retail sales index** is a relative measure of the dollar volume of retail sales that normally occur in each respective district. Based on the index selected, a quota is established using company sales volume as its basis. Actual sales from each region are compared with the established sales quota, and a dollar deviation is noted. It is desirable to express deviation in dollars rather than percentages because percentage figures tend to hide significant magnitudes of variation: for example, a 0.2 percent deviation may look insignificant, and it is if sales are $2,000, but it becomes very significant at a sales level of $20 million dollars.

Note the dollar deviations from the quota in Table 15.2. Apparently, the Pacific region has a problem. Perhaps the method of setting the quota should be scrutinized to determine whether the quota is reasonable. On the other hand, the Pacific region might be experiencing fierce competition from a regional firm; the sales force may be inadequate to handle the Pacific region's needs, and additional personnel should be hired; or the screening process may need strengthening. The sales manager probably will want to investigate further before reaching a conclusion.

An additional territorial breakdown shows that the problem may have been narrowed down (Table 15.3). The entire Pacific district is not noticeably inefficient; only the northern California district seems to be at fault. The marketing manager at this point might consider additional advertising in the northern California district or additional sales effort. Perhaps a memo aimed at stimulating sales effort should be sent to all sales reps in the district. Before taking this action, however, the sales manager may decide to analyze the performance of the four salespeople assigned to the northern California district.

TABLE 15.2

IMPERIAL HOME
APPLIANCE CORP.:
REGIONAL BREAKDOWN
OF SALES (THOUSANDS)

Region	Retail Sales Index[a]	Sales Quota	Actual Sales	Dollar Deviation
Midwest	99	$35,924	$36,075	+151
Southwest	95	34,473	34,449	−24
Southern	89	32,296	34,378	+2,082
Eastern	105	38,102	39,261	+1,159
Pacific	103	37,376	37,137	−239

[a]Or other relevant index.

TABLE 15.3

IMPERIAL HOME
APPLIANCE CORP.:
PACIFIC REGION
(THOUSANDS)

District	Quota[a]	Actual Sales	Dollar Deviation
Washington	$ 4,485	$ 4,497	+12
Idaho–Oregon	3,925	3,921	−4
Northern California	10,801	10,507	−294
Southern California	18,165	18,212	+47

[a]This quota can be established by company experience or by projected indexes.

SALES BY SALESPERSON   Assuming the sales manager has indeed defeated the iceberg principle and uncovered the problem, Table 15.4 shows that the salesperson with the poor performance is R. Stevens. Stevens's actual sales ($2,421) divided by his assigned quota ($2,792) results in a performance index of 87. Before firing Stevens for failing to achieve his sales goals, the sales manager might consider the possibility that some of Stevens's major accounts may be giving him trouble. Possible reasons for this could be bankruptcy of a high-volume customer or customers dropping their accounts due to a competitor's aggressive action.

SALES BY CUSTOMER CLASSIFICATION   Illustrated in Table 15.5 are selected retail outlets in the northern California district Stevens services. Only one account, Golden Gate Electric, appears to be doing well. Should Stevens be fired as a result of this discovery? It certainly does appear he has not been working to his potential as determined by the company.

Note that when classifications are made by customer, some firms find it more appropriate to break down sales volumes according to customer class. Examples of this, concerning the sale of washing machines, would be designations by institutions (schools, prisons, nursing homes), individual consumers, apartment complexes, or public services (self-service laundries, motels).

SALES BY PRODUCT   As a final move, the sales manager may decide to investigate the sales volume for each individual product line Stevens sold. It is evident from the information in Table 15.6 that Stevens's major problem is the dishwasher line. Sales analysis does not indicate *why* this is a problem. Is it a problem with the dishwasher line or with Stevens's lack of attention to this product line? Suppose subsequent analysis by the sales manager, including regional product breakdowns and investigation of retail outlets, indicated that the dishwasher line was having problems nationwide. High-volume sales in other successful product lines had hidden this fact. Without the extensive analysis that was performed, the sales manager might have taken inappropriate action to solve the problem, such as firing Stevens. With the aid of a thorough sales analysis, however, the real problem became apparent.

SALESPERSON	QUOTA	ACTUAL	DIFFERENCE	PERFORMANCE INDEX[a]
C. Black	$2,848	$2,896	$+48	102
R. Stevens	2,792	2,421	−371	87
B. Penn	3,006	3,023	+17	101
P. McGee	2,155	2,167	+12	101

[a]Actual Sales/Quota × 100.

TABLE 15.4

IMPERIAL HOME APPLIANCE CORP.: PACIFIC REGION, N. CALIFORNIA DISTRICT (THOUSANDS)

RETAIL STORES	QUOTA	ACTUAL	DIFFERENCE
Northstar Furniture Co.	$518	$378	$−140
Levitz, Inc.	488	365	−123
Golden Gate Electric	366	388	+22
San Francisco Furniture Outlet	588	515	−73
R.C. Wiley & Sons	227	200	−27
All Others	605	575	−30

TABLE 15.5

IMPERIAL HOME APPLIANCE CORP.: SALES PERFORMANCE BY CUSTOMER, R. STEVENS, N. CALIFORNIA DISTRICT (THOUSANDS)

TABLE 15.6

IMPERIAL HOME
APPLIANCE CORP.: SALES
PERFORMANCE BY
PRODUCT LINE, R.
STEVENS, N. CALIFORNIA
DISTRICT (THOUSANDS)

	QUOTA	ACTUAL	DIFFERENCE
Washing machines	$516	$522	$+6
Dryers	272	270	−2
Microwave ovens	104	117	+13
Ranges	549	548	−1
Refrigerators	763	808	+45
Dishwashers	588	156	−432

MARKETING COST ANALYSIS

A common myth used as a basis for marketing decisions is that the success of a given marketing program should be evaluated solely by the level of net sales volume generated. As emphasized earlier in this chapter, a comprehensive analysis of net sales volume is essential for effective sales control, planning, and personnel management. However, the true determinant of the acceptability of a given program is its ultimate effect on company profitability, which is a function not only of net sales volume but also of the expenses incurred in generating that volume. Controlling costs of production and distribution leads to a more desirable marketing mix. If costs can be lowered by an improved production process, this savings can be passed on to the consumer in the form of a reduced price, or the money saved could be used to improve product quality.

The following discussion of marketing cost analysis emphasizes the objectives of the analysis and reasons for it. In addition, basic techniques of cost analysis are introduced, as are some treatments of problems and applications.

WHAT IS MARKETING COST ANALYSIS?

Marketing cost analysis, or distribution cost analysis, is the analysis of costs that affect sales volume, with the purpose of determining the profitability of different segment operations. In a sense, marketing cost analysis extends beyond sales analysis; **profitability** is determined by sales volume and its associated costs and expenses, and analysis of these factors can help pinpoint the origins of waste and inefficiency.

Just as the marketing manager's ultimate goal should not necessarily be only to maximize sales volume, neither should the marketing manager strive only to minimize distribution costs. Rather, the marketing manager should seek to achieve a balance between sales volume and distribution costs that will maximize the company's profits and use the available resources most efficiently. This is indeed a difficult task because sales volume is stimulated to a different extent by each kind of marketing program expenditure. It is hard to determine whether available funds should be invested in additional advertising, improved packaging, or service expansion. In addition, sales force compensation and evaluations of management personnel can be problematic, because performance goals are often contingent on sales volume rather than on contribution to profitability.

In spite of the inherent problems in application, marketing costs analysis can be invaluable in determining answers to these questions:

1. Which customers/accounts are unprofitable because of order size or geographic location?
2. What is the minimum order size that can be filled profitably?
3. Which distribution channel will be the most profitable for the firm to use? (*Not* which channel is the cheapest to use?)
4. Which territories are potentially most profitable?
5. What profit contribution does each salesperson make?
6. Can cost improvements be made in physical distribution facilities?

7. Which product lines are unprofitable or could be improved in their profitability?

Uses of Marketing Cost Analysis

Marketing cost analysis is an integral part of the decision-making process. It is central to management decisions concerning sales force control and marketing-mix adjustments.

Although salesperson Smith, for example, may sell a larger volume of merchandise than any of his colleagues, Smith may be one of the company's least profitable salespeople because of reckless expenditures. Marketing cost analysis can identify this problem. All aspects of the marketing mix, such as the effects of fluctuations in the promotional effort on profits, changes in price levels, different types of physical distribution, and changing emphasis on different trade channels, can be studied.

Marketing cost analysis also serves as the basis for management decisions concerning products, the need for repositioning, and the determination of optimum order size and inventory levels.

Another primary reason for performing marketing cost analysis is accountability. Management is highly interested in the questions "Did the money allocated accomplish the purpose it was intended for?" and "If so, to what extent?"

An effective marketing cost analysis depends to a great degree on adequate communication between the sales manager and the marketing analyst and on their ability to translate accounting data into costs that can be fairly ascribed to the persons responsible. Once a sufficient amount of information is assembled, management must make decisions aimed at remedying the identified problem areas and at evaluating the progress of areas modified.

Objectives of Marketing Cost Analysis

The major objectives of marketing cost analysis are to determine the isolated contributions made to profitability and to evaluate the efficiency of all phases of the company's marketing structure in terms of corporate goals and objectives. If a firm's major goal is to increase return to shareholders, an appropriate marketing cost analysis should assist management in doing so.

Two important uses of marketing cost analysis are (1) determining which marketing strategies are the best of many alternatives and (2) isolating problem areas.

Assigning Marketing Costs

To determine the profitability of a specific sales volume, it is first necessary to relate it to the cost of the marketing activities involved. To arrive at a net profit figure for the entire firm, production costs are deducted from net sales, resulting in a gross profit margin. Operating expenses such as salaries, rent, administrative expenses, and so on, are then deducted to arrive at an aggregate net profit figure. Managers encounter problems, however, when using this approach to calculate the net profit contribution of an individual company segment, whether it is a specific product line, territory, or other identifiable division. They can determine gross profit margin easily enough by noting the cost of goods sold in each segment, but how do they then determine what portion of the total rent expenses should be allocated to, for example, the Northwest territory? Or what percentage of company salary expenses should be assigned to Product A to find its contribution to overall corporate profit?

At this point a distinction must be drawn between a marketing cost and a production cost. A **production cost** is the cost incurred by processing a product from its raw elements to a finished state. Common examples of production costs are direct materials, direct labor, and factory overhead. In contrast, a *marketing cost* is any cost incurred between the time a product comes off the production line and the time it reaches the hands of the ultimate consumer. *Marketing cost* is often referred to as **distribution cost.** Marketing, or distribution, costs can be broken down into two distinct categories: costs incurred by getting orders and those incurred by filling orders (Figure 15.1). Included in order-getting costs are those needed to induce the customer to buy: sales promotion, advertising, direct selling, and so forth.

Order-filling costs are incurred during and after the time the sale is made to effect the transaction and to physically get the product to the customer. Included here are physical distribution costs such as shipping, handling, transporting, and warehousing; credit and collection costs; and general marketing costs relating to clerical and office activities.

Although marketing cost analysis is related to production cost analysis, this chapter covers only marketing cost analysis. Techniques of production cost analysis are covered extensively in textbooks on cost accounting. It is important, however, to be aware of the relationship between the two analyses. The basic goal of each is to control the costs generated by a company's activities. Accountants have historically given more emphasis to controlling production costs, and similar analysis applied to the marketing function has largely been ignored.

This has traditionally been so for four major reasons. First, in most firms, a lack of communication exists between marketing management and accountants. Second, the accountant is primarily concerned with production as a controllable area for which standards have been established, as opposed to the far more complex and less controllable marketing environment. For example, x dollars invested in materials and labor will result in a predictable increase in unit production, but who can say exactly what effect x dollars invested in advertising will have on sales? Third, conventional methods of cost analysis are inapplicable to marketing. Production cost factors are becoming increasingly more standardized, while no hard and fast rules apply to marketing function costs. Fourth, comprehensive analysis of marketing data had been unavailable prior to the advent of the computer. Because marketing data are varied, the mass of data that must be analyzed is so large that hand calculations are prohibitive.

As production efficiency increases due to specialization, and as computer use becomes more viable for the small firm, an ever greater emphasis on marketing cost analysis is expected. With increasing production, marketing is becoming more important for stimulating product demand. The greater emphasis on marketing will make it even more crucial for firms to develop ways to control marketing costs, and the computer will aid them in this effort.

For cost analysis, marketing costs must be allocated to different sales volumes so comparable gross profit figures can be determined. With this approach, management can more readily discover areas of marketing inefficiency, unproductive regions,

FIGURE 15.1

CATEGORIES OF
MARKETING COSTS

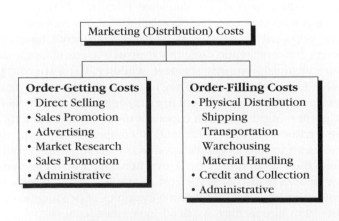

unprofitable product lines, and so on, and can adjust marketing policy accordingly. To allocate these costs, a reclassification of accounts by **functional marketing groups** (sometimes referred to as *activity groups*) is needed. These are different groups within the marketing operation that perform similar functions. First, a complete and detailed list of all the firm's marketing activities must be made. Examples of functional categories are warehousing, advertising, general administration, financial-clerical, sales promotion, and credit and collections. Costs must be assigned to each functional group. Accounting expenses are recorded as they are incurred in *natural accounts*; that is, companies keep records in categories that express the nature or purpose of the cost in question. Examples of natural accounts are wages, materials, office supplies, and rent. No subjective judgment is necessary to assign expenditures on a natural cost basis.

The natural cost basis, the traditional approach to accounting, must be modified for marketing cost analysis in order to properly assign expenses to functional cost groups. Given the many different natural accounts to be allocated to perform a segment analysis, it is imperative to exercise caution when choosing a relevant basis for allocation, and this decision should periodically be reevaluated. Some typical bases for allocating marketing costs to functional cost groups are listed in Table 15.7.

Different terminology is frequently used to describe classification of costs with reference to cost behavior. Commonly used cost classifications are defined in Table 15.8 (keep in mind that these cost categories are not necessarily mutually exclusive).

To summarize cost allocation: It is important to be able to trace the cost to the area that has direct responsibility for its occurrence, and this area of responsibility must have control; otherwise, the segment evaluation is based on factors beyond the manager's control.

METHODS FOR DETERMINING PROFITABILITY

Two basic approaches can be used to determine both overall corporate profitability and the profitability of identifiable segments. With the **full cost** (or *net profit approach*) **approach,** all costs (variable and fixed) are allocated among the market segments using the categories of goods sold (production costs) and operating expenses (nonproduction costs, including marketing costs). A segment's profitability is

FUNCTION[a]	BASIS FOR COST ALLOCATION
Warehousing and handling	Physical unit of goods handled (product, weight, or weighted factor), item handled, order line, or shipment
Transportation	Unit of product classes, weighted product unit, unit of product shipped as delivered, or dollar of shipments as delivered
Credit and collection	Account sales, credit sales transaction, or sales order
Market research	Time spent
Direct selling	Cost per customer served, cost per sales transaction, cost per sales order, or cost per product unit sold
Advertising and sales promotion	Prospect secured, sales transaction, or product unit sold

TABLE 15.7

SOME TYPICAL BASES FOR MARKETING COST ALLOCATION FOR SEGMENT ANALYSIS

[a]These functions can be broken down into more-specific categories and their costs allocated accordingly, if necessary. For example, clerical handling of shipping orders can be assigned to segments according to the number of shipments or orders.

Table 15.8

Commonly Used
Cost Classifications

- **Direct cost:** A cost that can be entirely identified with a particular segment and is totally separable. An example for a territorial analysis would be the salary expense employees incur delivering company products to retail outlets in a particular region only. Another example, for a product segment analysis, is a sales promotion campaign aimed at a particular product line only.
- **Indirect cost:** A cost that is common to more than one segment and therefore requires a basis for allocation among segments. Examples for both a territorial analysis and one for general administrative expenses would be media advertising campaigns that promote a specific product line nationally. Analysis of different types of segments requires different bases for allocation of certain costs. Consider expenditures for warehousing products when one warehouse services two or more territories. If product segmentation is selected, the warehouse expense charged to each product might be based on the percentage of floor space occupied by that product; whereas if segmentation by territory is selected, it would be more reasonable to use a basis such as the percentage of floor space all products for Territory A use.
- **Fixed cost:** A cost that remains unchanged for a given period despite wide fluctuations in activity. An example is the marketing manager's salary, because it remains basically the same regardless of the sales volume.
- **Variable cost:** A cost that changes in relation to changes in activity. Examples include commissions for salespeople, shipping expenses, and credit and collection expenses. The cost of each of these categories increases with an increase in sales volume.
- **Standard cost:** A predetermined or estimated cost for some type and amount of activity; for example, the estimated cost of direct materials for product A is $10 per unit. The "unit" standard is used to develop the company's budget. Standard costs are compared with actual costs incurred.
- **Controllable cost:** A cost over which management has some degree of control. An example is salespeople's expense accounts, because managers can influence the expenditures on direct selling by setting guidelines. Another example is the advertising cost, because management determines exactly how much to spend and where to spend it. Fixed costs, although controllable in the long run, are generally treated as uncontrollable in the short run. If a company invests in a new piece of major equipment, the manager will not have the option of investing in another item to perform the same task for a long time. Controllable costs are important because they are the only costs that must be used to determine a particular segment's contribution to profitability. These costs are included in the firm's entire profit picture but not in segmental analysis. Direct costs are controllable costs.
- **Uncontrollable cost:** A cost over which management has no control; that is, it originated outside the segment in question. An example would be the administrative costs the national office incurs. Managers should not be held responsible for inefficiencies resulting from uncontrollable costs. Indirect costs are uncontrollable costs.

determined by starting with its net sales, subtracting the cost of goods sold to produce gross margin, and then subtracting all operating expenses (controllable and uncontrollable) to arrive at the segment's net profit. The basic shortcoming of this approach is that it includes costs that do not affect marketing decisions and that the marketing division manager does not control. Therefore, its use is limited as a control device for management, and perhaps its most effective use is for external reporting purposes.

The other method of profitability determination is the **contribution margin approach** in which costs are separated according to controllability. The segment's controllable costs (variable and direct) are deducted from net sales to arrive at the segment contribution margin. The variable and direct costs are those that would be entirely eliminated if the segment did not exist and therefore pertain only to that particular segment.

An example of the full cost approach is given in Table 15.9. Net sales, cost of goods sold, and gross margin are shown for each of the five geographic regions of the Imperial Home Appliance Corp. Then all operating expenses are allocated to each region, using some arbitrary basis, and subtracted from gross margin to arrive at a net income figure for each region. Note the magnitude of difference between the net profit for the Pacific region and other regions.

Table 15.10 illustrates the contribution margin approach to an income statement. The Imperial Home Appliance Corp. is again segmented by region. Net sales are the same as they are with the full cost approach. Variable costs (those that fluctuate with net sales volume), including marketing and manufacturing costs, and assignable costs are first subtracted from net sales for each segment. This contribution margin is the amount each segment contributes to company overhead and to net profits. Nonassignable costs and fixed costs are not allocated to the segments. The contribution margins serve as measures of relative profitability. Note that the Pacific region, although still lowest in profitability, is not as low as when it was expressed as net income in Table 15.10. Note also that if we were to rank the regions in profitability, the eastern region would be the *most profitable* using the contribution margin approach. Contrast this with the full cost approach, where *only one region is shown as less profitable* than the eastern region. If the eastern region were totally eliminated, its $632,300 contribution to profit and overhead would have to be replaced by an additional contribution from other regions to maintain the firm's $3.78 million net income total.

In Table 15.10 every region is shown as making a positive contribution to net profits and overhead. If we discontinue our analysis here, the problem with the dishwasher product line never becomes evident. In Table 15.11, the contribution margin approach is extended to the product line. Now the unprofitability of the dishwasher line becomes more evident. It appears that the very profitable refrigerator line may be compensating for the dishwasher line's losses. We do not know from this analysis the reason for the dishwasher line's poor performance. Industry demand for

TABLE 15.9   IMPERIAL HOME APPLIANCE CORP. INCOME STATEMENT, FULL COST APPROACH (BY SEGMENT/IN THOUSANDS)[a]

	ENTIRE COMPANY	REGIONS				
		SOUTHWEST	SOUTHERN	EASTERN	PACIFIC	MIDWEST
Net Sales	$181,300	$34,449	$34,378	$39,261	$37,137	$36,075
Less Cost of Goods Sold	142,349	26,445	27,097	31,116	29,985	27,706
Gross Margin	$ 38,951	$ 8,004	$7,281	$ 8,145	$ 7,152	$ 8,369
LESS OPERATING EXPENSES						
Direct selling	$ 25,382	$ 5,070	$ 4,558	$ 5,126	$ 5,291	$ 5,337
Transportation and shipping	1,209	301	236	167	213	292
Warehousing	403	76	74	86	67	100
Credit and collection	907	187	176	193	140	211
Advertising	3,807	779	751	836	714	727
Sales promotion	1,436	288	280	318	277	273
General administrative	2,027	321	330	634	304	438
Total Operating Expenses	$ 35,171	$ 7,022	$ 6,405	$ 7,360	$ 7,006	$ 7,378
Net Income before Taxes	$ 3,780	$ 982	$ 876	$ 785	$ 146	$ 991

[a]Remember, other net profit breakdowns can be studied, such as product line, order size, and wholesaler channel.

TABLE 15.10   IMPERIAL HOME APPLIANCE CORP. INCOME STATEMENT, CONTRIBUTION MARGIN APPROACH
(BY SEGMENT/IN THOUSANDS)

	ENTIRE COMPANY	SOUTHWEST	SOUTHERN	EASTERN	PACIFIC	MIDWEST
Net Sales	$181,300	$34,449	$34,378	$39,261	$37,137	$36,075
LESS VARIABLE COSTS						
Manufacturing costs[a]	119,303	22,047	22,622	26,305	25,253	23,076
Marketing costs						
Sales commissions	5,768	1,171	1,031	1,253	1,337	976
Transportation and shipping	1,209	301	236	167	213	292
Warehousing	403	76	74	86	67	100
Credit and collection	907	187	176	193	140	211
ASSIGNABLE COSTS						
Salaries—salespeople	18,460	3,699	3,304	3,636	3,723	4,098
Salaries—marketing manager	1,154	200	223	237	231	263
Advertising	3,402	698	681	743	636	644
Sales promotion	1,436	288	280	318	277	273
Total Variable and Assignable Costs	$152,042	$28,667	$28,627	$32,938	$31,877	$29,933
Contribution margin	$ 29,258	$ 5,782	$ 5,751	$ 6,323	$ 5,260	$ 6,142
NONASSIGNABLE COSTS						
Institutional advertising	$ 405					
FIXED COSTS						
General administration	2,027					
Manufacturing[a]	23,046					
Net Income before Taxes	$ 3,780					

[a]These categories do not appear for a firm concerned with retailing only.

dishwashers may have declined, and the firm may not have anticipated this. The new model in Imperial's dishwasher line may have mechanical defects or poor aesthetic features. We cannot say, but we are sure that management should take appropriate measures to find out what the problem is. Had we not used this contribution margin analysis, the success of Imperial's other product lines could have hidden the problem.

TECHNIQUES OF COST ANALYSIS

A summary of the basic techniques of marketing cost analysis follows:

1. Direct expenses are measured and assigned to their respective segments.
2. Indirect expenses are allocated to functional cost groups.
3. Assignable fixed costs are included in the functional cost groups.
4. A variable activity is chosen for a cost allocation basis, and total variable activity is measured.
5. The variable-activity share of each of the functional cost groups is noted. (This indicates the total-cost share that should be borne by the segment.)
6. A segment's relative profitability is determined by gross margin less direct expenses and costs assignable to functional cost groups.

After contribution margin income statements are generated for specific segments, each of these segments can be further segmented and a contribution margin calculated for each subsegment. Primary segmentation can be done according to territory,

TABLE 15.11   IMPERIAL HOME APPLIANCE CORP. INCOME STATEMENT, CONTRIBUTION MARGIN APPROACH (BY PRODUCT LINE/IN THOUSANDS)

	COMPANY	WASHING MACHINES	DRYERS	RANGES	MICROWAVE OVENS	DISHWASHERS	REFRIGERATORS
Net Sales	$181,300	$33,450	$22,367	$35,176	$8,676	$22,057	$59,584
LESS VARIABLE COSTS							
Manufacturing	119,303	23,831	14,896	22,727	5,630	19,834	32,385
Marketing	8,287	1,458	1,326	1,581	266	1,424	2,232
Assignable Costs	24,452	4,075	3,827	4,388	1,000	3,232	7,930
Total Variable and Assignable Costs	$152,042	$29,364	$20,049	$28,696	$6,896	$24,490	$42,547
Contribution Margin	$ 29,258	$ 4,086	$ 2,318	$ 6,480	$1,780	$(2,443)	$17,037
Nonassignable Costs	405						
Fixed Costs	25,073						
Net Income before Taxes	$ 3,780						

and subsequently each territory can be further segmented by product line or wholesale channel. When further bases for breaking down contribution margins and segment income are identified, the only expenses used to calculate the contribution margin are those directly assignable to the segment chosen. Figure 15.2 illustrates how a segmented contribution income statement would be generated for Imperial Home Appliance Corp. Contribution margin and net income are first calculated for the entire company and then for each major product line. Each product line is broken down by regional data, and contribution margin and segment income are found for that small segment (for example, refrigerators in the Southern region). If refrigerators are doing well company-wide but are somewhat weak in one region, it might indicate that additional promotional effort is needed in that region. Had the company as a whole displayed a net loss, this could mean it should reallocate resources to more profitable segments, drop certain territories or product lines, or strengthen weaker segments with increased marketing effort. A modular approach such as that used in Figure 15.2 could pinpoint interrelationships that might be overlooked if segmentation is done by territory or product line alone. This approach greatly facilitates management control of planning.

Marketing cost analysis also can be performed by segmenting according to class, customer, or account size. Often firms refuse to service some accounts or decline orders below a specified minimum size. If a firm services a large volume of small orders, it incurs costs that may exceed the revenue the orders generate. Therefore, the firm may choose to eliminate that "unprofitable segment." Just as contribution margins were determined for territories (Table 15.10) and product lines (Table 15.11), the firm can calculate contribution margins based on account size. Management might keep the segment and hire intermediaries to handle smaller accounts, modify call schedules to trim the expenses of maintaining smaller accounts, or redistribute the marketing effort to concentrate on more-profitable classes of customers.

FIGURE 15.2   SEGMENTED CONTRIBUTION INCOME STATEMENT FOR IMPERIAL HOME APPLIANCE CORP.

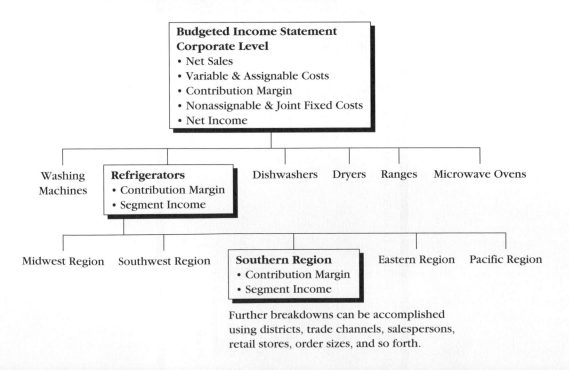

Cost analysis also can be used in conjunction with salesperson activity analysis (using information such as sales/active account and sales/call). For each account category, analysts can make calculations such as average gross profit/active account, average selling expense/active account, and average contribution/active account. This type of analysis can be useful for individual salesperson and account analysis; it is also used as a basis for comparison among larger segments (for example, districts).

RETURN ON INVESTMENT

Return on investment (ROI), also called *return on assets,* is a measurement firms use to determine how effectively the assets of a given operation are used. By definition:

$$\text{ROI} = \frac{\text{Net Profit}}{\text{Sales}} \times \frac{\text{Sales}}{\text{Total Assets Used}}$$

ROI is therefore the product of the profit margin on sales (net profit/sales) and its inventory turnover (sales/total assets). Because the contribution margin is a measure of profitability, the equation can be rewritten as follows for an isolated segment:

$$\text{ROI} = \frac{\text{Contribution Margin}}{\text{Segment Sales}} \times \frac{\text{Segment Sales}}{\text{Additional Assets the Segment Used}}$$

The additional assets the segment used are the new investment necessary to operate the segment, namely accounts receivable and inventory. Therefore, another measure of a territory's productivity is its return on investment. If the Southwest region of Imperial Home Appliance Corp. required an investment in accounts receivable of \$38,260 and an inventory of \$58,107, what would be its return on investment (see Table 15.10)?

$$\text{Solution: ROI} = \frac{\text{CM}}{\text{Sales}} \times \frac{\text{Sales}}{\text{Assets}} = \frac{5,782}{34,449} \times \frac{34,449}{96,367} = 6\%$$

Managers can generate ROI standards used for comparison from historical data or future projections.

INCREASING PRODUCTIVITY

The marketing manager is interested in the highest productivity from operations; therefore, he or she strives to maximize net profit. For any given production level, the

---

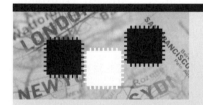

SELLING AND MANAGING GLOBALLY
COST OF A SALES FORCE VERSUS INDEPENDENT SALES AGENTS IN ITALY

The approximately 250,000 indirect sales agents and representatives in Italy provide an important link for Italian distribution systems. Manufacturers prefer to use independent sales agents because it saves them from the costs associated with maintaining their own private sales force. Small and medium-sized firms especially like to capitalize on the lower cost of outside sales forces, and they also benefit by having predictable costs since agents are paid a percentage of sales. Local sales agents also have the distinct advantages of market familiarity and well-established, ongoing buyer relationships.

Priorities are important to an Italian sales agent. Time is precious since customers are scattered over large geographical areas and the agent has many companies to call on. Dress, grooming, and attractiveness are also important. Appearance conveys success, and buyers like to deal with successful people. These sales agents must love the face-to-face give-and-take of putting a deal together because each sale involves negotiation.

Source: John Patterson, "Bristol-Myers Squibb Re-engineers Customer Service," *IIE Solutions* (September 1995): 60.

marketing manager also desires to minimize unit costs. Productivity may be increased for marketing operations in three ways:

1. *Sales increases.* By prudent use of advertising and promotional methods, for example, demand may be stimulated, thereby increasing the firm's sales revenues. If unit costs also do not rise, added profitability will result.
2. *Cost reductions.* If costs can be reduced while holding marketing effectiveness constant, profit margin will increase. For example, if the same target market can be reached at a lesser cost by advertising in the Houston *Chronicle* rather than in the Houston *Post,* a contribution can be made to the firm's profits.
3. *Eliminate or reduce emphasis on unprofitable products.* Sometimes firms must carry unprofitable products or cover unprofitable territories to supplement overall product offering. They should perform a cost-benefit analysis periodically to determine whether they should in fact continue to carry these unprofitable divisions or products. Also, more promotion and other forms of marketing emphasis should be placed on the more productive areas of the firm.

PROBLEMS IN COST ANALYSIS

As previously stated, marketing cost analysis is less exact than managerial cost accounting because, traditionally, it has been given less emphasis and because costs are much more difficult to allocate fairly, since functional classifications are used. An additional problem is the difficulty of predicting the effect on sales volume if a cost fluctuates, because cause-and-effect relations are not clearly established, and so many variables exist that their effects are difficult to isolate.

Effective cost analysis also is constrained by the marketing manager's limitations. Many times he or she is unsure of what data to request and how to use them. Finally, cost analysis can be expensive and time consuming. If a firm does not have access to computers, the extent of analysis possible will be seriously limited. In addition, the time marketing personnel must expend is extensive.

VARIANCE ANALYSIS

Until now, our major emphasis has been on cost analysis. Although cost control has been mentioned, primary consideration has been directed toward controlling

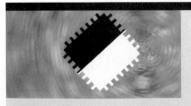

MANAGEMENT IN ACTION: ETHICAL DILEMMA
JURY DUTY OR VACATION?

One of your top salespeople, who had requested five days off for jury duty, served only three days and then was released from the jury. However, he took off the other two days without telling you. You have learned of his actions through one of your other salespeople.

WHAT DO YOU DO?
1. Nothing. Though you know what he did was wrong, he has been working very hard, often 60 hours a week. He

has earned a rest. But subtly let him know that you're aware of what he did, and imply if it happens again he will be disciplined.
2. Discipline him by taking the time away in vacation or sick days.
3. Immediately fire the salesperson as an indication that you absolutely will not tolerate dishonesty in any form from your employees.

marketing expenditures to obtain maximum profitability. For cost control analysis, a function's actual performance is measured against a predetermined standard, and the differences between actual and standard performance are investigated. Standard costs are established as bases for comparison with actual costs for this **variance analysis.**

Marketing costs are somewhat difficult to standardize because they often are generated from nonrepetitive activities. Note that in Figure 15.1, marketing costs are divided into order-getting and order-filling costs. Variance analysis is most effectively practiced with order-filling costs because they are somewhat repetitive, rather than with order-getting costs, for which the same amount of effort might result in differing sales volume.

A relationship must be established between the amount of each variable cost component and its resultant order-filling activity (for example, the clerical costs that can be expected for each shipment and the loading cost per pound loaded). Standards are determined for units of variability, the same bases that were previously used for cost allocation in segment analysis (Table 15.7).

Variance analysis identifies the factors that cause the discrepancy between standard and actual costs, with the ultimate goal of resolving the inefficiencies. The variances may be computed by price variances and quantity variances. They are determined as follows:

Price Variance = (Standard Price − Actual Price) × Standard Units
Quantity Variance = (Budgeted Work Units − Actual Work Units) × Standard Price

THE BOTTOM LINE

Net sales volume analysis and marketing cost analysis are useful to the marketing manager for planning and controlling the marketing program. Control helps the marketing manager uncover weak spots and develop strengths by isolating areas that need direct management intervention.

A marketing audit is a systematic appraisal of the marketing operation as a whole, which aids in effective control and in developing new strategies. Independent persons, either within or outside of the company, should bear the responsibility for conducting this audit. A sales force audit follows the same basic approach as the marketing audit but is designed to evaluate only one function within the marketing operation—the management of the sales force.

Misdirected marketing effort occurs when management ignores the effects of the 80/20 and iceberg principles. The 80/20, or concentration, principle, states that the majority of a firm's volume or profit may result from a small percentage of its customers, territories, or products. The marketing effort must be placed where it generates the most sales or profit. The iceberg principle warns that, although total sales or profit figures give some useful information about the firm's operations, underlying problems may be hidden. To minimize the effect of this principle, smaller identifiable segments must be analyzed, such as customer groups, individual territories, and product lines.

Sales analysis is the detailed analysis of a company's sales data and may incorporate breakdowns by account, customer class, territory, product line, and other categories. Sales analysis is used for evaluation of performance, planning, and direction of the sales effort. Segment performance can be analyzed by comparing actual performance with a predetermined standard, such as a quota, or with some type of sales index. Major deviations can be identified for management attention.

Sales volume analysis alone is insufficient as a basis for marketing decisions. The true determinant of a given program's accountability is its ultimate effect on company profitability, which depends on both net sales volume and associated expenses. Marketing cost analysis is the analysis of costs that affect sales volume, with the goal of determining profitability of different segment operations. The marketing manager's ultimate goal should be to maximize company profit while most efficiently using available resources.

Marketing cost analysis is primarily concerned with marketing costs (costs incurred between final production and ultimate consumption by the consumer), as opposed to production (or processing) costs. Marketing costs fall into two categories: order-getting costs incurred by inducing the customer to buy and the order-filling costs necessary to complete the transaction after the sale is made.

Accountants traditionally give more emphasis to production costs analysis because productive functions tend to be more repetitive and therefore more controllable, but marketing cost analysis is currently receiving more attention than ever before. For performing cost analysis, traditional ledger accounts (natural accounts) are reassigned to functional cost groups. Bases for allocation must accurately reflect a segment's ability to control those expenditures.

Commonly used cost classifications include direct versus indirect costs, fixed versus variable costs, standard costs, and controllable versus uncontrollable costs. Any combination of these terms may be referred to in current cost analysis literature.

Two separate approaches may be taken for determining aggregate or segment profitability. The full cost approach determines profitability by subtracting the cost of goods sold from net sales to produce gross margin and then subtracting all operating expenses to arrive at the net profit. The contribution margin approach separates costs according to controllability and then deducts only controllable costs from net sales to produce the contribution margin. This figure is then used as a basis of comparison among segments.

The productivity of marketing operations can be increased by minimizing unit costs and maximizing net profit. This can be accomplished by sales increases, cost reductions, and elimination of, or reduced emphasis on, unprofitable areas.

Variance analysis is useful for cost control. It is used to investigate deviations between actual costs and standard costs. These deviations are represented by price variances and quantity variances that alert the effective manager to problem areas.

■ KEY TERMS FOR SALES MANAGERS

Marketing audit, 364	Marketing cost analysis, 372	Contribution margin
Sales force audit, 364	Profitability, 372	approach, 376
80/20 principle, 365	Production cost, 373	Return on investment
Iceberg principle, 366	Distribution cost, 374	(ROI), 381
Sales analysis, 368	Functional marketing	Variance analysis, 383
Total sales volume, 369	groups, 375	
Retail sales index, 370	Full cost approach, 375	

■ MANAGEMENT APPLICATION QUESTIONS

1. Compare a marketing audit with a sales force audit. How are they different? How are they similar?
2. You are the sales manager for a large firm that has a wide product mix. One of the company's important products is not doing well in your area. Your regional manager has asked you to justify why the product should not be pulled from your sales area. What reasons might you use to justify why this product should be maintained in your product line?
3. How is the 80/20 principle similar to the iceberg principle?
4. What is a sales analysis? What is it used for?
5. A number of different levels of analysis can be done with a sales analysis. What are these levels, and what kind of information is supplied to the sales manager at each level?
6. What is a marketing cost analysis, and what is it used for?
7. What is the difference between a full cost approach and a contribution margin approach for determining profitability?
8. A variance analysis will normally have two components, a price variance and a quantity variance. Describe how these two variances are found and what they measure.

FURTHER EXPLORING THE SALES WORLD

Ask a sales manager to let you see a monthly sales report for the district. Discuss each item on the report with the manager. Find out how this information is used for evaluating performance of the district and individual salespeople.

SALES MANAGEMENT EXPERIENTIAL EXERCISE

COCKE'S OFFICE SUPPLY: CENTRAL CALIFORNIA DISTRICT'S PERFORMANCE APPRAISAL

"What in the world is wrong with Zank?" John Baker thought as he looked over the recent computer printout of his sales district's performance. The three territories in John's district are basically alike in size; consumer population and dispersion; number of present customers; number of prospects; consumer tastes, desires, and buying power; level and quality of competition; general economic conditions; and all other respects. Based on these factors, John established weekly quotas for the three territories by dividing the district's total weekly sales quota among high-profit product A, low-profit product B, and other miscellaneous products and accessories.

"I don't understand this," John said to himself. "I'd better go out and work with Zank to see what's happening. We cannot afford to have sales off by $1,950 in that territory."

QUESTIONS
1. What does an analysis of John's district's performance indicate?
2. What should John do?

CRITERIA	QUOTA	HERNDON	WARWICK	ZANK
Calls per week	75	90	45	55
Product A sales	$1,000	$400	$1,700	$ 250
Product B sales	2,000	3,500	1,600	1,350
Miscellaneous sales	1,500	1,000	1,800	950
Total dollar sales	$4,500	$4,900	$5,100	$2,550
Percentage of calls made sale	60%	40%	78%	47%
Average sales per call	$60.00	$54.44	$113.33	$46.36

DISTRICT **II**

CENTRAL CALIFORNIA
QUOTA VERSUS ACTUAL
PERFORMANCE

CASE 15.1

IOWA FARM SUPPLIES
Plans and Data Go Together

How could this be happening? A new field sales manager at Iowa Farm Supplies—one for whom you had the highest hopes—has difficulty following your instructions to target specific objectives. In fact, "has difficulty" is putting it mildly. Dick has become downright impossible as a planner. For example, you ask him for next year's forecasts for his territory. He responds late, with a single number and scarcely any data to support it. They're strictly bottom-line numbers; Dick volunteers nothing "above the line" to support them.

Good managers draw up clearly defined and detailed action plans for the short, medium, and long terms. Each level of the organization must have an internal action plan. Although each manager has his or her own name for this plan, to marketing managers it is a "marketing plan" and to sales managers a "sales plan." The details of each plan are "notched" so the plan will fit into the company's overall master plan.

Now you face your problem with Dick, who doesn't seem to have a clue about how to plan or why planning is so important. It's becoming embarrassing for you, and you shouldn't need to repeatedly ask Dick for the details that support his "total for the period."

Without data (including an expense budget and activity by specific account, salesperson, and products or services to be sold—all estimated for a time base), Dick's "report" has very little credibility. What's more, you can't include his bare-bones number in your own report. And where is his field plan that tells how his sales group will make his number? Does he use a rabbit's foot?

This isn't the first time Dick has given you a "nonplan." You've had it with his unfulfilled promises. Even worse, you've been burned before by accepting his last-minute revised forecasts, which turn out to be wildly inaccurate when compared later with the actual results.

He has a likable personality. He's popular. Dick's one heck of a productive salesperson—before you promoted him to field sales manager. But he is frustrating his salespeople.

Is his problem unwillingness, or is it an inability to do anything on a planned basis? Whatever the reason, something has to be done about it right away. He's taking a toll on your own work.

QUESTION
What would you do?

CASE 15.2

EXECUTIVE OFFICE SUPPLIES
Determining ROI

Sam Owens was the manager for Executive Office Supplies, a small regional manufacturer of general office supplies (for example, paper products, pencils, pens, and folders). Sam was in the process of examining some of his territories in order to determine the return from the assets committed to maintaining them. He was currently looking at a territory made up of northern Texas and several counties in southern Oklahoma.

Sales in the subject territory had been $400,000 last year. The company had maintained an average inventory of $45,000 to serve the area. In addition, $15,000 in cash had been kept handy to handle emergency transactions and to carry out day-to-day activities. The average accounts receivable for this territory had been $40,000.

Sam had found that the following costs or expenses could be directly traceable to the north Texas–south Oklahoma area:

Cost of goods sold	$331,100
Salespeople's compensation/benefits	44,400
Communications	1,075
Depreciation on automobile	1,300
Sales and delivery	2,510
Occupancy expense (lease)	2,150
Other expenses	3,025
Total	$385,560

It was Sam's hope that all sales territories would earn more than 15 percent on the assets committed to managing them. If possible, Sam wanted to accomplish closer to a 20 percent return.

QUESTIONS

1. Determine the return on investments managed for the north Texas–south Oklahoma territory.
2. What would the ROI be if sales could be increased by $5,000 without additional costs? By $10,000?
3. What would the ROI be if direct costs could be lowered by $2,000 without hurting sales?
4. What would the ROI be if the average accounts receivable or inventory were reduced by $10,000 without hurting sales? By $20,000?

Source: This case was developed by James L. Taylor of the University of Alabama.

CHAPTER 16

EVALUATION OF SALESPEOPLE'S PERFORMANCE

CHAPTER OUTLINE

LEARNING OBJECTIVES

Performance appraisals are excellent methods for building a strong and effective sales program. This chapter should help you understand:

■ What a performance appraisal involves.

■ The uses of performance appraisals.

■ Who does the evaluation and how often salespeople should be evaluated.

■ How performance criteria are developed.

■ The accuracy of performance appraisals and what can influence that accuracy.

■ The importance of evaluating the evaluation system.

One of the most important aspects of performance evaluation is knowing what kind of people to hire and when to fire an employee. According to Barry J. Farber, the best way to avoid firing employees is to put great care and attention into the hiring process. He suggests that one way to do this is to tell a candidate, "We like what we've seen so far. But right now we just don't feel you're right for our company." If the candidate gives no reply and seems to feel this is the interview close, then it indicates someone who may not have been suitable for the company. However, if the candidate has the desire and motivation to work for the firm, that person will use his or her best sales techniques in order to get the job.

Ellen Manzo-Ill is a general manager for AT&T and is based in Norwalk, Connecticut. She heads a sales organization that manages strategic relations between AT&T and global service customers. She also feels that the best way to avoid firing people is to make good decisions when hiring employees in the first place. Most of Manzo-Ill's salespeople work closely together on one or two large accounts. If she is seriously considering hiring someone, she will have the candidate meet with the customer for an interview. That is her way of deciding if the candidate and customer will be a good match.

After she hires a new sales rep, Manzo-Ill works closely with the new employee. "It pays to work very closely with new salespeople up front. I go shoulder-to-shoulder with them the first time they go on customer calls, the first time they put together new proposals, the first time they do anything new. It allows them to learn what my standards are. The next step in this process is to inspect and coach. There's a saying, 'You can't expect what you don't inspect.' You should always be inspecting, to make sure that everyone is keeping up to your standards of quality. When someone's performance is questionable, it's time to inspect even more," she says.

Manzo-Ill strongly believes inspection sets the pace. She will often follow up on a job she requests of her employees. "That way, they know what's expected of them, and they know that the boss is watching."

Farber is of the opinion that if problems start arising with a salesperson, it is crucial to be honest. Although he feels it is important to find the good in people, he says, it is also important to be straightforward in your criticism. Straightforwardness in a performance evaluation may not only be appreciated by the employee, but it also may help prevent a firing. ▪

This chapter reviews one of the most important elements of managing a high-performance sales team—the performance appraisal. As you read this chapter, think about how you would meet with someone. What are the main topics you should be prepared to discuss with the person? Will this be a friendly or hostile meeting? In addition, you might want to review Chapter 14 on leadership when forming your solution.

PERFORMANCE APPRAISALS AT J & J

"Once I hire an applicant, my job is to help make the person productive," Kevin Ryan, district sales manager for Advanced Care Products, a division of Johnson & Johnson, explains. "To be a successful sales manager, you have to motivate and develop your people. If they are successfully motivated and developed, they will have the knowledge and ability to develop the business potential in their sales territories. When they develop their business, sales will follow, and that's what we're here to do: sell more than we did last year and build our share of the market.

"As a manager," Ryan says, "my main focus is on the training and development of our people. We spend a great deal of time on performance evaluations and coaching our salespeople. We give them their formal evaluations annually, which cover the key areas of their job responsibilities. Their incentive compensation bonuses are based on their total performances. Total performance includes both sales quota attainment and achievement against their sales goals.

"In the performance appraisal, I sit down with our salespeople and review how well they are doing their jobs against performance standards." According to Ryan, this is one of the most important tasks managers have. "The performance appraisal gives them direction on how they can improve and allows for their feedback so agreement can be reached."

Ryan also believes it is just as important for sales reps to participate in the evaluations as it is for managers. "As a matter of fact, before we do performance appraisals, we send sales representatives the form in advance and let them rate their own performances. This allows them to evaluate their own strengths and weaknesses prior to the actual performance review with management. If you're doing a good job as manager, the sales representatives' evaluations should compare closely with your evaluation of them."

PERFORMANCE APPRAISALS—WHAT ARE THEY?

The performance appraisal is a time of reflection on the past and hope for the future. It is a time of decision that may have lasting consequences on an individual's career and life. In sales, the **performance appraisal** refers to a formal, structured system of measuring and evaluating a salesperson's activities and performance. It is part of a marketing audit. Management compares the results of a person's efforts against the goals set for that person.

THE PURPOSES AND IMPORTANCE OF PERFORMANCE APPRAISAL

As indicated throughout this book, productivity improvement of salespeople is of major concern to all organizations. What salespeople do or do not do influences their company's productivity. Salespeople's productivity can be measured and evaluated in relation to their job activities and sales quotas.

Numerous specific reasons for performance appraisals exist. The following are the more important reasons:

- *Compensation:* It helps determine appropriate pay for performance and equitable salary and bonus incentives based on merit or results.
- *Development:* It encourages continued successful performance and strengthens individual weaknesses to make salespeople more effective and productive.

- *Feedback:* It provides a format for dialogue between manager and salesperson and improves understanding of personal goals and concerns. This can lead to trust between the two people.
- *Goals:* It outlines what is expected from salespeople.
- *Legal compliance:* It helps establish the validity of employment decisions (for example, selection, compensation, promotions, and penalties) made on the basis of performance-based information.
- *Motivation:* It has a major impact on motivating salespeople.
- *Penalties:* It influences decisions on demotions, firing, and layoffs.
- *Personnel:* It allows for evaluating the recruitment and selection processes. Are they meeting their objectives? Why or why not?
- *Planning:* It provides information for planning such policies as employment, training, and rewards.
- *Promotion:* It helps determine who will be promoted.
- *Training:* It indicates training areas needed.

Because they need to create a high-performance sales group, managers must set high standards so sales reps can achieve outstanding results. The challenge to managers materializes when it comes time to evaluate each salesperson's performance. In order to help an average performer improve, managers use the performance appraisal to indicate where the individual falls below the preset benchmarks. Mike Ragan of W. R. Grace use profiles of the top performers as benchmarks to distinguish the top from the average employees. Once the new goals have been set, a secondary review is scheduled to cover what changes have been made. Managers usually have a positive attitude about helping as long as they notice improvement. Otherwise, as Ragan states, "if they're simply not putting in enough effort, then as a manager, you have to make a business decision to terminate."[1]

As you see, performance evaluation has some important purposes. Quite often, a single purpose is related to one or more other purposes. For example, compensation is related to motivation.

EVALUATE AND DEVELOP FOR MOTIVATION TO HIGHER PERFORMANCE

These many purposes can be condensed into two general categories: evaluative and developmental. The evaluative purposes include decisions on compensation, legal compliance, promotion, penalties, and personnel. The developmental purposes include development, feedback, goal setting, motivation, planning, and training.

A comparison of these types of appraisal is given in Table 16.1. Notice the differences in the comparison factors. For time, the evaluative role is concerned with past

TABLE 16.1

COMPARISON OF EVALUATIVE AND DEVELOPMENTAL ASPECTS OF PERFORMANCE APPRAISAL

COMPARISON FACTORS	EVALUATIVE ROLE	DEVELOPMENTAL ROLE
Time	Past sales performance	Future performance
Objective	Improve performance by rewarding based on performance	Improve performance through self-learning, e.g., taking selling courses
Method	Use of evaluation forms	Management by objective (MBO) approach to goal setting, career planning
Manager's role	Evaluate performance	Encourage and help salesperson
Salesperson's role	Explain past performance; react to evaluation	Active involvement in developing future career and performance plans

FIGURE 16.1   THE PERFORMANCE APPRAISAL'S INFLUENCE ON SALES PERSONNEL'S MOTIVATION, BEHAVIOR, AND PERFORMANCE

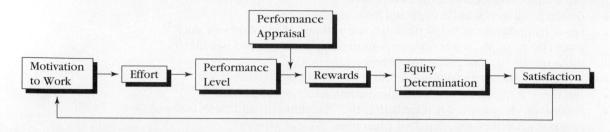

sales performance, the developmental with improving future performance. Can you now understand why performance evaluation is so important? It is critical to the success of creating and operating a high-performance sales group and organization due to its ability to motivate an individual to achieve higher levels of success.

THE PERFORMANCE APPRAISAL'S RELATIONSHIP TO BEHAVIOR

Where does performance appraisal become involved in the motivation of sales personnel? Take a look at Figure 16.1. As we discussed in Chapter 12, motivation is seen as the force influencing an individual to expend effort. Motivation thus leads to an individual's observed level of effort. Effort alone, however, is not enough. The **performance level** a salesperson attains results from a combination of the individual's effort and ability. Ability, in turn, reflects the individual's skills, training, information, and talents.

As the diagram shows, the performance level is then evaluated by the person's supervisor. Rewards are based on the appraisal's outcome. After determining the equity of—and satisfaction from—the rewards resulting from the appraisal, the individual again asks these four questions:

1. What is the probability of success?
2. Will I be rewarded for success?
3. Are the rewards worth it?
4. Are the rewards fair?

Answers to these questions influence the person's motivation to work, effort, behavior, and eventually the person's future performance level. As this cycle of performance to rewards occurs time after time, the actual experiences on the job, including the performance appraisal, serve to provide information that influences an individual's perceptions (particularly expectations). Thus, the performance appraisal also plays an important role in influencing salespeople's motivation, behavior, and performance.

PERFORMANCE APPRAISAL PROCESSES AND PROCEDURES

This chapter discusses the processes and procedures for appraising sales personnel's performance. The important relationships and appraisal purposes are summarized in Figure 16.2.

As shown in Figure 16.2, performance appraisal of any sales position is based on an analysis of the job. A job analysis defines the sales job through specific tasks or activities and determines the qualifications needed. A job description is then developed stating the job's specific nature, requirements, and responsibilities. Job specifications convert job descriptions into the people qualifications (for example, abilities,

FIGURE 16.2   THE SALESPERSON PERFORMANCE APPRAISAL SYSTEM WITH ITS NUMEROUS PARTS, PROCESSES, AND PROCEDURES

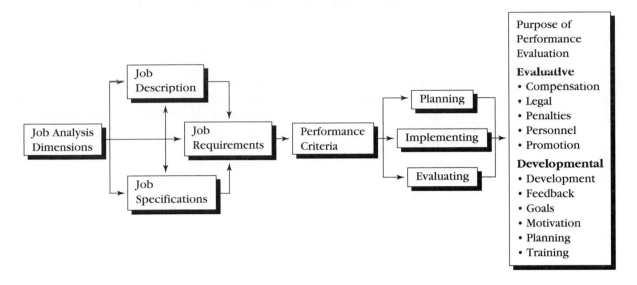

behavior, education, skills) the organization feels are necessary for successful performance of the job.

This gives the organization a clear picture of the job requirements. Specific performance criteria now can be developed. These criteria serve as the basis for evaluating each person in a particular sales job.

Now the important task of planning, implementing, and evaluating the performance appraisal system begins. This involves determining the following:

1. Who should evaluate salespeople?
2. When should salespeople be evaluated?
3. Are the criteria appropriate?
4. What forms should be used for gathering information?
5. What may influence the appraisal's accuracy?
6. How should the appraisal be conducted?
7. How can the appraisal process be evaluated?

Answers to these questions are discussed within this chapter. Let us begin by examining the first question.

WHO SHOULD EVALUATE SALESPEOPLE?

The primary evaluator should be the salesperson's immediate supervisor because this person has direct knowledge, having actually worked with the salesperson. For some companies, the immediate supervisor completes the entire evaluation including recommendations for pay raises and promotions. The evaluations and recommendations are then sent to the manager's immediate supervisor for final approval. The manager's supervisor accepts the recommendations without question.

In the majority of organizations, several managers evaluate each salesperson. The simplest approach is for the district manager and the regional sales manager to arrive at the evaluation. The other district managers in the regions also may express their opinion when the region's entire management group gets together periodically.

"Once a year, we have a formal evaluation conducted that is called the **Performance Development Review**," Kevin Ryan of J & J says. "This name was selected because the primary focus is to develop performance."

"The salesperson, manager, and the manager's supervisor are all present. At this session, we review the territory's performance, that is, sales against forecast to date for each brand," Ryan explains. "We also measure how the salesperson is doing compared to the unit and region's performance. We specifically review the sales opportunities in order to improve results by selling new distribution or gaining promotional support from our accounts in addition to other key management areas. Individual performance characteristics such as leadership and organizational ability, communication skills, and other personal attributes are also evaluated."

A few companies use the entire region's management group and a home-office personnel specialist to evaluate salespeople, as shown in Figure 16.3. The specialist presents the home-office viewpoint. The specialist also makes sure the evaluation procedures are followed and that each person is treated fairly.

WHEN SHOULD SALESPEOPLE BE EVALUATED?

Salespeople should be evaluated at the end of each performance cycle. A **performance cycle** is a period related to specific product goals or job activities. For example, consumer-goods manufacturers typically have certain products they want to emphasize periodically. They may have six performance cycles during the year. Every two months the sales force is given specific sales goals for five to ten different products. These goals should be compared with results after each cycle. In addition, salespeople are monitored monthly for the other products they sell.

What's an example of this? Kevin Ryan provides an excellent procedure to follow when doing a "work-with" evaluation.

"We work with our salespeople two to three days every month," Ryan says. "We usually make 10 to 13 calls a day. After each call, we go back to the car and review the sales call and presentation. Sometimes we'll role-play and review what was said by the buyer and the sales representative.

"It's my job to hear what the buyer and the sales representative said to properly review the call," Ryan continues. "If the sales representative said something that wasn't conducive to making a sale, I must directly point that out to the sales representative. This could include the way statements were positioned, attitude, or use of sales materials.

"After a field trip, I send the sales representative a 'field trip recap letter.' In this letter, I summarize what we accomplished on the field trip. Were our products well

FIGURE 16.3   POSSIBLE MANAGEMENT INPUT INTO THE SALESPERSON'S PERFORMANCE EVALUATION

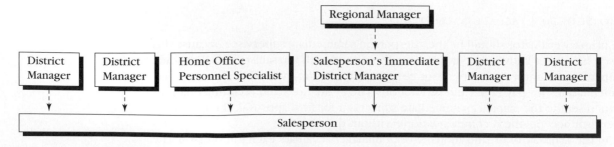

merchandised? Did we have any out-of-stocks? Was an order written? We'll cover most of these points in addition to other business matters in the follow-up letter.

"We try to get the letter to the sales representative within two days after the trip," Ryan concludes. "This provides direct feedback on what was observed during the field trip and what objectives we have set to accomplish by the next contact. When I return for the next field trip, I'll have the recap letter with me, and we'll discuss all the follow-up areas."

These periodic performance evaluations provide the input for semiannual and annual performance evaluations. They provide important feedback to both management and salespeople. A minimum of one formal evaluation should be completed yearly for each salesperson.

ARE THE PERFORMANCE CRITERIA APPROPRIATE?

First of all, what is a **criterion?** The dictionary defines it as a "standard" on which a judgment or decision may be based. In our case, firms determine what type of performance or standard they expect from their salespeople, and they determine how that particular criterion will be measured. Usually, companies use several criteria. This results in the development of a performance evaluation measurement instrument.

This may appear simple, easy to do, and straightforward. For many companies, it is relatively easy to develop a fair evaluation instrument. However, some companies have difficulty accurately and fairly judging a salesperson's true performance.

GUIDELINES FOR PERFORMANCE CRITERIA   Proper performance evaluation begins with the development of the proper criteria. Performance criteria should be measurable, practical, relevant, discriminating, and stable and should encompass both results and activities.

Measurable   The performance criteria should be measurable. For example, managers can measure actual sales volume easily and accurately. But can they accurately measure a salesperson's human relations ability, general personality, ability to communicate, and friendliness with customers?

Many companies do use these types of vague generalities. It may be easy to tell whether someone is extremely poor in communication skills, but these negative extremes are rarely found because people possessing them probably never would have been hired in the first place. How do you accurately measure this type of factor? It is difficult to do objectively and thus is done solely on a subjective basis.

Practical   The criteria should be practical. Most companies use sales as the major measure of job performance, but some companies do not. One national sales manager says, "We sell strictly through wholesalers. It is difficult to appraise directly a salesperson's dollar sales performance. An account in salesperson A's territory often orders products from a wholesaler in salesperson B's territory. The wholesaler will not provide us with information on specific sales to our various customers. Thus, using sales as a primary indicator of performance, salesperson B would get credit for salesperson A's sale. Therefore, dollar sales of the individual salesperson would be difficult to determine." This holds true for many companies in many different types of industries. Even though total sales for the district or region are measurable, sales as a criterion for measuring an individual's performance is not practical in such situations.

Relevant   A criterion should be relevant to job performance. Do not use a job activity as a criterion if it is not related and important to the behavior desired from the salesperson. This is particularly important today because of government guidelines on employment discrimination.

Firms often develop a list of three to ten specific activities under each general job category. Under the general category of territorial management, one company lists activities such as planning, use of time, records, customer service, or collections. Each salesperson ultimately can be evaluated on 50 to 100 items. Certainly, each activity is necessary. However, measuring them is impossible for the rater and the person being rated. On the job the salesperson identifies the most important activities of the 50 or so items and concentrates on them.

Typically, the manager also selects certain items, such as quotas met, and may perceive 3 to 10 items of the 50 or so on the evaluation form as the activities that should be evaluated. A point can be made that only the 3 to 10 items are actually used, and should be used, for performance appraisal.

Discriminating   A criterion should discriminate among poor, average, and excellent performance. After all, this is the major purpose of the evaluation. Even if all salespeople do a good job, it is still important to determine which ones are significantly above average.

Stable   A performance criterion may be measurable, practical, relevant, and discriminating and still not be usable if it is not stable. Stability means the criteria can be judged or evaluated by two or more raters and that they will agree on the individual's evaluation. If different managers rate the same salesperson on productive use of business time, for example, and one rates the person as excellent and the other rates the person as poor, then this criterion may need to be eliminated from the evaluation because it is a difficult criterion on which to obtain a consensus.

DEVELOPMENT OF PERFORMANCE CRITERIA   As noted, both a salesperson's results and activities should be used as performance criteria. Results criteria are objective, quantitative data such as total sales and percentage of sales increase. Activity criteria,

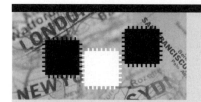

SELLING AND MANAGING GLOBALLY
ISRAEL—THE HOME-COURT ADVANTAGE

Rita Hunter was sent to Israel to establish a beachhead for her company in a region that finally seemed prepared to live up to its market potential.

After two weeks and three broken appointments at one company, she had begun to wonder if she would ever get her foot in the door. The next day she mentioned the problem to a local friend of hers, Sarit; she was surprised when Sarit called back to say that the appointment was set up for the following week. Hunter asked Sarit how she had arranged the appointment; Sarit explained her husband served in the same reserve unit as a manager at her target company. This manager set up the appointment for Hunter, and because the request came from in house, the appointment was kept.

Getting an appointment in Israel is not always this easy. However, given the geographical density, close family ties, local friendliness, military reserve duty, and workforce mobility, sometimes it is not too difficult to find somebody to act as a contact in an organization, either to set up an appointment or to find out who can set up the appointment.

Most Israelis are very social and friendly people. Their desire to be helpful enables them to assist others just for the intrinsic satisfaction of being able to help. They tend to make everybody's business their own so they can offer a solution. Perhaps one of the key reasons for this is the feeling that all Israelis face the same problems, and if they can't help each other, who else will help? On the other hand, their generosity and courtesy are not always extended to foreigners; thus, a local contact can ease the difficulty.

Not everyone, however, is willing to act as a go-between because this implicitly suggests an obligation. Although Israelis will usually go out of their way for friends, making friends locally is not always easy for a foreigner. Finding the right contact can sometimes consume more time than it is worth, and salespeople are encouraged to try the frontal approach as well.

Source: Written by Moshe Davidow.

many of which are subjective and qualitative, include factors such as precall preparation, paperwork in on time, and number of displays.

Quantitative Performance Criteria Of the two categories of performance criteria, the quantitative criteria are better for effectively evaluating performance. This criteria category represents end results or bottom-line, objective data such as:

1. Sales volume
   a. Percentage of increase
   b. Market share
   c. Quotas obtained
2. Average sales calls per day
3. New customers obtained
4. Gross profit by product, customer, and order size
5. Ratio of selling costs to sales
6. Sales orders
   a. Daily number of orders
      (1) Total
      (2) By size, customer classification, and product
   b. Order to sales-call ratio
   c. Goods returned

Qualitative Performance Criteria Many organizations use qualitative performance criteria because they represent the salesperson's major job activities, and they indicate why the quantitative measures look as they do. The evaluator should take care to minimize personal biases and subjectivity when evaluating qualitative performance criteria. Examples of such criteria follow:

1. Sales skills
   a. Finding selling points
   b. Product knowledge
   c. Listening skill
   d. Obtaining participation
   e. Overcoming objections
   f. Closing the sale
2. Territorial management
   a. Planning
   b. Utilization
   c. Records
   d. Customer service
   e. Collections
   f. Follow-up
3. Personal traits
   a. Attitude
   b. Empathy
   c. Human relations
   d. Team spirit
   e. Appearance
   f. Motivation
   g. Care of car
   h. Self-improvement

One sales manager says, "Qualitative performance criteria help explain quantitative performance results. If, for example, a salesperson's sales volume is low, poor methods used to close the sale may be the reason. Only by working with salespeople can I determine what's causing their numbers."

PERFORMANCE EVALUATION FORMS FOR GATHERING INFORMATION

Periodically each manager is supplied with performance appraisal forms for evaluating each salesperson. Several different types of appraisal forms exist, and each can have numerous variations. In this section, five basic forms for evaluating salespeople's performance are discussed: graphic appraisal scales, descriptive statements, management by objectives, behaviorally anchored rating scales, and 360-degree feedback.

GRAPHIC APPRAISAL SCALES   The **graphic appraisal scale** is the most commonly used form for evaluating salespeople's performance. Table 16.2 shows three formats for such scales. The manager fills out a form appraising all performance criteria. In this example, the manager is appraising a salesperson's selling skill. The first example uses two cues or anchor words with a five-point scale ranging from excellent to poor. This scale format is referred to as a *semantic differential* and uses opposite adjectives to express the extremes of each criterion. Numerical values are assigned to each possible level, and the manager can check any one of them. The better the salesperson's evaluation, the higher the score. In this case, an evaluation of poor selling skill would be given a "0" and of excellent selling skill would receive a "4." After all performance criteria have been evaluated, individual scores can be totaled to arrive at an overall performance evaluation score for each salesperson.

In the second example, four anchor words are used in a Likert-type scale. The manager can rate the salesperson as outstanding, above average, average, or below average. The same is true for example three. However, the manager also can rate the salesperson as improving, backsliding, or staying at the same level of selling skill.

Weights may be assigned to different criteria. For example, selling skill may have a higher value than car appearance. There may also be space provided for comments on each criterion.

DESCRIPTIVE STATEMENTS   The **descriptive statement** is a method of performance appraisal requiring the manager to provide a detailed, written description of each salesperson's performance. Typically, the manager has five to ten categories to evaluate, such as selling ability, management potential, goal attainment, general sales increase, and territorial management. The manager is often required to use these descriptive statements to rank the salespeople. This ranking serves to identify the best performers in the group.

Problems can arise when this method is used. Identifying either extremely good or poor performers may be easy, but the remainder tend to group in the center as average performers. A second problem involves the number of salespeople being evaluated. Companies evaluating a small number of salespeople can use this method, but it is difficult when large numbers of salespeople are involved.

Occasionally, a company uses a paired comparison method to overcome these problems. Each salesperson is compared with another. The manager with ten salespeople (N) would have 45 comparisons, as shown:

$$\text{Pairs} = \frac{N(N-1)}{2} = \frac{10(10-1)}{2} = 45 \text{ Comparisons}$$

TABLE 16.2

THREE EXAMPLES OF FORMATS FOR GRAPHIC APPRAISAL SCALES

1. Selling Skill Excellent ☐ ☑ ☐ ☐ ☐ Poor
   4 3 2 1 0

2. Selling Skill Outstanding Above Average Average Below Average
   ☐ ☑ ☐ ☐ Comments:
   4 3 2 1

3. Selling Skill +3 _____
   4 Outstanding _____
   3 Above Average
   2 Average
   1 Below Average
   + Improving
   − Backsliding
   * Same

This method also has a drawback because of the numbers involved. A manager may have difficulty accurately making 45 comparisons in order to rank salespeople from high to low.

MANAGEMENT BY OBJECTIVES **Management by objectives (MBO)** is a results-based evaluation program. Salespeople are given objectives, and their actual results are compared with the objectives to evaluate their performance on a performance index. This index is determined by dividing sales objectives by actual sales multiplied by 100. Table 16.3 illustrates how four performance criteria might be used for evaluation. This salesperson has reached objectives for three out of four criteria. The salesperson must explain to management why the specific product goal was not obtained and what is being done to make sure this objective will be reached in the future.

American Medical International, Inc. (AMI), uses the MBO technique with specific performance objectives. Managers then design performance appraisals to evaluate how well the objectives were met. The objectives are based on an overall strategy for a particular division. Steve Brown, director, says he feels that setting the right objectives is the key to successful management. However, Brown realizes that changes occurring in the health care industry affect these objectives. He and his staff need to be flexible, he says, toward redesigning the objectives to best fit AMI's business goals.[2]

BEHAVIORALLY ANCHORED RATING SCALES **Behaviorally anchored rating scales,** referred to as **BARS** or *behavioral expectation scales,* represent an attempt to improve evaluations that use descriptive cues or adjectives. With BARS, critical incidents distinguish among values on the scale, as illustrated in Table 16.4. In this example, salesperson Mac James has been evaluated as an above-average performer in reaching the company's individual product sales goals for the year. For this method, the manager must first determine how many product goals Mac was given and the number of goals he obtained. Next, Mac's performance for this particular criterion then is ranked in comparison with that of other salespeople in the group.

The BARS evaluation method makes each performance category easy for the manager to interpret because each includes a detailed explanation of exactly what the rating means. Such evaluation methods tend to be more reliable and valid, thus reducing rating errors. Also, the response categories directly represent job tasks. Thus, the manager can better explain the evaluation to the individual involved. The following is an example of Mac's district manager explaining the product sales goal to him.

Let's see, Mac, this year our district had 30 individual product sales goals. The average obtained by the district was 24, or 80 percent. You met 29 product goals, or 93 percent. That is a very good job! Because you consistently reached an above-average number of individual product sales goals, you received an evaluation score of 7. I hope you keep that up and can reach all product goals for the coming year. Now let's look at the remainder of our performance factors and see how you did.

TABLE 16.3

THE MBO PERFORMANCE EVALUATION METHOD

PERFORMANCE CRITERION	OBJECTIVE	ACTUAL ACCOMPLISHMENT	PERFORMANCE INDEX
Overall sales	$450,000	$520,000	115.5
Specific product goals obtained	42	40	95.2
Average number daily sales calls	6	7	116.6
New customers obtained	20	25	125.0

Table 16.4

A Behaviorally
Anchored Rating
Scale for Evaluating
Ability to Obtain
Individual Product
Sales Goals

Name: Mac James
Place X on Appropriate Rating Scale

Outstanding	_____	9	Salesperson reaches all individual product sales goals.
Above-average performance	X	7	Salesperson consistently reaches an above-average number of individual product sales goals.
Average performance	_____	5	Salesperson works to reach each individual product sales goal and can be expected to reach the district's average number of goals.
Below-average performance	_____	3	Salesperson has difficulty meeting the district's average number of individual product sales goals.
Poor performance		0	Salesperson reaches few, if any, individual product sales goals.

This method provides good performance feedback to the salesperson on what job factors are being evaluated, what is expected to achieve a high rating, and how the person was actually evaluated. It also makes the manager more comfortable with evaluating performance.

360-Degree Feedback   A new evaluation method that is becoming more popular among sales managers is called 360-degree feedback. Managers obtain feedback from an employee's peers, assistants, clients, and even the sales managers' supervisors in preparation for a performance review. At Trompeter Electronics, an electronics manufacturer in California, sales managers use 360-degree feedback to evaluate and advise their employees. As part of the review process at Trompeter, all staff members hand out surveys to clients and to people they work with internally. These surveys are filled out anonymously and then returned by mail to the evaluated employee, who can review and tabulate the results in private. During the actual evaluation, the employee reports on and discusses these results with the manager. Ray Calvin, vice president of sales and marketing for Trompeter, says, "The whole idea is not so much for me to know as for them [the employees] to know how others rate them. Then we can use this information as one of our discussion points. It's primarily to highlight areas of strength and let us know if any areas are below average."[3]

Influences on a Performance Appraisal's Accuracy

Certainly, establishing appropriate criteria and developing appraisal forms are important. However, the validity and reliability of the data are often influenced by the relationship between sales managers and their salespeople.

New Sales Managers   Since salespeople work by themselves most of the time, some managers, especially new ones, may not know what salespeople do in their jobs and thus not be able to truly evaluate them. This is especially true in sales jobs where objective sales data do not directly relate to a salesperson's efforts. This situation also occurs when a manager has a large span of control or too many responsibilities. It often happens in growth companies when managers are being "moved up" rapidly.

Managers may be in the management position for only 12 to 18 months before they are transferred to a better position. This may not be enough time to properly evaluate each salesperson. Kevin Ryan developed an effective method to handle this situation:

If you're a new manager, you might have some problems because you have not previously worked with the sales representative. You may have some input from the salesperson's former manager; however, you should make your own assessments. Often you are somewhat apprehensive about giving someone whom you have not personally observed a performance rating. What I do in that situation is to let the salesperson tell me what his or her strengths and opportunity areas are. I listen very closely and reserve judgment until I have observed the sales representative's performance over a period of time. It is very important not to make snap judgments or rate a sales representative based on others' opinions.

FALSE PERFORMANCE RESULTS   A second problem arises when even a knowledgeable sales manager does not have adequate performance standards for evaluating a person's performance. This can be compounded when managers think they understand all of the factors leading to good or bad performance and their information is incorrect. For example, sales may be down this year in a territory because last year was an exceptionally good year or sales forecasts were incorrect. As a result, salespeople may receive invalid (unfair) evaluations. Over the long run, this may not be a problem for a particular individual. Yet it can have the negative short-term effects of lower morale, lower performance, and possibly turnover for that particular salesperson.

PERSONALITIES ENTER IN   Another problem occurs when a sales manager uses inappropriate expectations and standards. The manager may allow personal values, needs, or biases to replace sales force values and standards. The result is the occurrence of any one of the following errors in an evaluation.

Central Tendency Errors   Managers may tend to rate all of their salespeople as average on all performance criteria. This rating is the **central-tendency error** illustrated in Figure 16.4. Such a narrow range makes it difficult to properly reward salespeople. This occurs more often when graphic rating sales are used.

Managers rate salespeople in the same way for three reasons. First, the manager honestly may not be able to distinguish among individuals. All salespeople may be performing at an average level. Second, performance may be so difficult to measure objectively that high and low performance cannot be judged. Third, the manager may have personal difficulty with rating people and may be unable to rank individuals as extremely high or extremely low. This type of manager is simply reluctant to take a stand.

Different Evaluation Standards   Somewhat similar to the central-tendency evaluation problem is the problem of different managers having different evaluation standards. At the heart of the problem is the fact two salespeople may actually perform the same; however, salesperson A is in a different sales district than salesperson B. Salesperson A has a manager whose idea of good performance is stricter than salesperson B's manager. Therefore, salesperson B receives a $2,000 annual raise, while salesperson A receives a $1,500 raise.

Managers may interpret the adjectives on rating scales differently. One manager may perceive "excellent" performance as meaning that a salesperson must meet 100 percent of a sales quota, whereas another manager views 90 percent achievement as "excellent" performance. Hard- and easy-to-judge rating distributions are illustrated in Figure 16.5.

When managers tend to give all of their salespeople favorable ratings, they are said to be committing an "error of leniency." An "error of strictness" is just the opposite.

The Halo Effect   A positive or negative "aura" may be associated with an individual. For example, assume a manager works with each salesperson one day each month. When he works with Pete, everything goes well. Everyone buys everything Pete is selling. This single experience can create a **halo effect** in the manager's eyes that all of Pete's days go this way, so Pete's shortcomings may be overlooked.

FIGURE 16.4

EXAMPLE OF
PERFORMANCE
EVALUATION CENTRAL-
TENDENCY ERROR

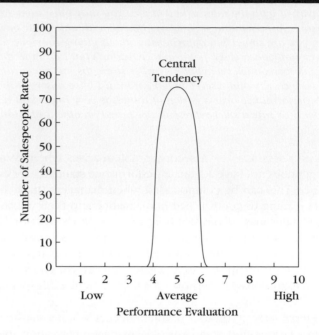

FIGURE 16.5

EXAMPLE OF DIFFERENT
STANDARDS USED IN
PERFORMANCE
EVALUATIONS

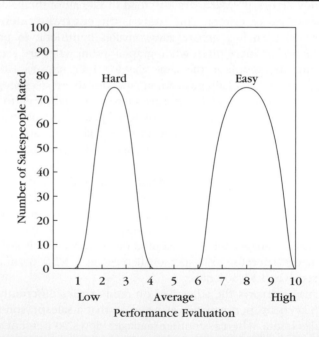

This manager views sales as the sole performance criterion. Pete's high sales-expenses ratio, low customer call average, high product return rate, and high customer complaints are overlooked. This halo may surround Pete for so long that, even when his sales decline, his past performance is remembered. Thus, he continues to receive high performance evaluations. He may even be promoted, resulting in the salesperson taking his place showing sales declines and being blamed for them.

Recent Performance Error   The **recent performance error** is a tendency to evaluate total performance on the last or most recent part of the individual's performance. Managers may forget the first part of the performance period and events that occur in a person's territory in an earlier sales period, remembering only recent performance. Salespeople are aware of this when they say, "We can be a bum today and a hero tomorrow."

THE MANAGER'S ATTITUDES   Another major problem relates to a manager's attitude toward performance evaluation. Some supervisors do not like—and where possible resist—making ratings, especially ones that need to be defended or justified in writing. The result is often inadequate or inaccurate evaluations.

SALESPEOPLE'S EXPECTATIONS   As we can see, the problems for managers in performance appraisal are many. However, salespeople also have problems regarding appraisals. First, people may not be performing well just because they do not know what is expected of them. They may have the ability; they just do not know how to apply it. This is true regardless of the difficulty level of their jobs and whether they work in hospitals, government agencies, or private organizations.

The second problem is that salespeople may not be able to do what is expected. This is especially true for the newer salespeople. This may be corrected by training or job matching, but it is not always easy to spot performance inabilities. Often the manager's supervisor (for example, a regional sales manager or a sales trainer) can play an important role in these cases, working in the field to spot reasons for performance deficiencies.

THE LEGAL ASPECTS OF PERFORMANCE APPRAISALS

The original purpose of performance appraisals was to enjoy their positive benefits—to evaluate the past, to motivate employees to seek higher productivity, and to "reward" good performance with a pay raise. The courtroom role came later. In today's complex work environment, increasing numbers of employees are exercising their rights to sue their employers for violations. It's a fact of life, and it's one that can't be ignored. In virtually every job-related legal action, the written records of the plaintiff's work history are of primary importance in making—and *winning*—cases.

So it's no wonder employees are on the defensive. Many, but not all, organizations have specific policies regarding performance appraisals. It's up to managers to carry out those policies with their sales employees. Managers have to develop certain skills so their appraisals will be effective and appropriate within the law and company policies.

RULES FOR PERFORMANCE APPRAISALS

Although performance appraisals require a great deal of thought and paperwork, clear, concise, and honest appraisal can be used as a management tool and, in extreme situations, as a legal safeguard in court. Whether or not appraisals are used to their full benefit potential is up to the managers. They must use a combination of the following guidelines in order to effectively communicate the good points of, and problems with, an employee's performance.

BE OBJECTIVE

Although it is natural to formulate personal opinions about someone, a performance appraisal is not the forum for those opinions, nor is it a review of a personality. Everything the manager says must center around the job and the job performance. Personal opinions (whether positive or negative) about an employee's character, beliefs, or work style must never be a factor unless they affect job performance.

SET GOALS AND STANDARDS

Managers need to clearly communicate their expectations and a plan to meet those expectations. Employees also should be encouraged to say what they need to improve their performance. Setting a time frame and providing a feedback system are crucial to employees' meeting their goals. Managers should allow time for adjustment to new procedures and meet regularly with those involved to give feedback on the proposed goals and standards.

BE HONEST

Whether or not the appraisal involves a manager and an employee who are friends or enemies, it will not be effective unless the true concerns of both people are discussed. All of the facts and, if possible, specific events should be considered, especially if poor performance is the issue. Although managers need to avoid rudeness or overcriticism, the tone always should remain business-like and professional.

BE CONSISTENT

It has been mentioned that a manager should be objective when reviewing an employee; that manager also needs to view performance objectively. Consistently good work should not necessarily be overshadowed or ignored because of a period of poor performance. Likewise, firing a person with documented good reviews is immediately suspect, as is promoting a person with a string of bad reviews.

USE PROPER DOCUMENTATION

Even with good reasons, a dismissal, disciplinary action, or even a promotion can appear unwarranted without a documented performance history. Managers should write down specifics, back up assertions, and record everything discussed in reviews where they plan to take action. Remember, these are the evidence courts look for should a lawsuit arise from this action. Vague references and poor or nonexistent records can return to haunt a company.

FOLLOW COMPANY POLICY

If a company's policy is, for example, three months of probation before a firing or two strong reviews before a promotion, any deviation will become suspicious, and motives will be questioned. "Going by the book" is the safest way to ensure that all concerns are addressed.

CONDUCTING THE APPRAISAL SESSION

Possibly the most challenging part of a manager's job is effectively conducting the performance appraisal session. A sales manager furnished this example of the basic guidelines he follows.

1. Both manager and salesperson should be prepared for the interview. The manager should collect all information on the salesperson's performance. The manager then should contact the salesperson and establish a time and place for the evaluation. The salesperson should be asked to review his or her past performance using the actual evaluation forms and to review the job description. This takes place before the formal meeting. Objective data should be used when possible.

2. Be positive: Both manager and salesperson must feel the evaluation is a positive method of helping the salesperson do the job better. The salesperson may feel required to defend rather than explain past performance. Two examples may help to illustrate the negative and positive approaches.

Manager: Well, Lou, it's that time of the year again.

Lou: I'm afraid it is.

Manager: I didn't have time to review your file, Lou, but I know you really messed up this year on the Goodyear account.

Lou: Well?

Manager: Well nothing! I really got chewed out by the regional manager over that.

Lou: Did you look at my total performance? Sales were up 5 percent above the district average.

Manager: All right, all right, so you're doing okay, but why did you lose the Goodyear account?

Here the manager was not prepared to talk with Lou. He puts Lou on the defensive from the very beginning. No wonder neither of them looks forward to this confrontation. Next is a more positive approach:

Manager: Lou, it's great we can get together and discuss your achievements and your goals.

Lou: I'm looking forward to it!

Manager: You know, I'm pleased with your sales. You're 5 percent above the district average; that's great! You're doing a good job managing your territory.

Lou: I'm glad you noticed. You know, I often feel I'm out there all by myself.

Manager: Well, Lou, you're not! Is there anything I can do to help you?

Lou: Well, things are going well.

Manager: What about the Goodyear account?

Lou: I sure hated to lose them. My competitor got the business with a low price. But they aren't happy with the service or the products. I'll have that account back in my pocket before you know it!

Manager: I know you will. Lou, we're here today to develop ways to make you the best salesperson in the best district, and this is the best district the company has.

Lou: Sounds great to me. What can I do?

Manager: Did you use the forms I sent you to evaluate your performance?

Lou: Sure did.

Manager: What did you find out?

Lou: Well, there are a few areas I need to look at.

Manager: Okay, but before we get to those, remember we're here to evaluate your performance. Certainly the score is important. It shows your strong points and, as you said, areas for improvement. You and I will work out a plan for this coming year that will allow you to continue to do the good job that you want to do. How does that sound?

Lou: In other words, ways to make me more money and maybe earn a promotion.

Manager: That's right. Ways for you to grow and prosper with our company.

These examples point to the need for both people to have a positive attitude toward the evaluation. The manager must believe in the positive effects this talk will have on

Lou's future performance and attitude toward his job. The manager has sold Lou on the purpose of their meeting. The evaluation has been prepared for and its purpose agreed upon by both the manager and the salesperson. Here are more guidelines:

3. Actually review performance. Again, the manager must be sincere and positive when discussing each performance criterion. Disagreements will occur. Research has shown people will tend to evaluate themselves better than their supervisor does. The following are important when reviewing performance:
   - An open discussion of each performance criterion.
   - The salesperson's discussion of performance.
   - The salesperson's evaluation of his or her own performance.
   - The manager's view of performance.
   - Mutual agreement on the performance level that must be established.
   - If disagreements occur, the manager's careful explanation of why the salesperson will receive a low evaluation in a particular performance area. Frequently, serious differences of opinion occur because the salesperson did not fully understand what was expected.
4. Finalize the performance evaluation. The manager should now review the evaluation of each performance area with the salesperson. Managers prefer to begin by reviewing the high ratings and then work down. The salesperson should understand clearly what has been decided on.
5. Summarize the total performance evaluation. The salesperson should be told how the manager views the person's past performance. For example:

   Susan, you have done above average this year. You are continuing to improve year after year and will receive a good raise. If you continue this level of performance, in a few more years you will be ready for a management position.

   Nancy, this is the second year in a row your sales have decreased while the district's increased. This has to change if you are to stay with the company. I don't want to do this, but you have six months to get your territory turned around.

   If someone needs to be terminated, follow the "do's and don'ts" in Table 16.5.
6. Develop mutually agreed-upon objectives. Performance and career objectives can be established now. Both manager and salesperson provide input.
7. Formalize the evaluation and objectives. Immediately after the evaluation session is over, the manager should write a letter to the salesperson restating the performance evaluation results and the objectives. A copy is sent to the manager's supervisor to go into the salesperson's permanent personnel file.

Guideline number 7 suggests that managers keep a copy of the performance review on file. In today's litigious society, it is increasingly important for companies to document such reviews. Many companies have fallen victim to heavy lawsuits or expensive court proceedings due to not having proper documentation of reviews designating poor or superior performance. Alpha Personnel, Inc., in Norton, Massachusetts, spent countless hours in court defending reasons behind an employee's termination. Alpha Personnel failed to keep any written documentation, signed or unsigned, pertaining to performance reviews. Even after acknowledging company warnings and discussions surrounding a falsified document, this employee sued on the grounds of discrimination. Alpha Personnel won the lawsuit but could have saved $3,000 and the time if it had kept proper documentation on file.[4]

Do's	Don'ts
■ Put everything in writing. Leave a paper trail. Use a witness to the discussions on unacceptable performance.	■ Don't leave room for confusion about the firing. Tell the individual in the first sentence that he or she is terminated.
■ Sit down one-on-one with the individual in a private office.	■ Don't allow time for debate during the termination session.
■ Complete a termination session within 15 minutes.	■ Don't make personal comments when firing someone; keep the conversation professional.
■ Provide a written explanation of severance benefits.	■ Don't rush a fired employee offsite unless security is an issue.
■ Provide outplacement services away from company headquarters.	■ Don't fire people on significant dates, like the 25th anniversary of their employment or the day their mother died.
■ Be sure the employee hears about his or her termination from a manager, not a colleague.	
■ Express appreciation for what the employee has contributed, if appropriate.	■ Don't fire employees when they are on vacation or have just returned.

TABLE 16.5

DO'S AND DON'TS ON TERMINATION

As you can see, much skill and knowledge are needed to effectively conduct a performance evaluation. To determine how well they have done, managers must evaluate the system.

EVALUATE THE EVALUATION SYSTEM

Evaluating the performance appraisal system is important. When used properly, few management tools are more valuable than an honest, objective-as-possible, well-kept, regularly reviewed, and consistent performance evaluation system. The system can take courage to do and to follow through with, but evaluating it can help improve managers. It also could be more help than you might believe should a manager ever face a discrimination charge from an employee. The specific evaluation of a sales force's appraisal system requires the examination of several aspects of the entire system. The following questions can provide an assessment of the specific components:

1. What does the sales force want its performance appraisal system to do? Does the firm have goals and objectives for the system?
2. Do procedures exist for gathering data to measure how well the goals and objectives are being met?
3. Do the appraisal forms really elicit the information to serve these goals and objectives?
4. Are the appraisal interviews done effectively?

By addressing these questions and taking corrective action when necessary, managers can ensure that a sales force's performance appraisal system is more likely to serve its purposes and the broader goals of productivity, quality of work life, and legal compliance.

So, what have you learned from this textbook? Did I hear someone say "Nothing!"? We know that is not true. You have come a long way, in a short time, in understanding the many challenges facing today's sales manager. It is a big job—one full of personal and financial rewards.

YOU HAVE ALMOST FINISHED THIS TEXTBOOK

Before finishing this chapter, take a look at the sales and marketing management model in Figure 16.6. You have learned about each of the model's elements and each element's relationship with other elements for managing a sales and marketing program.

You can see that we emphasize customers—we begin and end our sales and marketing model with the customer in mind. A company's first responsibility is to the people who buy and use its products and services. It must be dedicated to providing them with superior quality and value for their money.

How do managers know if they are accomplishing this goal? Marketing and corporate performance tells them—return on assets, sales, and market share. The right-hand portion of the sales and marketing management model relates to sales force management. As you have learned, what the sales team does is coordinated with the firm's total marketing effort and stems from it.

As you study Figure 16.6, look back through this textbook and your class notes to refresh your memory on the relationships shown in the model. What you see is a very simplified framework you can use to study for tests and, maybe in the future, as a road map for developing your own company's sales and marketing program.

THE BOTTOM LINE

Effective job performance is essential for organizations to stay in business and for salespeople to keep their jobs. Performance evaluations are periodically conducted with each salesperson to determine success or failure in meeting past goals and to develop plans for obtaining future goals. The primary evaluator is the salesperson's immediate supervisor.

Managers must be aware of the legal repercussions of performance appraisals. They should develop valid performance criteria and standards, as well as legal appraisal forms. The forms should demonstrate such information as the validity of criteria, the performance standards related to the job, and the legality of performance

FIGURE 16.6   THE RELATIONSHIP OF MARKETING TO SALES FORCE MANAGEMENT

Marketing Management

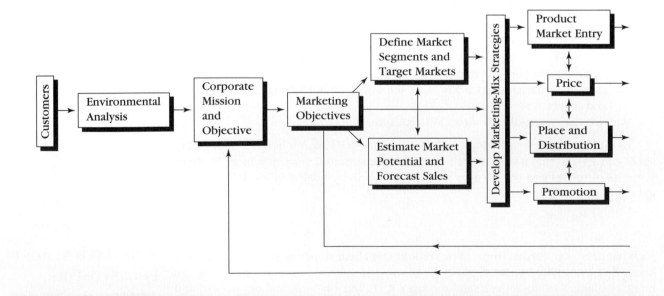

appraisal procedures. Salespeople must be told how they will be evaluated and should be given a copy of their completed appraisal.

Companies must develop performance criteria that are measurable, practical, relevant, discriminating, and stable. Firms use both quantitative and qualitative performance criteria. Evaluation methods must effectively measure performance. Managers need to be aware of the problems in evaluating salespeople, such as central-tendency errors, halo effects, varying standards, and referring only to the most recent performance behavior. Evaluations are often mishandled.

Performance evaluations serve to reward effective performers and penalize ineffective salespeople. Managers are often uncomfortable about dealing with ineffective personnel. One problem that frequently arises is that salespeople see their performance

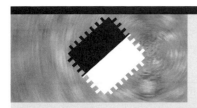

MANAGEMENT IN ACTION: ETHICAL DILEMMA
SHOULD YOU BE A WHISTLE-BLOWER?

As a regional manager, you frequently contact the doctors and hospitals hired by your company to conduct clinical research on your products. Today, you discover that a medical research group is falsifying results regarding the effectiveness of one of your company's products. Although the drug is safe, it doesn't work. Your company's president apparently knows about the situation but has not taken any steps to correct it.

WHAT DO YOU DO?
1. Nothing. You can't afford to compromise your position at the company.
2. Anonymously report to the appropriate governmental agency.
3. Make an appointment to discuss the situation with the president. If he does not agree to immediately rectify the situation, resign and contact the proper authorities.

FIGURE 16.6   THE RELATIONSHIP OF MARKETING TO SALES FORCE MANAGEMENT, *continued*

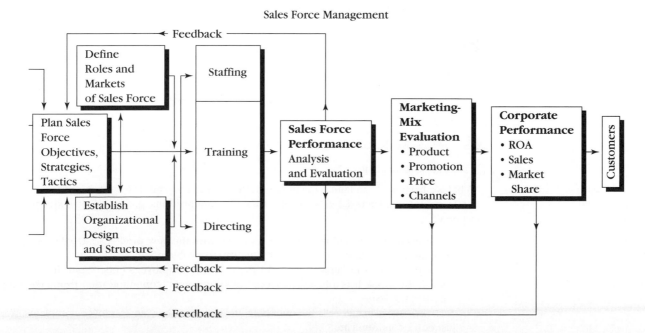

as better than their manager perceives it. A few salespeople may even feel they are next in line for a promotion when they are really not promotable.

Many difficulties can be corrected if performance evaluations are effectively conducted. The manager and salesperson must be prepared for the evaluation session. Both should view the evaluation positively. Performance should be honestly and openly reviewed. At the end of the evaluation, the manager should summarize the salesperson's past performance, and together they should outline future performance objectives. Finally the manager should write a letter to the salesperson restating the evaluation results. These procedures can lead to the salesperson's improved job performance and better attitudes toward the company and the work.

 KEY TERMS FOR SALES MANAGERS

Performance appraisal, 390
Performance level, 392
Performance Development Review, 394
Performance cycle, 394
Criterion, 395

Graphic appraisal scale, 398
Descriptive statement, 398
Management by objectives (MBO), 399
Behaviorally anchored rating scales (BARS), 399

Central-tendency error, 401
Halo effect, 401
Recent performance error, 403

 MANAGEMENT APPLICATION QUESTIONS

1. According to J & J's Kevin Ryan, why is a performance appraisal important, and to whom is it important?
2. Although performance appraisals may be used for a number of specific purposes, they can be grouped into two general categories. What are these categories, and what is the difference between them?
3. Discuss who should evaluate salespeople and why.
4. What are performance criteria, and how should they be used?
5. Two general categories of performance criteria exist. Discuss the difference between them, and explain why a sales manager needs to use both kinds.
6. The validity and reliability of the data on a performance appraisal can be influenced by the relationship between the sales manager and the salesperson. Describe at least two of these influences, and discuss what impact they may have on a performance appraisal.

 FURTHER EXPLORING THE SALES WORLD

Interview a sales manager to determine the process and procedure used to evaluate salespeople and the manager. What specific performance criteria are used for evaluations of both positions? For both positions, what does it take to be promoted?

SALES MANAGEMENT EXPERIENTIAL EXERCISE

A FAILURE TO COMMUNICATE?

"What we have here is a failure to communicate" goes a line from the movie *Cool Hand Luke*. But in reality, managers label a lot of issues "communications problems" that are not. For example:

- *Disagreements.* "My subordinates do not agree with the new pricing strategy," a vice president laments. "I guess we have a communication problem."
   In this case communication is not the problem. Employees understand the strategy; they simply think it is a bad idea. To call disagreements "communication problems" only confuses the issue.
- *Distrust.* "My manager tells me one thing and does another," an employee complains. "We just don't communicate."

No amount of communication will improve this relationship. It is a matter of trust, not communication. To improve this relationship, the manager must work on increasing trust among employees. A first step is to be open and direct with people.

■ *Information overload.* "I don't know why our people complain about communication. We provide them with stacks of reports," a manager says.

This organization bombards employees with tons of data, but employees can care less about most of the details. The few items of interest are often buried deep. Again, more communication will not reduce employees' frustration. But a newly designed, more effective management information system probably would help.

Management Quiz

Assume you have ten points to allocate between each pair of statements. Allocate the points according to the strength of your belief.

1. a. Communication is a major problem today.
   b. Communication is a symptom of other issues.
2. a. Words are more important than actions.
   b. Actions are more important than words.
3. a. Listening is more important than telling.
   b. Telling is more important than listening.
4. a. Human relations are more important than logic.
   b. Logic is more important than human relations.
5. a. Effective communication is persuasive.
   b. Effective communication is understanding.
6. a. Disagreements represent communication problems.
   b. Disagreements represent conflict problems.

Total the points allocated to the following: 1b, 2b, 3a, 4a, 5b, and 6b. A score of 40 or higher suggests an effective communication philosophy.

CASE 16.1

MICHIGAN SECURITY SYSTEMS
Promote Me or Else!

Charlie Daft is a winner! Just ask him. He is truly an outstanding salesperson for Michigan Security Systems, always meeting or beating quota. The trouble is, Charlie is not as great as he would like to believe. Charlie feels he deserves to be promoted to a manager's position. The company grapevine is spreading the rumor that a new slot for a district sales manager is opening. Charlie will want—no, he'll demand—the promotion. He genuinely expects to get the job. You, as Charlie's supervisor, feel trouble is coming, because you are not convinced Charlie is ready to manage others.

Although Charlie is a top-notch salesperson, one of the best, he is also a loner. In your opinion, he is not at all ready to manage a group of sales reps. Also, this time, the grapevine is wrong. No district sales manager's job is opening soon, nor is one anticipated to open. However, you've just received a letter from Charlie that makes it quite clear you're dealing with a crisis. The letter is direct and unambiguous: "I have been a sales rep for this company for several years and have always been the top producer, meeting and often beating my sales quotas. I have built every one of the accounts assigned to me to a higher sales level, and I have opened more new accounts than anyone else in the department. In performance reviews you have rated me 'excellent.' You, your boss, and others have often told me I am an exceptional sales rep.

"I have no complaints at all about the salary, the commission, or the bonus plans. I want you to recognize that I feel I am completely ready for the next available sales manager's job. It is important for me to tell you that if this company can't use my talents, I will have only one choice: I will have to go to work with a competitor."

Charlie expects a promotion—if not now, then soon.

QUESTION
What are you going to do?

THE DUNN CORP.
What Should Be Done with a Low Performer?

Robert Head, the newly appointed sales manager for the Dunn Corporation, had completed a review of the sales force he inherited. He knew he had an important decision facing him regarding one of his sales representatives, John Little.

COMPANY BACKGROUND

The Dunn Corporation, with headquarters in Tuscaloosa, Alabama, produced and sold asphalt roofing products and other building materials throughout the southeastern United States. The primary market area consisted of Alabama, Tennessee, Georgia, Florida, and Mississippi. It also had selected accounts in Kentucky, Indiana, and South Carolina. Five sales representatives covered the primary marketing area, with each representative having one of the states assigned as a territory. The selected accounts were assigned to the sales representatives at the sales manager's discretion.

Historically, Dunn's management had pursued a conservative growth strategy with particular emphasis on achieving maximum return on investment. In order to keep costs down, it gave capital expenditures for replacement of worn-out or obsolete equipment low priority. This led to such a drop in efficiency at the company's Tuscaloosa plant that production was unable to keep pace with demand. Thus, from 1991 to 1995, company sales were limited by the product's availability. However, despite these difficulties, the company had been profitable and had built an excellent reputation in the construction industry for service and quality

The company had initiated successful capital improvement programs during 1994 and 1995; consequently, the company's production capacity had been greatly increased. No longer would Dunn's sales performance be hindered by lack of product availability. Robert Head recognized that this increase in production capacity would require some revisions in the sales force's duties. More time would have to be spent seeking new accounts in order to fully realize this new sales potential.

One of the first tasks Head had undertaken as sales manager was a review of the field operations and performance of each salesperson. Head traveled with the sales reps for a week in order to obtain as much information on each one as possible. He also spent two days with each person compiling a territorial analysis. This analysis broke each salesperson's district into trade areas that were then analyzed in terms of established accounts, competitive accounts, potential of the trade territory, market position of competitive manufacturers, and selection of target accounts. Head believed a properly prepared territorial analysis could reveal whether the sales reps really knew and worked their districts. Some pertinent statistics uncovered by the analysis are reported in Exhibits 1 and 2.

JOHN LITTLE'S PERFORMANCE

Head concluded, after reviewing the results of the territorial analysis, that John Little's sales performance could be improved. Little had been with the company for more than 20 years. A tall, handsome man with a polished, articulate manner, he appeared to be a perfect salesperson, yet his performance never seemed to equal his potential.

While evaluating Little's accounts, call reports, and expense accounts, Head uncovered a pattern of infrequent travel throughout Little's district. Little sold only 34 active accounts, well below the company average of approximately 55. With the low number of accounts and a daily call rate of two, it appeared Little simply was not working very hard. When Little's sales performance was compared to his district's estimated potential, it appeared Little was realizing only about 60 percent of his area's potential sales. When compared with the other

---

EXHIBIT 1   SALES PERFORMANCE OF INDIVIDUAL SALESPERSONS: 1999–2000

SALES REP	SALES VOLUME	
	1999	**2000**
Peters	$2,732,464	$2,636,832
Little	1,366,232	1,315,916
Homer	1,639,420	1,879,880
Cough	2,368,136	2,443,844
Stiles	1,001,903	1,127,928
Total	$9,108,155	$9,404,400

Source: This case was developed by Professor James L. Taylor, Department of Management and Marketing, University of Alabama. The company name has been changed.

EXHIBIT 2   RESULTS OF TERRITORIAL ANALYSIS

SALES REP	NUMBER OF ACCOUNTS	NEW ACCOUNTS IN 2000	AVERAGE DAILY CALLS
Peters	63	3	4
Little	34	0	2
Homer	52	2	5
Cough	78	4	2
Stiles	47	2	3
Average	54.8	2.2	3.2

territories, Little's district ranked last in terms of sales volume per 1,000 housing starts and sales volume per 100,000 population.

Head had questioned Little concerning coverage of his Georgia district. Head recalled part of their conversation:

Head: John, it appears that you simply are not calling on the potential customers in the outer areas of your district. For example, last month you spent 12 out of 20 days working in Atlanta. I know you live in Atlanta, and people have a tendency to work closer to home, but I believe that we are missing a lot of business in your area simply by not calling on people.

Little: Look, I have been selling roofing for a long time, even when the plant couldn't produce and ship it. Why get upset when we have a little extra product to sell?

Head: Look, John, we have increased production by 20 percent. You will have all the product you can sell. This means extra income to you, better services to your accounts, and more profit to the company. I will be happy to assist you in working out a plan for coverage of your district.

Little: Bob, don't you ever look at the volume of our customers? If you did, you would know that the Republic Roofing Supply in Atlanta is the second largest Dunn account. Upchurch, the owner of Republic, is very demanding concerning my servicing Republic on ordering, delivery, and product promotion. It has taken a long time, but I have gained the trust and respect of Upchurch. That is why he looks to me to take care of the account. The reason that we have not lost the account to our competitors is that I give the type of service Upchurch demands.

Head: John, I agree that service to all of our accounts is extremely important. However, service does represent a cost, not only in terms of an outlay of money but also in the potential loss of business from other accounts. I seriously question the profitability of spending approximately 40 percent of your time with one account.

Little: What do you mean, profitability? My district has always made money. Just because we have new management, why does everything have to change?

Head had continued the conversation by suggesting that he and Little meet at some future date for the purpose of laying out a travel schedule. It was Head's intention to structure the schedule so Little could make a minimum of four calls per day. Little, however, refused to even consider setting up a schedule or to increase the number of calls per day. His refusal was based on the contention he needed at least two days a week to service Republic properly. Little further stated that if Dunn would not allow him the two days a week to service Republic, other roofing manufacturers would.

Robert Head pondered his decision regarding John Little and the Georgia territory. He felt he had three options: (1) He could simply fire Little with the possibility of losing the Republic account. Because Republic was Dunn's second largest account, Head realized this might be a dangerous course of action. (2) Head considered rearranging Little's district by transferring some of the outer counties to other sales reps. (3) Head realized he could simply accept the situation and leave things as they were now. He remembered once being told by a close friend with years of management experience that sometimes a "don't rock the boat" strategy is the best way to handle difficult situations.

QUESTION

What should Robert Head do regarding John Little and his Georgia territory?

SALES FORCE EXPERIENTIAL EXERCISES

SALES TEAM BUILDING EXERCISE

You and your sales team were flying from Chicago, Illinois, to Fairbanks, Alaska, when your plane crash-landed in the woods somewhere in the Canadian Yukon.[1] It is 10 A.M. in January. The single-engine plane and the bodies of the pilot and co-pilot were completely destroyed except for the airplane's frame. No one in your sales team was injured.

The plane was struck by lightning causing it to crash instantly. The pilot was unable to radio for help. The storms in the region caused the plane to change course several times. Immediately before the plane was struck by lightning, the pilot announced the plane was about 90 miles from the nearest town.

You are in a wooded area with numerous lakes, rivers, and mountains. It is −10 degrees now and night-time temperatures are expected to be −30. The group is dressed in casual clothes appropriate for living in a city—jeans, shirts, street shoes, and overcoats.

Before the plane caught fire, your group was able to salvage the 15 items listed in Exhibit A. You are to rank these 15 items in order of their importance to your survival, starting with "1" as the most important to "15" as the least important.

You can assume the number of survivors is the same as the number on your team; the team has agreed to stick together; and all items are in good condition.

ASSIGNMENTS

- First, on their own, each member of the sales team is to individually rank each item in order of importance to survival.
- Second, rank each item as a team. It is critical no one changes his or her individual rankings once discussion starts within the group.

SELL YOURSELF ON A JOB INTERVIEW

You will play the roles of a sales job applicant and as a recruiter.[2] You may choose to interview with any organization, but the hope is that you would choose an organization with which you would like to interview for a job sometime in the future. For your role as an applicant, develop a one- to two-page, professional-looking résumé. Before you are to be interviewed, turn in to your instructor a copy of the résumé to give to your interviewer to go over before the meeting. Also give the instructor a one- to two-page description of the company at which you are applying for a beginning sales job. Assume this is your first interview with the company, and you have never met the recruiter. It will last approximately five to eight minutes.

EXHIBIT A

ITEMS	STEP 1 YOUR INDIVIDUAL RANKING	STEP 2 THE TEAM'S RANKING	STEP 3 SURVIVAL EXPERT'S RANKING	STEP 4 DIFFERENCE BETWEEN STEPS 1 AND 3	STEP 5 DIFFERENCE BETWEEN STEPS 2 AND 3
Compress kit					
Ball of steel wool					
Cigarette lighter					
.45-caliber pistol					
Newspaper					
Compass					
Ski poles					
Knife					
Sectional air map					
Piece of rope					
Chocolate bars					
Flashlight					
Whiskey					
Shirt and pants					
Shortening					
Totals (The lower the score the better)					
				Your Score (Step 4)	Team Score (Step 5)

			TEAM NUMBER					
Please complete the following steps and insert the scores under your team's number.			1	2	3	4	5	6
Step 6	Average Individual Score—Add up all the individual team members' scores (Step 4) and divide by the number on the team.							
Step 7	Team Score (Step 5 above)							
Step 8	Gain (Loss) Score—The difference between the Team Score and the Average Individual Score. If the Team Score is lower than Avg. Ind. Score, gain is "+"; if higher, gain is "−".							
Step 9	Percentage Change—Divide the gain (loss) by the Average Individual Score.							
Step 10	Lowest Individual Score—on the team.							
Sep 11	Number of Individual Scores—lower than the team score.							

RECRUITER. Create a business card to give to the applicant sometime during the interview.

RÉSUMÉ. Bring an original copy of the résumé with you to the interview. During the interview, be prepared to point out one or more selling points in the résumé that relate to the interviewer's question(s) or to major point(s) you will discuss about yourself during the interview.

PERSONAL BUSINESS CARD. Here are several format ideas for your business card. On the left side have a head-and-shoulder photograph of yourself. This should be a professional pose. On the right side, have your name in boldface type. Underneath your name, have your address, telephone number, e-mail address in a regular typeface. Skip a line and have the name of your school in bold, followed with your degree (such as B. B. A. in Marketing), and graduation date. On the card's back have a bulleted list of items such as your overall and major grade point average, courses relating to job, and main job(s). You are creating a creative mini-résumé.

PORTFOLIO. Create a bound portfolio of school projects you have completed during your coursework. At the appropriate time during the interview, go over one or more of the projects that best relate to this job. If you have no projects, use a fake portfolio. Make up facts related to the project(s) for discussion with the recruiter.

The résumé and course portfolio serve as visuals that aid in creating the image of you as a creative, highly motivated person who has thoroughly prepared for this interview and is very interested in obtaining a job with the organization. You will leave both the résumé and portfolio with the interviewer. They will be returned to you after the interview. You are encouraged to develop other creative elements for your presentation.

I WANT THE JOB. Before the interview is over, consider letting the recruiter know "you are very interested in this job." The interviewer may not feel this is true if you do not show knowledge about the organization and job. However, if you can demonstrate in-depth knowledge about the company, job, products, and customers—such a statement will be taken positively by the recruiter. Some organizations will not hire someone unless they state: "I want this job." If true, you would declare this in a later interview.

GRADE BEGINS–ENDS. Your grade for this exercise begins when you knock on the door to enter the recruiter's office and ends when you leave the office and close the door behind you. You should act in a professional manner this entire time.

FOLLOW-UP. After the interview, create a professional "thank you" letter. In order to know the interviewer's address, ask for a business card sometime during the interview. Within one day after the interview, mail or e-mail the "thank you" letter to your instructor. For the letter's inside address and salutation, use the recruiter's name as shown on the business card. If you send a thank you by e-mail, consider sending an electronic greeting card "thank you." Bluemountain, Amazon, Hallmark, and others have free electronic greeting cards that you can use on the Internet for this part of the assignment. Select a professional "thank you" card to e-mail to your recruiter.

Five to seven days after the interview, send a follow-up e-mail to your recruiter. Use the recruiter's name in the e-mail (To: Mrs. Smith). The e-mail actually goes to your

This exercise was created by Professors Charles M. Futrell of Texas A & M University and George Wynn of James Madison. Copyright © 2000.

EXHIBIT B   PLAN YOUR INTERVIEW APPEARANCE

Name:

The most successful people in customer-contact jobs claim mental sharpness means communicating a positive self-image. Like an actor or actress, interacting with others requires you to be on stage at all times. Creating a good first impression is essential. Also important is understanding the direct connection between your attitude and how you look to yourself. The better your self-image when you encounter customers, clients, or guests, the more positive you are.

Rate yourself on each of the following grooming areas. If you write 5, you are saying improvement is not required. If you write a 1 or 2, you need considerable improvement. Be honest.

	EXCELLENT	GOOD	FAIR	WEAK	POOR
Hairstyle, hair grooming, fingernails (appropriate length and cleanliness)	5	4	3	2	1
Personal cleanliness habits (body)	5	4	3	2	1
Clothing, piercings, and jewelry (appropriate to the situation)	5	4	3	2	1
Neatness (shoes shined; clothes clean, well pressed, etc.)	5	4	3	2	1
Fragrances, tattoos, and makeup	5	4	3	2	1
General grooming: Does your appearance reflect professionalism on the job?	5	4	3	2	1

When it comes to appearance on the job, I would rate myself as follows:
☐ Excellent   ☐ Good   ☐ Need Improvement

instructor. Assume you have not heard anything back from the recruiter after the interview, and you want to know if the recruiter has received your follow-up letter and has any other questions to ask of you. Also, assume you are interested in being further considered for the sales job and that the recruiter said she or he would let you know if you are still being considered for the job within two weeks after the interview.

PS.   For both the letter and the e-mail, please have a "PS:" stating your class day and time. The PS will ensure you receive proper credit for this important learning exercise.

YOU ARE SELLING.   Whether you are an applicant or an interviewer, imagine that you are placed in a sales situation. As an applicant, you are selling yourself. As an interviewer, you are not only selling yourself but also your company and the sales job as well.

Interviewers are looking for indications that the applicant can sell or can be trained to sell. How can you—the applicant—apply basic selling procedures to the job interview situation?

You can look, dress, groom, and have the attitude of a successful person. Showing the interviewer you have prepared for the interview indicates how you might prepare to make a sales call on a customer. Using the résumé and portfolio during the interview helps to distinguish you from others interviewing for the job. Finally, you should "close" the sale by asking for the order (job).

CLOSE THE SALE.   An applicant typically goes through several interviews before being offered a job. Consider this your first interview. What is your sales call objective for the first interview? It is to be asked back for a second interview! The end of the interview is an excellent time for you to illustrate your sales skills.

FUTRELL'S CLOSING SEQUENCE.   One way to demonstrate your sales skills is by using "Futrell's Two-Question Interview Closing Sequence." At the end of most first interviews, the recruiter will ask something like, "Do you have any questions?" You should respond,

- "Yes, I have two questions. What is the next step in the interview process?" Wait for the reply. Then ask,
- "Based upon my background, résumé, and what we have talked about to-day, what is my chance of being asked back for a second interview?"

Should the interviewer *not* ask if you have a question, you should say something such as, "I have two questions," or "May I ask two questions before I go?"

PLAN YOUR INTERVIEW APPEARANCE QUESTIONNAIRE.   After your interview, com-plete the Interview Appearance Questionnaire in Exhibit B. Give the completed ques-tionnaire to your instructor.

WHAT'S YOUR STYLE—SENSER, INTUITOR, THINKER, FEELER?

Individuals differ in the way they interact with others and the way they gather and evaluate information for problem solving and decision making[3]. Four psychological functions identified by Carl Jung are related to this process: sensation, intuition, think-ing, and feeling.

Before you read further, complete the Problem-Solving Diagnostic Questionnaire (Part A), and then check the scoring key that appears in Part B. It has no right or wrong answers; just read each item carefully, and then respond with your answer.

According to Jung, gathering information and evaluating information are separate activities. People gather information either by *sensation* or *intuition* but not by both simultaneously. People using *sensation* would rather work with known facts and hard data and prefer routine and order while gathering information. People using *intuition* would rather look for possibilities than work with facts and prefer solving new prob-lems and using abstract concepts.

Information evaluation involves making judgments about the information a per-son has gathered. People evaluate information by *thinking* or *feeling*. These represent the extremes in orientation. *Thinking* individuals base their judgments on impersonal analysis, using reason and logic rather than personal values or emotional aspects of the situation. *Feeling* individuals base their judgments more on personal feelings, such as harmony, and tend to make decisions that result in approval from others.

PART A: QUESTIONNAIRE TO DETERMINE YOUR STYLE

Indicate your responses to the following questionnaire on a separate sheet of paper. None of these items have right or wrong responses.

I. Write down the number and letter of the response that comes closest to how you usually feel or act.

1. I am more careful about
   a. People's feelings
   b. Their rights
2. I usually get on better with
   a. Imaginative people
   b. Realistic people
3. It is a higher compliment to be called
   a. A person of real feeling
   b. A consistently reasonable person
4. In doing something with many people, it appeals more to me
   a. To do it in the accepted way
   b. To invent a way of my own

5. I get more annoyed at
   a. Fancy theories
   b. People who do not like theories
6. It is higher praise to call someone
   a. A person of vision
   b. A person of common sense
7. I more often let
   a. My heart rule my head
   b. My head rule my heart
8. I think it is a worse fault
   a. To show too much warmth
   b. To be unsympathetic
9. If I were a teacher, I would rather teach
   a. Courses involving theory
   b. Fact courses

II. Write down the letters of the words in the following pairs that appeal to you more.

	a.	b.
10.	compassion	foresight
11.	justice	mercy
12.	production	design
13.	gentle	firm
14.	uncritical	critical
15.	literal	figurative
16.	imaginative	matter-of-fact

According to Jung, only one of the four functions—sensation, intuition, thinking, or feeling—is dominant in an individual. However, the dominant function is usually backed up by one of the functions from the other set of paired opposites. Part C shows the four problem-solving styles that result from these matchups.

PART B: SCORING KEY TO DETERMINE YOUR STYLE

The following scales indicate the psychological functions related to each item. Use the point-value columns to arrive at your score for each function. For example, if you answered *a* to the first question, your *1a* response in the feeling column is worth zero points when you add up the point-value column. Instructions for classifying your scores follow the scales.

SENSATION	POINT VALUE	INTUITION	POINT VALUE	THINKING	POINT VALUE	FEELING	POINT VALUE
2 b ___	1	2 a ___	2	1 b ___	1	1 a ___	0
4 a ___	1	4 b ___	1	3 b ___	2	3 a ___	1
5 a ___	1	5 b ___	1	7 b ___	1	7 a ___	1
6 b ___	1	6 a ___	0	8 a ___	0	8 b ___	1
9 b ___	2	9 a ___	2	10 b ___	2	10 a ___	1
12 a ___	1	12 b ___	0	11 a ___	2	11 b ___	1
15 a ___	1	15 b ___	1	13 b ___	1	13 a ___	1
16 b ___	2	16 a ___	0	14 b ___	0	14 a ___	1
Maximum point value:	(10)		(7)		(9)		(7)

Classifying total scores:

- Write *intuition* if your intuition score is equal to or greater than your sensation score.
- Write *sensation* if your sensation score is greater than your intuition score.
- Write *feeling* if your feeling score is greater than your thinking score.
- Write *thinking* if your thinking score is greater than your feeling score.

Part C: The Four Styles and Their Tendencies

Personal Style	Action Tendencies
Sensation-thinking	■ Emphasizes details, facts, certainty ■ Is decisive, applied thinker ■ Focuses on short-term, realistic goals ■ Develops rules and regulations for judging performance
Intuitive-thinker	■ Shows concern for current, real-life human problems ■ Is creative, progressive, perceptive thinker ■ Emphasizes detailed facts about people rather than tasks ■ Focuses on structuring organizations for the benefit of people
Sensation-feeling	■ Prefers dealing with theoretical or technical problems ■ Is pragmatic, analytical, methodical, and conscientious ■ Focuses on possibilities using interpersonal analysis ■ Is able to consider a number of options and problems simultaneously
Intuitive-feeling	■ Avoids specifics ■ Is charismatic, participative, people oriented, and helpful ■ Focuses on general views, broad themes, and feelings ■ Decentralizes decision making; develops few rules and regulations

Questions

1. Look back at your scores. What is your personal problem-solving style? Read the action tendencies. Do they fit?
2. Studies show that the sensation-thinking (ST) combination characterizes many managers in Western industrialized societies. Do you think the ST style is the best fit for most jobs in today's society?
3. Also look at Part D, Guidelines to Identify Personality Style. Compare yourself and others you know to the guidelines. Do you find a match between you and the individual style? What about your roommate, spouse, parents, or your brother or sister?
4. How can you use this information to improve your communication ability?

PART D: GUIDELINES TO IDENTIFYING PERSONALITY STYLE

GUIDELINE	THINKER	INTUITOR	FEELER	SENSER
How to describe this person	A direct, detail-oriented person; likes to deal in sequence on *his/her time*; very precise, sometimes seen as a nitpicker; fact oriented	A knowledgeable, future-oriented person; an innovator who likes to abstract principles from a mass of material; active in community affairs by assisting in policy making, program development, etc.	People oriented; very sensitive to people's needs; an emotional person rooted in the past; enjoys contact with people; able to read people very well	Action-oriented person; deals with the world through his/her senses; very decisive and has a high energy level
The person's strengths	Effective communicator, deliberative, prudent, weighs alternatives, stabilizing, objective, rational, analytical, asks questions for more facts	Original, imaginative, creative, broad gauged, charismatic, idealist, intellectual, tenacious, ideological, conceptual, involved	Spontaneous, persuasive, empathetic, grasps traditional values, probing, introspective, draws out feelings of others, loyal, actions based on what has worked in the past	Pragmatic, assertive, directional results oriented, technically skillful, objective—bases opinions on what he/she actually sees, perfection seeking, decisive, direct and down to earth, action oriented
The person's drawbacks	Verbose, indecisive, overcautious, overanalyzes, unemotional, nondynamic, controlled and controlling, overserious, rigid nit-picking	Unrealistic, far-out, fantasy bound, scattered, devious, out of touch, dogmatic, impractical, poor listener	Impulsive, manipulative, overpersonalizes, sentimental, postponing, guilt ridden, stirs up conflict, subjective	Impatient, doesn't see long range, status seeking, self-involved, acts first then thinks, lacks trust in others, nit-picky, impulsive, does not delegate to others
Time orientation	Past, present, future	Future	Past	Present
ENVIRONMENT				
Desk	Usually neat	Reference books, theory books, etc.	Personal plaques and mementos, family pictures	Chaos
Room	Usually has a calculator and computer runs, etc.	Abstract art, bookcases, trend charts, etc.	Decorated warmly with pictures of scenes or people, antiques	Usually a mess with piles of papers, etc.; action pictures or pictures of the manufacturing plant or products on the wall
Dress	Neat and conservative	Mod or rumpled	Current styles or informal	No jacket; loose tie or functional work clothes

YOUR SALES APTITUDE

CUSTOMER A

You are a salesperson for the Sport Shoe Corporation.[4] Upon arrival at your office, you find a letter marked "urgent" on your desk. This letter is from the athletic director of Ball State University and pertains to the poor quality of basketball shoes you sold him. The director cited several examples of split soles and poor overall quality as his main complaints. In closing, he mentioned that since the season was drawing near he would be forced to contact the ACME Sport Shoe Company if the situation could not be rectified. What actions on your part would be appropriate?

A. Place a call to the athletic director assuring him of your commitment to service. Promise to be at Ball State at his convenience to rectify the problem.

B. Go by the warehouse and take the athletic director all new shoes and apologize for the delay and poor quality of the merchandise.

C. Write a letter to the athletic director assuring him that SSC sells only high-quality shoes and that this type of problem rarely occurs. Assure him you'll come to his office as soon as possible but if he feels ACME would be a better choice than Sport Shoe he should contact them.

D. Don't worry about the letter because the athletic director seems to have the attitude that he can put pressure on you by threatening to switch companies. Also, the loss in sales of 20–40 pairs of basketball shoes will be a drop in the bucket compared to the valuable sales time you would waste on a piddly account like Ball State.

CUSTOMER B

Sam Gillespie, owner of Central Hardware Supply, was referred to you by a mutual friend. Gillespie had been thinking of dropping two of their product suppliers of home building supplies. "The sales should be guaranteed," your friend has stated.

Your friend's information was correct, and your presentation to Gillespie convinces you he will benefit from buying from you. He comments as you conclude your presentation: "Looks like your product will solve our problem. I'd like to think this over, however. Could you call me tomorrow or the next day?" The best way to handle this would be to:

A. Follow his suggestion.

B. Ignore his request and try a second close.

C. Probe further. You might ask: "The fact that you have to think this over suggests that I haven't convinced you. Is there something I've omitted or failed to satisfy you with?"

CUSTOMER C

In order to convince your customers that your product's benefits are important, you must show how your product's benefits will meet their needs.

Suppose your customer says: "I need some kind of gadget that will get me out of bed in the morning." Check the statement below which best relates your product feature, the G.E. Clock radio's snooze alarm, to this customer's need:

A. "Ms. Jones, this G.E. Radio has a snooze alarm which is very easy to operate. See, all you do is set this button and off it goes . . ."

B. "Ms. Jones, the G.E. Radio is the newest radio on the market. It carries a one-year guarantee and you can trade in your present radio and receive a substantial cut in the price."

C. "Ms. Jones, since you say you have trouble getting up in the morning, you want an alarm system that will make sure you wake up. Now, G.E.'s snooze alarm will wake you up no matter how often you shut the alarm off. You see, the alarm goes off every seven minutes until you switch off the "early bird knob."

CUSTOMER D

You are planning to call back on Mr. Pride and the president of his company to sell them several of your electric carts. The company's manufacturing plant covers some 200 acres, and you have sold many companies smaller than this one up to ten carts. Since Mr. Pride is allowing you to meet with his company's president, and maybe other executives, you know he is interested in your carts.

You are determined to make a spellbinding presentation of your product's benefits which will make use of visual aids and a demonstration of the cart itself. Mr. Pride raised several objections on your last presentation which may be brought up again by other executives. Your challenge is to develop a dramatic, convincing presentation. You plan to give a "live" demonstration of the cart to show how effective it is to move around the plant. Which of the following is the best technique for the demonstration?

    A.   Get Mr. Pride and the president involved by letting them drive the cart.
    B.   You drive letting them ride so they will listen more carefully to you.
    C.   Leave a demonstrator and check back the next week to see how many they will buy.

CUSTOMER E

You are also planning to use your ten-page visual "presenter" to guide Mr. Pride through your benefit story. This selling aid is in binder form and contains photographs of your cart in action, along with its various color options, guarantee, and testimonials. Should you:

    A.   Get Mr. Pride to participate by letting him hold it.
    B.   Handle it yourself, letting him watch and listen while you turn the pages and tell your story.

CUSTOMER F

Picture yourself as a Procter & Gamble salesperson who plans to call upon Ms. Hansen, a buyer for your largest independent grocery store. Your sales call objective is to convince Ms. Hansen that she should buy your "family" size of Tide detergent. Her store now carries the three smaller sizes. You have developed a marketing plan that you feel will help convince her that she is losing sales and profits by not stocking Tide's family size.

You enter the grocery store, check your present merchandise, and quickly develop a suggested order. As Ms. Hansen walks down the aisle toward you, she appears to be in her normal grumpy mood. After your greeting and handshake, your conversation goes like this:

> **Salesperson:** Your sales are really up? I've checked your stock in the warehouse and on your shelf. This is what it looks like you need. [You discuss sales of each of your products and their various sizes, suggesting a quantity she should purchase based upon her past sales and present inventory.]
>
> **Buyer:** OK, that looks good. Go ahead and ship it.
>
> **Salesperson:** Thank you. Say, Ms. Hansen, you've said before that the shortage of shelf space prevents you from stocking our family-size Tide—though you admit you may be losing some sales as a result. If we

	could determine how much volume you're missing, I think you'd be willing to make space for it, wouldn't you?
Buyer:	Yes, but I don't see how that can be done.
Salesperson:	Well, I'd like to suggest a test—a weekend display of all four sizes of Tide.
Buyer:	What do you mean?
Salesperson:	My thought was to run all sizes that are regular shelf price without any ad support. This would give us a "pure" test. Six cases of each size should let us compare sales of the various sizes and see what you're missing by regularly stocking only the smaller sizes. I think the additional sales and profits you'll get on the family size will convince you to start stocking it on a regular basis. What do you think?
Buyer:	Well, maybe.

At the end of your conversation, Ms. Hansen said, "Well, maybe." Which of the following should you do now?

A. Continue to explain your features, advantages, and benefits.
B. Ask a trial close question.
C. Ask for the order.
D. Back off and try again on the next sales call.
E. Wait for Ms. Hansen to say "OK, ship it."

Customer G

Before making a cold call on the Thompson Company, you did some research on the account. Barbara Thompson is both president and chief purchasing officer. In this dual capacity she is often so rushed that she is normally impatient with salespeople. She is known for her habit of quickly turning down the salesperson and shutting off the discussion by turning and walking away. In looking over Ms. Thompson's operation, you notice that the inefficient metal shelving she is using in her warehouse is starting to collapse. Warehouse employees have attempted to remedy the situation by building wooden shelves and reinforcing the weakened metal shelves with lumber. They have also begun stacking boxes on the floor, requiring much more space.

You recognize the importance of getting off to a fast start with Ms. Thompson. You must capture her attention and interest quickly, or she may not talk with you. Which of the following attention-getters would you choose?

A. "Ms. Thompson, I'd like to show you how Hercules shelving can save you both time and money."
B. "Ms. Thompson, can you spare a few moments of your time to talk about new shelving for your warehouse?"
C. "Ms. Thompson, how would you like to double your storage space?"

Customer H

This is your fourth call on Ace Building Supplies to get them to begin carrying and selling your home building supplies to local builders. Joe Newland, the buyer, has given you every indication that he likes your products.

During the call, Joe reaffirms his liking for your products and attempts to end the interview by standing up and saying, "We'll be ready to do business with you in three months—right after this slow season ends. Stop by then and we'll definitely place an order with you."

Under these circumstances, which one of the following would you do? Why?

A. Call back in three months to get the order as suggested.
B. Try to get a firm commitment or order now.
C. Telephone Joe in a month (rather than make a personal visit) and try to get the order.

CUSTOMER I

You work for the Lanier Pager Equipment Corporation selling pagers and other equipment. Imagine yourself as just entering the lobby and reception room of a small manufacturing company. You hand the receptionist your business card and ask to see the purchasing agent. "What is this in reference to?" the secretary asks, as two other salespeople approach. Which of the following alternatives would you use and why?

A. Give a quick explanation of your equipment, ask whether the secretary has heard of your company, or used your equipment, and again ask to see the purchasing agent.
B. "I would like to discuss our paging equipment."
C. "I sell paging equipment designed to save your company money and provide greater efficiency. Companies like yours really like our products. Could you help me get in to see your purchasing agent?"
D. Give a complete presentation and demonstration.

CUSTOMER J

Skaggs Omega, a large chain of supermarkets, has mailed you an inquiry on hardware items. They specifically wanted to know about your hammers, screwdrivers, and nails. Upon your arrival, you make your presentation to the purchasing agent, Linda Johnson. You start out by stating that you had visited several of their stores. You discuss your revolving retail display which contains an assortment of the three items Johnson had mentioned in her inquiry and relate the displays, advantages, and features to benefits for Skaggs.

During your presentation, Johnson has listened but has said very little and has not given you any buying signals. However, it does appear she is interested. She did not object to your price nor did she raise any other objections.

You are approaching the end of your presentation, and it is time to close. Actually you have said everything you can think of. What is the best way to ask Johnson for the order?

A. "How do you like our products, Ms. Johnson?"
B. "What assortment do you prefer, the A or B assortment?"
C. "Can we go ahead with the order?"

CUSTOMER K

As you drive up into the parking lot of one of your best distributors of your home building supplies, you recall how only two years ago they purchased the largest opening order you ever sold. Last year their sales doubled, and this year you hope to sell them over $100,000 worth.

As you wait, the receptionist informs you that since your last visit your buyer, John Smalley, was fired and another buyer was transferred in to take his place. John and you had become reasonably good friends over the past two years, and you hated to see him go.

As you enter the new buyer's office, she asks you to have a seat and then says: "I've got some bad news for you. I'm considering switching suppliers. Your prices are too high." Under these circumstances the best way to react to this objection would be:

A. "It's certainly a good idea to compare prices, because price is always an important consideration. When you add up all the benefits we offer, however, I think you'll find that our prices—over the long haul—are actually lower than the competition's."

B. "Would you mind telling me exactly why you're considering this move?"

C. "Gee, I'm really surprised at this move. After all, we were the ones who originally got you interested in handling home building supplies. Our service has been good, and most importantly, you've derived excellent profits from our line."

Customer L

This is a cold call on the warehouse manager for Coat's Western Wear, a retailer with four stores. You know most of the manager's work consists of deliveries from the warehouse to the four stores. Based on your past experience, you suspect that the volume of shipments to the warehouse fluctuates with certain seasons of the year being extremely busy.

As a salesperson for the Hercules Shelving, you want to sell the manager your heavy-duty gauge steel shelving for use in the warehouse. Since this is a relatively small sale, you decide to go in cold, relying only on your questioning ability to uncover potential problems and make the prospect aware of them.

You are now face-to-face with the warehouse manager. You have introduced yourself, and after some small talk, you feel it is time to begin your approach. Which of the following questions would serve your purpose best?

A. Have you had any recent storage problems?

B. How do you take care of your extra storage need during your busy seasons such as Christmas?

C. Can you tell me a little about your storage problems?

Customer M

You have been working for two months on an industrial account to obtain a firm commitment for a $185,000 computer system. Over the past three years, this particular firm has purchased $575,000 worth of computers from your company. If you can land the order today, you will become eligible for a quarterly commission bonus of $2,500. To meet your competitor's lower price, your manager decides to give you special authorization to offer your client a $9,000 package consisting of free software, specialized operation training, and extended-service contract terms. Similar incentives have been offered on special occasions in the past. All customers are eligible for the package. You feel this sweetened offer will bring you below your competitor's rock-bottom price. You know your customer is a price buyer.

As you drive to your customer's office, you get tied up in a huge traffic jam. You call your client from your car phone and ask her secretary if it would be okay to come about 30 minutes later than scheduled. He tells you not to worry.

As you are ushered into the buyer's office, you greet your customer with a smile, ready to announce the good news. She informs you that she signed a contract with your competitor just ten minutes ago. Upon your insistence, she shows you the bottom line on the signed contract. You realize that by purchasing your system, she could have saved as much as $12,000. What do you do?

A. Compare the two offers for the buyer, and ask her to cancel the signed contract.

B. Tell her about your proposal, but do not suggest she cancel the signed contract.

C. Say nothing. Keep your cool—act professionally. Otherwise, you will lose the customer forever. Accept the loss in a gracious and courteous manner.

CUSTOMER N

Afer a two-hour drive to see an important new prospect, you stop at a local coffee shop for a bite to eat. As you are looking over your presentation charts, the coffee spills on about half a dozen of them. You don't have substitute presentation charts with you. What should you do?

A. Phone the prospect and say that you'd like to make another appointment. Say that something came up.
B. Go ahead and keep the appointment. At the start of your presentation, tell the prospect about the coffee spill, and apologize for it.
C. Go ahead with your presentation. But don't make excuses. The coffee stains are barely noticeable if you're not on the lookout for them.

CUSTOMER O

Using your knowledge of negotiation, which of these methods would be the best way to handle a prospective new-car purchaser and why? A customer has told you she is only looking, prices are too high, and she cannot afford a new automobile at this time.

A. Agree with her; then proceed to the next available customer.
B. Show the customer a cheaper model of the same car.
C. Explain to the customer how payments can be tailored to fit almost anyone's budget.
D. Ask her why she is wasting her time looking at new cars.

CUSTOMER P

You have just learned that one of your customers, Tom's Discount Store, has received a shipment of faulty goods from your warehouse. The total cost of the merchandise is $2,500. Your company has a returned-goods policy that will only allow you to return $500 worth of your product at one time unless a reciprocal order is placed. What would you do?

A. Call Tom's and tell them you will be out to inspect the shipment in a couple of days.
B. Ask Tom's to patch up what they can and sell it at a reduced cost in an upcoming clearance sale.
C. Send the merchandise back to your warehouse and credit Tom's account for the price of the damaged goods.
D. Get over to Tom's as soon as possible that day, check the shipment to see if there are any undamaged goods that can be put on the shelf, get a replacement order from Tom's manager, and phone in the order immediately.
E. Call your regional sales manager and ask what to do.

EXPLORING SALES FORCE TECHNOLOGY

SALES WORLD WIDE WEB DIRECTORY

The Sales World Wide Web Directory contains some of the URLs (Universal Resource Locators) for the Sales World Wide Web exercises found in the next section. Also included are organizations with the largest sales forces in the United States. The **URL** is a standardized naming, or addressing, system for documents and media accessible over the Internet.

An Internet address, or URL, tells you a lot. Let's use http://www.microsoft.com as an example and break down a URL. The **http** means "Hypertext Transfer protocol" and refers to one way that data from Web pages is transmitted on the net. **WWW** means "World Wide Web" and consists of graphic pages of information that can be viewed by Internet browsers such as Netscape. The name of the Web site is **microsoft.com.** This site belongs to the software company Microsoft. The **com** means this is a commercial site. Other types of sites include **gov** (governmental), **edu** (educational), and **org** (organizational—often not-for-profit) sites. Additional information after the "com" points to specific Web pages in a particular site.

For each URL, you can locate the Home Page of these organizations. The **Home Page** is the name for the Web site's main page where users can find links to other pages in the site. **Hyperlinks** are an icon, graphic, or word in a file that, when clicked with the mouse, automatically opens another file for viewing. World Wide Web pages often include hyperlinks that display related Web pages when selected by the user.

These URLs help you learn how to apply the WWW to the sales job by guiding you to sites for answering the Sales World Wide Web exercises in the next section. They also help you find out information about American organizations having large sales forces. Thus, you can find information on each company, its products and customers. There may be a hyperlink to career opportunities with the companies. URLs are an excellent place to start researching an organization or industry. This can also help prepare you for a job interview with the company.

| AUTHOR'S SITE | http://futrell-www.tamu.edu |
| Publisher's Site | http://www.harcourtcollege.com |

SEARCH ENGINES	
Alta Vista	http://www.altavista.digital.com
Essential Links	http://www.el.com
Excite	http://www.excite.com

Infoseek	http://www.infoseek.com
Lycos	http://www.lycos.com
Magellan	http://www.mckinley.com
Open Text	http://www.opentext.com
Webcrawler	http://www.webcrawler.com
Yahoo!	http://www.yahoo.com

CAREERS

Sales Staffers International, Inc.	http://www.salesstaffers.com
Career Site	http://www.careersite.com
Career Mosaic	http://www.careermosaic.com
Hot Jobs	http://www.hotjobs.com
Monster Board	http://www.monster.com
Online Career Center	http://www.occ.com
Career Path	http://www.careerpath.com

DATABASES, INDEXES, AND LISTS

Society of Competitive Intelligence Professionals	http://www.scip.org
Fuld & Company	http://www.fuld.com
Hoover's Online	http://www.hoovers.com
Individual Inc.	http://www.individual.com
Companies Online	http://www.companiesonline.com
Manufacturer's	http://www.mfginfo.com
Franchising Opportunities	http://www.franchise1.com
Relocation	http://www.homefair.com

ETHICS

Business Ethics Magazine: Online	http://condor.depaul.edu/ethics/bizethics.html
Marketing Ethics	http://www.lan.unt.edu/mktg/faculty/pelton/mesig/other.html
Association for Practical and Professional Ethics	http://php.indiana.edu/~appe/home.html
American Marketing Association	http://www.ama.org/about/ama/ethcode.esp
Center for Applied Ethics	http://www.ethics.ubc.ca/papers/business.html
National Association of Sales Professionals	http://www.nasp.com
The Better Business Bureau	http://www.bbb.org

FIND, LOOKUP, AND MAPS

Internet Airfares	http://www.air-fare.com
American Airfares	http://americanair.com

Expedia	http://www.expedia.com
Microsoft Expedia	http://www.expedia.msn.com
Continental Airlines	http://www.flycontinental.com
Southwest Airlines	http://iflyswa.com
Map Quest	http://www.mapquest.com
Trip Quest	http://tripquest.com
Sales Leads USA	http://lookupusa.com
Weather Channel	http://www.weather.com
People Finders	http://www.411.com
SwitchBoard Directory	http://www.switchboard.com
Big Yellow	http://www.bigyellow.com
Big Book	http://www.bigbook.com

Organization Finders

Industry.net	http://www.industry.net

Government

SEC's EDGAR file	http://www.sec.gov/cgi-bin/srch-edgar
Census	http://www.census.com

Individual Sites

Videoconferencing	http://cuseemeworld.com/guide

Personal Finance

Bloomberg	http://www.bloomberg.com
Fidelity Investments	http://www.fidelity.com

News Sites

Deja News	http://www.dejanews.com
Newsworks	http://www.indosite.com/coba.html
NewsBot	http://www.newsbot.com
NewsTracker	http://nt.excite.com

Personality Sites

Tests	http://www.2h.com
Keirsey Temperament Sorter	http://keirsey.com/cgi-bin/keirsey/newkts.cgi
Emotional Intelligence	http://www.utne.com/cgi-bin/eg

Sales Magazines and Publications

Sales and Marketing Management	http://www.salesandmarketing.com
Selling Power	http://www.sellingpower.com

SALES ACADEMICS

American Marketing Association	http://www.ama.org
American Marketing Association Sales SIG	http://mkt.cba.cmich.edu/salessig
Journal of Personal Selling & Sales Management	http://mkt.cba.cmich.edu/jpssm
National Conference in Sales Management	http://mkt.cba.cmich.edu/ncsm

Go to www.harcourtcollege.com for more sales-related URLs.

ACT! AND GOLDMINE HELP CREATE CUSTOMERS FOR LIFE!

ACT! and GoldMine are two top-rated, best-selling contact managers (CM). This software allows you to manage your business relationships. The CMs store information on all of your customers, such as your previous contacts, sales, business conversations, calls to make, meetings to attend, and action items to complete. In addition to data entry, you can write letters, e-mail, fax, use calendars, and organize contact groups.

Both CMs have demonstration products you can use to become familiar with the software before buying it. You can go onto their Web sites and download the demo onto your computer or fill out a request to have the demo mailed to you.

- ACT! is a product of Symantec. Their Web site is: http://www.symantec.com.
- GoldMine is a product of GoldMine Software Corporation. Their Web site is: http://www.goldmine.com.

WHY REVIEW AND LEARN CONTACT MANAGER SOFTWARE?

When viewing Symantec or GoldMine's main Web page, look for the word *demo*. Most companies have their salespeople use some type of customer software. When you interview for a sales job, it is a selling point for you if you mention to the recruiter that you are familiar with ACT! or GoldMine. If you are in sales now, you probably need to be using contact manager software. This is a great way of determining if ACT! or GoldMine can help you be more productive.

SALES WORLD WIDE WEB EXERCISES

FIND OUT ABOUT A CAREER IN SALES!

Looking for a job? Would you consider a sales job? Want to find out more about a sales career? The answers to these questions are found on the World Wide Web. In fact there is so much career information on the Web that one wonders where to send you.

The easiest place to start is to enter the word "career" into your favorite Web search engine. The term **search engine** is computer lingo for a Universal Resource Locator (URL) site you can use to perform a keyword search by developer or subject name. As with everything on the Internet, these search tools change daily and new features are constantly added. Here are several URLs for the major search engines:

www.el.com

www.yahoo.com

www.altavista.com   www.lycos.com

www.excite.com   www.search.com

www.infoseek.com

If you still need to find out more about a career in sales, you can try URLs created specifically to help people looking for a job. These include:

www.salesstaffers.com   www.monster.com

www.careersite.com   www.occ.com

www.careermosaic.com   www.careerpath.com

www.hotjobs.com

Take a look at your school's home page. Many schools refer you to career opportunities. You should also go to the Web site of a specific company. Many companies have hyperlinks from their home page to their job openings. Try finding career opportunities for several of the organizations listed in the Sales World Wide Web directory.

CAN THE WORLD WIDE WEB HELP BUILD RELATIONSHIPS?

The ultimate outcome of relationship selling is the building of a partnership between the seller and the buyer. More and more companies are using the Web to stay in touch with customers. Pick several organizations listed in the Sales World Wide Web directory to see what information they provide to people.

Look for documents such as annual reports that describe their sales, profits, markets, and customers. Check to see if they are collecting information from you, such as having you complete a questionnaire. Then write a report to your boss discussing your findings. Include your suggestions on how an organization can use the Web to build long-term relationships with their customers and attract new customers.

WHAT IS ETHICAL IN THE WORLD OF SALES?

Ethical behavior refers to treating others fairly. This is an easy definition to understand. Yet what seems ethical to one person may not seem ethical to another person. Salespeople must deal with various job dilemmas and issues that fall squarely in the domain of ethics. Beginning with your favorite WWW search engines listed in the Sales World Wide Web Directory, research the topic of ethics. Also see if these URLs have information:

Business Ethics magazine: Online
www.condor.depaul.edu/ethics/bizethics.html

Marketing Ethics: Ethics, Associations, Organizations, and Institutions of Interest www.lan.unt.edu/mktg/faculty/pelton/mesig/other.html

Association for Practical and Professional Ethics
www.ezinfo.ucs.indiana.edu/~appe/home.html

Corporate Watch www.corpwatch.org

American Marketing Association Code of Ethics for Marketing on the Internet www.ama.org/ethcode.html

Center for Applied Ethics www.ethics.ubc.ca/papers/business.html

National Association of Sales Professionals www.nasp.com

Sales & Marketing Management magazine www.salesandmarketing.com

The Better Business Bureau www.bbb.org

Your computer search should turn up names of organizations mentioned in articles. Go directly to several of the companies to see if they have:

1. A code of ethics.
2. An ethics committee.
3. An ethical ombudsman.
4. Procedures for whistle blowing.

WHAT IS YOUR PERSONALITY?

Salespeople need to be good communicators. Communication skills help people do a better job of relating product benefits to customer needs. This increases the salesperson's productivity. An essential part of having good communication skills is to better understand your own personality.

To better understand yourself, first complete the exercise "What's Your Style—Sensor, Intuitor, Thinker, Feeler?" This exercise uses an adaptation of the Myers–Briggs Temperament Indicator. The Keirsey Temperament Sorter URL, listed below, asks you to complete a more comprehensive Myers–Briggs-type indicator.

To further your understanding of "the real you," go to these sites and complete several of the personality exercises you feel are important for salespeople:

www.2h.com (IQ, personality, and entrepreneurial tests)

www.keirsey.com/cgi-bin/keirsey/newkts.cgi
(the Keirsey Temperament Sorter)

www.el.com (type in *personality test*)

www.yaoo.com (type in *emotional intelligence*)

Write a short report summarizing what the personality tests uncovered about you. Do you feel the tests accurately assessed your personality and the real you?

BUSINESS INTELLIGENCE: CAN THE WEB HELP?

On its way to transforming the world of sales, the World Wide Web is triggering a revolution: It is having a radical effect on the way marketers get the business intelligence they need. There are whole new categories of information available now. A few clicks of the mouse can provide an avalanche of free—but priceless—information about competitors. Useful Web sites include:

Companies Online www.companiesonline.com

Deja News www.dejanews.com

Farcast www.farcast.com

Fuld & Company www.fuld.com

Hoover's Online www.hoovers.com

Individual Inc. www.individual.com

NewsBot www.newsbot.com

NewsTracker nt.excite.com

Newsworks www.newsworks.com

SEC's EDGAR file www.sec.gov/cgi-bin/srch-edgar

Society of Competitive Intelligence Professionals www.scip.org

Research one or more companies you have an interest in working for or that you know or have worked for in the past.

PLANNING YOUR
SALES CALL ON
DELL COMPUTER:
LOCATION, TRAVEL,
MAPS, AND
RESEARCH

You've recently acquired a significant lead on a possible sale to Dell Computer Corporation. Being your company's top sales rep of novelty items such as sweatshirts, T-shirts, and sports gear, you have been chosen to pursue the account.

It was just pure luck that at a computer convention yesterday in Las Vegas, the national sales manager for Dell stopped by your booth and mentioned she wanted to have a company create a motivational program that centers on sportswear and gear. She asks you to be in her office next Wednesday at 3:00 P.M.

At this time though, your secretary is on vacation and you are responsible for making your own travel arrangements. Your secretary has told you that there are Web sites where you can make travel arrangements from your computer and not have to make any phone calls. To make your airline reservations, hotel arrangements, and car rental all in one stop, visit the following sites:

www.previewtravel.com   www.americanair.com

www.expedia.com   www.flycontinental.com

www.expedia.msn.com   www.iflyswa.com

www.air-fare.com

But hey! Where is the headquarters for Dell Computer? You have heard the name Dell Computer and you know they make computers, but that is about all. First things first. Check out www.dell.com. Click on company information, then investor information, and finally contact information to find their geographical location. You need to go to your favorite search engine(s) and research Dell. Also search the sites:

www.mfginfo.com   www.bigbook.com

www.companiesonline.com   www.el.com

www.bigyellow.com

You saw an article in *Sales & Marketing Magazine*, www.salesandmarketing.com, October 1997, titled "The Dell Way." You had better read it.

Since you may be driving your own rental car, you will need specific directions so as not to get lost. Go to:

www.mapquest.com

www.lookupusa.com

www.el.com (click on phone/address and review travel)

www.tripquest.com

Also check the weather forecast at: www.weather.com. Finally, check the correct time at www.el.com by clicking on USNO. Then write a memo to your boss outlining your travel schedule. Print out appropriate URL screens and place in the appendix of your memo.

FINDING PEOPLE,
ORGANIZATIONS,
MAPS, AREAS,
PHONE, AND
ADDRESS

Opposition or resistance to information or to the salesperson's request is called a *sales objection*. Objections often arise because the salesperson has not researched the individual or organization. Some types of selling require a tremendous amount of research to create a sales presentation. The better your research, the fewer objections, and thus the more likely you are to make the sale. The following are URLs that can help you in your research:

PEOPLE FINDERS

www.four11.com

www.bigyellow.com

ORGANIZATION FINDERS

www.bigyellow.com

www.bigbook.com

www.companiesonline.com

www.mfginfo.com

www.bnet.att.com

www.industry.net

MAPS

www.lookupusa.com

www.mapquest.com

E-MAIL

www.el.com (see phone/address)

Of course, also use your favorite search engines to find out more about people, organizations, markets, and geographical areas.

WHAT IS THE BEST METHOD TO DETERMINE FEEDBACK?

Providing service after the sale to customers is important, no matter what type of company, product, or service you represent. Customer service refers to the activities and programs provided by the seller to make the relationship satisfying for the customer.

Some organizations specialize in analyzing a company's customer's satisfaction, such as J. D. Powers in the automobile industry. Their URL is www.jdpower.com.

For this assignment, determine how one or more companies determine the satisfaction of their customers with their products and services. Find a company that has people answer a satisfaction questionnaire over the Internet.

One way to begin is by using your favorite search engine. Type "customer satisfaction" into the search field and, if possible, add "selling" to the search.

Write a brief report to your boss on your findings. State what you feel would be the best way for a company of your choice to determine their customers' satisfaction.

RESEARCH PAYS OFF IN THE SALES GAME!

This exercise is to help you gain first-hand experience in the process of researching a company. Pick an organization you might like to work for, or your present employer. Using your favorite search engine, the organization's Web site, major competitors' Web sites, articles, and governmental information, write a report to your boss that includes:

1. Company Analysis:
   a. List the company mission statement.
   b. Analyze the company's sales and profits as compared to its industry.
2. Customer Analysis:
   a. Who are their customers?
   b. How many, what type (segments), and what is the location of their customers?
3. Competitor Analysis:
   a. Who are their competitors?
   b. How many competitors are there, and where are they located?
4. Market Trend:
   a. What is happening with their customers, sales, profits, competitors?
   b. What technology affects the industry?

Write a three- to five-page report to your boss detailing your findings. In your conclusions state if this is a company you would want to work for. Why?

Time is Money, So Make Every Minute Count!

It is said that "time is money." Wasted time trying to find a prospect's address and location can cost a salesperson valuable time. For this assignment you are to imagine you work for an organization. Find three potential customers within a 50-mile radius of the city where you presently live. Choose another two potential customers located in two states bordering the state you live in. Using the following geographic information mapping tools found on the Web, create a travel schedule that would allow you to contact these five potential customers in a two-day period. The URLs are:

MapQuest www.mapquest.com

Tiger Map Server www.census.gov/main/www/access.html

Also look at the www.el.com search engine for maps and information on finding organizations and individuals. For example, under "references" click on "Tools!" See if the Phone/Address site has anything useful for you in this assignment. Finally, since time is money in sales, click on "USNO" under "Clock" to get the correct Naval Observatory time. You do not want to be late to your appointments!

Write a memo to your boss showing the addresses of each potential customer, plus the route and day you will be at that customer's business. Print out the appropriate maps showing locations of customers.

Comparing Places to Live for Your Salespeople

As a newly appointed sales manager, you will often hire people for different geographical locations within the United States. To help you better understand moving and living in other areas of the country, use www.homefair.com to help you compare the city you live in with two other cities no closer than 500 miles from you.

Click on all appropriate functions, such as the Salary Calculator and the Moving Calculator, to make a comparison between the city you presently live in and the two other cities. Do not forget to also click on our favorite search engines for information on the three cities.

How Does Your Money Grow in a Retirement Fund?

As a sales manager, one of your greatest challenges is to effectively compensate your salespeople. Your employer pays salespeople a base salary and commission and has a great benefits package. One of the problems new salespeople always have is whether or not to participate in the company's 401(k) retirement package. Salespeople can contribute up to 6 percent of their salary each month, and the company will match whatever percent the employee invests. The individual salesperson controls the retirement money by picking the organization and the mutual fund(s) in which to invest the money.

Your assignment is to create an investment example for a new salesperson showing what can happen to the invested funds over a 20-year period. Go to www.fidelity.com. Click on an item that refers to a "calculator." This might be called a "retirement planning calculator" or "investment growth calculator." Answer the questionnaire by making up the data you feel is appropriate for the time.

Compensation Plan for College

Assume you have four children whose ages are one year apart. Their ages are 1, 2, 3, and 4, all born in the month of June. All will attend a public university in your state.

Part one of your assignment is to determine the estimated cost of college for all children using: http://personal461.fidelity.com/toolbos/college/collegequiz.html (or you may use a similar URL).

Use the default values provided by Fidelity (or whatever information service you use) for pre-tax rate of return and college inflation rate. Make your own assumptions according to your personal experience regarding the average annual cost of college. For the number of years of college planned, assume that it will take each of your children five years to finish. Be sure to make the average costs increase by 5 percent, for each child, for each year in school.

Begin the assignment by estimating your present cost of college for one year. Be sure to consider such items as the following:

1. Tuition and books.
2. Having a vehicle—including insurance, parking, traffic tickets, wreck(s).
3. Clothes for class, work, interviews, social events.
4. School-related supplies—computer, calculator, tutor(s), etc.
5. Travel allowances—home, breaks, personal and school trips.
6. Health care and insurance.
7. Unexpected expenses.
8. Organizational costs—fraternity, sorority, etc.
9. Food.
10. Rent and related expenses such as utilities, furniture, TV, cable, etc.
11. Entertainment.
12. Miscellaneous.

Part two of your assignment is to create a compensation plan for your children. For this part of the assignment, assume the first child will enroll in the fall of 2001. They all want to know now what they can expect from you for support. Assume you have the money to implement your "child compensation plan for college."

Based upon your and others' experiences in school, you want to have a program that is fair, rewards performance, and ensures you are not taken advantage of by one or more of your children. Your goal is for each child to have a reasonable amount of compensation if they do acceptable work. They will receive more or less pay based upon their performance in school. Performance is demonstrated by their grade point average (G.P.A.) and the number of credit hours completed each term.

All four children are to be on the same pay plan. Your pay policy must be set now in order to be fair for all children and cannot be adjusted at any time until all four children have graduated with their undergraduate degrees. Assume your financial situation will not change during the time period estimated for each child to graduate from the university. The plan must contain the following elements:

1. Monthly base pay.
2. Commission.
3. Bonus.

For the monthly base pay, you will need to come up with a set amount of money that you think will be enough for your child to pay for necessities such as food, rent, books, tuition, and so on. After you come up with this amount of money, you will then need to decide the minimum G.P.A. and number of hours your child must reach in order for him or her to receive the monthly base pay amount. Once you have decided on this amount, you will need to fill in the chart for G.P.A. and hours completed. To do this, you start by putting 100 percent in the column or row that has the number of hours and G.P.A. that your child must complete to receive all of his or her base pay. To fill in the rest of the chart you will need to decide how much money your child will receive extra if he or she completes more hours or has a higher G.P.A. than the one set or how much money will be taken away if he or she does less. For example, you might set the base for your child at 12 to 15 hours completed with a 2.75 G.P.A. If your child completes over 15 hours and has a 4.00, then you might increase the child's pay by $500.00 a month. However, if your child only completes three to six hours with a 2.00 then you might decrease the child's pay by $500.00 a month. Be sure to fill in the whole chart. The amount of money that you add or take away from the child is his or her commission.

You will also need to write a paper explaining all aspects of your compensation plan. Include in the paper the maximum and minimum amount of money you are willing to pay your child once the commission is added in. Also, include in your paper what you would consider to be a bonus. A bonus might include such things as a new car, stereo, trip to Hawaii, and so forth. Be sure to tell what conditions must be met for your child to receive a bonus, how much you are willing to spend on a bonus, and how often you will give a bonus. Also, in the paper tell why you think a compensation plan for your children would (or would not) be a good idea.

NOTE: Consider whether you should factor in the child's responsibility—if any—for earning money for school through employment during and outside the school term, such as during Christmas and summer breaks. Be sure to consider what you will do if the child drops out of school in the middle of the term or completes a low number of hours during a term.

COMPREHENSIVE CASES

ZENITH COMPUTER TERMINALS, INC. (A)
Development of a Total Business Plan

Juan Mendez, president of Zenith Computer Terminals (ZCT), has recently promoted Rob Zwettler as his assistant. Rob has been a salesperson and then a sales manager for the past four years. Rob's main job is to work at different levels of the organization to help implement the firm's objective-setting process. Rob has to work with all the department managers to assist them in determining their objectives.

In brief, Juan's major corporate objective for next year is to increase profits to $1 million (before taxes). It is now late December, and below is a simplified profit-and-loss statement for the current year (including a projection for the balance of the year).

Sales		$10,000,000
LESS EXPENSES		
Sales	$1,500,000	
Production	6,000,000	
Marketing	1,300,000	
Administration	500,000	
Service	250,000	9,550,000
Net Profit		$ 450,000

In discussions with the president and five department managers, Rob has learned a great deal that should help him in establishing budget (expense) objectives for each department.

First, Juan feels that sales must be raised to the $12 million level if the profit objective is to be met. All of

the department managers concur and think this a realistic and challenging objective for next year. They also have committed to freeze their salaries and those of their staffers for the year in order to meet the profit objective.

In conversations with the national sales manager, Rob has learned the following facts, which should aid him in determining an objective for the sales department budget:

- Currently 20 sales reps are in the sales force.
- A sales rep costs an average of $75,000 per year for salary, travel expenses, and the cost of supervision.
- Last year, each rep produced, on average, $500,000 in sales. A new rep, although costing the same as an experienced one, will produce about $300,000 the first year. Obviously, the sales force must be expanded to meet targeted sales of $12 million.
- In a normal year (next year is projected as normal), the sales volume from sales reps will grow at a rate of 10 percent assuming the sales manager can work with each rep at least four days per year.

Although the major objective of the sales department related to attaining sales volume within its budget, supporting objectives must be set by the sales manager, with your help. In addition to the background information previously supplied, here are some other facts Rob uncovered.

- Hiring a sales rep normally takes about a month. It is desirable to recruit and hire all the new sales reps at one time.

- Training of new sales reps takes four weeks of classroom time followed by a month of on-the-job coaching in the field. The sales manager must handle the classroom segment but can delegate three of the field training weeks to senior sales reps, as long as he personally handles at least one week of coaching during the new sales reps' first month in the field.

- The sales manager must not neglect his existing sales staff on a long-term basis. Ideally, the sales manager should average four days a year with each rep supporting his or her efforts and upgrading performance.

THE PRODUCTION DEPARTMENT

Rob also met with the production department and learned some significant facts about the operations and projections for the future. Last year, production turned out 10,000 units at a total production cost of $6 million. To achieve the new sales goal of $12 million, production will have to be increased to 12,000 units (computer terminals). At present, ZCT has four production lines, which can produce 2,500 units each per year. New production equipment to support an additional production line will cost $400,000 (amortized cost for next year) plus an additional $125,000 for labor and $325,000 for materials used in production. The fifth production unit will be able to produce 2,500 units, also.

The late date for setting objectives for the coming year (end of December) creates a problem in ordering the necessary equipment for the production line. The equipment order cannot be placed until January 1, and it will take three months for delivery and installation. However, the production target for the year must be achieved, regardless. The production manager feels that this can be accomplished by running the existing four production lines on a second eight-hour night shift (in addition to the day shift) for as long as necessary to compensate for the delay of the new production line. From a budget standpoint, the cost of paying overtime can be absorbed by the savings of not having to purchase the equipment for three months.

Two weeks will be needed to recruit and select ten additional workers for the new production line, and another two weeks will be needed to train them on existing equipment. The necessary production equipment and materials will be automatically ordered by the purchasing administration.

As far as objective setting is involved, neither Rob nor the production manager needs to be concerned about the planned 1,000 newly designed terminals projected to be sold during the fourth quarter. Even though the terminals may be booked during the fourth quarter, they will not be produced and delivered until the first quarter of the following year.

THE MARKETING DEPARTMENT

Rob's meeting with the marketing manager to discuss the department's needs was equally productive. The marketing department is responsible for advertising, promotion, and new-product development. The marketing manager has a staff of 15 people with a related overhead (projected for next year) of $600,000. In addition, the manager normally budgets about 5 percent of projected sales for direct mail and advertising to support the sales force activities. Further plans call for the introduction of the new terminal by the fourth quarter of next year. (The president stressed that this is critical and, as noted, hopes to sell 1,000 units before year-end.)

The following new-product budget is required during the year:

- $250,000 for product development.
- $25,000 for sales aids.
- $25,000 for training and introduction.

The training will be budgeted through the marketing department, but the sales department will plan and implement a one-week workshop in late September to introduce the new terminal to the sales reps.

One of the most important functions of the marketing department is providing direct-mail support for the sales force. Last year the direct-mail efforts produced 6,000 leads (inquiries for the sales staff) from 12 monthly mailings, each consisting of 50,000 pieces of direct mail. This represents a 1 percent return, which probably cannot be improved on. However, the size of the mailings must be increased to accommodate both the enlarged sales objective (20 percent) and the expanded sales force.

A second important item on the marketing manager's agenda is the development of the new terminal. This is normally done on a contract basis with an outside consulting firm, and the new product has been tentatively named the Alpha Terminal. Basically, the consultant will modify one of the existing products, updating both the design and styling to meet or exceed competition. Two months will be needed to select a vendor for this, and about six months' lead time will be required to develop a production model. A sales brochure to accompany this introduction cannot be started until the new product is about one-third finished, and this brochure will require three to four months to write and print.

THE ADMINISTRATION DEPARTMENT

The following is what Rob learned from the administration manager regarding the department's needs. Based on an efficiency study, three clerical jobs can be safely eliminated, and Rob has convinced the administration manager that the payroll should be cut accordingly. Last year's budget breakdown looked like this:

7 managers	$240,000
12 clerks	200,000
General overhead	60,000
	$500,000

The administration department literally services the other departments at ZCT, handling finances and paperwork and providing internal systems backup. The administration manager, although agreeing to the suggested cutback in clerical staff, felt that it would be desirable to stagger the release so a heavy strain is not incurred at one time; this also would permit other people to be trained to pick up the slack. Rob agreed to this but emphasized the need for all changes to take place as soon as possible. About two weeks of training (on the job) will be needed for the staff to absorb the tasks and assignments handled by the three clerks scheduled to be terminated.

Further, one of the seven managers in the administration department is currently considered marginal. The manager in question, Joe Wallace, has been aboard about a year and has failed to meet expectations. His weaknesses may become a big liability as these clerical cutbacks take place, and a decision on him should be made as soon as possible. If necessary, a plan should be made to replace him immediately. This evaluation should take about a month.

To support the new sales growth, Juan Mendez feels that the entire administrative function must be computerized during the next two years. Consequently, he has asked the administration manager to do an internal study, with a task force from the staff, and to present a report by December 1 of the coming year. Based on Rob's discussions, Rob estimates that the task force will need a month for each of the four other departments, a month for interviewing computer vendors, and two months to write a comprehensive report.

THE SERVICE DEPARTMENT

Rob's final conference was with the service manager to discuss the objectives for the coming year. Basically, the service manager feels a strong need to increase service support to the sales force. Customer complaints are on the rise because the service staff growth has not kept pace with sales. Each of five service reps is budgeted at $40,000 for salary and travel expenses. Supervision and other expenses run about $50,000. In the past, a four-to-one ratio of sales to service reps was adequate, but now that the quantity of terminals has grown, the service manager wants the ratio to be three to one and is determined to implement this strategy next year. Rob tends to agree with him. In addition to these expenses, the service manager estimates he will need $30,000 for new servicing tools and equipment.

One of the big problems the service department manager faces is the heavy load of service calls that must be handled within 24 hours, especially with projected increased sales. This could be alleviated by additional service reps.

The service manager feels that, in addition to staffing up, the total number of service calls can be cut significantly by having the staff sell maintenance contracts to customers. This will provide some additional revenue, but a planned maintenance program will head off service calls before they occur and, equally important, will enable the staff to plan their schedules more efficiently. Right now, the service manager's staff is handling about 7,400 calls per year, and this will rise in proportion to the projected sales increase. However, if the sales manager can achieve this new maintenance program and get it implemented, he feels strongly that the overall number of calls required can be cut by 25 percent.

The sales manager anticipates needing about six months to design the program and kick it off. The manager is also planning to hire the new service people immediately; about a month will be needed to hire and train them.

QUESTIONS
1. Develop a new budget based on how the ideal profit-and-loss statement should look if it reflects the president's bottom-line objective for ZCT. Justify your expenses for each of the five budgeted expense areas.
2. What would be the net profit if sales
   a. Remained the same, at $10 million, and budgeted expenses increased to the projected levels?
   b. Increased to $14 million and budgeted expenses increased to the projected levels?
3. Determine the four most important objectives for each department. Specify in detail what should be done and the time frame for reaching the objective.
4. Write up your recommendations to Juan Mendez, the president, in a memorandum format.

CASE 2

ZENITH COMPUTER TERMINALS, INC. (B)
Strategic Business Plans Fail—Sales Decline

As the year was coming to a close, Rob Zwettler saw that sales were not going to increase to the planned $12 million. In fact, sales were going to decrease by $500,000.

He could not understand it. Yes, it was true that their big national competitors had increased their promotional efforts, hired more salespeople, and implemented several price reductions. Several competitors introduced some new terminals. Yet, this was nothing new for Zenith. Competition always had been tough. "What should we do?" Rob thought. "Because sales have decreased, we can't afford to increase our advertising, hire more salespeople, or reduce prices."

Rob asked each department to review its operations. All departments were told to stay with their present budgets. At a meeting of all department heads and Zenith's president, Juan Mendez, Rob said. "Folks, we may be in a crisis situation. If sales don't increase shortly, we'll begin laying people off. We could be out of business this time next year!"

Rob went around the room asking each department head what his or her group could do to cut costs and increase sales. Rob was surprised when everyone basically said, "We have problems because marketing and the sales force are not doing their jobs." Henry Baker, the sales manager, blamed the problem on competition. "We don't have enough salespeople," Henry said. "We have 24 salespeople covering the entire United States."

"Well, there is no way we can hire more salespeople," Rob said. "Those big plans of yours for 100 salespeople in two years are out until sales improve. Henry, I want you to develop a detailed plan on how to increase sales with what you have. Your first step is to carefully analyze past sales and sales potentials. Henry, all of Zenith's employees are counting on you and your people. Juan and I know you can do it!"

The next day, Henry's assistant handed him a report that contained Exhibit 1. While reviewing the sales figures, Henry remembered the good old days when sales were increasing year after year. Henry was one of the first people to go to work with Zenith. The company was formed by Juan eight years ago after he graduated from MIT with a master's in electrical engineering. Headquartered in Denver, the company first expanded into the central states, then to the West and East coasts.

Zenith's four regional managers have been with the company almost as long as Henry. They are all friends, and Henry always has given everyone the same budget. Each region has the same number of salespeople.

QUESTIONS

1. Forecast next year's total sales volume using both the naïve and the three-year, moving-average forecast methods.
2. Henry has been told to increase sales to $12 million, regardless of past sales. Based on the information presented, what actions could Henry take to increase sales?

EXHIBIT 1

PERCENTAGE OF SALES
FOR EACH REGION

	WEST	WEST CENTRAL	EAST CENTRAL	EAST	TOTAL SALES
Previous year	0%	100%	0%	0%	$ 250,000
Previous year	0	75	25	0	750,000
Previous year	15	50	25	10	2,100,000
Previous year	30	20	20	30	6,500,000
Previous year	30	20	25	25	8,000,000
Previous year	40	15	15	30	9,000,000
Last year	30	30	20	20	10,000,000
Present	30	20	20	30	9,500,000
Forecast (%)	—	—	—	—	_____
Forecast ($)	—	—	—	—	$_____

ZENITH COMPUTER TERMINALS, INC. (C)
Redesigning Sales Territories

Henry Butler, Zenith's vice president of sales, has consistently said "no" to redesigning sales territories. "Redesigning in other companies has resulted in firing people, demoting managers, and all sorts of unprofessional things," Henry said in a meeting with Rob Zwettler. "These regional managers are my friends, Rob. I'm not going to see them hurt."

"Henry," Rob said, "as the assistant to the president, I know Juan is concerned about the west central region's performance. We're having too much turnover. When sales dropped, salespeople's commission also decreased. Between you and me, Henry, in the past three months salespeople have left faster than we've been able to train new ones. This is really happening all over the country."

"What can we do?" Henry asked.

"Your hunting buddy, Bill Cron [the east central regional manager in Dallas], wants to handle some of our present customers in those states by telephone. If a customer is big enough or we get a hot prospect, a salesperson or the regional manager can fly in and out of the state. Bill wants to transfer or not replace salespeople who quit in the Dakotas, Nebraska, Kansas, Iowa, Wisconsin, and Arkansas [see Exhibit 1]. He will use those people in areas that have higher sales potentials [see Exhibit 2]. Bill said he's so tired of people quitting, hiring new ones, and training them that he really would like to stop replacing people. He mentioned three people he'd like to fire," Rob said.

"I hate to hear that," Henry said. "We've always been a family. A great company to work for. But if we don't do something soon, there's not going to be a company."

Rob suggested, "What if we do this: Let's redesign all regions so each regional manager could have approximately equal sales, budgets, and people. We can use Bill's suggestion."

"That sounds like we'll have to fire some salespeople," Henry said.

"We may," Rob replied, "but if Bill fires his 3, and we don't replace the 2 that quit in the west central region

EXHIBIT 1   ZENITH COMPUTER TERMINALS'S SALES REGIONS

EXHIBIT 2

SUMMARY OF SALES
PERCENTAGES BY STATE[a]

STATE	SALES %	STATE	SALES %
Alabama	0.5	Nebraska	0.5
Arizona	3.0	Nevada	0.5
Arkansas	0.5	New Hampshire	0.0
California	19.0	New Jersey	2.5
Colorado	8.5	New Mexico	2.0
Connecticut	0.0	New York	10.0
Delaware	0.0	North Carolina	1.0
Florida	3.5	North Dakota	0.5
Georgia	1.0	Ohio	2.0
Idaho	0.5	Oklahoma	1.0
Illinois	2.5	Oregon	5.0
Indiana	2.0	Pennsylvania	3.0
Iowa	0.5	Rhode Island	1.0
Kansas	0.5	South Carolina	0.0
Kentucky	0.0	South Dakota	0.5
Louisiana	2.0	Tennessee	0.0
Maine	0.5	Texas	8.0
Maryland	0.0	Utah	5.0
Massachusetts	0.0	Vermont	0.0
Michigan	4.0	Virginia	0.0
Minnesota	1.0	Washington	5.0
Mississippi	0.5	West Virginia	0.0
Missouri	1.0	Wisconsin	0.5
Montana	0.5	Wyoming	0.5

[a]Percentages rounded to nearest half percent.

last week, we're down to 19. I can call all managers and tell them there is a freeze on hiring. We would have to reduce our selling costs some way."

"Yes, but sales are going to be hurt!" yelled Henry, who was now getting emotional. "OK, OK, do what's needed, Rob. Redesign our sales regions. Use the sales forecast of $9,500,000 to determine sales areas. Maybe once we get past this crisis we can begin to expand again. But remember, Rob, we want all regional man-agers to be treated fairly and equally, no matter what your plan."

QUESTIONS
1. Redesign Zenith's sales territories following Henry's and Bill's guidelines.
2. What are the advantages and disadvantages of the new design?

CASE 4

ZENITH COMPUTER TERMINALS, INC. (D)
Setting Quotas Facing Decreasing Sales

Alice Tanner was so excited about her new job. She was recently transferred from Dallas to New Jersey to take over as the eastern regional sales manager. Alice had broken all performance records by increasing sales more than 435 percent during her three years with Zenith. Juan Mendez, Zenith's president, refers to Alice as "a born salesperson. She's someone people believe in and listen to. Alice has a great natural communications ability. She's dedicated, often working 60 to 70 hours a week—week after week."

"That is why Alice was promoted," Jeff Sager, western regional sales manager, says. "She's going to have to have more than sales ability to turn around the performance of her region. We all are!"

Alice agreed with Jeff. In her mail today were last year's sales results for the eastern sales region (see Exhibits 1, 2, and 3). As she looked over the information, Alice wondered what to do first.

Last year the region was $750,000 short of its sales goal of $3 million. This year the region's goal was set by Juan at $4 million. That is an increase of $1,150,000 over last year's sales of $2,850,000. Sales are down, and Alice has to turn things around. Her first step is to set new objectives and quotas for her region.

QUESTIONS

1. Determine the types of quotas Alice should set.
2. Re-create Exhibits 1, 2, and 3 assuming that Alice's six salespeople's efforts for the year resulted in the information in the following table. Assume the costs of goods sold remained at 80 percent of sales.
3. Each salesperson's sales percentage of the region's $2,850,000 sales is shown in Exhibit 2. Set a sales quota for each person by multiplying the $4 million sales quota by that percentage. Calabrese's new quota would be $600,000 (15% × $4,000,000). Calabrese's territory did 15% of the $2,850,000 in sales shown in Exhibit 2 ($427,500/$2,850,000). Create the sales quotas needed to reach your sales goals of $4 million. Recalculate Exhibits 1, 2, and 3 using your forecasted sales.
4. This is one way to calculate the new quotas. Is anything wrong with this method? What other way(s) could be used? Why?
5. Can Alice be expected to increase sales to $4 million without increasing other data shown in Exhibits 1, 2, and 3? Why or why not?
6. What can Alice do to help her salespeople reach their sales quotas?

	ACTUAL SALES	EXPENSES	NUMBER OF CALLS	NUMBER OF ORDERS
Calabrese	$550,000	$66,000	1,500	1,050
Gonzalez	620,000	65,000	1,475	1,300
Wong	675,000	60,000	1,450	1,300
Rao	625,000	65,000	1,500	1,200
Stark	550,000	90,000	1,200	650
Williams	450,000	90,000	1,100	575

EXHIBIT 1   EASTERN REGION'S SALES AND PROFITS FOR THE YEAR

PERSON	CALABRESE	GONZALEZ	WONG	RAO	STARK	WILLIAMS
Sales	$427,500	$556,000	$527,500	$456,000	$470,000	$413,000
Cost of Goods Sold[a]	342,000	444,800	422,000	364,800	376,000	330,400
Gross Margin	85,500	111,200	105,500	91,200	94,000	82,600
Expenses	65,000	65,000	53,000	70,000	89,000	91,000
Net Profit	$ 20,500	$ 46,200	$ 52,500	$ 21,200	$ 5,000	$ −8,400
Sales/Net Profit Ratio (%)	4.80[b]	8.31	9.95	4.65	1.06	−2.03

[a]Equals 80 percent of sales.
[b]($20,500/$427,500) × 100 = 4.80%

EXHIBIT 2   EASTERN REGION'S YEARLY SALES VOLUME

PERSON	SALES % OF REGION[a]	SALES QUOTA	ACTUAL SALES	DOLLAR DIFFERENCE	PERFORMANCE INDEX
Calabrese	15.0	$ 540,000	$ 427,500	$112,500	79.16
Gonzalez	19.5	576,000	556,000	20,000	96.53
Wong	18.5	540,000	527,500	12,500	97.69
Rao	16.0	576,000	456,000	120,000	79.16
Stark	16.5	720,000	470,000	250,000	65.27
Williams	14.5	648,000	413,000	235,000	63.73
Total	100.0	$3,600,000	$2,850,000	$750,000	80.26

[a]Based on actual sales.

EXHIBIT 3   CUSTOMER ACTIVITIES FOR THE EASTERN REGION

	NUMBER OF CALLS	NUMBER OF ORDERS	ORDER/CALL RATIO	ACTUAL SALES	AVERAGE ORDER SIZE
Calabrese	1,350	945	70%[a]	$ 427,500	$452.38[b]
Gonzalez	1,500	1,275	85	556,000	436.08
Wong	1,400	1,260	90	527,500	418.65
Rao	1,450	1,015	70	456,000	449.26
Stark	1,100	660	60	470,000	712.12
Williams	1,000	500	50	413,000	826.00
	7,800	5,655	71%	$2,850,000	$549.08

[a](945/1,350) × 100 = 70%.
[b]($427,500/945) = $452.38.

WALLIS OFFICE PRODUCTS
Defining New Sales Roles

As he looked across the desert horizon from his Phoenix sales office, John Stevens, vice president of sales for the Southwest region of Wallis Office Products (WOP) felt good about his latest results.[5] "This has been a good year," he thought. "O'Brien will do cartwheels when she sees these year 2000 sales numbers." As John closed the third quarter report, Margaret O'Brien, WOP's national sales manager, passed John's door. "Maggie!" John shouted. "Come get a look at these numbers. With the bonus I'm delivering you this year, you'll be able to buy back the old St. Louis Cardinals and bring them home."

"That football team hasn't won a thing since they came to Phoenix anyway," said O'Brien as she walked into John's office. "And with the news I just got, you may want to save your sales for January."

O'Brien had just spoken with WOP's president and CEO, Phillip Plimpton, about the company's 2001 sales goal. "He gave me some of that corporate babble about the stockholders and return on investment," said O'Brien, "and then he laid a $1.5 billion sales goal on me! That's up 25 percent from this year . . . and we'll do well to make this year's number!"

John joked about squeezing water from a stone, but O'Brien was in no mood to joke and was rushing out to get her flight back to St. Louis. On the way to the airport, she called John to voice her appreciation for the year he was having. "You do another $350 million, plus 50 percent next year, and I'll give you your own football team," said O'Brien, knowing she would need John to have a great 2001 for her to reach $1.5 billion.

After O'Brien's call, John began thinking what his region's sales goal would be if WOP had to do $1.5 billion in 2001 . . . and he didn't like the numbers he came up with. His region had been having a good year, in fact, the best year since he had been promoted to vice president of sales for the Southwest four and a half years ago. He knew that in a few weeks O'Brien was going to give him and the other four regional vice presidents their 2001 sales goals. "Now I know why they never ask us for our input," thought John. "The regional VPs would never volunteer $1.5 billion."

COMPANY BACKGROUND

A sister and brother from Missouri, Phyllis and George Clemens founded Wallis Office Products in 1948. The company began to thrive in the mid-1950s and built a reputation in the Midwest as a quality producer of a variety of business forms. Phyllis handled the creation and production of the forms, and George did the selling. In the early 1960s, George attended a trade show on the future of the forms business. There he met a young entrepreneur Roberto Martinez who sold George on an idea.

Roberto believed that American business was "fed up with you and all your forms." He told George that growth in the forms business was going to slow down once technology took off and that new ideas would be needed if the Clemenses were going to continue to grow their business. Roberto proposed a new service for Wallis Office Products: document storage and record keeping. "Essentially," said Roberto, "the business will remotely store documents electronically that aren't needed regularly. When someone needs a stored document, you'll retrieve it and send it to the customer."

Roberto believed that this service would eliminate thousands of file cabinets in government offices and large companies, and it would free employees to spend their time on more valuable work than moving old files and archiving unneeded documents. In return, companies would pay for each document stored and a monthly storage charge.

In 1962, Phyllis and George Clemens were persuaded by Roberto Martinez and made an agreement that changed Wallis Office Products forever. Roberto joined the company, and growth in Wallis Office Products' document storage business in the 1960s shot up faster than an Apollo rocket.

Over the next 30 years, the business grew to become a billion-dollar corporation. Their core business became document storage and record keeping. In the mid-1980s, the U.S. Supreme Court ruled that film document reproductions were acceptable as court evidence, and this contributed to the growth of the electronic document storage business. Wallis Office Products divested itself of the forms business because of declining margins and slow market growth and concentrated on document storage. The company had national distribution, with an account base of over 900 customers. In 2000, revenues were expected to be $1.2 billion. WOP had over 8,000 employees in 32 offices (primarily sales and local operations). Headquarters remained in St. Louis, where most functions were centralized, including finance, human resources, and marketing. Regional sales and operations offices were in New York, Atlanta, Phoenix, San Francisco, and St. Louis.

PRODUCTS AND SERVICES

In 2000, WOP's core product was a relatively manual, paper- and microfilm-based document storage service. Typical contracts (which were renewed annually) called for WOP to provide the following:

- Document pickup.
- Document indexing.
- Document storage (which could include microfilm, paper copies, or both).
- Document retrieval on demand (that is, companies called an 800 number to request specific paper copies of documents).

Customers pay WOP based on two types of fees:

- Processing fees per new document (that is, the number of picked up, indexed, and retrieved pages)
- Storage based on the volume of documents stored and document format (paper, microfilm, or both).

Annual revenues per customer range from $100,000 to $10 million with most accounts generating between $500,000 and $1,500,000 in revenue. With some customers, up to 85 percent of WOP's revenues are storage charges.

WOP offers multiple "value-added services" on top of the plain vanilla offering (for example, reporting services relative to retrieval, consultative document management services, and the like). The add-on services have been very lucrative for WOP—they produce 10 percent of revenues and 13 percent of profits—and management is looking into ways to expand this market. In 2000, Margaret O'Brien estimated that 88 percent of WOP's sales revenue would come from a version of the traditional business (excluding value-added services). Although 2000 was shaping up to be a good year, O'Brien knew that the market wasn't growing as quickly as it had in the late 1980s, and it was only a matter of time before WOP's traditional product could no longer meet the company's growth goals.

In 1997, WOP introduced an automated document retrieval system called SARS (Safe Automated Retrieval System) 1000. The system is computer based and offers customers online, real-time document retrieval. In addition to providing document pickup and storage services, SARS 1000 gives customers immediate access to all their stored documents. The system requires a significant investment in computer hardware and software for the user (up to $100,000). In 2000, WOP introduced a more powerful version of SARS called Document Flash, which has online storage capability in addition to retrieving documents.

Sales have been disappointingly slow for SARS 1000. O'Brien had forecasted $50 million in sales for this product in 2000 (by converting 15 existing buyers and selling 10 new customers), but actual sales were only projected to be $20 million. Strong sales of the traditional product, and another good year in the Southwest, looked like they would get O'Brien to her goal. But O'Brien knew her future success was tied to SARS 1000.

BUSINESS OBJECTIVES

In 1983, Wallis Office Products made its initial public offering (IPO), and officially changed the name of the company to WOP. After 35 years as a family-held business, WOP quickly became a hot stock on Wall Street. On the one-year anniversary of WOP's IPO, the Supreme Court ruling sent the company's stock soaring to $40 per share, 250 percent of its initial price.

Since the company went public, WOP had promised stockholders a 20 percent annual return on their investment. It has met this goal every year except 1992. That was the year Phyllis Clemens retired as CEO and chairman of WOP. Pushed by Wall Street analysts, WOP hired an outside executive, Phillip L. Plimpton, to replace Clemens. Plimpton wasted no time putting his mark on the company, reorganizing the management team and cutting costs throughout the organization. The field sales organization was reduced from eight regions to five (at that time John Stevens gained responsibility for southern California as part of the Southwest), and Margaret O'Brien was put under increased pressure to grow the business's top line.

Plimpton's objective was to grow profits 8–10 percent in 1999, 2000, and 2001. He knew he met his goal in 1999 based on the cost cutting completed from 1997 to 1998 and the company's record of retaining 83 percent of its customers. In 2000 and 2001, however, Plimpton was counting on revenue growth of 25 percent each year, for $1.5 billion and $2 billion goals, respectively. Plimpton believes the market for his traditional document storage services is mature and fully penetrated. Since he feels growth in the traditional business is flat, he believes WOP needs new-product sales (for example, SARS 1000 and the Document Flash product being introduced in 2000) and value-added services to meet his revenue goals. In addition, Plimpton is not convinced that the sales and marketing organizations have effectively used the available distribution channels, which will be necessary in order to reach these goals.

SOUTHWEST REGION

John Stevens is one of the rising stars of WOP. First as an account executive and now as a vice president of sales in the Southwest, he consistently exceeds the goals the company gives him. Plimpton is impressed by John's ingenuity and willingness to try new ideas.

John's organization consists of 14 account executives and 16 service representatives in 6 offices. His account executives average ten years of industry experience and are very knowledgeable on traditional document storage services and the marketplace. John and his organization have been particularly effective in retaining customers, which he believes is the key to his success. John is so committed to this strategy that he established on-site service for his largest customers. His is also the only region that has more service representatives than account executives. John is concerned, however, that his sales organization has sold only five SARS 1000 systems.

John's market is large in comparison to other regions, by both customer numbers and sales revenue. With the addition of the Los Angeles, Orange County, and San Diego territories, John estimated sales of $350 million (versus a goal of $310 million) in 2000 on a base of 253 customers. Many of his customers are government agencies, law firms, and financial services companies. Unlike the other regions, John proactively targets specific industry accounts. Of John's 253 customers, many represent a single site or department. In 2000, his region lost only 21 customers, most of whom generated less than $1 million in revenues.

As John thought about the sales target O'Brien would give him for 2001, he wondered how she would determine the final number. He figured he would be penalized for having a great 2000 and be asked to do more than his fair share in 2001. "I've got to figure out a better way to deploy my people," John thought, "not only to increase their sales productivity but to improve the sales of the new products and services."

QUESTIONS

1. Formalize the sales strategy and quantify the sales opportunities that exist.
2. Map out the sales process associated with the different products/services and the roles of current sales and service personnel in the process.
3. Use the five w's (who, what, where, when, and why) to determine if the sales process requires different sales roles. For example:
   a. Who is the customer?
   b. What is your offering?
   c. Where can customers purchase the products?
   d. When do customers buy and how frequently do they make purchases?
   e. Why should a customer purchase your product? What is the value proposition?
4. Determine the gaps that exist between the current sales process and the desired sales process.
5. Formulate new sales roles for each sales position.

CASE 6

BRIGGS INDUSTRIAL SUPPLY COMPANY (A)
Determining Who and How Many to Hire

Briggs Industrial Supply Company is a general-line industrial distributor. The company sells a wide range of industrial goods to manufacturing industries. As the year is drawing to a close, Jay Anderson, general manager of Briggs, is reviewing the performance of his sales force over the past year.

THE COMPANY BACKGROUND

Briggs Industrial Supply Company was founded in 1940 in a town outside of New Orleans. The local people thought of the business as a hardware store. Yet the company had a distribution emphasis from the start. The company served primarily the petroleum refining and manufacturing industry, supplying it with industrial tools and supplies to meet its specific needs.

A gradual decline of the oil industry began in 1990. The company began to see an influx of nonoil-related industry into the states it served, such as manufacturers of electronic components, clothes, glass, and plastic pipe.

During the past five years Briggs witnessed a rapid growth of widely diversified manufacturing industries. The company still has some large customers in the oil-related industry, but recent growth and potential are credited to supplying the other manufacturing industries moving into the area.

THE DISTRIBUTION INDUSTRY

In many instances the forerunner of the industrial distributor was the general store, and in others it was the hardware store. As local industry grew, presenting these businesses with demands for specialized tools and supplies, one of the stores frequently came forward with the required service. This agent evolved into the industrial distributor, identifiable as a distinct marketing function. The functions that the distributor performs have not changed a great deal over the years. A full-service distributor such as Briggs performs these eight functions:

1. Buys
2. Sells
3. Stores
4. Delivers
5. Finances
6. Takes risks
7. Provides product information
8. Services

The distributor takes possession of and stores the products, thus taking risks of obsolescence, theft, fire, and so forth. The distributor sells the products to customers on credit and then bills the customers either weekly, semimonthly, or monthly. The distributor services the products after the sale and provides technical and product application information. The distributor bases its existence on the value-added concept. By performing these eight functions for customers, it adds value to the products. The distributor's complete stock runs the gamut of industrial products. In short, the distributor is a central stockroom for industry. Briggs stocks 11 major product classifications listed in the table. Briggs's competitors also carry about the same assortment of products.

MAJOR PRODUCT CLASSIFICATIONS

- *Abrasives:* grinding wheels, abrasive paper, etc.
- *Cutting tools, saws, and files:* drills, mills, inserts, etc.
- *Hand tools:* tape rules, screwdrivers, socket sets, hammers, etc.
- *Power tools and accessories:* drill presses, lathes, milling machines, band saws, etc.
- *Pumps, valves, compressors:* for air and fluid power systems
- *Fasteners:* bolts, rivets, washers, screws, nuts, etc.
- *Power transmission:* V-belts, pulleys, sheaves, gears, chains, etc.
- *Industrial rubber goods:* hoses, sheet rubber, etc.
- *Material handling equipment:* hand trucks, carts, wheelbarrows, forklifts, etc.
- *Precision measuring tools:* Micrometers, calipers, scales, etc.
- *Fluid power:* Valves, cylinders, fittings, etc.

EXHIBIT 1   BRIGGS INDUSTRIAL SUPPLY COMPANY ORGANIZATIONAL CHART

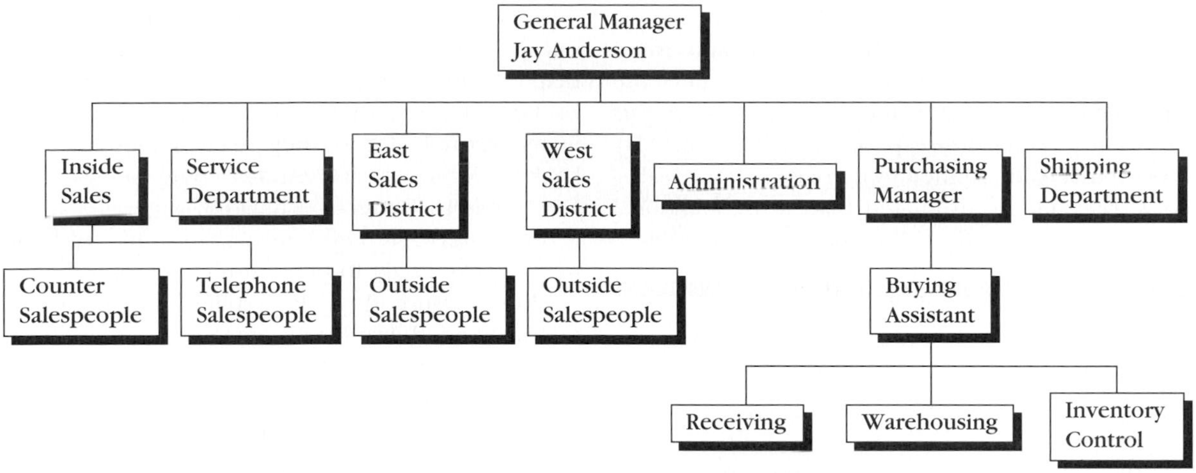

COMPANY MANAGEMENT STRUCTURE

Exhibit 1 shows Briggs's organizational structure chart. The structure is set up primarily along functional lines. Each functional area—sales, purchasing and inventory control, administration (bookkeeping), shipping and delivery, and the service department—reports directly to the general manager, Jay Anderson. After completing his bachelor of business administration degree in marketing in 1993, Jay took a position with Briggs. During his one-year training period, he worked in various operations of the company—shipping, receiving, stocking, and inventory. He also spent time in telephone sales and made some outside sales calls. The company then bought a smaller general-line distributorship. Jay spent 18 months there setting up systems (inventory, receiving, purchasing, warehousing, and so on), and he also did some selling. He then came back to Briggs and worked as sales manager for about eight months. In 1997 he was made partner and general manager of the operation.

THE CURRENT SALES FORCE AND ORGANIZATION

The company currently has 3 inside counter salespeople, 3 inside telephone salespeople, and 15 outside salespeople. The counter and telephone salespeople are managed by Ross Burns. Ross is a telephone salesperson and has been with the company for 10 years. He has held various positions in the company and once spent a year in outside sales. In addition to telephone sales, he has other duties and responsibilities. The business demand at the sales counter varies from time to time during the day. When the counter salespeople are over-loaded, the telephone salespeople step in to help. At times all telephone salespeople are busy and a counter salesperson takes the call. Ross's job is to coordinate these efforts. He also trains counter salespeople who look promising for telephone sales positions.

The company's large customers are assigned to both an outside salesperson and an inside telephone salesperson. When a particular company telephones, the call is handled by the telephone salesperson assigned to that account. The telephone salespeople and outside salespeople, therefore, work as a team serving customers they jointly handle. Each outside salesperson is responsible for a number of local customers and also has an assigned out-of-town geographic territory. The outside salespeople spend about two days a week out of town, but they are rarely away from home at night.

The salesperson's selling approach varies depending on the size of the customer being called on. When calling on large customers, the salesperson usually will talk to purchasing people who buy primarily on the basis of service. In a recent survey, many large customers stated that price is not a major consideration.

When calling on small and medium-sized customers, the salespeople attempt to get in the "back door" and talk to shop personnel, supervisors, engineers, and so on. In such companies, these people tend to influence the buying decision. Loyalty and friendship with the salesperson are usually more important buying motives than they are with the large customers.

OUTSIDE SALESPEOPLE

The outside sales force is divided into two districts. The western district manager has ten salespeople covering

Texas, New Mexico, and Oklahoma. The eastern district has five salespeople. Salespeople are paid a base salary of $40,000 a year plus 5 percent commission on all sales. They also receive $500 a month to cover their expenses, such as for an automobile, motels, and entertainment. Unless measures could be taken to reduce the costs of goods sold, estimated at 65 percent of sales, this is all Jay felt he could pay salespeople. Over the years Jay has noticed that sales seemed to increase as more salespeople were hired. He estimated that hiring additional people would generate the following volume of sales:

ADDITIONAL SALESPERSON	ESTIMATED ADDITIONAL SALES VOLUME
16	$380,000
17	300,000
18	225,000
19	165,000
20	100,000
21	95,000
22	83,000

Jay was considering hiring six more salespeople. He determined that sales of $95,000 would cover the salesperson's base salary, expenses, and commission, leaving a profit of $44,250. If he hired a seventh salesperson, sales would increase $83,000. However, he was unaware if this would cover the salesperson's fixed and variable costs. Once the present geographic areas' sales increased as predicted, Jay felt more salespeople might be hired to move into the new territories of Alabama, Tennessee, Missouri, and Kansas.

As Jay looked back on the year, he judged the sales force performance as having been pretty good. He added to himself, "The sales force has performed well, but I have a couple of problems."

The sales force is directly responsible to Jay. He has made sales calls with the salespeople, but, in his estimation, too rarely. "I haven't kept as close a contact with the salespeople and their accounts as I should," he thought. "Maybe this is the reason for the 15 percent turnover each year."

Jay monitors each account monthly. He looks at the gross margin and sales of each account and of each salesperson.

THE PRESENT SITUATION

During this year, the company experienced a dollar growth in sales of 34 percent more than last year's revenues of $6,540,000. Jay was guessing that next year the company would see 25 percent growth. The company has experienced some problems with such a growth rate.

The sales force has complained of not enough inside backup help. When meeting with Ross to discuss his plans, Jay said, "I feel this is a legitimate gripe because sales have grown so much that it is hard to keep up. The salespeople are not being given the amount of time and help they need, both outside in the field and from inside backup. Because of the increased sales and the projected growth, I feel they need a more coordinated backup. Maybe new methods could be used. At least they could be better coordinated."

Ross interrupted his conversation and said, "Does this mean you're going to pirate my salespeople?"

"I'm not sure, Ross," Jay replied. "You know we also will need another sales manager."

"Well, I don't want the job, Jay! My wife would leave me if I had to travel as much as they do," Ross said. "Besides, I don't know how to hire outside salespeople. What do you look for in a person?"

"Don't worry about that, Ross. I'm going to have a personnel consultant help us create a staffing system. I've made contact with a university professor who works with companies in the sales area. You and I are going to meet with him tomorrow."

"What does he do?" Ross asked.

"Well, for one thing he gives them a sales aptitude test, the Strong–Campbell interest test, and the Wonderlic test. The first two relate directly to sales, and the last test measures intelligence. You know, like that high school SAT test you made such a low grade on. The higher the scores, the better the candidate's chance of success. He also gives a personality test. I think that's a sophisticated program."

"How do you know that's true?" Ross asked. "We've never done anything on hiring other than you, and sometimes the DMs, interviewing the people who just walk in. Then you just seem to use your gut reaction to the person. Most of the time you hire someone already employed. Like one of my inside salespeople. We would have never hired our minorities if they hadn't worked here in the summer while in school or worked their way up into inside sales."

"That's true, Ross. I'm still not sure women and the other minorities can make it here. I'm certainly not planning on hiring any more."

"You didn't answer my question, Jay. How do you know the consultant can do what he says?"

"Well," said Jay, "I had him give the tests to all of our salespeople. Then the DMs supplied the other information you see on this report [see Exhibit 2]. It appears that our best performers are young males who have a 'senser' type of personality. I'm going to study this some more. However, the consultant is suggesting we hire only young (under 35) white married males who have scored equal to our present salespeople in the upper one-fourth of the entire sales force."

"What about Kane, Dacy, Kurtin, and Spahn? They seem to be doing all right."

"Yes, but they are in the minority," Jay said. "And some of their success could be due to luck. You know it's easy to meet quota when a company is growing as fast as ours. We only have a few people who have low performance levels."

"Once you hire these people, where are you going to put them?" Ross asked. "You know it's getting competitive out there."

"That's exactly why we have to hire more people. The more we hire, the more we sell," Jay answered. "I've asked the DMs for their recommendations, and I'm examining the situation."

QUESTION
What should Jay Anderson do?

EXHIBIT 2   SALES FORCE CHARACTERISTICS

SALESPERSON	OVERALL PERFORMANCE	AGE	MARITAL STATUS	SEX	YEARS OF SELLING EXPERIENCE	PERSONALITY TYPE	SALES APTITUDE	STRONG-CAMPBELL INTEREST TEST	WONDERLIC TEST
Cahill	120	29	M	M	5	Senser	55	33	32
Everest	115	26	M	M	3	Senser	60	55	36
Billings	110	34	S	M	10	Senser	32	38	38
Kane	110	55	M	M[a]	15	Intuitor	35	43	38
Dacy	109	25	S	F[a]	3	Intuitor	65	35	41
Kurtin	105	41	S	M[b]	19	Senser	56	54	34
Manus	104	46	M	M	20	Senser	33	42	28
May	102	62	S	M	32	Thinker	55	42	28
Russell	100	49	S	M	20	Intuitor	68	48	39
Spahn	99	24	S	M[a]	2	Thinker	63	43	38
Walter	96	24	M	F	1	Intuitor	63	41	29
Smith	91	27	S	M	5	Thinker	43	49	36
Head	85	38	M	M	9	Senser	61	43	23
Holmes	78	36	M	M	11	Feeler	71	46	28
Reasor	77	52	S	M	10	Thinker	55	39	28

[a]African-American.
[b]Mexican-American.

CASE 7

BRIGGS INDUSTRIAL SUPPLY COMPANY (B)
Creating Recruitment and Selection Procedures

THE NEXT DAY

Jay and Ross were waiting in the company's conference room when Jim Hise walked into the room. "Ross, have you met Dr. Hise?" "Nope!" said Ross. "Dr. Hise is the personnel consultant I have helping us with improving our hiring procedures. He is here to tell us what we should do in interviewing people for these sales jobs. You have always said we hire based upon our gut reaction. Let's hear what the good doctor has to say."

"Let me begin," said Dr. Hise, "by going over a few interesting points research has shown on selecting and interviewing people. We know that if you have 100 applicants, and you randomly select 10 people, 4 of these people will be successful. So with no selection process we can have a 40 percent batting average.

"By considering an applicant's education we can increase the possibility of selecting successful people to 47 percent. If we consider their training and experience, we further improve our batting average to 49 percent. Fifty percent if we consider interviewing, 58 percent using good reference checks, and 78 percent if we use personnel tests. We have begun using all of these selection tools except creating the proper interviewing procedures.

"Research has shown that highly structured interviews greatly improve the ability to select successful people. Structured interviews are excellent predictors of supervisory ratings of job performance after the person has been employed for at least 18 months. The best-structured interview method is the panel interview. It's referred to as a panel interview because two or more people conduct the main interview with each applicant. Retail chains have been using the panel interview for years. Sales human resource managers have only recently started using this procedure.

"You have determined that the four key activities of your salespeople are customer service, negotiating with others, obtaining new customers, and selling skills. The interview questions should be designed to measure each applicant's ability in these four skill areas. Here is how the procedure works. The panel picks a team leader who asks each of the questions. After answering a question, each panel member scores the applicant's response by marking a score from one to nine at the bottom of the page. After all questions have been asked, and the applicant leaves the room, the panel members discuss each question's response and come up with a consensus score for each question. This individual question score is recorded on the 'applicant evaluation summary' sheet. The four questions' consensus scores are totaled. You calculate an average score by dividing the total consensus score by four—the number of interview questions. You end up with an overall score, such as four or eight. This indicates if the applicant's performance was unsatisfactory, satisfactory, or excellent.

"I recommend you do the panel interview before you send the applicant to me for testing. This will save you my $400 a person fee. There is no need to test if the applicant has a low score on the interview.

"Once we have used the panel interview form for 18 months or so, I will correlate the interview score with each person's manager's evaluation to see if the interview is helping to pick successful salespeople. How does this sound?"

"Sounds great," said Jay. "But I'm not sure our sales managers will do it. They want to make their own minds up about hiring someone rather than have a score on a form make the decision for them. How do we get them to use all of these new procedures?"

"What has worked for me," said Dr. Hise, "is to have the sales managers help create the forms for the interview questions. What people help build, they will support. So, at next week's sales managers' meeting, have them create the forms for negotiating with others and obtaining new customers. I have created the forms for customer service and selling skills as a guide, plus the applicant evaluation summary sheet. Be sure and have the managers create questions that have each applicant discuss the situation, the action taken, and results of the action. You'll see that I did not do that with the selling skills question. That will be all right for this one question. Plus, managers like to ask this question in the interview. The question is easy to score.

"Now, the last element of your sales staffing program is to create a recruiting program," said Hise. "Where are you going to find the people to interview and hire?"

"Let me see if I have this correct," said Jay. "You want us to determine how many people to hire, what personal characteristics to look for in an applicant based upon your current tests, create an interview procedure around the panel interview, and come up with ways to find applicants. Is that right?"

"Yes, those are some of the main items for your staffing program," said Hise. "However, you should review everything you know about staffing and see what else can be done to hire people who will be successful with Briggs."

CUSTOMER SERVICE

- Addresses the willingness of the applicant to provide a high level of service and ensures that customers are satisfied with products and service. Relevant skills include the ability to be courteous, tactful, and attentive to customer needs.

SITUATION QUESTION

At times, our people have to deal with a customer who is upset or angry. Think of when someone was angry with you. What was the situation?

ACTION QUESTION

What did you do?

RESULTS QUESTION

What were the results?

NOTES

EVALUATION BASED ON THIS FACTOR ONLY

Unsatisfactory			Satisfactory			Excellent		
1	2	3	4	5	6	7	8	9
Applicant demonstrated little or no ability to provide customer service.			Applicant demonstrated a satisfactory level of skills in being able to handle customers.			Response showed excellent skills in effectively handling customers.		

SELLING SKILLS

■ Addresses the individual's ability to sell. Includes the abilities to "think on one's feet"; interact effectively; and communicate in an organized, positive, and effective manner using negotiation and persuasion skills.

SITUATION QUESTION

You're applying for a sales job. Yet I have never seen you sell anything. I want you to sell me this _____. (pencil, pen, chair, coffee cup . . .) Hand it to the applicant.

NOTES

EVALUATION BASED ON THIS FACTOR ONLY

Unsatisfactory			Satisfactory			Excellent		
1	2	3	4	5	6	7	8	9
Applicant showed unsatisfactory ability to sell. Does not meet our high standards.			Response shows satisfactory ability to sell. Meets our high standards.			Excellent ability. Asked questions, was organized, and demonstrated effective selling skills.		

APPLICANT EVALUATION SUMMARY

Applicant's Name: _____
Applicant's SS#: _____
Date Interviewed: _____

GUIDELINES
The panel should now discuss the applicant's qualifications for the job. Review your ratings on each selection criterion. As a group, come to a consensus on the qualifications of this person for success at our company. Place an ("X") representing the group's decision for each criteria in the appropriate box below.

Excellent — 9, 8, 7

Satisfactory — 6, 5, 4

Unsatisfactory — 3, 2, 1

Customer service	Negotiating with others	Obtaining new customers	Selling skills

RATING AND RECOMMENDATION

Based upon the above ratings, what is the panel's evaluation of this applicant's qualifications for a job with our company? (check one)

_____ Unsatisfactory   _____ Satisfactory   _____ Excellent

RECOMMENDED NEXT STEP IN INTERVIEW PROCESS

_____ Continue;   _____ Test;   _____ Prospect File;   _____ Stop
A   A   B   C

Interviewer's Signature _____ Date _____

Interviewer's Signature _____ Date _____

Interviewer's Signature _____ Date _____

CASE 8

UNITED COSMETICS, INC.
Creating a Staffing Program

It was Al Kantak's first day on the job, and he was anxious to get started. Al knew that what he needed to do would be one of the biggest challenges of his life. Al's job title was Field Sales Employment Manager for United Cosmetics, Inc. (UCI). UCI is a national manufacturer and marketer of consumer goods sold primarily to retail grocery stores.

As Al began unloading boxes in his new office, the telephone rang. "Al, this is Sparky [the company's executive vice president of sales]. Come on up to my office, and let's discuss some ideas to help you get started, and let's talk about the employment information received this morning from our regional sales managers."

As soon as Al entered the office, Sparky started in. "Al, as you know, I asked our four regional managers to send in a report on employment activities and costs for their areas. You'll find this interesting.

"We have sales territories sitting vacant for a great deal of time while the district managers go out and recruit, hire, and train new people. This year, I calculated that there will be 2,700 days of vacant territories. Someone said this represents as much as $10 million in lost sales opportunities. I just cannot believe that, but I do feel we are losing sales due to having vacant territories.

"This year we will have 68 new hires, with 55 found through employment agencies. This is costing us $5,000 for each person. That's too much money to spend on these people. Many of them quit after a short period of time.

"I feel the worst thing about all of this is the drain on the DMs' time and the way people are trained to take over their new territories. Each time someone leaves, the DM has to recruit, hire, and train an individual. With the number of new hires we have each year, many of the DMs are spending too much time training the new people. Managers are not spending enough time working with others in their district. Some salespeople are complaining that their managers only work with them a few times a year. The new person is often left to 'sink or swim' after being trained, and many people are quitting because of this.

"We don't have a centralized training program. We could have ten managers individually training ten people at the same time in ten locations. This is inefficient and costly and results in some salespeople not being properly prepared to operate their sales territory.

"Al, I'm not even sure our DMs know how to properly screen and interview people. They get almost no training in this area. Maybe this is the reason for so much turnover. I'm not sure. I do know that sales are rapidly increasing, and we need to begin expanding the size of our sales force.

"This is what I want you to do. [Sparky began writing this list on a blackboard.] As quickly as humanly possible:

- Begin to decrease the cost per hire.
- Establish a uniform recruitment program.
- Increase the quality of new hires.
- See that our managers spend less time recruiting.
- Decrease the number of vacant territory days per year.
- Eliminate our dependence on employment agencies.

"Al, don't waste any time getting started; we need a new employment program yesterday. We may be losing millions of dollars in sales each year due to vacant territories. The cost of recruitment, training, and our managers' time also may run into the millions. I'm afraid to calculate that figure.

"If I can help you in any way, if you need more money, let me know. Your program will directly impact our bottom line. Keep me up to date on your progress. We have a meeting of the regional sales managers in three weeks. I want you to present your ideas on what we should do."

"Sparky," Al said. "I can't do this overnight. It is too big a project. What I have in mind is to develop a five-year plan. At the end of five years we will have accomplished everything you have asked for and more. However, we will see major results in just a few years. To hire the number of people needed, we'll have to recruit primarily on college campuses throughout the United States. To plan and implement a national sales employment program is a big undertaking."

"Okay, Okay, Okay," said Sparky. "I understand. But at this meeting I want you to outline what we will do. We'll get input from the regional managers and see what they think. The field sales managers will have to believe in this program or it will be a hard row to hoe."

When Al got back to his office, he asked his assistant to hold all of his telephone calls. He might as well start outlining his new sales employment program.

QUESTION

Assume you are Al Kantak. What would be your recommended college recruitment program?

CASE 9

FARM MACHINERY FOR AMERICA
The Selection of a Salesperson

It was Monday morning, November 27, 2000, and Mr. Randall (Randy) Garvin was eagerly waiting to begin a new week at work, fully rested from his Thanksgiving holiday. As he stepped from the elevator and into the sales department of Farm Machinery for America (FMA), Garvin's high spirits were dampened by an uneasiness in the air. His instincts told him something as he entered his office, where a letter was awaiting his review; one more salesperson had left FMA for a sales position in another industry.

Garvin, regional sales manager for the southern region of FMA, has had resignations from many salespeople this year. A change in FMA's sales compensation plan and the foreign competition that was cutting into its sales were thought to have had some influence on the departures, but Garvin had long thought that the salespeople were quitting because the company's recruiting program was hiring the wrong people to sell farm equipment. Whatever the reason, a new salesperson for the central Texas sales territory needed to be selected immediately to minimize lost sales. So Garvin had his secretary notify the FMA personnel department in the home office to send a list of applicants for sales positions.

COMPANY BACKGROUND

Farm Machinery for America, located in the Midwest, was one of the major producers of agricultural equipment in the United States. The modern tendency toward mechanization of agriculture had resulted in the production of large, expensive agricultural equipment used for efficient handling of crops. Consequently, many lines of agricultural tractors; crop harvesting machines such as grain combines and cotton pickers; crop production equipment such as plows, harrows, planters, and cultivators; hay, cane, and forage harvesting equipment; and lawn/garden tractors for commercial, residential, and recreational use were made by FMA.

FMA distributed equipment and service parts through nine farm implement sales regions in the continental United States to a network of 3,680 retail dealers, all of which were independent with the exception of 20 retail stores owned and operated by the sales branch of FMA. Garvin's sales region included all of Texas, Louisiana, Arkansas, and Oklahoma. Each sales region was divided into sales territories, to which salespeople were assigned. The central Texas sales territory was vacant, and selection of a new salesperson would proceed through the usual company recruiting procedures.

FMA RECRUITING PROCEDURES

FMA identified four important steps in recruiting and selecting a sales force:

1. Determine sales personnel needs.
   a. Job Analysis
   b. Job Description
   c. Job Specification
2. Identify sources from which good salespeople might be obtained.
3. Locate and recruit prospective salespeople.
4. Select prospects with highest probability of success.

FMA job analysis for salespeople was done several years ago by questioning sales personnel on the specific job roles or activities that a potential salesperson should have to succeed. This job analysis resulted in a job description that formally stated the nature, requirements, and responsibilities (for example, expected sales volume, product lines sold, customers) of the job (see Exhibit 1).

FMA's job specification, developed from the FMA job description, listed the personal characteristics (for example, skills, knowledge, capacity, and attributes) the organization deemed necessary for successful performance in sales potential:

1. Energetic, forward, and friendly.
2. Self-confident.
3. Hardworking.
4. Independent.
5. Competitive.
6. Good physical appearance.
7. Likable.
8. Professional.
9. Good memory.
10. Good communication skills.
11. Intelligent.

Through experience, FMA has identified potential sources of good sales candidates. This source list was prepared by keeping records of successes and failures of past salespeople. FMA encourages potential sales personnel to apply by running advertisements in local newspapers, presenting FMA programs at colleges and universities, and by word of mouth. A list of the sources with the most potential for yielding good salespeople follows:

1. Sales personnel from competing firms.
2. Educational institutions.
3. Nonsalespeople within the company.
4. Recommendations.

All applicants for sales positions submit résumés and application forms to the FMA personnel department, which screens all potential salespeople, weeding out those who obviously do not qualify according to the job specifications. Those who do qualify are given a short, initial interview. The personnel department interviewers then further weed out those who do not meet FMA's standards. All remaining sales applicants are given a regional sales office interview.

Garvin received information (see Exhibits 2 through 4) on 3 sales applicants out of a field of 29 that FMA home office personnel executives recommended as good sales prospects. Along with this list, the personnel department sent a booklet from the EEOC on hiring guidelines and a number of shorter pamphlets on interviewing tips. While Garvin did not have time to read all of these, he did take note of one that appealed to him and decided to try it for the upcoming interviews.

This pamphlet suggested that the interviewer write down the questions that he or she wanted to ask the applicant, then number them according to the order they should be asked. This way the interviewer would be sure to ask the important questions first. This allows the interviewer time to see more applicants or do other work.

Garvin spent the next hour reviewing each applicant's résumé and company application. From this he developed a list of questions he wanted to ask each applicant (see Exhibits 5 through 7). Garvin then scheduled the interviews to take place as soon as possible.

The three people who came through his office in the next few days could not have been more diverse. One was a well-dressed, though portly, man who appeared to be in his late 30s. Then there was a small, attractive, fashionably attired woman. The last interviewee was a man of about 45, dressed in a Western-style suit. He looked as though he might have been a basketball player when he was younger. Garvin wondered if any of the applicants would go to the World Wide Web and research the industry and competitors such as John Deere, International Harvester, and Caterpillar.

QUESTIONS

1. Review the questions Garvin plans to ask each person (found in Exhibits 5, 6, and 7). Which would you choose to ask? In what order? Why?
2. Who would you hire? Why?

EXHIBIT 1   JOB DESCRIPTION FOR AN FMA SALESPERSON

POSITION: SALESPERSON
REPORTS TO: REGIONAL SALES MANAGER

DEPARTMENT: SALES
DATE: JANUARY 15, 2000

NATURE OF JOB

- Responsible for servicing the needs of independent dealers in respective sales territories; develop new accounts.

PRINCIPAL RESPONSIBILITIES

SALES

- Make regular calls to independent dealers
- Sell the line, demonstrate products
- Inform dealers of new products
- Check dealer inventory
- Field questions
- Estimate customers' needs
- Emphasize quality
- Explain FMA policies on price, delivery, and credit
- Get the order, send to regional warehouse

SERVICE

- Report product weaknesses and complaints
- Handle questions for credit
- Analyze local conditions for customers

TERRITORY MANAGEMENT

- Arrange efficient route for best coverage
- Balance sales efforts to customers' potential volume

SALES PROMOTION

- Develop new accounts
- Distribute sales literature and brochures
- Talk with customers' sales personnel

EXECUTIVE

- Make daily work plan for next day
- Organize sales trips for minimum travel and maximum calls
- Report to home office on trends
- Investigate reasons for lost sales
- Attend sales meetings
- Collect overdue accounts

GOODWILL

- Counsel customers on problems
- Be loyal and respectful of FMA
- Attend trade shows

EXHIBIT 2

DYANNE LONG
2312 Loma Linda Drive
Austin, Texas 77546
(512) 820-0823

EMPLOYMENT HISTORY

1986–Present   Neiman-Marcus Department Stores

1994–Present   Buyer—Junior Dresses

- Managed a business for Neiman-Marcus that did $20 million in sales volume per year
- Placed the orders necessary to sustain this business with the vendors
- Was responsible for an increase in inventory turnover from 5 times per year to 6 times per year
- Reported to the divisional merchandise manager
- Received an award for the most profitable department in the division for fiscal year 1995
- Had management responsibility for two assistant buyers
- Was promoted to this position in August 1994

1990–1994   Assistant Buyer—Junior Tops, Misses Dresses

- Worked closely with the buyer of the department in selecting and evaluating merchandise
- Did monthly counts and balancing of inventory in the stores to achieve maximum sales potential
- Was responsible for coordinating all return-to-vendor merchandise activities
- Was promoted from assistant in a department that did $3.5 million a year to one that did $25 million a year in sales volume
- Was promoted from department manager in May 1990

1987–1990   Department Manager—Children's, North Park

- Had management responsibility for 18 salespeople
- Assisted in training all new salespeople with regard to the merchandise, as well as company policies and procedures
- Managed a department that did $2.5 million a year in sales volume
- Responsible for achieving a 20-percent increase in sales each year in the department
- Coordinated with the buyers to achieve maximum effectiveness of the merchandise and supporting advertising
- Was promoted to this position from management trainee in January 1987

1986–1987   Management Trainee

- Joined the company in July 1986 after graduating from University of Houston

Farm Machinery for America—Huntsville, Texas

- Worked in my father's FMA dealership all through high school and during summers when in college

EDUCATION

B.B.A. in Marketing, University of Houston, 1986
   Graduated with honors.

EXHIBIT 3

SCOTT HARRISON
701 Eisenhower
College Station, TX 77823
(512) 623-9877

WORK EXPERIENCE

1994–Present   International Harvester—Tractor Division
Sold tractors to farm implement stores in the eastern half of Texas and western Louisiana. Position was eliminated in the sale of the division to John Deere.

1990–1994   Caterpillar—Construction Equipment Division
Sold heavy construction equipment to construction companies in east Texas.

1988–1990   Courtesy Ford—Bryan, TX
Sold new and used automobiles. Was the number two salesman for the year 1989–90.

1987–1988   John Deere Dealer—Navasota, TX
Sold new and used farm equipment. Dealership went out of business

1985–1987   Central Hardware—College Station, TX
Was in charge of the plumbing department for the hardware store. Was promoted from a sales position in this store.

1980–1984   Various part-time jobs while attending school.

1976–1979   Served in the Army.
Was honorably discharged with the rank of corporal.

EDUCATION

B.B.A. in Accounting, Texas A&M University, 1984

PERSONAL

Married with two children. In good health.

EXHIBIT 4

WILLIAM LENNON
4409 Grand
Austin, Texas 77509
(512) 824-4094

WORK HISTORY

1975–Present   *Farm Machinery for America*

I started out as a dispatcher for FMA in 1975. I am presently employed as the warehouse manager of the same warehouse that I started working at. I have held five different positions at FMA during these years. After two years as a dispatcher, I was promoted to a shift supervisor. I worked there for three years before being promoted to head of transportation, shipping, and receiving. I ran that area until I was promoted to assistant warehouse manager five years later. I was assistant manager until three years ago when I became warehouse manager.

EDUCATION

I graduated from the University of Texas in 1974 with a bachelor's degree in management.

CLUBS

I have been an active member of the Longhorn's Club for almost 20 years.

EXHIBIT 5   QUESTIONS FOR MS. LONG

1. You seem to have had an excellent career going at Neiman-Marcus. Is there any particular reason why you left them?
2. Do you know anything about the equipment we sell here at FMA?
3. You have never been in a straight sales position according to your résumé. Do you think you would like an outside sales job?
4. Are you planning to have children in the near future?
5. You majored in marketing in college. What made you choose that major?
6. What did you like most about your jobs that you had at Neiman-Marcus?
7. What did you like least about your jobs at Neiman-Marcus?
8. What would you like to be doing ten years from now?
9. Were you satisfied with your earnings at Neiman-Marcus?
10. You have an excellent academic record. Did you enjoy your college experience?
11. Do you have any questions about the job that you would like to ask me?
12. What are your strengths that you feel you would be bringing to our company and this job in particular?
13. Since all of our present dealerships are owned by men, do you feel that you would have any trouble dealing with them?
14. Why the industry change now? You have an excellent record in retail; why are you willing to switch to industrial sales?
15. Would you mind the traveling that is involved in a position like this?

EXHIBIT 6   QUESTIONS FOR MR. HARRISON

1. I see you majored in accounting at college. Any particular reason for this?
2. Why didn't you pursue an accounting career when you graduated?
3. You have been in sales for a number of years now. Do you like selling?
4. Physically you are a rather large man. Are there any health problems that we need to be concerned with because of your weight?
5. You seemed to be doing a good job selling cars at the Ford dealership. Why did you leave that job to go to work for Caterpillar?
6. Why did you leave Caterpillar to go to work for International Harvester?
7. What did you enjoy most about your jobs with both Caterpillar and IH?
8. What did you like least about your jobs with both Caterpillar and IH?
9. Did you gain anything from your military service?
10. What would you like to be doing ten years from now?
11. Did you enjoy your first job that you had after you graduated from college?
12. Do you have any questions about the job that you would like to ask me?
13. Do you know anything about the equipment that we sell here at FMA?
14. What clubs or organizations do you belong to?
15. Were you satisfied with your earnings while you were with IH?

EXHIBIT 7   QUESTIONS FOR MR. LENNON

1. You've worked for our company for a long time now. Do you like your present job with the firm?
2. Were you born and raised here in Texas?
3. On your application it says that you received your bachelor's degree from the University of Texas. What year was that?
4. What was your first job here at FMA?
5. With all your experience here at FMA, you must know a great deal about our products. How do you think you would do selling these products?
6. How do you think you would adjust to having a commission instead of a straight salary?
7. What do you like least about your present job at FMA?
8. If I were to ask the employees you supervise to describe you, what do you think their response would be?
9. Have you been happy with your career so far here at FMA?
10. What do you like most about your present job at FMA?
11. How would you feel about being on the road a great deal of the time?
12. If you aren't chosen for this position, how will you feel about FMA?
13. Do you have any questions about the job that you would like to ask me?
14. Why now? Why have you decided to change your direction in the company after 20 years?
15. What would you say are some of your strengths that you would be bringing to this position?

CASE 10

MEAD ENVELOPE COMPANY
Is a New Compensation Plan Needed?

Mead Envelope Company, a $100 million division of a large, diversified paper products company, manufactures and markets standard and customized envelopes.[6] It is a real company, but we have changed the name, the industry, and certain identifying details. Mead sells to both direct accounts—banks, insurance companies, utilities, direct mail services—and distributors. Until 1997, the division achieved relatively steady sales growth in the range of 5–6 percent a year. Top management believes and marketing research supports the opinion that the division could achieve annual sales growth in the 10–12 percent range.

As a first step to that growth, management hired a new vice president of sales, whom we'll call Hal Jones. Jones toured the field to meet with key customers and the sales force to learn firsthand why the company was growing at only about half the rate of the estimated potential. Jones observed the following people.

CUSTOMER VISITS

The customers he visited, particularly the large accounts, said they were pleased with Mead's product quality and customer service and with the relationship with their account executive.

ACCOUNT EXECUTIVES

Mead has 45 geographically deployed account executives who call on customers of widely different sizes, ranging from community banks to large direct-mail marketers. The company has no national or major accounts program. The salespeople told Jones that their account planning is "informal," and Mead offers no training in how to develop complete account plans for customers, regardless of size. Overall, the account executives appear to be hardworking in the face of the competition from both national and local competitors. Mead compensates account executives with a salary and a sales commission. On average, their W-2 earnings are 50 percent salary, 50 percent commission. The company pays a commission at the rate of 3 percent of all sales over a base. The firm defines the base as the prior year's actual sales plus an upward adjustment for price increases. The average account executive earns $70,000 in total compensation while the annual pay among all salespeople ranges from $40,000 to $150,000.

CUSTOMER SERVICE REPRESENTATIVES

Fifteen customer service representatives handle accounts that account executives cannot reach on a regular basis, either because they are too busy or because there does not appear to be enough business in the account to justify on-premises sales calls. Typically, these accounts call the customer service representatives to reorder, to ask about incomplete orders and billing problems, or to inquire about new products. Some customer service representatives told Jones they did not have enough to do, so they are telephoning customers that their account executive has turned over to them. Mead pays customer service representatives a salary; it does not include them in the sales commission plan.

FIELD SALES MANAGERS

The three field sales managers spend the majority of their time working with account executives on major sales opportunities. They spend a relatively small amount of time on sales analysis and planning. They appear to be good trainers, motivators, and coaches for their people. Two of the field sales managers told Jones they believe sales results would be higher if their people specialized in certain types of accounts: direct-mail companies, for example, or utilities. The company pays field sales managers a salary plus a 1 percent commission (that is, an override) on the sales of their people over the sales base. The W-2 earnings for the field sales managers averaged $125,000 last year.

WHAT DOES THE PRODUCT MANAGER THINK?

When Jones returned from his field tour, he asked Mead's product manager to meet with him. The product manager for the standard product line indicated that the current sales "run rate" was on plan for the year, and she was satisfied with the sales force's efforts this year and last. The product manager for the customized product line was not satisfied. He noted that sales results for his products were, on average, 50 percent below plan. He pointed out that Mead made significant investments last year in manufacturing and envelope design capabilities to support the sale of customized products. This product manager is concerned that the sales force is not comfortable with computer-based envelope design—an essential part of sales process—at accounts where significant new sales have been booked. He pointed out that in virtually every large account where Mead has won new, customized business, he has had to play a role in the sale, particularly in analysis of the need, design of the solution, and the business case for the pricing.

A BRIEF ANALYSIS OF SALES

After meeting with the product managers, Jones looked over his sales numbers for the year and the growth projections that top management had given his predecessor for next year. What he saw was discouraging. The sales force was well behind its $106 million goal for the year. Standard product sales, which represented 80 percent of the business, appeared to be on plan; but customized product sales, projected to be $21 million, were well below plan. In fact, as the product manager had pointed out, actual sales were running at about half of the year's goal. What Jones found particularly disturbing was that, while customized projects were projected to be 20 percent of the current year's business, next year's forecast showed they were supposed to be 30 percent of the business, and the total goal for the business was set at $118 million. This meant that the customized product goal would be $35 to $36 million, or slightly more than three times greater than the current sales rate.

With his previous employer, Jones found everyone felt that any sales performance problems were always related to compensation. At least today, Hal is unsure of the way to improve sales. "I do not see how pay is the problem here," thought Jones. Just then the telephone rang in Hal's office. It was his boss's secretary saying that he wanted to see Jones next Monday at nine in the morning. Hal was hired to improve sales growth. What is he going to tell his boss?

CASE 11

McDONALD SPORTING GOODS COMPANY
Determining the Best Compensation Program

The annual sales volume of the McDonald Sporting Goods Company (MSG) for the past three years had ranged between $7,200,000 and $7,650,000.[7] Although profits continued to be satisfactory, Hudson McDonald, president and chief operating officer, was concerned because sales had not increased appreciably from year to year. Consequently, he asked a consultant in New York City and the officers of the company to submit proposals for improving the salespeople's compensation plan, which he believed was the basic weakness in the firm's marketing operations.

THE PRODUCTS

MSG's factory and warehouse were located in Albany, New York, where the company manufactured and distributed sporting equipment, clothing, and accessories. Hudson McDonald had organized it in 1990 when he learned that the market for sporting goods would grow because of the predicted increase in leisure time and the rising level of income in the United States.

Products of the company, approximately 700 items, were grouped into three lines: (1) fishing supplies, (2) hunting supplies, and (3) accessories. The fishing supplies line, which accounted for approximately 40 percent of the company's annual sales, included nearly every item needed to fish, such as fishing jackets, vests, caps, rods and reels of all types, lines, flies, lures, landing nets, and creels. The hunting supplies line contributed 30 percent of annual sales; it consisted of hunting clothing of all types, safety garments, shell holders, whistles, calls, and gun cases. The accessories line, which made up the balance of the company's annual sales volume, included items such as compasses, cooking kits, lanterns, hunting and fishing knives, hand warmers, and novelty gifts. Although the sales of the hunting and fishing lines were very seasonal, they tended to complement each other. The period from January to April accounted for the bulk of the company's annual volume in fishing items, and most sales of hunting supplies were made during the months of May through August. Typically, the company's sales of all products reached their lows for the year during the month of December.

The McDonald's sales volume is $7,529,806 for the current year, with products manufactured by the company accounting for 35 percent of this total. Imported products, which come primarily from Taiwan, comprise 50 percent of the company's volume. Items manufac-

tured by other domestic producers and distributed by MSG account for the remaining 15 percent of total sales.

McDonald reported that wholesale prices to retailers were established by adding a markup of 50 to 100 percent to McDonald's cost for the item. This practice is followed on products manufactured by MSG as well as on items purchased from other manufacturers. The resulting average markup across all products is 70 percent of cost.

THE SALES FORCE

The McDonald's market area consisted of the New England states, New York, Pennsylvania, Ohio, Michigan, Wisconsin, Indiana, Illinois, Kentucky, Tennessee, West Virginia, Virginia, Maryland, Delaware, and New Jersey. The area over which MSG could effectively compete was limited to some extent by shipping costs, because all orders were shipped from the factory and warehouse in Albany.

McDonald's salespeople sold to approximately 6,000 retail stores in small- and medium-sized cities in its market area. Analysis of sales records showed that the firm's customer coverage was very poor in the large metropolitan areas. Typically, each account was a one- or two-store operation. McDonald stated that he knew for a fact that McDonald's share of the market was very low. For all practical purposes, he felt the company's sales potential was unlimited. McDonald believed that, with few exceptions, McDonald's customers had little or no brand preference, and in the vast majority of cases, they bought hunting and fishing supplies from several suppliers.

McDonald felt that the pattern of retail distribution for hunting and fishing products had been changing during the past ten years as a result of the growth of discount stores. He thought that the proportion of retail sales for hunting and fishing supplies made by small- and medium-sized sporting goods outlets had been declining as compared with the percentage sold by discounters and chain stores. An analysis of company records revealed that MSG had not developed business among the discounters, with the exception of a few small discount stores. Some of MSG's executives felt that the lack of business with discounters might have been due in part to the company's pricing policy and in part to the pressures that current customers had exerted on company people to keep them from calling on the discounters. No one knows if people would buy their products through the mail or over the Internet.

MSG's sales force for the current year totaled 11 full-time people. Their ages ranged from 23 to 67, and their tenure with the company ranged from one to ten years. Salespeople, territories, and sales volume for the previous year and the current year are shown in Exhibit 1. Duvall, Edwards, and Logan's territories were created when all territories were redesigned around state geographical boundaries.

The company's sales force played the major role in its marketing efforts, since MSG did not use magazine, newspaper, or radio advertising to reach either the retail trade or consumers. One advertising piece that supplemented the work of the salespeople was MSG's merchandise catalog. It contained a complete listing of all the company's products and was mailed to retailers who were either current accounts or prospective accounts. Typically, store buyers used the catalog for reordering.

Most accounts were contacted by a salesperson two or three times a year. The salespeople planned their activities so that each store would be called on at the beginning of the fishing season and again prior to the hunting season. Certain key accounts were contacted more often.

THE COMPENSATION PLAN

The salespeople were paid straight commissions on their dollar sales volume for the calendar year. The commission rate was 5 percent on the first $675,000, 6 percent on the next $225,000, and 7 percent on all sales over $900,000 for the year. Each week, the salespeople could draw all or a portion of their accumulated commissions. McDonald encouraged the salespeople to draw commissions as they accumulated, because he felt the salespeople were motivated to work harder when they had a very small or zero balance in their commission accounts. These accounts were closed at the end of the year, so the salespeople began the new year with nothing in their accounts.

The salespeople provided their own automobiles and paid their traveling expenses, of which all or a portion were reimbursed per diem. Under the per diem plan, each salesperson received $101.25 per day for Monday through Thursday and $47.25 for Friday, or a total of $452.25 for the normal work week. No per diem was paid for Saturday or Sunday nights in the territory.

In addition to the commission and per diem, the salespeople could earn cash awards under two sales incentive plans that were begun two years earlier. Under one, called the Annual Sales Increase Awards plan, a total of $23,400 was paid to the five salespeople who had the largest percentage increase in dollar sales volume over the previous year. The awards were made at the January sales meeting, and the winners were determined by dividing the dollar amount of each salesperson's increase by his or her volume for the previous year, with the percentage increases ranked in descending order. Earnings under this plan for the current year are shown in Exhibit 2.

EXHIBIT 1   McDONALD SPORTING GOODS SALES FORCE

SALESPERSON	AGE	YEARS OF SERVICE	TERRITORY	PREVIOUS YEAR	CURRENT YEAR
Allen	45	2	Illinois and Indiana	$ 371,548	$ 370,368
Campbell	62	10	Pennsylvania	1,341,216	1,552,770
Duvall	23	1	New England	—	466,488
Edwards	39	1	Michigan	—	471,842
Gatewood	63	5	West Virginia	403,344	403,370
Hammond	54	2	Virginia	466,802	466,570
Logan	37	1	Kentucky and Tennessee	—	638,684
Mason	57	2	Delaware and Maryland	725,662	928,224
O'Bryan	59	4	Ohio	611,920	643,942
Samuels	42	3	New York and New Jersey	829,152	927,532
Wates	67	5	Wisconsin	417,050	384,976
Salespeople terminated in previous year				2,057,418	
House account				289,556	275,040
Total				$7,513,668	$7,529,806

Exhibit 2   Earnings and Incentive Awards for the Current Year

| | SALES | | ANNUAL SALES INCREASE AWARDS | | WEEKLY SALES INCREASE AWARDS | |
| | | | PERCENTAGE | | | |
SALESPERSON	PREVIOUS YEAR	CURRENT YEAR	INCREASE IN SALES	AWARD	TOTAL ACCRUED	EARNINGS[a]
Allen	$ 371,548	$ 370,368	—		$ 2,307	$ 45,000[b]
Campbell	1,341,216	1,552,770	15.773	6,750(2nd)	5,049	92,943
Duvall	—	466,488	—	—	5,049	45,000[b]
Edwards	—	471,842	—	—	—	45,000[b]
Gatewood	403,344	403,370	.007	900(5th)	2,484	20,169
Hammond	466,802	466,570	—	—	957	45,000[b]
Logan	—	638,684	—		—	45,000[b]
Mason	725,662	928,224	27.914	9,000(1st)	7,749	49,230
O'Bryan	611,920	643,942	5.233	2,250(4th)	3,402	32,193
Samuels	829,152	927,552	11.865	4,500(3rd)	2,925	50,796
Wates	417,050	384,976	—	—	1,377	19,251
Totals	5,166,694	7,254,786		23,400	31,299	489,582

[a]Exclusive of incentive awards and per diem.

[b]Guarantee of $900 per week or $45,000 per year.

Under the second incentive plan, the salespeople could win Weekly Sales Increase Awards for every week in which their dollar volume in the current year exceeded their sales for the corresponding week in the previous year. Beginning with an award of $9 for the first week, the amount of the award increased by $9 for each week in which the salespeople surpassed their sales for the comparable week in the previous year. If a salesperson produced higher sales during each of the 50 weeks in the current year, he or she received $9 for the first week, $18 for the second week, and $450 for the fiftieth week, or a total of $11,475 for the year. The salesperson had to be employed by the company during the previous year to be eligible for these awards. A check for the total amount of the awards accrued during the year was presented to the salesperson at the sales meeting held in January. Earnings under this plan for the current year are shown in Exhibit 2.

The company frequently used "spiffs" to promote sales of special items. The salesperson was paid a spiff, which usually was $18 for each order obtained for the items designated in the promotion.

For the past three years, in recruiting salespeople, McDonald had guaranteed the more qualified applicants a weekly income while they learned the business and developed their respective territories. During the current year, five salespeople—Allen, Duvall, Edwards, Hammond, and Logan—had a guarantee of $900 a week, which they drew against their commissions. If the year's cumulative commissions for any of these salespeople were less than their cumulative weekly drawing accounts, they received no commissions. The commission and drawing accounts were closed on December 31, so each salesperson began the year with a zero balance in each account.

The company did not have a stated or written policy specifying the maximum length of time a salesperson could receive a guarantee if his or her commissions continued to be less than his or her draw. McDonald felt that the five salespeople who currently had guarantees would quit if these guarantees were withdrawn before their commissions reached $45,000 per year.

McDonald was convinced that MSG's salespeople's annual earnings had fallen behind earnings for comparable selling positions, particularly in the past six years. As a result, he felt that the company's ability to attract and hold high-caliber, professional salespeople was being adversely affected. He strongly felt that each salesperson should be earning $90,000 annually.

In December of the current year, McDonald met with his comptroller and production manager, who were the only other executives of the company, and solicited their ideas concerning changes in the company's compensation plan for salespeople.

The comptroller pointed out that the salespeople who had guarantees were not producing the sales that had been expected from their territories. He was concerned that the annual commissions earned by four of

EXHIBIT 3   COMPARISON OF EARNINGS IN CURRENT YEAR UNDER EXISTING GUARANTEE PLAN AND EARNINGS
UNDER THE COMPTROLLER'S PLAN[a]

SALES-PERSON	SALES	COMMISSIONS	EXISTING PLAN GUARANTEE	EARNINGS	COMPTROLLER'S PLAN COMMISSIONS	GUARANTEE	EARNINGS
Allen	$370,368	$18,522	$45,000	$63,522	$18,522	$22,500	$41,022
Duvall	466,488	23,328	45,000	68,328	23,328	22,500	45,828
Edwards	471,842	23,590	45,000	68,590	23,590	22,500	46,090
Hammond	466,570	23,328	45,000	68,328	23,328	22,500	45,828
Logan	638,684	31,932	45,000	76,932	31,932	22,500	54,432

[a]Exclusive of incentive awards and per diem.

the five salespeople on guarantees were approximately half or less than their drawing accounts. Furthermore, according to the comptroller, several of the salespeople who did not have guarantees were producing a relatively low volume of sales year after year. For example, annual sales remained at low levels for Gatewood, O'Bryan, and Wates, who had been working four to five years in their respective territories.

The comptroller proposed that guarantees be reduced to $450 per week, plus commissions at the regular rate on all sales. The $450 would not be drawn against commissions, as was done under the existing plan, but would be in addition to any commissions earned. In the comptroller's opinion, this plan would motivate the sales force to rapidly increase sales, because incomes would rise directly with sales. The comptroller calculated the incomes of the five salespeople who had guarantees in the current year as compared with the incomes they would have received under his plan (Exhibit 3).

From a sample check of recent shipments, the production manager had concluded that the salespeople tended to overwork accounts located within a 75-mile radius of their homes. Sales coverage was extremely light in a 100- to 150-mile radius of the salespeople homes. The coverage seemed to result from the desire of the salespeople to spend most evenings during the week at home with their families.

He proposed that the per diem be increased from $101.25 to $121.50 per day for Monday through Thursday, $47.25 for Friday, and $121.50 for Sunday if the salesperson spent Sunday evening away from home. He reasoned that the per diem of $121.50 for Sunday would act as a strong incentive for the salespeople to drive to the perimeters of their territories on Sunday evenings rather than use Monday morning for traveling. Further, he believed that the increase in per diem would result in a more uniform coverage of the sales territories and an overall increase in sales volume.

The consultant from New York City recommended that the guarantees and per diem be retained on the present basis, and he proposed that McDonald adopt what he called a Ten Percent Self-Improvement Plan. Under the consultant's plan, each salesperson would be paid, in addition to the regular commission, a monthly bonus commission of 10 percent on all dollar volume over sales in the comparable month of the previous year. For example, if a salesperson sold $90,000 worth of merchandise in January of the current year and $81,000 in January of the previous year, he or she would receive a $900 bonus check in February. For salespeople on guarantees, bonuses would be in addition to earnings. The consultant reasoned that the bonus commission would motivate the salespeople, both those with and those without guarantees, to increase their sales.

He further recommended discontinuing the two sales incentive plans currently in effect. He felt the savings from these plans would nearly cover the costs of his proposal.

QUESTION
Which of these plans, if any, should the company use to compensate its salespeople? Why?

CASE 12

BURDITT CHEMICAL CORPORATION
Analysis of Sales and Marketing Costs

Scott Cate had just come into his office when the telephone rang.[8] "Scott, this is John Zinc." Mr. Zinc is Scott's boss. "Did you get the information I sent you? You should have received six exhibits."

"Yes, it arrived this morning," said Scott. "But I haven't looked at it yet."

"Well, take a good, close look, Scott, because your district's sales and profits don't look so hot. Be sure and

EXHIBIT 1   BURDITT CHEMICAL CORPORATION: SALES AND PROFITS, 1994–1998

	1994	1995	1996	1997	1998
Sales	43,758,000	47,762,000	41,932,000	48,356,000	52,558,000
Production expenses	26,254,000	29,693,400	26,835,600	29,946,400	32,038,000
Gross profit	17,503,200	18,068,600	15,096,400	18,409,600	20,519,400
Administrative expenses	5,733,200	6,351,400	6,142,400	6,435,000	6,833,200
Selling expenses	4,452,800	4,930,200	4,694,800	5,002,800	5,277,800
Pretax profit	7,317,200	6,787,000	4,259,200	6,971,800	8,408,400
Taxes	3,326,400	3,053,600	1,738,000	3,137,200	3,779,600
Net profit	$ 3,990,800	$ 3,733,400	$ 2,521,200	$ 3,834,600	$ 4,628,800

EXHIBIT 2   INDIVIDUAL DISTRICT SALES QUOTAS AND RESULTS, 1998

DISTRICT	NUMBER OF SALESPEOPLE	SALES QUOTA	SALES—ACTUAL	GROSS PROFIT QUOTA	GROSS PROFIT—ACTUAL
1	7	$ 8,536,000	$ 8,593,200	$ 3,414,000	$ 3,495,800
2	6	8,250,000	8,228,000	3,300,000	3,363,800
3	6	8,030,000	7,493,200	3,212,000	2,725,800
4	6	7,414,000	7,299,600	2,965,600	2,849,000
5	5	7,260,000	7,062,000	2,904,000	2,609,200
6	5	6,886,000	7,051,000	2,754,400	2,593,800
7	5	5,984,000	6,831,000	2,393,600	2,882,000
		$52,360,000	$52,558,000	$20,944,000	$20,519,400

EXHIBIT 3   INDIVIDUAL DISTRICT SELLING EXPENSES, 1998

DISTRICT	SALES REP SALARIES[a]	SALES COMMISSION	SALES REP EXPENSES	DISTRICT OFFICE	DISTRICT MANAGER SALARY	DISTRICT MANAGER EXPENSES	SALES SUPPORT	TOTAL SELLING EXPENSES
1	$389,620	$42,737	$123,816	$46,530	$73,700	$25,212	$152,900	$ 854,515
2	315,084	41,140	111,672	46,886	74,800	26,475	156,904	772,961
3	346,236	37,466	119,759	48,690	77,000	27,240	154,022	810,414
4	331,056	36,498	108,029	48,409	71,500	24,211	146,234	765,937
5	277,090	35,310	93,984	46,453	72,600	24,470	168,520	718,428
6	274,670	35,783	91,344	46,182	73,700	25,142	147,620	694,441
7	252,670	38,566	98,340	49,467	69,300	25,615	129,250	663,208
								$5,279,903

[a]Includes cost of fringe-benefit program.

EXHIBIT 4   INDIVIDUAL DISTRICT CONTRIBUTION TO CORPORATE ADMINISTRATIVE EXPENSE AND PROFIT, 1998

DISTRICT	SALES	GROSS PROFIT	SELLING EXPENSES	CONTRIBUTION TO ADMINISTRATIVE EXPENSE AND PROFIT
1	$ 8,593,200	$ 3,495,800	$ 854,515	$ 2,641,197
2	8,228,000	3,363,800	772,961	2,590,839
3	7,493,200	2,725,800	810,414	1,915,036
4	7,299,600	2,849,000	765,936	2,083,063
5	7,062,000	2,609,200	718,428	1,890,772
6	7,051,000	2,593,800	694,441	1,899,973
7	6,831,000	2,882,000	663,208	2,221,393
	$52,558,000	$20,519,400	$5,279,903	$15,242,273

EXHIBIT 5   SOUTHEAST (#3) AND SOUTH-CENTRAL (#7) DISTRICT SALES AND GROSS PROFIT PERFORMANCE BY ACCOUNT CATEGORY, 1998

DISTRICT	(A)	(B)	(C)	TOTAL
	SALES BY ACCOUNT CATEGORY			
Southeast	$2,013,000	$3,698,200	$1,782,000	$7,493,200
South-Central	1,652,200	3,744,400	1,434,400	6,831,000
	GROSS PROFIT BY ACCOUNT CATEGORY			
Southeast	$ 783,200	$1,370,600	$ 572,000	2,725,800
South-Central	726,000	1,595,000	561,000	2,882,000

EXHIBIT 6   POTENTIAL ACCOUNTS, ACTIVE ACCOUNTS, AND ACCOUNT CALL COVERAGE: SOUTHEAST AND SOUTH-CENTRAL DISTRICTS, 1998

DISTRICT	POTENTIAL ACCOUNTS (A)	(B)	(C)	ACTIVE ACCOUNTS (A)	(B)	(C)	ACCOUNT COVERAGE (TOTAL CALLS) (A)	(B)	(C)
Southeast	180	762	1,270	126	420	626	2,594	6,102	4,236
South-Central	120	772	998	84	364	432	2,060	5,236	2,598

study the exhibits comparing your district (the southeast district) and the south-central district (district 7). South-central is one of the best I have. Call me, Scott, as soon as you have gone over the material," said Mr. Zinc as he hung up the telephone.

THE COMPANY

The Burditt Chemical Corporation manufactures and sells a line of chemical products purchased by dry cleaning retail outlets and industrial organizations. They have several thousand customers. Salespeople call on retail buyers, purchasing agents, and chemical engineers. Almost no advertising and other promotion efforts are used. The success of the sales force determines the success of the company. Company sales in 1998 had reached a new high of $52.56 million, up from $48.36 million in 1997. Net pretax profit in 1998 had been $8.408 million, up from $6.338 million in 1989.

Despite their success, there is a high degree of competition. The company's product line is as follows:

Product	Price per Unit	Margin
BIC	$160	$56
LOW	152	68
OHH	152	68
VIC	160	70
ABC	440	180
X12	240	88

The Sales Force

The Burditt sales organization consisted of 40 sales representatives operating in seven sales districts. Sales representatives' salaries ranged from $30,800 to $52,800 with fringe-benefit costs amounting to an additional 20 percent of salary. In addition to their salaries, Burditt's sales representatives received commissions of 1 percent of their dollar sales volume on all sales up to their sales quotas. The commission on sales in excess of quota was 2 percent.

In 1996, Mr. Zinc had developed a sales program based on selling the full line of Burditt products. He believed that if the sales representatives could successfully carry out the program, benefits would accrue to both Burditt and its customers:

1. Sales volume per account would be greater and selling costs as a percentage of sales would decrease.
2. A Burditt's sales representative could justify spending more time with such an account, thus becoming more knowledgeable about the account's business and becoming better able to provide technical assistance and identify selling opportunities.
3. Full-line sales would strengthen Burditt's competitive position by reducing the likelihood of account

loss to their plating chemical suppliers (a problem that existed in multiple-supplier situations).

Mr. Zinc's 1996 sales program had also included the following account call-frequency guidelines:

- A accounts (major accounts generating $26,400 or more in a yearly sales)—two calls per month.
- B accounts (medium-size accounts generating $13,200–$26,399 in yearly sales)—one call per month.
- C accounts (small accounts generating $13,200 yearly in sales)—one call every two months.

The account call-frequency guidelines were developed by Mr. Zinc after discussions with the district managers. Mr. Zinc had been concerned about the optimum allocation of sales effort to accounts and felt that the guidelines would increase the efficiency of the company's sales force, although not all of the district sales managers agreed with this conclusion.

The Pressure Is On!

Three days after their first talk, Scott called John Zinc. After a minute or so Mr. Zinc said, "It appears your people may be misallocating their sales efforts, Scott. See if you are calling on customers incorrectly and if you are concentrating on selling the less profitable products. You need to turn things around. Scott, I want you to carefully examine everything, and let's talk more next week. Pay particular attention to gross profit quota. The company is interested in 'profitable' sales, not just sales."

Questions

1. Evaluate the southeast district's performance. Consider such performance bases as sales volume, gross margin, and contribution to profit.
2. Where can the southeast district improve its performance? Do they really need to do better?
3. What should be done to improve areas of low performance?

DEER TRACTORS, INC.
Analyzing Sales Data

Deer Tractors, Inc. (DTI), manufactures six major product lines: push lawn mowers, power lawn mowers, riding mowers, garden tillers, lawn tractors, and garden tractors. The company is divided into five geographic regions. As shown in Exhibit 1, annual sales have steadily increased to $725.6 million as of 2000. In fact, sales have increased at a more rapid rate than industry demand, and the company's market share has been increasing.

Jim Tanner, national sales manager, takes great pride in these figures and has always felt his group was working at its maximum potential.

MARKET DECISION SUPPORT SYSTEM

At the beginning of 2000 a market decision support system (MDSS) was installed to provide a continuous audit of the firm's marketing operation. It was hoped the MDSS would help the firm allocate time and dollars for generating higher sales volume and net profits by concentrating market effort in the most profitable areas. The company wanted to examine market segments and determine which were producing the majority of sales and profits so management could divide the total marketing resources in the most efficient manner.

Because different net profits and sales are often contributed by different product lines, price lines, and geographic areas, management wanted to direct the majority of marketing expenditures at areas where the profit, sales, or a profit–sales ratio of return per marketing dollar spent was the highest. As one manager said, "We must allocate our funds where we get the most bang for the buck." MDSS was expected to aid in such tasks as sales forecasting, evaluating market position, production planning, inventory control, sales force planning, and appraising, pricing, advertising, sales promotion, and distribution strategies.

An important part of MDSS is the computer-generated data used to assist the sales analyst. Corporate management wanted to examine the extent to which the so-called 80/20 principle was operating. Managers realized that a major part of the company's sales and profits may directly result from a small number of customers, products, or geographic areas. They felt that some marginal or unprofitable products, geographic areas, or customers should be carried to complement the existing product line and to encourage sales volume in the more profitable areas. Furthermore, MDSS could examine the effect that averaging, summarizing, and aggregating data have on the true sales or profit picture. Management did not want to assume that just because sales were increasing, the company's operations could not be improved.

	COMPANY SALES VOLUME (MILLIONS)	INDUSTRY DEMAND (MILLIONS)	SHARE OF MARKET (%)
YEAR			
1992	$530.2	$32,300.2	1.64
1993	560.0	34,400.0	1.63
1994	574.0	34,578.4	1.66
1995	588.8	34,840.4	1.69
1996	606.8	36,119.2	1.68
1997	630.4	37,082.4	1.70
1998	674.8	39,472.4	1.71
1999	681.6	39,859.6	1.71
2000	725.6	41,678.0	1.74

EXHIBIT 1   DEER TRACTORS, INC. SALES

FINANCIAL ANALYSES

One of the first reports MDSS generated was the income statement shown in Exhibit 2. The contribution margin approach, rather than the full cost approach, was used to prepare the income statement. As shown, variable costs (those that fluctuate with net sales volume), including marketing and manufacturing costs, are first subtracted from net sales for each segment. This contribution margin is the amount each segment contributes to company overhead and to net profits. Nonassignable costs and fixed costs are not allocated to the segments. The contribution margins serve as measures of relative profitability. Tanner noted that the western region was the lowest in profitability. He also observed that, if regions were ranked by profitability, the eastern region would be the most profitable.

Management was pleased to see that every region was making a positive contribution to net profits and overhead. Several managers suggested that the firm did not need to continue the analysis. However, Tanner asked that this contribution margin approach be extended to product line (Exhibit 3). He was somewhat surprised to see that the lawn tractor line was unprofitable. It appears from certain territorial analyses that the very profitable garden tractor line may be compensating for the lawn tractor line's losses. He could not tell from this analysis alone the reason for the lawn tractor line's poor performance. Industry demand for lawn tractors may have declined, and the firm may not have anticipated this economic fact; or the new model of lawn tractor may have mechanical defects or poor aesthetic features. "We don't know, but what I am sure of is that management should take appropriate measures to find out what the problem may be. Maybe MDSS is better than I first felt it was because, without this analysis, the success of our other product lines may have hidden this from us," Tanner stated.

REGIONAL SALES ANALYSIS

Tanner requested a regional breakdown of company sales volume. Last year he had developed a retail sales index to serve as a relative measure of the dollar volume of retail sales that normally occur in each region. Based on that index, he had established quotas for the sales regions, districts, and individual territories. As shown in Exhibit 4, all except the western region were meeting quotas. Tanner did not know why sales were down. He called John Anderson, the western regional sales manager, and asked him to look into the matter and report back to him in two

EXHIBIT 2   DEER TRACTORS, INC. INCOME STATEMENT, CONTRIBUTION MARGIN APPROACH

	ENTIRE COMPANY (000)	SOUTHWEST (000)	SOUTHERN (000)	EASTERN (000)	WESTERN (000)	MIDWEST (000)
Net sales (thousands of dollars)	$725,200	$137,796	$137,512	$157,044	$148,548	$144,800
Less variable costs:						
Manufacturing costs	477,212	88,188	90,488	105,220	101,012	92,304
Marketing costs:						
Sales commissions	23,072	4,684	4,124	5,012	5,348	3,904
Transportation and shipping	9,836	1,204	944	668	852	1,168
Warehousing	1,612	304	296	344	268	400
Credit and collection	3,628	748	704	772	560	844
Assignable costs:						
Salaries—salespeople	73,840	14,796	13,216	14,544	14,892	16,392
Salaries—marketing manager	4,616	800	892	948	924	1,052
Advertising	13,608	2,792	2,652	2,972	2,544	2,576
Sales promotion	5,744	1,152	1,120	1,276	1,108	1,092
Total variable and assignable costs	608,168	114,668	114,508	131,752	127,508	119,732
Contribution margin	117,032	23,128	23,004	25,292	21,040	24,568
Nonassignable costs:						
Institutional advertising	1,620					
Fixed costs:						
General administration	8,108					
Manufacturing	92,184					
Net income before taxes	15,012					

EXHIBIT 3   DEER TRACTORS, INC. INCOME STATEMENT, CONTRIBUTION MARGIN APPROACH (BY PRODUCT LINE)

	COMPANY (000)	PUSH MOWERS (000)	POWER MOWERS (000)	RIDING MOWERS (000)	GARDEN TILLERS (000)	LAWN TRACTORS (000)	GARDEN TRACTORS (000)
Net sales (thousands of dollars)	$725,200	$133,800	$89,468	$140,704	$34,704	$88,188	$238,336
Less variable costs:							
Manufacturing	477,212	95,324	59,584	90,908	22,520	79,336	129,540
Marketing	33,148	5,832	5,304	6,324	1,064	5,696	8,928
Assignable costs	97,808	16,300	15,308	17,552	4,000	12,928	31,720
Total variable and assignable costs	608,168	117,456	80,196	114,784	27,584	97,960	170,188
Contribution margin	117,032	16,344	9,272	25,920	7,120	(9,772)	68,148
Nonassignable costs	1,620						
Fixed costs	100,292						
Net income before taxes	15,120						

EXHIBIT 4   DEER TRACTORS, INC. REGIONAL BREAKDOWN OF SALES

REGION	RETAIL SALES INDEX	EXPECTED SALES (000)	ACTUAL SALES (000)	DOLLAR DEVIATION
Midwest	99	$143,696	$144,200	+504
Southwest	95	137,892	137,896	+4
Southern	9	129,184	137,512	+8,328
Eastern	105	152,408	157,044	+4,636
Western	103	149,504	148,548	−956

EXHIBIT 5   DEER TRACTORS, INC. WESTERN REGION SALES

DISTRICT	EXPECTED SALES (000)	ACTUAL SALES (000)	DOLLAR DEVIATION
Washington	$17,940	$17,988	+48
Idaho-Oregon	15,700	15,684	−16
Northern California	43,204	42,028	−1,176
Southern California	72,660	72,848	+188

weeks. Anderson knew sales were slow; however, he had not been that concerned until now.

WESTERN SALES REGION

To examine the $956,000 Tanner used the district sales breakdown shown in Exhibit 5. It was very apparent that the northern California sales district was experiencing problems. He called Kurt McNeal, the district manager, and asked him why sales were down. McNeal said, "John, I was just about to call you. I'm getting ready to fire Leslie Stark. His sales are down. You know he is in the process of getting a divorce, and his personal life must be getting in the way of business."

"Have you talked to him?"Tanner asked.

"Yes, he claims competition is using that area as a test market for a new line of garden tractors. However, I suspect he is not working very hard, and the competition is stealing our business. You know we have some large retail-chain accounts there, and we cannot afford to lose that business. So let's replace him."

"Before you do, Kurt, look over some of the data I'm mailing to you, and then talk to Leslie. After this, if you still feel you should let him go, you have my permission. I'm not sure he's doing so badly compared with the rest of you."

Until this time McNeal had been working with total sales figures and figures salespeople developed on their own, so it was difficult for him to break out sales data. In fact, he really did not want to do it. He felt it was the company's job and not his responsibility. If sales were

down, they would let him know. Until recently he always had met his overall sales quota. Several days after the conversation with Tanner, McNeal received the data shown in Exhibits 6, 7, and 8. It was amazing to him to see this much detail in the data. When he saw that Stark was the only person selling below quota and in fact making the district's performance look bad, he made up his mind to fire Stark.

QUESTIONS

1. What do you feel is the main purpose of a firm's marketing decision support system? Do you feel KTI has an adequate MDSS?
2. Do you agree with McNeal's decision to fire Stark? Why?
3. What action, if any, should John Anderson take? For example, should he let McNeal handle the problem of low sales in the district?

EXHIBIT 6   DEER TRACTORS, INC. WESTERN REGION, N. CALIFORNIA DISTRICT SALES

SALESPERSON	EXPECTED SALES (000)	ACTUAL SALES (000)	DIFFERENCE	PERFORMANCE INDEX[a]
J. Boles	$11,392	$11,584	+192	101
L. Stark	11,168	9,684	−1,484	86
J. Dozzier	12,024	12,092	+68	100
A. Penny	8,620	8,668	+48	100

[a](Actual Sales/Quota) × 100.

EXHIBIT 7   SALESPEOPLE'S DOLLAR GAIN OR LOSS OVER EXPECTED SALES

PRODUCTS	J. BOLES EXPECTED SALES (000)	J. BOLES ACTUAL SALES (000)	L. STARK EXPECTED SALES (000)	L. STARK ACTUAL SALES (000)	J. DOZZIER EXPECTED SALES (000)	J. DOZZIER ACTUAL SALES (000)	A. PENNY EXPECTED SALES (000)	A. PENNY ACTUAL SALES (000)
Push mowers	$ 1,878	$ 2,018	$ 2,064	$2,088	$ 1,998	$ 2,016	$1,176	$1,210
Power mowers	1,260	1,218	1,088	1,080	1,942	1,960	1,372	1,404
Riding mowers	414	320	416	468	1,792	1,800	1,696	1,702
Garden tillers	2,144	2,224	2,196	2,196	2,582	2,590	1,746	1,716
Lawn tractors	3,340	3,404	3,052	3,232	1,466	1,470	1,270	1,304
Garden tractors	2,356	2,400	2,352	624	2,244	2,256	1,360	1,332
Total	11,392	11,584	11,168	9,684	12,024	12,092	8,620	8,668

EXHIBIT 8   SALESPEOPLE'S PERCENTAGE GAIN OR LOSS

	PERCENTAGE GAIN OR LOSS OVER LAST YEAR		
	TERRITORY	DISTRICT	REGION
J. BOLES			
Push mowers	7.0	8.9	7.6
Power mowers	−3.4	−1.5	3.7
Riding mowers	−44.3	41.4	3.8
Garden tillers	3.6	−14.8	−4.2
Lawn tractors	1.9	8.2	11.5
Garden tractors	10.1	−18.6	−9.1
L. STARK			
Push mowers	11.0	8.9	7.6
Power mowers	−2.2	−1.5	3.7
Riding mowers	.4	41.4	3.8
Garden tillers	−8.2	−14.8	−4.2
Lawn tractors	15.2	8.2	11.5
Garden tractors	−46.3	−18.6	−9.1
J. DOZZIER			
Push mowers	9.0	8.9	7.6
Power mowers	1.0	−1.5	3.7
Riding mowers	1.7	−41.4	3.8
Garden tillers	5.2	−14.8	−4.2
Lawn tractors	1.6	8.2	11.5
Garden tractors	21.6	−18.6	−9.1
A. PENNY			
Push mowers	8.6	8.9	7.6
Power mowers	3.1	−1.5	3.7
Riding mowers	.8	41.4	3.8
Garden tillers	−15.4	−14.8	−4.2
Lawn tractors	−10.5	−8.2	−11.5
Garden tractors	−4.0	−18.6	−9.1

HARVARD CASES

CASE 14

WESCO DISTRIBUTION, INC.

Late in June 1997, Jim Piraino, VP marketing for WESCO Distribution, Inc. (see Exhibit 1), was preparing for a yearly review meeting with his CEO Roy Haley. At the top of the agenda was the performance of the National Accounts (NA) program during the first half of 1997 (see Exhibit 2). Haley had ambitious plans for WESCO over the next five years. He had charted out a course that called for an annual growth rate of 6 percent to 8 percent in sales, and more important, an annual increase of 12 percent to 16 percent in profitability. "In 1996, we were a $2.2 billion company with an EBIT of around 3 percent. I want us to be a $3 billion company with an EBIT of over 5 percent by the year 2000. This target is very much achievable. In the last few years, our customers have made significant changes to their business processes. These changes provide us a unique opportunity to provide greater value to our customers while improving our market position and profitability. I want WESCO to be recognized as a leader in learning, adapting, and responding to changes in customer needs," said Haley.

Although acquisitions of other companies were expected to contribute over half the revenue growth, most of this business was not expected to exceed current profitability levels. WESCO's current NA program, which had been initiated in 1994 as a response to the changing market dynamics, was expected to deliver the additional revenue growth and obtain the desired increases in profitability.

Yet, as of mid-1997, the NA program had not delivered the expected increases in sales and profitability. Haley had now asked Piraino to examine the NA program and present recommendations for improvements.

"We need to get more out of our NA effort. This is our best growth avenue with existing customers and new prospects. We have to generate significantly better results with this program," Haley had told Piraino.

PREPARING FOR THE NA REVIEW MEETING

In early May, Piraino had spoken with WESCO national account manager (NAM) Mike McKinley about one of his NA customers, who had signed an agreement in late 1996. During the first five months of 1997, the account had generated only 40 percent of its target sales volume, with gross margins falling a full 2 percent from the prior year.

Piraino reflected on the meeting:

From our account analysis prior to signing the agreement, this was a very promising NA customer offering immediate, exclusive access to their 28 U.S. plants. We thought we could increase their existing $1.5 million annual purchases from us by a factor of ten. However, ever since implementation began in January, we have discovered an unexpectedly poor alignment between the customer's local and corporate interests. This was their first national purchasing agreement, and it turns out that despite corporate enthusiasm, some of their plants were reluctant to abandon local

Exhibit 1   The WESCO Executive Organization Chart

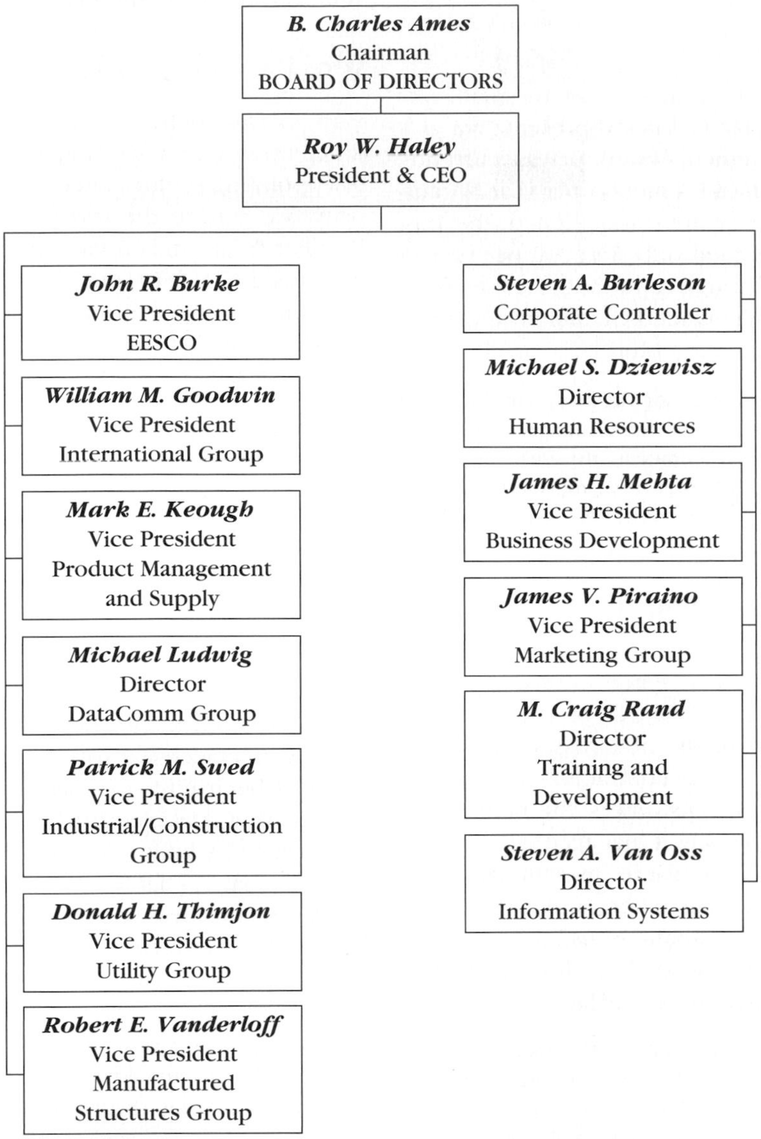

B. Charles Ames
Chairman
BOARD OF DIRECTORS

Roy W. Haley
President & CEO

John R. Burke
Vice President
EESCO

William M. Goodwin
Vice President
International Group

Mark E. Keough
Vice President
Product Management
and Supply

Michael Ludwig
Director
DataComm Group

Patrick M. Swed
Vice President
Industrial/Construction
Group

Donald H. Thimjon
Vice President
Utility Group

Robert E. Vanderloff
Vice President
Manufactured
Structures Group

Steven A. Burleson
Corporate Controller

Michael S. Dziewisz
Director
Human Resources

James H. Mehta
Vice President
Business Development

James V. Piraino
Vice President
Marketing Group

M. Craig Rand
Director
Training and
Development

Steven A. Van Oss
Director
Information Systems

Source: Company records.

Exhibit 2   Sales to National Accounts ($ Millions)

Class of Account	Number of Customers	1996 Sales	YTD Sales May 1997
Key	50	180	89
Focus	100	52	25
Other	150	34	14
Total	300	266	128

Source: Company records.

distributors with whom they had developed very strong relationships. We are now being charged with the responsibility of developing the program up from the local level. Managing headquarters has turned out to be only half the task.

The second conversation that came to mind was with John Whitney, a WESCO sales representative at a $30 million per year branch. Whitney was currently serving the local plant of a $5.4 million per year NA customer. Once the NA agreement was signed, the customer plant, which generated only $50,000 per year in sales and which was located two hours away from WESCO's branch, had demanded semi-monthly calls. Whitney described his situation bluntly:

> They may be a good customer for the company. But from my perspective, they and other NA customers demand a lot of service that is not commensurate with their sales volume—either current or potential. Unless compelled, I wouldn't call on NA customers in my region even without the long commute they usually require. The opportunity costs of serving these customers are way too high—both for me and for the branch. I would rather spend my time selling to other customers.

The third conversation that Piraino considered was with Larry Worthington, a WESCO branch manager whose branch had traditionally obtained a major portion of its sales from electrical contractors. In order to serve recently acquired NA customers, the branch had been forced to change the way it managed its business. Worthington was concerned: "We're investing an awful lot of resources to serve NA customers, and it's tempting our contractor customers to abandon us."

Piraino realized that he needed to develop a clear plan for the upcoming meeting with Haley.

> We must isolate the root cause of the NA program shortfall. If we are trying to market a new way of doing things that our customers don't really understand or appreciate, then it's time to make some hard decisions. Will it make more sense to promote this program proactively to our customers, or to be passive and offer the NA program only when customers show a legitimate interest? In addition, if the issue is one of improper implementation at our end, then we'd better get our act together very quickly, before we lose important customers.

THE ELECTRICAL EQUIPMENT AND SUPPLIES BUSINESS

Electrical equipment and supplies (EES) referred to any products needed for channeling and using electricity. (Exhibit 3 provides details of the different products that formed the EES market.) Most manufacturers of EES products had specialized product lines, but customers generally had to buy a range of products made by several manufacturers in order to manage their electrical needs. Like other EES distributors, WESCO represented many EES manufacturers and offered customers the convenience of one-stop access to all of their EES needs.

WESCO DISTRIBUTION, INC.

WESCO Distribution, Inc. was founded in 1922 as the distribution arm of Westinghouse. Following a period of disappointing performance in the early 1990s, the company was sold to the investment company of Clayton, Dubilier & Rice in February 1994, with Roy Haley taking over as CEO. Under Haley's leadership, the company had rebounded from an annual revenue run rate at purchase of $1.4 billion to become the third largest full-line wholesale EES distributor in the United States by 1996 with over $2.2 billion in sales globally (see Exhibit 4) of which U.S. sales were a little over $1.6 billion.

CUSTOMERS

WESCO had three types of customers: Electrical Contractors, Industrial Customers, and Commercial/ Institutional/Government (CIG) Institutions. (Exhibit 5 provides more details on the nature of WESCO's business in each of these customer segments.)

Electrical Contractors Electrical contractors installed lighting and electrical systems for construction projects and had been WESCO's primary customer base in the past. In 1996, the electrical contractor market was estimated at $17.9 billion and accounted for $465 million of WESCO's sales. This was commonly referred to as bid-and-quote business. Contractors obtained business by bidding for contracts. Very few contracts required a bill of materials that covered all parts of the EES system as shown in Exhibit 3. After winning a bid, contractors requested quotes from several EES distributors for the required bill of materials. Next, due to inflexible contracting timetables, the contractor short-listed those distributors that appeared capable of delivering all the materials on time. The contractor then generally negotiated with the short-listed distributors and placed the final order with the distributor who offered the lowest overall price.

Industrial Customers Industrial customers accounted for slightly more than $1 billion of WESCO's sales in 1996 and were expected to grow in importance. Industrial customers had an ongoing need for EES products in their Maintenance, Repair, and Operations (MRO) activities such as replacing a safety switch that did not work, repairing a worn out motor before it failed, and upgrading a lighting or drive system to make it more energy efficient and reduce costs. In order to facilitate their MRO activities, industrial customers maintained inventories of EES products. Under Haley's direction, WESCO was currently pursuing customers in several industry segments

EXHIBIT 3   THE EES MARKET

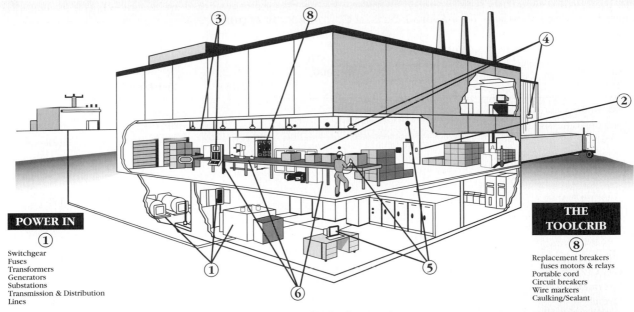

POWER IN
①
Switchgear
Fuses
Transformers
Generators
Substations
Transmission & Distribution
Lines

THE TOOLCRIB
⑧
Replacement breakers
  fuses motors & relays
Portable cord
Circuit breakers
Wire markers
Caulking/Sealant

CURRENT CARRIERS ②	**PROTECT & DIRECT** ③	**LIGHTING & LOADS MOTORS** ④	**COMPUTERS & COMMUNICATIONS** ⑤	**INDUSTRIAL CONTROL** ⑥	**TOOLS OF THE TRADE** ⑦
Compression & Mechanical Connectors	Rigid Hubs	Hi-Bay Lighting	Hubs	Timers	Lockout/Tagout Identification Products
Terminals	Liquidtight Cord Connectors	H.I.D. Fluorescent & Incandescent	Raceway & Struts	Programmable logic controllers	Electricians' Supplies
Wire & Cable	Cable Tray	Floods & Wall Packs	Voice and data cabling and related supplies	Motor controls	Tool boxes
Bus duct & related equipment	Cable Ties	Roadway Lighting & Parking Lot Lighting	Signaling Equipment	Motor control centers	Multimeters
Wiring Devices	Metal Framing	Hazardous Environment Lighting Fixtures	UPS systems	Variable-frequency drives	Cable-pulling lubricant
GFCI equipment	Enclosures	Motors	Surge suppressors	Relays	Electrical tape
	Explosion proof equipment	Industrial fans, heaters, and blowers	Bar coding equipment	Pushbuttons	Electricians' tools
	Engraved signaged for control stations	Lamps, ballast and lighting fixtures	Building management systems	Proximity sensors	
		Reflectors		Photo eyes	
		Occupancy sensors			
		Exit Lighting			
		Lighting Fixtures			

Source: Company records.

EXHIBIT 4   SELECTED FINANCIAL INFORMATION ($ MILLIONS)

	FISCAL YEAR ENDED DECEMBER 31		
	1994	**1995**	**1996**
Revenues	$1635.8	$1857.0	$2274.6
EBITDA	29.9	63.1	79.1
Operating Income	21.2	55.7	68.2
Sales Growth	4.1%	13.5%	22.5%
Operating Margin	1.3%	3.0%	3.0%
Pro Forma			
Net Working Capital	$196.5	$ 222.5	$ 291.6
Long-Term Debt	$180.6	$ 172.0	$ 260.6
Debt/Equity	1.7x	1.4x	1.7x
EBITDA/Total Interest	1.9x	4.0x	4.3x

Source: Company records.

Note: As of 12/31/96, total long-term debt was $260 million.
      As of 12/31/96, common equity was $158 million.

EXHIBIT 5   PRICE, COST, AND VALUE-ADDED INDICES BY CUSTOMER SEGMENT (FOR 1996)

CUSTOMER TYPE	SALES ($ MILLIONS)	FORECASTED ANNUAL GROWTH 1996 TO 2000 (%)	PRICE INDEX[a]	COST INDEX[b]	CUSTOMER VALUE INDEX[c]
INDUSTRIAL CUSTOMERS					
NA Customers	266	15–19			
Key NA Customers	180		90	80	120
Focus NA Customers	52		93	110	105
Other NA Customers	34		95	100	100
Other Industrial Customers	721	1–3	100	95	95
Industrial Contractors	465	2–4	93	105	105
CIG Customers	148	2–4	105	90	90
International	675	1–3	105	110	95
Overall	2,275		100	100	100

Source: Company records.

[a]*Price Index* refers to average prices obtained from customers in a specific customer segment. The weighted average price across all customer segments is 10 (the weights used being sales to a customer segment).

[b]*Cost Index* reflects WESCO's average costs to serve a customer segment. The weighted average cost across all customer segments is 100.

[c]*Customer Value Added by WESCO Index* is an indicator of the average differentiation created by WESCO compared to other EES distributors. An index value below 100 means that WESCO has below-average opportunity to add value to this customer segment. It does not mean that WESCO is at a disadvantage with respect to competition in its ability to differentiate itself from other competitors.

including utility, manufactured structures, pulp and paper, lumber, petrochemical, mining and metals, and transportation. (See Exhibit 6 for a breakdown of top industrial segments.) WESCO's NA program was designed to serve large, high-potential industrial customers.

Commercial, Industrial, and Government (CIG) Customers WESCO's CIG business was substantially smaller than the contractor and industrial businesses. In 1996, this market was estimated to be just over $5.9 billion, of which WESCO had a 2.5 percent share. Commercial customers such as hotels and motels, and institutional customers such as hospitals and universities were small, stable, and low-potential customers to WESCO. Government, on the other hand, was more concentrated in demand and was a source of very large orders.

MANAGING THE DIFFERENT CUSTOMER TYPES

Piraino perceived several difficulties in managing the various kinds of large customers:

The conflict lies in the different business styles across customer types. For instance, industrial customers require a steady flow of EES products and are therefore more likely to negotiate long-term contracts. They often demand a high level of service. Electrical contractors, on the other hand, have a project and they often define their relationship with us transaction by transaction. Because contractors usually win orders by offering low prices to their customers, they want us to give them the best possible quote every time, keeping our margins low. There is no guarantee of business here and we find it very tough to forecast sales accurately.

Such different businesses require different management approaches. Our sales reps need to be hunters when it comes to the contractor business. Every day, they need to find the contractor who has won a project bid, give a quote, negotiate a deal, and move on. The hunt for a new customer is always on. By contrast, in order to serve our industrial customers, our sales reps need to be farmers. They know exactly who the customer is, and once they have a contract it is usually for the long haul. The primary mode of interaction is to ensure satisfactory service and educate customers about new products and services that become available over time. Managing these customers is all about cultivating relationships and being a good materials manager. Traditionally, we served the contractor business. Many of our sales reps and branch managers have the hunter

EXHIBIT 6   WESCO'S MARKET SHARE OF THE INDUSTRIAL CUSTOMER MARKET SEGMENT

INDUSTRIAL TOP SEGMENTS	HIGH MARKET POTENTIAL ($ BILLION)	WESCO SHARE (1996)
Utility	3.4	8.5%
Manufactured Structures	0.6	35.9
Machinery	4.0	2.5
Electrical Equipment	2.5	3.7
Primary Metals	0.9	7.0
Mining	0.7	7.3
Petroleum & Chemicals	0.8	5.8
Transportation	0.4	10.8
Pulp & Paper/Lumber	0.5	7.5
Food	0.6	3.7
Instrumentation	0.5	1.9
Other MRO	1.8	3.0

Source: Company records.

mentality. It is not easy for them to become farmers, as they seek rewards in the constant pursuit of new opportunities.

SUPPLIERS

On the other side of the distribution equation, WESCO maintained strong ties with over 150 suppliers, the largest of which were Cutler-Hammer, Thomas & Betts, Philips, and Leviton. Piraino said:

There are several reasons why it makes sense for EES suppliers to go through distributors like us. First, most suppliers make only part of a customer's total EES requirements while customers prefer a one-stop solution. Second, the relatively small volume of business from each customer can make direct sales economically unfeasible for the EES supplier. Third, and most important, we add a lot of value to all stages of the sales process. We call this the WESCO selling story (see Exhibit 7).

COMPETITORS

WESCO had traditionally functioned in three competitive arenas: specialization, geography, and peer (see Exhibit 8). First, along with other full-line distributors, WESCO shared a market with both product specialists and retail generalists. Specialty distributors focused on small product niches such as alarms or lamps. Retail generalists, such as hardware stores and home centers, sold simpler products to homeowners and small contractors. They carried a broad range of supplies, though without the depth of full-line distributors.

Second, as a national chain, WESCO competed with regional chains and local distributors. Local distributors competed with individual WESCO branches for local business. Piraino pointed out, "although they lack our national size and the breadth and buying power that goes with it, these guys can often be formidable competitors. They have developed excellent, long-term relationships with major customers in their markets. Making inroads can be a daunting task."

WESCO also faced competition from regional chains. Piraino explained,

Although regional distributors are significantly smaller than us, their sales are more concentrated than ours in the regional markets in which they compete with us. Based on revenues, this usually makes them one of the top two distributors in their local markets.

Within its peer group, WESCO competed with several major national distributors, among which it placed third in sales volume in 1996 behind W. W. Grainger, a broad-line distributor of MRO products, and Graybar, the largest electrical/telecommunication products distributor. These competitors were pursuing similar customer management strategies to WESCO.

BRANCH OFFICE ORGANIZATION

WESCO was organized into 279 U.S. branches. Each branch maintained its own inventory, had its own P&L responsibility, and enjoyed substantial autonomy in its own territory, including the authority to prospect for customers. In 1997, one-third of WESCO's branches served customers in a specific industry. These branches carried inventory that was tailored to meet the needs of that specific customer segment, and it affected their ability to serve other customers in their region. WESCO had found that the disadvantages of these branches serving a narrower customer base were heavily outweighed by their ability to serve the chosen customers better

EXHIBIT 7   THE WESCO SELLING STORY

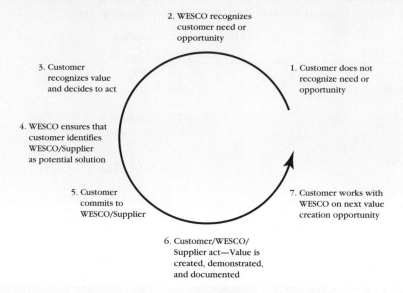

Source: Company records.

EXHIBIT 8   DISTRIBUTOR CHANNELS

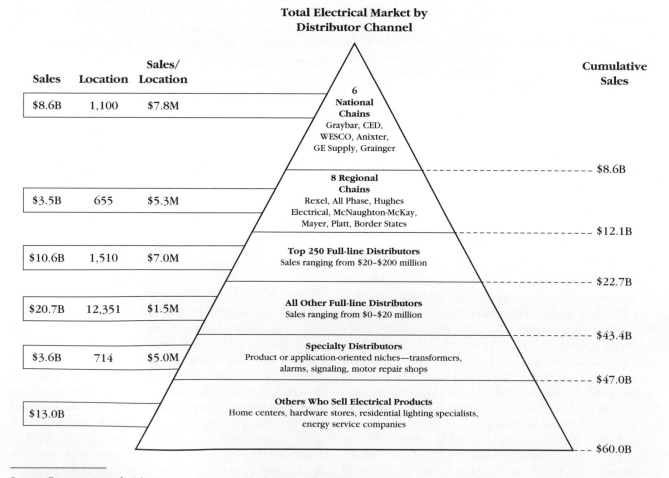

Source: Company records. Adapted from *Electrical Wholesaling*, June 1997.

than anybody else. Currently, WESCO had no plans to change the orientation of these branches. Amongst the other two-thirds of WESCO's branches, the typical WESCO branch had $9 million to $10 million in sales, with about 40 percent to industrial customers, 40 percent to contractors, and the balance to CIG customers. Direct cooperation between branches was limited because each branch operated in its own markets.

In addition to the branch manager, a typical WESCO branch had four outside sales reps, four inside sales reps, one warehouse specialist, one administrative officer who was also in charge of inventories, and one office manager who managed the branch's policies, procedures, training, and office maintenance. Outside sales reps served 20 to 40 customers with a total market potential of $10 to $30 million. These reps were responsible for visiting customers regularly, identifying new sales opportunities, and developing solutions together with customers. For each outside sales rep, there was a corresponding inside sales rep whose job was to process new orders, expedite existing orders, and provide all necessary service and support. Broadly, outside sales reps acquired customers, and inside sales reps ensured their retention. In the past, sales reps would shuttle between inside and outside sales positions before becoming a branch manager. This pattern had been fading recently, however, as each job required increasingly specialized skills. Currently, sales rep compensation had both a fixed salary component and a variable commission component. Commissions were the same regardless of whether sales were made to industrial customers, contractors, or CIG customers.

TRENDS IN THE EES INDUSTRY IN THE 1980s AND EARLY 1990s

During the late 1980s, the EES industry, like other component and supplies industries, had witnessed a dramatic change in the way many large customers dealt with suppliers and distributors. In order to bridge the quality gap with international competition and improve their overall competitive stance, American companies implemented stringent supplier/distributor quality programs while demanding price reductions as well. In the process of implementing these programs, customers pared their lists of suppliers/distributors, and signed long-term contracts with those that remained. These few suppliers/distributors felt compelled to make substantial investments in order to provide the higher level of service and quality now demanded.[1] At the same time, the growth of reengineering in organizations had encouraged customers to examine their procurement costs, i.e., the costs of placing and following orders, and monitoring and managing suppliers/distributors (see Exhibit 9). In order to improve supply chain efficiency, customers reduced inventory, which necessitated a Just-In-Time (JIT) procurement policy in which suppliers/distributors, carried inventory and provided components on an as-needed basis (see Exhibit 10).

---

[1]Not making such investments meant risking the sales volume provided by these large customers. More importantly, once an opportunity was missed, it could be several years before a distributor had another shot at doing business with that customer.

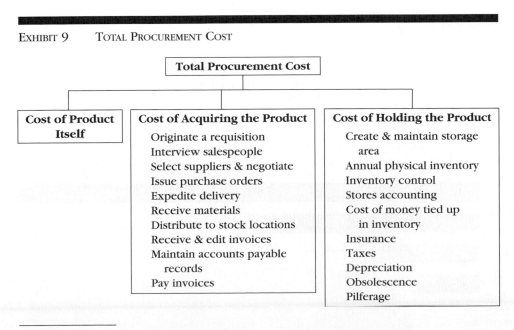

EXHIBIT 9   TOTAL PROCUREMENT COST

Total Procurement Cost

Cost of Product Itself

Cost of Acquiring the Product
Originate a requisition
Interview salespeople
Select suppliers & negotiate
Issue purchase orders
Expedite delivery
Receive materials
Distribute to stock locations
Receive & edit invoices
Maintain accounts payable records
Pay invoices

Cost of Holding the Product
Create & maintain storage area
Annual physical inventory
Inventory control
Stores accounting
Cost of money tied up in inventory
Insurance
Taxes
Depreciation
Obsolescence
Pilferage

Source: Company records.

EXHIBIT 10   VALUE-ADDED SERVICES

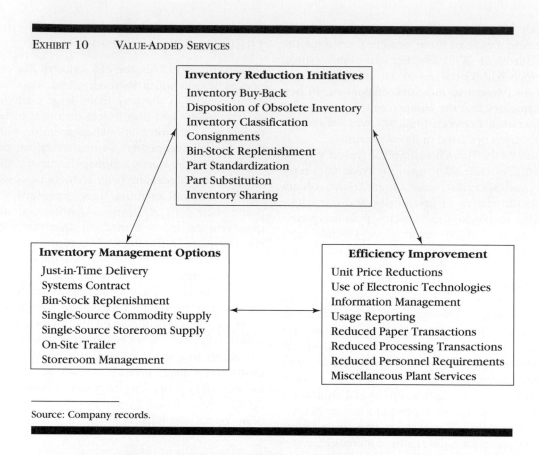

Inventory Reduction Initiatives

Inventory Buy-Back
Disposition of Obsolete Inventory
Inventory Classification
Consignments
Bin-Stock Replenishment
Part Standardization
Part Substitution
Inventory Sharing

Inventory Management Options

Just-in-Time Delivery
Systems Contract
Bin-Stock Replenishment
Single-Source Commodity Supply
Single-Source Storeroom Supply
On-Site Trailer
Storeroom Management

Efficiency Improvement

Unit Price Reductions
Use of Electronic Technologies
Information Management
Usage Reporting
Reduced Paper Transactions
Reduced Processing Transactions
Reduced Personnel Requirements
Miscellaneous Plant Services

Source: Company records.

EXHIBIT 11   THE RANGE OF CUSTOMER NEEDS ACROSS MARKET SEGMENTS

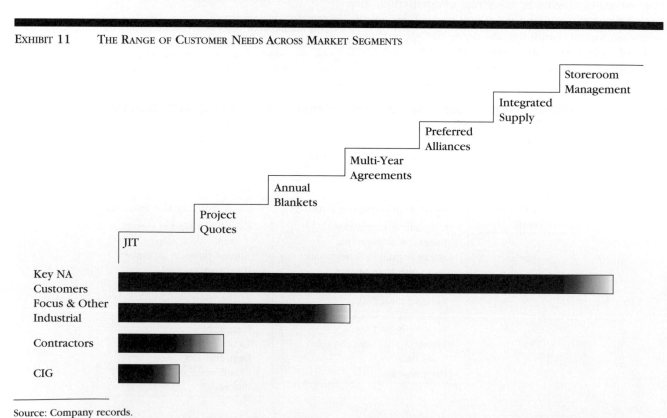

Source: Company records.

To make matters more complicated, the move toward long-term collaborative JIT contracts with a select few suppliers/distributors was not universal among customers. Piraino explained:

> Many of our industrial customers still prefer to do business the old way—simultaneously maintaining arms-length, bid-oriented relationships with multiple EES distributors. (See Exhibit 11 for the evolution of customer needs). Periodically, they send a "request for quotation" (RFQ) for all their requirements to several EES distributors, selecting the one with lowest overall prices. These customers do not appear to be interested in streaming procurement processes in collaboration with their EES distributors and are more resistant to change.

WESCO's NATIONAL ACCOUNT PROGRAM

WESCO's National Account (NA) program had been established under the premise that large contracts could mean significant savings for both customers and WESCO. In exchange for giving their EES business to WESCO, NA customers received competitive, year-long national pricing regardless of volume. In the early stages of the NA program, most contracts pertained to individual products. Art Hersberger, WESCO's Director of National Accounts, described:

> In years past, before the time of WESCO's new ownership, all of the major customer agreements were for single products. In fact, over 80 percent of these agreements were just for lamps. These agreements were essentially product driven and required minimal value-added services. We had hoped that customers who signed such agreements would buy their national EES needs from us exclusively, as per the contracts. What we learned was that customers treated these agreements as non-exclusive. Many even signed contracts for the same products with other national EES distributors.

By 1997, there were 300 customers in the NA program. Piraino classified these 300 customers by sales volume and commitment into three groups: key, focus, and others.

Key customers were the top fifty NA customers by sales volume. With each of these customers, WESCO had moved beyond a single-product, single-site relationship[2] and implemented some form of a multi-site agreement. In many instances, WESCO now also supplied multiple EES products at each of these sites, and some customers were even asking WESCO to supply non-EES products as well. "Sales to these 50 customers were a little over $180 million in 1996, giving us an average of a little less than $4

million per customer. In most of these cases, we can now supply about 60 percent to 90 percent of the customer's EES needs. While we count on these relationships as our successes, we still don't have total compliance from all of these customers," said Piraino. He continued:

> The story is very different with the next 250 NA customers. Our focus customers, comprising the 100 accounts below our key accounts, have yet to use us to fill a major portion of their needs. These customers give us an average of $500,000 annually. Despite pockets of compliance, most of these relationships are still single-product agreements and they are very often restricted to a single site.

The bottom half of the NA customers were like "hunting licenses," said Hersberger: "In return for getting a low price from us, these customers have given us permission to find opportunities to sell within their organizations. On average, these customers purchase less than $250,000 annually. They are typically the non-exclusive, product-only accounts, and we have a long way to go before we tap their full potential."

NAM SALES ORGANIZATION

In addition to the branch sales force, WESCO had 18 national account managers (NAMs) based across the country, with half reporting to the director of national accounts, Art Hersberger, and the other half reporting to Jim Piraino. Each of the 18 NAMs was responsible for a particular industrial segment, with a complement of 10 to 15 customers plus 15 to 20 prospects. NAMs were expected to call on prospective customers, lead the active selling and implementation processes with new NA customers, and maintain long-standing relationships with existing NA customers.

For current NA customers, NAMs were responsible for volume and profitability targets. They were expected to meet regularly with the customer's corporate purchasing staff, ensure compliance to the volumes agreed upon in the NA contract, build relationships with local plant personnel, and facilitate relationship building between WESCO's branch sales reps and the NA customer's local plant personnel. With each NA customer having anywhere from 5 to 20 sites all over the country, NAMs were not able to spend much time at the local level and focused more on the NA customer's corporate offices where the NA agreement was usually negotiated and monitored. Consequently, it was the branch sales reps' responsibility to build relationships at the local level.

Most of WESCO's NAMs had been successful branch managers prior to their current jobs. Since building a relationship with an NA customer could take a long time and demanded extensive technical skills, selecting a NAM was a very difficult and painstaking process. The need for industry expertise, a good understanding of

[2]An NA customer that purchased lamps at one plant exclusively from WESCO would be an example of a single-product, single-site relationship.

WESCO's business, and the ability to get the support of sales reps to build local relationships with NA customers made it very difficult to find suitable NAM candidates from the outside. Currently, only a couple of WESCO's NAMs had come from outside.

NAMs received commissions for all sales to their customers. At the same time, the branch sales rep assigned to the account also received commissions for sales to the NA customer's local plant or facilities within their territory. This double counting of sales credit ensured that branch office personnel did not see any threat from NAMs visiting their NA customers in the local area. In fact, NAMs were in great demand at the branches since sales reps saw this as an easy way to get sales.

Building NA Agreements

The process of building NA agreements involved several stages. During the initial prospecting stage, NAMs called on customers that had high-potential EES sales. They made presentations to the customer's corporate purchasing group on the total cost of ownership and how WESCO's national accounts program might enable companies to reduce procurement costs. Bill Lawry, a National Account Manager (NAM) explained:

> The average MRO order from an industrial customer ranges from $100 to $135. Each purchase order itself, however, can cost the customer $150 to generate and process. Even the very best purchasing agent can only get a price reduction of maybe three to five percent. If you're in charge, you want to get rid of the $150-a-shot purchase orders, not nickel and dime at the margin. Reducing these costs incurred in purchasing is a compelling proposition, but not every organization is prepared to make the sort of changes that our NA program requires. Many of our presentations are just to get our prospects thinking.

When a prospect expressed a strong interest in WESCO's proposals, the account could be moved into an active selling phase. During the usual six to nine months of this phase, the NAM made presentations to the purchasing staff and other executives in each plant, matched WESCO branches with potential customer branches, addressed customer concerns about staffing, inventory, emergency service, and so forth. This period of intensive selling could demand between 30 percent and 40 percent of a NAM's time.

When the selling effort succeeded, the signing of the NA contract initiated an even more intensive implementation phase, requiring half of the NAM's time for the first several months. The NAM became part of WESCO's national implementation team (NIT), which included the director of national accounts and national sales support services. As part of this team, the NAM worked with a counterpart in the customer's NIT. These two representatives traveled to each customer site, meeting with local implementation teams (LITs) to help implement NA di-

rectives and to work on any initial stumbling blocks. Hersberger explained: "A NAM might travel for 30 to 60 days with the customer counterpart after the contract is finalized. This allows them both to meet with all the branches as well as to iron out between them any major decisions that arise during the meetings. Within 90 days, if implementation succeeds, the NAM will have obtained from each branch a list of items to be sourced from WESCO, a detailed inventory management plan, and target areas for value-added services."

Once the major initiatives were implemented, the account moved into a maintenance or development mode. Maintaining a national account meant continuing to hold NIT meetings to resolve any difficulties that could not be solved on a local level, and presenting new cost saving initiatives. An average account in this mode required at least 15 percent of a NAM's time, with large customers demanding much greater time commitments. For instance, NAM Mark Houston estimated that he spent 75 percent of his time in 1996 maintaining two large key NA customers, one with $20 million and the other with $9 million in annual sales.

By the time the account reached maintenance level, WESCO could decrease its costs to serve these customers and sufficiently improve gross margins to over 20 percent, compared to contractor accounts, which earned from 11 to 18 percent. In addition, WESCO could offer its lowest prices to these customers; Piraino explained, "since we take part in planning procurement, we can obtain better prices ourselves and pass the savings along." If the process stalled at the implementation phase, however, WESCO had found that it could be stuck with high costs and low margins.

A Success Story

One NA program success story was WESCO's partnership with an industrial customer in the paper segment managed by NAM Walter Thigpen. This customer has undertaken extensive communication and training programs at all management levels as part of a cost management initiative, ensuring support for the supplier reduction effort and working at the senior management level from day one. Thigpen explained:

> Even though we had done relatively little business with this customer before, they asked us to compete for their EES business in 1995. During the selection process, we used questionnaires to develop details of programs they had proposed to reduce the customer's inventory and energy costs. We determined that we could currently serve all but three of their plants. In order to serve these three plants, we decided it would be best to purchase the current local distributors to two plants and to open a new branch near the third. Hersberger and I made presentations to the selection committee, and by the time we secured the account in June 1996, we had a good idea of what implementation would look like.

As soon as the agreement was signed, we formed NITs and held a national rollout meeting to begin implementation. During the next few months, we moved toward compliance at each customer plant, agreeing to hold monthly NIT meetings to address LIT concerns at various mill sites. As planned, we acquired two distributor branches and opened one new branch. We conducted a complete energy audit and recommended more energy efficient systems for all their plants. We also reduced inventory and implemented EDI procurement.[3] With the exception of a few small difficulties in setting up information systems, the process moved like clockwork. Everyone in their organization seemed to know exactly what to expect of the process and how to manage change.

By June 1997, the intensive implementation phase was over. Sales had increased tenfold from the year before, reaching $1 million per month (see Exhibit 12). Be-

[3]Electronic Data Interchange (EDI) was a standardized system for electronic purchasing and information exchange between companies.

tween transaction cost reductions, energy savings, and inventory reduction, WESCO was able to document over 20 percent cost savings to the customer, far more than expected (see Exhibit 13).

COMMON CHARACTERISTICS ACROSS SUCCESSFUL NA RELATIONSHIPS

Piraino summarized the results of a recently conducted in-depth analysis of all the key NA customers. He said:

Several pieces need to be in place to develop a successful relationship with an NA customer. First, we need to be in the sweet spot of our customer's procurement strategy. For most of our customers, over 70 percent of the annual procurement budget is accounted for by the top five to ten suppliers. It is with these suppliers/distributors that customers are usually interested in developing a relationship based on value more than price (see Exhibit 14 for the purchase profile of this customer). The purchase dollar volume and effort involved in these relationships makes customers willing to go beyond transaction prices and focus on the total cost of procurement and ownership. They are open to

EXHIBIT 12   A TYPICAL NATIONAL ACCOUNT DEVELOPMENT AND PROGRAM IMPLEMENTATION

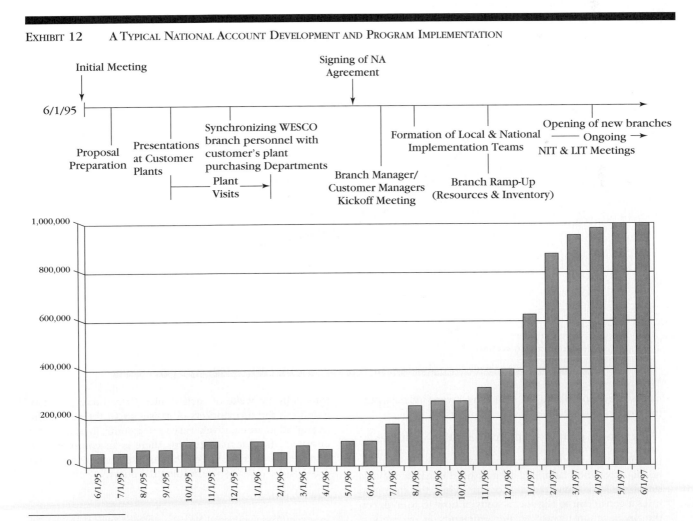

Source: Company records.

EXHIBIT 13   CUSTOMER COST SAVINGS BY CATEGORY FOR A SUCCESSFUL
               NA IMPLEMENTATION

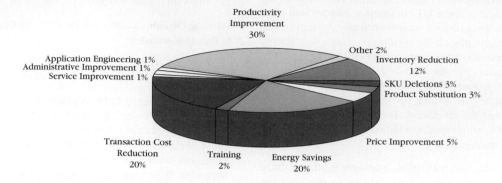

Source: Company records.

EXHIBIT 14   COMMODITY AND MRO PURCHASE PROFILE OF A HIGH-POTENTIAL
               NA CUSTOMER

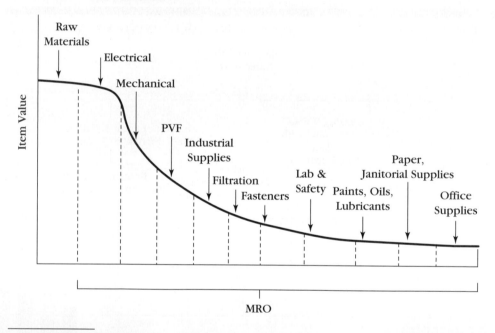

Source: Company records.

national-level proposals for managing inventory, maintaining storerooms, and coordinating supplies.

"That is only part of the picture," Piraino continued:

It is also important that top management at the customer's headquarters be committed to making this happen. Many times, we have found that this occurs when the customer hires a consultant to conduct a study of how to re-engineer the organization toward greater efficiency in operations, manufacturing, and service. Some of the most successful national accounts have begun with requests from cus-

tomers in the wake of such studies. Once there is a mandate from the top, pockets of resistance in the rest of the organization are relatively easy to overcome. Even among a customer's senior management, there is an enormous difference between a VP of Purchasing championing our cause and the CEO spearheading the effort.

Lawry added:

In several less successful NA relationships, unanticipated differences in procedures and purchases across customer sites have made implementation difficult. In some cases, a local plant's bill of materials has turned out to be very different from the list covered by the NA agreement. The local WESCO branch has ended up having to resolve all matters locally, often with no cooperation from the customer. In these cases, you can try as hard as you want, but it just won't make a difference. The customer's corporate staff accuses us of not working hard enough. Their local purchasing and materials management folks will not cooperate because they would need to make changes to their systems. Our people get caught in the middle, quickly losing interest in the face of implementation headaches, and small potential sales volumes. Even the NAM shifts focus to accounts that might be easier to manage. With no champion on either side, the NA agreement has almost no chance for recovery.

"Local ties can make all the difference," explained Piraino:

In all our success stories, our branch managers and field reps had existing relationships with the customer's local personnel, making local compliance relatively simple for both sides. It's funny the way it works. Our main weapon to fight local and regional EES distributors is to offer an NA customer the opportunity to standardize procurements and reduce costs. This is very attractive to the customer's corporate procurement staff. But this is not what the plant level purchasing staff want. Their power base has been built on managing their own suppliers and developing relationships that are good for the local plant. When you go into these accounts with an NA contract, unless they know you, their first reaction is to throw you out. The NA contract erodes their power and can affect their position. Who in their right mind would want that to happen?

THE NA CUSTOMER OF THE NEXT MILLENNIUM

INTEGRATED SUPPLY AND THE "NEW AGE OF PROCUREMENT"

As part of their effort to win sole-source agreements, WESCO had offered customers a set of value-added services such as inventory analysis and reduction programs. Although demanding and labor intensive for WESCO, these programs produced substantial savings to NA customers time and again, savings that justified the margins WESCO realized on sales to these customers.

Recently, however, the tables had turned and several of WESCO's key NA customers had demanded an increased service commitment. Bill Cenk, WESCO's Director of Integrated Supply, explained:

We have found that two to three years after establishing successful partnerships with their top 5 to 10 suppliers/distributors, NA customers typically reach a stage at which the cost of monitoring and managing these top suppliers/

distributors drops to 10–20 percent of their total procurement costs.[4] In effect, the top 10 supplier/distributors now account for over 70 percent of the customer's MRO purchase dollars, while demanding less than 20 percent of the customer's procurement costs.

The hundreds of other suppliers/distributors from whom these customers buy now account for just 30 percent of the customer's purchasing dollars yet over 80 percent of the procurement costs. These customers next try to reduce their costs of purchasing further by asking one of the top 5 to 10 supplier/distributors to manage and monitor the smaller supplier/distributors. In effect, these customers are creating "supplier tiers" (see Exhibit 15). Suppliers in the highest level of the hierarchy are referred to as "primary" or "first tier" suppliers/distributors. They make money by marking up the products and services provided by "second tier" suppliers/distributors. The customer does not mind paying a higher price because the price increase is more than offset by the decrease in procurement costs.

As early as 1994, soon after he arrived, Haley had anticipated these trends in outsourcing and had been preaching this approach internally as well as to WESCO's major customers. In fact, one of the main reasons why Haley had developed WESCO's National Account program was to develop a path for the organization to become capable of offering these integrated solutions (IS) systems to customers.

Cenk added:

Right now, when NA customers and prospects ask us to take business that is different from our traditional activities, the decision to do it or not is made in Pittsburgh. We have a detailed process to analyze costs and potential benefits from the relationship. First, using publicly available information on product prices and discount structures,[5] we estimate the revenue stream from this additional business. Next, based on past experience, we estimate how much it will cost us to serve the customer. If the products/services involved are things that we have never handled before, then for a reference or benchmark, we look for existing products/services in our portfolio that are closest to the new ones. We also take into account the availability of the concerned NAM's time. Overall, here in Pittsburgh, I think we do a pretty good job of estimating revenues and costs involved in each of these situations.

Yet, to many in our company, this is still an ad hoc process. For example, in the last six months, we have been asked to shovel snow for one customer, manage janitorial supplies for another, and manage the industrial gases requirements for a third. This is not to say that it is wrong in principle to do these types of things. If the margins are good, then it makes sense. Especially under Haley's definition of integrated supply, it is something that we shouldn't

---

[4]Procurement costs are the costs of placing orders and monitoring and managing suppliers/distributors. These are different from costs of the products and services themselves.

[5]In many consumables and supplies industries, third party organizations published product specifications, pricing information, volume discounts, and special terms from various manufacturers. This information was publicly available and easy to use. For example, in the EES business, the *NEMA Publications and Materials Catalog* published by the National Electrical Manufacturers Association served as an industry reference book.

EXHIBIT 15   DIFFERENT MRO PROCUREMENT MODELS

Single-Source Commodity Supply

Some customers are reducing their supply base to one distributor per product category . . .

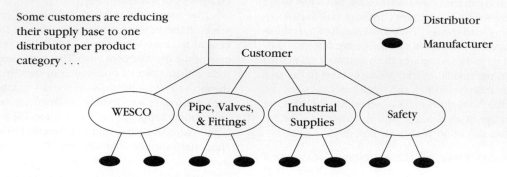

Multi-Source Commodity Supply

Some customers elect to use one or more integrators to reduce their supply base even further . . .

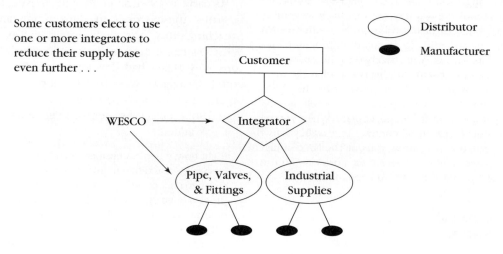

Alliances & Consortiums

Some customers are choosing to contract with an alliance of noncompeting distributors . . .

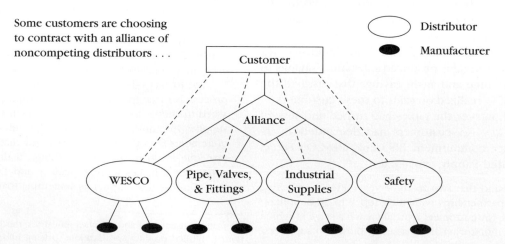

Source: Company records.

shy away from. We add value to a customer's MRO procurement process and that's the bottom line. The issue is whether we should standardize on what we want to do when each customer comes to us with a unique set of needs. We need to have some quick answers here since every major player in the EES business has now started talking about managing their customer needs with an IS philosophy.

Another area of concern for Cenk was another new trend amongst large NA customers:

A few NA customers have taken a cost reduction route that is a little bit different from tiering. These customers are talking about forming alliances and consortia of non-competing distributors (see Exhibit 15). They want groups of MRO suppliers and distributors to partner and offer the customer a one-stop solution (see Exhibit 16 for a profile of the MRO purchases of this customer type). They expect us to share warehousing facilities with other distributors, create common billing formats, develop integrated product/service solutions, and so forth.

The question that we face here is how to plan for these customer migration paths. Without the benefit of tiering-related profits, each player will have to invest in learning about the others' businesses and integrating logistics functions and systems. What if each customer comes up with a dif-

ferent set of suppliers and distributors for their alliance? Developing these systems can be prohibitively expensive unless we can replicate the process across customers. Yet, if WESCO tries to establish itself as the leader of its own alliance, offering customers solutions before they ask, then we risk losing their confidence if they disapprove of our partners. We also risk taking on new forms of competition, since we will have to compete with competitors of our alliance partners.

Jim Piraino had also recently become concerned that integrated supply solutions were putting WESCO in a position to compete with some of its traditional customer base of electrical contractors. Donald Mitchell, a WESCO branch manager, saw this happening in the process of branch-level implementation:

In our NA program, we have been telling our industrial customers that we can add significant value by auditing their electrical systems and suggesting ways in which they could improve the quality and efficiency of these systems. These customers now want us to apply the same skills to new projects. So, if we want their MRO business, we also need to get involved in the specification and installation of new systems—the electrical contractor's traditional business. In these situations, the electrical contractor could now see us as a competitor and could decide to stop buying their EES needs from us.

EXHIBIT 16   COMMODITY AND MRO PURCHASE PROFILE OF A CONSORTIUM CUSTOMER

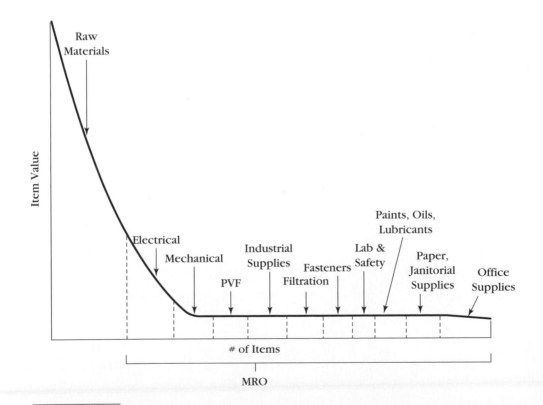

Source: Company records.

Going Ahead: What Should WESCO Do?

Piraino had to find answers to several questions. With a budget of $12 million in 1998, the decision of whether or not to continue the NA program was a non-trivial one. Piraino said: "If we decide to drop the program, most of the $12 million goes straight to the bottom line. I need to make a strong case if we are to proceed." Was this the right time to scale back the NA program? Should WESCO take a proactive stance in developing NA customers, or should it simply react to explicit customer demand? If the decision was to be proactive, how should WESCO define its approach? What should the firm do about supplier/distributor tiering and supplier/distributor alliances? How should they manage the demands of their traditional customer base during this period of change?

Being proactive, said Piraino, could require substantial investments:

Seeking out new national accounts is wasteful unless we know how to optimize our existing NA relationships. Strong individual partnerships have brought us to where we are and they may even be able to keep us going for some more time. Do we now need a better approach to managing our current NA customers? Do we need a better model to anticipate customers' needs? Can we manage the migration path of an NA customer? How will this help us make reasoned decisions about what services we really want to provide our NA customers while recognizing that every customer is different? How should we plan to handle the new trends in NA customer behavior? Do we need to reorganize our company's structure?

The reactive model had the advantage of attracting only those customers interested enough to seek out WESCO's services on their own. Piraino's only concern here was that WESCO could start losing potential key customers very quickly. There were cases already where this had happened.

We are already in a second tier relationship with one of our best customers who used to purchase substantial levels of EES products from us. This customer should have been one of our "key" national accounts. Although we used to deal directly with the customer, during the last twelve months, the picture has changed. Now, we sell to Smith Industries, a distributor of power transmissions, who in turn sells our product to this customer after marking up our prices. We have lost touch with this customer.

Professor Das Narayandas prepared this case with the assistance of Research Associate Sara Frug as the basis for class discussion rather than to illustrate either effective or ineffective handling of an administrative situation.

SALESOFT, INC. (A)

In September 1995, Gregory Miller, the president and CEO of SaleSoft was faced with the question of whether or not to introduce a Trojan Horse[1] product. Trojan Horse (TH) could potentially distract SaleSoft from its primary objective of becoming a leader in the high end of the Sales Automation (SA) software industry. In addition, there was a risk that it would cannibalize sales from the PROCEED product that SaleSoft was currently marketing. Finally, TH could potentially prevent SaleSoft from forming relationships with consultants whose support was critical to the success of PROCEED. Yet TH might offer an easy way for SaleSoft to get into new customer accounts, gain quick sales, and generate much needed revenues.

Greg Miller had founded SaleSoft in June 1993 with the objective of marketing PROCEED, a Comprehensive Sales Automation System (CSAS). In the past 18 months PROCEED had received very favorable responses from prospects. However, converting interest to actual sales was taking a long time. With limited funds and the need to show performance before seeking additional venture capital, Miller and Bill Tanner, executive vice president and CFO, had to decide whether to continue trying to sell PROCEED to select customers, or to make an all-out effort to launch TH to a much larger customer base.

Further, the best place to launch TH would be the Sales Automation Conference in December that was expected to attract more than half the prospective customers for SA products. To have a demonstrable version of TH for the conference, SaleSoft would have to devote all its efforts in the next few months to TH.

---

[1]The term 'Trojan Horse' refers to an object or action used to gain easy entry into areas that might otherwise be difficult to access. The Trojan War is the subject of Homer's *Iliad* and is thought to reflect a real siege of Troy by the Greeks in 1200 B.C. The fall of Troy is recounted in Virgil's *Aeneid:* according to Virgil, the Trojans, having held out against the Greeks for 10 years, were tricked into hauling inside their city walls a large wooden horse (the so-called Trojan Horse) left as a gift for the Trojans by the Greeks. The belly of the wooden horse was full of Greek soldiers who, once inside the walls, opened the city gates at night and thus let in their compatriots to sack Troy.

THE SALES AUTOMATION INDUSTRY

Sales Automation (SA) could be broadly defined as any system that automated some or all processes used in the sales order cycle from lead generation to post-sales service. This included marketing functions such as telemarketing, direct mail, and other modes of direct communication with the customer; sales functions such as account management, team selling and sales force management; and customer service functions such as complaint tracking, service reports, and repurchase details. International Data Corporation, a respected market research organization, estimated the 1995 SA market at around $1 billion, and expected it to grow at over 40 percent annually over the next five years.

The rapid growth in SA was due to significant changes in three areas. The first was the dramatic drop in laptop computer prices with enhanced processing speed, increased storage capacity, color displays, and light weight. The second was the introduction and continuous enhancement of powerful and user-friendly software, including operating systems such as Microsoft Windows, groupware such as Lotus Notes, that allowed for easy sharing of information, and networking software such as Novell's Netware for easy information transfer. The last was developments in communication technology that allowed remote laptop computers to link with central databases.

The potential U.S. market included over 9.2 million salespeople. The Gartner Group, a leading authority in SA, estimated current SA penetration at 2.4 million or 26 percent of the market. There were over 300 vendors that offered solutions addressing one or two SA areas. Most of them were small niche firms that had annual sales less than $5 million. Only a couple of vendors, such as Sales Technologies with sales over $50 million and Brock Control Systems with $25 million, were considered big players. These firms had been well established in the mainframe environment. However, the major shift from mainframes to PC-based client/server systems had recently forced these firms into the PC world where most SA action was now concentrated.

There were no integrated solutions currently available that addressed the complete automation of any customer. One industry expert stated,

You cannot buy everything in an integrated fashion from one vendor. Although the industry is moving in that direction, it will be a long time before that's possible. So the customer will be forced to act as her own integrator and force different vendors to work together to provide a customized solution. (*Datamation*—May 1, 1995.)

One reason for this was a general belief that there was no standardized approach to the sales order cycle:

People in sales are not willing to realize that the way they sell is similar to the way someone else sells, so we are not seeing the development of cross-industry SA applications. (*Datamation*—May 1, 1995.)

The time to sell and install a typical SA project took anywhere from 22 to 30 months. The extended time frame of implementation, high level of customization, and the rapid change in technology stretched the resources of small SA vendors and affected their ability to stay competitive and survive. In fact, seven out of ten SA vendors were forced out of business by three years after start-up. This high failure rate had led to a great deal of skepticism amongst potential customers.

Types of SA solutions

There were a variety of SA solutions available in the market ranging from simple Contact Management Systems (CMS) at the low end to Comprehensive Sales Automation Systems (CSAS) at the high end.

Over 80 percent of all SA efforts in the early 1990s were projects where the salespeople had been equipped with simple contact management software. Contact managers or Call Reporting systems allowed the user to maintain, access, and update details of the contact person (customer) in a database that resided in the salesperson's laptop computer. Typically, salespeople maintained customer names, telephone numbers, addresses, and personal details.

It was common to find salespeople within a firm using the same CMS in radically different ways. This restricted the usefulness of CMS. As one CEO put it:

The bottom line of our SA initiative is that we provided our salespeople with an electronic card file costing $3,500 instead of a $100 paper organizer . . .

Most *Fortune* 1000 firms had initiated their SA effort by equipping their salespeople with CMS. Several hundred SA vendors offered proprietary versions of contact managers that did not allow for integration with other databases or software. The most popular CMS was ACT, sold by Symantec Corporation. Unlike most CMS vendors, Symantec was a large PC software company that offered a suite of productivity software for enterprise-level corporate computing and had over 1,500 employees worldwide. ACT had an installed base of close to 1 million users and cost from $200 to $500 per user.

With an emphasis on providing individual products that performed one function in the sales and marketing process, CMSs lacked integration across all marketing, sales, and service functions. This severely limited the scope of CMS projects and reduced their bottom-line impact. As one vice president (Management Information Systems) put it,

Neither did the CMS help management leverage the market information to which our sales people are privy, nor did it help our sales reps and sales managers improve their management of the sales process/order cycle . . .

A New Wave in Sales Automation

As an answer to inherent limitations in CMS, and in response to growing customer needs, several firms had announced development of Comprehensive Sales Automation System (CSAS) solutions that took a process view to automating the sales order cycle. These solutions were expected to (1) provide sales, marketing, and service personnel with a suite of integrated tools to enable them to communicate better and to perform their jobs more efficiently and effectively; and (2) provide management with back-end decision support systems to enable them to manage marketing, sales, and service resources more proactively. Overall, the main objective was to increase productivity by improving efficiency and effectiveness, and reducing order cycle time. (See Exhibit 1 for more details.)

CSAS solutions were expected to provide greater value where there was greater variance and uncertainty in the sales order cycle. Tanner said,

We do not see the next generation of SA products being used in all situations. They are not useful in simple selling situations. Our ideal customer profile would face pressures to predict revenues correctly all the time, have a dispersed sales force with a team selling approach—perhaps, multi-level or even cross-functional, and have made significant investments in their salesforce.

This narrowed the focus for CSAS solutions to industries that involved large-ticket items with long, complex sales order cycles and/or that involved consultative team selling. The complexity of CSAS made it easier to implement in industries with computer-literate sales force. Exhibit 2 gives more details on the market potential for SA. Larger firms in most of these industries had installed CMSs like ACT with varying degrees of success in the first phase of their SA effort. Their salespeople were known to "swear by" and "swear at" CMS.

In June 1994, there were no integrated CSAS products available. Towards the end of 1994, several vendors announced their intent to develop and sell such systems. Some had even established beta[2] test sites by

---

[2] It was a common practice to install early software versions at a few select customer sites for test. These were referred to as "beta" test sites.

EXHIBIT 1   BENEFITS OF CSAS

EFFICIENCY BENEFITS

- Effective and timely distribution of sales leads and marketing literature to the field.
- Increased customer contacts and face-to-face selling time.
- Improved visibility to identify salesperson's weaknesses and developmental opportunities.
  More effective management by exception via sales process metrics for each rep, district, region, and for the entire company, including:
    - Overall average sales cycle.
    - Average number of days in each segment of the sales process.
    - Yield by each segment of the sales process.
    - Win/loss rates.
- Lower salesperson turnover and retraining costs.
- Decreased paperwork and reporting (administrative) time.
- Improved account planning and customer service.
- Increased communication.

EFFECTIVENESS BENEFITS

- Improved accuracy of forecasting.
- Complete visibility into the buying cycle for each customer.
- Immediate insight into all customer activity for entire sales team and management.
- Improved timeliness and visibility of order cycle status and ability to effect closure.
- Shorter nonproductive time for new hires.
- More effective sales management, training, and reinforcement of sales methodology.
- Timeliness of correspondence, quotations, and proposals with fewer mistakes.
- Easier territory maintenance.
- Better and timely competitive information updates.

ORDER CYCLE BENEFITS

- Reduced order cycle times because of greater efficiency and effectiveness.

Source: Company product literature.

early 1995. By mid-95, more than a third of the vendors had dropped out. Exhibit 3 provides more detail on firms currently in the market with preliminary CSAS solutions.

A TYPICAL CSAS BUYING CYCLE

The inefficiencies within and across most current sales, marketing, and service systems affected all levels from the CEO right down to the salesperson. Trying to undertake a selling effort that involved educating a potential customer at all levels on the benefits of a CSAS system was beyond the resources of most SA vendors (see Exhibit 4 for some of the important issues raised by the affected constituencies). It was easier for SA vendors to pursue prospects that had already decided to implement a CSAS solution.

A typical customer buying cycle involved several steps. First, was the realization by senior management that CSAS might solve some of the existing sales, marketing, and service problems. Having reached this stage, it could take a customer another twenty-one to thirty months to implement CSAS.

It was rare for firms to automate all processes at the same time. Thus, the second step in the buying cycle was to evaluate the potential to automate existing processes and to specify the order of functions to be automated. Customers were usually not equipped to do this in-house. It was common for SA consultants to help them. SA consultants typically specialized in implementing SA in one or a few vertical industry markets like healthcare, pharmaceuticals, etc. Their deep understanding of the industry and their skills and experience made them the best option for this step, which took three to four months.

In the third step, the customer decided how the different functions to be automated were related, and determined how data was to be collected, stored, and analyzed. This again was usually done by SA consultants with the support of the customer's information systems department, and usually took two to three months to complete.

The customer decided the type of SA software and hardware to be purchased, at this point, the fourth step. Here again, the customer relied heavily on the

EXHIBIT 2   MARKET POTENTIAL FOR CSAS

INDUSTRY	TOTAL # OF FIRMS WITH 50+ SALES REPS	ESTIMATED NUMBER OF EMPLOYEES	ESTIMATED NUMBER OF SALES REPS
SOFTWARE INDUSTRY			
Computers; Periph. Equip; Software	46	68,642	6,864
Computer Programming Services	49	67,241	6,724
Prepackaged Software	54	116,095	11,610
Aggregate Total	149	251,978	25,198
COMPUTERS, OFFICE EQUIPMENT			
Aggregate Total	137	1,211,601	121,160
COMMERCIAL BANKING			
National Commercial Banks	1,097	1,954,088	1,074,748
State Commercial Banks	1,299	781,603	429,882
Other Banks	44	34,583	19,021
Aggregate Total	2,440	2,770,274	1,523,651
DIVERSIFIED SERVICE COMPANIES			
Computer Programming, Data Processing, Other Computer-Related Services.	113	427,393	21,370
Accounting, Auditing, Bookkeeping	19	218,998	10,950
Management Consulting Services	66	314,224	15,711
Aggregate Total	198	960,615	48,031
ELECTRONICS, ELECTRICAL EQUIPMENT			
Aggregate Total	479	2,043,614	143,053
SCIENTIFIC, PHOTO, & CONTROL EQUIP.			
Aggregate Total	263	1,309,515	78,571
DIVERSIFIED FINANCIAL COMPANIES			
Aggregate Total	547	891,611	276,399
LIFE INSURANCE COMPANIES			
Aggregate Total	370	1,049,653	293,903

Note: SIC stands for Standard Industry Classification.

consultant. Short listing[3] and selecting vendors typically took six to eight months. Even at this late stage in the buying cycle, it was not uncommon for CSAS vendors to face concerns about SA at all levels of the customer organization (see Exhibit 5 for a list of concerns and benefits sought).

[3]Detailed evaluation of all available products was a very expensive and time-consuming process. Therefore, based on preliminary analysis, business customers with the consultant's help would identify a few select vendors that were likely to meet their specific needs. This reduced set of vendors was called a "short list." In the next stage, extensive comparative analysis across vendors in the short list was done prior to selecting a vendor for the project.

After choosing the vendor, the fifth step was to pilot test the CSAS after customizing it to meet the customer's specific needs. It usually took three to five months to implement this step.

The sixth step was to modify the CSAS software in response to feedback from the pilot test, which took three to four months. Full-scale roll-out, the final step, typically took another four to six months.

RECENT TRENDS IN PARTNERING IN THE SALES AUTOMATION INDUSTRY

Recently, several CSAS vendors had announced partnerships with SA consultants. Partnering with consultants helped a CSAS vendor in two ways. First, it allowed the CSAS vendor to access the consultant's customers while

EXHIBIT 3 LIST OF CSAS COMPETITORS

COMPANY/ LOCATION	SALESOFT, COLUMBUS, OH	ACTION SYSTEMS, GOLDEN, COLO.	SALESBOOK SYSTEMS, PITTFORD, NY	SALES TECHNOLOGIES, ATLANTA	SARATOGA SYSTEMS, CAMPBELL, CA	PENULTIMATE, IRVINE, CA
Product	PROCEED	Heatseeker	SalesBook	SNAP for Windows	SPS (Windows version)	SalesForce
Client/user base	5/500	7/1,700	5/3,000	27/1,500	80/3,200	15/1,600
1993 Estimated/ 1994 Projected Revenues	$0/$0.3 million	?/$8.5 million	?/$5 million	$50/$50 million	$5/$10 million	$0/$3.5 million
Average Price 200 Users	$480,000	$250,000	$250,000	$400,000	$250,000	$260,000
Process- or data-driven application	Process	Process	Data; optional process module avail 6/94	Process	Data	Process
Primary system focus (account or opportunity mgmt.)	Opportunity and Account	Accounts	Accounts	Accounts	Accounts	Opportunity
Customization	Vendor-customized, client-customized (PowerBuilder source code is provided) or third parties (e.g., Affiliates) can customize.	Vendor-customized	Vendor-customized, or clients can add pieces using Visual Basic PowerBuilder, etc.	Proprietary. Configurator tool for client customization, or vendor customized.	Proprietary. Saratoga Tools for client customization, or vendor-customized.	Proprietary tool for client customization, or vendor-customized.
Back-end System	Novell, Windows NT, OS/2, Unix	SQL Server, Windows NT, or any ODBC compliant database server	Back-end implementation available through mix of base product and customization	Unix, OS/2, Novell via NLMs	MVS, DOS, Windows under DOS, SCO Unix, OS/2, AIX	Windows NT (OS/2 and Novell available via NLMs)
Remote Communications Strategy	MAPI, VIM, (Microsoft Mail, CC Mail), Xcellenet	Remote LAN connectivity software (e.g., Microsoft's RAS, DCAs Remote LAN Node	Any network gateway product as a default, or any specialty product like Xcellenet or Intel	Xcellenet for OS/2 back end, proprietary for Unix back end, or standard E-mail packages	Proprietary or left to client's selection	Xcellenet; Microsoft's RAS for NT users; IBM's LAN Distance for OS/2 users

Source: Company records.

Exhibit 4   Typical Issues Raised by Decision-Making Unit as Regards to Order Cycle and Possible Solutions

Who?	Issue	Possible Solution
Entire Organization	It is impossible to keep track and schedule everyone's time. If a meeting requires several people, we have to schedule it way into the future. If the meeting topic cannot wait, we end up making decisions without everyone's input.	Group calendar. Time management.
CEO	Sales, Marketing, and Service have their customer information systems. None of them have a complete understanding of what is occurring in the account.	Sales, Marketing and Service activities are integrated into one database. This system shows every activity that has occurred with the account in the same format.
CEO	My manufacturing cycle is greater than the customer backlog. Therefore, manufacturing tries to anticipate customer product demand and they always forecast wrong. We end up with too much of some products and not enough of the products we need to meet demand.	Detailed product forecast with trend analysis and confidence indicators.
CEO	I cannot tell if sales are doing their job.	Sales management gives anyone the visibility to see everything that is going on in the sales cycle.
CEO	Channel conflict is hurting my profits. When we do not effectively communicate amongst channels, we usually end up giving the customer two prices. In effect, we lose face with the account even if we win the business.	Give your channel the same system. Allow salespeople in the channels to have visibility to each other's activities.
CEO/CFO	Sales and marketing cannot identify their constraints with the demand and sales cycle. Therefore, resources are being allocated to perform the wrong activities.	Order cycle management.
VP Sales	We are not sure if the sales reps are using a sales process.	Sales and Marketing method/process steps.
VP Sales	When a salesperson leaves us, it takes a year before we can effectively manage the territory again. This ends up costing us a lot money in training and lost revenue during the start-up period.	Develop a database that has a complete history of event by account and opportunity. This in combination with the marketing encyclopedia system will get new reps up to speed faster.
VP Sales	We do not have a means to understand our wins or losses. Therefore, we cannot learn from either.	Record the wins and losses for each opportunity. Use the information gained to enhance the appropriate areas of the system.
VP Sales	The sales cycle is getting longer and longer and we are not sure why. This forces us to make decisions to close business that is not in our best interest.	Measure each step in the sales cycle. Understand early on if the opportunity is taking too long or if the step is not being responsive.
VP Sales/ Sales Managers	We are not sure the reps are taking the right step to move the account through the pipeline.	Process and activity review by opportunity.
VP Sales/ Sales Managers	Forecasting and call reports are the only way I can see what activities are taking place in the field. These items consume too much time away from selling.	These items are a by-product of the salesperson using the system to do time management.
VP Sales/ Sales Managers	It takes us too long to acknowledge the receipt of an order from a customer. The customer thinks we are being unresponsive.	Print a copy of the order acknowledgment for the customers to sign before you leave their offices.
VP Sales/ Sales Managers	Sales reps must come in to the office to get access to the information to do their jobs.	Provide them with a store and forward remote client server platform. This platform allows the rep to do business anytime, anywhere.

Who?	Issue	Possible Solution
VP Marketing	Telemarketing sends leads to the salesperson and never hears anything about them again.	Give the telemarketers visibility into the sales cycle. This allows them to understand status without getting the rep involved.
VP Marketing	Sales reps do not know which accounts are in their territories. They end up wasting resources on opportunities that belong to a different channel.	Populate the local databases of all the accounts in each territory. This provides the ability to perform account, contact, and territory management in one system.
VP Marketing	Competitor information is out of date before it can be distributed.	Marketing Encyclopedia System.
VP Marketing	We cannot measure the effectiveness of our marketing dollars or the messages they send. We know we are wasting resources, but where? and why?	Keep track of each campaign, response rates, costs. Record this information by account. Allow the user to review before and after pipeline status.
Sales Reps	We spend too much time verifying and chasing down expense reports and commission checks.	Provide status of these items on their local database.
Sales Reps	Every year the company raises my quota, which forces me to do more to keep my compensation the same. We need the ability to manage more opportunities at one time.	Give the salespeople tools that allow them to manage more tasks. Address their administrative needs.

Exhibit 5   Typical Concerns Regarding CSAS Solutions

Who?	Typical Concerns	Benefits Sought
CEO, CFO	■ Are the costs justified? ■ Who else is using it? Give us a reference list. ■ What's the guarantee that you will be around after a few years? ■ Can you prove that it will work in our selling environment?	■ SG & A cost reductions. ■ Process control and improvement. ■ Sustainable competitive advantage. ■ Reduced sales force turnover. ■ Reduced sales cycle. ■ Increase in opportunities addressed.
VP MIS	■ Is the system compatible with our existing systems? ■ Can you customize reports to our formats? ■ Who is going to maintain the system? ■ What is the guarantee that the system will work? ■ How do you know that our salespeople will use the system the right way? ■ Can you guarantee that sales will give us all the information required?	■ Integrated with our other systems to allow for bi-directional information transfer. ■ Transportable to the new hardware computing environments that we plan to buy in the future. ■ Minimal increase in load on MIS department to support these systems.
VP Sales and Sales Managers	■ Will my reps use it? ■ Will my salespeople use all the functions? ■ Will they spend all their time playing with it rather than using it properly? ■ Will my salespeople censor information that they need to report?	■ Improved visibility of opportunities. ■ Better forecasts. ■ Better sales management. ■ Improved work habits of salespeople. ■ Improved coaching tools through exception reporting. ■ Reduction in paperwork.
Sales Reps	■ Will this lead to management trying to keep an eye on everything I do? ■ Is this extra work? ■ If I give away information about my customers, then the firm will not need me anymore. ■ What is in it for me? ■ I do not need to be told how I should handle my customers. ■ I like working on my own and I do not like intrusion into my privacy. ■ As long as I deliver results, why should they care?	■ More freedom through better and more efficient forecasting, call reporting, and account reviews. ■ Better information flow on team accounts, new leads. ■ Better and prompt customer service. ■ Ability to identify areas/skills that need to be developed.

Source: Company records.

potentially locking out other CSAS vendors. Second, it took care of training issues.[4] It was common for consultants to either have in-house training skills or long standing partnerships with specialized training firms. The main drawback of partnering was that it could potentially alienate the CSAS vendor from other consultants

and their customers. This was amplified by the fact that consultants expected the CSAS to be customized to proprietary specifications.

Currently, SaleSoft did not have any partnerships with any consultant. In preliminary discussions with Miller, several consultants had indicated that they needed to see a complete CSAS solution before they would even think about partnering.

---

[4]Training was a critical factor in CSAS vendor evaluation given product complexity and minimal prior user experience. In addition to using the CSAS system, users also had to be educated on using laptops, linking to central databases to transfer information, printing reports, and using application software such as word processors, spreadsheets, and electronic mail. Customers expected CSAS vendors either to have in-house training skills (which was usually not the case) or to partner with firms that specialized in training.

THE PROCEED SMRP® (SALES AND MARKETING RESOURCE PLANNING) SYSTEM

SaleSoft's CSAS product, called PROCEED SMRP®, allowed customers to automate their entire marketing, sales, and customer service operations. PROCEED had eight modules:

SALES SYSTEM	MARKETING SYSTEM	SERVICES SYSTEM
■ Field Sales	■ Campaign Management	■ Incident Tracking
■ Opportunity Management	■ Marketing Encyclopedia	■ Relationship Management
■ Sales Management	■ Literature Fulfillment	

Currently, only the three modules in PROCEED's Sales System were ready. Miller estimated that it would cost a million dollars to develop and roll-out the remaining five over the next eight months.

Sales System The PROCEED Sales System consisted of three modules.

The *Field Sales* module recorded and displayed on an easy-to-use scheduling system all customer information, personal appointments, meetings, and "To Do" activities. It was designed to minimize keyboard and mouse entry to make it easier for salespeople to use. It also created a common database using information input from each salesperson that allowed the entire sales team to view the availability, allocation, and coordination of resources throughout the organization. The data collected in this module was the only input into the Opportunity Management and Sales Management modules reducing the "paperwork" burden on salespeople, an activity they generally despised.

The *Opportunity Management* module organized the flow of each prospective sale into pipeline segments. Each segment contained a user defined set of sales activities involving the sales person and/or other sales team members. When all activities in a segment were completed, an opportunity was automatically moved to the next pipeline segment. Exhibit 6 gives one example of an opportunity pipeline. Used in conjunction with the Field Sales module, it allowed each sales-

person to constantly view her sales opportunities and the progress made toward closure.

The *Sales Management* module continuously updated and consolidated information by opportunity and provided up-to-date pipeline status on all opportunities. It also included a decision support and executive information system that allowed management to plan efficient resource deployment.

Marketing System The three modules in this system automated and integrated all the marketing processes within a firm.

The Campaign Management module automated telemarketing, direct mail, and advertising campaigns. It provided an effective and efficient means for rapidly transferring qualified leads to field sales. It also provided management with data for evaluating the cost/benefit of each campaign, including "what if" campaign analysis.

The *Marketing Encyclopedia* module was a central repository for maintaining and updating all product information, pricing schedules, new product launch announcements, press releases, and other marketing material. This ensured consistency and timely availability of all marketing and sales support information.

The *Literature Fulfillment* module automated the identification, accumulation, and distribution of literature requests from all sources—within the organization, customers, and prospects. It also tracked the usage and inventory of marketing resources.

EXHIBIT 6   OPPORTUNITY PIPELINE MANAGEMENT IN THE PROCEED SALES SYSTEM

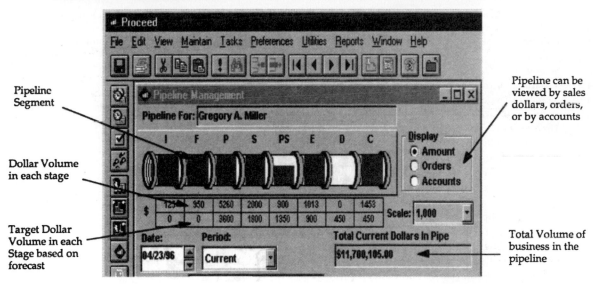

Note: This pipeline is for Gregory Miller as of 23rd April 1996 for the current quarter. The pipeline has 8 segments labeled I, F, P, S, PS, E, D, and C respectively. Currently, Miller has opportunities worth $125,000 in the first segment (labeled I) against a target of $0. Similarly, he has opportunities worth $900,000 in segment PS against a forecast of $1.35 million.

For each opportunity, its current status in the pipeline, all associated current activities, and the probability of converting this opportunity into a sale can be input into PROCEED. For the example shown below, the opportunity is currently in pipeline segment E and has a 50 percent chance of being converted into a sale.

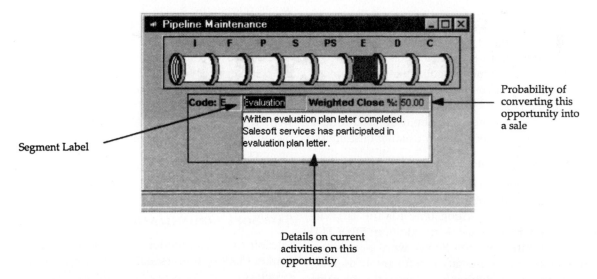

The number of pipeline segments, the name/label of each segment, and the probability of closing the sale can be specified based on user requirements.

EXHIBIT 7   PROFILE OF TWO PROSPECTS FOR PROCEED

		COMPANY A	COMPANY B
1	Industry	Financial Services	Computer Hardware
2	Annual sales	$120 million	$350 million
3	Selling costs (% of revenues)	30%	35%
4	Variable component of sales expense (e.g., commissions)	10%	4%
5	Number of sales reps	120	250
6	Annual rep turnover (%)	20%	35%
7	Time for new reps to become productive	60 days	90 days
8	Number of PROCEED users	250	600
9	PROCEED license fee	$600,000	$1,440,000
10	Implementation and training costs in the first year	$180,000	$430,000
11	Annual software support and maintenance (% of license fee)	20%	20%
12	Hardware costs	$1,500,000	$3,600,000
13	Project start-up costs	$200,000	$450,000
14	Annual cost of internal resources	$150,000	$350,000
15	Current selling cycle	120 days	180 days
16	Estimated reduction in sales cycle using PROCEED	6 days	15 days
17	Estimated reduction in start-up time for a new sales-person using PROCEED	14 days	20 days
18	Estimated % reduction in rep turnover using PROCEED	10%	15%

Source: Company records.

Note: Costs and benefits were estimated by the customer in each case.

Service System The customer service system was made up of two modules.

The *Incident Tracking* module captured all customer service issues and tracked them through to ultimate resolution. By maintaining information online, it provided management with continuous feedback from customers.

The *Relationship Management* module provided a repository for all customer contacts, activities, commitments, and correspondence that could be used to generate new sales opportunities from existing customers.

PROCEED SYSTEM DESIGN

PROCEED was developed to run on Microsoft Windows, an industry standard operating system. This was expected to shorten the learning time for the large installed base of Windows users. In addition, PROCEED was integrated with common E-mail, word processing, fax, spreadsheet, and presentation software. It used advanced software technologies that allowed the sales person to use the complete functionality of the system unattached to the host system. The sales person could, at any time, connect to the host to transfer data to and from a central corporate database.

CURRENT PROCEED SALES

To date, SaleSoft had sold the three existing modules of PROCEED to five customers in the computer software industry and had an installed base of just under 300 users. SaleSoft had committed to these customers that it would release the remaining modules on a staged basis by June 1996.

SaleSoft was also pursuing sales opportunities with over 20 prospects in computer software and hardware, financial services, and banking. The number of users varied from 200 to 600 per prospect. Exhibit 7 gives more details on two of them. In each case, the customer wanted to see the total PROCEED product before making any purchase commitments. Barring any delays in product development, Miller felt at least a quarter of the current prospects would buy PROCEED over the next 12 to 15 months.

SALESOFT ORGANIZATION

SaleSoft Inc. was founded in July 1993, to develop and market CSAS systems (see Exhibit 8 for the organization structure).

Greg Miller, the president and CEO of SaleSoft, had spent over 12 years in the application software industry including positions in sales and marketing, product development, services, and general management. Before founding SaleSoft, Miller was president of Symix Computer Systems, Inc., a $30 million public company that developed and marketed manufacturing software. Prior to Symix, Miller was vice president of Sales and Marketing and the third employee at a software company that

EXHIBIT 8   ORGANIZATION CHART

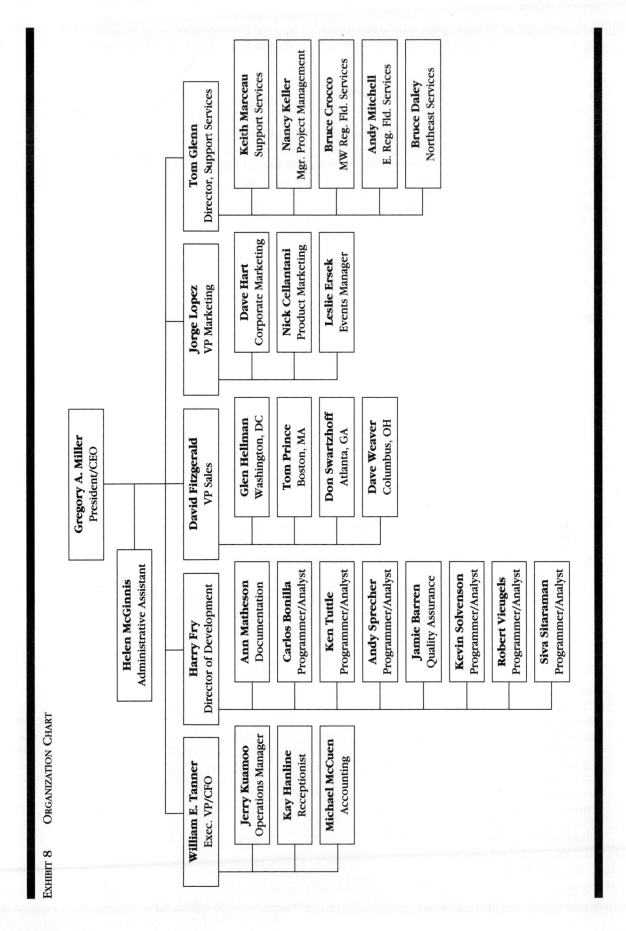

developed and marketed one of the first integrated Manufacturing Resource Planning (MRP) systems. His experience in automating manufacturing environments convinced Miller that there was a tremendous opportunity for a solution that integrated a firm's sales, marketing, and service functions.

We were able to bring order to chaos in manufacturing and provide customers with huge savings by reducing wasted effort. I am sure that PROCEED will prove as effective as MRP packages that I have sold in the past.

Very few firms have any control over customer management processes. They are held hostage by their salespeople. By using CSAS, our customers will be able to drive out inefficiencies in their sales, marketing, and service cycles, and reduce their SG&A costs.

The benefits are so great that customers will be eager to adopt these systems at the earliest. If you thought MRP systems led to a revolution in manufacturing, wait till you see what CSAS will do to selling, marketing, and service.

William Tanner, the executive vice president and CFO, had over 14 years of work experience in finance and management of technology based businesses. Tanner's experience and contacts had been instrumental in SaleSoft's ability to get venture capital funding.

THE FINANCIAL SITUATION

By 1994, Miller and Tanner and a few other promoters had invested just over $800,000 in equity. This was supplemented in early 1995 with $2 million of venture capital. To support the firm's expenses through 1997, Miller and Tanner felt they would need to raise another $2 million in early 1996 (see Table A for a summary of projected revenues and market share for SaleSoft).

TABLE A   SUMMARY OF REVENUES AND MARKET SHARE FOR SALESOFT

YEAR	REVENUE ('000 $)	NET INCOME ('000 $)	TOTAL MARKET (MILLION $)	SALESOFT'S MARKET SHARE
1993	0	(104)	600	0%
1994	305	(658)	780	0.1
1995[a]	2,000	(1,328)	1014	0.2
1996[a]	6,750	(413)	1318	0.5
1997[a]	15,000	1,395	1713	0.9
1998[a]	30,000	3,197	2227	1.3

[a]Projected.

EXHIBIT 9   STATEMENT OF OPERATIONS

	1993	1994	1995[a]	1996[a]	1997[a]	1998[a]
REVENUES:						
License Fees	0	203	1,659	4,813	10,500	21,000
Services	0	102	350	1,937	4,500	9,000
Total Revenues	0	305	2,009	6,750	15,000	30,000
EXPENSES:						
Cost of License Fees	0	0	143	546	1,155	2,310
Cost of Services	0	0	377	1,146	2,700	5,400
Sales & Marketing	3	192	1,527	3,524	5,700	10,500
Product Development	90	384	516	1,007	2,100	4,200
Interest Expense	2	4	0	0	0	0
General & Admin. Exp.	8	288	774	940	1,950	3,000
Total Expenses	103	868	3,337	7,163	13,605	25,410
Income Before Taxes	-103	-658	-1,328	-413	1,395	4,590
Provision for Income Taxes	0	0	0	0	0	-1,393
Net Income (Loss)	-103	-658	-1,328	-413	1,395	3,197

Source: Company records.

[a]Projected.

Exhibits 9 and 10 give more details of the financial projections for SaleSoft. As of September 1995, expenses were running at projected levels. Year-to-date revenues, however, were a little over half a million dollars.

THE TROJAN HORSE OPPORTUNITY

On several occasions, salespeople had told Miller that a large number of prospects, who were not ready for PROCEED, were desperately looking for a system to manage their sales forecasting process. These firms were involved in long, complex selling cycles that made it difficult to forecast revenues and affected overall operations including revenue planning, inventory management, capital equipment budgeting, and human resource development. As sales VP put it:

> Our selling cycle is long and uncertain. Most of the time, until the order is in, I have no idea of what is going to happen and when it is going to happen. There are many cases when a sure-shot lead was left unanswered because the salesperson was chasing a low-probability opportunity. There are other times when the salesperson did not push

the customer along to the next stage in the buying cycle. This delayed the order and sent our forecast right out the window. Right now, it takes my team months to gather the data and by the time I get the information, it is too late to do anything.

I hate to go to management meetings with no clue of what is going to happen, when it's going to happen, and worst of all, why it did not happen. I want reports that will give me up-to-date status on every lead generated in the past 18 months. That will reduce my high blood pressure dramatically.

In my ideal world, my people can log onto their systems every morning and look at a plan for the day, week, month, quarter, and year. This would include the status of each opportunity, and what they need to do to close each sale. If we have this information available online, then we should be able to improve our selling effectiveness, reduce our selling time cycle by 2 to 3 percent, and impact our bottom line significantly.

I know I need more than a CMS. I also know that I do not need CSAS. I am not going to try to convince marketing and service about integrating their functions with sales. Give me a solution that will help *me* manage the sales pipeline better.

EXHIBIT 10   BALANCE SHEET

	1993	1994	1995[a]	1996[a]	1997[a]	1998[a]
CURRENT ASSETS:						
Cash	171	146	330	1,300	281	365
Accounts Receivable	0	50	750	2,118	4,726	9,452
Other Current	8	7	10	40	121	242
Total Current Assets	179	203	1,090	3,458	5,128	10,059
Equipment & Improvements:		6	169	381	1,206	2,856
Less Accumulated Deprn	0	0	−43	−145	−386	−957
Net Equip. & Improvements	0	6	126	236	820	1,899
Capitalized Software, Net	0	0	0	0	0	0
Other Assets	1	9	9	16	122	182
Total Assets	180	218	1,225	3,710	6,070	12,140
CURRENT LIABILITIES:						
Acts Payable & Accr. Expenses	5	25	254	481	1,379	2,645
Income Taxes Payable	0	0	0	0	0	557
Customer Deposits	0	0	80	302	300	600
Deferred Revenue	0	17	193	681	750	1,500
Total Current Liabilities	5	42	527	1,464	2,429	5,302
Debt	180	110	0	0	0	0
Stockholder Equity:						
Common Stock & Paid-In Capital	99	829	2,789	4,749	4,749	4,749
Retained Earnings	−103	−763	−2,091	−2,503	−1,108	2,089
Total Stockholder Equity	−4	66	698	2,246	3,641	6,838
Total Liabilities & Equity	180	218	1,225	3,710	6,070	12,140

Source: Company records.

[a]Projected.

Miller knew that some of the functions currently available in the three modules of PROCEED's Sales System could serve as the basic building block to develop a product that provided answers for the Sales VP's problems. Tanner called this the Trojan Horse. Miller added:

> Over the last couple months, we did try to push the current Sales System modules of PROCEED to various prospects. The response from these sales VPs was very discouraging. None of the prospects that saw the current product were even remotely serious about buying the product as it is today. They all said they needed a lot more functionalities than what we have right now. Frankly, I agree that PROCEED's sales system needs substantial work before it can be sold as a stand-alone Trojan Horse (TH) product.
>
> Unfortunately for us, when developing the sales system modules, we never thought they would be sold as stand-alone products. A lot of functions that the prospects want to see in TH are ones that we had planned to build into the other two systems of PROCEED. In order to add these functions and interfaces, we have to put in substantial effort in software design and development. Without this additional work, we do not have an adequate solution that will interest sales VPs.
>
> I wish we had known right in the beginning that we needed to develop TH. By now, for the same costs that we have already incurred in developing the three sales system modules of PROCEED, we would have developed TH as well. But what's the point in crying over lost chances. We need to look ahead and make some decisions now. The most important question facing us is whether or not we should develop the TH product.
>
> If done right, using information provided by the salespeople for all their accounts, TH will allow a sales manager to review expected close dates of all opportunities and the probability of closing them on time. The sales manager can anticipate any shortfall in sales and set up early and timely intervention programs to manage the gaps in performance. Further, by archiving data over time, a sales manager will be able to track and review previous wins and losses, associated sales activity, and competitive behavior to improve sales force performance.

Selling Cycle for TH versus PROCEED

Selling TH was different from PROCEED in several ways. First, unlike PROCEED, TH was focused only on sales. This significantly reduced the number of people involved in the buying cycle. Second, it was easier to quantify the benefits of TH. This simplified the selling process for TH. Miller estimated that selling TH would take a third of the time to sell PROCEED. Finally, TH needed minimal customization. This included changing the number and names of segments in the opportunity pipeline and could be done at a fraction of the cost of customizing PROCEED.

Tanner believed that selling TH would be more like selling CMS. "We can go after this market by ourselves. We do not have to partner with SA consultants or other firms. Further, with low customization costs, we can afford to go after a much broader market than our current approach for PROCEED," he said.

The Decision

Miller and Tanner had to decide whether or not to go ahead with the launch of TH. Miller thought,

> PROCEED and TH will be targeted to different markets. Customers that are convinced about implementing CSAS are not going to be interested in looking at only TH.

Another issue that concerned Miller was the sales force.

> We do not have the resources to have separate sales forces for the two products. At the same time, I fear that if we ask our people to sell both, most of them will land up pushing TH rather than PROCEED. It gets worse if the customers of TH are unlikely to consider PROCEED in the long run.
>
> Pricing TH low to get entry into an account does not make sense. I do not think we will ever sell the whole system once we launch TH. If we decide to launch TH, we need to price it high. In addition, if the customers are really excited about TH, then they will be willing to pay almost any price for it.
>
> PROCEED is priced at $2,400 per user and I think we should charge at least $1,000 per user for TH. At that price, we will extract a substantial part of the value of TH to a customer.

Tanner, on the other hand, felt that they should use TH to open customers' doors. He preferred a low price approach for the TH.

> Setting a high price for TH will make it difficult to sell and will demand a lot more customer education effort on our part. It will put off potential customers who recently have spent a lot of money on hardware and software.
>
> TH should be priced at the same level as CMS. That is the reference customers will use to evaluate TH. A price of $400 is about right. At this price, our sales force will have to just go out and pick up orders. There is nothing more important to us today than orders in the book.
>
> I also believe that once we get into an account, it will just be a matter of time before we sell PROCEED. I realize we might not have PROCEED ready if we go ahead with TH. I do not think we will lose our first-mover advantage if we were to pull out of the CSAS market for a couple of years.
>
> In fact, if we do well with TH, then we should have the resources to get back to PROCEED after a few years. That will be the right time to convert TH users to PROCEED.

Miller responded:

> I agree there is a crying need for TH. However, I do not share Tanner's feeling that customers will line up to buy TH. Further, I do not agree with his thought that we will not relinquish the CSAS market to others by temporarily pulling out of it.
>
> And then there is the issue of costs. I estimate that developing and fine-tuning TH will take the entire develop-

ment team three months and cost about $200,000. This does not include marketing costs that could be very high.

Educating customers about TH will demand a broad-based marketing strategy that could cost us half a million dollars over the next six to eight months. Once we create

general awareness for TH, I estimate marketing costs per TH user will be a third that of PROCEED.

THE CHANGING COMPETITIVE ENVIRONMENT

Recently, several things had changed at the low end of SA. Giants like Microsoft[5] and Lotus[6] had announced major strategic thrusts into this area. In addition, CMS vendors had announced their intent to upgrade existing CMS capabilities to allow users to hook onto networks, share information, and manage sales opportunities. This would make the TH market extremely tough and competitive very quickly.

Staying on course and trying to sell PROCEED had its advantages. This market was less crowded with all CSAS vendors being small start-ups. And this was not expected to change very soon.

---

[5] The maker of DOS and Windows operating system software and other application software such as Word, a word processor, and Excel, a spreadsheet software.

[6] The maker of Lotus 1-2-3 spreadsheet software and Notes groupware.

Professor Das Narayandas prepared this case with the assistance of Professor Benson P. Shapiro as the basis for class discussion rather than to illustrate either effective or ineffective handling of an administrative situation.

CASE 16

ARROW ELECTRONICS, INC.

INTRODUCTION

In the spring of 1997, Jan Salsgiver, president of the Arrow/Schweber (A/S) group, a subsidiary of Arrow Electronics, reviewed the Express parts Internet Distribution Service proposal with her colleagues Skip Streber, senior vice president for sales at A/S, and Steve Kaufman, CEO of Arrow (see Exhibit 1). Express had developed an Internet-based trading system that would allow distributors to post inventories and prices on a bulletin board that customers could access to compare prices and place orders. By including distributors like A/S, Express planned to use the Internet to offer customers large and small an opportunity to shop for prices.

Express offered A/S an opportunity to sell to new customers and gain quick sales. Yet it also could potentially affect Arrow's relationship with its current customers. It was quite possible that A/S's current customers would switch to buying part of their needs from Express rather than from A/S. In the process, Arrow's customers would be able to cherry pick products from different channels at the best possible prices. In addition, Express could also affect Arrow's relationship with its suppliers. It was possible that if A/S's suppliers saw Express as a legitimate option, they could decide to go directly to Express and dis-intermediate[1] Arrow from their distribution channel.

"As a distributor, amongst others, we need to know three things: how we create value for our customers for the prices we charge, how this value is different from what our suppliers can provide to our customers, and whether firms like Express can offer the same value or more for lower prices," commented Salsgiver. She continued, "We have a successful business model that is based on a portfolio of products and services that we

---

[1]Dis-intermediation refers to the removal of a channel member (or intermediary) from a distribution channel.

Copyright © 1998 by the President and Fellows of Harvard College. To order copies or request permission to reproduce materials, call 1-800-545-7685 or write Harvard Business School Publishing, Boston, MA 02163. No part of this publication may be reproduced, stored in a retrieval system, used in a spreadsheet, or transmitted in any form or by any means—electronic, mechanical, photocopying, recording, or otherwise—without the permission of Harvard Business School.

EXHIBIT 1   ORGANIZATION CHART

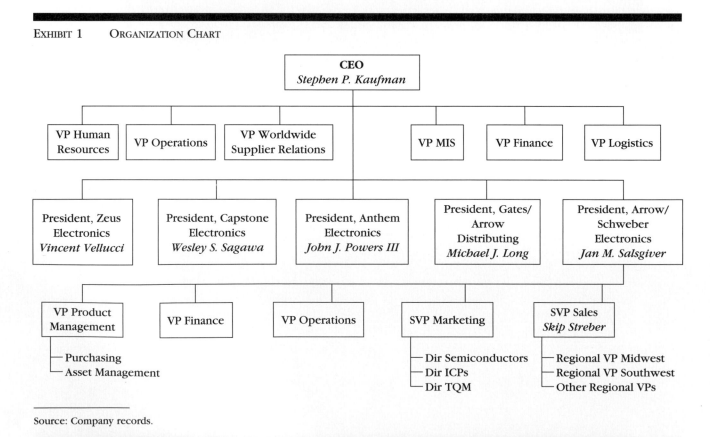

Source: Company records.

offer our customers. Our customers come back to us because they get most value from us for the prices they pay. If Express is going to change this equation, then we need to adapt our business model to accommodate the changes."

Salsgiver realized that she needed answers to several questions before she could decide on the Express proposal: How many of A/S's customers were likely to switch some of their purchases to Express? How would this affect A/S's sales and profitability? How would A/S's suppliers react to Express? And overall, was Express a threat or an opportunity to A/S?

THE ELECTRONICS INDUSTRY

In the six decades between Arrow's beginnings and the latter 1990s, the electronics industry evolved rapidly, incorporating numerous technological advances as they were developed. The advent of the transistor in 1947 signaled the beginning of a transition toward computers as a central product focus, with developments such as the integrated circuit in the late 1950s and the microprocessor in the early 1970s driving the change. Practical applications followed increasingly quickly upon the heels of technological advances, leading to a climate of planned obsolescence.

It was common for semiconductor and electronic component manufacturers like Intel and Motorola (hereafter referred to as suppliers) to deal directly with large original equipment manufacturers (OEMs). Suppliers franchised small numbers of distributors to manage sales to customers that they could not serve directly, whether because of diminutive size or voluminous service requirements. Between 65 percent and 75 percent of suppliers' sales were made directly by suppliers to their largest 200 customers. The remaining 25 percent to 35 percent of sales went through the distribution channels.

During the 1980s and early 1990s, as chip technologies developed and inventory became more rapidly obsolete, inaccuracies in demand estimation were increasingly exaggerated. Compounding this problem were a series of economic downturns during these years. Although by the mid-1990s the U.S. economy had improved, the industry was still characterized by volatility. Between August 1994 and February 1996, supplier shortages made it nearly impossible to live up to delivery commitments. Kaufman remembered: "Lead time stretched to 30–48 weeks—nearly every commodity was in short supply. However, this problem did not last very long. In February 1996, the situation reversed and the bottom dropped out of the memory market, producing vast oversupplies. Declines in dollar volume of sales across the board resulted from and in turn exacerbated excess inventory." Distributors suffered the effects of what one trade magazine called "a year best forgotten" in the semiconductor industry, during which Intel was the only top-five semiconductor manufacturer to increase sales, reflecting the precipitous drop in memory prices.

ARROW ELECTRONICS

Arrow Electronics was a broad-line distributor of electronics parts, including semiconductors and passive components. Founded in 1935 to sell radio equipment, the company had undergone a number of major changes in its history. In 1968, three Harvard Business School graduates teamed up and acquired a controlling interest in the company, which they grew to a number-two position by 1980, largely through acquisitions. The latest management era had begun in the aftermath of a hotel fire in December 1980 that claimed the lives of five of the company's top six officers and eight other Arrow executives. During a shaky regrouping period coinciding with an overall economic recession, Stephen Kaufman became President in 1982 and the CEO in 1986. Under Kaufman's leadership, however, Arrow had reached the number-one position among electronics distributors by 1992.

Also by 1997, consolidation throughout the distribution world had allowed a small number of large companies to capture the top tier of the market. Arrow's closest competitor was Avnet Inc., which trailed it by over 20 percent in sales in 1996, though it had grown by 14 percent as opposed to Arrow's 10 percent during that year. The largest of the next group of competitors was only one quarter the size of Arrow in total sales volume, earning less than Arrow's largest operating group. This competition included foreign entrants Rabb Karcher and Future Electronics as well as longtime rivals Pioneer-Standard, Wyle, and Marshall Industries. In 1996, Arrow had performed solidly in a less than solid market, reaching over $6.5 billion in sales. (See Exhibit 2 for financial information.) In the comparatively more stable first half of 1997, Arrow saw an increase in sales compared to the first two quarters of 1996, but a decrease in net income.

Headquartered in Melville, NY, Arrow's North American operations were managed by a corporate marketing and purchasing group, finance and accounting, credit, human resources, MIS, operations, and senior management (see Exhibit 1). Sales and marketing functions were divided among five distinct operating groups, each of which had its own P&L responsibility and maintained its own asset management and materials management. These operating groups were distinguished according to product and strategy concerns. Three groups, Arrow/Schweber, Anthem Electronics, and Zeus Electronics sold semiconductors, differing in customer base. Zeus sold to military and aerospace customers, while Anthem

EXHIBIT 2   CONSOLIDATED STATEMENT OF INCOME (IN THOUSANDS EXCEPT PER SHARE DATA)

FOR THE YEAR	1996	1995	1994
Sales	$6,534,577	$5,919,420	$4,649,234
Costs and expenses			
Cost of products sold	5,492,556	5,919,420	4,649,234
Selling, general, and administrative expenses	604,412	574,166	487,982
Depreciation and amortization	36,982	33,299	27,759
Integration charges			45,350
	6,133,950	5,496,211	4,393,260
Operating income	400,627	423,209	255,974
Equity in earnings (loss) of affiliated company	(97)	2,493	
Interest expense, net	37,959	46,361	36,168
Earnings before income taxes and minority interest	362,571	379,341	219,806
Provision for income taxes	144,667	153,139	91,206
Earnings before minority interest	217,904	226,202	128,600
Minority interest	15,195	23,658	16,711
Net income	$ 202,709	$ 202,544	$ 111,889
Per common share			
Primary	$ 3.95	$ 4.21	$ 2.40
Fully diluted	3.95	4.03	2.31
Average number of common shares and common share equivalents outstanding			
Primary	51,380	48,081	46,634
Fully diluted	51,380	51,123	50,407

Source: Company records.

and A/S sold to industrial customers. Using product-driven strategies on the other hand, Gates/Arrow Distributing sold mostly computer systems, peripherals, and software, while Capstone Electronics sold passive components.

ARROW/SCHWEBER

Arrow/Schweber was the largest of Arrow's working groups, with sales of $2.07 billion in 1996. A/S president Jan Salsgiver had assumed the helm in 1995 and worked at headquarters with the sales and marketing VPs as well as VPs in charge of demand creation, value-added services, and account development. As president of A/S, Salsgiver had been leading the operating group toward higher levels of technological expertise through technical certification for its field sales representatives and dedicated investments to enhance product management.

A/S's local operations were serviced through a branch structure. Each branch was headed by a General Manager and included Field Sales Representatives, Inside Sales Representatives, Product Managers, and Field Application Engineers. In addition, branches maintained administrative personnel, plus one or two other managers depending upon branch size. Six Regional VPs oversaw A/S's 39 branch managers.

PRODUCTS AND SUPPLIERS

The Arrow/Schweber line card (i.e., the set of products for which A/S was a franchised distributor) consisted of two categories of chips: standardized and proprietary. Standardized products were interchangeable chips produced by multiple suppliers. Proprietary products, on the other hand, were manufactured by only a single supplier. Only a franchised distributor could sell a supplier's standardized or proprietary products.

In an industry in which the top 10 suppliers provided 80 percent of the products on distributors' line cards, the A/S supplier list was long, including 56 suppliers in the spring of 1997 and increasing continually.

One of A/S's largest suppliers was Altera, a manufacturer of proprietary programmable logic devices (PLDs) that required a lot of value-added programming before a customer could use the product. As was typical in the industry, this manufacturer did virtually no programming themselves. Roughly 20 percent of Altera's products were purchased directly by customers who had in-house programming skills. Altera sold the remaining 80 percent of their products through two franchised distributors. Each of these distributors had built capabilities to provide all the value-added programming required by each customer.

Intel, a semiconductor manufacturer, was another large supplier for A/S. Like Altera, Intel supplied mostly proprietary products, though its most popular line, the x86 chip, did not demand the sort of value-added support and programming or engineering that A/S provided for Altera's PLDs.

Texas Instruments and Motorola, the other two of A/S's "big four," balanced the line card by selling a 75/25 mix of standardized and proprietary products.

CUSTOMERS

Mid- and small-sized Original Equipment Manufacturers (OEMs) were A/S's traditional customer base and accounted for 56 percent of A/S's sales in 1996. Unlike large OEMs that purchased directly from suppliers, these OEMs often purchased through distributors because they were simply too small for the supplier to serve directly. However, suppliers still wanted to serve these customers, so they appointed franchised distributors to consolidate demand from the smaller OEMs. Suppliers allowed limited return privileges and price protection to these franchised distributors.

Franchised distributors offered customers the opportunity to order in small quantities and with short lead times,[2] a facility that suppliers were not willing to provide. Another important function provided by the distributor was credit. Suppliers had chosen not to build the structure to support credit management for all their customers. It fell upon the distributors to offer this benefit. In addition to the massive inventories distributors carried, they created value-added services for customers who needed more than just specific parts shipped against scheduled orders. Examples included the ability to receive all products necessary for a specific manufacturing run in a single shipment, as well as releasing products to shipment, based only on a forecast, not previously entered firm purchase orders. Kaufman explained, "This is very important to customers that have adopted JIT procurement systems. These customers want to be very sure that they have everything they need at the right time and in the right quantities. If not, they run the risk of having to stop their production lines."

Distributors' up-to-the-minute knowledge of available products could also be extremely valuable to OEMs in designing their equipment for manufacture.

Even when an OEM was large enough to purchase direct, a distributor could be attractive for particular value-added services. Salsgiver explained: "When a customer gets large enough, they want to buy only direct from the supplier, who can provide them with the technical support and low prices they want. As time passes, however, these customers begin to reach a stage where they want to hand off materials management as well. Most suppliers are not capable of providing this service, and, more important, are not interested in getting into this business. They don't want to take on any activity that does not have the high margins that electronic parts and components usually provide.[3] At this time they can become good distributor customers."

A second and growing new market was the Contract Manufacturers (CMs), who were in the business of building circuit boards or industrial computer systems for OEMs. OEMs would outsource the production of a prototype or even a whole product run to the CM, who would procure the components and assemble the piece. Between 1992 and 1996, the CM business had grown at 30% per year. During the same period, the percentage of A/S business going through the CM channel grew as well, reaching 20 percent of A/S's total sales by 1996. Said one A/S field sales representative: "Five years ago, the only CMs were small mom and pop operations used for overflow or testing demand. A few of them have grown to be multi-billion dollar enterprises. However, there still are a large number of mid- and small-sized CMs. CMs tend to be very price sensitive. They selectively use our value-added services such as programming and supply chain management, in addition to our quick delivery service. But they don't need our engineering services at all."

A/S served two other major customer segments. Amounting to 11 percent of A/S business were customers who purchased Intel x86 chips exclusively to manufacture PC clones. These customers could be differentiated from the traditional OEM customers insofar as they purchased in a purely commoditized fashion. The major value A/S could offer to these customers was credit that was unavailable through suppliers or other financial institutions.

The last segment was made up of customers who purchased industrial computer products. These customers were involved in various industries and tended to buy entire systems or at least assemblies from A/S. Streber explained: "These are computer product subassemblies that are used as a component inside industrial equipment such as elevators or medical equipment. For example, the heart of a blood gas analyzer is an

---

[2]In a business where the margins on a personal computer were typically less than a couple of hundred dollars, OEMs could have their margins wiped out completely when the supplier dropped the price of microprocessors by more than a hundred dollars, a phenomenon that usually happened two to three times a year. Customers therefore maintained minimal inventories and preferred to order products at the last minute and in small quantities.

---

[3]For example, Intel's gross margin was over 55 percent in 1997, and was expected to stay above 50 percent in 1998 and 1999.

Intel-based PC that we supply to the manufacturer of this equipment. These customers tend to order in smaller quantities and need highly customized solutions."

"OUR SUPPLIERS ARE OUR CUSTOMERS"

To a far greater extent than in most other industries, electronic component manufacturers made distributors responsible for demand creation. This tendency, Salsgiver explained, resulted from the nature of the electronics business:

> Suppliers have two fundamental needs from us. They need us to win business in their commodity products to help them grow and gain both profit and market share. They also need us to represent their new technologies and products to our customers. It's obviously critical for both of our future success to help customers design our suppliers' new proprietary devices into their products. Suppliers tend to price commodity products based on the competitive nature of the market. Our gross margins on standardized products run above the company average, in the range of 20 percent to 25 percent. However, suppliers are careful to try to ensure that our margins on the proprietary products run equal to or greater than commodity products, in an effort to reward us for our design work with our customers. This doesn't always work out.
>
> First, they franchise select distributors to sell their products and provide financial incentives such as price protection and limited return privileges to only these franchised distributors. More pointedly, suppliers refuse to honor warranties of products purchased through channels other than the ones they have designated.
>
> Second, many suppliers ship their proprietary products to us at list price or marginally below it. For example, one of our suppliers sets our book cost at a constant 5 percent below their list price. When we get a request for a price quote from a customer, we call the supplier back and give them the details of the customer and the opportunity. The supplier then decides how much of an additional discount they will provide us on this request. In this manner, they know exactly what we are doing, and they are also able to control prices. The level of discount provided varies depending on whether it is our *design win* or a *jump ball*.

DESIGN WIN

A/S, like other electronics distributors, generated demand by helping customers engineer their end products and making A/S suppliers' chips integral to these designs. Suppliers kept track of which distributors did design work by assigning a number to the distributor/ customer partnership. Explained Streber:

> When we start working on an opportunity and invest resources in a customer's project, we will call our supplier and give them all the details. The supplier then assigns a design number that recognizes the work we have done. This is called "design registration." Next, when the order materializes, and the customer shops across distributors for price, the supplier offers a much higher discount to the distribu-

tor credited with the design registration as compared to any other distributor. Unless another distributor is willing to take a hit, they will not be able to serve this customer since only the distributor with the design registration will be able to earn an acceptable margin at the suggested resale price.

JUMP BALL

In some cases, the customer purchased according to manufacturer reputation or price, with no distributor doing any design work. These instances were called "jump balls" in the business. The supplier offered every distributor the same margin, which was significantly lower than the margin given with a design win. Jump balls could also occur when a customer switched from direct purchasing to distribution. Salsgiver explained:

> In these cases, the supplier has already created the demand for the product by doing the design work themselves, so they see the distributor's value only in credit and fulfillment, and they compensate minimally for these services.

MANAGING THE RELATIONSHIP WITH SUPPLIERS

"Our suppliers are able to control our destiny in many ways," commented Kaufman. He continued:

> In the case of jump balls, our suppliers inform the customer about the various distributors they can buy from. Suppliers usually don't exclude a distributor from the list. But they do control the order of names in a list. This is an important factor. Being the first name on that list increases the chance of getting the sale. It is the supplier's way of rewarding one distributor over another.
>
> Another way suppliers manage demand flow is in the order in which they inform the distributors about an opportunity. Getting to know about an opportunity even a few minutes or hours before anyone else can give our sales reps all the time they need to secure the sale.
>
> Finally, suppliers can manage the flow of orders by managing the time they take in responding to a distributor's request for prices. The norm is that the supplier needs to get back within 24 hours of a request. If you have a good relationship, or if the supplier wants to reward you, you might get a response a lot faster. If you are not in the good graces of the supplier, you could be the victim of an overloaded sales rep who was so busy that it took all of 24 hours for them to process your request.

Kaufman continued:

> This does not mean that the distributor has no power. Usually, for the standardized products we will carry several lines. We can also favor one supplier over the other by recommending a particular supplier's product. If suppliers use jump balls to keep distributors in check, distributors are able to use design wins and competitive standardized products to counter-balance supplier power.
>
> In my mind, our relationships with our suppliers are as important as our relationships with any of our customers. Our suppliers are our customers.

Salsgiver further explained the relationship with suppliers:

Suppliers want A/S and other distributors to get technology into the hands of the right customers. In this business, demand points are not always known. An operation in someone's garage this year could be the multi-billion dollar giant five years from now. Our suppliers want us to identify these growth opportunities and lock them in before anyone else does. Our job at A/S is to know our customers well enough to create demand for our suppliers' products. We maintain a separate account development group, calling on small companies and opportunities of the future. This is our ace of spades when it comes to managing our relationship with our suppliers.

ARROW'S SELLING EFFORT

BOOK AND SHIP (BAS)

A/S maintained 300 branch-based sales and marketing representatives (SMRs), who handled the daily phone calls from customers checking delivery, availability, and current price levels. One way a customer might order would be simply to request a quote directly from the SMR, in which case the representative would try to secure the business and arrange to ship the product. This was called a book and ship transaction. SMRs exercised pricing authority for daily orders. They obtained discount levels from the supplier and quoted prices to their assigned customers based on their knowledge of the customer's buying patterns, trends in that local market, and the current cost levels and availability of inventory on hand.

Each SMR used a computer terminal linked to a comprehensive real-time, online computer system (similar to an airline reservation system), which tracked the costs, prices, and movements of the 300,000 different part numbers in inventory, as well as the detailed ordering (A/S handled over 10,000 transactions a day) patterns and sales history for each of the company's 50,000 customers.

VALUE ADDED (VA)

Alternatively, an order could arise through field engineering facilitated by a field sales representative (FSR)—the typical design win situation. In this case the customer's purchasing agent would speak to the SMR only to solidify details of the transaction. These transactions represented the culmination of tremendous effort and expenditure of resources. Field sales representatives, of which there were approximately 400, traveled to their customers (usually 10–20 customers per FSR), spending time with customers' design engineers to understand their current projects and to explain and promote the new products being introduced by Arrow's suppliers. They also spent time with customer purchasing personnel to build relationships, negotiate major

contracts, and resolve any problems that might be arising in the flow of orders and deliveries.

FSRs worked hand in glove with Field Application Engineers (FAEs), who served as technical support for the sales force when customers wanted detailed design assistance or problem solving on specific product design issues. They were in heavy demand from suppliers, who wanted Arrow to help smaller customers design in their proprietary parts. FAEs were salaried and generally expensive to maintain.

Product Managers (PMs) were manufacturers' advocates, ensuring that the FSRs and SMRs were up-to-date on the suppliers' latest product and marketing programs, and that the sales force was meeting its supplier-by-supplier sales budgets. The PMs also worked closely with the suppliers' local personnel to follow up on leads and referrals that came to A/S from the suppliers, as well as working with Arrow's corporate marketing department to make sure low-volume or unusual products were being ordered on a timely basis.

Streber pointed out that much of the involvement with the customer revolved around the changing understanding of value added:

The meaning of value added has continuously changed in our business. In 1977, value added meant nothing more than providing an inventory buffer for the customer. In 1987, it meant altering components to meet customer needs, either by programming, packaging, or kitting[4] parts. In 1997, for our most important customers, it means building virtual organizations with us, through in-plant stores and the like. Today the true value added is in order cycle management. In 1977, about 2 percent of our sales had a value-added component. By 2000, this number can reach as high as 80 percent (see Exhibits 3 and 4).

PHANTOM INVENTORY

One of the results of the system of debits-to-cost used by suppliers was what Salsgiver called "phantom inventory." (See Exhibit 5 for the overall Arrow inventory figures).

"As strange as it sounds, the way our business works, we buy product all day long at a dollar per part, sell it at sixty cents, and make a decent profit." Salsgiver explained that because of the way the suppliers managed pricing, distributors ended up with inventory on the books at high costs, when in fact what they ended up paying was a much lower figure. Nevertheless, this system made it look as though inventory never turned, making day-to-day management, not to mention projections, more difficult.

---

[4] "Kitting" meant gathering all the parts needed for a job into a single package, or kit. The customer would submit a bill of materials, and A/S would provide the complete set. Streber explained that this procedure worked well during the late 1980s, when customers were building to forecast, or in a "push manufacturing" environment, but had fallen off in popularity during the current "pull" (build-to-order) climate.

Exhibit 3   Value Added from Arrow/Schweber

Transaction Cost Reduction

Total Cost of Ownership Analysis
In today's competitive environment, the need to identify all the costs in a company's supply chain process is becoming increasingly important. Companies that understand their "total cost of ownership" find they are better prepared to make complex "make versus buy" and supplier selection decisions. Using Activity Based Costing (ABC) methodologies, Arrow/Schweber's Total Cost of Ownership financial model helps companies identify the total cost associated with a particular activity or process.

Automated Replenishment
Arrow CARES® is our PC Windows®-based automated inventory replenishment system. A user-friendly materials management solution that can be easily and economically installed, CARES automates the purchasing and receiving process while dramatically reducing inventory and associated carrying costs. Designed to support high-volume repetitive purchase items, CARES operates in a multiple bin, kanban environment using "pull" processes to replenish materials. Operating from the customer's stockroom or at point-of-use, CARES uses bar code technology to scan empty kanban bins. CARES then sends a replenishment signal to designated suppliers via EDI or fax transmission. While material is pulled from a second kanban, a replenishment bin is being shipped to support ongoing production requirements. Flexible, efficient, and user-friendly, Arrow CARES provides an automated inventory management solution for our customers' entire supply base.

Electronic Data Interchange
As an integral part of all of Arrow/Schweber's value-added services, EDI allows us to move information faster and more accurately, driving cost out of the supply chain. EDI provides increased productivity and, as a result, makes our customers more competitive while reducing overhead, lowering inventory, and shortening cycle times. Whether sharing forecast information, placing purchase orders, or looking for advanced shipping notification, Arrow/Schweber supports the ANSI X.12 transactions our customers require.

In-Plant Terminals
By providing direct access to Arrow/Schweber's online, real-time computer system, our Customer Staffed Terminal enables our customers to check inventory availability, place purchase orders, cross parts, or view component specifications. A simple and easy way to access information makes Arrow/Schweber's customer staffed terminal a valuable tool for engineering and purchasing. For added value our Arrow/Schweber Staffed Terminal provides on-site materials management for customers that handle high levels of order processing. On-site support for planning, purchasing, and engineering departments provides increased productivity and reduces acquisition costs.

Planning the Material Pipeline

In-Plant Stores
An Arrow/Schweber In-Plant Store provides on-site staffing to help manage material requirements. We maintain and manage a warehouse, stocked with the components our customers require, on-site at the customer's manufacturing facility. The In-Plant Store personnel are responsible for planning, purchasing, receiving, stocking, and fulfilling production and engineering requirements. Customers only take ownership of material once it has been delivered to them providing a significant reduction in inventory carrying costs.

Turnkey Service
Arrow/Schweber's Turnkey service provides complete management of a customer's printed circuit board assembly requirements. We combine our expertise in materials management with those of our certified turnkey partners to provide a flexible manufacturing strategy customized to meet our customer's unique requirements.

Our Turnkey service provides dedicated program management to support and facilitate our customers' production requirements, from prototype to production, decreasing a product's time-to-volume and time-to-market.

Improving Logistical Efficiency

Production Kitting
Arrow/Schweber's kitting service provides our customers prepackaged kits for delivery to a production facility designated by the customer. Our ISO 9002 Kitting division resides in Sparks, Nevada in one of our Primary Distribution Centers (PDC) providing customers with access to our extensive line card and inventory. Our dedicated Kitting project management oversees programs from quoting through delivery—managing ECO, pricing, and forecast changes. By supplying kits in a Just-In-Time (JIT) delivery process, we help reduce inventory-related expenses such as stockouts, component obsolescence, and inventory carrying costs.

EXHIBIT 3   VALUE ADDED FROM ARROW/SCHWEBER, *continued*

Device Programming
As the leading distributor of programmable products in North America, we do more than provide our customers with the industry's broadest line card. We are also uniquely positioned to provide solutions for every PLD application by offering a comprehensive resource of silicon and design support.

We serve our customers from four primary ISO 9002 certified programming centers. Each center is linked to a single network to provide an optimal means of matching demand to capacity, providing faster turnaround for our customers. Programming with Arrow/Schweber eliminates the need for costly capital equipment expenditures and reduces product obsolescence due to last-minute firmware changes.

Complete Supply Chain Management

Business Needs Analysis
Arrow/Schweber's Business Needs Analysis provides an analysis of a customer's existing materials planning, acquisition, handling, and inventorying processes. After gaining a thorough understanding of a company's existing capabilities and desired goals, Arrow/Schweber is better able to make practical recommendations that provide sustainable results to our customer's bottom line.

Custom Computer Products (CCP)
Offering the most comprehensive computer customization capabilities in the industry, our ISO 9002-certified Custom Computer Products (CCP) Division is the premier nationwide source for complete system and subsystem integration, assembly, and testing. A valuable resource for design and development assistance, CCP is staffed by an in-house support team of engineers and technical personnel who offer total project management services, from concept to completion.

CCP offers this total project management from a facility certified by Intel for hardware and software design and product integration. Applications provided through CCP include disk drive formatting and custom drive configurations; software configuration and customization; custom packaging, painting, and labeling; run-in and diagnostic testing; complete functional, diagnostic, environmental, and confidence testing; extended warranty; local installation and on-site training; and nationwide field service programs. Using Arrow/Schweber's CCP service lowers production costs, reduces time to market, and enhances our customer's cash flow.

Source: Company records.

EXHIBIT 4   PERCENT OF ARROW SALES WITH VALUE-ADDED CONTENT

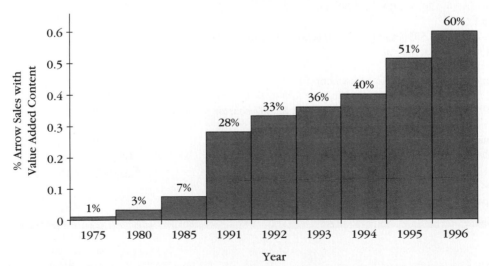

Source: Company records.

EXHIBIT 5   CONSOLIDATED BALANCE SHEET (DOLLARS IN THOUSANDS)

DECEMBER 31,	1996	1995
ASSETS		
Current assets		
Cash and short-term investments	$ 136,400	$ 93,947
Accounts receivable, less allowance for doubtful accounts ($39,753 in 1996 and $38,670 in 1995)	902,878	940,049
Inventories	1,044.841	1,039,111
Prepaid expenses and other assets	36,004	31,610
Total current assets	2,120,123	2,104,717
Property, plant, and equipment at cost		
Land	8,712	14,527
Buildings and improvements	77,527	63,857
Machinery and equipment	127,633	112,883
	213,602	191,267
Less accumulated depreciation and amortization	98,377	73,932
	115,225	117,335
Investment in affiliated company	34,200	36,031
Cost in excess of net assets of companies acquired, less accumulated amortization ($57,802 in 1996 and $48,085 in 1995)	388,787	379,171
Other assets	52,016	63,762
	$2,710,351	$2,701,016
LIABILITIES AND SHAREHOLDERS' EQUITY		
Current liabilities		
Accounts payable	$ 594,474	$ 561,834
Accrued expenses	180,129	207,738
Short-term borrowings, including current maturities of long-term debt	71,504	117,085
Total current liabilities	846,107	886,657
Long-term debt	344,562	451,706
Other liabilities	68,488	68,992
Minority interest	92,712	97,780
Shareholders' equity		
Common stock, par value $1		
Authorized—120,000,000 and 80,000,000 shares in 1996 and 1995		
Issued—51,196,385 and 50,647,826 shares in 1996 and 1995	51,196	50,648
Capital in excess of par value	549,913	530,324
Retained earnings	805,342	602,633
Foreign currency translation adjustment	8,753	18,398
	1,415,204	1,202,003
Less: Treasury stock at cost (1,069,699 and 22,297 shares in 1996 and 1995),	49,065	24
Unamortized employee stock awards	7,657	6,098
Total shareholders' equity	1,358,482	1,195,881
	$2,710,351	$2,701,016

Source: Company records.

In addition to getting discounts for design wins on proprietary products, Arrow was sometimes able to negotiate with the supplier on an order-by-order basis for a special discount. A supplier that was anxious to fill its production lines for standardized products could "buy an order." This led to higher margins for Arrow on that order.

RELATIONSHIP WITH CUSTOMERS

Some customers chose to work with A/S on a transaction-by-transaction basis. These customers would place a request-for-quote (RFQ) for one or a few products with several distributors. The distributors would obtain current pricing information from their suppliers and offer a price to the customer. These customers could require several rounds of negotiations to obtain the best price.

SMRs expressed some ambivalence about transactional customers. Explained one SMR: "I spend a good portion of my day speaking to these sorts of customers. They always know the current prices and will list grey market distributors' prices when I give my quote."

Added an FSR who called exclusively on CMS:

We are currently able to provide credit and short delivery lead times on small orders to contract manufacturers, which they cannot receive either from the suppliers or from the non-franchised distributors otherwise known as brokers. This means that when an OEM asks a CM to build a board, the CM has an incentive to purchase through us. But CMs can design in our manufacturers' products just as easily as we can. If our suppliers decide to reward CM demand creation the way they reward such distributor activities, then it's going to be really tough to compete.

Kaufman commented:

Roughly 25 percent of our sales today come from transactional customers. Typically, a majority of these sales are of the book and ship (BAS) type. We cannot afford to ignore this group for several reasons. In addition to accounting for a significant portion of our current sales, this customer segment is also a major source of relationship customers in the long run. Most of our relationship customers today started out as transactional customers. Customers want to check us out and monitor our performance over several orders before they are willing to get into any sort of agreement that goes beyond the transaction level. We are generally able to convert at least half of our transactional customers into relational customers over the long haul.

Other customers attempted to establish long-term relationships with a small number of distributors. Salsgiver explained:

Most of our relationship customers do more than half of their business with their top distributor. These customers want the convenience of submitting an entire bill of items for a quote, finding it more valuable to have a steady partner than the rock bottom price over the long haul. That doesn't mean that they don't care about prices. It is very common for them to maintain a relationship with one or two other distributors in order to ensure continuous availability of products and to keep their primary distributor in check.

Most of our relationship customers buy a basket of products from us that includes BAS and VA products. Given the competitive nature of this business, we have found that it is difficult to get close to a customer through the "book and ship" business. Our approach is to use the value-added products as the first step to building a relationship. We provide customers with the best-in-class support in this category. Once the customer gets a chance to interact with us, they are able to see the true benefit of doing business with us rather than any other distributor.

Now comes a peculiar trait in our business. You would expect that the customer pays us high prices for the value-added services we provide. Well, that doesn't happen. The customer knows that there are several distributors that can provide these value-added services. They then use the threat of switching to other distributors to make sure that we don't charge too much of a premium for our services. While we try to demonstrate tangible financial benefits to justify our prices, there are times when we practically give away the value that we create for them and recover our profits in other areas. Our gross margins on value-added products run below the company average, in the range of 10 percent to 15 percent. We cross-sell our other products to these customers by offering them significant breaks on the value-added products in return for their commitment to buy the book and ship products exclusively from us. In a way, in these relationships the commodity products subsidize the specialty products.

Finding the right customers with which to develop a long-term relationship was very important. It was not uncommon for some customers simply not to appreciate the work done by A/S or even honor their own commitments. Martha Moranis, an SMR, related:

We had been pursuing a prospect for some time when a request came in from them for a highly allocated proprietary chip manufactured by one of our major suppliers. We saw this as a great opportunity to break into the account and establish a long-term relationship, and we agreed to obtain this product for them at a favorable price. In return, they promised to purchase one of their major needs exclusively from us at a price that allowed us a good margin. We jumped through flaming hoops to deliver on our side of the bargain, but once they had received their shipment, they seemed to change their mind about the agreement. When it came time for them to place their standing order, they tried to lower the price we had agreed upon and finally placed the order with another distributor. We could not do anything with the supplier because they saw it as a jump ball. In hindsight, we would have been better off not serving this customer at all.

The same set of actions on our part will get a very different response from some of our good customers. We have found that the best way to strengthen a relationship that is already strong is by helping our customers in their times of need. Our good customers will always remember what we did for them and usually reward us at a later date.

Long-term relationships had their own perils. One FSR related:

I once called on a customer who had a gatekeeper for a purchasing manager. This buyer had been there for 15 years and had fallen into a routine of placing the same orders with the same distributors all the time. For some reason, he did not want to deal with us. We rotated this account through some of our best reps with no success. This buyer was "anti-Arrow" and we had no clue why. We tried to go around the buyer and work with engineering. This made things worse for us. We were told by the buyer that we could not design in any product that they currently purchased through our competition. This made it really tough to maneuver. Our chance arrived when a new buyer came in. This buyer was willing to work with us, and we ended winning significant amounts of business from this customer.

This process can work in reverse as well. We can establish a solid relationship with a customer that is utterly obliterated when a new buyer with a different set of connections replaces the person with whom we used to work.

"There is another angle to building a relationship with a customer," added Kaufman. He continued:

I think we need to go further to make the relationship virtually unbreakable. We need to get the customer to invest along with us in systems and processes that enable us to provide value-added services.

It is easier for us when we are dealing with value-added products like PLDs where the customer has to have invested in product related systems and processes that are customized to match our programming skills. But even with commodity products, where there is little that can be done at the product end, a customer that invests in supply chain management initiatives along with us is very unlikely to terminate their relationship with us.

The trend toward greater demand for value-added services is our best bet to counterbalance the high-price sensitivities of our customers and the relational "cheating" that takes place in our business.

A/S AND THE INTERNET

During the early to mid-1990s, many electronics distributors had set up home pages on the Internet through which to present their companies, give line card information, and even sell products. In the move to the Internet, the prominence of independent, nonfranchised distributors on the landscape was unmistakable. These companies were seen by many franchised distributors as well as customers as being less than legitimate. They purchased their products from others' overstock, and because they lacked authorized reseller agreements, they could not use the manufacturers' warranties.

Although Arrow had established a closed system to allow its customers to obtain fixed price and availability information from a terminal in the customer plant, Arrow had been reluctant to establish a presence in the public domain. Preferring instead to watch and wait while others tested the waters, eventually Arrow had put up home pages for the company as a whole and its operating groups. Nevertheless, purchasing capability was not a feature of Arrow's new Web sites. Instead, they functioned as information centers with material about the various suppliers, searchable lists of parts, and news.

Potential customers were directed from the Web page to the national 1-800 number for the group in question.

EXPRESS PARTS, INC.

Express parts, Inc., was a new independent distributor. The company had developed an Internet-based trading system that revolved around a multi-distributor bulletin board. Express said that its search engine could quickly cross-reference equivalent parts from multiple manufacturers based either on any manufacturer's part number or a technical description, and it estimated that over 50,000 OEMs across the U.S. would have access to the service. By gaining access to such a large market, Express proposed, A/S could increase its sales at less than half the cost of their existing branch network. The program worked as follows:

1. A/S would transmit its full list of available inventory and prices to Express each night. This list would be combined with similar lists from a limited number of other distributors.

2. Express would allow customers to sign onto its service via the Internet and search by part number or description. Upon making a selection, the customer would see a screen showing all products matching the search criteria, along with the quantity available for shipment and the price at which each distributor was prepared to sell. The customer would not actually know the distributor's name, since on the Internet screen used by the customer, each distributor would be identified only by an arbitrary letter. (See Exhibit 6)

3. The customer could select any supplier/distributor combination, enter the quantity desired, and click the mouse to place the order. The order would instantly be transmitted to Express. Express would review the order, perform a credit check, accept and acknowledge it to the customer, and then send it electronically to the appropriate distributor.

4. After receiving the order, the distributor would pick the parts and "drop ship" the order on behalf of Express directly to the customer.[5] The distributor would then notify

_____

[5]"Drop Ship" was a process by which one company, in this case Arrow, would ship a product to a customer as an agent for a middleman, in this case Express, making it look as though the product came from the middleman. Legally, Arrow had "sold" the product to Express, who instantly resold it to the customer. Express was thus the legal party responsible for the transaction, did the billing and collecting, and was responsible for paying Arrow.

EXHIBIT 6 EXPRESS PARTS SAMPLE

EXPRESS PARTS, INC.

PART NUMBER REQUESTED: SN74LS244N   **PART DESCRIPTION: LS OCTAL BUFFER/LINE DRIVER**

| | | | | | | | | DISTRIBUTOR | | | | | | | |
| | | A | | B | | C | | D | | E | | F | |
MANUFACTURER	PART NUMBER	QTY	$	QTY	$	QTY	$	QTY	$	QTY	$	QTY	$
Texas Instruments	SN74LS244N	62,507	.31	83,200	.28	5000	.72	30,250	.67	89,660	.45	45,000	.62
Motorola	SN74LS244N	30,245	.42	77,700	.49	89,500	.25	82,300	.58	94,200	.26	145,000	.22
Natl Semiconductor	DM74LS244N	59,000	.30	12,400	.67	64,500	.53	73,000	.50	100,000	.23	2,200	.70
SGS Thomson	T74LS244B1	29,800	.55	28,000	.54	73,250	.59	62,900	.66	78,780	.39	40,245	.49
Philips	N74LS244N	76,400	.24	25,975	.62	25,000	.48	10,000	.70	47,120	.58	50,800	.55

Click on the price you want

Quantity _____

Quote _____

Order _____

Customer: _____

Name: _____

Address: _____

Email Address: _____

Source: Company records.

Express electronically that the shipment had been made, and Express would bill the customer.

5. A/S would be paid by Express 30 days later with no credit risk, minus Express's fee of 6 percent.

DECISIONS

Express's proposal had stirred significant debate among the A/S management team, which had now been discussing it for nearly a month. Express had told Salsgiver that they needed a decision within the week. This was, they said, because they were only going to ask a limited number of distributors to join, in order to avoid having too many duplicate and competitive lines.

Kaufman had asked Salsgiver to evaluate the impact that Express would have on A/S's business under different scenarios. "We need to have some idea of what this is going to do to our business," he had told Salsgiver. Salsgiver had commissioned a detailed study to look at this issue under different settings. Two outcomes were considered in this study. In the optimistic scenario, all transactional customers were assumed to switch purchases of their products from A/S to Express. In the pessimistic scenario, all transactional customers and roughly 40 percent of relationship customers were assumed to switch their purchases from A/S to Express in the future. These percentages were arrived at through a detailed bottom-up account product analysis. Exhibit 7 provides the results of this study, which had stirred a lot of debate and little agreement. Salsgiver realized that this analysis only provided some direction but not all the answers she needed to make her decisions.

Salsgiver now considered the words of her colleagues as she composed her thoughts.

Kaufman:

It is very important that we keep in mind our corporate objectives. With expenses at 11 percent, we cannot afford our overall gross margins for A/S to fall below 15 percent. We certainly don't want to accelerate the downward trend in margins that we've been seeing any more than is necessary.

Ultimately, I think the Internet will never be anything more than an invitation to bargain. In the worst-case scenario, all our current customers will get the lowest price from the Express system and use it as a starting point to bargain with us. I have yet to meet an industrial buyer who does not believe that he can do better by bargaining, especially on a price open to the public. With Express as a competitor, I think we will have to learn how to sell against "going out of business" prices on a regular basis. We have to have a much stronger value-in-use sales story than ever before.

Streber:

I think Express gives us access to sales that would never have come our way in the past. I agree that any time the only value A/S brings to the table is in price and delivery, we are vulnerable to the Internet for competition. My feeling is that we will lose little or none of our business with relationship customers and about half of our business with transactional customers. But, if we do it right, this loss will be more or less compensated for by the additional business we get from Express. Express does not look like an attractive competitor, but it might give us one advantage. I would use it to sell to those customers that we cannot sell to using our current business model.

Currently, our SMRs spend a tremendous amount of time and energy trying to build new customers. When many of these customers call, we spend a lot of time trying to figure out whether we can build a relationship with

EXHIBIT 7   MARKET SEGMENT MIX[a]

MARKET SEGMENT	MARKET SEGMENT (% AND $ OF TOTAL BUSINESS)		VALUE-ADDED BUSINESS[b]		STANDARD PRODUCT BOOK & SHIP BUSINESS		OPTIMISTIC CANNIBALIZATION OF BAS BUSINESS		PESSIMISTIC CANNIBALIZATION OF BAS BUSINESS	
	%	$	%	$	%	$	%	$	%	$
Core										
— CM	20	460	57	262	43	198	30	59	70	139
— OEM	56	1300	72	936	28	364	25	91	60	218
X86	11	250	2	5	98	245	50	122	80	196
ICP[c]	13	300	80	240	20	60	35	21	80	48

Source: Company records.

Note: [a]Calculations assume that value-added business is immune to Internet cannibalization.
[b]Includes scheduled orders and forecast sharing.
[c]Industrial Computer Products.

them. We have found that most of the time, these customers are not interested in going beyond the transaction—all they want is to shop around for the lowest price. We could ask these customers to go to Express or possibly our own Internet site. For these price-sensitive, low-loyalty customers, the opportunity to offer standardized pricing over the Internet can minimize our efforts and even make it worthwhile for us since we might be able to significantly cut our costs to serve them. Finally, as long as we are the lowest, we will always get the sale.

By maintaining strong relationships with our suppliers, we will still be able to sell at competitive prices for design wins. As long as our suppliers believe that we create demand for them, they will give us the most favorable pricing. Express only responds to demand. I think if we quote anonymously on their system, given our ability to get the lowest prices, we might be able to hang onto a bit more of the business than our models indicate.

Salsgiver, however, was pessimistic:

We all agree that Express will get the customer who is less likely to think long-term and is more likely to want to return to the old price-and-availability business. With Express, we are quite vulnerable in highly commoditized products

---

Professor Das Narayandas prepared this case with the assistance of Research Associate Sara Frug as the basis for class discussion rather than to illustrate either effective or ineffective handling of an administrative situation. This case is based in part on a case developed by Stephen P. Kaufman, CEO of Arrow Electronics, for in-house executive training. Some proprietary data have been disguised.

like memory, for which it's very visible to any customer what a good price will be.

I also think we are erring in making the absolute association between commodity products and transactional behavior on the one hand, and value-added products and relational behavior on the other. Although these generally line up, it does not always happen. This goes back to the point that Steve made. Even our relationship customers are going to use this as a tool to get lower prices from us. In the future, I think they will not appreciate what we do for them as much as they have in the past. The one thing that is in our favor over the long haul is the flux in the business. When product is scarce, a market may be good, but a friend is better. Our customers will be better off maintaining their relationship with us. We need to remind our customers of this.

I also wonder how the Express proposal affects our suppliers. Suppliers franchise us because we add value for them. Arrow pays the bills for them—we stock products and schedule orders with enough size and scale. Currently, 70 percent of our commodity product sales to transactional customers are of products manufactured by our "big four" and other larger suppliers. To these suppliers, the Internet can mean lost control. For example, they can lose control over the point-of-sale information we currently can give them. In addition, they see a chance that prices for commodity products will fall down faster than they would like. Remember, it is the commodity product margins that is a major source of revenues for them. They use the money they make here to support the value-added and new proprietary products.

Salsgiver wondered, "How should we leverage all this information to our advantage?"

ALADDIN KNOWLEDGE SYSTEMS
(www.aks.com)

On May 26, 1996, Yanki Margalit, founder, president, and CEO of Aladdin Knowledge Systems, a leading Israeli developer of antipiracy hardware, software security, and smart cards, announced Aladdin's $59 million share-swap acquisition of its German competitor, FAST Software Security AG. Later on May 30 the company announced the $5.1 million cash acquisition of Glenco's software security business in the USA. As a result, Aladdin became the market share leader in Europe and strengthened its number two position in the United States.

An important challenge for Margalit was to determine whether and how to integrate the worldwide marketing, sales, and distribution of the firm's two overlapping software security product lines: the Aladdin HASP (Hardware Against Software Piracy) line and the FAST AG Hardlock line. Within the firm, executives voiced three different strategies. The first group felt that HASP should be developed as a global brand, and that the Hardlock name should be quickly phased out on the grounds that one voice would perform better than two in an already very cluttered market. The second group advocated analyzing the distribution capabilities and relative strengths of each brand in each country market, picking a winner and going with it on a country-by-country basis. The third group, however, suggested that since the two brands were serving different customers, the two product lines should continue to compete side by side in order to maximize Aladdin's market share against the firm's competitors in each country market.

COMPANY BACKGROUND

Like his high-tech peers in the Silicon Valley, Margalit left school in the late 1970s and began building computers in his home outside of Tel Aviv. The scarcity of computer hardware and software in Israel at the time meant that both items, when they were available, were astronomically priced. As a result, Israel was labeled a "one-diskette" country to satirize the notion that a single diskette, effectively pirated, could serve an entire popu-

lation. Israel was fertile ground for many who, like Margalit, had a talent for decoding the occasional piece of software that came his way. Between 1980 and 1983, while doing his military service, Margalit applied his talents to artificial intelligence (AI), writing specialized software to assist handwriting experts in their analysis of penmanship samples.

In 1985, at age 22 and with less than $10,000 in start-up capital, Yanki Margalit established Aladdin Knowledge Systems with his brother, Dany, and a few friends. His objective was to market the handwriting analysis software, and to develop new knowledge-based applications in the areas of education, banking, insurance, and agriculture, using the original AI package as the core. Once Margalit found his own software being pirated, he set about devising a means of protecting software that would not inconvenience legitimate users the way that traditionally copy-protected diskettes often did. Margalit became the first person to conceive of a hardware plug to protect software. The result of this idea, the HASP product line, was launched. In 1987, the next generation HASP-II was released and Margalit spent most of the young company's available cash on placing a quarter-page black and white ad in *Byte* magazine, the leading international trade journal for software developers. This single ad generated numerous inquiries from distribution companies seeking to represent Aladdin in a variety of country markets. By the end of 1987, distributors had been appointed in five countries. By 1988, Aladdin had sales of $353,000 and began to focus its marketing and development efforts on software security keys rather than expert-system software packages.

In late 1993, with annual revenues having reached $4 million, Aladdin launched an independent public offering (IPO) on NASDAQ (ticker ALDNF) that helped give the company the capital and the recognition it needed to crack the all-important U.S. software security market. In Margalit's words: "The IPO had the extra benefit of forcing us to develop a clear vision for the company's future." In the year following the IPO, net revenues increased 75 percent, but Aladdin's stock price, like those of many smaller Israeli companies floated around the same time, suffered. From the offering price of $4.66, the share price soon fell to an all-time low of $2.66. Margalit announced a dividend payout to increase interest in the stock. By early 1995, the share price had risen to $17.30, and the firm was well known to Wall Street analysts for having the youngest management team of all NASDAQ-listed companies.

In March 1995, Aladdin made its first acquisition. The target was Eliashim's software security business, an Israeli competitor in the field of software security with sales about one-fifth those of Aladdin. This acquisition enabled Aladdin executives to gain experience for their future mergers and acquisitions.

In 1995, Aladdin's sales were almost $11.5 million, as shown in Exhibit 1. Almost 95 percent of these revenues were from sales of software security products. However, sales growth in this area was slowing. Aladdin management decided that Aladdin's future depended on a two-pronged strategy—first, to consolidate Aladdin's market position in the software security business. The acquisition of FAST was intended to achieve this goal. A 1996 income statement for Aladdin, incorporating the costs of the FAST acquisition, is also included in Exhibit 1. Second was to expand Aladdin's research and development and marketing efforts in the fast-growing smart card and license management markets in which Aladdin had already launched some proprietary products.

PIRACY AND SOFTWARE SECURITY PRODUCTS

Software piracy occurred in the following ways: by end-users making unauthorized copies of software at work or home; by retailers selling illegal copies; by computer dealers loading illegal copies onto their customers' hardware; by bulletin board operators and subscribers offering software for illegal copying; and by commercial counterfeiters offering illegally copied software for sale. A trade association estimated that software piracy, defined as the unauthorized use of copyrighted software programs, cost software development companies $13.1 billion worldwide in 1995.[1] As indicated in Table A, the

TABLE A   PERCENTAGE OF WORLDWIDE REVENUE LOSSES DUE TO SOFTWARE PIRACY, BY REGION (1995)

REGION	PERCENTAGE OF WORLD TOTAL ($13.1 BILLION)
Western Europe	26.7%
Eastern Europe	5.7
United States	22.1
Latin America	8.4
Asia-Pacific	29.8
Middle East and Africa	4.0

Source: Software Publishers Association, 1995.

[1]The piracy estimates cited in this case are from studies conducted by the Business Software Alliance and the Software Publishers Association. They covered piracy committed in commercial settings of business applications, namely, fonts, screen savers, utilities, spreadsheets, word processors, databases, statistical analysis, and graphing packages. These estimates did not include home and school copying nor did they include the illegal copying of educational software, games, or other consumer software.

EXHIBIT 1   ALADDIN INCOME STATEMENTS: 1995 AND 1996

	1995 ($000) ALADDIN ONLY (PRE-MERGER)	1995 ($000) COMBINED (POST-MERGER)	1996 ($000) COMBINED (POST-MERGER)	1996 ($000) EXCLUDING ONE-TIME MERGER-RELATED EXPENSES
Sales	$11,345	$24,831	$28,701	$28,701
Cost of sales	2,988	6,887	8,184	8,184
Gross profit	8,357	17,944	20,517	20,517
R & D	1,149	2,208	2,669	2,669
Selling and marketing	2,852	4,270	7,677	7,677
General and administrative	1,237	2,640	3,196	3,196
Combination and Reorganization Expenses	0	0	5,360	0
Operating (loss) income	3,119	8,826	1,615	6,975
Net finance income	491	976	885	885
Other income (expenses)	(19)	(6)	(7,350)	104
Income (loss) before taxes	3,591	9,796	(4,850)	7,964
Taxes on income (benefit)	207	3,779	(1,702)	1,080
Net income (loss)	$3,384	$6,017	$(3,148)	$6,884

Source: Company records.

Note: 1996 figures include the costs associated with acquiring FAST's software security business. Aladdin's fiscal year was the calendar year.

United States, Japan, and Germany accounted for 41 percent of these losses.

The prevalence of software piracy varied by country. Exhibit 2 summarizes the number of software applications sold in 1992 and 1993 per personal computer for selected country markets. It also reports software expenditures per PC sold, as well as software revenues and piracy rates for these markets. The world average in 1993 was 3.6 software packages per PC sold; the North American average was 5.4; the rest-of-the-world average; only 2.0. The Software Publishers Association stated: "It is hard to imagine that sophisticated businesses are gaining maximum utility from their hardware purchases with an average of only two software packages per PC sold."[2]

In the early days of software development, programmers protected their innovations through a variety of highly technical and often unreliable mechanisms, such as the key-disk method. Over time, software security acquired a hardware component in the form a "key" and dongle, which were attached to the printer port, and analogous to an anti-theft system for a car. The objective of a dongle was to encode a program already in its production phase so that it could be decoded, and thus operable, only in the presence of a particular software program code. Because a dongle processed information only upon appropriate activation, one measure of a don-

gle's quality was the number of different values it could receive and/or produce.

The most advanced dongles operated with ASIC[3] chips contained encryption algorithms for the integrated memory. With 128 bytes of storage capacity, products were differentiated according to the manner in which this capacity was allocated. FAST's Hardlock, for example, devoted 96 cells to "read only" encryption functions, leaving 32 to the software developer. Rainbow Technologies' Sentinel Super Pro, the market leader, divided its memory into 64 16-bit cells. Aladdin's HASP offered up to 496 bytes of internal memory, which the developer could allocate accordingly. Values were attached to these memory cells with passwords which, together with the "read only" serial number and manufacturer code, secured the software.

Dongles varied primarily on the basis of their ASIC technology and memory allocation, with different dongles addressing different developers' needs. Developers generally looked first at the level of computer language compatibility offered by a particular dongle, and then at any other special features which a security product might have. FAST's Hardlock line was rated by some industry experts as the most secure device; however, it was also among the most expensive. The T-Lock, manufactured by Microdevices, was considered by many to

[2]Report on Global Software Piracy, 1993:13. The Software Publishers Association noted that the above ratios included software applications purchased for newly purchased computers only, and excluded installed computers.

[3]Application Specific Integrated Circuits (ASIC) enabled the design of an integrated circuit to be independent from the manufacturing process. The main security advantage of ASIC circuits was that the contents of its cells could not be read, even with an electronic microscope.

EXHIBIT 2   SOFTWARE SALES AND APPLICATIONS PER PC IN SELECTED MARKETS: 1992–1993

COUNTRY	1993 SOFTWARE SALES ($000)	1993 SOFTWARE SALES PER PC ($)	SOFTWARE PACKAGES SOLD PER PC 1992	SOFTWARE PACKAGES SOLD PER PC 1993	LEGALLY ACQUIRED SOFTWARE 1993
United States	3,868,950	$329	4.0	5.4	67%
Germany and Austria	707,795	503	2.7	3.9	67
United Kingdom and Ireland	523,224	450	2.8	3.8	73
France	369,356	349	1.5	2.4	48
Nordic Countries	107,502	249	1.5	1.9	38
Japan	674,253	269	0.8	1.6	53
Brazil	24,963	57	NA	0.7	11
India and Pakistan	5,400	32	NA	0.3	5
Weighted World Average/Total	8,000,000	NA	NA	3.6	53

Source: Adapted from Software Publishers Association, Report on Global Software Piracy, 1993.

TABLE B   RANKING OF LEADING SOFTWARE PROTECTION SYSTEMS (OUT OF 10)

SCORING CATEGORY	ALADDIN HASP	RAINBOW SENTINEL	GLENCO/FAST HARDLOCK	SOFTWARE SECURITY ACTIVATOR
Security	9.3	6.3	6.9	6.2
Ease of Learning	9.1	7.1	8.8	7.7
Ease of Use	8.3	7.2	6.8	6.3
Versatility/Features	10.0	8.7	8.8	8.6
Compatibility/Power Consumption	6.7	6.5	6.6	7.4
Speed of API Calls[a]	0.9	1.2	10.0	4.1
Final Score	8.5	6.5	7.5	6.6

Source: NSTL, October 1995.

[a]The speed of API calls was the speed at which the system responded to a verification query. A lower speed would mean that the system responded more slowly. A score of 0.9 was still satisfactory in that the software response was not lowered so much that it was noticeable to the user in terms of speed of system response. A slower speed of API calls also meant that it would take longer for someone to break into the security system. So what might appear to be a weakness in HASP was, in fact, a competitive advantage.

be the most user-friendly, inexpensive dongle, and provided sufficient security against most amateur pirates. Aladdin's HASP product line offered a much higher degree of security and flexibility at a somewhat higher price and was therefore rated the most cost-effective dongle on the market.

A 1995 study by National Software Testing Laboratories, the leading independent testing facility for the microcomputer industry, announced that Aladdin's HASP product outscored three competing products. The report compared the flagship dongles of the industry's four leading software protection vendors: Aladdin's MemoHASP, Rainbow Technologies' SuperPro, Glenco Engineering/FAST Electronic Hardlock,[4] and Software Security's Activator. The results, reported in Table B, confirmed previous comparative studies which rated HASP as the highest-quality software protection system on the market, in terms of both the security it offered and its support for a broad range of operating systems and network environments.

By early 1996, hardware-based software security solutions, which accounted for 80 percent of the software security market, were experiencing slower growth. The hardware-based software security market grew by over 25 percent in 1996 but was less than the previous year. Interest was also increasing in software-based license management solutions, whereby the security software was built into the operating system software that ran

the PC. Software-based solutions were less expensive than dongles. Industry experts expected software-based solutions to be used more widely in the future. They also expected software-based solutions to have shorter life cycles and lower prices than hardware-based solutions. Aladdin and its principal competitors were already selling software-based solutions by May 1996, but no clear leader had yet emerged in this segment of the market.

MARKET SIZE AND COMPETITION

The market for antipiracy hardware-based and software-based solutions reached $120 million (at manufacturer prices) in 1995 and was expected to grow to $150 million in 1996. Forty percent of unit sales were made in the United States, 25 percent in Europe, and 25 percent in Asia-Pacific. Sales growth was faster in North America and Asia than in Europe.

The leader in market share was Rainbow Technologies, headquartered in Orange County, California. Established in 1984, one year before Aladdin, Rainbow soon dominated the North American market. The company's 1995 revenues of $72.6 million, 70 percent of which were sales of software security products, yielded a net income of $9.8 million. Rainbow claimed to be the "leading provider of cryptographic technology for software antipiracy, Internet security, and satellite and telecommunications security." More than half of Rainbow's revenues came from U.S. sales. Rainbow lagged Aladdin in network solutions and in code security applications. However, with twice as many salespeople, expertise in cold calling and telemarketing, and a larger

[4]Glenco Engineering was FAST's authorized distributor in the United States.

marketing budget, Rainbow held 40 percent of the U.S. market.

After Aladdin, the third largest competitor was FAST Software Security AG, founded in 1985 in Munich, Germany, by Matthias Zahn. By 1991, the company had expanded beyond software security products into multimedia and, two years later, the multimedia business surpassed the software security business in annual sales. Early in 1994, FAST was split into two companies to facilitate a possible spin-off of its software security business. FAST's software sales were forecast to be $13 million in 1996, 5 percent higher than in 1995. Around $10 million of these sales were made in Europe, around $9 million in Germany alone.

The fourth competitor, U.S.-based Software Security, Inc., was rumored to be in merger discussions with Rainbow Technologies. Software Security's UniKey and Activator product lines were among the strongest selling hardware-based security solutions in the United States. The combined market share of these products in the United States was 12 percent. Around 80 percent of Software Security's sales were generated in the United States.

MARKETING MIX

PRODUCT LINES

The HASP product line was based on a hardware key that contained a unique electronic code which the protected software could "recognize." It offered transparency to the computer user and compatibility with different languages, compilers, and hardware platforms. The software developer who purchased the hardware and licensed the software would simply insert "checks" for the HASP key into the source code so that when the system was running, the protected program could check whether the correctly coded HASP key was connected to the user's computer. The software would run only if this code was confirmed. HASP was the only protection key on the market to be designed, manufactured, and marketed entirely in-house.

In 1996, Aladdin launched its highest-tech line of HASP products, called the HASP R3. The advantage of the HASP R3 over competing software-based protection programs was its transparency to the user, connecting an exterior plug with interior software in a one-time installation that did not require code words and other cumbersome protection methods. This new version of the HASP key and dongle was lauded by experts as the new industry standard since the ASIC chip behind HASP R3's power featured state-of-the-art micron technology. Not only did the HASP R3 offer the highest level of security than competing software security products, it was also compatible with earlier generation HASP products, allowing developers to upgrade their systems without incurring the cost of a total system overhaul.

The HASP R3 manufacturing process made the product even more reliable than its predecessors. As Aladdin's vice president of production noted a short time after the release of R3, "To date we have shipped over 25,000. Our quality control department has received back only 35 faulty units, a return rate of just 0.014 percent. This makes the new HASP the most reliable software protection key on the market by far."[5]

The Hardlock product line was narrower than HASP's, since it relied on a generic product that was shipped to clients and customized on-site by software developers themselves. FAST executives felt that, since nearly anyone had the capacity to make a key (software), the real security came from the quality of the dongle technology. The Hardlock dongle was considered the most sophisticated on the market, meaning that it had the largest capacity for data encryption. Hardlock brochures touted on-site customization, stating, "You make your own key to ensure that no one else, anywhere else, has the code to your safe."

CUSTOMERS AND THE BUYING PROCESS

The purchasers of software security products were publishers and developers of expensive software packages, ranging from Microsoft to small companies developing specialist, vertical industry software, which together accounted for 70 percent of sales; vertical market software developers (e.g., Marketplace Information), which together accounted for 15 percent; and multinational corporations (e.g., Hewlett-Packard that packaged software with hardware), which also accounted for 15 percent. The shift from hardware-based to software-based and licensed management solutions was thought likely to increase the importance of the second and third categories. In this event, companies like Aladdin would have to market directly to a broader array of corporations rather than just to the software developers.

Most purchasers looked at no more than two software security product lines before settling on a single manufacturer. They rarely mixed security technologies from several vendors since, once installed, the dongles could not easily be retrofitted to fit alternative programs. The additional forming market for license management, software-based solutions was expected to stimulate reappraisal of existing vendor-customer relationships. However, complex, highly priced software programs (selling for $1,000 or more) would still require and justify the added security of hardware-based protection measures.

By May 1996, Aladdin had sold HASP products, either directly or through distributors, to some 12,000 customers. The corresponding figure for FAST's Hardlock

---

[5]*Business Wire,* July 25, 1996.

line was 8,000. In 1995, 60 percent of HASP unit sales came from 10 percent of the company's customers.

In smaller firms, the decision to invest in software security protection was usually made by presidents or sales managers, whose own bonuses were especially vulnerable to the impact of piracy. In larger firms, technical specialists typically gathered information on and tested alternative software security products. In both cases, the selling price of the software package had to be sufficient to warrant the extra cost of including the security dongle as part of the bundled price.[6]

Decision makers were reached through a variety of communications methods, ranging from trade shows to magazine advertising and direct mail. Salespeople could justify calling on only the largest customers. Aladdin spent almost $1.75 million on worldwide marketing communications for its software security products in 1995, broken down as shown in Table C.

Direct-mail efforts involved card deck mailings of postcard size advertisements being sent to subscribers of software magazines such as *Byte* and *PC,* inviting inquiries about Aladdin's products. Examples of Aladdin's corporate advertising, U.S. advertising for HASP, and by Aladdin's Italian distributor are presented in Exhibits 3–5. Aladdin made its advertisements and brochures available to all international subsidiaries and distributors. Most translated the material and published it locally; some simply issued the brochures in English; others invested in developing their own local advertisements and collateral.

Once a prospect contacted Aladdin, (s)he was sent an information packet and an order form for a $15 developer's kit. This was more than a mere "demo," since it actually included one unit of the product (a hardware key, a manual, and the software) and could be integrated into an existing software program. In 1996, 5,000 kits were

---

[6]Software security products were rarely offered as a separate purchase option by software developers.

sent to prospective customers. Approximately 30 percent of the kits that were sold resulted in follow-on orders within 4–8 weeks. It was evident that more software developers needed to protect their software and more of them were choosing HASP. Aladdin's management speculated that half of those who purchased the developer's kit, but did not place subsequent orders, did so more out of curiosity than a need to protect software. The remainder ended up purchasing products from Aladdin's competitors.

In the software security business, selling the dongle was just the beginning of a long-term relationship with a customer. Margalit clarified:

> When a new piece of software or a new version of an existing software is introduced, without any protection, there is a very quick ramp in piracy rates. By incorporating HASP, our customers delay this process significantly and protect their revenue streams.
>
> In order to protect our customer investments in the dongle, we regularly provide them with software upgrades. These upgrades are like changing the insides of a lock and the combination key required to unlock it. Currently, a purchase of an Aladdin dongle also includes the right to upgrades. Giving the latter away is an industry practice and we offer them free to our customers.

The company offered free technical support for its products. Requests for assistance could be faxed, e-mailed, or telephoned in. Because most purchasers were sophisticated software developers, demand for after-sales service was low.

The communications mix for FAST's Hardlock line was similar in size and breakdown to that for HASP. However, Hardlock was less heavily advertised. Sample Hardlock magazine advertisements from the United States and Italy are presented as Exhibits 6 and 7. A greater emphasis was placed on generating qualified leads through trade shows, personal selling, and direct mail, rather than through advertising. In the United States, Rainbow Technologies successfully used telemarketing representatives to cold call prospective

---

TABLE C   ALADDIN COMMUNICATIONS BUDGET FOR SOFTWARE SECURITY PRODUCTS: 1995

VEHICLE	EXPENDITURES
Magazine advertising (*Byte, PC,* etc.)	$1,100,000
Trade shows	350,000
Brochures and collateral	75,000
Direct mail	160,000
Mailed samples	100,000
Cooperative marketing (with distributors)	120,000
Public relations	50,000

Exhibit 3   Aladdin Corporate Magazine Advertisement: 1996

EXHIBIT 4   ALADDIN HASP MAGAZINE ADVERTISEMENT: 1996

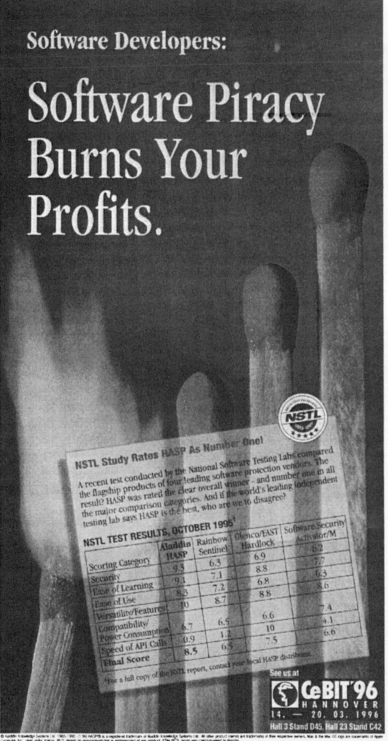

EXHIBIT 5   HASP ITALIAN DISTRIBUTOR MAGAZINE ADVERTISEMENT: 1996

Anche per MAC!

HASP: LA CHIAVE DEL SOFTWARE
Ora protegge anche le reti di sistemi

Se vuoi proteggere il tuo software, cioè il tuo lavoro, la tua creatività, i tuoi investimenti, puoi farlo in modo semplice ed economico. HASP è un dispositivo Hw di piccole dimensioni che va applicato alla porta parallela del PC o PS/2, ed ora anche del MAC, e che inibisce l'utilizzo non autorizzato di qualunque programma se non si è in possesso della chiave d'accesso memorizzata nel dispositivo stesso. Tutti i dispositivi HASP sono trasparenti al software e non ostacolano minimamente il normale funzionamento della stampante.

● **HASP-3** dispone oggi di 2 passwords e si avvale di una nuova tecnologia di protezione per una completa trasparenza. E' possibile proteggere direttamente un programma compilato (.Exe, .Com) oppure inserire delle call in tutti i programmi usati. Funziona in ambienti MS/DOS, XENIX, UNIX, AIX, WINDOWS 3 e OS/2. Un codice di accesso, preinserito (firmware) nella chiave, viene assegnato in esclusiva a ciascun cliente.

● **MemoHASP**, oltre a tutte le caratteristiche del precedente, dispone di una memoria di 496 bytes dove puoi registrare il codice da te scelto e altri dati riservati. Il programma applicativo può modificare tale memoria che può così fungere, per esempio, da contatore d'uso del pacchetto, inibendone l'accesso oltre certi livelli di utilizzo.

● **NetHASP**, infine, protegge anche il software in rete, limitando inoltre l'accesso alle sole stazioni abilitate.

Le varie versioni di HASP sono serializzabili, per cui più dispositivi possono essere utilizzati contemporaneamente. La Versione HASP-3 costa solo **69.500** lire; quindi, se vuoi proteggere il tuo software puoi farlo, noi ti diamo il modo di metterlo sotto chiave.

partner data s.r.l.
Servizi e Prodotti Informatici

20145 Milano - Via Prati, 4 - Tel. 02/33101709 (r.a.) - Fax 347564

EXHIBIT 6   FAST HARDLOCK U.S. MAGAZINE ADVERTISEMENT: 1996

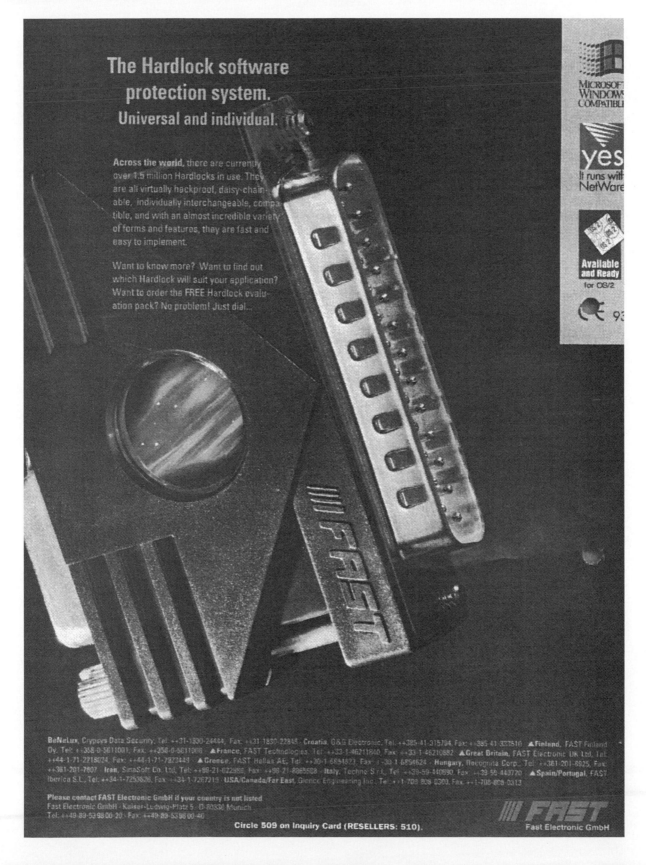

customers directly as well as the other communications methods.

PRICING

The price a customer was willing to pay for software security depended upon the value of the software to be protected. The more expensive the software, the more the customer would pay for extra levels of security.

The HASP line included four levels of progressively more sophisticated and expensive products ranging from $20 to $100. Unit variable costs of materials and direct labor ranged from $5 to $10. While single unit orders were accepted, a quantity discount schedule offered discounts of up to 50 percent from the unit price on large orders. All prices were quoted in U.S. dollars. Payments could be made by credit cards, wire transfers, checks, and cash. Delivery within four business days was normal.

Any industry shift towards software-based solutions would have, it was believed, significant effects on pricing. Glassman commented:

> Traditionally, we've made our profit on the hardware and "given away" the accompanying software, manual, and follow-on upgrades. As developers sell and download their software to purchasers via the Internet, we'll need to add software-based solutions. That means we'll have to charge for the software as well. I'm not sure we'll be able to charge the same prices that we do today. On the other hand, lower prices will expand our market.

The most price competitive markets for software security products were the United States and the United Kingdom. In general, unit prices were higher in Europe than in North America. The Hardlock line was priced around 20 percent higher than the HASP line in most markets; Hardlock advertising emphasized the line's robustness, premium product quality, and German manufacturing. HASP products were positioned as the total best solution and value priced on the price performance curve at, on average, 5 percent to 10 percent below equivalent Rainbow products.

INTERNATIONAL DISTRIBUTION

Exhibit 8 summarizes the subsidiaries, joint ventures, and distributors through which Aladdin and FAST went to market with their software security products in the ten most important world markets. Around 70 percent of HASP units were sold in Israel, exported direct from Israel or sold through Aladdin's subsidiaries in the United States, United Kingdom and Japan. The remaining 30 percent were made through 40 authorized foreign distributors. HASP distributors typically marked up the prices they paid Aladdin by 40–50 percent. Hardlock distributors followed a similar policy.

According to Glassman, the best HASP distributors were sometimes the smaller companies specializing in software security products for whom the HASP line represented a significant portion of their sales. Aladdin signed one- or two-year agreements with foreign distributors, renewable if agreed upon sales targets were reached. Distributors had to have both a full-time salesperson and technical specialist on staff dedicated to HASP sales and service. They had to submit an annual marketing plan and customer list and attend an annual Aladdin management conference. In return for not representing a competing software security company, most independent distributors received product training and cooperative marketing support from Aladdin headquarters.

United States The United States was the most important software security market in the world, in large part because the opinion leaders and magazines which reviewed the industry's products were published in the United States and circulated worldwide. Both HASP and Hardlock, as two of only a handful of foreign-made protection systems, faced stiff competition in a price-sensitive market dominated by Rainbow Technologies. Rainbow was expected to sell over a million units, more than half its volume, in the United States in 1996. In 1989, FAST's U.S. distributor, Glenco Engineering, headquartered in Chicago, had approached both Aladdin and FAST to become distributor for one or the other's software security systems. Glenco's deal with FAST gave it distribution rights for Hardlock products in Latin American and Asia-Pacific as well as North America. Aladdin then established its own subsidiary. By the time of the acquisition, Hardlock sales accounted for four-fifths of Glenco's total sales. However, HASP was outselling Hardlock by more than two-to-one in the United States.

Asia-Pacific In Japan, South Korea, and New Zealand, Aladdin's HASP products dominated the security market, outselling Hardlock by five-to-one. HASP reached Japanese customers through a 51 percent owned subsidiary and, because of its greater compatibility with a broader range of compilers and operating systems, claimed 20 percent market share against Hardlock's 5 percent. Hardlock products were redistributed in Asia by Glenco, FAST's U.S. distributor, via a cumbersome two-step process.

Europe *Germany*—With a 75 percent market share, Hardlock was the uncontested leader in the German market, where its reputation for superior quality commanded a higher price than in other markets. HASP held a 10 percent market share and competed on price, occasionally obtaining large volume orders from experienced, price-sensitive customers.

France—Aladdin owned 10 percent of its HASP distributorship, but the principals of this firm had other commercial interests which distracted them from

EXHIBIT 8   INTERNATIONAL DISTRIBUTION ORGANIZATION FOR ALADDIN AND FAST: MAY 1996

Sales Rank	Countries	Aladdin Subsidiary/Distributor	Type	Software Security Sales as % of Total Sales	FAST Subsidiary/Distributor	Type	Software Security Sales as % of Total Sales
1	Germany	Computer Security Service, GmbH	D	45%	FAST Software Security AG	S	95%
2	U.S.A.	Aladdin Knowledge Systems, Inc.	S	90	Glenco Engineering Inc.	D	75
3	Israel	Aladdin Knowledge Systems, Ltd.	—	90	—	—	—
4	France	Aladdin France SA	JV—10%	80	FAST Technologies	JV—50%	80
5	Japan	Aladdin Japan Co., Ltd.	S	95	1. CRC Technical Co. 2. Suncarla Corporation	D	40
6	Russia	Aladdin Software Security R.D., Ltd.	D	75	Kasi	D	40
7	U.K.	Aladdin Knowledge Systems U.K., Ltd.	S	95	FAST Electronic U.K., Ltd.	JV—50%	75
8	Italy	Partner Data, srl.	D	40	Techne Security srl	D	55
9	Spain	PC Hardware, SL	D	75	FAST Iberica, SL	JV—50%	85
10	Benelux	Aladdin Software Security Benelux BV	D	75	CrypSysData Security BV	D	40

Source: Company records.

Note: D = Independent Distributor; S = Subsidiary; JV = Joint Venture.

concentrating on selling the HASP line. The FAST acquisition gave Aladdin a stake in the Hardlock distributor. However, following the lead of FAST headquarters, the latter had been focusing more on multimedia than on the software security line.

Russia—When Aladdin acquired Eliashim's software security business in 1995, it licensed Eliashim's Russian distributor to sell the HASP product line. HASP held a more than 60 percent market share in Russia. Hardlock sales were minimal.

United Kingdom—Aladdin's wholly owned subsidiary had developed an 18 percent market share for the HASP line in this highly price competitive market. The Hardlock market share was 7 percent despite FAST's 50 percent stake in its distributor. The Hardlock distributor was concentrating more sales effort on FAST's new multimedia product line.

Italy—Despite some local manufacturing assembly of HASP products, the HASP distributor had achieved only a 5 percent market share. The Hardlock distributor, Techne, on the other hand, had achieved 10 percent market share and was considered capable of also distributing Aladdin's new line of smart card products.

Spain—HASP and Hardlock unit sales were similar. An executive at the Hardlock distributor had already complained that high transfer prices and lack of marketing support from Germany impeded his ability to grow sales.

Benelux—HASP sales were growing 60 percent annually versus Hardlock's 10 percent.

THE FAST SECURITY AG ACQUISITION

Discussions between Aladdin and FAST commenced in mid-1994. Margalit commented:

There seemed to be a good cultural fit. Both companies were very entrepreneurial and run by young management teams. We also looked at Software Security Inc., the American company, but their products seemed inferior to FAST and their management team less in line with our culture. Also, acquiring Software Security would not have taken us to number one in the United States, let alone in Europe. By merging with FAST, we would become the share leader in Europe and a much stronger number two in the United States. At the same time, we suspected Rainbow was also looking to boost its share through one or more acquisitions, so we had to consider their likely next move when deciding our own.

A minority of Aladdin executives questioned the wisdom of the acquisition on the grounds that the software security market was maturing, and that smart card technology and license management was where Aladdin should be investing for the future. Margalit believed, however, merging with FAST to boost Aladdin's world unit market share in software security by about 100 percent would prove a sound investment.

At a meeting on May 30, 1996, following the announcement of the acquisition, Margalit sat down with David Glassman, Aladdin's director of marketing and sales, Steffi Koerner, FAST's expected new chief executive, and Shai Saul, Aladdin's VP for business development, to discuss how to integrate the Aladdin and FAST product lines, marketing efforts, and distribution systems worldwide. As preparation for the discussion, Glassman had developed the chart shown in Exhibit 9 which summarized (a) how Aladdin and FAST went to market with their software security products in the ten countries with the highest combined sales and (b) the unit sales and market shares achieved by the Aladdin and FAST distributors, joint ventures, and subsidiaries in the ten most important markets.

The discussion proceeded as follows:

Margalit: The terms of the acquisition have been negotiated. We have announced the deal. Now the hard work begins. We have to build trust and get the two organizations to work together. Our goals are to increase HASP and Hardlock worldwide sales by 30 percent by the end of 1996. At the same time we would like to make sure that we do not upset our current customer and distribution channels. Have you guys come up with a marketing integration plan to enable us to achieve these goals?

Koerner: No, but we're going to have to move quickly. I have heard from several FAST distributors that they have been approached by competitors telling them that their distributorships are going to be canceled by Aladdin and inviting them to switch.

Glassman: Another issue is that some of the FAST distributors and subsidiaries have also been distributing and, in fact, concentrating on selling FAST's new multimedia products. They may just prefer to hand the Hardlock line over to the HASP distributor in the same market.

Koerner: Wait a minute. Many of these Hardlock distributors have been very loyal and as effective at pushing software security products as they could be, given the shift in FAST's corporate strategy to multimedia. David and I have found no more than a 5 percent overlap between Hardlock customers and HASP customers in the same country markets, so surely it makes sense to keep two brands and two distribution channels to compete against Rainbow.

Margalit: The economics of the acquisition require that we find some synergies. As you know, we're going to unite Hardlock and HASP manufacturing to take advantage of government tax incentives. We should be able to cut Hardlock unit manufacturing costs by 20 percent. The research and development groups at FAST and Aladdin have already begun to coordinate their efforts, so we'll save some money there. But surely we can generate some hard dollar savings and increase our clout in the marketplace by consolidating distribution in some country markets, especially the smaller ones.

Saul: It all depends on how we decide to position the two brands and whether we feel it's necessary for the same brand positionings to be followed in all markets worldwide. I believe that, if the two brands are positioned

EXHIBIT 9   ALADDIN AND FAST SOFTWARE SECURITY SALES PERFORMANCE BY COUNTRY: 1996 (ESTIMATED)

SALES RANK	COUNTRIES	ALADDIN UNIT SALES[a] (000)	FAST UNIT SALES[a] (000)	COMBINED UNIT SALES[a] (000)	COMBINED MARKET SHARE (UNITS)	ALADDIN UNIT PRICE[b]	FAST UNIT PRICE[b]
1	Germany	80	320	400	80%	$30	$35
2	U.S.A.	585	230	815	30	25	45
3	Israel[c]	100	5	105	90	20	30
4	France	45	35	80	20	35	45
5	Japan	100	20	120	25	50	55
6	Russia	25	5	30	60	20	35
7	U.K.	85	30	115	25	25	35
8	Italy	20	35	55	15	30	40
9	Spain	20	20	40	50	25	45
10	Benelux	10	15	25	30	30	40
Total	—	1,070	715	1,785	—	—	—

Source: Company records.

[a]Unit Sales in hardware-based software security products only.

[b]Manufacturer prices before quantity discounts. Average realized prices were one-third lower.

[c]Includes some direct shipments to end customers in countries outside of Israel where there were no authorized distributors.

differently, say Hardlock as a premium brand and HASP as a value brand, the same organization can easily sell both.

Koerner: Surely, it's the reverse. If you have two brands positioned differently, you need to go to market through two distribution organizations. You need to have separate booths at the trade shows and separate Internet sites. You need to continue separate advertising campaigns. Our FAST distributors and subsidiaries will be demotivated if they're all merged in with the Aladdin organization. That's especially true in Germany where we dominate the market. We also need to reassure our Hardlock end users around the world that the acquisition isn't going to affect our product availability and service.

Glassman: I agree. We have to find the best way of building the combined sales and profitability of HASP and Hardlock in each country market. However, our resources are limited, so it doesn't make sense to me to try to advertise both brands; let's focus our efforts behind one in each market.

Margalit: Perhaps we shouldn't be looking for a standardized solution in all country markets. Why don't you two put your heads together, analyze the strengths and weaknesses of the two brands and how they are distributed in each of our important country markets, and develop a set of recommendations. Where consolidation looks appropriate, we do have some funds to either buy back distribution rights from those distributors whom we terminate or to increase our equity stakes in others. Do not forget that it is extremely important for us as a company to guarantee the continued satisfaction of both our HASP and Hardlock customers. Also bear in mind that we are dealing with people who have been loyal to us for years. We should not forget that.

Research Associate Robin Root prepared this case under the supervision of Professor John A. Quelch as the basis for class discussion rather than to illustrate either effective or ineffective handling of an administrative situation. Confidential data and certain protagonist names have been disguised.

NOTES

Chapter 1

1. Malcolm Fleschner, "Signed, Sealed, Delivered," *Selling Power* (April 1999): 43–46.
2. Andy Cohen, "Practice Makes Profits," *Sales & Marketing Management* (July 1995): 24.
3. Michael Hammer and James Champy, *Reengineering the Corporation* (New York: Harper Collins, 1993).
4. Kevin Waters, "H-P's Sales Soar," *USA Today* (April 10, 1996): C1.
5. Bill Fromm and Len Schlesinger, *The Real Heroes of Business* (New York: Currency Doubleday, 1993): 95–114.
6. Based on a 1996 survey by the author.
7. Personal interview with the author.
8. Adapted from Susan Harte, "When in Rome, You Should Learn to Do What the Romans Do," *Atlanta Journal-Constitution* (January 22, 1996): D1, D6. Also see *Lufthansa's Business Travel Guide/Europe,* 1995.
9. Frank Pacetta, *Don't Fire Them, Fire Them Up* (New York: Simon & Schuster, 1994): 70.
10. Frank Pacetta, *Don't Fire Them,* 71.

Chapter 2

1. Melinda Ligos, "Too Old to Sell," *Sales & Marketing Management* (June 1998): 50–55.
2. James Srodes, "Corporations Discover It's Good to Be Good," *Business and Society Review* (Summer 1990): 57–60.
3. Emily Barker, "DuPont Tries to Clean Up Its Act," *Business and Society Review* (winter 1995): 36–41.
4. Jim Rogers, "Ethics in America," *Newsweek* (June 1996): 52.
5. Based on L. Kohlberg, "Moral Stages and Moralization: The Cognitive-Development Approach," *Moral Development and Behavior: Theory, Research, and Social Issues,* ed. T. Lickona (New York: Holt, Rinehart, and Winston, 1976). Also see Jerry R. Goolsby and Shelby D. Hunt, "Cognitive Moral Development and Marketing," *Journal of Marketing* (January 1992): 55–68.
6. Also see Thomas R. Wotruba, "A Comprehensive Framework for the Analysis of Ethical Behavior, with a Focus on Sales Organizations," *Journal of Personal Selling & Sales Management* (Spring 1990): 29–42; and Michael A. Mayo and Lawrence J. Marks, "An Empirical Investigation of a General Theory of Marketing Ethics," *Journal of the Academy of Marketing Science* (Spring 1990): 163–172.
7. Also see Leslie M. Dawson, "Will Feminization Change the Ethics of the Sales Profession?" *Journal of Personal Selling & Sales Management* (Winter 1992): 21–32; Anusorn Singhapakdi and Scott J. Vitell, "Marketing Ethics: Sales Professionals versus Other Marketing Professionals," *Journal of Personal Selling & Sales Management* (Spring 1992): 27–38; and Shay Sayre, Mary L. Joyce, and David R. Lambert, "Gender and Sales Ethics: Are Women Penalized Less Severely than Their Male Counterparts?" *Journal of Personal Selling & Sales Management* (Fall 1991): 50–65.
8. Andy Cohen, "Is Stealing against the Law?" *Sales & Marketing Management* (July 1995): 101–103.
9. M. Galen, "Ending Sexual Harassment: Business Is Getting the Message," *Business Week* (March 18, 1991): 98–100.
10. Joseph A. Bellizzi and Robert E. Hite, "Supervising Unethical Salesforce Behavior," *Journal of Marketing* (April 1989): 36–47.
11. Jeffrey A. Fadiman, "A Traveler's Guide to Gifts and Bribes," *Harvard Business Review* (July–August 1986): 122–136; I. Frederick Trawick, Jr., and John E. Swan, "How Salespeople Err with Purchasers: Overstepping Ethical Bounds," *The Journal of Business and Industrial Marketing* (Summer 1988): 5–11; and I. Frederick Trawick, Jr., John E. Swan, and David Rick, "Industrial Buyer Evaluation of the Ethics

of Salesperson Gift Giving: Value of the Gift and Consumer vs. prospect Status," *The Journal of Personal Selling & Sales Management* (Summer 1989): 31–37.

12. Also see Rosemary R. Lagace, Robert Dahlstrom, and Jule B. Gassenheimer, "The Relevance of Ethical Salesperson Behavior on Relationship Quality: The Pharmaceutical Industry," *Journal of Personal Selling & Sales Management* (Fall 1991): 39–47; and Gary Minkin, "The Bait and Switch Pyramid," *Insurance Sales* (February 1990): 14–19.

13. Also see Karl A. Boedecker, Fred W. Morgan, and Jeffrey J. Stoltman, "Legal Dimensions of Salespersons' Statements: A Review and Managerial Suggestions," *Journal of Marketing* (January 1991): 70–80.

14. Federal Trade Commission, *Trade Regulation Rule: Cooling-off Period for Door-to-Door Sales,* 1982, 16 C.F.R., pt. 429.

15. Also see Alan J. Dubinsky, Marvin A. Jolson, Masaa Ki Kotabe, and Chae Un Lim, "A Cross-National Investigation of Industrial Salespeople's Ethical Perceptions," *Journal of International Business Studies* (Fall 1991): 561–670.

16. "Corporate Ethics: A Prime Business Asset," *The Business Roundtable,* 200 Park Avenue, Suite 2222, New York, NY 10166, February 1988.

17. Sean Armstrong, "The Good, the Bad and the Industry," *Best's Review* (June 1994): 35–39, 114.

18. Based on Bart Victor and John B. Cullen, "The Organizational Bases of Ethical Work Climates," *Administrative Science Quarterly.*

CHAPTER 3

1. Don Peppers and Martha Rogers, Ph.D., "Growing Revenues with Cross-Selling," *Sales & Marketing Management* (June 1999): 24.

2. Peter D. Bennett, *Dictionary of Marketing Terms* (Chicago: American Marketing Association, 1988): 115.

CHAPTER 4

1. Sarah Lorge, "Learning to Love Change," *Sales & Marketing Management* (May 1999): 63.

2. George Webster, "Big Blue Reorganizes," *Newsweek* (November 1992): 24–28; and John Lewis, "H-P Reorganizes," *USA Today* (November 5, 1993): A4.

3. Ravi S. Archrol, "Evolution of the Marketing Organization: New Forms for Turbulent Environments," *Journal of Marketing* (October 1991): 77–93.

4. For background on other classifications of sales jobs and the empirical development of sales-position taxonomies, see William C. Moncrief, III, "Selling Activity and Sales Position Taxonomies for Industrial Salesforce," *Journal of Marketing Research* (August 1986): 261–270.

5. Kate Bertrand, "Reorganizing for Sales," *Business Marketing* (February 1990): 30.

6. Abe Krone, "Corporate Sales Knows Their Powers," *Business Week* (July 1996): 101–106.

7. Joseph P. Vaccaro, "Organizational Issues in Sales Force Decisions," *Journal of Professional Services Marketing* (March 1992): 69–80.

8. Ibid.

9. "Follow the Leader," *Sales & Marketing Management* (April 1996): 34.

10. Malcolm Fleschner, "Anatomy of a Sale," *Selling Power* (January/February 1999): 79–82, 84.

CHAPTER 5

1. Sarah Lorge, "Why It Pays to Be Curious," *Sales & Marketing Management* (August 1998): 76.

2. William Keenan, Jr., "Numbers Racket: Are Your Salespeople Contributing to the Effort to Predict Tomorrow's Business Results?" *Sales & Marketing Management* (May 1995): 64–76.

3. Thayer C. Taylor, "The Right Platform, Uh-Huh," *Sales & Marketing Management* (December 1994): 41–42.

4. Tracy Peverett, "Ault Foods Finds a Recipe for Success," *Computing Canada* (October 26, 1995): 24.

5. Charles M. Futrell, *ABC's of Relationship Selling* (Burr Ridge, IL: Richard D. Irwin, Inc., 1997): 56.

Chapter 6

1. Melinda Ligos, "Point, Click, and Sell," *Sales & Marketing Management* (May 1999): 51–52, 54, 56.

2. Melissa Campanelli, "A New Focus," *Sales & Marketing Management* (September 1995): 56–58.

Chapter 7

1. Don Peppers and Martha Rogers, Ph.D., "Growing Revenues with Cross-Selling," *Sales & Marketing Management* (June 1999): 24.

2. Nancy Arnott, "Leading Edge," *Sales & Marketing Management* (July 1994): 11.

3. Adapted from Sergy Frank, "Global Negotiation," *Sales & Marketing Management* (May 1996): 64–69.

4. John Apple, "Fasten Up Your Salespeople," *Business Week* (April 15, 1996): 118.

5. Wilson Harrell, "Down with Sales Budgets," *Success* (July/August 1995): 104.

Chapter 8

1. Malcolm Fleschner, "Signed, Sealed, Delivered," *Selling Power* (April 1999): 43–46.

2. Adapted from Bill Fromm and Len Schlesinger, *The Real Heroes of Business— and Not a CEO among Them* (New York: Doubleday, 1994): 112–113.

Chapter 9

1. William Keenan, Jr., "Professionally Speaking," *Sales & Marketing Management* (September 1995) 31–36.

2. "Finding Top Reps on Campus," *Sales & Marketing Management* (March 1995): 38.

3. Weld F. Royal, "From Socialist to Sales Rep," *Sales & Marketing Management* (August 1994): 63.

4. "Agents: What Characteristics Do You Consider Most Important When Hiring Salespeople?" *Agency Sales Magazine* (August 1994).

5. Adapted from Charles M. Futrell, *ABC's of Relationship Selling* (Burr Ridge, IL: Richard D. Irwin, Inc., 1996), 35.

Chapter 10

1. Melinda Ligos, "Point, Click, and Sell," *Sales & Marketing Management* (May 1999): 51–52, 54, 56.

2. Sally Johns, "Re-engineering Training," *Training* (April 1996): 102.

3. Wayne Bland, "Sales Training Pays Off," *Engineering* (April 1996): 102.

4. Personal conversation with the author.

5. Personal conversation with the author.

6. William Keenan, Jr., "Getting Customers into the A.C.T.," *Sales & Marketing Management* (February 1995): 58–63.

7. Melissa Campanelli, "Can Managers Coach?" *Sales & Marketing Management* (July 1995): 59–66.

8. Stephanie Ducker, "Training Costs Run into the Billions," *Business Week* (February 15, 1996): 15–18.

9. Ben Former, "Business Goes Multimedia," *Technology* (January 1996): 57–58.

10. Personal visit to company.

CHAPTER 11

1. Melinda Ligos, "Point, Click and Sell," *Sales & Marketing Management* (May 1999): 51–52, 54, 56.
2. Developed by Pushkala Raman.
3. Adapted from Charles M. Futrell, *ABC's of Relationship Selling* (Burr Ridge, IL: Richard D. Irwin, 1977).
4. Lisa Rodriguez, "The Cutting Edge," *Sales & Marketing Management* (February 1999): 15.
5. Barrett Joyner, "Success Sure Is a Lot of Fun," *Sales & Marketing Management* (January 1999): 59.
6. Portions of this section were adapted from George W. Colombo, *Sales Force Automation* (New York: McGraw-Hill, 1994).
7. Rochelle Garner, "The E-Commerce Connection," *Sales & Marketing Management* (January 1999): 42.
8. Andy Cohen, "Going Mobile, Part 2," *Sales & Marketing Management* (June 1994): 5.
9. For more information, see Ronald and Douglas L. Fugate, "Using Trust-Transference as a Persuasion Technique: An Empirical Field Investigation," *The Journal of Personal Selling and Sales Management* (August 1988): 1–7; Daniel H. McQuiston and Rockney G. Walters, "The Evaluative Criteria of Industrial Buyers: Implications for Sales Training," *The Journal of Business and Industrial Marketing* (Summer/Fall 1989): 667–675; and Jon M. Hawes, Kenneth E. Mast, and John E. Swan, "Trust Earning Perceptions of Sellers and Buyers," *The Journal of Personal Selling and Sales Management* (Spring 1989): 1–8.
10. Joe Mullich, "Copying Xerox's Style: Sales Strategy Duplicated at Other Firms," *Business Marketing* (November 1994): 1, 48.
11. Ginger Trumfio, "Cultivating Your Network," *Sales & Marketing Management* (January 1994): 57.
12. Malcolm Fleschner, "Signed, Sealed, and Delivered," *Selling Power* (April 1999): 43–46.
13. Weld F. Royal, "Unearthing Hard-to-Find Prospects," *Sales & Marketing Management* (November 1995): 92.
14. Arun Sharma, "The Persuasive Effect of Salesperson Credibility: Conceptual and Empirical Examination," *Journal of Personal Selling and Sales Management* (Fall 1990): 71–80.
15. For a discussion of improving sales approach and training effectiveness, see Thomas W. Leigh, "Cognitive Selling Scripts and Sales Training," *The Journal of Personal Selling and Sales Management* (August 1987) 39–48.
16. Michele Marchetti, "That's the Craziest Thing I Ever Heard," *Sales & Marketing Management* (November 1995): 77–82.
17. James C. McElroy, Paula C. Morrow, and Sevo Erogle, "The Atmosphere of Personal Selling," *Journal of Personal Selling and Sales Management* (Fall 1990): 31–42.
18. Tom Dellecave, Jr., "Now Showing: New Multimedia Tools Put Sound, Video, and Graphics at Your Sales Reps' Fingertips," *Sales & Marketing Management* (February 1996): 68–73.
19. Chad Kaydo, "Making Online Sales Presentations," *Sales & Marketing Management* (September 1998): 16.
20. Thayer C. Taylor, "It's Better to Show than Tell," *Sales & Marketing Management* (April 1994): 47–48.
21. Steve Martin, "Visual Tools," *Sales & Marketing Management* (April 1996): 82.
22. Adapted from Phillip R. Cateora, *International Marketing* (Burr Ridge, IL: Richard D. Irwin, Inc., 1996): 524–525.

CHAPTER 12

1. Erin Strout, "Just Rewards," *Sales & Marketing Management* (May 1999): 37–40, 42.
2. Personal conversation with the author.
3. Edward C. Tolman, *Purposive Behavior in Animals and Men* (New York: Appleton-Century-Crofts, 1983); Kurt Levin, *The Conceptual Representation and the Measurement of Psychological Forces* (Durham, NC: Duke University Press, 1938); Victor H. Vroom, *Work and Motivation* (New York: John Wiley & Sons, 1964); David C. McClelland, *The Achieving Society* (New York: Van Nostrand, 1964); and John W. Atkinson, *An Introduction to Motivation* (New York: Van Nostrand, 1964).
4. Caroline Bollinger and Liza Rodriguez, "Which Rep Stacks Up?" *Sales & Marketing Management* (August 1998): 63–64.
5. Erika Rasmusson, "What the Little People Want," *Sales & Marketing Management* (June 1999): 14.
6. Personal conversation with the author.
7. Malcolm Fleschner, "Team Up to Sell," *Personal Selling Power* (March 1995): 74–75.

CHAPTER 13

1. Michele Marchetti, "Helping Reps Count Every Penny," *Sales & Marketing Management* (July 1998): 77.
2. Personal conversation with the author.
3. Michele Marchetti, "Compensation Is Kid Stuff," *Sales & Marketing Management* (April 1999): 55.
4. Vincent Alonzo, "Money Isn't Everything," *Sales & Marketing Management* (January 1999): 28, 30.

CHAPTER 14

1. Erin Strout, "Just Rewards," *Sales & Marketing Management* (May 1999): 37–40, 42.
2. Malcolm Fleschner, "Signed, Sealed, Delivered," *Selling Power* (April 1999): 43–46.

CHAPTER 15

1. John Patterson, "Bristol-Myers Squibb Reengineers Customer Service," *IIE Solutions* (September 1995): 60.

CHAPTER 16

1. Andy Cohen, "Lighting a Fire under Average Performers," *Sales & Marketing Management* (January 1996): 27–28.
2. Lance B. Eliot, "Cooperative Goal Setting Makes the Difference," *Incentive* (July 1995): 42–43.
3. Minda Zetlin, "Up for Review," *Sales & Marketing Management* (December 1994): 82–86.
4. Zetlin, "Up for Review," 82–86.

EXERCISES, TECHNOLOGY, AND COMPREHENSIVE CASES

1. This exercise copyrighted by Charles M. Futrell, 2000.
2. This exercise was created by Professors Charles M. Futrell of Texas A & M University and George Wynn of James Madison University. Copyright © 2000.
3. Carl Jung, *Psychological Types* (London: Routhledge and Kegan Paul, 1923); Adapted from I. Myers, *The Myers-Briggs Type Incicator* (Princeton, NJ: Educational Testing Service, 1962).
4. This exercise copyrighted by Charles M. Futrell, 2000.
5. Adapted from Jerome A. Colletti and Mary S. Fiss with Wally Wood, *Compensating: New Sales Roles* (New York: AMACOM), 58–62.
6. Adapted from Jerome A. Colletti and Mary S. Fiss with Wally Wood, *Compensating: New Sales Roles* (New York: AMACOM), 26–28.

7. Based upon the work of Zarrell V. Lambert, Professor of Marketing, Southern Illinois University, and Fred W. Kniffin, Professor of Marketing, Emeritus, University of Connecticut. Assistance provided by Professor Charles M. Futrell.

8. Assistance provided by Professor Charles M. Futrell. Based upon the work of Robert W. Witt of The University of Texas, Arlington.

GLOSSARY

Ability Skills, knowledge, experience, and performance of the individual.

Activity quotas Objectives set for job-related duties useful toward reaching salespeople's performance targets.

Advertising Nonpersonal communication of information paid for by an identified sponsor such as an individual or an organization.

AIDA approach Sales presentation using a structured series of steps: attention, interest, desire, and action.

Application blank An orderly, convenient method of collecting necessary information for determining an applicant's minimum qualifications.

Approach Also called the *sales opener,* first major part of the sales presentation.

Assessment center Centralized organizational unit within the firm that evaluates all applicants in a comprehensive and uniform manner.

Behavioral anchored rating scales (BARS) An evaluation program in which the manager determines a salesperson's performance in very specific areas, compares it with others, and rates the performance, providing feedback to the salesperson.

Behavioral objectives Objectives that identify the goals of the training program for both the trainer and trainee.

Behavioral training A type of training that involves instructing salespeople how to change their customer interaction habits.

Bonus system A formal plan for giving salespeople compensation in addition to what they normally make, usually over an extended period.

Boundary position Position that salespeople are placed in between meeting the needs of their company and those of the customer.

Breach of warranty Legal cause of action similar to misrepresentation but differing in requirements of proof and types of damages awarded.

Breakdown approach Method of determining the quantity of sales territories needed to sell and service a firm's market sales by considering population or number of customers.

Career counseling Help in understanding future with organization.

CCC GOMES An acronym referring to eight important stakeholders in an organization.

Centralized training Training conducted at a central location for all salespeople.

Central-tendency error The tendency of managers to rate all of their salespeople as average on all performance criteria.

Ceremonies and rites The elaborate planned activities that make up special events and often are conducted for the benefit of an audience.

Closing Step in the selling process in which the salesperson helps the prospect make a decision about the product to conclude the sale.

Coaching The process of training someone on the job intensively through instruction, demonstration, and practice.

Code of ethics A formal statement of a company's values concerning ethics and social issues.

Coercive power The ability to influence others through one's authority to punish or to recommend punishment.

Combination salary plan A type of compensation plan in which a portion of the pay is guaranteed and the rest is incentive pay.

Company sales potential The maximum estimated or potential sales a company may reach in a defined period under given conditions.

Compensation message The communication to salespeople about pay and management's expectations.

Conceptual and decision skills Refers to the cognitive ability to see the organization as a whole and the relationship among its parts.

Contribution margin approach Method of determining profitability in which costs are separated according to controllability.

Controlling Monitoring sales personnel's activities, determining whether the organization is on target toward its goals, and making corrections as necessary.

Conventional moral development level Level of moral development in which an individual conforms to the expectation of others and upholds legal and moral laws.

Cooling-off laws Laws that provide for a specified period in which the buyer may cancel a contract, return merchandise, and obtain a full refund.

Cooperative acceptance The right of employees to be treated fairly with respect to race, sex, national origin, physical disability, age, or religion while on the job.

Coordination The quality of collaboration across groups.

Counseling Helping a person become a better adjusted human being within the work environment.

Criterion A standard on which a judgment or decision may be based.

Cross-functional teams Teams composed of a defined group of individuals bringing together expertise from different parts of the supplier organization to capture, retain, and increase business with customers.

Curbstone conferences Brief post-sale call discussions about what has just occurred at the customer's place of business.

Curiosity approach An approach technique in which the salesperson asks a question to make the prospect curious about the product or service.

Customer benefit approach An approach technique in which the salesperson asks a question that shows the product can benefit the prospect in some way, such as saving money.

Customer contact plan Plan that involves scheduling sales calls and routing a salesperson's movement around the territory.

Customer satisfaction A customer's feelings about any differences between what is expected and actual experiences with a purchase.

Customer Satisfaction Index An index usually compiled of all customer satisfaction data rated into one number or percentage.

Decentralized training Primary means of training that may be conducted anywhere.

Deliberated structure An adopted system in which tasks are divided, and the responsibility for their performance is assigned to organization members.

Delphi method A survey method that entails administering a series of questionnaires to panels of experts.

Descriptive statement A method for performance appraisal requiring the manager to provide a detailed written description of each salesperson's performance.

Difficulty analysis A process used to uncover and analyze problems experienced by salespeople.

Directive guidance Gives manager an active role in the counseling session.

Discretionary responsibility Highest criterion of social responsibility that is purely voluntary, guided by a company's desire to make social contributions not mandated by economics, laws, or ethics.

Distribution The channel structure used to transfer products from an organization to its customers.

Distribution cost Also called *marketing cost,* cost incurred in getting and filling orders.

District sales manager These managers are responsible for usually three to ten salespeople in one district.

Drawing account A type of compensation plan that combines the incentive of a straight commission plan with the security of a fixed income by enabling the salesperson to borrow against future commissions.

Education Amendments Act of 1972 Legislation that entitles employees in executive, administrative, or professional capacities, as well as outside salespeople, to equal pay.

80/20 principle Theory stating that 80 percent of a firm's sales comes from 20 percent of its customers. Also called the *concentration principle;* the majority of a company's sales (or profits) may result directly from a very small number of the company's accounts, product or price lines, or geographic area.

Employee rights Those rights desired by employees regarding the security of their jobs and treatment administered by their employer while on the job.

Equal Employment Opportunity Act of 1972 Legislation that prohibits discrimination based on race, sex, religion, or national origin.

Equal Employment Opportunity Commission (EEOC) The principal government agency responsible for monitoring discriminatory practices.

Equal Pay Act of 1963 Legislation applied to private employers that prohibits discrimination on the basis of sex for substantially equal work.

Equity theory A way of determining if rewards are fair by developing a ratio of inputs into a job to outcomes from it that is compared with the salesperson's perception of other salespeople's ratios.

Ethical behavior Behavior centered on treating others fairly.

Ethical committee A group of executives appointed to oversee company ethics and provide rulings on questionable ethical issues.

Ethical ombudsperson An official given the responsibility of corporate conscience who hears and investigates ethical complaints and keeps top management informed about potential ethical issues.

Ethics A code of moral principles and values that govern the behaviors of a person or group with respect to what is right or wrong.

Executive forecasting A qualitative sales-forecasting method done by an individual(s).

Exit interviews A series of questions asked when people quit their jobs to determine attitudes toward the job.

Expectancy The salesperson's estimate of the probability that expending a given amount of effort on a task will lead to an improved level of performance on some dimension.

Expectancy theory Theory based on the assumption that salespeople have expectancies about what they should receive from their employer as a result of their work efforts.

Expense plans A system that reimburses salespeople for their food, lodging, travel, entertainment, and auto expenses to allow them to maintain a good "business" standard of living.

Expense quotas A target aimed at controlling costs of sales units.

Expert power The ability to influence others because of special knowledge or skill regarding tasks performed by lower-level employees.

Exponential smoothing A time-series projection method similar to the moving-average forecast method, but it allows consideration of all past data, and less weight is placed on data as it ages.

External recruitment sources Sources where potential job applicants may be found outside the organization.

Extrinsic outcomes Rewards an individual obtains from the environment.

Eyeball fitting Information-series projection method in which data are plotted on a graph and used to estimate a linear trend.

Failure analysis A process used to determine the reasons low-performing salespeople fail to achieve their sales goals.

Firm An organization that produces goods and services.

Forecasting process A series of procedures used to forecast.

Formal compensation process The process of establishing a formal written plan for compensation and rewarding of salespeople.

Full cost approach Sometimes called *net profit approach,* a method of determining profitability in which all costs are allocated among the market segments using the categories of goods sold (production costs) and operating expenses (nonproduction costs), including marketing costs.

Functional marketing groups Sometimes called *activity groups,* different groups within the marketing operation that perform similar functions.

Functional organizational design Organizational structure in which work is grouped according to its characteristics; sometimes called *line* and *staff organization.*

Goal directed Designed to achieve some outcome, such as profit, educated people, meeting spiritual needs, or providing health care.

Good A physical object that can be purchased.

Government An organization that has two functions: the provision of goods and services to households and firms and the redistribution of income and wealth.

Graphic appraisal scale A way of evaluating salespeople's performance in which the manager fills out a form appraising all performance criteria.

Green River ordinances City ordinances that require persons selling directly to consumers to pay a fee and be licensed by the city in which they are doing business if they are not residents.

Gross margin quota A quota determined by subtracting cost of goods sold from sales volume.

Halo effect A positive or negative "aura" associated with an individual.

Household A decision-making unit buying for personal use.

Iceberg principle The distorting effect that averaging, summarizing, and aggregating data can have in presenting the true sales or profit picture and underlying problems.

Incentives Aspects of the environment that appeal to the salesperson's motives and have enough worth to motivate purposeful behavior to obtain them.

Incremental method Method of determining the quantity of sales territories a firm needs by adding territories until the incremental profit contribution of the last territory added equals the territory's incremental cost.

Individual wage The salary for a specific salesperson determined on the basis of personal background and abilities as they relate to job characteristics.

Industry sales forecast The estimated sales for all sellers in the entire market or industry over a specified period and under given conditions.

Instrumentality The salesperson's estimate of the probability that achieving an improved level of performance will lead to increased attainment of a particular reward or outcome.

Internal recruitment sources Sources where potential job applicants may be found inside the organization.

Intrinsic outcomes Type of outcome that occurs purely from the performance of a task.

Introductory approach The most common approach a salesperson uses by stating his or her name and business.

Job adjustment counseling Help in adjusting to the job.

Job analysis The formal study of jobs to define specific roles or activities to be performed in sales positions, for example, and to determine the personal qualifications needed for the jobs.

Job descriptions Formal written statements describing the nature, requirements, and responsibilities of a specific sales position.

Job satisfaction Refers to feelings toward the job.

Job specifications Qualifications that the organization feels are necessary for successful performance of the job.

Joint sales call The main element of a coaching session in which the manager accompanies a person on a sales call.

Key account sales position Senior position in which the salesperson contacts the larger, more important customers.

Leadership The ability to influence other people toward the attainment of objectives.

Leading The ability to influence other people toward the attainment of objectives.

Leads People and organizations that the salesperson knows nothing, or very little, about.

Learning A relatively permanent change in behavior occurring as a result of experience.

Learning attitude An important trait for new managers, consisting of a willingness to learn, change, adapt, and seek help when needed.

Learning curve A graph that indicates the extent the rate of learning changes with or without training and practice.

Least squares technique A time-series projection using the past to predict future sales.

Legitimate power The ability to influence others that comes from a formal management position in an organization and the authority granted to that position.

Line authority Formal power given to those in management positions that allows them to direct and control their next lower-level employees.

Management The attainment of organizational goals in an effective and efficient manner through planning, organizing, staffing, directing, and controlling organizational resources.

Management by Objectives (MBO) An evaluation program in which salespeople are given objectives and their actual results are compared with the objectives to evaluate performance on a performance index.

Market factor Item related to the demand for a product.

Market index A market factor expressed in quantitative form relative to some base figure.

Market share A company's share of the estimated sales for an entire industry, usually stated as a percentage.

Marketing audit A tool designed to evaluate the degree of integration of the entire marketing function with company operations in a systematic and comprehensive manner.

Marketing cost analysis Sometimes called *distribution cost analysis,* the analysis of costs that affect sales volume with the purpose of determining the profitability of different segment operations.

Marketing Decision Support System (MDSS) An ongoing, future-oriented structure designed to generate, process, store, and retrieve information to aid decision making in an organization's marketing program.

Marketing mix Consists of four main elements—product, price, distribution or place, and promotion—used by a marketing manager to market goods and services.

Mathematical methods Quantitative sales forecasting methods.

Misrepresentation Legal cause of action in which an injured party seeks damages arising from erroneous statements or false promises salespeople made regarding a product's characteristics or capabilities.

Mission The basic purpose and values of the organization, as well as its scope of operations.

Motivation The arousal, intensity, direction, and persistence of effort directed toward job tasks over a period of time.

Motivational mix The various methods and techniques sales managers use to influence the arousal, intensity, direction, and persistence of salespeople's behavior.

Moving averages A time-series projection method that allows consideration of all past data with less weight placed on data as they get older.

Naïve method A time-series projection method based on the assumption that what happened in the immediate past will continue to occur in the immediate future.

Needs assessment The process of determining the training needs of the sales force and setting objectives for satisfying those needs.

Net profit quota A quota determined by subtracting cost of goods sold and salespeople's direct selling expenses from sales volume.

Network organization A collection of independent, mostly single-function, firms.

Nondirective guidance Asks open-ended questions to help employee through counseling session.

Norms Standards established by the group.

Objection Opposition or resistance from the prospect to information or requests the salesperson presents.

Objective-based thinking A means of prioritizing activities in which everything the sales force does is aimed at achieving stated objectives.

Open sales territories Those territories left vacant until new salespeople are assigned to them.

Operational learning A type of learning that involves procedures that will be instantly used on the job and will quickly become habit.

Operational, or first-line, managers Type of managers who are directly responsible for sales of goods and services.

Operational planning A type of planning that identifies the specific procedures and processes required at low levels of the organization.

Order getters A type of salesperson who obtains, retains, and increases business with customers.

Order takers A salesperson who waits for the customer to place an order.

Organization A social system that is goal directed and deliberately structured.

Organizational design The formal, coordinated process of communication, authority, and responsibility for sales groups and individuals.

Organizational effectiveness The degree to which the organization achieves a stated objective.

Organizational efficiency The amount of resources used to achieve an organizational goal.

Organizational structure The relatively fixed, formally defined relationship among jobs within the firm.

Organizing The deployment of organizational resources to achieve strategic objectives.

Orphans Customers whose salesperson has left the company; company records provide the only information about these past customers.

Partnering A level of relationship marketing in which the seller works continually to improve its customer operations, sales, and profits.

People planning Process of determining the number and type of people to hire.

People skills The manager's ability to work with and through other people and to work effectively as a group member.

Performance appraisal A formal, structured system of measuring and evaluating a salesperson's activities and performance.

Performance counseling Helping salesperson better understand his or her performance.

Performance criteria Job requirements that determine the type of information to obtain from applicants and often the method used to gather that information.

Performance cycle A period related to specific product goals or job activities.

Performance development review A formal evaluation conducted to determine how well an individual, group, or territory is performing and that focuses on developing and improving performance.

Performance level Level a salesperson attains as a result of or combination of effort and ability.

Personal adjustment counseling Help with personal life's situation.

Personal interview One-on-one, face-to-face meeting of an applicant and a recruiter.

Personal selling A personal communication of information to persuade a prospective customer to buy something—a good, service, idea, or something else—that satisfies an individual's needs.

Placement A process concerned with ensuring that job demands match an individual's skills, knowledge, and abilities, along with preferences, interests, and personality.

Planning The conscious, systematic process of making decisions about goals and activities that an individual, group, work unit, or organization will pursue in the future.

Polygraph test Test that measures physiological responses to questions to determine if the subject is lying.

Power The ability to influence the behavior of others.

Preapproach Step in the selling process in which the salesperson investigates the prospect in greater depth and plans the sales call.

Preconventional moral development level Lowest level of moral development in which individuals act in their own best interest, following rules only to avoid punishment or receive rewards.

Predictors A set of factors common to the success of the firm's specific salespeople.

Presentation Part of the approach in a sales presentation that provides knowledge to the prospect about the product.

Price The value or worth of a product that attracts the buyer to exchange money or something of value for the product.

Principled moral development level Highest level of moral development in which an individual lives by an internal set of morals, values, and ethics.

Problem solving The manager becomes active in suggesting ways out of the problem.

Process A series of actions or operations conducted toward an end.

Product Bundle of tangible and intangible attributes, including packaging, color, and brand, plus the services and even the reputation of the seller.

Product approach An approach technique in which the salesperson places the product on the counter or hands it to the customer, stating nothing, and then waits for the prospect to begin the conversation.

Production cost Cost incurred in processing a product from its raw elements to its finished state.

Productivity The level of contribution a person makes to the organization.

Profit quotas A performance target based on profit for a sales unit, product, or customer.

Profitability Measure of efficiency determined by sales volume associated with cost and expenses.

Promotion A part of the marketing mix that increases company sales by communicating product information to potential customers.

Proof statements Part of a sales presentation in which the salesperson substantiates claims made about the product.

Prospect pool A group of names gathered from various sources.

Prospecting The act of finding the people who need and can buy the product.

Publicity Nonpersonal communication of information not paid for by an individual or organization.

Pure line organization Organizational structure in which the chief executive, usually the president, does the decision making for the firm.

Pygmalion effect Situation in which a manager believes a new salesperson will do well and conveys that belief to the salesperson, who in turn responds by meeting the manager's expectations.

Qualified prospect A prospect who has the financial resources to pay, the authority to make the buying decision, and a desire for the product.

Quality of work life (QWL) A program that creates a workplace that can enhance sales personnel's well-being and satisfaction.

Quota An expected performance objective routinely assigned to sales units such as individuals, regions, or districts.

Recent performance error A tendency to evaluate total performance on the last or most recent part of an individual's performance.

Reciprocity Agreement between two parties that they will buy products from each other.

Recruitment The set of activities and processes used to legally obtain a sufficient number of individuals that takes the people's and the sales force's best interests into consideration.

References Names of persons from whom information can be obtained regarding an applicant's ability and character.

Referent power The ability to influence others because of personality characteristics that command identification, respect, and admiration.

Referrals People or organizations salespeople know little about other than what they learn from the referral.

Regional sales manager Level of sales management responsible for three to five districts.

Regression analysis Statistical method used to incorporate the independent factors thought to influence sales units into the forecasting procedure.

Relationship behavior A way of relating to employees in which a manager uses two-way communication by listening, providing clarification, getting to know the individual's motives and goals, and giving positive feedback.

Relationship marketing The creation of customer loyalty.

Relationship selling A level of relationship marketing in which the seller contacts customers after the purchase to determine if they are satisfied and have future needs.

Retail sales index Relative measure of the dollar volume of retail sales that normally occur.

Return on Investment (ROI) Also called *return on assets,* a measurement firms use to determine how effectively the assets of a given operation are used.

Reward power The ability to influence others that stems from the leader's authority to bestow rewards on other people.

Role ambiguity Feeling experienced by salespeople when they do not have enough information to adequately perform their jobs.

Role conflict Feeling experienced by salespeople when they receive conflicting, inconsistent, or incompatible job demands from two or more people.

Role playing A training method in which a trainee acts out the sale of a product or service to a hypothetical buyer.

Sales analysis A detailed examination of a company's sales data, involving assimilating, classifying, comparing, and drawing conclusions.

Sales contests Special sales programs offering salespeople incentives to achieve short-term work goals.

Sales culture The set of key values, ideas, beliefs, attitudes, customs, and other capabilities and habits shared or acquired as a member of the sales group.

Sales force audit Involves the same six factors measured by the marketing audit but is designed to evaluate selling strategy and to improve the overall effectiveness of the sales force.

Sales force budget Amount of money available or assigned to the sales force for a definite period, usually a year.

Sales force composite An approach to forecasting that obtains the opinion of sales personnel concerning future sales.

Sales force objectives Goals for a company's sales force in a specified territory based on contribution to profits, sales/cost ratios, or market share.

Sales forecast The estimated dollar or unit sales for a specific future period, based on a proposed marketing plan and an assumed market environment.

Sales human resource management (SHRM) Activities undertaken to attract, develop, and maintain effective sales force personnel within an organization.

Sales leakage Lost sales due to sales position vacancy and the time required for a new salesperson to produce at average.

Sales management The attainment of sales force goals in an effective and efficient manner through planning, staffing, leading, and controlling organizational resources.

Sales manager A person whose job is the management of sales resources such as people and budgets.

Sales process A sequential series of actions the salesperson takes that lead toward the customer taking a desired action.

Sales promotion Involves activities or materials used to create sales of goods or services.

Sales reward system A system of measuring and rewarding salespeople's performance.

Sales skills development A process by which salespeople learn to apply their sales knowledge to prospects and customers.

Sales territory An individual segment of a company's market composed of a group of consumers or a geographic area.

Sales training The effort an employer puts forth to provide salespeople job-related culture, knowledge, and attitudes.

Sales training evaluation The process of collecting, tabulating, and analyzing data related to a program's objectives.

Sales volume quotas A performance objective that includes dollar or product unit objectives for a specified period.

Scheduling The process of establishing a fixed time when the salesperson will be at the customer's place of business.

Selection Process of choosing the best available person for the job.

Selection tools Series of steps used to aid managers in choosing the applicants best suited for a position.

Selling by objectives (SBO) A process in which the manager and salesperson jointly identify common goals, define major responsibility areas, and agree on the results expected.

Semistructured interview Type of interview that allows for interaction and collection of information of interest to both parties.

Service An action or activity done for others for a fee.

Service quality A subjective assessment that customers arrive at by evaluating the service level they perceive being delivered.

Simulated test market (STM) Mathematical forecasting method that consists of monitoring a preselected panel of consumers for their reaction to the test products.

Slogans Specific sayings used to convey special meaning or to communicate the organization's culture to employees.

Social An organization or system made up of two or more people that is designed to achieve an outcome.

Social adjustment counseling Helping to fit into the sales team.

Social responsibility Management's obligation to make choices and take actions that will contribute to the welfare and interests of society, as well as to those of the organization.

Socialization Process by which salespeople learn the sales culture and behaviors appropriate for their roles in the organization.

Split credit A situation that results when more than one person or department is involved in a sale and all parties receive a portion of the incentive pay.

Staff authority Power given to those in staff positions that allows them to advise, recommend, and counsel in their areas of expertise.

Staffing Refers to activities undertaken to attract, develop, and maintain effective sales personnel within an organization.

Stakeholder Any group within or outside the organization that has a stake in the organization's performance.

Stories Narratives based on true events that are frequently shared among salespeople and told to new sales reps to inform them about the organization.

Straight commission plan A way of compensating employees for their work in which they are paid entirely on the basis of what they sell.

Straight salary plan A way of compensating employees for their work in which they are paid a specific dollar amount at regular intervals.

Strategic alliance A formal relationship created with the purpose of joint pursuit of mutual goals.

Strategic goals Major targets or end results that relate to the organization's long-term survival, value, and growth.

Strategic, or top, managers Managers at the top of the hierarchy who are responsible for the entire organization.

Strategic plan The company's mission, vision, values, objectives, strategies, and tactics.

Strategic planning Involves making decisions about the organization's long-term goals and strategies.

Strategic vision An idea that moves beyond the mission statement to provide a perspective on where the company is headed and what the organization has become.

Strategy A pattern of actions and resource allocations designed to achieve the organization's goals.

Structured interview Type of interview in which the recruiter asks questions, often from a standard form.

Success analysis A process used to identify factors that appear to make salespeople successful.

Supervision The actual overseeing and directing of the day-to-day activities of salespeople.

Survey methods Qualitative sales forecasting methods.

Symbol One thing that represents another thing.

System A set of interdependent parts that processes inputs into outputs.

Tactic Operational means by which an organization intends to reach its objectives.

Tactical, or middle, managers Managers who work at middle levels of the organization and who are responsible for major groups.

Tactical planning Plans that translate broad strategic goals and plans into specific goals and plans relevant to a definite portion of the organization, often a functional area like marketing or human resources.

Task behavior A way of relating to employees in which the manager describes the duties and responsibilities of an individual or a group.

Team-based organization The most responsive type of organization due to the use of work teams as a basic building block.

Technical skills The abilities to perform a specialized task that involves a certain method or process.

Telemarketing A marketing communication system using telecommunications technology and trained personnel to conduct planned, measurable marketing activities directed at target groups of consumers.

Termination-at-Will Rule Rule established and upheld by the courts that allows an employer to terminate an employee at any time for any reason.

Territorial control The establishment of performance standards for an individual territory in the form of qualitative and quantitative quotas or goals.

Territorial manager A salesperson who plans, organizes, and executes activities that increase sales and profits in a given territory.

Test markets Mathematical forecasting method that measures consumer acceptance of new products.

Tests Various pieces of information gathered about applicants and used to make selection decisions.

Tie-in sale Situation in which a buyer is required to buy unwanted goods in order to purchase a particular kind of merchandise.

Time series projections A mathematical tool for forecasting sales that uses chronologically ordered, raw data.

Total sales volume The starting point for a sales volume analysis; the total sales for a specific period for a company, region, product, or customer.

Transaction selling A level of relationship marketing in which customers are sold to and not contacted again.

Trial close Step in the selling process in which the salesperson checks the attitude of the prospect toward the sales presentation.

Turnover When employees leave their present job.

Unstructured interview A free-form interview using few preplanned questions.

Valence The value a salesperson places on a reward.

Values Represents a firm's mode of conduct toward others and itself.

Variance analysis A method of identifying factors that cause a discrepancy between standard and actual costs with an ultimate goal of resolving inefficiencies.

Wage level The amount of compensation established for salespeople in comparison with the industry average.

Wage structure The pay differential among different sales levels within an organization.

Work withs A manager's routine visits with each salesperson.

Workload Quantity of work expected from sales personnel.

Zone sales manager Level of sales management responsible for three to five regions.

INDEX